D0938495

Four Men

FOUR MEN

LIVING THE REVOLUTION
An Oral History of Contemporary Cuba

Oscar Lewis
Ruth M. Lewis
Susan M. Rigdon

UNIVERSITY OF ILLINOIS PRESS
Urbana   Chicago   London

In order to maintain the anonymity of the subjects of this study, the names of all informants, members of their families, their friends, and their neighbors have been changed. Places of birth, hometowns, details of work histories (but not salary or skill levels), as well as some streets, stores, hotels, and other public places, have also been changed. The names of historical figures and public officials have not been changed except in those cases in which a public figure or official had a personal relationship with one or more of the subjects in this study.

LIBRARY OF CONGRESS CATALOGING IN PUBLICATION DATA

Lewis, Oscar, 1914–1970.
  Living the revolution.

  Bibliography: p.
  CONTENTS: v. 1. Four men.
  1. Cuba—Social conditions. 2. Cuba—Poor.
3. Cuba—Politics and government—1959–   4. Family
—Cuba—Case studies. I. Lewis, Ruth M., 1916–
joint author. II. Rigdon, Susan M., 1943–
joint author. III. Title.
HN203.5.L48 1977   309.1′7291′064   76-54878
ISBN 0-252-00628-3

Contents

Nine   Life Goes On   298

             PART III   NICOLÁS SALAZAR FERNÁNDEZ

One   *Papá*'s Burden   319

Two   Struggling Along   340

Three   Beginning to Understand   350

Four   Flora Mir Monte   369

Five   Politics and Personal Problems   391

Six   They Just Don't Understand   408

Seven   Getting Ahead   425

Eight   Our Socialist Society   440

             PART IV   GABRIEL CAPOTE PACHECO

One   Abandoned   451

Two   Ernesto, Rita, and My Old Man   469

Three   I Found My Way   482

Four   Fina and My Children   497

Five   They Made Me a Militant   511

Six   More to Lose Now   521

             Abbreviations   529

             Glossary   531

             Selected Bibliography   533

Foreword[1]

IN EARLY 1969, DESPITE THE U.S. economic blockade of Cuba and the antagonism between the two countries, my husband, Oscar Lewis, with my assistance and that of others, undertook a three-year research project in Cuba. This was not the first time a North American university professor had done research in post-revolutionary Cuba, but the broad scope of the project and the fact that it was being done at the invitation of Fidel Castro and the Cuban Academy of Sciences, with the consent and cooperation of the U.S. State Department, aroused some curiosity and suspicion on both sides. There were those who believed the State Department's special concessions for extensive travel to Cuba could only mean Oscar was working for the CIA, while others assumed he was a communist because he had been invited by Castro and was being allowed to do independent research. Then, when the project came to an abrupt halt in June, 1970, less than a year and a half later and six months before Oscar's death, there were more questions and rumors. I would like, therefore, before presenting the results of the field work, to review briefly the background of the project, why and how it came about, how it fared in Cuba, and, finally, how it ended.

From the very beginning of the Revolution, Oscar had wanted to do research in Cuba. As an anthropologist and a humanist with a long-time interest in socialism, he believed it important to study the revolutionary process—the transformation of an entire society, the impact of new institutions and cultural values with all the conflicts and hopes they engendered—and to record these experiences at the very time they were happening. To a social scientist familiar with its language and culture, Cuba seemed to promise unusual possibilities for research.

Oscar's interest in Cuba began in the summer of 1946,[2] when he was

1. I am very much indebted to Susan Rigdon for her help in writing this Foreword. For their editorial suggestions, I would also like to thank Joseph Casagrande, Alan J. Booth, Douglas Butterworth, Elizabeth Kelly Fry, Zunia Henry, Judith Lewis, Gene Lewis, and Mitchell Morris. RML.
2. The date of the Cuban visit incorrectly appeared as 1947 in the Introduction to *La Vida* (all editions) and *A Study of Slum Culture: Backgrounds for La Vida*.

invited to teach the first course in anthropology offered by the School of
Social Work at the University of Havana. As part of that course, he and
his students visited Las Yaguas, a shantytown slum in Havana, and did a
two-month survey of social and economic conditions in Melena del Sur, a
sugar-mill community approximately 90 miles southeast of the capital.
He had hoped to go back to Cuba to study both of these communities,
but as it turned out, this wasn't to happen until fifteen years later, after
the Revolution.

Early in 1961, when travel to Cuba (and also to China, North Korea,
and North Vietnam) was restricted by the U.S. State Department, Oscar
applied for permission to go to Cuba for an extended period to explore
the possibilities of doing research. This was just before the Bay of Pigs
attack in April, and his request was, of course, turned down. He did
succeed in going to Cuba for five days in August of that year, to write an
article for *Harper's* magazine. With research in mind, he went to the
sugar *central* in Melena del Sur and was pleased that some of the families
and informants[3] he had interviewed in 1946 still remembered him and
gave him a warm reception. He also revisited the slum in Havana and
wrote in his notes that neither community had changed much physically
but there were new communal facilities and some organizational changes
that would be interesting to study. It was a short visit, though, and he was
able to make only a few preliminary inquiries at the University and the
Academy of Sciences.

In February, 1968, he visited Cuba again for two weeks at the invitation of the Instituto del Libro, the major Cuban publishing house, which
had just brought out his study of the Mexican village Tepoztlán and
was preparing to publish *Pedro Martínez*. Oscar also carried with him an
invitation from the Cuban Academy of Sciences to do family and community studies in Cuba. He wanted to explore this prospect further,
although he had already decided not to undertake such a project unless
the invitation came directly from the Prime Minister. In a centrally controlled, highly politicized system such as existed in Cuba, sensitive research would, at the very least, need support and approval from the
top to have some chance for success. With this in mind, Oscar met with a
number of university professors, with José Llanusa Gobel, then a
member of the Central Committee of the Communist Party and Minister
of Education, with Armando Hart, member of the Political Bureau, and,
finally, with Fidel Castro.

The meeting with Castro took place early on the last morning of
Oscar's stay, at a predesignated spot on a highway somewhere outside of

---

3. The word *informant* is widely used by anthropologists for persons who are sources of
information about the native society and culture, and should not be confused with *informer*.

Havana. Castro was waiting in a jeep, with two other jeeps full of armed guards, and for the next six hours he drove Oscar, José Llanusa, and two men from the Cuban Department of Agriculture through the countryside, talking at length about plans for the reorganization of agriculture, the improvement of the cattle industry, problems of underdevelopment, and many other subjects.

It was after dark when the jeep pulled up before a small pine cabin, one of Castro's country homes. Here they were joined for dinner by Rolando Rodríguez, head of the Instituto del Libro, and Dr. René Vallejo, Castro's physician and close companion. Dr. Vallejo later became quite important to the project, not only for his interest in it but also by serving as our main contact with Fidel Castro. For the rest of the evening, the conversation centered on the proposed research project.

Castro told Oscar he had read *The Children of Sánchez* and said it was a revolutionary book, "worth more than 50,000 political pamphlets." He had apparently also read *La Vida* and was familiar with the studies of peasants in Mexico and India and with the concept of the culture of poverty. After discussing the *Sánchez* book, he said, "Why don't you come and do research like that here in our country?" He did not believe, he went on to say, that the results would be of any direct help to the Revolution, but it would be an important contribution to Cuban history to have an objective record of what people feel and think. He said Cuba did not have the time or personnel for such a study and he was convinced Oscar would do an honest job.

Oscar pointed out that some Mexicans and Puerto Ricans had resented his portrayal of life in their slums and he wondered whether a similar study focusing on internal problems and on poverty would be acceptable to the Cuban government at this difficult time of transition. Fidel Castro said, "Oh yes, you should come. Cuba is different. We won't give you the hard time the Mexicans did. This is a socialist country and all we are concerned with is that you do an honest job." He added that there was nothing to hide, that Cubans were a talkative people and there were no complaints or grievances he hadn't already heard. He agreed, however, that it would give a more balanced picture if families representing other sectors of society were included. He said that for a really well-rounded study of the effects of the Revolution on Cuban family life, it would be necessary to study those who had left Cuba as well as those who had remained. Oscar explained that he had already begun interviewing members of ten emigré families in New York City.

Dr. Vallejo then suggested the study include some former millionaires who had remained in Cuba to become active revolutionaries. Castro agreed and added that rehabilitated prostitutes would also make an interesting study. The question of representative types was discussed, as well as research methods and techniques and the need for objectivity in gathering data. Castro did not, at that time at least, take the position frequently expressed in Latin-American leftist circles, especially since Project Camelot, that social science research initiated in capitalist countries was to be distrusted. Indeed, Castro asked if Oscar would be willing to train a group of Cuban students in his methods of research. The answer was yes, provided the group was kept small.

Finally, Oscar said he would be glad to undertake the research project if certain basic conditions were guaranteed. These were, in summary: (1) freedom of investigation, that is, the right to decide what and whom to study, without censorship or intervention by the government, including the right to take taped interviews, manuscripts, and other materials out of Cuba without having them read or inspected; (2) assurance that the government would not harm or punish any of the subjects for cooperating with the study, and a recognition of the need to maintain their anonymity; (3) permission to bring in necessary equipment and supplies and a non-Cuban staff to help maintain confidentiality and independence. To this end, the project would also pay for food and rent.

Castro agreed to everything but seemed to be taken aback by these conditions. He may have had some second thoughts about the implications of independent research, for at one point he said, "We are probably the only socialist country in the world that would allow you to do your kind of studies with the complete freedom you need." The agreement was, of course, an oral one, witnessed by Castro's three associates: Dr. Vallejo (who died in August, 1969), José Llanusa,[4] and Rolando Rodríguez.

We had doubts of our own about the wisdom of the undertaking. We were not under the illusion that freedom, as we knew it, existed in Cuba, but we did hope for an atmosphere of relative freedom that would allow us to work on a more than superficial level. We thought that if Fidel Castro, for reasons of his own, was ready to guarantee personally the independence we needed, field work in Cuba would be feasible even under prevailing security conditions. We also realized that the project might be halted at any time the leadership decided that changes in internal conditions warranted it.

Oscar had nowhere in print raised the ethical questions posed by doing family studies and tape-recording life stories. However, because of our continued interest and involvement in them it is fair to say that we had committed ourselves, at least implicitly, to the position that the knowledge and insights gained from this kind of research outweighed the consequent invasion of privacy and the risk to the informants and to ourselves. Even though we believed greater risks existed in Cuba, we did not change our attitude.

4. In 1970 Llanusa was replaced as Minister of Education; he is now director of the Matanzas cattle-breeding project.

Why Castro was interested in having this research done in Cuba and agreed to the guarantees requested is a matter for speculation. We believed it was a genuine, if impulsive, gesture on his part, to show that his government had no fear of revealing internal problems, and that, unlike other socialist countries, Cuba had a certain climate of free inquiry.

After his twelve-hour meeting with Castro, Oscar returned to the United States and immediately applied to the State Department for special travel permission, which he received after a short delay. For reasons which we can only guess, the government of the United States agreed to lift its restrictions temporarily and the project thus became a possibility. Carried along by enthusiasm for the research and curiosity about life in Cuba, we seized the opportunity to go.

First, it was necessary to raise funds to finance the project. Long before, in 1960, Oscar had unsuccessfully applied to the Ford Foundation for support of research in Cuba, but in 1968 the Foundation's board of trustees voted to approve support for such research, and several grants for that purpose were made that year. Ours was a three-year grant, to be supplemented by funds of our own. As it was important to get clearance on the Cuban side, we sent a letter via the Cuban Embassy in Mexico, informing Dr. Vallejo of the Ford Foundation support. About ten days later, Dr. Vallejo telephoned from Havana to Urbana, Illinois, approving the arrangement.

The general purpose of our project in Cuba was to study the impact of a revolution-in-progress upon the daily lives of individuals and families representing different socioeconomic levels in both rural and urban settings. Using the technique of tape-recorded autobiographies, the study would, in effect, be an oral history of contemporary Cuba as well as of the Cuban Revolution. We also hoped to observe the mass organizations and revolutionary institutions as they functioned at the local level and to evaluate, albeit tentatively, the degree of success or failure in achieving some of the goals of the Revolution.

Because of our interest in comparative studies of the culture of poverty, the research design provided for a special study of slum families under the revolutionary government. We wanted to study, in the context of a socialist system, the relative stability or vulnerability to change of some of the basic traits of the culture of poverty, such as consensual marriage, illegitimacy, abandonment, violence, authoritarianism, alcoholism, mother-centered families, present-time orientation, fatalism, and so on.

On February 20, 1969, we left by plane for Havana via Mexico City, carrying with us 750 pounds of luggage, most of it in equipment—tape recorders, typewriters, cameras, books, spare parts, and office supplies. We had U.S. passports stamped "Valid for Travel to Cuba," and Cuban visas that we were to pick up at the Cuban Embassy in Mexico City. Our non-Cuban staff consisted of a secretary-typist, who was from Puerto Rico, and a total of seven assistants—four North Americans, one Italian, and two Mexicans—who joined us during the following year and a half.

I should make clear that in Cuba support of Castro's decision concerning the project came principally from a few of his close associates, namely, Dr. Vallejo, Armando Hart, Haydée Santamaría, heroine of the Revolution and president of the publishing house Casa de las Américas, as well as Dr. Antonio Nuñez Jiménez, José Llanusa, Argeliers León, head of the Institute of Ethnology and Folklore of the Academy of Sciences, and several others. We learned soon after our arrival that a number of members of the Central Committee, the Cuban Department of State Security, some of the younger university faculty, and other individuals were strongly opposed to having a foreign "bourgeois professor" do unsupervised, unrestricted research in Cuba. After some debate they yielded to Castro, but apparently did not view favorably either our project or the fact that it was being financed by the Ford Foundation.

While we were en route to Havana, the Cuban government made public a decision not to cooperate directly or indirectly with organizations such as the Ford Foundation, which they considered an agency of the CIA and of North American imperialism. This decision was made partly in response to pressure from a group of leftist students in Argentina who had requested a policy statement on the question of whether or not Latin-American Marxists should accept grants-in-aid originating in the United States. The position taken by the Cuban government made our arrival an embarrassment and presented them with the problem of what to do with us. There were top-level meetings those first weeks, during which time we were visited occasionally by Dr. Vallejo or Comandante Manuel Piñeiro Lozada, head of Security and member of the Central Committee of the Communist Party, who kept us advised of the discussion. Oscar explained his position as an independent scholar vis-à-vis the Ford Foundation, declaring that the source of support did not in any way affect the nature of his research or publications. Comandante Piñeiro, for one, refused to believe this could be possible and apparently never changed his point of view. Finally, however, it was decided that because the grant had not been given directly to us but rather to the University of Illinois, the project would be permitted to continue as planned.

Anthropological field work in socialist Cuba was a profoundly unique experience for us, although some of the differences were subtle and not immediately perceived. It is not feasible to consider them systematically here, but a discussion of the Cuban staff, the details of our living arrangements, the way the project was set up, and a few of the problems we encountered will indicate the distinctive nature of the situation.

I can say flatly that there was not a single important aspect of the field work that was not affected in some degree by the great societal changes in Cuba, above all by the ubiquitous presence of the state. In non-socialist countries, anthropologists doing research are normally on their own and, whether in an urban or rural or jungle setting, must spend a good deal of their time, energy, and funds establishing themselves in the field. In Cuba such self-reliance was impossible. Although we made the basic decisions concerning whom and what to study, there were many things we could not do or get on our own. With the government as the source of all goods and services, we were unavoidably dependent upon them for material things such as food and housing. Almost everything had to be done through the proper channels, a process involving a good deal of bureaucratic red tape. To speed up action, many Cubans rely on informal personal contacts with friends, relatives, associates, or anyone willing to help them. These strategically placed persons are known as *socios,* and the use of them exists to such a degree that some Cubans jokingly call their system *socioismo* instead of *socialismo.*

To facilitate our work and avoid red tape, the government assigned a trusted militant as project *responsable* to administer to the needs of the project and its staff and act as intermediary with the government and its agencies. He met us at the airport when we arrived, obtained identification papers, plane tickets, furniture, and supplies for the office, arranged appointments, repairs, helped hire additional employees, etc. He also introduced Oscar to the local authorities in places where community studies were to be conducted. The *responsable* was indispensable to the project and undoubtedly made it possible for us to devote most of our time and energy to the research itself and thus gather a great deal of data in a short period.

On the whole, project-related problems were usually solved rapidly. There were times, however, when for one reason or another the *responsable* was ineffectual, and then Oscar would step in and try to resolve the problem. Had he been more passive, or easily intimidated or discouraged, the project would have foundered or he would have lost control of it. When a bottleneck occurred, he would go directly to José Llanusa (the project had been placed under the guidance of the Ministry of Education); if that didn't work, he would not hesitate to go to other persons in positions of authority.

For example, the Ministry did not assign us three Cuban typists as promised and the taped interviews were piling up untranscribed, threatening to bring the project to a standstill. Oscar therefore went to the Union of Cuban Writers and Artists, which helped him locate an excellent typist. Later, someone at the Mexican Embassy recommended another typist. Unfortunately, these women were not revolutionaries or government workers and it was considered undesirable to employ them.

Our *responsable* was able to get permission to do so only because government typists were unavailable. Liberated Cuban women, we were told, no longer wanted to be typists (Cuban men apparently never did), and all the secretarial schools had been closed. True or not, we weren't able to get more than one government typist assigned to the project.

The entire matter of getting settled in our living quarters had been taken care of by our *responsable* and by various other persons representing the Ministry of Education and INIT, the National Institute of the Tourist Industry. The large, furnished house we rented from the government included a staff of four government employees—a cook, two assistants who worked in shifts, and a cleaning woman, all of whom we felt obliged to add to the project payroll. A temporary chauffeur and car were placed at our disposal until two small cars we had ordered were delivered from Canada. We were assigned to certain diplomatic stores where we could buy foods and other items that were unavailable to most Cubans. In short, we received many courtesies that put us in a privileged position compared to Cuban citizens. Although not unappreciated by us, we were always acutely aware of the differences in our living standards, which, I believe, may have had a negative effect on our rapport with some Cubans.

To provide an office for the project and living quarters for the non-Cuban staff, we rented two additional houses. Later, because traveling to informants' homes by public bus was too slow, the project was given a small bus of its own, with a full-time chauffeur and a permit to buy all the gasoline we needed, despite the limited supply. The government was equally generous in lending us tables, desks, and chairs for the office, and in providing us with paper and other supplies we weren't able to bring with us.

Despite this cooperation, or perhaps because of it, we were constantly questioning their motives, as they must have ours, a situation that created some tension. Because the threat to national security was very real, we knew that project personnel would be subject to security checks. We assumed, for example, that our household staff would be observing us and that the telephones would be tapped, even though we had no evidence of this until the very end of our stay. In any case, we had no motives other than the ones we had declared, and we did not feel under excessive restraint or scrutiny. If there was surveillance it was done discreetly, and we were on friendly terms with everyone throughout our stay.

The first few months were spent in training the field staff, then consisting of two of our own assistants and an *equipo* or team of ten Cuban students, five men and five women. Six other assistants requiring training arrived within months from the United States and Mexico, and one year later Douglas Butterworth, an anthropologist from the University of Illinois, joined us to take over the task of training the Cuban students and supervising their field work.

My work on the project consisted mainly of evaluating, editing, and organizing the transcribed interviews and checking the translations. I made frequent visits to the families involved in *Neighbors* and periodically supervised the work of the staff there. I also interviewed other informants and recorded their life histories, and, with the assistance of Olivia Hernández, did a pilot study of a Miramar nursery school.

The original agreement to train Cuban students was made in the interest of maintaining good relations with the government and out of a real desire to contribute to the development of anthropological research in Cuba. The *equipo* of students assigned to the project, however, was larger than we had expected. We had hoped for two or three university graduates trained in social science, but of the ten volunteers only two had been university students and the remaining eight had graduated from various teacher-training schools. All had had some teaching experience and their fields of special training included history, biology, and geography, but no social science research of any kind.

The Cuban students ranged in age from nineteen to twenty-five. All but one had participated in the student-teacher brigades of the Literacy Campaign of 1961, and, like other *brigadistas,* they became the "darlings of the Revolution," completing their high school and advanced education with full scholarships and many other considerations. Most of them were members of the Communist Youth and were fully integrated "*patria o muerte*" revolutionaries. They had volunteered for the *equipo* for "the good of the country" and to improve their skills, admittedly without fully understanding the project's objectives.

The task of training them in a short time appeared formidable. It seemed unlikely that these young people, who were entirely unfamiliar with social science, let alone anthropology, and whose own education was so highly politicized, would be able to confront and report facts and opinions that might have anti-government implications. At first some of the students doing field work would scold their informants who complained about poor housing. One member of the *equipo* went so far as to attack verbally an elderly informant who mentioned that he had once supported Batista. Detachment as a methodological tool is difficult to learn, especially so soon after a revolution, and it is certainly not an attitude that is encouraged in Cuba. After six weeks of lectures in basic anthropology given by Oscar, and with several months of additional training and field work doing surveys, interviews, and life stories, most of the Cuban staff began to adopt a stance of detachment toward their informants.[5]

5. In September, 1969, after seven months of work, Oscar wrote of the Cuban students in a letter to a colleague: ". . . all of them . . . have reached the point where they are making a real contribution to the project."

Field-work training began with preliminary surveys of seven new housing settlements inhabited by former residents of the old Las Yaguas slum, which had been razed by the government in 1963. The new settlements differed somewhat from each other in their degrees of integration, i.e., their identification and involvement with the Revolution. With this in mind, Oscar wanted to compare a well-integrated settlement with a poorly integrated one. He began with a pilot study in the Buena Ventura housing project, which was a poorly integrated community. The 100 families who lived in this development were studied continuously until the end of our stay in Cuba. The study of the well-integrated community, Bolívar, was, unfortunately, not completed, and it was impossible to do a comparison of the two.

An important part of the training of the *equipo* was the preparation of questionnaires to be used in the community studies. There were eight questionnaires covering basic background information, work history, education, participation level, and so on. With the help of the *equipo*, the questionnaires were administered to almost all of the families in Buena Ventura and then analyzed. The *equipo* went on to study other aspects of the community and, finally, to interview individuals in preparation for family studies.

The field work expanded in several other directions to include a broader segment of Cuban society. Families that represented different socioeconomic levels were sought out for study; others were met by happenstance. Still others were referred to us by their friends or relatives. By the end of the first six months we were intensively interviewing ten unrelated individuals and many members of their families. Of these, the life stories of four men and four women have been selected for publication in two separate volumes.

During our second month in Cuba, we began a separate study of five families living in an apartment building in the suburb of Miramar, Havana. To understand how the distribution system for goods and services functioned on a day-to-day basis on the local level and the extent to which the families participated in mass organizations, the research design included a study of the block and the neighborhood. We were also interested in the children living in the building because they represented a generation reared under the Revolution, but we were unable to complete this aspect of the study before the project was halted. The volume based on this small community is concerned with the past and present lives of the five married couples, how they came from different regions and socioeconomic backgrounds to live in Miramar, and how they related to each other and to the new community.

The entire rural part of the project, which we intended to carry out in Melena del Sur, was to take place during the second half of our stay. We made a preliminary trip with some of the Cuban assistants to Melena del

Sur to arrange for housing and to renew contacts with former informants. Field work was to begin in September, 1970, but the project
ended before that date.

To explain how and why the project ended, it is necessary to review
some of the events occurring in Cuba at the time. The most important
development was the failure to meet the goal of the 10-million-ton sugar
harvest and the negative effect of the concentrated nationwide effort
upon the rest of the economy. This was summed up in great detail by
Fidel Castro in his report on the Cuban economy given in a speech on
July 26, 1970. It was a discouraging report and a great blow to the
leadership and to the Cuban people.

According to Castro, none of the annual production goals had been
met—except for fish, nickel, electric power, and eggs—and production
in some areas had declined. Sugar production was a special case, because
although they had not attained their goal, the harvest of 8½ million
tons was the largest Cuba had ever achieved. The rice ration was increased, but the supply of many important foods, as well as consumer
goods and services, had declined. Housing continued to be an acute
problem. Castro was equally open in his explanation of the production
failures, attributing them to a long list of problems—transportation and
port difficulties, delays in import deliveries, shortages of key raw
materials, currency and market problems, power and labor shortages,
absenteeism, general inefficiency—and to the ignorance, semiliteracy,
even illiteracy of many men in responsible positions. He frankly admitted
his own responsibility and blamed it on ignorance and inexperience.

In addition to great economic stress, Fidel Castro and other Cuban
leaders had come under severe criticism from foreign writers, some of
whom were sympathetic to socialism. The critics were denounced forth-
with as enemies, although only a little later, in his July 26 speech, Castro
himself made equally critical disclosures on the state of the economy. At
that time, he exhorted the people to welcome embarrassing criticism,
even from "the enemy." He said, "We couldn't care less about the
enemy. . . . The embarrassment will be welcome if we know how to turn
this shame into strength. . . !"

But Castro did care about what his critics were saying. The books that
most infuriated him were *Cuba: Est-il Socialiste?* by René Dumont and
Guerrillas in Power by K. S. Karol, published in early 1970. Dumont, a
French agronomist, and Karol, a Polish-born, Russian-educated Parisian
journalist, had both been invited to Cuba by Castro, and, to some extent,
he had to accept some responsibility for the two publications. With the
prospect of yet another possibly embarrassing publication coming out of
our research, it is easy to see how Castro would change his attitude and
take the position of those who had opposed our project from the start.

On June 25, 1970, a day before we were to leave for a summer in

Urbana, Oscar received a call requesting him to appear at the office of Dr. Raúl Roa, the Foreign Minister. Oscar was delighted, because he had wanted to discuss the present status of the project with Fidel Castro and had been unsuccessfully trying to contact someone who might arrange another meeting. From mid-April on it had been impossible to reach anyone, presumably because they were preoccupied with the harvest. At Dr. Roa's office, however, Oscar was to learn that it had been a deliberate attempt to isolate us while we were under intense surveillance.

At the Foreign Minister's office, Oscar was shocked to be formally notified by Dr. Roa that Project Cuba, as they called it, had been suspended by the government. Reasons were given in the form of a list of alleged breaches of the original agreement. Oscar was charged, in brief, with accepting funds from the Ford Foundation, hiring nonintegrated typists, and studying middle-class and counterrevolutionary families in Cuba and in New York, as well as members of the Army and the Communist Party. There was also a charge that Oscar was a difficult, demanding person and that complaints against him had been made by two non-Cuban staff members whom he had asked to leave the project.

Whatever we did in Cuba, beginning with our acceptance of the Ford Foundation grant, was open and aboveboard and well known to the authorities. Not only would it have been unwise for us to hide a significant move, such as hiring an employee, for example, but it would have been impossible to do so.

According to the original agreement, there was no sector of society we could not study. Thus it was not forbidden to interview members of any rank in either the Army or the Communist Party. Indeed, in 1968 Armando Hart had personally contacted two leading Party members at the provincial level and had urged them to talk freely to Oscar about their lives. We did not, however, do such a study, and we have only incidental data on the Army and Party from informants who were selected for other reasons. In the case of the Army, many citizens in Cuba are involved in the defense of their country and it would be difficult to locate representative informants who did not, sooner or later, mention this experience.

The one counterrevolutionary family the charges might refer to was the X family, whom we met four months before the end of our stay. Mr. and Mrs. X had read some of Oscar's books and sought him out to offer him their life stories. Mr. X was opposed to the government but Mrs. X was in conflict about her position because her mother and sister were ardent revolutionaries. It was an interesting situation to study and Oscar immediately began to interview them.

Mr. X, we learned, had been known as a *gusano*[6] since the Bay of Pigs

---

6. Literally "worm," used in Cuba to refer to anyone who does not support the Revolution, from passive opponents to active counterrevolutionaries.

attack in 1961. At that time he was among the thousands rounded up and detained for three days in the Stadium. But there had been no charges against him, and after his release he moved steadily upward in his profession. He was the only informant who had asked about the confidentiality of the materials and the question of his personal safety before undertaking the study. Our explanation of the agreement with Fidel Castro and the good record of the government in observing it during the preceding year had apparently reassured him. It may be more accurate to say that his great desire to talk to someone overcame his apprehensions.

Mr. X expressed quite strong opposition to the system, but to our knowledge he had never done anything more active than complain and avoid voluntary labor. During the interviews he criticized the shortages, his colleagues, the "new elite," and the difficulties in developing himself personally and professionally because of travel restrictions and the lack of foreign journals. He was individualistic, materialistic, and admired the United States, the consumer society, Nixon, South Vietnam's fight against communism, and he blamed Castro for the break in Cuban-U.S. relations.

As the interviews progressed, Mr. X became increasingly excited and vociferous. At various times we said it might be dangerous for him to record his life story and that he should stop. He agreed about the danger, and although he was generally suspicious and had often expressed the belief that our house was bugged, he insisted on continuing.

During this time, a high-ranking government official, related to the X family and with some indiscretions of his own to conceal, learned of the study, saw it as a threat, and apparently decided to get the Department of State Security to stop the entire project. It is considered very important in Cuba that the public image of heroes and government and Party leaders remain untarnished, and this simple fact may well have been the immediate cause for the ending of the research. In addition, in this case Comandante Piñeiro, head of Security, was a close personal friend of the official concerned.

In a different category, there was another charge involving the use of the diplomatic pouch of a foreign country. Late in October, 1969, a set of corrected galleys for a new book of Oscar's, the contents of which were not connected in any way with Cuba, was sent to him from Mexico. It was, unfortunately, lost in the mails and his publisher urgently needed to get a new set to him. Because of the blockade, mail service between Cuba and the United States took from four to six weeks, making it impossible to meet the printer's schedule. Very much disturbed by this, one evening at a social gathering Oscar explained the situation to an official of the Israeli consulate, who observed that his country's diplomatic pouch arrived from New York once a week. Not knowing it might be considered a violation of protocol, Oscar asked if his publisher might send the galleys via the pouch; the Israeli diplomat agreed and the galleys arrived in a few days. They were corrected and returned the same way. The pouch was used two or three times after that, to send other urgent personal correspondence to Cuba from the United States.

Israel had reasonably good relations with Cuba in 1969–70, and had twice sent technical advisory teams there. Nevertheless, Oscar was charged with having used the diplomatic pouch of an "enemy capitalist, imperialist country," thereby raising suspicions about his activities in Cuba. The whole transaction had been made with no attempt at concealment and was openly discussed on the telephone and in the presence of our household staff. In retrospect, it was, of course, a naiveté much to be regretted and apologized for, but in no way did it demonstrate anything more than lack of experience in diplomatic rules. The Cuban government could not have taken it very seriously themselves because it wasn't until seven months later that they mentioned it.

We did not question the right of the government to reverse its position and close down Project Cuba, but we were dismayed at the reasons given for doing so. Oscar was upset at the thought of stopping when the research was in high gear, with a better-trained, more efficient staff and with the *equipo* eager to begin the rural phase of the study. It is true, however, that for almost sixteen months the government had lived up to the conditions of the original agreement, and in many ways had cooperated far beyond our expectations.

During that time neither we nor our staff nor any of the informants had been questioned or approached in any way, nor were we prevented from going anywhere or doing anything we wished. Between us we made ten trips to the United States, each time taking out of Cuba tapes, typed interviews, and copies of everything except certain charts and questionnaires that could not be easily carried. Not once was a suitcase of ours opened for inspection upon leaving. Our *responsable* always accompanied us to the airport to be certain of this. Even in the office, where copies of many but not all of the interviews were kept in locked files, they were, to my knowledge, never read by the *responsable* or by any government bureaucrat, or even by members of the *equipo*, who saw only their own material or that being discussed.

After leaving Dr. Roa's office, Oscar was followed by several men who identified themselves as State Security agents. Ramón de la Paz, our first *responsable* and a Party member in the Ministry of Foreign Affairs, was with them. They entered and confiscated all our manuscripts, interviews, tapes, personal papers, photographs, and so on. Approximately 10,000 pages were taken, only half of which we had duplicates of in the United States. Among the confiscated papers were all our copies of interviews done in the last three months with family X. In addition, carried off were our only copy of the field notes of the 1946 study of

Melena del Sur, and some manuscripts on Mexico and Puerto Rico. Ignoring my husband's protests and his request for an inventory of what was being taken, they proceeded to the office and the staff house, where they sealed the files and confiscated other documents, including all the completed questionnaires of the Buena Ventura study, totaling approximately 25,000 additional pages.

That evening Comandante Manuel Piñeiro arrived, repeated the charges, and discussed them with us at some length. He said we must remember that Cuba was a small country whose security was constantly threatened by U.S. imperialism, and that as Oscar had never broken his ties with the Ford Foundation, he came under suspicion.

The Comandante went on to advise us that the Dumont and Karol books had been "very irritating" to Fidel and under the circumstances the authorities could take no chances with ours. They were frankly concerned about the "negative data" we were finding in Buena Ventura and the "conflictive" nature of the X family study. Piñeiro therefore questioned the wisdom of publishing these and had decided to examine all of our material. Oscar protested strongly and said the Comandante was making a serious error. Piñeiro said he hoped they *were* mistaken but that would be determined by the kind of books Oscar wrote on Cuba.

When Piñeiro left, Oscar wrote a letter to Celia Sánchez, Minister of the Presidency, member of the Central Committee, and close associate of Castro, requesting an appointment to see the Prime Minister. Within ten minutes after it was delivered to her house, Comandante Piñeiro telephoned to say he had received it and an appointment with Castro would not be possible.

On Saturday Piñeiro visited us once more. He and his assistants had read a good deal of the material on the X family, and he said he was thereby convinced that Oscar was not a CIA agent. He also said he admired our method of interviewing and our thoroughness and patience with even so unworthy a subject as "this counterrevolutionary worm, Señor X." Piñeiro's anger and contempt for our informant, whose story he persisted in seeing as "conflictive," was very disturbing, particularly since the day before, Mr. X had told us he was certain he was under surveillance. When we expressed our concern to Piñeiro and reminded him of the promise of confidentiality and safety for all our subjects, he assured us the information would go no further because his assistants in Security were the best-trained men in Cuba, dedicated to their job. Our informants would not be endangered in any way, he said. "We are not fascists here!"

Before the Comandante left the house that afternoon, we again requested the return of the confiscated materials and were told to submit a list of those most urgently needed. That very evening some of our personal papers and a few manuscripts on the list were returned, with the promise of others before our departure on Monday morning. The second batch was not delivered, and our associate, Douglas Butterworth, remained in Cuba for two additional weeks in the hope of receiving them. However, only a few documents, randomly selected by Security, were given him just before he was scheduled to leave the country.

In retrospect, apart from the charges and the confiscation, we were treated with much patience and restraint. Piñeiro spent a good deal of time explaining the government's action and assuring us they had no wish to harm us personally. They were, of course, aware that we had already taken much of the data out of the country and this was probably an attempt to mollify us. We were urged to stay on as tourists and were even given return-trip plane tickets that were good for one year. More important, Comandante Piñeiro promised to invite us to Cuba in September to discuss the return of the rest of the materials. This promise was never fulfilled.

One week after we left Cuba, we learned by telephone that Mr. X had been arrested for suspicious behavior. Apparently fearing arrest, Mr. X had left his job and gone to live, or, as the government said, to hide, in his mother's house just outside Havana. The authorities denied that the arrest was related to the project and no one else connected with the X family or with the project had been threatened in any way.

The news of the arrest affected us deeply. We felt personally responsible and kept in touch with the X family by telephone and mail. In an effort to have Mr. X released, Oscar tried to contact Fidel Castro and other authorities, still hoping that if he could personally explain the situation, he would be able to resolve the problem. At first he thought Castro had not been properly informed about the project by the men around him, but later Oscar came to accept the view that Castro had full knowledge of what had taken place and that it had been his political decision to scrap the project.

Without having succeeded in freeing Mr. X or saving the project, Oscar died less than six months later. Mr. X, according to my last reliable information in April, 1971, was still a prisoner, although it was hoped at that time he would soon be given a visiting pass and possibly even be released. He had been transferred to a prison farm where he did agricultural labor, mostly cutting cane. He was in good health; his wife, who saw him regularly on visiting days, was receiving an adequate income from the government; and their children were attending school on scholarships.

A letter from Cuba in 1973 informed me that the project *equipo* members were all either teaching or participating in research programs. One was directing a survey and another was taking a doctorate at the University of Havana.

Why was the project ended in this manner when it would only have been necessary to ask us to leave? The immediate, obvious motive was to prevent publication of the data, particularly on the X family, not necessarily because of anti-government statements but to protect a high-ranking leader's public image. In previous research, we had found that family studies and life stories told by even the humblest, least powerful people were often seen as very threatening by those above them. This was true in Mexico, Puerto Rico, in our own country, and now again in Cuba. The range and depth of topics touched upon in the autobiographies, the direct and indirect expression of opinions and attitudes on controversial matters, the reference to public figures and private matters, the involuntary involvement of relatives, friends, neighbors, and other persons whom the informant wishes to talk about, and the simple personal account of daily life with its frustrations, anxieties, and social injustices—all these make the data unpredictable and hazardous, sometimes explosive in effect, with far-reaching repercussions.

The closing of Project Cuba, although triggered by the study of the X family and several other factors, seems to have been also, in part, the result of a general crackdown on foreign intellectuals that summer of 1970. The "turn" in attitude, brought about by serious economic setbacks and the strong criticism from outsiders sympathetic to socialism, has since become the official government policy. At the First National Congress on Education and Culture in Havana, April 23–30, 1971, a strong attack was made on "cultural colonialism" and on those foreign critics who supposedly were implementing it. The Congress's declaration said, "We reject the claims of the Mafia of pseudo-leftist bourgeois intellectuals to become the cultural conscience of society...."[7]

To protect Cubans from exposure to such negative influences, the Congress also declared it to be necessary "to establish a strict system for inviting foreign writers and intellectuals, to avoid the presence of persons whose works or ideology are opposed to the interests of the Revolution, especially in formation of the new generation, and who have participated in ideological diversionist activities encouraging their local flunkeys."

At the close of the Congress, Fidel Castro said, "Now you know it, bourgeois intellectuals and bourgeois libelants, agents of the CIA and intelligence services of imperialism, that is, of the intelligence and espionage services of imperialism: you will not be allowed to come to Cuba! just as UPI and AP are not allowed to come. Our doors will remain closed indefinitely, ad infinitum!"[8]

Apoliticalism was especially denounced in the declaration of the Con-

7. The text of the Declaration on Education and Culture appeared in *Granma Weekly Review*, May 9, 1971, pp. 5–6.
8. The text of Castro's closing speech was reprinted in *ibid.*, pp. 7–9.

gress and was described as "nothing more than a reactionary and shamefaced attitude in the cultural field." To this Fidel Castro added in his closing speech: "... the value of cultural and artistic creations is determined by their usefulness for the people.... Our standards are political."

In the late 1960s many high government officials already held the view that artistic and intellectual skills must be subservient to the needs of the people and the state. By 1969, a time of much personal sacrifice for Cubans, the freedom and privileges extended to Project Cuba caused it to stand out as an exception and probably made it a threat to some individuals or at least a source of resentment and concern. The fact that the exception was granted to a foreigner from a hostile capitalist country only made it more difficult for them to accept. In a sense, the special position of the project helped bring about its end.

In 1972, in a speech on problems of internal security, Raúl Castro Ruz, Vice-Premier, Minister of the Revolutionary Army, and younger brother of Fidel, elaborated upon the general theme of "cultural colonialism" and dangerous foreigners.[9] In this speech, two years after we left Cuba, Oscar, along with others, was portrayed as a secret agent:

> A certain part of the visitors from the capitalist countries—sociologists, professors, newspapermen, sailors, and tourists—must be secret agents or collaborators with the enemy information agencies.
>
> One North American sociologist, now dead, connected to the Ford Foundation, established ties with counterrevolutionary elements before arriving in Cuba. Once here, he carried out sociological studies departing from the proposals he had made to the Cuban authorities. He dealt with 327 informants, among whom were militants of the Party and of the Youth [Union of Young Communists], administrative functionaries, and members of mass organizations, who unconsciously volunteered interesting data. There were also anti-socialists and elements who are enemies of the Revolution who offered it consciously. He availed himself of taped interviews, inquiries, conversations, written reports, pamphlets, and materials he solicited about political organizations, mass organizations, the educational system, and biographical data of our leaders. And he even tried subtly to obtain facts about FAR [Revolutionary Armed Forces] and MININT [Ministry of the Interior].
>
> This isn't the only case of intellectuals who, under the pretext of coming to give lectures or to make specific studies, have conducted political, economic, social, cultural, and military espionage, making use of their progressivist facade. And always, they appear very generous in their relations, very flexible in the face of our difficulties, and very understanding of the circumstances of our revolutionary process. And, as we have said on another occasion, they receive people kindly with good meals, gifts, and drinks, and in that climate of confraternity they criticize the Revolution subtly and they acquire information and they praise the consumer society.

9. The text of this speech is in *Educación*, July–Sept., 1972, pp. 21–35. *Educación* is a journal published in Havana by the Ministry of the Interior.

This has been possible, of course, because they have approached comrades incapable of seeing beyond the outward appearances.

When the conditions agreed upon beforehand become accusations, when standard research techniques are called espionage, and when customary social behavior is described as a facade to dupe unwary citizens, there is little room left for discussion. It is clear from this and from the fate of our project that the freedom needed for our type of broad, open-ended research is not consistent with prevailing Cuban views. This is not to say, however, that other research did not fare better. As a matter of fact, in 1969–70 there were in Cuba several individuals from U.S. and European universities doing studies of economic, education, and housing policy, as well as studies of the Committees for Defense of the Revolution and the People's Courts. To my knowledge, none of them ran into difficulties with the government. In our case, whatever the role of personality and other factors, I believe it is fair to say that the sensitive nature of our research played a large part in the sudden end of the project.

II

When our stay in Cuba was over, we had in our possession a little less than 21,000 pages transcribed from tape-recorded life-history interviews, and approximately 3,500 pages of assistants' reports on special subjects such as budgets, material inventories, genealogies, impressions of the informants and of home environments. These 24,500 pages represented the data gathered in the thirteen-month period of active field work before April, 1970. As we have explained above, all work done after this date, as well as certain earlier materials for which there were no duplicates, were lost to us.

After Oscar's death, I decided to publish the life stories and the Buena Ventura study because they have, in fact, carried out to a limited extent the objectives of the original research design and can, I believe, contribute to a general understanding of life in contemporary Cuba. Preparation of the materials for publication was begun in January, 1971, with the help of a staff that included a project secretary and several editorial assistants, typists, and translators.

In September, 1972, Susan M. Rigdon joined the staff, to organize and write up *Neighbors* and do the difficult work of researching and writing the footnotes for the entire series. In addition, she wrote the Introductions to *Four Men* and *Four Women* and shared with me the work of organizing the editing the life stories of the men and women presented in them.

Some of the materials had to be discarded—unfinished surveys and reports, case histories that were too fragmentary or in which the informants' identities could not be adequately concealed, materials that had been half-confiscated, and so on. The remaining data were translated, edited, and organized to make up this series and several additional publications.[10]

The process of editing the life-history materials is difficult if not impossible to describe without going into tedious detail. In general, we followed the same method used in *The Children of Sánchez* and other family studies. Most of the changes made in the materials were to conceal identities, reduce repetitions, delete the investigator's questions as well as uninformative material, and to bring order and readability to the text. As in all translation and editing, there is some room for error and for the expression of personal judgment, taste, and style. Although we tried to preserve the individuality of expression of each informant, we were less successful for some than for others. Many informants were imprecise about dates and the passage of time; obvious errors in the sequence of personal events were deleted, and other important factual errors were corrected in footnotes.

The separate studies carried out in Cuba will be discussed in the Introduction to each volume. Here we would like to make some general observations that apply to the project as a whole. There were, for example, certain factors within the Cuban system that significantly affected informant-investigator relations. One such factor was the Cuban informants' direct dependence upon the government for jobs, food, housing, and basic services. This was in sharp contrast to non-socialist countries, where our informants, particularly the slum dwellers, depended little upon their governments and received few benefits from them. Their loyalties and dependencies were almost entirely focused upon their families, who were usually in no position to fulfill their most pressing needs. Informants such as these tended to accept an anthropologist who expressed a personal interest in them, and they often saw him or her as a benevolent figure who offered much-needed aid, moral support, and an outlet for expression. In Cuba we did not encounter a need for this type of dependency relationship, and on the whole Cuban informants demonstrated a greater sense of security and self-respect.

In Buena Ventura, too, among those reared in the culture of poverty we found many who were assertive, self-reliant, time-conscious, work-oriented, future-minded. They displayed an unprecedented loyalty to

10. See Douglas Butterworth, "Grass-Roots Political Organization in Cuba: A Case of the Committees for the Defense of the Revolution," in Wayne A. Cornelius and Felicity Trueblood, eds., *Latin American Urban Research: Anthropological Perspectives on Latin American Urbanization*, vol. IV (Beverly Hills, Calif.: Sage Publications, 1974). Also soon to appear is the study of the Buena Ventura community.

the government, which, in effect, had become a kind of father figure to all. They did not need the anthropologist or any other outsider to help them with the basic necessities, or with money, medical advice, work, or education for their children. Although the majority of our informants in Buena Ventura cannot be described as "integrated" in the Revolution (Oscar estimated that only about one-third were), nowhere did we observe the degree of alienation, isolation, despair, or marginality we had seen among the very poor in other countries. Whether Cubans joined the unions, Committees, or other mass organizations as token or participating members, or did not join at all, they knew those groups were ready and eager to accept them, and that there were jobs to be had for the asking.

As a result of their busy work schedules and relative independence, informants in Cuba were less generous in granting us their time. Often some of them could not or would not make or keep appointments or allow for unhurried interviews. It was also true of women, the majority of whom did not hold outside jobs but who spent much time standing in queues and doing household chores without benefit of labor-saving devices. Nevertheless, almost everyone expressed a willingness to cooperate with us, and there was, in fact, remarkably little resistance to answering questions once an interview was under way.

Informants understood that we were there with the blessings of the government and may have felt obligated to work with us. Some may have even believed we were there on official government business, although this did not mean that they responded under coercion or fear. Rather, I would say that because of their positive view of the government, the tendency to identify the project in this way gave informants greater confidence in us. Such an initial response to the investigators as authority figures was not unique to Cuban informants, however, and in most cases was soon replaced by genuinely cordial relations that permitted the establishment of good rapport.

There were, of course, other motives for cooperating with the project, such as a desire to explain the Revolution to the outside world, or because of personal vanity or opportunism. Money, however, was not a motive and we did not pay our informants. Most of them had no great need of it; more important, government officials and the Cuban students on the staff disapproved of such compensation and insisted upon a purely moral motivation for participation in the project. For the same reason and also because of the possible disruptive effect upon the system of rationing, it was not advisable to give substantial gifts. In practice, however, we felt the need to reciprocate in some way, and we occasionally gave informants minor gratuities, such as cigarettes or candy, and coffee to replenish what they served us out of their rations. We also expressed our thanks when we returned from trips to the United States by bringing, like many foreign visitors, small gifts of clothing, transistor pocket radios, flashlights, batteries, vitamins, and other scarce items.

Despite the shortage of goods and the keen competition for certain services, very few Cubans made requests of us, either for material things or for favors. Three middle-class informants and friends asked for books or subscriptions to U.S. professional journals, and four other requests for aid came from people who were confused by the bureaucracy or who did not know how to travel about the city. They specifically asked for help in locating a psychiatrist and for appropriate schools for their problem children. These particular requests posed no problems, but in general, because of the popular emphasis upon egalitarianism, it was important to avoid seeking special treatment for informants.

Finally, was it possible to record an honest, believable life history in socialist Cuba? With the government as a major source of rewards and punishments, how did this affect the Cuban informant's life story? Did he feel the need to present himself as "a revolutionary" or in some other stereotyped role? With every Cuban being urged to become the "new man," that is, to work for the common good and for future generations, for moral rather than material rewards, was this the image we tended to get from the informant? Did he speak in slogans or repeat phrases he might not understand or really believe? To what extent did fear of being labeled "counterrevolutionary" control what an informant said? How did we know when he was being sincere and when he was not?

Taking into consideration the personal, cultural, social, and political limitations that informants everywhere are subject to, and recognizing the special conditions existing in Cuba, we believe the life stories presented here, whatever their other failings, are as honest and revealing as those we have recorded elsewhere. One of the advantages of a long autobiography is that it allows the basic personality and outlook of the informant to emerge, making inconsistencies or false statements stand out by contrast. Wishful thinking, deception, or manipulation may be attempted, but these are difficult stances to maintain. In telling their personal life experiences, informants generally become too caught up in their own emotions to be concerned with systematic cover-up, or with labels and effects.

From the texts it is apparent that our informants expressed themselves on a wide variety of subjects, and even the most ardent revolutionaries spoke out against those things they did not like. No matter how prejudiced or narrow the informant, he or she exposes the reader to a great number of individuals, each with his or her own point of view, adaptations, conflicts, and anxieties about the past, present, and future, and thus to a broader, more balanced picture of life in Cuba.

For the most part, the deficiencies in the material stem not so much from the specific field-work conditions or informants in socialist Cuba as from the limited time available to us. Since it was not possible to do the number of interviews required for each informant, there is considerable variation in the length, depth, and interest of the different life stories. That many of the stories covered the full life span in spite of the abrupt halt of the research was due to our policy of encouraging informants to recount their lives more or less chronologically from birth to the present. Only then did we review the material for clarification and elaboration. A satisfactory story is literally built up through very specific questioning in repeated interviews over a period of months or even years, as in the case of the Mexican family studies. Given a good informant, there is a direct positive relationship between the number of interviews and the depth and quality of the autobiography.

The lack of time in the field also accounts for the absence of a comparative rural community study and of whole family studies. Several family studies were begun, but there is no family in which *all* the members were interviewed. Because these studies were meant to illustrate how revolutionary institutions function on the neighborhood, family, and personal levels, we are especially conscious of shortcomings in information in this area.

The three volumes of this series together contain fifteen long life stories and thirteen short or partial ones. The Buena Ventura study will provide survey data on approximately 100 families. All four of these sources present a cumulative, detailed picture of the impact of the Revolution on a wide variety of Cubans. Each study illustrates different aspects of the great social, economic, and political changes and the effects of these upon individual informants and their families, particularly on the relationship between family backgrounds and levels of participation in the major revolutionary institutions.

The autobiographies are rich in Cuban history as the informants viewed it. They spoke of slavery, the struggle for Cuban independence from Spain, U.S. political and economic penetration, important public figures and events, the conditions that led to the overthrow of Batista, and many of the significant occurrences during and after the Revolution. Because of the many historical references that may be confusing or unknown to readers, we have included in the texts a large number of footnotes, even though the reader may find them intrusive. We have also used footnotes to indicate the significant economic and social changes that have occurred since 1970.

There is, throughout these volumes, much information on a variety of important topics, such as the status of women and children, changes in man-woman relations, racial attitudes, rural life, education, labor, rationing, the different mass organizations, the Roman Catholic Church, Afro-Cuban religions, attitudes toward the U.S.S.R., the United States,

Cuban leaders, and so on. These topics are dealt with in greater detail in some autobiographies than in others, depending upon the experiences and interests of the informants, but by following any one theme through all the volumes, much basic information on the subject can be found.[11]

The inclusion in the texts of many prosaic details on problems of daily life—rationing, buying and selling, household management—reflects our conviction that through such information we get a truer, i.e. more complete, picture of what it is like to live under revolutionary conditions. It is important, too, to see the information in the context of the informant's background and known attitudes and biases; the inclusiveness of the text helps to keep the individuality of each informant in sharper focus.

One of the broader objectives of all of Oscar Lewis's research was to show the wide range of variation in individual behavior and personality and in family types within any one society or community, in order to provide a better basis for comparison and generalization. In 1959 he wrote that "the more homogeneous (and superficial) the picture we get of a single society, the more contrasting will it appear in comparison with other societies. The more we know about the range of behavior within any society, the more readily can we perceive the cross-cultural similarities as well as the basic human similarities."[12] The use of personal histories does just that for Cuba, by helping us to see the rich diversity that makes that country different from other socialist and non-socialist systems, and also that which makes it similar. It prevents us from making easy generalizations and from thinking of the revolutionary process as a uniform experience. Although our sample was relatively small and heavily weighted toward the least-prepared and most-deprived sector of the population, these studies give some appreciation of what the Revolution means to the people as well as an understanding of the internal obstacles to change.

RML

11. A summary of our findings and impressions on these and other topics can be found in an Epilogue to *Neighbors*.

12. "Family Dynamics in a Mexican Village," in *Marriage and Family Living,* Aug., 1959, p. 226.

Acknowledgments

SINCE 1969, WHEN FIELD WORK for this project was begun in Cuba, we have incurred many obligations which we would like to acknowledge. We thank the Ford Foundation for the original research grant and for a subsequent grant to write up the data. We also thank the University of Illinois Graduate College Research Board and the Center for International Comparative Studies for additional financial support, and the university's Department of Anthropology for office space and other services. We are grateful to the Cuban Academy of Sciences for its early interest in the project and to the many Cuban citizens and government officials whose cooperation made the research possible.

The completion of this series involved many people whose contributions will be acknowledged in the volumes in which they appear. For *Four Men* we would like first to express our gratitude to the four informants and the members of their families who so generously participated in the research. We would also like to thank the following persons: Maida Donate, Rafael Salinas Madrigal, Enrique Vignier Mesa, Elsa Barreras López, Nisia Aguero Benítez, and Paola Costa, for interviewing one or more of the informants presented here; Dr. Alilí Jordán, psychologist with the Instituto de Neurofisiología in Havana, for administering psychological tests; Muna Muñoz Lee, for translating the bulk of the Spanish materials, and Asa Zatz and Claudia Beck, for additional translations; Deborah Kolditz Vera, Cecilia Behague, and Theodore Macdonald, for organizing some of the Spanish materials. For the preliminary editing and organizing of the long stories, we are grateful to Cecilia Coles, Barbara J. Sewell, Binnie Williams, and Jane McClellan; for other editing we thank Elizabeth Spence, Phoebe Stone, and Phyllis Murphy Hobe; and for the difficult work of changing the original names to pseudonyms and for many clerical tasks, Nina Díaz-Peterson.

For their skillful typing we thank Lorraine Glennon, Barbara Anderson, Josephine Ippolito, Shirley Lee, and Betty Victor. Transcription of the original Spanish tapes was completed in Cuba and we are grateful to

Carmen Graxirena and to the several Cuban women who performed this difficult task.

For reading early versions of three life stories and for making helpful suggestions, we thank Jorge Cela. We would also like to thank Professor John O. Stewart for his comments on the story of Lázaro Benedí Rodríguez. For their many critical comments and helpful suggestions on all three volumes in the series we are very grateful to Diane Levitt Gottheil, Susan Welch, and Alan J. Booth. We would especially like to express our deep gratitude to Fern M. Hartz, secretary to Oscar Lewis since 1959 and to the Cuba research project since its inception. Finally, we wish to thank Elizabeth Dulany of the University of Illinois Press for her painstaking editing of the final manuscript.

Introduction

IN 1961, ON HIS FIRST TRIP to Cuba after the Revolution, Oscar Lewis wrote (in unpublished notes), "I am primarily interested in how the poor react to this kind of revolution." Basically, that is what this book is about. It contains the life stories of four Cuban men raised in poverty, three of them from Las Yaguas, a well-known Havana shantytown. The fourth man lived in a poor barrio in a small town in Oriente Province until he was eleven and then spent the next ten years in Havana, moving from one poor barrio to another.

As indicated in the Foreword, Lewis's interest in studying the poor of Las Yaguas began in 1946, during his first visit to Cuba. He was unable to return, however, until August, 1961, at which time Las Yaguas was already in the process of being dismantled as part of the Revolution's massive slum-clearance program.[1] Residents were being relocated in groups of 100 or more families, preparatory to total eradication of the slum. In his notes, Lewis described his visit to the area and some of the changes he found.

> The thing that impressed me most of all is the slum in Havana called Las Yaguas, one of the worst I have ever seen. It consists of approximately 1,000 shacks and is primarily a Negro slum. It is built on a hill and the houses are at various levels [see pls. 1–6]. I went there with a guide from the Department of Education. He was born in Havana and had lived there all his life, but had never been to Las Yaguas. He was frightened stiff and thought that before we went into the slum we should somehow identify ourselves. So we went to see some members of a Defense Committee[2] who lived in a nearby barrio.
>
> Afterwards, as we walked through the endless alleyways of open sewage and filth [in Las Yaguas], and [saw] kids who still seemed to me to be undernourished, with swollen bellies, and all the rest you see in any slum

1. In 1963, the Cuban anthropologist Aida García Alonso did a study of Las Yaguas published under the title *Manuela, la Mexicana* (Havana: Casa de las Americas, 1968).

2. In 1961 the Committees for Defense of the Revolution (CDR) functioned primarily as a people's militia or vigilance organization; their activities and responsibilities have since been greatly expanded and are discussed at length in the life stories. (See Benedí, n. 80.)

anywhere, we met a man who was rather well dressed. He was there for the
government, doing a census of illiterates, and he was very suspicious of my
presence. He stopped and wanted [to see our] identification. The guide I
was with was dressed in civilian clothes and [had been] driving an unmarked
car, but when he showed his identification, everything was all right.

It is interesting that it wasn't one of the inhabitants of the slum who
stopped me.... The first thing they asked was whether I was Czech or
Russian. When I told them I was from the United States, their first reaction
was one of great surprise. They wanted to know why I was there, but they
let us go on.

I tried to get some notion of how long people had lived there. The slum
seemed to date back to 1925, and some people have lived there all those
years.[3] The houses are just little shacks, made of tin, wood, cardboard, and
what they called *yaguas* (bark from the royal palm tree) [see pl. 7]. What
amazed me about the whole thing was that each of the families—I must
have talked to about eight or ten of them—spoke with great hope about the
future, with great love for Fidel Castro, telling me about the plans for new
housing for them and saying that now they had no unemployment. For the
first time in my twenty years of research among the poor, I heard no gripes
against the government leaders. I have never experienced that in a slum
before. The usual reaction, if you ask them "What do you think about the
government?" is, "*Ay,* they are all thieves. They don't do anything for us;
they don't help." In any slum in Mexico, if you ask about the PRI[4] they tell
you that it isn't worth a damn, that there are no honest elections, that
everybody knows what the results will be, and so on. I felt I'd like to go back
to Cuba to compare Las Yaguas with a Mexican slum.

The general attitude in Las Yaguas was very hopeful and positive, and
later on, when I saw the nursery school they had built on top of the hill
(Loma del Burro), a beautiful new school, I could understand why [see pls.
8–9]. Toward the upper part of the settlement, there was also a temporary
cement-block building that was the center of the literacy program [see pls.
10–11]. I talked to a number of teachers and volunteer high school students
who were carrying out *alfabetización;* they said they had "alphabetized"
eighty people in the past two and a half months. After spending about two
hours there, talking to the schoolteachers and watching the children, the
contrast between this lovely school and the filthy slum was just awful.

The president of the Defense Committee in Las Yaguas was a fascinating
old Negro who spoke fluently and with wisdom and dignity. He told me his
father had been a slave. This man was a wonderful character. I enjoyed him
very much and felt he was a capital subject for a life history. I asked him
about the new housing that was going to be built. I still didn't know how
they were going to select these families. Were they all going to be put
together in some new location? He said no, a hundred families at a time
would be resettled among different housing projects. Then he gave his
explanation of why they were going to be split up: "You know, when there is
poverty, there is much hatred among neighbors."

Then they took me to see the new houses [see pls. 12–13]. It was a
settlement of about 120 homes, all of which were being built with govern-

3. In 1969 it was learned that some informants had moved to Las Yaguas as early as 1920
and that a number of houses had already been built on this tract of land by that time.

4. *Partido Revolucionario Institucional* (Institutional Revolutionary Party), the dominant
party of Mexico.

1 Las Yaguas, overlooking a main street where men are gathered in front of a local store, 1961.

2   Entrance to Las Yaguas.

3 A street in Las Yaguas.

4 Las Yaguas, looking north toward Havana.

5 Another street in Las Yaguas.

6 Las Yaguas street scene.

7   Houses constructed of *yaguas* and scrap materials.

8   Nursery school built in Las Yaguas after the Revolution.

9   Nursery school (interior).

10 Literacy center in Las Yaguas.

11 Literacy Campaign slogan painted on roof of Las Yaguas house.

12 New homes under construction for Las Yaguas residents in August, 1961.

13 Homes in another housing development in 1969; occupied by former Las Yaguas residents since 1963.

ment funds, with engineers and architects supplied by the government, but with volunteer labor from the slum. The buildings were in very good taste, I thought; the poured concrete and the way they worked with color was very beautiful. The new settlement had been going up for about seven months and was still not inhabited. They said it would be another four months before the families could move in.

When government representatives began making the housing survey in Las Yaguas, many residents, fearing they would be left homeless, claimed they were content where they were and did not want to move. To them government was government, and it had never done anything for them before. Moreover, in the 1940s there had been many attempts to evict them, sometimes with promises of other housing or small amounts of money. To add to their skepticism, it appeared at the outset of the new government that Las Yaguas residents were to be regarded as outcasts and criminals, as they had been in the past. In February, 1959, just a month after the Revolution, police came into the barrio, rounded up all the men—"herding us into trucks" as one informant said—and took them to the nearest precinct station. (Evidently no women were arrested.)

The government was primarily interested in ending arms and drug trafficking in the barrio, and after some arrests were made, most of the men were released. By razing the slum and dispersing the residents throughout the city, the government was not only trying to make decent housing available to everyone but was also attempting to break up the informal social networks which were potential arms markets for saboteurs and which the government felt fostered a climate conducive to criminal and "antisocial behavior."

It was not until Las Yaguas residents actually began to work on construction of the new developments that they believed they would receive new housing. The Self-Help and Mutual Aid program (*Esfuerzo Propio y Ayuda Mutua*), under whose authority the housing projects were begun, was designed to help eliminate all of Havana's shantytown slums, as well as the worst slums in other Cuban cities. It provided credit toward the purchase price of the new homes for those families who participated in the construction. All members of a family who could work a minimum of twenty-four hours each week were eligible.[5] Remuneration was at the rate of 2.50 *pesos* a day,[6] plus lunch and dinner, and credit for the hours worked. The remainder of the purchase price (or all of it for those who did not work on the construction of the homes) was paid in monthly installments set at not more than 10 percent of household income.

In 1962 Las Yaguas families began moving to the first of the com-

---

5. *Cuba Review*, Mar., 1975, p. 6.
6. Cuban currency was maintained by the Castro government at the pre-1959 rate of 1 *peso* = 1 U.S. dollar until 1974, when the rate was changed to 1.25 *pesos* = 1 U.S. dollar.

pleted projects. Relocation continued for a year and a half, dispersing
residents to the different housing projects in groups ranging from 100
to 126 families. Another 100 families received housing through the
Urban Reform Office, which was responsible for allocating all formerly
private urban rental property as well as some vacated or confiscated
housing.

Each housing project consisted of a cluster of dwellings, for the most
part single-family units, built within an established middle-class residential neighborhood. In deciding to build low-cost housing in such neighborhoods, the Cuban government apparently faced opposition similar to
that confronting such projects in the United States. Fidel Castro warned
those middle-class critics of the projects that if they were not able to live
next door to former slum dwellers they should find someplace else to live.
Despite Castro's moral support for the people of Las Yaguas, the government had approved architectural designs for the developments that
tended to enhance some residents' feelings of isolation from the larger
neighborhood. The Buena Ventura project, for example, was architec-
turally distinct from the older section of the *reparto,* which was located on
a rise surrounding, and literally looking down upon, the new houses.
Some of the newcomers claimed that the old residents, with whom they
shared a grocery store and some community facilities, received them with
hostility. One informant said, "Up the hill they call this *Las Yaguas de
mampostería.*" In other words, although the houses in the Buena Ventura
project were made of concrete, the people had not changed. Six years
after moving to the new community, many of those from Las Yaguas
were still made to feel like intruders.

Las Yaguas had been even more of an enclave, but it had been largely
self-contained, and its residents had almost no social contact with
middle-class Cubans. With a population of 3,412, Las Yaguas had been
in itself a small town.[7] The community was built on a separate 6,250-
square-meter tract of land that had been part of an abandoned farm.
When the former owners tried to evict the Las Yaguas residents, the
latter, with the help of university students, fought in the courts and won
claim to the land. Henceforth the land belonged to the squatters. This,
together with an awareness of their isolation, shared social status, and
dependence upon one another, helped create a real, though amorphous,
sense of community that did not develop in Buena Ventura.

I

Lázaro Benedí Rodríguez,[8] the first of the "Four Men" of this volume,
was the elderly Defense Committee president whom Lewis had encoun-

---

7. The 1960 census data are quoted in García Alonso, *Manuela,* p. 11.
8. In Cuba (and most Spanish-speaking countries), children take the surnames of both
parents, with the father's name coming first. The mother's name is sometimes dropped.

tered in Las Yaguas in 1961 and described as "a capital subject for a life history." In 1969 Lewis located Benedí in the Bolívar housing project and asked him to participate in the research project. He was more than willing to have his life story recorded and published, and even expressed a desire to have it appear under his true name. He made every effort to keep his appointments, dressing for them in a starched cotton shirt-jacket and his best straw hat. Slow-moving and dignified, he projected an image of a purposeful man with a sense of his own importance. When telling his life story he did not like to be interrupted and tended to lecture and to intellectualize, using large words and formal, pompous expressions. Although he rambled and repeated himself, his memory was remarkably good.

Benedí was born in 1900 in Cayo Hueso, a poor working-class neighborhood of Havana. His parents, both born into slavery, lived together for thirty-seven years and had nineteen children, nine of whom died in infancy. Benedí's father was a coachman and had a small carriage-repair shop where he also built and sold new carriages. Benedí dropped out of school in the third grade, at age twelve, to work as a houseboy for 5 *pesos* a month. In 1915, after working three years as an apprentice to an ironsmith, he learned carpentry, a trade he practiced for the next five decades.

In 1933 Benedí was evicted from his one-room apartment for non-payment of rent and he moved to Las Yaguas, where land was rent-free and a few *pesos* were enough to build a small shanty. During the twenty-eight years he lived there, he came to be, as one of his wives said, a "top dog" in the barrio. This was due in part to the fact that he read books and newspapers, knew something of current events, history, and political philosophy, and in part to his active involvement in Afro-Cuban religion. This was especially important because Las Yaguas, a predominantly black slum, was a stronghold of the Afro-Cuban sects.

Benedí worked with Communist Party members in Las Yaguas (but was never a member himself) and joined a number of ad hoc political groups and movements. Occasionally in Las Yaguas, there arose land disputes and other crises that affected the barrio as a whole and could be resolved only by dealing with municipal or national authorities. At those times, Benedí and a few others with political contacts outside of Las Yaguas were the only persons the slum dwellers could rely upon to help them.

Arrested several times for his political activities, Benedí, under questioning, always denied being a communist. He was usually released after a short detention, although at the time of the 1935 strike he served six months in jail. The formal charge was violation of the public-health code, but apparently he was detained for discussing the strike with workers in Las Yaguas. All in all Benedí was not a revolutionary; he eschewed violence for the tactics of the liberal reformer. He organized demonstrations and self-help groups, wrote letters of protest, and relied on the courts and the electoral process. He supported the old Communist Party (PSP) when it chose the path of cooperation with the Batista government and of withholding public support from Castro until his victory was at hand. That Benedí was a "book radical" and a dreamer is evident in the naiveté which, over a period of thirty years, allowed him to believe that each new Cuban dictator would live up to his promises.

Predictably, given his faith in organized political activity, Benedí had been integrated in the Revolution since 1959. He joined the militia, did guard duty and voluntary productive labor, and helped establish Las Yaguas' provisional Committee for Defense of the Revolution, serving as its first president. As head of the Committee's Education Front, he helped with the campaign against illiteracy in 1961, and formed a program of his own to encourage neighborhood children to stay in school.

Benedí said that his political work in Las Yaguas was greatly aided by his "power as a *santero*," a priest-practitioner of *santería* (*Regla Ocha*), an Afro-Cuban religious cult. He was also a baptized Roman Catholic and was, at one time or another in his life, associated with two other Afro-Cuban sects, *Palo Monte* or *Mayombé* (*Regla Conga*) and the all-male *Abacuá* society. As a *santero* he had participated in many rituals with his neighbors and had worked as a diviner and curer, usually for a donation of a few *pesos* or *centavos,* or just a cup of coffee. His reputation for working cures gained him entrance to many homes in the barrio and gave him an audience for his political ideas. As he said, "You can make a lot of friends by trying to help others."

As a husband and father Benedí had little success. He had six free-union marriages, none lasting longer than five years, although he had hoped to spend his life with one woman. His two sons, one born in 1923 during his first marriage, the other in 1948 during his fourth, were a disappointment to him. His relationship with them began to deteriorate when they did poorly in school, and as they grew older he was often not on speaking terms with them. Both sons went through periods of juvenile delinquency, and the younger one was twice sentenced to prison farms. A daughter was born to his second wife, Eloisa Bermúdez, but he denied paternity, saying the girl was too light-skinned to be his. Because Eloisa had worked as a prostitute, at least until the time of her marriage to Benedí, it is possible that there was a question of paternity.

Benedí, like the other men in this volume, was an undisguised sexist. He showed little interest in women except in service to men, for sexual satisfaction, childbearing, and homemaking. He was a very jealous man and watched his wives closely, although he never expressed himself with physical violence. He was opposed to women (particularly his wives) working outside the home, and he was against birth control. Despite this,

Benedí was quite timid in his relations with women and was attracted to those whom he felt he could dominate intellectually and "improve." He married two prostitutes, both of whom were ill at the time and unable to care for themselves. Three of his other four wives had been abandoned and/or left with small children and little or no money to support them. His main assets in courting were the security he offered through his home and a steady, however small, income.

Benedí was himself dominated by his mother until her death. She was a harsh disciplinarian who left him in a state of permanent intimidation. He allowed his mother to intrude in his personal affairs well into his adult life and reported that during his first marriage she presided over all his marital quarrels, as "judge, advocate, and prosecutor."

The voices of four of Benedí's six wives are included in his story. The women were not sought out as subjects for independent life stories and we have used only those parts of their accounts that add perspective to Benedí's autobiography. In general, the women respected Benedí's work and standing in the barrio, his stability and lack of "vices," and they especially admired his ability to speak well. Three of the four wives interviewed, however, complained about him as a sexual partner, about his jealousy, and about his tendency to lecture and look down on them. Overall, the women presented images of themselves that differed from Benedí's, exposing a certain lack of sensitivity on his part to their true feelings about their relationships with him.

Benedí's sixth union, to Amalia Carranza, was in its third year at the time of the interviews. This marriage was strictly one of convenience for both. Amalia, a short, thin, black woman of forty-six, was deeply involved in Afro-Cuban religion, and as a *santera* followed the practice of covering her head with a kerchief or turban. During interviews Amalia was cheerful and expressed herself in a livelier, more direct style than Benedí. She was active in the CDR, serving as finance chairman and in the Public Health Front, and she was also a member of the Federation of Cuban Women. She frequently volunteered for agricultural labor and would have liked a regular, paid job but did not apply for one because Benedí was opposed to it.

In his seventieth year Benedí was ordered by a doctor to retire from his job. He was also removed from his position as CDR block organizer because the Committee believed he could no longer keep pace with the demands of the work. Having lost his positions of responsibility and authority, it is quite possible that at the time of the interviews Benedí was experiencing a sense of inadequacy, even failure. This must have been intensified by the fact that it came as those around him seemed to be gaining a greater sense of efficacy. With so many of his neighbors becoming incorporated into revolutionary organizations and emerging as social and political activists, Benedí's skills were rapidly becoming less unique and his status as a community leader was diminished.

Benedí was not born into desperation poverty, but neither was opportunity knocking on his door. He seemed, however, to have had sufficient
resources to keep him out of a shantytown like Las Yaguas. Benedí was
intelligent and wanted to learn; he had a skill and believed in working
hard and steadily. A cautious man, he was not given to excesses such as
heavy gambling or drinking. But under the old system, Benedí might
never have significantly improved his economic position. Being black was
a significant barrier for him, especially to his political aspirations, and the
twenties and thirties were not good years for Cubans who wanted to
work their way upward, or even to hold their own economically. The
"dance of the millions" crisis, which brought chaos to the sugar industry
and the Cuban economy, was followed by the Great Depression.

Although these economic conditions may have forced Benedí into the
slum, it is not equally clear that they were responsible for his staying
there until 1962. The longer he lived in the barrio and the more firmly
he established himself as a community leader, the more he retreated
from life outside the slum. During his first years in Las Yaguas, Benedí
found most of his jobs in workshops outside the slum, but by the 1950s
(and until the Revolution) he was doing only such carpentry work as he
could find within it. Having established himself there as a community
leader, Benedí may have realistically concluded that he could never find
similar status in the larger society, and therefore he may have chosen to
remain a "big fish in a small pond."

Although Benedí lived among Las Yaguas residents, defended them
against attacks from outside the community, and remained deeply
rooted in black culture, many of his basic values—formal education,
hard work, and the need for a defined social order and central political
institutions—were those of the dominant culture. Straddling both worlds
as he did, Benedí gave the appearance, prior to the Revolution, of being
a professional poor man. In 1970 this exceedingly complex man was still
living in two worlds, with one foot in the realm of "scientific socialism"
and one in the realm of superstition and mysticism.

II

Alfredo Barrera Lordi was a tense man of medium height and weight,
olive skin, and dark brown hair and eyes. During interviews he rarely
relaxed and sometimes complained of severe headaches. Although he
appeared to be wary at times, he seemed to value his contact with the
reseach project and made an effort to keep his appointments. Barrera was
born in Las Yaguas in 1932 and at the time of our study was living in
Buena Ventura, which was the subject of a community study by Lewis and
his staff from March, 1969, to June, 1970.[9] Barrera was the eldest of the

9. See the Foreword for a discussion of this research.

eight surviving children of his parents' free-union marriage, and in addition had three half-sisters and one half-brother. Barrera's father, also named Alfredo, was a mulatto; his mother, Argentina Lordi, was the daughter of immigrants from Sicily and the United States. Argentina's marriage to a man of Negro ancestry caused a bitter split in her mother's family, but the union lasted from 1930 until Barrera's death, of cirrhosis of the liver, in 1954. Although an alcoholic, old Alfredo Barrera was a steady worker, mayor of Las Yaguas, and, by the unanimous agreement of his wife and children, a good husband and father. Old Barrera worked as a janitor at the nearby La Corona cigar factory, where he collected discarded *yaguas* used for packing and transported them by horse and cart to Las Yaguas. There he added to his income by selling the *yaguas* for building materials and by helping construct new houses and move furniture. When times were hardest, Argentina Lordi worked as a seamstress and laundress.

On his father's side young Alfredo was part of a close-knit family that included his two aunts, Constancia and Dalia. His Aunt Constancia had worked her way out of Las Yaguas and later started a small business in her home, selling canteen lunches to workers at the cigar factory. When his father was ill or out of work, young Alfredo's aunts helped support the family, so there was always enough money for the most basic essentials. Like his aunts, Alfredo wanted very much to get ahead, and from childhood on felt great shame at his association with the slum community.

For a time in his youth Barrera was convinced that old Alfredo was not his real father, and in the initial taping of his autobiography he represented himself as the son of his mother's first husband, a white man. This fantasy apparently had its origin in teasing by his mother and sisters that he was too light-skinned to be the son of a mulatto,[10] and that he had been found in a garbage can. Revenge against his mother was undoubtedly a factor in the misinformation given in Barrera's early interviews. Throughout his story he maintained a stance of unrelenting hostility and resentment toward her, constructing a caricature of her as a mother that was rejected by every other member of the family interviewed.

For her part, Alfredo's mother, Argentina Lordi, whose voice is included in Barrera's story, dismisses her son as "crazy." Señora Lordi, fifty-eight, was a small, spry, swarthy woman with the same tense appearance as her son. She was a *santera* of the *santería* cult and usually dressed in white, with a white kerchief tied, turban-style, about her head. Except for participating in religious meetings, Señora Lordi rarely left her home. She was proud of her housekeeping and of the new house she had

10. The source of this information was Barrera's sister Angela, whose interview is not included in this account.

received in the Algeria project, where she lived with her fourth husband and her youngest daughter. The fact that she had married twice after the death of old Alfredo was another source of discord with her son. As an informant Señora Lordi was decisive and self-confident, but she tended to be short of speech and to regard what she said as definitive.

Alfredo Barrera had dropped out of Roman Catholic primary school at age fourteen after having failed third grade several times. He left Las Yaguas to live with his aunts, for whom he was working part-time, delivering lunch pails to their customers in the cigar factory. In addition he shined shoes, sold newspapers and bottles, and worked as a cook in a restaurant. From 1954 to 1959 he worked primarily as a plasterer for a construction company.

Prior to the triumph of the Revolution, Barrera was marginally involved with the activities of the Popular Socialist Party (the old Communist Party), which he claims to have joined in 1956. In this he was influenced by his uncle's many communist friends, who gave him Marxist literature to read, and also by a cousin, who was killed by Batista's police in 1956. Through a friend Barrera became involved on the periphery of the Havana underground, running errands and buying guns and ammunition for them.[11] However, there is reason to believe he performed the latter service primarily for personal profit, since there is nothing in Barrera's story to indicate he was in any way committed to ideology or principle.

Barrera's political ambivalence is reflected in his attitude toward the present Cuban government. His positive observations about the Revolution were invariably offset by positive comments about the United States, just as he offset his favorable impressions of Cuban leaders with remarks about their shortcomings and failures. He was only nominally integrated in the Revolution. He belonged to the Committee but was inactive, stood guard with the militia only when he could not get out of it, and in general did no more than the "officially designated" duties. He was a volunteer in the 1960 cane harvest for a short period but found the work too difficult and never went again. According to Barrera, in 1967 he was sent to work on a construction project in Oriente Province "to punish me for complaining."

Barrera married for the first time in 1958, when he was twenty-six. It is indicative of his embarrassment at having grown up in the slum that he

---

11. That there was ample opportunity to buy guns in Las Yaguas was made clear in a 1968 interview Oscar Lewis had with a former Las Yaguas resident who had been imprisoned for selling arms in Havana after the Revolution. According to this informant, prior to the Revolution soldiers and policemen in need of money sometimes came into Las Yaguas to sell their weapons to certain local residents who made a small business of arms-dealing. To use the informant's example, a pistol might be bought for as little as 5 *pesos* and then resold to one of the many rival underground political organizations for as much as 40.

represented his first wife, Martita Puyada, as a country girl he had met at a village fiesta in Matanzas. In fact, Martita had spent part of her life in Las Yaguas, and it was there, according to her grandfather, that Alfredo met her. After their marriage in a civil ceremony, the couple lived first in Las Yaguas with Martita's grandfather, then in the small town where her maternal relatives lived. In 1962, shortly after the birth of their second child, Martita died in a tuberculosis sanitarium and Barrera moved back to Havana, boarding his two sons in Las Yaguas with Esperanza Llera, a friend of his sister's. In 1963 Alfredo also moved in with Esperanza, becoming her husband in free union. Both of Barrera's wives, like his mother, were spiritists and actively involved in the *santería* sect.

In 1970 Barrera was living with Esperanza Llera in the Buena Ventura house she and her family had received through the relocation program. Barrera himself did not receive a house, because at the time the government assigned new housing he had already bought a house in Matanzas Province. Because Alfredo and Esperanza have never legally married, he has no claim to ownership of her house, although he has established some rights of residency. Should the couple ever want to separate, it would probably be impossible for Barrera to be evicted.

Alfredo Barrera and Esperanza Llera had three children together, in addition to two each from their previous marriages. Their household of twelve also included two of Esperanza's brothers and one sister, all listed in the family ration book although they lived there only occasionally. Barrera worked at various plastering and maintenance jobs from 1963 until 1967, when he got his current job as a garbage collector at 200 *pesos* a month. Esperanza, a member of the Committee and the Federation of Cuban Women, was not employed outside their home.

In 1970 Barrera was unhappy in his marriage and in his work, and was in many ways frustrated by the revolutionary ethic. The selflessness, austerity, hard work, and service to the community demanded by the new order were not Barrera's strong points. In the past, almost all of his energies and creativity had gone into trying to get his "fair share." In this pursuit Barrera was sometimes imaginative, certainly cunning, and almost always a good provider for his family. Of the three Las Yaguas men in this volume, he was the only one to get out of the slum on his own initiative.

Under the new system it was more difficult for Barrera to put his kind of ambition to work to improve his economic position. He could not understand—or perhaps he had not resigned himself to the fact—that his old hustler's tricks would not work under the new government, at least not easily or without great risk. For example, his plan for making extra money through the sale of counterfeit U.S. travelers' checks backfired when the 1961 currency exchange went into effect, leaving him unable to exchange several thousand *pesos*.

In the 1940s and 1950s Barrera had learned that in his impoverished position he stood little chance of getting ahead except by trying to beat the system. Despite this, he preferred the old system because he believed it was one he understood and one in which his talents were of some use to him. Although the new government was working for him to the extent of trying to ensure him full employment and basic material needs, Barrera, who trusted no one but himself, was unwilling to sacrifice the little independence his entrepreneurial skills gave him in exchange for complete dependence on the state. The Revolution offered him a solution to his problems, a remedy for his malady, but he was not willing or able to take the cure. He had no interest in investing his energy in long-range efforts to improve his future, such as going back to school or learning a new skill. He wanted most to improve his present. Unlike Benedí, Barrera cared little for the welfare of society at large. His basic approach to every undertaking was to ask, "What's in it for me?"

The Revolution did not make Alfredo Barrera the way he is—his character was well developed before 1959—but through decisions on the degree to which it will help, punish, or just tolerate or ignore men and women like Barrera, the government does set limits on the extent to which he can continue in his old way of life. Barrera's behavior, which included absenteeism, changing jobs without permission, black-marketeering, illegal slaughter of animals, avoidance of civic obligations, and general complaining, was well within the realm of what the government considered "antisocial behavior," yet he had never faced forced rehabilitation in a prison or work camp. During the first decade of the Revolution, the government, of necessity, tolerated at least some small-scale black-market activity and some absenteeism. Since 1970, however, they have cracked down on both by passing an anti-loafing law in 1971, and by raising prices of some consumer goods and extending amortization payments for housing in order to absorb the excess cash in circulation. To further control the black market, tighter controls were placed on food grown on private plots. Fear of prosecution under these laws, however, would probably not in itself be enough to deter Barrera or others like him who had lived a good part of their lives in defiance of the law.

In 1959, when the police made large-scale arrests in Las Yaguas, they sifted out the hard-core criminal element and released the remaining men. The government apparently hoped that given a start in a new life, with the help of mass organizations and the threat of severe sanctions, those who had been on the margins of criminality would not drift back into it. Beyond that, what they did with their lives was largely a question of personal initiative. But employment, housing, and educational opportunities are not in themselves sufficient to bring men and women like Alfredo Barrera within the mainstream of socialist life and morality.

Some personal assistance, guidance, and rehabilitation are needed. This the government may clearly understand, but with far-ranging social and economic objectives and limited resources, the Revolution has placed primary emphasis on the development of children, who are, Guevara said, "the malleable clay from which the new man can be shaped without any of the old faults."[12]

As of 1970 Barrera still did not show any inclination toward self-improvement. He felt thwarted and was diverting his best qualities—imagination and initiative—into unethical and/or illegal activities. It is possible that, allowing for his past, the government will overlook indefinitely his illegal activities, so long as they are minor and without ideological content.

Alfredo Barrera is a deeply neurotic and confused man. He felt rejected by his family, was hostile to his mother, and was very aggressive and self-serving in all his relationships, save, perhaps, for his children. While he was viciously critical of others, he was very defensive about his own behavior. This has resulted in a number of contradictions in his autobiography; some we have clarified in footnotes, and some are countered by the voices of his mother and his elder half-sister, Anita Valverde Lordi. Many disparities still remain, and to remove them would have been to make Barrera a different man than he is. We believe, however, that Barrera's life and his personality are accurately portrayed in his story and that the fate of such a man is an important part in any accounting of the Revolution.

III

Nicolás Salazar Fernández, thirty-two, was, like Alfredo Barrera, met by project staff members while taking a census of the Buena Ventura housing project. Salazar, a thin, pale man who appeared to be in poor health, was born in Las Yaguas in 1938, and with the exception of two years spent in a neighboring barrio, lived in the slum until it was razed. His father was an unskilled laborer who for a time had earned about 2 *pesos* a day working in construction and as a car washer and chauffeur. When Nicolás was about eight, his mother abandoned him and his three brothers. She continued to live in Las Yaguas with her third husband but showed little interest in her children and took no responsibility for raising them. Nicolás and his brothers lived with their father, who remarried and eventually had three more children.

About a year after Nicolás's mother had left him, his father sold his

12. George Lavan, ed., *Che Guevara Speaks: Selected Speeches and Writings* (New York: Merit, 1967), p. 135.

voting card to a local *político* to get Nicolás and his brother Ernesto into a boarding school. It was there, Nicolás said, that he learned "correct manners," how to eat at a table, use utensils, brush his teeth, etc. Six months after they enrolled, the politician was out of office, the boys were out of school, and their father had lost his construction job. From that date, in 1948, until 1959 Salazar's father was a beggar, and because small children often fared better than adults, he forced his sons to beg with him. Nicolás was deeply humiliated, but when he refused to beg he was beaten by his father.

At ages twelve and thirteen respectively, Nicolás and Ernesto were arrested for sleeping in doorways in the Havana business district, where they went each day to shine shoes. They were sent to Torrens Reformatory for one year, then transferred to the Casa de Beneficencia, an orphan asylum which, although very regimented, was cleaner and more benevolent than the reformatory. According to Salazar's account, the Beneficencia was almost pleasant. It was here that he received most of the little formal education he had.

When he was sixteen Salazar lapsed into a period of passivity and severe depression during which he was unable to look for work. He fed himself by scavenging food from the streets of the outdoor market. It was only with the help of a neighbor that Salazar was able to begin working, collecting and selling bottles. Later he peddled flowers and homemade candy and worked in a restaurant. He also lived, in part, off the earnings of his first wife, a Las Yaguas prostitute. Soon after the Revolution, at age twenty-two, he got his first steady, full-time job as a kitchen helper with a government reforestation project in Pinar del Río. During the following five years he worked harder and more steadily than ever before in his life, but he continued his practice of walking away from work that did not suit him, and in 1962 even returned to selling bottles for a year.

Salazar's integration in the Revolution began in 1960, when he joined the militia and volunteered to stand guard duty. After moving to Buena Ventura in 1963 he became very active in the Committees for Defense of the Revolution, first as chairman of the Public Health Front and later as finance chairman. His story contains a good firsthand description of the way in which block Committees were first organized, and of the general malaise that overcame much of the CDR organization during the preoccupation with the 10-million-ton sugar harvest in 1969. Salazar also volunteered for productive labor, and in 1966, 1967, and 1968 signed up to cut sugar cane, twice staying the full harvest season (January-June). After 1965 Salazar took a job with the Carpentry Enterprise, became a fairly stable worker, and was promoted to carpenter's apprentice, although he still had an absentee problem.

Prior to his present marriage Salazar had three free-union marriages, two to Las Yaguas prostitutes and one brief liaison with an abandoned mother of six. Since late 1966 Salazar had been living with Flora Mir Monte, age twenty-three, who was a niece of his stepmother and a native of Guines, a small town outside Havana. Flora had borne two children and was pregnant with a third at the time she married Salazar; at least two of the children were by her elder brother Cirilo. This was the only confirmed case of incest we encountered during the course of the project, and it had occurred not in Buena Ventura but in Guines, in rural Havana Province. On learning of the relationship, their parents ordered Flora and her brother to leave their home, whereupon they moved in with their Aunt Ramona, who was married to Salazar's father.

We have used excerpts from Flora Mir's life story to establish her personality more clearly and to present her own account of her rather controversial life. In her interviews Flora Mir showed no interest in, and little understanding of, anything beyond her immediate needs. She spoke almost exclusively and without inhibition about sex, clothes, and food, revealing a childhood of unusual indulgence by her parents despite their poverty.

According to Salazar, Flora Mir worked as a prostitute after she went to live with her aunt and his father. Flora, however, apparently accepted and even sought out these relationships with men, whether or not she was paid. In fulfilling her needs, Flora was not restrained by any moral standards or judgments; she seemed unable to understand or absorb them, and in this sense they were largely irrelevant to her life.

Flora once left Nicolás for another man; when she returned to her husband, he tried to gain complete control over her daily life by using physical punishment and by confining her to their home. He later encouraged her to join the Women's Federation and take a full-time job. After some difficulty in coordinating their work schedules, and unable to place the children in nursery schools, Salazar quit his job to take care of them and do the household work.

At the time of this study, Nicolás, Flora, and her two younger children were living in the one-bedroom home Salazar had received through the relocation program. She was pregnant with Nicolás's first child and had quit her job. As the interviewing began, Nicolás was returning to his job with the Carpentry Enterprise, at a wage of 110 *pesos* a month.

After all his efforts to improve life for himself and his family, Salazar was disappointed that he had been unable to advance more quickly in his work and to increase his wages. He was hurt by the reaction of the many neighbors who ridiculed him for living with a woman who had been unfaithful to him and for staying home to care for the children while she worked. He was also discouraged by the apathy of his neighbors toward the mass organizations and by factionalism among CDR officers. His block CDR had stopped functioning in 1969, and Nicolás was no longer performing his official duties. That same year, when his experience cutting sugar cane would have been valuable to the great 10-million-ton harvest effort of 1969–70, he was so wrapped up in his family problems and so fearful of leaving Flora alone at home that he did not volunteer.

Back at work again, Salazar seemed to be making a recovery from the period of disillusionment that had engulfed him in the previous year. He seemed more optimistic about his personal life and his chances for advancement. He was also hopeful of receiving organizational help from the CDR sectional to revitalize the block Committee.

After 1959 Nicolás Salazar gradually integrated into the political and economic mainstream; he held a full-time job with all the health, retirement, and other fringe benefits, he participated in community-action programs, he was aware of and sympathetic to the major programs of the Revolution, and he identified, at least on a verbal level, with the Cuban nation. He stated, perhaps with more wishfulness than conviction, that he was working for the good of all and not just for himself. This change in social and political consciousness may not constitute a personal transformation, but it is significant in a formerly marginal man like Salazar.

Compared with Lázaro Benedí and Alfredo Barrera, Nicolás Salazar is a simpler, less ambitious man, both in his work and in his personal life. As poor as the other two were, Salazar was still poorer and had suffered worse degradation and humiliation. He was never headed anywhere in particular, so that, in contrast to Barrera, everything that has come to him under the Revolution has been well received. Barrera had material ambitions beyond both his pre-Revolution and post-Revolution opportunities, just as Benedí had intellectual and political ambitions beyond his opportunities. The hopes that Barrera and Benedí may have had for crossing over into "respectable" society were absent in Salazar. Whether for this reason or another, Salazar lacked the pretensions of Benedí and Barrera and told his story in a more simple and direct manner. Compared to Barrera's story, Salazar's account has a feeling of greater openness and honesty, and compared to Benedí's, more earthiness and vitality. This is apparent in Salazar's description of Las Yaguas, with which we have chosen to begin his story. He discussed the barrio from the perspective of one who was very much in touch with its daily life—the location of stores and basic services, the availability of credit and part-time work, the layout of neighborhoods, relations among neighbors, street life—including the role of police—and so forth.

Benedí, on the other hand, discussed Las Yaguas in terms of its relationship to major political and historical events, and the effect upon it of what was happening in the country at large. In talking about his role in the barrio, Benedí seems at times to be almost detached from the daily life of Las Yaguas. This accurately reflects his greater concern for intellectual than for physical needs.

Benedí looked on residents of the slum with a kind of paternalistic

LIVING THE REVOLUTION: Four Men

affection, as though he were not really one of them. He did not share
their skepticism for the society at large or for government, politicians, or
reform movements. He was untiring in recruiting volunteers, in persuading Las Yaguas residents to contribute their scarce resources to
radical causes, and in lecturing his neighbors on the beauties of self-
improvement and the need for reform. While Benedí accepted many of
the values of the dominant culture, at the same time he maintained his
credentials as a man marginal to that culture. He lived in a shantytown,
rejected civil marriage for a series of consensual unions, and remained a
devoted practitioner of Afro-Cuban religion, with all its anti-rational
elements, including sorcery and divination, sacrifice of animals, punishing initiation rites, and the expenditure for religious rituals of substantial sums of money needed for essentials.

Unlike Benedí and Salazar, Barrera looked at Las Yaguas with contempt. He was ashamed to live there and to associate with its residents.
His discussion of his neighbors, whom he divides into three classes, is
scathingly critical. Although all three men were sensitive to the ways in
which outsiders characterized Las Yaguas residents as criminals and der-
elicts, Salazar and Benedí considered the stereotyping an injustice and
did not join in ridiculing their neighbors.

In Chapter 7 of his story, Salazar compares the Buena Ventura housing project with Las Yaguas, with no small measure of nostalgia for his
old way of life. He missed the ambience and quality of life of the slum,
and was particularly disappointed over the loss of neighborliness and
mutuality.[13]

Conditions in Las Yaguas were such that neighbors were forced into
frequent contact with one another. The crowded conditions and the
tentative construction of the dwellings exposed the residents and their
households to passersby. Some of the most private functions were performed in public places. The barrio as a whole became living space for
everyone, extending from front doorsteps or porches to the streets, and
to bars, restaurants, and grocery stores, many of which were in the
owners' homes.

The new community in Buena Ventura was a strong contrast to Las
Yaguas. The physical appearance in itself struck a completely different
mood, with houses uniformly constructed along cement sidewalks,
paved, lighted streets, public utilities and sanitary facilities, a community

13. For a similar response, see Cruz Ríos's comparison of life in a San Juan housing
project with life in La Esmeralda slum in Oscar Lewis's *La Vida* (New York: Random
House, 1965), pp. 661–69. For similar findings in North American housing projects, see
the work of Chester Hartman on Boston's West End, "The Limitations of Public Housing:
Relocation Choices in a Working Class Community," *AIP Journal*, Nov., 1963, pp. 283–96,
and "Social Values and Housing Orientations," *Journal of Social Issues*, Apr., 1963, pp.
113–31.

center, and a small central park. It was a neighborhood planned for residential use; small family businesses, peddlers, and street vendors were outlawed. This new, no-nonsense order was offset somewhat by residents who converted their yards into small family gardens, turned out animals to graze in the park or empty lots, and enclosed their yards with variegated fences made from imaginative combinations of scrap materials.

As the haphazard design of Las Yaguas was replaced by structural uniformity, so was the moral ambivalence of the slum being forcibly displaced by a new, strongly defined morality. The state virtually eliminated the old street life, abolishing organized prostitution,[14] gambling, and drug sales, and prohibiting cockfighting. To the extent any of these still existed, they operated on a very small scale in private homes. The state also broke up youth gangs, closed taverns, and rationed liquor.

The heart of the new morality, however, was not in the absence of old vices but in the insistence on new virtues: elementary education was compulsory, and full-time employment for adult males was all but mandatory, as was membership in at least one of the mass organizations. Most workers were obliged to join unions, attend study meetings, do guard duty or minimal voluntary productive labor. Couples living in free union were urged to legalize their marriages in civil ceremonies and to stabilize family life. Contrary to the isolation of Las Yaguas, the state and the dominant culture were never far from view in Buena Ventura. Committee and Federation activists, social workers, and lay courts came into the new community to enforce public-health and sanitary codes, oversee truancy and vagrancy problems, referee family quarrels and cases of child abuse or neglect, and in general to monitor the social behavior of the community.

As the state took over responsibility for providing material necessities, employment, and basic social services, the interdependence of the former slum dwellers began to disappear, and some of the underlying hostilities came to the surface. For many, the move to better housing in a middle-class neighborhood presented the opportunity to change their life-styles and to disassociate themselves from people they had not been able to avoid in Las Yaguas. The increasing demands of housekeeping, jobs, volunteer labor, meetings, and other civic functions left far less time to spend with neighbors. Furthermore, the sturdily built houses of

14. In a 1970 interview with Oscar Lewis, Armando Torres, head of the agency responsible for eliminating prostitution, said, "There may be girls here and there who go out on their own, but prostitution as a social phenomenon has disappeared. There may be isolated cases of girls trying to obtain scarce articles—portable radios, silk stockings, things like that—who resort to such practices at times. I don't think that can be called prostitution, but such cases are subject to prosecution, in part because of the personal corruption involved in hunting down consumer goods that way."

Buena Ventura could be closed tight against the outside world, permitting families a privacy they never had before. People tended to retreat indoors and confine their living space to their homes.[15] The small park, which was meant to be a gathering place, was used instead for grazing animals and for drying laundry, and the community center was occupied for several years by families left homeless after a hurricane.

Life in Buena Ventura was more regimented, more impersonal, and in some ways more demanding than life in Las Yaguas, for if the pre-revolutionary system pronounced itself all but free from responsibility for the poor, the poor also felt free from obligation to society. Within the physical boundaries of the slum and within their own material limitations, they had had more freedom to order some aspects of their daily lives than they did in Buena Ventura. In Las Yaguas there had been no pressure to conform to a work ethic or to rigid moral precepts. Although there was less money, there was greater opportunity for spontaneity of expression, for instance, in the elaborate, exhaustive religious rituals of the Afro-Cuban sects, or in the frequency and length of celebrations. There was, in general, a broader range of recreation and of immediate gratification, including, for example, the availability of alcohol, marijuana, and other drugs. In return for restrictions on their old freedoms, these former slum dwellers have been given a new set of freedoms that are basic to life: freedom from hunger, from inadequate clothing and shelter, from epidemic diseases and poor health care, from unemployment and illiteracy. While it is probably true that not more than a handful of them would trade their new freedoms for the old, this does not preclude their missing the old and wanting both.

At times, the people of Buena Ventura appeared baffled by the modus vivendi of the revolutionary system. For many, it was the first time they had had to deal with formal institutions and procedures. Nicolás Salazar, for example, did not know how, and sometimes was not willing, to avail himself of the services offered. When Flora Mir became pregnant, neither he nor she entirely understood the procedures for requesting maternity leave or a transfer to a lighter work load. As a result, she quit her job. Salazar had also walked off his job without getting correct authorization or without applying for a leave or transfer. It was not that he was unaware that procedures existed but that he preferred to come and go as he pleased, as he had in the past, no matter how much greater the sanctions or smaller the benefits he received. Such lapses from the new

15. In discussing residents of Boston's West End who had been relocated in new housing projects, Chester Hartman wrote that the environment of their old neighborhood "seemed to define and delineate degrees and types of contact and to provide a clear sense of available human resources. In the absence of these bases for social relationships, other people tend to be treated as an undifferentiated crowd, and for many working-class people, the better part of wisdom under such circumstances is to remain suspicious and aloof." ("The Limitations of Public Housing," pp. 285–86.)

morality of course do not generally reflect conscious opposition to the government, but rather reversion to handling problems in familiar ways. When faced with the frustrations of coping with the strange and different, the comfort of the familiar looms very large. The number of old habits that persisted in the new barrios in 1970—absenteeism, vagrancy and frequent job changes, gambling, truancy, black-marketeering—not only helped to reduce the strangeness of the new life, but were also ways of retaining some measure of personal freedom.

Since 1959 the revolutionary government has tried to bring slum dwellers into the mainstream as forcibly as the old order cast them out. For the very poor there has been little room for choice in either system. Under the pre-revolutionary system, there was a certain toleration of so-called social excesses and deviations by the poor, so long as they were confined to the slum community. Under the revolutionary government's policy of incorporation and assimilation, however, there is a lower tolerance threshold, because the objective is not to isolate but to eradicate the subculture in favor of a new, all-pervasive (not just dominant) culture and belief system.

IV

There are many responses to poverty, depending not only upon personality but on how and where poverty is experienced. Gabriel Capote Pacheco is significantly different from the other three men in this volume in that he never lived in a self-contained slum like Las Yaguas. After growing up in a small town in Oriente Province, Capote lived in several poor working-class neighborhoods in Havana, never experiencing the sense of territoriality or of belonging that Benedí, Salazar, and even Barrera felt for Las Yaguas. Not having access to the resources of a slum community, where a communications network and other mechanisms, however informal and unstructured, helped the poor meet their daily needs, Capote's family was almost solely dependent on their own abilities. Furthermore, they often lived close to more prosperous families and were thereby exposed to humiliating contrasts. The help Capote and his family received from their neighbors was not simply sharing among equals, as it would have been in Las Yaguas, but the kind of charity that suggested inequality.

As an informant Gabriel Capote was modest and somewhat timid; apparently unaccustomed to speaking about himself, the initial interviews cost Capote much effort and had to be cut short because of his fatigue. However, he persevered and after a time seemed to want the opportunity to express his thoughts. Capote was always carefully dressed, usually in his waiter's uniform of white shirt, black trousers, and bow tie. His wife, Fina Frías, was a small, fragile-looking woman, darker-skinned

than Gabriel and less well groomed. In Gabriel's presence she was generally quiet, but toward the end of the study, after Gabriel abandoned her,
she spoke very rapidly and heatedly about her domestic and marital
problems. Due to technical difficulties with the tapes, Fina Frías's interviews could not be transcribed.

Fantasy and misinformation play a role in Capote's story as they do in
Alfredo Barrera's, but the discrepancies are not of the same significance.
Capote's fantasy was also about his father, but it did not have the vicious,
paranoic, and destructive aspects that Barrera's had. It was more of an
elaborate daydream, perhaps to make life more interesting, or more
significant, or to bolster the image of a father who had abandoned his
family. Taking a few basic facts about his life—that his paternal grandmother's surname was Batista and that she had lived in the same town
as the family of the dictator Fulgencio Batista—Capote greatly em-
bellished them, creating a foster relationship between his father and the
dictator. He further claimed that when Batista came to power, he made
his father, Ernesto Capote, Minister of Public Works. Gabriel's mother,
whose voice appears in his story, told interviewers that her former
mother-in-law had worked as a laundress for Fulgencio Batista's mother
and that several members of the Capote family, including Gabriel's
father, had received small sinecures. The two families, however, were
not related by blood or through a foster relationship. Nevertheless, Capote seemed to believe in the little fantasy he had constructed, and he
enjoyed it. In fact, we found a tendency in a number of the informants
to exaggerate or even to manufacture experiences with famous Cuban
leaders, especially meetings or associations with heroes of the Revolution.

Gabriel Capote, the youngest of three children, was born "around
1941" in Banes, Oriente. His father, a soldier, had abandoned the family
shortly after Gabriel's birth, and the children's mother, Ana María
Pacheco, had supported them by working as a domestic and a prostitute. When Gabriel was seven or eight, Señora Pacheco left him with
her mother and went to Havana to find work. Poorly fed, half-clothed,
infested with lice, Gabriel lived for the next several years in the squalor
of his grandmother's one-room, palm-thatched hut.

When he was eleven, his mother returned for him and took him to
Havana to live. In the city the family's economic fortunes went up and
down with the success of Señora Pacheco's free-union marriages. There
were two short periods during which they lived in lower-middle-class
neighborhoods, but most of Capote's adolescence was spent in one or
another of Havana's poor barrios. Between liaisons his mother worked
as a cook, laundress, and spiritist.

Although the father, Ernesto Capote, had abandoned his family, he
was still a presence in their lives, primarily because the children sought
him out. While still a young boy, Capote and his older brother located

their father in Banes, Oriente, and from then until his death in 1963 they visited him intermittently. He never contributed to their support but on occasion bought something for them or gave them small amounts of money. More important, insofar as his influence on Gabriel is concerned, Ernesto Capote was insane and spent part of his life in the Mazorra asylum for the mentally ill. Gabriel and his brother often saw their father in fits of rage, and sometimes they and their mother were the targets of his violent outbursts.

As with most children of his background, Gabriel began working at a very young age, holding down a number of part-time jobs, selling empty bottles, newpapers, candy, and lottery tickets. At fourteen he got his first full-time job at a coffee stand, working ten hours a day, seven days a week, for 75 cents a day. He had never attended school and was so deficient in the rudimentary skills that he could not make change for customers or add a sum if someone bought several items. Capote worked at the stand for almost six years, until 1961, when the owner left Cuba and the shop was closed.

In 1961 Capote began working for the National Institute of the Tourist Industry (INIT) as a hotel janitor, earning 86 *pesos* a month, plus partial room and board, free laundry, and thirty days of paid vacation each year. After completing a sixth-grade equivalency course in night school, he was promoted to a waiter's job, a position he continued to hold in various INIT hotels up to 1969–70, when his story was taped. At that time he was earning 175 *pesos* a month.

Capote's work history differs significantly from the employment patterns of the other three men in this volume, particularly from those of Salazar and Barrera. He did not suffer from the stereotypes that shadowed residents of Las Yaguas, who, having moved there because they had lost their jobs, were then denied access to jobs because that slum was regarded as the home of vagrants and criminals. This destructive cycle helped establish or perpetuate the erratic work habits of many slum residents. The fact that Capote was not subjected to these environmental influences undoubtedly was important in the development of his stable work habits. It would have been the exception, not the rule, for someone from Las Yaguas to have worked full-time for almost six years at one job, especially at such low pay. Capote demonstrated the same steadiness and consistency in his second job, having worked for INIT for nine years as of 1970.

Not only was Capote amenable to permanent, full-time employment, but he actually enjoyed his work and always tried to improve his performance, approaching it with an enthusiasm and ambition that were unknown to Barrera and Salazar. His overall outlook on life was much less cynical than theirs. This was apparent in Capote's earlier, more thorough integration in the Revolution. Barrera and Salazar had a tendency to adopt a wait-and-see attitude while Capote was much more eager to please. In the mid-1960s he took on increasingly greater responsibilities even though he was considerably worse off materially than Barrera and Salazar.

Capote's integration began when he joined the militia and was called up for active duty during the October missile crisis. He joined the CDR, and in 1964 worked in the sugar-cane harvest. In 1967 he was elected a Vanguard Worker and admitted to the Union of Young Communists (UJC). He spent many hours doing voluntary productive labor, and in the late 1960s was chosen to lead a work brigade in Havana's greenbelt.

In 1963 Capote married (in free union) Fina Frías, seventeen, a country woman who had come to the city to work as a domestic. After the birth of their first child, the couple legalized their marriage in a civil ceremony. Capote considered Fina a poor, ignorant country girl and showed little respect or affection for her as a person. In fact, he cared so little for her at first that he had sexual relations with her without telling her he had a venereal disease. He did, however, have respect for the role of wife and mother. This, and his devotion to his children, held the union together.

Capote's sexism is so intense that by comparison it dims even Benedí's antifeminist views. Gabriel took pleasure in what he claimed was Fina's ignorance and he enjoyed being able to dominate her. The reason he loved her, he said, was "because she doesn't contradict me. She accepts all my decisions without a word." He was against Fina working outside their home or doing voluntary agricultural labor; he said he would never "allow" her to be away from him for "even a few days." Women were "weak," he said, and would be unfaithful to their husbands as soon as they were away from home. "The closer she stays to [her husband], the more children she bears him, the better.... She owes herself to me and the children." All in all, he considered her a good wife, describing her as unexciting and inept but "properly" submissive. He also approved of her attitude toward the Revolution, which he summed up by saying, "She's so revolutionary she never complains about anything."

Capote believed he was a good husband in every way; he worked steadily and hadn't abandoned the family; he didn't drink and he chased women "only after 9:00 or so, when the kids are asleep." In 1970 he was having an affair with Margarita, one of Fina's best friends, a woman who lived across the hall.

In addition to his extreme sexism, Capote was a hard-core racist. In contrast to his belief that some of his sexist attitudes were shared by the Party, he recognized that his racism was contrary to the Party's official position. He was convinced, however, that it was too late for him to change.

At the time we met him, Capote had a serious housing problem. He was living with his wife and four children in a very small furnished room. The room had no kitchen facilities, and the bathroom was shared with eight other families. At first the room was a considerable improvement over their previous housing arrangements, but as the family grew it became unsuitable. The building was located on a narrow, busy street with no safe place for the children to play, and their mother kept them indoors every day. Only when they went to nursery school, or on Capote's vacations or days off, did they go out for any period of time. If their mother had to go on some errand, she tied the children to the beds. These conditions were at least a contributing factor to the serious emotional and nervous disorders suffered by the three eldest children. Their teachers in the primary and nursery schools they attended complained that they were unable to concentrate and were very restless, causing problems in discipline. The schools recommended psychiatric care for all three children. Capote was unsuccessful in securing such care and managed only to have the children's names placed on a long waiting list. Meanwhile he concentrated his efforts on finding better housing.

Failing to get a new housing assignment, Capote tried to draw attention to his problem by refusing a temporary two-year transfer to the Centennial Youth Column, a paramilitary agricultural work force. He said in a letter that he would not leave his family to go to the countryside until his work center satisfied his housing needs. He supported this ultimatum by returning his Communist Youth membership card. When he refused to attend a hearing of his case he was expelled from the UJC. This occurred shortly before we met him, and he was still upset over what he believed to be the insensitivity of the Party organization to his situation, especially to his duty as a father. In retrospect, however, he expressed regret at refusing to attend the hearing.

Capote was a deeply conflicted man. The extreme poverty in which he grew up had been complicated by abandonment by his father and temporary abandonment by his mother. He felt obligated to his mother for the great personal sacrifices she had made to support her children, but he felt rejected by her and resented her for leaving him. He was very grateful to the Revolution for his education, his job, and his new status as Vanguard Worker and Youth member, but he was greatly angered by what was happening to his children, who were really the focal point of his affection. During the interviews he spoke of his deep frustration and sometimes voiced a fear of losing his mind. In 1970, not long after completing the taping of his story, Capote, without informing his wife of his intentions or of his secret relationship, abruptly left her and the children to live with Margarita.

Four Men

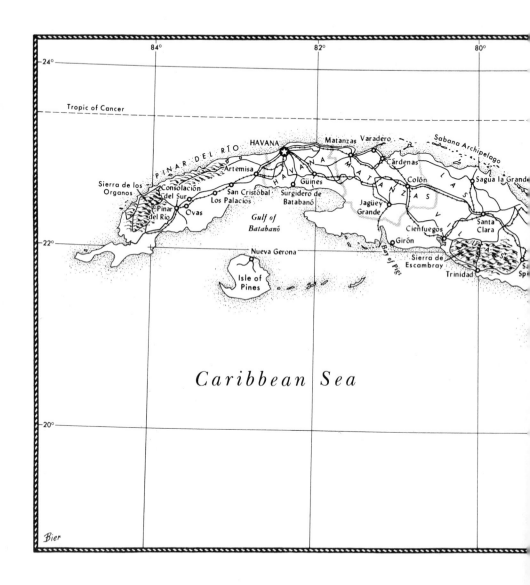

24°

Tropic of Cancer

84°   82°   80°

PINAR DEL RÍO   HAVANA   Matanzas   Varadero   *Sabana Archipelago*

Sierra de los
Organos   Artemisa
        Consolación
        del Sur   San Cristóbal   Surgidero de   *H A V A N A*   Güines   *M A T A N Z A S*   Cárdenas   *L A S*   Sagua la Grande
        Los Palacios   Batabanó   Colón
Pinar
del Río   Ovas   Jagüey   *V I*
                    Grande   Santa
        Gulf of   Cienfuegos   *L*   Clara
        Batabanó   *L*   *S*

22°   Nueva Gerona   Girón   Sierra de   *A*
                                        Escambray   *S*
                Isle of   *Bay of Pigs*   Trinidad   *S*
                Pines   Sp

Caribbean   Sea

20°

Bier

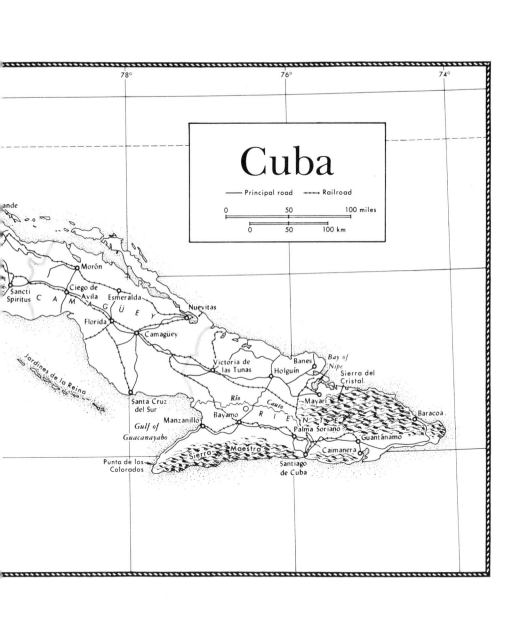

Cuba

—— Principal road ++++ Railroad

0   50   100 miles

0   50   100 km

ande

Morón

Sancti
Spiritus C A M Ciego de
Avila Esmeralda

A   Nuevitas
Florida G Ü E Y

Camagüey

Jardines de la Reina

Victoria de
las Tunas Banes Bay of
Nipe

Holguín Sierra del
Cristal

Santa Cruz
del Sur Río Mayarí Baracoa

Manzanillo Cauto O

Bayamo R I E N T E Palma Soriano Guantánamo

Gulf of
Guacanayabo Sierra Maestra Caimanera

Punta de los
Colorados Santiago
de Cuba

PART I

Lázaro Benedí Rodríguez

Chapter One

Very Black and Very Poor

I'VE NEVER BEEN a pessimist. Men can get what they want if they work for it. That I have never doubted. Never, not even when I heard one hypo-crite after another fill his mouth with promises . . . false promises, empty promises. I'm seventy years old and have lived to see what I always longed for and knew would happen. Why do I say this? Because I knew that someday a man must arise who would make live the ideals throbbing in my breast.

I have always wondered why, for what cause or reason, there should be such poverty and illiteracy in Cuba, a tropical country with a suffi-ciency of productive land. Why should we import products that we could grow or make ourselves? Why, when all was told, were the Cuban people mortgaged—yes, mortgaged—and forced to live in submission to some-body else's will? There are plenty of Cubans who mouthed patriotic phrases but they always acted in subjection to the will of the Americans.

How often I held back the words I longed to shout for all the world to hear! I wanted to say, publicly, openly, that only when the Cuban people understood this and cast off the American yoke could our problems be solved. But these words on the lips of a humble workingman like me would have meant nothing. And why? Because the great majority of the Cuban people were illiterate workers. All you could do was hope that someday things would change. But years passed, years . . . and nothing changed.

As a boy it was my dream to go to the University and study mechanical engineering. I liked to make small models out of paper or cardboard,

Lázaro Benedí's autobiography is based upon 1,054 pages of transcribed notes gathered in twenty-two interviews by Oscar Lewis and Maida Donate, a member of the team of Cuban research assistants assigned to the project. Another interview was done by Maida Donate with the Cuban assistant Elsa Barreras López. Four of Benedí's six wives were interviewed by Oscar Lewis and Maida Donate, resulting in 486 additional pages. Benedí's son Yara as well as two of his ex-wives' husbands and two of their children were also interviewed.

and when I showed them to a mechanic he would say, "That's real good, *chico,* you should study to be an engineer."

"I'd like to study," I'd say, "but I must work to help my family. We are so many and so poor." It was for that reason that I never studied beyond the third grade.

I daydreamed sometimes. I would sit somewhere alone and think of what I could and should be. But even in my dreams I had to face the reality that the obstacles in my path were too many and too great. Money mostly, and my family's need of me. How could I have ever managed to put my ideas into practice?

I have been constantly and wholly an enemy of poverty, but I never felt superior to somebody simply because he was poorer than I. On the contrary, when I met someone who was destitute, I saw it as an opportunity to help another human being, a person like me, who should not have to suffer so. My most vulnerable spot in regard to extreme poverty is children—all children. I have always cherished Martí's[1] precept: "Children are born to be happy." But for thirty years I lived in Las Yaguas and saw children suffer miserable poverty, sleeping on doorsteps, going from door to door with a tin can, begging a little food at each house.

In Las Yaguas I had my little carpenter shop. I had plenty of good opportunities to make money but I rejected that as an aim. I have never worked to make myself rich. Wealth meant nothing to me. What's the point? I have always asked myself, "Does the rich man lead a happy life?" What does he—or most of them—have in his life except the drive to make more money, gain more and more privileges? On what does he base his self-respect? On nothing, except a feeling of superiority to those who are poorer than himself. I want none of that. To be at peace with myself, that is my aspiration. Ambition? I have none. I saw to what extremes we laborers were pushed by men who had accumulated large amounts of money. The idea of ordering other men around and getting rich with their work repelled me. That was not my aim. My only ambition was to study and help mankind.

I love and respect faith, any faith. Religion is something you accept on faith and faith grows through desperation. By means of religion I have been able to save many people. In dreams I am shown dangers that lie in wait for others, and so I am able to remove the obstacles from their path.

The African religion has a philosophy of its own and a profound logic. It is the African belief that each region has its own god, and sometimes the same god has different names in different regions. In Cuba the

1. José Martí y Pérez (1853–95), poet, philosopher, and Cuba's most famous nationalist, was an organizer of the Cuban independence movement. He died in battle against Spain in May, 1895.

region is very important too. Oriente has its Maceo[2] and its Fidel; Havana has its Martí. It is the same thing; just as each province has its commander-in-chief, so each land has its god.

Fidel has never said that *santería*[3] is an archaic matter which does not fit into the present. On the contrary, he wants *santería*, like all other religions, to be respected—provided, of course, that we serve it in a proper way. This is what I have always tried to do. Not long ago my CDR[4] sent me to the town of Guines, where I know many *santeros*[5] and members of the religion, to start a movement of vigilance against sabotage at the sugar mill. But we also carried out some rituals to divine which spirits were holding up the sugar production, and we tried to get their blessings for the 10-million-ton harvest.

For me, there is no conflict between religion and revolution. At home I have a bust of Lenin and an altar to Yemayá.[6] To us Lenin is a god. Why do we love Lenin when we never met him? Because he was one of the many men who fought for the rights of man and against exploitation. Christ, too, tried to redeem mankind and was the very pioneer of communism. I don't remember reading anywhere that he bowed to class privileges or discriminated against anyone because of the color of his skin.

My father was a slave. I know very little about his parents, but both were Africans and slaves too. *Papá* died free, but the pain of slavery never left him. Some slaves were well treated, that is true; but for many, slavery meant nothing but cruelty and exploitation. A black was held to be lower than a dog. Why should any man be allowed to enslave another, or exploit and mistreat him? Is his white skin and the other's black one a reason? Does his wealth and the other's poverty give him that right? *Papá* had no knowledge of books, but in his own words he explained these things to us, and we understood the message.

My father told us a little about his life as a slave, and when he spoke the pain showed. He had no visible scars, although on his back there were marks that he used to show to us. "These are my souvenirs of

2. General Antonio Maceo y Grajales (1848–96), a mulatto, was a principal military leader of the War of Independence (1895). He and his brother José, both killed in battle, were commanders of the predominantly black *mambí* army.

3. An Afro-Cuban religious cult that combines Yoruban (*lucumí*) and Roman Catholic beliefs and traditions. Widely practiced in Cuba, this cult is also known as *Regla Ocha*.

4. The Committees for Defense of the Revolution (see n. 80).

5. Priest-practitioners of the *santería* cult, also called *babalorishas*.

6. An African goddess identified with the *Virgen de Regla*, the protector of Cuban sailors. Yemayá is worshipped as the goddess of rivers and springs, the spirit of fertility, and the Prime Mother of all things. The colors blue and white are associated with Yemayá. (Jahnheinz Jahn, *Muntu: An Outline of the New African Culture* (New York: Grove Press, 1961), p. 65.

slavery, the marks of floggings," he said. He didn't really say "flogging"
though, because he wasn't the kind of man to use words like that. He'd
just say, "These are from the blows they gave us. There were many of us
slaves in that place and we even formed groups to resist working. They
beat us to force us to work." His stories made me burn with indignation.

Papá was absolutely illiterate but he forced us to improve ourselves by
studying and working. He'd say, "You must find a way to lead a different
kind of life from the one I led." Then he would remind us of his scars.
We appreciated *papá*'s nobility of heart. We knew he expected us to rise
above the system of slavery and not regress.

I've often wondered, "How did a man with no education at all have
such obsessive ambition for his children?" My old man couldn't explain it
because he wasn't that good with words. Here in Cuba ignorant people
were taught to be submissive and there was no way they could assert
themselves and say, "I want to be myself."

In his youth *papá* married a slave girl who bore him a son, Gaspar. I
didn't meet my half-brother until we were both grown men. When he
visited our home he was not on familiar enough terms with *papá* to call
him *tú*, much less with *mamá*, even though he was eight or ten years older
than she. He addressed them both formally and *mamá* expected us to do
the same with him. People were very strict about good manners in those
times.

I think my parents met during a trip of *papá*'s to Havana, and that's
where they got married. Whenever they got into an argument, as married people will, *mamá* would say to him, "I was a mere child of fourteen
when you took me from my home." But that was as far as she'd go. They
remained together for thirty-seven years and she bore him nineteen
children. Nine of them died before I was born. At present only three of
us are still alive.

I was born in the barrio of Cayo Hueso in Havana on February 28,
1900. *Mamá* told me that *papá* wouldn't even look at me in my cradle
because my skin was lighter than theirs. He really thought it was possible
I wasn't his son, so he never picked me up or showed any fatherly
feelings for me. When I cried, he'd look at me indifferently and walk
away. He was beside himself because one of his *compadres*[7] had said to
him, "But Tomás, are you sure this child is yours? Look at his color!"
And when in the course of a conversation *papá* happened to say, "My
wife, the mother of my children . . . ," there was always somebody present who would laugh and say, "*Ay,* that Tomás . . . he's blind!"

Papá was a good family man, but those jokes made him uneasy. He
couldn't help wondering if what they were saying might be true. *Mamá*

7. *Compadre* and *comadre* are terms used by a child's parents and godparents to address
or refer to each other.

told me about *papá*'s doubts because she was deeply hurt by them. I thought, "Well, I'll keep an eye peeled." However, as time went on, I got to be so much like *papá* physically that he was finally convinced I was his son. He didn't come right out and say so but I noticed the change. The time came when if he took his children out somewhere, he always called me first: "Come on, Zarito." I became his favorite. His feeling for me was more than predilection, it was an obsession.

I remember *papá* with all the affection that a son can feel for his father. Although I have no photographs of him, I can see his image clearly. His name was Tomás Benedí and he was born in Remedios, Cuba, around 1842. His eyes were large, like mine, with the same blue ring around them that I have now because of old age. He had a heavy beard, a mustache, thick lips, and a nose like mine—not thin, but not flat either. His hair was clipped very short. He wasn't the kind of man to have a stylish haircut or a fancy mustache.

Mamá was a little slip of a woman, about 2 inches shorter than *papá*. She wasn't hunchbacked or anything, but hard work had bent her figure. Her hair was short and her eyes were round, very prominent, and black, like her skin. Her nose and lips were somewhat thinner than *papá*'s. She had the habit—or the vice—of smoking cigars, keeping the thing in her mouth long after it had gone out. She couldn't stand being idle, so when she didn't have anything to do at home, she took in laundry.

Mamá was not a happy woman, though she kept her sorrows to herself. Her parents were slaves and had bought her freedom, but being their liberated daughter did not relieve her from any obligations toward the slaveowner.[8] A freed slave still had to obey his master's voice.

I know more about *mamá*'s side of the family than about *papá*'s, though I never met my maternal grandmother. She was called Ana Rodríguez, taking the surname of the owners of the sugar mill where she worked. She had four daughters and one son, and while she worked as a slave she bought her children's freedom.

We lived in Havana and *mamá* kept talking of making a trip to visit her mother some day. But *mamá* was always working to make ends meet, so she kept postponing it from month to month and from year to year and none of us children ever met our grandmother. The eldest of my

8. The 1880 law for the gradual abolition of slavery in Cuba established an eight-year state of tutelage (*patronato*) for all slaves liberated by the law. Since the legislation included no provision for indemnities to slaveowners as had been promised earlier, the *patronato* system was offered as a form of compensation to the owner. A slave could buy his way out of the *patronato* for the near-prohibitive price of 30–50 *pesos* a year for each of the eight years of the tutelage period. With the formal abolition of slavery by a royal decree from Spain, the *patronato* system ended in 1886. (See Philip S. Foner, *A History of Cuba and Its Relations with the United States*, II (1845–95) (New York: International Publishers, 1963), 292–95.)

grandmother's children, Lázara, came to Havana now and then. She dressed like the humble country woman she was, with long skirts and loose white blouses. We liked to have her visit us because we'd been brought up with the idea that one must love one's relatives. But Aunt Naomi was the aunt we knew best and who helped *mamá* the most. She was the most daring of the lot. She'd take things into her own hands and *mamá* never objected.

My grandmother practiced *santería*. It would be strange if she hadn't. It was a rare African in Cuba who didn't have some knowledge of those things. The religious beliefs of my family have always been founded on tradition. We felt a profound respect for the *santos* and customs of our ancestor's religion.[9]

Mamá never got around to explaining why she set out the glass of water and the flowers for the dead, but she believed that the dead tell us things. She was devoted to Yemayá, though she didn't go in much for that sort of thing, and always prayed to the *Virgen de Regla,* who had cured her once. If she had cured my *mamá* only *half* a time it would have been enough to make me feel more than a son or a slave of the *Virgen de Regla* forever!

We were Catholics because we were baptized in the Catholic Church; *mamá* believed an unbaptized child turned into a Jew, but she wasn't a strict observer of Catholicism. As for *papá,* I never heard him talk about religion at all.

Mamá practiced both Catholicism and spiritism, but she was no fanatic. The choice between Catholicism and spiritism is simply a matter of faith. In Cuba, people were so illiterate they believed what anybody told them. But poor people, who couldn't contribute large amounts of money to the Catholics, belonged mostly to the spiritist religion and to the African religion.

Within "the religion" there are three different orders: *Abacuá, santería,* and *Mayombé.*[10] They were brought to Cuba by the black slaves. From the sixteenth through the nineteenth century Cuba was one of the places where the largest number of slaves landed. Their religious strength

9. The word *santo* is used to refer to both the African *orishas* or spirits and Roman Catholic saints.

10. The all-male secret societies of *Abacuá* (or *ñáñigo*) are, according to David K. Booth, "unique to Cuba ... though they appear to be modelled on the secret societies of the Cross River ports of modern Eastern Nigeria and draw heavily upon Efik mythology." *Mayombé* is also known as *Regla Conga* or *Palo* (the stick), and is derived from the traditions of the Bantu-speaking people of the Congo and northern Angola. For a definition of *santería*, see n. 3. (David K. Booth, "Neighbourhood Committees and Popular Courts in the Social Transformation of Cuba" (unpublished Ph.D. thesis, University of Surrey, 1973), pp. 241–42. Also see Lydia Cabrera on the *Regla de Mayombí* in *El Monte* (Miami: Rema Press, 1968), pp. 21–22.)

almost overshadowed Catholicism.[11] But the more intelligent Catholics, seeing that their power was being undermined, tried to teach the blacks that these beliefs were fetishisms and even downright criminal. They convinced people that Yoruba devotees killed children to give their blood to the *santos*. That's a lie. From all I've ever heard, when the *santos* were to be fed, only animals were killed.

Aunt Naomi was a strong practitioner of *santería*. It was through her and my other maternal aunts rather than my parents that the influence of the African religion reached me. I was devoted to Naomi and followed her about. I've always liked anybody who had ability and a strong personality without being a bully. I was still a child, not old enough to think up questions on religion, but I listened to what she said.

Aunt Naomi was never presented to a *santo*[12] because it was not the custom then. But they said she could do anything a man could do; all that was required for women was to have some knowledge and interest in *santería*. I do know that she felt a profound adoration for *Palo Monte*,[13] which was generally a matter for men. In that regard she *was* a man.

Aunt Naomi died because of a quarrel she had with some *santeros* in her town. She thought she was the strongest woman in the world, and the quarrel started when she said she had more powers than anybody else. She threatened one of the men by declaring, "What you do, I can eat."

The day she made that remark, the man's only answer was, "All right, try it." Later, at a party, they served chocolate and Naomi's cup was doctored ahead of time. After she drank it she developed chills and got colder and colder until she died. Later on it was discovered that she'd been poisoned. I didn't hear this story until I was a grown man because they didn't discuss things like that with children.

My relatives have always been on very good terms with one another, always keeping a certain distance, of course. *Papá* treated his in-laws rather ceremoniously. There was no intimacy, but there was a great deal of mutual respect. Even Naomi, as eccentric as she was, treated him with respect. It was this family respect that kept a man from one day saying "This is my woman" and the next day exchanging her for another woman.

When *papá* first came to Havana, his older brother Octavio got him a

11. The slave population of Cuba rose from 44,333 (or 20 percent of the total population) in 1774 to 370,553 (or 26.5 percent of the total population) in 1861. (Hugh Thomas, *Cuba: The Pursuit of Freedom* (New York: Harper and Row, 1971), p. 169.) There were also well over 100,000 free black and mulatto people, many of whom probably practiced an African religion. (See also Philip Foner's interesting chapter on "'The Africanization of Cuba' Scare," in *A History of Cuba*, vol. II.)

12. Ceremony whereby the novice in *santería* calls upon an *orisha* and becomes its spiritual descendant.

13. Another name for *Mayombé* (see n. 10).

job working in a carriage shop. It was clear from the way *papá* worked and organized his life that his aim was to earn enough money to support his family. He never believed in accumulating money, though eventually he had his own little workshop to make carriages, which he then hired out. He also worked as a coachman, driving his own coach.

Papá was a man who liked a good time and women—all women. He was a woman-chaser. But he wasn't lacking in tenderness. At home he acted like a saint, like somebody dropped from heaven and set up on a pedestal. That's how he kept *mamá* under control. She was jealous and would argue with him about women but he always shrugged it off, saying, "So that's what you believe? Well, all right."

Papá would never permit me to ask where he was going or to say, "Wait, I'll go along with you." Not he! From the time we were small we knew we had to respect him. But sometimes he would say to me, "Let's go for a ride." We'd drive around a bit, then he'd stop in front of some house and say, "I think I'll go in here and have a cup of coffee." So he'd go in while I waited for him in the coach. When he came back, there'd always be a woman with him who'd gush, "Oh, Tomás, is this your son? Well, if he's yours, he's mine too!"

Naturally a kid observes things and wonders. These visits, the way the women talked. . . . For instance, in a merely friendly visit there's no need to kiss a person every single time. I observed it all and drew my own conclusions.

When I'd get home, *mamá* would ask me suspiciously, "Where did your father take you?"

"Oh, we just drove around."

"Did you visit a woman's house?"

"No, *mamá*."

"You know more than you're telling me!"

"No, *mamá*."

Papá knew he could trust me to keep my mouth shut so he took me to visit different houses. He'd say, "You don't have to tell her, that's all." *Mamá* preferred to have me go along with him, thinking that I'd scold him if he went into bars with women. Me! Why should I scold him? So he wouldn't take me out anymore?

Mamá wasn't one of those women who went out spying on their husbands, nor did she let neighbors bring gossip about *papá*. She fully understood and often said that a woman's place is in the home. Of course, in those times such things could happen, because men were more humble and women more modest. Now women are far too provocative.

Papá could never feel jealous about *mamá* because she was the very prototype of chastity. She didn't enjoy chatting with other men or going out with them as I have seen some women do. Her home and her children were her whole world. Within the four walls of the house, *mamá* was the boss; my father simply spent his time working to make money for his family. He had nothing to say on household matters other than, "Jacinta, here is the rent money." *Mamá* managed everything else.

I remember my mother as a strong, domineering woman. She loved each of her children dearly for what he was—Tomás as Tomás and Andrés as Andrés. She had eighteen sons and only one girl and never showed any favoritism. "You are all my children," she'd say. Sometimes she paid more attention to one and we'd decide that she loved him more. But then we'd stop and think, "She treats him in a special way because he's the smallest or the weakest." It was clear to all of us that our sister was her darling. After my sister, her favorite was Octavio, but he married and left home early.

Mamá was very stern. I never saw her caress one of us. She never sweet-talked us or spoiled us, as mothers do nowadays by calling to their children, "Come here, darling." She wasn't mean but she'd never call a son "Tomasito" instead of "Tomás." To *mamá*, petting a son was one of the most dangerous things in the world. She was an illiterate woman but she raised her sons as men, with a man's character. From the time we were little she told us, "You must learn to do everything in this life." By that she meant helping with the laundry. Her upbringing was a bit hard on us boys, but no woman ever loved her children more or took better care of them.

We children got gifts for the Day of the Three Kings only if we deserved them. *Mamá* taught us that we had to earn a gift by good behavior even six months before the holiday. If she heard a single complaint about us from any of the neighbors, we wouldn't get the toy horse or other trifle on that day. We didn't have the lavish gifts children have now. But those little gifts were a great treat for us.

When we needed something *mamá* could afford, she gave it to us with the explanation, "I don't give you this because you are my son but because you have earned it with your good behavior." We respected her and did all we could to earn the reward. Often it was a *medio*[14] for the movie, and another *medio* for candy.

My father was more affectionate and attentive to his children than *mamá*, but he was no fonder of kissing than she was. "Men don't kiss each other," he'd say. He would show his affection by asking us things like, "Are you going to the movies today? Did you behave yourself? I'll ask Jacinta how you behaved." Then he'd ask her and give us money to go to the movies.

During the first ten years of my life we lived in a house next door to *papá*'s coach workshop. It was an old, two-room wooden house with a packed-earth floor and tarpaper roof. The kitchen was in the back and

14. Five *centavos*.

led out to a large backyard. In the yard there was a small shed divided in half, with the latrine on one side and a place to bathe on the other. We got our water from a well in the yard. Electricity was hardly known in Havana. For light we used a *chismosa,* a can with a wick dipped in kerosene. In spite of being country people, my parents had little interest in raising animals. All they had was a couple of chickens and one pig.

From that house we moved just a block away to a *solar.*[15] We had a room with a kitchen. A bathroom was out in the patio. Conditions there were different. *Mamá* had us boys do the family laundry in the patio and the other boys would stand around yelling at us, "Sissies, sissies!" We couldn't talk back to them because *mamá* wouldn't allow it. We just had to burn inside.

Mamá had five or six of us boys working on the wash at the same time, some washing, some hanging up the clothes. We hated that. Well, what boy wouldn't! But she'd say to us, "I know you don't like it, but in the future you'll find it may come in handy. When your wife doesn't wash your clothes right you can show her how."

Time, of course, is the best teacher. As we grew older we realized *mamá* had been right. Suppose a man gets a wife who can't even cook a pot of rice and he doesn't know how to do anything either? How is that going to end? In tragedy for the home, of course. I can say that *mamá*'s training has served us well. When I had to live alone for a while, I never had to beg favors because I did everything for myself.

My mother's discipline was based on blows. She'd hit us for anything, but always with good reason. She'd tell everybody, "If you see any of my kids misbehaving, slap them if you have to and then bring them to me."

Once when I was six or seven years old, someone told her that I called Paco the grocer *tú.* She followed me to the grocery store and heard me say, "Hey you, Paco, *gallego,*[16] I want some service." She slapped my face so hard I thought the store had fallen in on me! That was sixty-odd years ago, but it's one lesson I've never forgotten.

Mamá asked my old man for a three-finger-wide leather strap to whip us with. She never hit my sister the way she did us boys because that girl lived in terror of her. It's only natural for boys to feel superior, so we were a lot more daring. When we were bigger, sometimes we'd get home at 11:00 or 12:00 at night thinking *mamá* would be fast asleep. We'd tiptoe in and there she'd be in a rocking chair. She'd lock the door and hit us with the strap. No matter how it hurt we didn't let out more than a sob. She'd say, "Shut up, don't scream, you'll wake the neighbors." When

15. A low-rent multiple-family structure commonly built in quadrangular form and composed of single rooms or small apartments opening onto a central patio. It is usually one story high, but may have as many as four.

16. A person from Galicia, Spain; often used in the vernacular to refer to light-skinned people whether or not they are of Spanish descent.

she was through, she'd say, "Go to bed now and don't you dare complain."

We had to control ourselves. God help us if we made an instinctive gesture to ward off the blows! She'd hit us three times harder. We soon found out it was better not to cover our heads but just stand there with our arms hanging, letting her do as she liked. She hit us mostly on the face because, she said, when people saw us with a black eye or swollen lips and asked what happened, we'd have to tell the truth and suffer the shame. She'd hit us on the back, too, but was careful not to let the strap fall below the shoulders because it can affect the lungs. She knew what she was doing but we didn't until much later. We might have died of T.B. and she didn't want that weighing on her conscience.

Another way she punished us was to make us stay home, take off our clothes, and wear a jute sack with *pica-pica*[17] in it. *Mamá* never took back anything she said, and nobody dared talk back to her. If one of us so much as said, "Heck, *mamá*," it was best to get out of her reach as fast as possible.

"If one doesn't keep a tight rein on one's children," she'd explain, "they'll grow up to be hooligans, men with the souls of convicts." We felt then that she was being dictatorial, but to avoid it would have meant leaving home and that was no joking matter. Anyway, time convinced us that she was right.

As a child, my temper varied according to the occasion. I was a bit quarrelsome and ready to stand up for my rights. You know how boys talk, challenging each other. But if any of the boys said, "I'll tell your mother on you," I'd keep my distance no matter how mad I was. Now, after facing a great many problems, I've come to the conclusion that sudden action is stupid, and I'm able to react to quarrels with a certain amount of indifference.

In our barrio there were several small gangs of boys, and we thought we were better than the boys in the next barrio. Once, when I was about ten, we went to the movies and the other gang was waiting for us. We called each other names and suddenly I felt a strong blow on my right arm and thought they had pulled it right out of its socket. I couldn't use it, so the others said, "Stand aside, get out of the way, don't try to fight this time." I didn't tell *mamá* why my arm hung limp. If I had, she'd have hit me again on that very arm.

I started smoking when I was about fourteen. One day a group of us were in Neptune Park and one of the boys said, "Let's see who can smoke the most." I was always wary about things like that because *mamá* was apt to pop up like a ghost where I least expected her. She didn't find out I smoked until I was married and my oldest son was two and a half months

17. A powdered substance from a plant, *pica-pica* produces itching.

old. I took advantage of one of her hometown trips to write her a letter saying, "I'm going to surprise you when you come back."

The day she returned, I left an empty box of matches on her table. When she found it, she thought, "Ah, this must be the surprise Zarito was talking about!"

I didn't dare go back until three days later for fear she'd be angry. Without her noticing, I lit a cigarette, took one puff, and left the butt there. When I was about a block away, I stopped and called back, "*Mamá*, look for the surprise—it's a cigarette butt."

She smoked, but she didn't think any of us should. As a result, I never smoked in front of her. She didn't allow us any liberties. Why, even on Christmas Eve we weren't allowed to drink at the table in her presence. After supper, though, we could go outside, where anything might happen.

I got drunk the first time on Christmas Eve, when I was fifteen. I was celebrating at the home of some friends, drinking wine, and the second glass went to my head. I lay down to rest and the other fellows began to tease me, "Well, do we have a man here or don't we?"

Then they sent one of the girls. "Ah, come on, have another one," she urged me. Nothing was more humiliating than to have a girl imply that you were a coward. So I snatched the glass from her and gulped down the wine. I got drunk and was afraid to go home. Of course that was just a passing phase, because absolutely nothing can drag me into vice.

When I was about eight, I went to the first grade in the barrio public school. "Behave yourselves at school," *mamá* told us. "I don't want your teachers to come here complaining about you." When she enrolled us in school, *mamá* told the teachers, "At home I am my children's mother, and their father is the one who brings home the food. But here in school, if they misbehave hit them as much as you have to." She did this to make us respect our teachers.

I was very fond of my first teacher, Susana Echemendía. She was an older woman, gray-haired, stout, very affectionate, and an excellent teacher. She and another teacher often chatted about which of their pupils were intelligent and had a future. She mentioned me because I was interested in studying and learning. Having seen the trouble *papá* and *mamá* had in their life because they were illiterate, I decided that a person who cannot read or write is like a blind man—ignorant and easily impressed because he has no knowledge to judge others.

My older brothers felt the same. They wanted to improve us younger ones, so they'd often deprive us of our play and make us study. We'd get home from school or from work planning to play at Neptune Park, and instead we'd have a pencil and a primer thrust into our hands. Some of my brothers were pretty rough with me, and I had no defense because they were acting under *mamá*'s orders. Octavio didn't interfere with us younger ones and he was my favorite. He believed it wasn't right to do as *mamá* asked.

I stayed in school four years and got as far as the third grade. I learned a bit of Cuban history and read Martí's sayings and liked them immensely. Those were rough years for me because I could see how destitute my folks were. I wanted to stay in school and learn a trade to help them out. As it was, we boys could never hope to be economically independent. If we found a *centavo* we had to say, "Look, *mamá*, I have a *centavo.*" Even after we were married, sometimes *mamá* decided how our money was to be spent.

Mamá did the laundry for a family who lived across the street from the University. One day they asked her if she knew of a boy who could clean house and run errands. *Mamá* said, "I have a boy who's in school now. He might do."

"Send him over," the man of the house said. So *mamá* took me there. He told me, "As a houseboy your pay will be 1 *centén* a month." That was the equivalent of 5.30 *pesos.* I got all excited and quit school right away. I was twelve years old.

Shortly after I got the job, the family I worked for had a master smith make a wrought-iron fence all around their yard. I was so enthusiastic about his work that sometimes I'd drop whatever I was doing and go outside to sweep the front yard and watch him. One day he asked me, "Do you like this kind of work?"

"Oh, yes!"

"Would you like to work with me and learn how to be an ironsmith?"

"I sure would, but I'll have to ask *mamá* first."

I talked it over with *mamá.* "That way I'll probably earn more," I argued. She discussed it with the owner of the smithy and agreed to let me work there. At the end of the first week, he handed me 1 *peseta.*[18] There's a lot of difference between earning 1 *centén* a month and 1 *peseta* a week. I didn't like that! What boy would? I didn't say a word, though, because if I had protested to my old lady I'd have been in trouble for sure. I simply showed her the *peseta* and said, "Look, *mamá*, this is all I earned this week."

"That's all right," she answered. "Are you learning?"

"Yes."

"Good. But don't think you can keep that *peseta.* Every week, when you get paid, I expect you to bring me your wages."

So every Saturday I gave *mamá* the entire *peseta.* As I was eager to learn the trade and earn more money for *mamá*, I worked hard. Every week the smith raised my wages by 1 *peseta* as a reward for my improved work. When I left in 1915, I was earning 1.50 *pesos* a day.

18. A coin worth one fifth of a *peso,* or 20 *centavos.*

People began to treat me like a man when I was fourteen, but I was still wearing short pants and it mortified me. When I begged to wear long pants, *mamá* always answered, "You're still a child. If we put you into long pants, you'll think you're a grown man and we'll start having problems with you."

But *mamá* had saved the money I earned and she gave it to me to buy pants. I think getting the first pair of long pants is the most impressive moment in a man's life. *Mamá* told me, "Now don't get these all muddy, or torn in a fight," and when I finally wore them, I didn't want even a breeze to touch them.

In the beginning of 1916, the master smith to whom I was apprenticed said to me, "You know the trade now, and the best advice I can give you is to get a job at some other smithy where you can earn more." I went to Amistad Street, to a workshop owned by the Díaz brothers, and told them I was a smith. That was hard to say, and even harder to prove. I lied, but I was sure I'd figure out how to do the job from the blueprints.

They said, "All right, can you take the measurements for a job on a porch and a flight of steps we're about to do?" I was young and ambitious, so I agreed.

When I went back to the workshop they said, "The porch is all right but what about these steps?" I wanted to make them think the error arose from something done in the workshop, but the man knew his work and suggested that we go back to check the measurements. On the way over he said, "Look, *chico*, the trouble is that you don't know enough yet."

This time I answered sincerely, "The truth is that I have to earn money for my family." He corrected the measurements. I improved rapidly and they kept me on until I decided to look for another job where I could earn more.

In 1918 the ironsmith's work was on the way down because it was becoming fashionable to build houses with cement porches. Seeing that, I decided to take up another trade with a better future, like carpentry. I talked with Pepe, a friend of mine who was in charge of a carpentry shop on Esperanza Street. It was owned by a Spaniard, Ramón, who was a nice fellow with charming manners. I knew nothing about carpentry except how to take measurements, but they hired me as an assistant at 2.25 *pesos* a day. I became so skilled at making tables and chairs that the owner handed the blueprints directly to me. Having progressed that far, I found a better-paying job near my home, at a furniture workshop called Loma de San Rafael.

During my childhood many great events took place in Cuba. I still remember them even though I was very young, because my older brothers, especially Tomasito, talked a lot about politics.

In 1912 the Independent Colored People's Movement was started. All I understood then was that the blacks were forming a political party to represent their race and to wage civil war.[19] The aim of the struggle was to federate the eastern provinces of Las Villas, Camaguey, and Oriente into a republic for the blacks. The western provinces were to be the white man's country. The war began in Oriente, the province with the largest black population, where the first slaves were brought ashore in Cuba. The leaders were Ivonet and Estenoz. They and 3,000 other blacks were killed at La Maya.

I myself was nothing but a black, but I disagreed with the Independent Colored People's Movement because under our Constitution all Cubans were equal. Therefore we blacks should never join a movement representing only one race. As a child I admired Maceo because he was black and defended us blacks. He said many times that his people should not ask for anything on the basis of race, but only on the basis of right and reason.

Years later I learned that the president of the Senate at that time, Martín Morúa Delgado, was a black man himself, as was Senator Juan Gualberto Gómez, and they both had opposed such a division. They asked how, in a country where Martí's white hand joined with Maceo's black one in love of Cuba and in the interests of all Cubans, it was possible to create such a division!

José Miguel Gómez, a Liberal called "the Shark," was the President of Cuba then.[20] He tried by every means to keep the blacks under his leadership. My family always liked the word "liberal" better than the word "conservative." Besides, my brother Tomasito was a political agent of the Liberal Party. The Liberals appealed to us blacks because they permitted a lot of freedom in our religion. For instance, they gave the blacks permission to play their music out in the street to celebrate the Day of the Three Kings. That really helped the integration of blacks since we are so fond of our religion and our drums.

In 1913 Menocal rose to power.[21] He belonged to the conservative class, the *mayorales*. He was a President of the bourgeoisie, the capitalists, an enemy of the poor, a man drugged by ambition. I hated him because his politics favored his group. If he ever did anything for the fatherland

19. *The Movimiento de Independientes de Color* was founded in 1907 and led by Pedro Ivonet and Evaristo Estenoz, a former member of the Liberal Party. Creation of the party prompted the passing of the Morúa Law prohibiting the formation of any party with membership based on race or color. In May, 1912, an uprising began across the island but was quickly suppressed, except in Oriente Province, where the movement had some military success. The U.S. government sent troops to help the Cuban Army defeat the black insurgents. (E. E. Chapman, *A History of the Cuban Republic* (New York: Macmillan, 1927), pp. 308–12.)
20. 1909–13.
21. General Mario García Menocal, President of Cuba 1913–21.

it must have been earlier, during the War of Independence. Beyond that, he was interested only in piling up capital for himself. He used to say that the needier a man was, the better the opportunity to exploit him. And in those days we blacks were very black—and poor. He believed a black had no right to be wealthy. Not that we wanted to be wealthy; we just wanted to live independently and enjoy our rights.

At that time black society was practically primitive and we lived in a terrible state of savagery. The carnivals reflected our background. They used to be great celebrations here, completely different from the Day of the Three Kings. During the carnival season many societies gave parties and the government gave every organization a chance to form its own *comparsa*.[22] I belonged to the Society of Youth of Cayo Hueso, which even had its own band.

In Havana the entire organization of the *Abacuá* came out during the carnival, and rivalries arose between the groups. For instance, the people of Los Pinos would sing satirical songs about the inferiority of the *comparsa* Aldabó. In this situation, the position of the *Abacuá* and the other groups was, "I will defend my group." This disrupted the friendly spirit of the carnival and many fights developed.

Another cause of problems was that everybody came out masked. This served as a cover for many crimes. For instance, if you bore a grudge against somebody, you might go out disguised as Death, in a skeleton costume and a death's-head mask. You could cut up or even murder a person and it would be very difficult to identify you afterward.

Various administrations took steps to stop these things. Gradually people modified their violent customs and diverted their energies to different channels. Antagonistic groups realized they were losing the respect of society as a whole and endangering the prerogatives they had. They also realized that we are all brothers and should avoid the excesses detrimental to our religion. Conditions improved even long before the Revolution.

During 1916 presidential elections were held; November 1 was an official holiday, but the campaign for votes began six months earlier. Political agents of the different parties went around visiting families. When people complained about something, the agent would say, "If you

22. A group of costumed, masked dancers. In Cuba the *comparsas* traditionally took part in the processional festivities of the annual carnival on Epiphany (January 6, the Day of the Three Kings). The *comparsas* date back to the nineteenth century, when it was the policy of the Spanish colonial government to receive in procession official delegations of the *cabildos de nación*, mutual-benefit associations of native Africans. The *comparsas* were banned at the time of the War of Independence and re-emerged in the twentieth century in the carnivals of Havana and Santiago. In Cuba today, this form of African expression takes place largely in the *Conjunto Folklórico Nacional* under the National Council of Culture. (Booth, "Neighbourhood Committees and Popular Courts," pp. 240, 241, 259.)

want to solve your problems you should join our party. How many voters are there in this family?"

The families were more concerned about their own pressing needs than about any party's program. "How much will you pay us?" was their one question.

"Well, it depends. If all five of you promise to vote for us, we could let you have as much as 25 *pesos*."

Agents took advantage of people's miserable poverty. They'd promise an unemployed man a job, any job. Oh, how happy it made the family if the man of the house got a job paying 20 or 40 *pesos!* It also served as propaganda to impress other families.

At home Tomasito influenced us, so my first vote, at the age of sixteen, was cast for Zayas.[23] I saw Zayas as an unprejudiced man who'd welcome any qualified black into his government. I was not legally old enough to vote, but in former times the political agent would arrange with the barrio polls official to forge a certificate. In return for such favors, the agent received a sum of money from his candidate or was appointed to a post.

I never asked Tomasito how much he got paid for my vote. I knew he had influence, because when any member of our family quarreled with someone, he'd get a lawyer from his party. The only payment they demanded was the man's vote and the votes of his relatives. I didn't mind cheating because I knew I was helping my brother. In fact, I wanted to vote again right away in another polling place so that Octavio and Tomás could keep their jobs.

Tomasito started a newspaper, *The Arrow*, with money given to him by a politician. The paper's name really fit because my brother's criticisms were as keen as darts. I helped by writing short articles. We managed to publish the paper only twice. Before the third copy could be printed, it was closed down because certain vested interests were opposed to it.

The Liberals couldn't accept Menocal's re-election, so in 1917 there was conflict between Liberals and Conservatives over the establishment of a government by José Miguel Gómez.[24] That incident was called "La Chambelona,"[25] after a popular song with a very catchy tune that the blacks liked. Most blacks will follow any drum they hear, without a thought to spare for freedom. So the Liberals, realizing that blacks were

23. Alfredo Zayas, the Liberal Party candidate, was defeated by incumbent President Menocal of the Conservative Party.

24. Protesting Menocal's return to office through a fraudulent election, José Miguel Gómez, with the support of other Liberal Party leaders such as Zayas, Gerardo Machado, and Carlos Mendieta, tried to take over the government by force. President Menocal, a U.S.-educated engineer who had managed a U.S.-owned sugar mill, crushed the rebellion with U.S. government support that included the sale of arms.

25. "The Lollipop," a conga, sung during the Liberal campaign.

a great force in this country, were able to get large numbers into their party. After that, when someone wanted to insult a black, he'd say, "Look at this *negro chambelonero!*" From a political point of view this conflict was racist, just like the one in 1912, but it ended with a call for goodwill and Menocal remained President for a second term.

During that period two of my brothers, Tomás and Diego, were put in jail, supposedly not for political reasons, but at bottom politics did have something to do with it. Tomasito was very emotional, not self-controlled like the rest of us. He was arrested three times. The first time was when he had a fight with a man in barrio Galiano. The man had once said, "That fellow thinks he can lord it over everybody just because he's Tomás Benedí. Well, the day he tries to interfere with me, he'll get what's coming to him."

It wasn't like my brother to let anyone get away with such talk. The next time they met, Tomasito had had a beer and was aggressive, so he said to the man, "You've been making threats, eh?" My brother carried a knife. The other man had a revolver, but Tomás didn't stop to think that he was outmatched. He lunged at the man, snatched the gun from him, fired *bang, bang,* just like that, and the bullet hit its mark! He stayed in jail about three months. In those times it was merely a question of getting someone with influence to put in a word for you.

The second arrest was because a woman, Elena, talked too much. Tomasito wasn't a womanizer but he did need a woman to wash and iron his clothes and cook his meals, and he didn't bother to find out if she was good or bad. Elena was a . . . well, at first they lived together secretly and later they started living together openly. She was the kind of woman who boasted that her husband didn't dare talk back to her. "The day Tomás gets into an argument with me, I'll fight it out with him," she added.

That annoyed my brother. He said, "I'm a man who respects other men and demands that same respect in return. How can I allow a woman to say that she can order me around?" Because of that, they separated. She said that if she ever ran into my brother, she'd fight him. Tomás got wind of it and said, "Very well, we'll see."

He started to look around for someone who could lend him a couple of revolvers. When he couldn't get them, he tried to borrow two knives. Everybody refused him the knives too. Finally he settled for two razor blades and began searching for Elena all over the place. One night someone told him, "I think I saw your wife at El Chino's fritter stand." What hurt Tomasito most was to have that woman called his wife.

He hurried over and found her still there, buying fritters. He touched her shoulder, "Hey, you, is it true you've been saying that you're going to fight me?"

She could only say, "Who, me, Tomasito?"

"Yes, you. Take one of these blades because I'm going to kill you."

"Oh no, no!" she protested.

"Oh yes!" he said. And, *pa!* he slashed her from her ear down to her chest. El Chino's stand was at a busy intersection, and when he saw Tomasito cut Elena he ran out screaming, "Tomasito Benedí killed a woman!" A crowd gathered immediately to see what had happened.

Tomasito was in jail three or four months, but once again he got out by means of influential politicians. Besides, Elena decided not to press charges against him. She talked it over with her family, who told her, "You should never talk about a man as you did about Tomasito. If you want to leave him, leave him, but don't say nasty things about him, much less challenge him to a fight."

The third time, he landed in jail after some man told everybody that my brother was an *Abacuá* and was a coward, too scared to fight. But that man knew there weren't any *Abacuás* in our family precisely because we wanted to avoid such gossip and quarrels. So the fight started and Tomasito wounded the other man with a knife.

Diego was like Tomás, though he was not a politician. He was first jailed because of a fight beginning with a trivial argument. Diego was lucky enough to strike the first blow and was jailed for six months. The second time it was for murder. He was passing a store and a drunk ran out and lifted his hand to hit him. In that situation Diego had no choice but to kill the man. That time my brother was sentenced to seventeen years, but before going to prison he managed to run away.

He spent some time in Yaguajay, where he had two or three friends who were policemen, so he joined the police force as if nothing had happened. He was all right until he arrested a prostitute who'd formerly worked in Havana. She said to him, "Aren't you Diego Benedí?"

"And what's that to you?"

"You'll find out. You'll be sorry you arrested me. I remember that you killed a man in Havana, that's all."

As soon as the woman returned to Havana, she went straight to the police and squealed on him. Since he was a fugitive from justice he had to serve out every single day of his sentence. After he got out, he died of cancer.

How my mother suffered during those seventeen years, waiting for her son. I never saw her shed one single tear though. She suffered silently, as mothers do. People asked her, "But Jacinta, how did it happen?" And she was such a brave woman she'd simply shrug her shoulders and say, "Oh well, such is life!"

I was making furniture at the shop at the time my father died. At 4:00 in the afternoon I received a phone call: "Listen, your father is seriously ill." I dropped what I was doing at once. By the time I got to the *solar,* there were lots of people milling around there. *Papá* was dead and my old lady was tying up his jaw with a kerchief when I came in the door. Think what a shock his death was for her!

Mamá never found out about my father's mistresses until the day he died. Several women showed up at the wake, one of them a girl who couldn't have been more than eighteen, weeping and crying aloud, "Oh, my Tomasito, my Tomasito!" *Papá* had taken me to visit her once, but at the wake she didn't give any sign at all that she'd seen me before. She just wept for her Tomás and wailed, "*Ay*, it's all over for me, he's gone!" Then she sat down quietly, and after a while she gave her condolences to my old lady, said goodbye, and left.

Even though *papá* had just died, *mamá* made a fuss about it. People tried to calm her down: "Don't worry about such things now, *chica;* they aren't important. She's just some girl Tomás passed the time with." *Mamá* brooded and brooded over it. My brothers and I tried to get her mind off it, and she calmed down a bit but could never really accept the idea.

My father's wake only lasted twenty-four hours. In those days it was the custom to burn lots of candles, four at the very least and occasionally eight. We didn't pray much, though *mamá* did say some prayers, right or wrong. I spent the night at some distance from my father's body, writing a poem about the way he died. People came up to me to express their condolences but I was absorbed in the poem I was writing.

Papá's death has been the greatest sorrow of my life. We all felt it so much we never again celebrated Christmas Eve together. He was the center of unity in our family, so all his children would celebrate it with him as the great fiesta in our home. But we were growing up by then, and afterward each of us went his own way.

Our family's situation was very depressing. Every one of us had the ambition to be somebody. But what happened? We had too many children and too little money. If one of us had some *centavos*, he had to help the rest of the family. Not one of us had failed to learn to read and write at least a little and to learn a trade, because that was what our parents wanted, but we could go so far and not one step further. There just weren't any great opportunities then. We had to make do with whatever crumbs fell from above. Jobs were very scarce. It really seemed as if the capitalists were conspiring: "The needier a man is, the more we'll deny him a job, until he'll work as cheaply as possible."

If I'd had an opportunity . . . who knows? I might be something different now, because I had the drive. My greatest ambition was to own enough property to give me some peace of mind and security. Some of my brothers hoped for more than I did. Octavio did pretty well, thanks to a bit of luck. He bought one of the first Fords in Cuba with 4,000 *pesos* he won in the lottery. He made good money driving it because it was a novelty here at the time. He worked as a chauffeur for Zayas for a while, so naturally he developed some political inclinations, like buying votes. But he was never a spokesman for any party or politician. Octavio wasn't the kind to spend money as fast as he earned it. He saved most of it.

Octavio was calm and even-tempered. He was very fond of dancing, and a dance was always a good place to get into a fight. But for all the dances he went to, nobody in the barrio could ever say that Octavio had been involved in so much as a heated argument. He had the good sense to leave whenever it looked as if a quarrel were about to start.

I won't say that Octavio's death was a mystery, since we're all born to die. But it was mighty strange. I saw him one minute full of life, and the next dead. He was living with a woman on Peregrino Street and at first I was suspicious and thought she might have caused his death. But the doctor certified that he died of a heart attack. Your heart can kill you without your even realizing it; anything—a strong emotion, a sudden joy—and you are dead. Octavio had problems just like everybody else, but he kept them to himself, and they finally killed him.

My sister Irene started working as a tobacco stripper. She realized later that to get ahead in this life you need an education, so she studied to be a nurse and became a midwife. She had a different approach to life. She liked to have lots of clothes and wanted to be somebody. She didn't marry until she was about thirty-seven, and she insisted that her daughter get an education before she married. The girl wanted to be a midwife but there wasn't enough money for that, so Irene advised her to study typing and shorthand instead. "Once you get your diploma," she said, "you can get a job and save up until you have enough money to study whatever you please." Irene had quite a strong character, just like *mamá*.

Years later, after *mamá* died, Irene was a second mother to us. We were all grown men then, so she never dared lift her hand against us. But she did put her foot down when necessary. Sometimes we felt it wasn't right for a woman who wasn't our *mamá* to be ordering us around. But we'd talk it over among us and finally agree, "*Chico*, she's right. She's simply following *mamá*'s example. Where would we all end if we started doing as we pleased simply because we are men? A woman, even if she has a strong personality, is much more tender in giving advice than any man could be." So we allowed her to lay down the law.

My brother Andrés was younger than I and died of tuberculosis in his twenties. He worked hard to become a sculptor and carver, and wanted to have a workshop of his own. He did good work and was in demand as a highly skilled and disciplined worker. But he didn't eat enough and he got sick. We just couldn't get ahead, any of us, because our family was so poor.

My brother Federico was a carpenter. He died of heart disease. Next to him in age was Jacinto. Only two of my brothers are still alive, Carlos and Javier. There are strong bonds between us but at the same time we're independent and don't see one another often. We don't have time for visiting. The youngest, Javier, works for JUCEI,[26] often staying out in the cane three, four, and five months at a stretch. He visits me when he comes to Havana.

The other one, Carlos, is both a housepainter and a builder. I haven't seen him for years. He's a Vanguard Worker[27] now and his family is very revolutionary. In fact, he's so absorbed in the revolutionary process that he has no time to visit his relatives. We're completely different anyway and I don't take any particular interest in seeing him.

Carlos was luckier in life than me. He had a steady job and the good fortune to marry a country girl who is very much like him in personality. In our home we weren't allowed to have one sweetheart today and a different one tomorrow, much less one wife today and a new one tomorrow. Having been brought up in that atmosphere Carlos brought home this girl and never brought another. And he never wavered in his loyalty to his wife, which is more than I can say about myself.

I'd wanted a wife, a home with every comfort, children and grandchildren like Carlos has, but I always put *mamá* first. I was very attached to her. After the others were gone, they all contributed toward the rent, but I stayed on and took care of her even after I was first married. Toward the last, though, *mamá* lived with Carlos.

26. *Juntas de Coordinación, Ejecución e Inspección* (Boards of Coordination, Execution and Inspection), a network of regional agencies which supervise implementation of state policy on provincial and local levels.

27. The Vanguard Worker program was part of a new system of union organization introduced in 1965–66, following the founding of the present Communist Party and the establishment of Party cells in all work centers. Requirements for Vanguard Worker status were similar to those for Party membership, so these workers provided a reservoir of potential Party candidates. In fact, membership in the Union of Young Communists was often awarded conjointly with Vanguard Worker status. (The Vanguard Worker program is discussed by Lionel Martin in the *Guardian* in a series of six articles beginning in the issue of May 10, 1969, and ending on July 5, 1969.) After 1970, this merger of Party and union functions for Party membership selection was abandoned, but the Vanguard Worker status was retained.

Chapter Two

Full of Illusions

LIFE IS NOT WHAT one wishes it to be and it brings grief and mental upsets that make us sometimes judge mankind wrongly. About the time *papá* died, I had some trouble with my first real sweetheart.

I'd had other women before. I'd even had a little sweetheart when I was about fourteen, but it was only a young fellow's flirtation. I'd stand on a corner with my hat tilted to one side and a cigarette in my mouth, just to show off. One day she walked by and I said to her, "From now on, you are my sweetheart."

"What, just like that?" she exclaimed.

And half seriously, half in fun, we became sweethearts. She was the first girl I ever kissed. I don't even remember her name or where she lived.

I started having relations with women when I was sixteen or seventeen. A bunch of us used to run around the different barrios. The "zone of tolerance," where most of the professional prostitutes were to be found, was in barrio Colón. Another was in barrio San Isidro, down by the docks, where so many foreigners landed. But in barrio Colón the zone was a bit more careful, more refined. The streets and houses were cleaner and the owners of establishments gave the women a kind of seminar on the way to treat clients. And if they had to spend a few *pesos* on a hairdo and clothes, they spent them. Quite a business!

I fell into San Isidro, the worse of the two. That was an education for me. Then I remembered my mother's advice about loose women and infections and I began worrying. A fellow runs around, urged on by the hot blood of youth, and all of a sudden he finds himself infected. Seventy-two hours passed with no symptoms, but I was still uneasy because there's a type of venereal disease that's very tricky. So I made up my mind not to go back to that kind of place. "I'll pick up a woman who I know is healthy, even if it costs more," I decided.

Things were different with the girl who was my sweetheart. We were serious. We'd been going together for about a year and we planned to get married soon. But my love for her died in the simplest, most painful way. My sweetheart was pregnant! *I* didn't make her so, that's for sure. Pregnant by another man! I don't know whether my eyes got green or yellow, whether my skin changed color, or what, but I controlled my temper and said, "She isn't worth getting angry about," and I left her.

I've always been grateful that it's my nature never to lose my temper over someone else's lack of conscience, dignity, or respect. Of course things like that hurt me deeply, but freedom meant so much to me that when something unpleasant happened I always kept above it all.

Youth is so impulsive! I decided I could pick up my life and forget the loved ones I had lost. Besides, I wanted to keep on reading so that I could become a writer some day. That's how my first marriage came about. Trying to get material for a novel at a dance, I got involved with María del Carmen.

It was at a costume party given by an association. I danced with a masked girl and was eager to know what she was really like. I could hardly wait for midnight and the order, "Off with the masks!" I was curious to know if there really was a woman under that costume. I wanted to judge her figure, her personality, her education. Led by my curiosity, instead of making the usual small talk I brought up the subject of Cuban history. Everybody else's mind was on nothing but dancing and drinking! I said, "Think of it, we live in a society where people are completely alienated from one another."

"What do you mean by that?" she asked.

"Well, take this dance. You find nothing but black faces here, dark skin. Why?"

"Because that's the way things are."

"All right. But really looking at it, in what way is a white person worth more than a black person?"

"*Chico,* I can't answer that. I have black skin myself but the way society is set up, a white skin does have value."

"But, look, physiologically speaking, what's the difference between one woman and another?"

"I don't see any difference except the color of their skin."

"Well, for me that has no importance." Then I took advantage of the occasion to bring up a related subject. "Take you, for instance," I said. "You're an ugly woman, yet you're attractive."

"Oh no, I have no attraction."

"You have attracted me."

When the dance was over I asked, "May I see you home?"

She said yes and that's when we started to talk lovers' talk. Strange as it may sound, I court a woman to find out how much I can trust her, and that's how I decide whether to live with her.

Love is a mysterious thing. Sometimes people think only of the physical aspect. They believe a man can love a woman at first sight, perhaps because of some very insignificant trait. But not me. I don't fall for a woman merely because she's pretty. When I see a pretty woman, I look her over from the top of her head to the tip of her toes but I pay special attention to two parts of her—her belly to see whether she eats a lot and her head to find out what's in it. There are a lot of women who know how to think but aren't the least bit pretty. Their beauty is inside. For me, a woman like that is worth more than one who covers herself with makeup from head to foot. I'll admit that, everything else being equal, I prefer a pretty woman. And if she can also think, so much the better.

María del Carmen hadn't had much schooling but she was the kind of woman you could talk to. When I met her she was living in the home of her former husband's mother. She had a two-year-old daughter. I don't know why María and her first husband separated. I felt it was unimportant and indelicate to pry. The more one questions, the more lies one may provoke.

I was very considerate of her former husband from the beginning, realizing that we men have our pride. I didn't insist on visiting her at her mother-in-law's house, because if that had happened to me I wouldn't like it. I usually met her someplace else between 8:00 and 8:30 P.M. Sometimes we'd stand and talk, other times we'd go somewhere. That way we got to know each other well before we decided to live together.

María del Carmen's husband, Manolo, pursued her insistently to get her back, and even went so far as to threaten that if he ever saw her with me, he wouldn't answer for his actions. I was effervescent with youth and love and my reaction was, "Well, *chica,* if that's what he said, I should ask him what he meant by it."

On May 1 we had the day off, and María and I were standing outside talking when Manolo walked up and said to María, "Hey, I've come to see you."

María just stood there staring at him. I said, *"Chico,* you're Manolo, aren't you? You told María you were going to make a decision the day you found us together. Well, this is it. Here I am, now do whatever you were thinking about doing."

"Then come on, step aside and let's have a man-to-man talk," he said.

We walked to the corner. I said, "This has to be settled right away. You've said that one of these days you were going to get me. Well, here I am."

"Ah, *compadre,"* he said, in a conciliatory tone, "you can't let yourself be led by woman talk."

"You didn't deny it in front of her, so it seems we do have something to talk over."

"No, no. Look, men's problems are something else again. There's no woman in the world worth fighting for!"

When he said that, I realized what a weakling he was and decided not to push him any further. The only thing I said was, "Well, don't bother María again, understand? I've decided that she will be my wife and must be respected."

I was still living with my mother, and before making my decision I took María to meet her. Right away *mamá* asked me, "How do you plan to treat her?"

"Well, *mamá*, as long as she's good, I'll be good to her, but if she turns out bad I'll separate from her."

"Aha, did you hear that, María? That means you have to look after him, too. I don't want to hear any complaints." Then she threatened to intervene if anything went wrong with our marriage.

I never met María's *mamá* but I met her *papá*, who was a musician. My family liked music, but there were no musicians in our family because it gave little opportunity to advance or to earn enough to support a family. María's *papá* had relationships all over the place and didn't bother much about his children's upbringing. He was as careless of his daughters as of his sons. María wasn't a loose woman though. She was a pleasant, amusing girl who loved to dance and didn't care where she did it. If you wanted a wife with strict manners you had to pick a girl who had been brought up in the country.

We waited about one year before we began living together, though we'd been having intimate relations ever since we met. As soon as I asked her, María agreed to move in with me, bringing her little daughter. The child's father wanted to keep his daughter, but María . . . well, you know how mothers are. "The child goes with me!" she said.

"All right," he agreed. "Just take good care of her and don't let Lázaro mistreat her." Me mistreat her? Impossible! I wanted that child to be my own daughter so that I could forget the failure of my first love affair. Besides, the child was completely obedient and already had plenty of clothes so she wouldn't be any great expense. The only thing she lacked was a bed, but a friend of mine gave us a crib a few days later.

María and I lived first in a room in barrio Cayo Hueso. It was in a *solar,* two stories high, with a metal roof. Each floor of the *solar* had about eight rooms and one bathroom, so our room didn't have a private bath.

Before we moved in, the landlord whitewashed the room and we fixed it up. I was still doing carpentry, and the owner of the workshop let me make my own furniture there, using bits of left-over wood. They also let me have cane for the seats and a mahogany-colored varnish. It took me two months to make a set of six chairs, two rocking chairs, and a bedside table. I was earning about 15 *pesos* a week and they discounted 3 *pesos* a month from my wages until it was all paid up.

I bought an iron bed for 15 *pesos* and a cotton quilt to use as a mattress. I got it from a friend for 3 *pesos,* which I paid out little by little. We had a charcoal stove in the room since we were forbidden to cook outside. One by one I bought the pots and pans and other utensils we needed.

I refused María permission to bring along her bedding. *"Chica,"* I said, "by making a small sacrifice, I can buy new bedding. I think it's my duty to do it." I also wanted to avoid problems with her former husband. Men are likely to have certain selfish or stupid reactions, like, "I don't want them to lie on the bed I bought or to cover themselves with my sheets."

I said, "If we have no sheets, we'll cover ourselves with hemp sacks." There was no need for that, though, because María had a job too, earning 15 *pesos* a month as a domestic.

I've always been against women working. I demand a lot in the way of housekeeping, and a woman who is holding an outside job can't tend her own house as she should. Besides, I wanted to give María del Carmen a completely different kind of life. Not only that, I was afraid if my wife worked outside, another man might fall in love with her. I know that's silly. If a woman's going to fall for another man, she'll fall in love even if you keep her locked up behind iron bars. Anyhow, as soon as things settled down, María and I decided to live on what little I earned.

The day we finally moved she said, *"Chico,* why go to work today? Please stay home. I want to talk to you." It was only a piece of feminine coquetry, something a man needs, but I've always hated to be short of money so I explained to her that a day without work meant a day without pay. "I'd be so upset about missing a day's pay, I'd spend the whole time quarreling." That was the kind of honeymoon we had, a working one. I make strict demands on myself as I like to give my wife everything she needs.

We began our marriage full of illusions, María thinking that now she had her own home, and I believing our love would last forever. I was a romantic because I'd read so many novels. If there was a spot on her dress, I looked for the most tactful way of telling her, "Here, take a bit of alcohol and rub out that spot." I even picked out her underclothes, but I always asked first if she liked them because I didn't want to impose my wishes on her.

María was very agreeable and eager to please me. She always had clean clothes laid out ready for me. She was a good manager of money and never spent a cent on things we didn't need. Even though she was always clean and neat, she had the coquetry to ask me if she looked all right. "Yes, you do look nice," I'd answer. Then of course we'd kiss and make plans to go to the movies or to a dance that night. She only had to express a wish and I would agree, to please her. We left the child with one of María's women friends. She was the sociable type and made lots of friends right away.

Duties and obligations were discussed, never quarreled about. If I did something wrong, I always gave her the opportunity to express her point of view and claim her rights. But I watched over her comings and goings jealously. I was afraid that some day she might make a slip, and quite often I put my foot down. If she happened to go to *mamá*'s house, she was careful to note what time she left and when she got there. "Jacinta," she'd say, "don't forget what time I got here in case Lázaro asks you. You're my best witness if he should want to know."

Many times I deliberately tried to annoy María to see how she'd react. Sometimes when I got home and found her deep in thought, I'd say to her, "What are you thinking about, the other man?"

"But Lázaro," she'd protest, "why should you think such a thing?"

"Well, you looked so thoughtful."

"And couldn't I be thinking about you?" That was all she'd say at the moment. When I annoyed her like that, she'd respond with silence. But when she saw I wasn't angry anymore, she'd ask me, "Why do you treat me that way? Why do you even bring up such things? Why?"

We hadn't been living together a year when María became pregnant. It happened in an impulsive moment, I don't know how. After that I worried about her all the time. It was her second child but my first. To me nothing was too much to assure her a safe delivery, especially after I was told the baby would be a boy. I didn't even want her to laugh, because she'd be exerting herself and the baby might come out prematurely. Whenever I passed a store selling baby things, I'd buy rattles, milk bottles, or baby clothes. The crib was a gift from my brother Tomás. My whole family was preoccupied with the birth of my first child.

In her eighth month of pregnancy María lost the baby as a result of lifting something heavy. She'd been warned not to because her womb was too low. But it's a defect in women that they'll always do the opposite of what they're told. That day, when I got home from work, María complained she wasn't feeling well. "I think the baby's coming," she told me.

I fetched the midwife, then I waited and waited for the baby's first cry, but no cry came. I was desperate. Finally the midwife came out and gestured. "What happened?" I asked.

"The baby was born dead," she answered. "It was premature."

I just stood there and stared. I guess the midwife realized what I was feeling because she said, "Don't worry, you can have another child. Your wife is in very good condition."

When I heard why she had miscarried I was like a wild beast, a brute. I screamed at her, "Listen, if you kill my next child, I swear I'll kill you!" I knew I shouldn't have threatened her like that, least of all at that moment, but I was so upset I couldn't help myself.

Afterward I talked this over with my sister, who later became a midwife herself. She explained that a woman has seven wombs. Any one of these can accept a man's semen. If for some reason the remaining six wombs lack the strength, they close up and the baby occupies only the womb in which it was conceived. If the baby is carried in the lowest of the seven, it's easier for it to come out if the woman slips and falls or over-exerts herself. Even a scare can make her miscarry.

In 1920 the crash came because some financial negotiations fell through and the price of sugar sank so low that stores sold it at 1 *centavo* a pound.[28] Only the rich owners escaped ruin. The Cuban people were helpless. They flocked to take their savings out of the banks and a law was made to delay it. I found out about it, but by the time I got there my money was lost.

I'd been putting all my extra money in the International Bank and had saved up 200 *pesos*. I didn't really like to squander money so I put it in the bank instead of carrying it around in my pocket. Most black Cubans spend more of their money on amusement than on their real needs. That was proved when blacks began to work in construction. How many white owners were there and how many black, eh? But I saved my money, and look what happened to me. In one day I lost all that I'd worked so hard to earn!

In 1920 Zayas ran against Gómez for President and won. By then I knew pretty well what was going on in Cuban politics. I was in favor of Zayas because he respected men's rights and followed Martí's doctrine. I hoped that as chief executive of the nation, Zayas would get together with his Council of Ministers and do something about Cuba's general poverty. Eventually I realized he was as ambitious as he was intelligent. His aim as a lawyer was not to serve mankind but to get rich by defend-ing criminals.

During the Zayas administration the Veterans' and Patriots' Associa-tion was organized,[29] to defend everyone's interests I thought. This was easy to believe, considering that each of them had made sacrifices for our country's independence. But there were many lawyers, doctors, and professionals who very cleverly utilized this movement for their own political ends. That made me think hard about the whole business. I decided to remain a sympathizer but not get involved in propagandizing

28. This decade, beginning with a period known as the "dance of the millions," when the world sugar price fluctuated rapidly, was a disastrous one for Cuba's sugar industry. The world market price fell from 22.5 cents per pound in May, 1920, to 3.75 cents by De-cember, 1920. As supply exceeded demand, prices rose and fell throughout the decade and many persons in the sugar industry were financially ruined. (Thomas, *Cuba: The Pursuit of Freedom*, pp. 536 ff.)

29. Founded in 1923, the Association was a short-lived attempt to fight corruption in the Zayas government. It was headed by Carlos García Vélez, son of the War of Independence hero General Calixto García, but he denounced the Association when it launched a mili-tary expedition against the government. It was quickly put down and the Association disbanded.

until I saw how it developed. I was more ambitious than anyone suspected and I didn't want to get mixed up with anything losing prestige. My real preoccupation was with social, not political, problems.

I often talked with my friends in the barrio about Cuba's problems and discussed the news we read. My favorite newspapers were *El Mundo* and *La Prensa*. I liked Ramón Vasconcelos's articles in *La Prensa* against racist discrimination.[30] He also wrote some important articles examining international problems in depth. Next to Vasconcelos, I liked the classified ads because it made looking for a job much easier.

I was out of a job! I lived by stretching 2 *pesos* as far as I could. I nicknamed myself "the 2-*peso* man," because no matter what work I did I always got paid 2 *pesos* a day. María said, "*Chico*, it looks as if I'm a stumbling block in your path, because when we first started we were much better off. Let's go to a spiritist to see if you can find out why you're having such a streak of bad luck."

"Don't go telling the spiritist all our troubles first," I warned her. "If you do, she'll only repeat everything you told her. I can see through their tricks." At that time I didn't believe in anything, not even the sun that shined on me. I didn't allow María to have an altar or anything like it in the house.

But then *mamá* got sick and asked me to go. In spite of being a devout Catholic, she had to have some African rites to get better. She was from the country, where people treated everything with herbs because it was difficult to get to a doctor. And people did get better.

So María and I went to a spiritist and found her sitting there with her eyes shut. We sat down and right off she told me a lot of things which, unfortunately, were all true. At first I wasn't impressed because I thought María must have told her about them on the sly, but later everything she predicted happened just as she said. From that moment on, I began to feel a great respect for spiritism. I even started to set out water offerings to the spirits.

Because of my financial problems, I moved to no. 250 Virtudes Street, where I had to pay only 10 *pesos* a month for rent. I was practically without work then and not liking it a bit. To fill up my time, I often went to a barbershop on San José Street, to watch the barbers and learn how to cut hair. I got several customers among the young fellows in the barrio. That way I managed to survive until I found a job.

María got pregnant again. This time she gave me the news timidly,

30. A journalist who held diplomatic and cabinet positions under the governments of Gerardo Machado, Carlos Prío, and Fulgencio Batista. Hugh Thomas refers to Vasconcelos as a "mentor" of Fidel Castro: Vasconcelos nominated Castro for the House of Representatives and many times printed Castro's articles in his newspaper, *Alerta*. (*Cuba: The Pursuit of Freedom*, p. 820.)

afraid I would yell at her. I was still upset over my first loss, so I said, "Listen, if picking things up can make you lose this baby, don't pick up anything, not even a box of matches. If cooking is too much for you, don't cook. There's no need to take such risks."

I took her to the doctor regularly for five months. At the end of that time he told me, "Your wife is all right now, but she shouldn't lift anything heavy." I treated María as if she were a baby herself.

On January 14, 1922, my first child was born. When they told me it was a boy, I was so wildly happy I forgot all my problems. We called him Octavio after my eldest brother. María nursed the baby for two years. We both loved him dearly. He was an adorable child and *mamá* came often to see him.

I'd felt sure all the time that my firstborn would be a boy. That's what every man egotistically wants. I even went to the extremes of egotism, or stupidity, I don't know which. I had a friend with whom I kidded all the time. One day when I ran into him, I was carrying my child very proudly. I don't know why he teased me then, but he stopped and said, "So you think the kid is yours?"

Something came over me. I held the child tighter and lifted him with every intention of throwing him at the guy's head. A man who was walking along behind him realized what I was about to do and snatched the baby from me just in time. Then my friend said, "*Chico, compadre,* can't you take a joke?"

"Not about my son I can't. This child means everything to me. In my anger, I was fool enough to risk losing him and going to jail because of your joke. Don't you dare kid me like that again!" After my first outburst of rage I understood he was only joking, but that was the end of our friendship.

I can't figure out exactly how women manage to get the upper hand, but a man with many children is a slave. If his wife knows he loves children, she's bound to use that fondness to enslave him even more. For that reason, and because I thought that if we had more children we'd be robbing our son of affection, I tried to keep María from getting pregnant again. That was pure ignorance on my part, I must confess. With time I came to the opposite conclusion. An only child cannot bring happiness to the home because his parents live with the fear, "What if we should lose him? What's left to us then?"

I always associate my son's birth with an adventure I had one time as I was strolling through Central Park with some friends. We met a group of girls who were also out for a walk. In typical manly fashion, I paid a compliment to them. All I said was, "*Ay,* what a pretty sight!" Some compliment, eh? Why, it didn't mean a thing! But one of them turned right around and smiled at me. What struck me most about Marta was her smile. A smile accompanied by a coquettish look means a woman is willing to answer if you start a conversation. So when that happens, we men press on.

Marta was eighteen or nineteen years old. She told me I was the first man she'd known and I believed her. I knew the signs that show if a girl is a virgin because I had questioned my older brothers, who had more experience. "Why *chico*, it's simple," they said. "When you deflower a girl there's always a little spot of blood."

Well, I couldn't go snooping around to find out whether she bled or not. That's why I've never bothered about a woman's being a virgin, especially when I'm just having a casual affair with her.

Marta and I kept meeting in secret, and one day she said, "Oh Lazarito, I'm pregnant!"

"Very well," I told her. "If it turns out that you're right, you can be sure I won't abandon you."

But when her folks noticed her condition, they said, "We're going to move right back to Santiago. This can't go on." And it didn't. Marta didn't even write me after she left. The only thing I ever learned was that she gave birth to a girl.

María never found out about it. I loved and respected her too much to be indiscreet. It seems she looked upon me as some kind of a god. She was noble-hearted; I think I conquered her heart and her feelings. Some people might say, "If you loved María that much, why did you have an affair with Marta?" Well, like anyone else, I won't risk having any woman say I'm something less than a man. It was a mere adventure. But María had her outbursts of violence, and if she had ever found out about Marta, I don't know where I'd be now. A woman whose feelings have been hurt is more dangerous than a man, because women are jungle beasts disguised as human beings.

The truth is, I deceived María del Carmen only when I had a chance with some other woman. But she was always jealous and thought it proper to take her complaints to *mamá* so that the three of us could sit down and talk them over. *Mamá* was judge, advocate, and prosecutor. She usually leaned toward María's side because in her opinion women are always right and men are always rascals. She'd say that just because we were her sons we needn't expect her to let us browbeat our wives.

It seemed to me that María was bribing *mamá* with gifts so that when she went to her with some complaint, *mamá* would remember and say, "María's always good to me." When I protested María only said, "I'm very fond of your mother." Then I'd say, "If you're trying to buy her, kindly remember she's my mother, not yours."

My separation from María del Carmen came about because I loved her too much. When you love someone deeply, your mind gets fogged. I can't explain what made me worship María, but I was so madly in love with her that, young and free as I was, I could never look at another woman as a woman. I felt I had all I needed right at home. But in spite of her good points, we separated because I had a stupid jealous fit.

María's first husband had gotten into the habit of hanging around the street corner near our house. I didn't like that, so I said to him, "Look, when you want to see your daughter, you don't have to wait for my permission. Go up to the house. That's something I cannot forbid you to do."

Even after that he kept on hanging around. Then I told María, "When he comes here, let him in, even if I'm not home. That child is his daughter. If you and I ever separate and another man tries to prevent me from seeing my child, I'll hold you responsible."

She was very nervous about the whole business and I don't know whether she forgot or didn't have a chance to tell him. But one day I came home from work and found him standing there on the corner. I got really angry so I didn't say a word to him. But as soon as I walked in the door, I said to María, "This is precisely the kind of thing I don't want. I bet you two have been standing there making signs at each other." I made a terrific fuss and ended up by telling her, "This is the end of our marriage."

"But Lázaro," she pleaded. "What's wrong? What upset you?"

"Nothing. I didn't see anything and I don't want you to tell me anything about it, either. My mind is made up."

If there's one thing I can't stand, it's a disobedient woman. Although, frankly, I don't know whether María disobeyed me this time or not. All I know is it bothered me. I told her, "I'm going to live at *mamá*'s house. You stay here. You'll have no problems as you'll always be sure of a place to live and money to support the children." From that day on, we never again lived together.

María tried to come back to me. She was very hurt, of course, and kept visiting *mamá*, whom she truly respected and loved. She'd give *mamá* her version of things, then *mamá* would scold me without letting me explain my reasons. She simply said it was all my fault and it was useless to argue. She never said, "You, Lázaro . . ." or "You, my sons . . ." but always, "You men . . . !" María and *mamá* had become so attached that even before the separation *mamá* nagged me constantly, "Don't you ever leave María, not for anything in the world. You men treat a woman carelessly and María is a noble-hearted woman who deserves a lot better than you."

I sincerely confess that breaking up with María made me terribly unhappy. It was the hardest blow I ever received. An understanding grows between a man and a woman, so that he comes to think of her not as a wife but as a sister, a person who is concerned about him. When that happens, he gets equally concerned about her.

After I cooled off I asked myself what she'd done wrong and why I had been so violent. I suffered and wept and wanted her back. My life had been loving her, though I don't know whether she was that much in love with me.

One day we ran into each other and she called me a coward. Her words disarmed me, physically disarmed me. I thought, "What's she up to? She's probably trying to make me angry and violent to get me in trouble."

I couldn't understand myself. How can I explain what it is to hate a woman, yet to love her so much that you feel jealous if another man so much as looks at her? I knew it would be very hard to find another who would compare with her. You may ask then, why did I leave her? Well, when a man no longer trusts a woman, it's best to break up. In my mind I keep the woman and the female apart. They both belong to the same sex, but what a difference between them!

If María del Carmen had been the kind to stop and think for just one minute, it might have been enough to keep us together until now, some forty-odd years later. It would have been a treat, me walking around, leaning on a stick, with grandchildren and even great-grandchildren growing up around me.

Two years after we broke up, María took up with another man. I couldn't expect anything else, after all. She was only twenty-four. She had waited long enough, especially considering that it was impossible for her to support herself and the children on the little I gave her. If only it had been a first love for both of us, it might have ended quite differently.

María's a little old woman now. I visit her house and talk with her husband and the children she bore him. Sometimes I can tell she wants to bring up the subject of our marriage. But, after all, she's a grandmother now and it just isn't proper to discuss the past. When she sighs, "*Ay*, Lazarito!" I say to her, "No, old girl, look, many years have passed. You've grown old and so have I. We can't scramble around and try to dig up the past. What's done is done and we might as well forget it. If you tried to revive our old feelings, you'd be setting a bad example for your children."

MARÍA DEL CARMEN MÉNDEZ:

I met Lázaro at a dance given by a club named Youth of the Golden Arm. It must have been about 1921, shortly after I had separated from my little girl's father. My daughter, Benita, and I were still living in my mother-in-law's house, next door to the club. My mother-in-law was very good to me. She took care of the little girl so I could work.

Lázaro began to visit me at home, and my aunt said, "Look here, girl, rather than go looking for a bad man, here you have one who at least you know is good." And so I accepted him.

I never told Lázaro anything about my separation from my first husband, Manolo Gutiérrez. It wasn't necessary. Lázaro was a little jealous but has always been a very correct man, sweet and affectionate, never rude or a user of bad words. My first husband wasn't vulgar either. He came to the house to visit after we separated and I went to his house, too.

I was working in a tobacco factory when I first met Manolo. My father hadn't wanted me to work, but when I was twelve my step-mother said, "Well, there isn't enough money so let her become independent and get a job." My own mother had wanted me to study, but after your mother dies nothing is ever the same. I only went through the second grade. My stepmother wasn't concerned about such a thing as education, but, poor woman, she did treat me well and never beat me. She'd tell me, "You see, women have to learn to be practical, to clean the house and all that."

I began to work deveining tobacco leaves, a trade I had learned from my *mamá*. The tobacco poisoned her but she had to work to bring me up. I used to take the leaves away from her and start helping, but then she'd get angry and scold me a lot. She finally got a lung disease and died in 1911 when she was thirty-five years old. I was nine.

Three years later I got a job in a tobacco factory. I worked from 6:00 A.M. to 4:00 P.M. and had lunch right there in the shop, in a canteen where they served thick soup, meat, and tubers or rice for 15 *centavos* a day.

I earned 6.25 *pesos* a week. I'd never had so much money of my own. I took my first pay envelope to my stepmother, and I'll always remember that from my first week's money she and my father took 2 *pesos* and bought me a pair of boots trimmed with patent leather. I thought it was a real extravagance. Later I earned more money, 10.50 *pesos* a week, in another factory.

Then I met Manolo, and he told my stepmother that he wasn't interested in playing fast and loose with me but wanted to set up a home of our own. In those days people didn't marry. My stepmother came to see us and she made me clothes, so even though we were poor, we had enough of everything.

Our little girl was born a year later when I was sixteen. I was happy the day I had my child. I was quite well off and had the money to pay the midwife. In those days they charged 15 *pesos* for a delivery.

I don't know whether Manolo was jealous, but after we got married he wouldn't let me work and was awfully particular about me not going out to do the shopping. He'd buy the groceries himself every fifteen days, when he got paid. We'd go out with the baby every Sunday, but I never went anywhere alone because Manolo didn't like it.

I was happy but I had to leave Manolo because he had another woman. The girl next door started to flirt with him and he began courting her. I found out about it because I saw them coming out of the bath together, and you aren't going to share your bath with a man you don't know, are you now? Naturally, I really got mad. So I told him, "I don't care for this sort of thing and we're through."

Love can't be shared by two because that is hypocrisy. If you really love, you love only one, but if your love isn't real, you may care for two or three. A man like that will always be deceiving either one or the other, and I don't like to be deceived. So I went to my aunt's house and later I went back to his mother's.

Manolo's *mamá* was really a mother to me. Even my other children call her Grandmother. She felt very bad about the separation, but she said to me, "Daughter, he has the same habit his father had. It's better for you to separate, because if he shows this lack of respect for you today, tomorrow he'll make you leave and bring someone else into your house."

So I told my *papá*, "Look, Manolo and I are going to separate." And my *papá* said, "Then I don't want you talking with him on the street. Either you stay separated or go on living together." And I answered, "No, I give you my word that I won't go back to him again."

Later Manolo wanted me to go back to him, but I'd given my word to my *papá* and I had to respect that. Things were different then; if you made a promise to your elders, you had to keep it.

When I was about to get engaged to Lázaro I informed Manolo. "Well," he answered, "if you don't want to continue with me, it's your funeral. I'll look for another wife."

When Lázaro and I began living together, he was working as a carpenter in a furniture factory. We got along nicely because he treated my little girl well and so did his mother, Jacinta.

My daughter Benita liked yellow rice very much and would say, "Jacinta, cook me some rice with goat meat because I like it so much." It was really pork with pork bones, so the old woman would laugh and laugh and go ahead and do it to make the child happy.

Lázaro's mother was black. She took in laundry, but was very refined and well-bred. She was nice to me from the start, really treating me like her daughter. She said, "I only had one daughter, now I'll have two." She went everywhere with me. If she went to the movies, she took me. But she beat her sons and didn't have much of a way with other people.

Lázaro didn't like me to go out even with his mother because he was very jealous. When I got ready to go somewhere, he'd ask, "Where are you going?" If I took my daughter to visit her grandmother, he'd remind me, "Watch the time, now." He'd look at his watch and keep track of when I went out and when I came back. I'd say, "You're crazy. There's nothing between Manolo and me now. He has his wife just as I have my husband." And it's true, Lázaro never had any problems with my first husband.

A year after we began living together I got pregnant, but I miscarried. A little girl pulled a bench out from under me and I fell. I never told Lázaro the truth about it because he was so furious. He was crazy to have a child. He thought I didn't want any more children. But I told him, "No, this wasn't on purpose, it was an accident." Later, when Octavio was born, he was very happy.

If Lázaro wasn't in love with me, he certainly acted as if he were. And it was the same with me, I was sincere with him. But in this respect I had bad luck with him, too. I had to leave him because of another girl.

They used to sell ice cream in carts on the street, and if you went to the creamery at night you could buy the left-over ice cream. They gave large portions, and since I got out of work at 11:00 P.M. I'd buy ice cream for Lázaro and his mother. Well, this girl Eva came to Jacinta's house all the time, making up to him. She'd say, "Let me have just a taste of yours."

I said, "Lazarito, what's this all about?" And he said, "Nothing, it's friendship, nothing more." But that friendship was carried on half naked and that didn't look good. Jacinta always told me, "That one's a hussy." Lázaro didn't dare talk back to his mother because he knew how strict she was.

One day he said to me, "Listen here, don't bring ice cream to my mother at 11:00 at night anymore, because that's no hour for any woman to be on the streets." But I went on bringing the ice cream, and once I ran into them talking with their heads together in a dark corner. It looked suspicious, so I went to his mother and said, "Look, Jacinta, my love for Lazarito goes up to this point and no further, because as things are I'm not staying with him."

That was at the beginning of 1924. Octavio was still a baby. He must have been just a little over one year old when we separated. I went to stay with my aunt and got a job in the tobacco factory. At the end of the same year I got together with my present husband, Pedro. I'd known him for a long time because he lived in the neighborhood. So when I was left alone for the second time, he came over and began to talk with me. Who could be better than a man I'd known for such a long time? I accepted him and moved to Saravia Street with him and the two children.

At that time Pedro was a longshoreman and he didn't earn more than 2 *pesos* a day. I went on working until I gave birth to Pedro's eldest child. After that, I'd go to work once in a while when things were slow at the docks. I had thirteen children with Pedro, but I lost six.

BENEDÍ:

In 1924 Machado[31] ran for President as a Liberal and won. I voted for him because the Liberal Party had established a number of small industries here in Cuba. They were limited but at least they were Cuban. First came the shoe industry, then the cement factory, and then, I think, the paint factory at Rancho Boyeros. This industrial development kept alive the hope that my relatives and friends and I would have an opportunity to work. In his first few years of office, Machado won the people's confidence and affection, but unfortunately things got worse later.

By then I was twenty-four and felt I knew enough to manage my own workshop. I was working for Pepe Ruiz and I told several of the other workers, "Look, *chicos*, I know we can earn more than we do here." At the time, a carpenter named Sierra, who owned a workshop, had been put in charge of all the carpentry for the jail. Our group worked for him as a brigade, "at a thousand and ten miles an hour," we said. Sierra was enthusiastic about our work and raised our wages several times. After a while I was earning 3 *pesos* a day, which really meant something then. We kept on working there until one of the fellows ran into our former boss, Pepe Ruiz. Ruiz said we had all acted very badly, leaving in a bunch like that. The young fellow was a weakling. He replied, "Oh, it wasn't my fault, Lázaro suggested it."

"He did?" said Ruiz. "Well look, the rest of you fellows come back to work with me and I'll pay you more than whatever you're earning now. Only make sure Lázaro doesn't come back to my shop."

Four men were all for going back to Ruiz, but the rest of us were satisfied to stay away, knowing that Ruiz only offered higher wages to get us back. So we divided up.

Around 1925 we got interested in the international labor movement. Some of the men argued, "But *chico*, we don't have the strength to carry out those aims."

"All right, we don't," I admitted. "We have to build up our own strength. If we can get a good number of workers to join the movement, you'll see how we can work for our class." So three of us, Juan Aranal, who worked as a linotypist, Miguel Quesada, a stonecutter, and I, decided to found the Trio of International Workers. Miguel was a mulatto, Juan was white, and I, black.

Then began the movement to unionize the trades. In organizing unions and fostering the workers' struggles at that time, we gave our

31. General Gerardo Machado, President 1925–33, was one of Cuba's most notorious dictators.

greatest energy to Havana workshops. But we were so ignorant! We lacked understanding of the working class. People here felt you had to be on the side of your boss. It's easy to see why. The workers would outdo themselves so that on Christmas Eve the boss would say to them, "Here's an extra 5 *pesos* for you," or "10 *pesos*," and they'd be very pleased.

Communism was making its start in Cuba under the leadership of Mella[32]—this was in 1925—and all who were involved were persecuted. It went hard with us. We were attracted to the Communist Party because they had no prejudice against race or color. We didn't know much about communism, but we understood those things instinctively. When I say "we" I mean myself. "I" is a pronoun I hate and avoid.

Our interest in the labor movement contributed toward Mella's campaign. We'd always heard about the Americans and how they could destroy us any time they felt like it, so we had developed a patriotic conscience but not a proletarian one. We knew nothing about our rights as workers. Mella came forward to focus on some of the problems. Being a man of clear intelligence, he foresaw that Machado's administration would weaken under the thrust of imperialism, so he created the Anti-Imperialist League. In 1925 he went on a hunger strike in protest against the government. The papers carried news of it every day, and it turned into a public scandal because he almost died.

I didn't actively collaborate with Mella's League. It was one of those organizations where people had to pass through a sieve, so to speak. Only a carefully selected few were fully informed. I like to know all the problems in depth, and I refused to belong to an organization just because someone said, "Join this because it's good" or "Take a gun and shoot in that direction." I won't follow a cause blindly. When I fight, I want to understand what I'm fighting for.

I saw Mella in 1926 or 1927. I was standing with some others at a crossing and one of the group said, "Look, there's Mella." He was one of those men whose mere presence is attractive. What a splendid, athletic figure he had! He seemed to be from another world. It's like painting a picture of God and loving Him. Absolutely! By that I mean that his attitude, his amiability and understanding, his manners, his natural and honest selflessness in pursuit of a cause, made him loved by men. The way he spoke! And his actions proved the sincerity of everything he said.

In 1928 Machado decided to abolish the vice-presidency and give

32. Julio Antonio Mella (1905–29), a leader of the university student movement in the twenties and one of Cuba's most famous martyrs. Mella helped found the Cuban Communist Party in 1925 and was a member of the Party's first Central Committee. In 1927 Mella went into exile in Mexico, where he became involved in the international communist movement. He was assassinated in Mexico in 1929, apparently on order from Cuban President Machado.

himself another six-year term of power without re-election.[33] At first we didn't understand that this was motivated by imperialism. As I saw it, his administration had done some good things and had some nationalistic ideas, but the men around him were personally ambitious. They wanted to get rich by exploiting the working people and preventing them from being organized. Things began to look bad. As soon as he postponed the election and announced his intention of remaining in power, Machado's attitude became, "Whoever doesn't agree with me is a burden on the earth." And he started having people killed for protesting. We long-suffering Cubans had to accept him as President or else. What a way to live!

As a worker my own interests were involved, so two or three comrades and I decided that, poor as we were, we weren't going to stand for it. We believed it should be the people who should decide. In spite of all their faults, the Cuban people have always been clear-sighted enough to realize that what is forced on them is not good. I couldn't accept such things, so I protested publicly. That made me subject to persecution, and I had to clear out. I left my job and my home and had to sleep in doorways. It was a disaster!

Because of the economic depression, one by one we lost our jobs, and when we fell behind one month in the rent, the landlord immediately began eviction proceedings. My family had been living in the same place fifteen years, paying 15 *pesos* a month regularly! My brothers and I figured out that in all those years we must have paid enough to reimburse the owner for his original investment. I confronted him and said, "I don't mind sleeping on a park bench, but it's inconceivable that my mother should be driven into the street. Let me tell you one thing: if you dare bring a court official here, I'm going to blow your brains out. I'll kill you like a dog if you commit such an injustice."

He filed charges anyway, and in due time he showed up with the bailiff and the court official. Then I suffered the worst pain I ever felt in my life—seeing my mother's furniture in a heap out in the street. The shame of it!

As it happened, the bailiff was a white boy who'd been my playmate in childhood. "But Lázaro, if you had told me ahead of time, we could have prevented this."

"Don't worry," I told him. "It's going to stop right here. The landlord is within the law. I respect the laws and believe they should be kept. But I

---

33. In April, 1928, a constitutional convention was convened to abolish the vice-presidency and to extend the term of office for the presidency from four to six years. Without calling new elections, Machado was given a six-year second term in office that was to have ended in 1935. In 1933 he was overthrown in a military coup ("the sergeants' conspiracy") led by Fulgencio Batista Zaldívar. (Thomas, *Cuba: The Pursuit of Freedom*, pp. 586 ff.)

also believe a man's word must be kept, and I've promised to blow his brains out if he goes through with this."

The court official heard me and, well, we lost our room, but with the condition that we could look for a place to live before we had to move. I finally found one on San Nicolás Street. The landlord, Rogelio Díaz, was my friend because we belonged to the same religion. He told me, "The only problem is that it has two rooms."

"That's fine. One room for *mamá* and one for the rest of us."

We lived awhile there, paying 2 *pesos* a month rent for each of the two rooms. But things got worse and worse. We didn't want to make problems so we said, "All right, Rogelio, if we have an opportunity, we'll move."

Shortly after I lost my job—sometime around 1929—Armindo López, a friend of mine, said to me, "*Chico,* you can work with me if you want to."

"If I want to! How could I not want to?" I answered.

We worked from Monday through Friday making little chairs. On Saturday and Sunday we'd go out and sell them. We didn't become millionaires but at least we made a living. There were times when we earned 8 to 10 *pesos* a week, but other times it was only 5. Of course if we had had a contract with a furniture store, that would have brought us a fixed income. But we didn't, and the lumber was a problem too. We had to look for the wood and never knew how much we'd have. If we'd bought it from a lumber mill, we'd have known how many chairs we could make.

After I started working with Armindo, some members of the Liberal Party made me all sorts of propositions, asking me to take part in the government because they knew I was an intense fighter. They tried to bribe me by offers of jobs and favors. It may sound strange, but I was never interested in their offers. I knew their political motives and I wanted nothing from people who didn't believe in the common good as I did.

In one instance, a Liberal Party leader who was in charge of municipal construction offered me a job through a friend of mine. I told my friend, "*Chico,* he wants me to accept putting my name on his payroll to earn 1 *peso* more than other Cubans. I won't accept wages under those circumstances." And I didn't. Investigate and examine every government payroll since the establishment of the Republic and you won't find my name on one of them. If we were going to struggle for the good of the community, we had to think of everyone.

Once I was offered employment as a special policeman. I didn't accept, of course. One of my friends in the police argued, "What's wrong with being a policeman? Earning money, that's what's important!"

I explained to him, "Don't assume that an oppressive government can ever be a stable one. This government is going to fall sometime, maybe soon, and the first ones to suffer the consequences will be you police-men. You know your mission is to browbeat the people and that isn't exactly popular. Unless you eliminate every single person who's against the current government, or make sure nobody can point you out when the government falls, you're out of luck."

Chapter Three

The Move to Las Yaguas

AFTER MY SEPARATION from María del Carmen, I couldn't seem to find a compatible woman. I gave lots of advice to married people, but for myself I was utterly disappointed. I don't know who said past times were always better; for me, remembering the past sometimes makes me want to die.

I think that the truest and most sincere love is that of a man for a woman, not that of the woman for the man, because men are willing to go to any extreme, even self-sacrifice, for their women. When a man falls in love, he's like an artist trying to paint a beautiful picture. He forgets to eat, bathe, or make himself look presentable. He cares only about making his picture as perfect as possible, then he takes care of it and shelters it. And if the portrait turns out to be a bit colorless, he retouches it. He makes the image of that woman the core of a great illusion. And when the idol is broken, he grieves for the loss of it. Ah, we men weep.

A woman merely says, "I was once everything to this man but now it's over and what do I care." That's why I believe a woman's love is much less than a man's. I hope the ladies will forgive me for saying so, but men are slaves to real sacrifice. When a woman goes down the street leaning on your arm and another man pays her a compliment, you can see how she swells with pride. Women are so egotistical that you can't even smile because they'll think you're smiling at another woman. Now that socialism has come, women are more jealous and irritating than ever because of the liberty they've been granted by the Revolution.

There's a constant state of war between men and women, and it's the women who make it so. They can never believe that men are good. They claim that once a man is out of his home and in the street, he'll always cut up. If they only knew what a slave a man is, in or out of the home, when he has real faith in his woman! But most women are too domineering. Analyzing my own case over the years, it's always been my lot to get involved with the domineering type. A few women are submissive, but all women think they aren't sinners and that men have no right to criticize them.

During the years I lived alone, I did my own cooking, but there was always some neighbor I could ask, "Would you wash these clothes for me and then tell me how much I owe you?" Some of them wouldn't even accept pay. They'd tell me, "No, *hombre,* just give me the soap to wash them with."

A good home life is important to me, so I waited eight years and gave the matter a lot of thought before I asked another woman to share my home. I had my adventures, but I always feared getting involved in the kind of conflicts women are apt to create. Because I was in contact with certain persons, I didn't want to risk introducing some woman as my wife only to have her turn out to be a tramp. Yet in spite of all my precautions, I did get involved.

There was a girl called Eloisa Bermúdez living in the back room of my *solar.* She had a boyfriend, a stevedore, who helped her out but didn't live with her. One day I heard her moaning, so I knocked on her door and asked, "What's the matter, neighbor?"

"Oh, I feel so sick. See how swollen my legs are with these worms?"

"You should see a doctor."

"Even if I did, how could I pay for the medicines?"

"But doesn't the young fellow you're living with look after you?"

"Yes, but he works and is married and has a home of his own, so that doesn't leave him much time for me."

"But look, if he pays for your food I'm sure he'd pay for your medicine."

That was enough to make her lover jealous. I don't know who told him she and I were friendly but one day he showed up, demanding to know just what there was between us. Eloisa was crying and yelling and all the neighbors ran out to watch.

I answered quietly, "If you hear someone moaning, it seems only human to see what you can do for her. Think what you please but so far there's been nothing between us."

"You'd better be telling the truth because I'm the fighting kind."

I've never been a coward, but I wasn't such a fool as to pick a fight with an armed man. I told him, "Think carefully, because you're the one who will be sorry if you pull out that knife, not I. I can see you're obsessed to the point of madness."

Eloisa had no family because she had lived a disorderly life and her folks had thrown her out. In my opinion, a man may enjoy every freedom, get involved in any kind of trouble if he chooses, but it's different for a woman. That was Eloisa's problem. Her family had abandoned her because she took off with a man. She had little fighting spirit, and after he left her some man convinced her to become a prostitute. She was about sixteen at the time. He cared nothing for her and made her walk the streets even when she had a fever. One day she met up with her boyfriend and he got a room for her. But then she got sick and didn't have the courage to go out and get money. Alone and without money, she felt no one cared for her and lost all desire to live.

That's the way she was when I met her. I told her, "You're young, you can remake your life if you want to. First, you must make a complete break with the past. Count on me. I'll help you all I can."

"*Ay!* That's what I needed, someone like you!" she burst out. After that I felt what a man feels when he sees a certain nobility in a woman. I resented the men who'd mistreated and abandoned her. We were close but she still lived in her room and I in mine. It may sound paradoxical but sometimes you fall in love with a woman because she needs you. I couldn't see Eloisa's misery and destitution without trying to remedy them.

One day I said, "Well, Eloisa, would you like to be my wife?"

As abruptly as I had asked my question, she gave her answer. "All right."

Love and marriage are things one finds along the way. Frankly, I never courted a woman for her lovely face or voluptuous figure. I study her character and I think of her needs. My first wife was my goddess, the second, my protégé. I took up with her out of compassion, something few men would do. After we married, Eloisa recovered her health, and then she attracted me as a woman.

I was already thirty-three years old and Eloisa was only seventeen. I've always chosen young women, because the older ones have acquired bad habits and are very jealous. Young women are easier for a man to dominate—I mean persuade. Eloisa had a noble character, and as I look for beauty in a woman's feelings, I became attached to her. At first she was obedient and spoke little. She wasn't very lively—there was always a sadness about her which was only natural, considering her past life. Now and then she was affectionate. She never quarreled or tried to dominate me because, frankly, I'm not the kind who lets himself be dominated easily.

The *solar* where Eloisa and I first lived was a mess, and we were in danger of being evicted any minute. Our rent came to 2 *pesos,* and in those times, when you paid 2 *pesos* a month for rent you were as good as out in the street. Like many landlords, the owner of the *solar* was only interested in profit. There was no running water and the place wasn't even sanitary. It had two patios and in the middle of each was a tank where all the tenants got their water. The rooms were shanties made of any kind of wood that was handy. Anybody who turned up and said, "Hey, I've got a bit of wood," could sell it to the landlord, and he'd build another room out of it. He didn't care who he rented to as long as they paid him.

I suggested to Eloisa, "Let's move to Las Yaguas because we can't establish ourselves properly here." Besides, her former husband kept pestering us and I knew we'd end up fighting. If he bothered us in Las Yaguas, we could call the police and they'd ask him why he wasn't in his own barrio. I wasn't worried about myself but I wanted to protect Eloisa. She said, "All right, I'll go to Las Yaguas or anywhere you say."

Camilo Beltrán, a friend of my aunt's, let me know about a vacant house in Las Yaguas. It was nothing but four posts with a roof, marking off a tiny plot of land. It cost me 2 *pesos.*

I had a folding bed and Eloisa had another. Aside from that we had our other "luxurious" furniture to move—two wooden packing cases to sit on, another that we used as a bedside table, and some boards that we set up as a dining table. We cooked on charcoal in a large tin can with a grill on top.

My good friend Armindo asked me, "How are you going to move your things?"

"In your handcart, how else?"

"Do you mean to tell me that you're going to push those things all the way to Las Yaguas?"

"What else can I do? I can't afford to pay 4 *pesos* for moving them. I'll walk slowly. Don't worry, I'll make it."

Eloisa helped me load the cart. Afterward she went on the Route 5 bus. She didn't know very much about going on a bus by herself, but I told her to get off at Hijas de Galicia, ask the way to Camilo Beltrán's house, and keep on asking until she got there. I waited until it was dark because I was embarrassed about being seen pushing that junk down the street.

Camilo was already there, waiting for me. "All right," I said, "let's get to work." I laid down my load and went to get some *yaguas* and sticks from Felo, who got them from La Corona cigar factory. He charged 5 and 10 *centavos* for them. Camilo helped me build the house. We worked day and night to get it finished because I didn't want to leave my so-called furniture out in the open. It took two days to build. The walls and roof were of *yaguas* and thatch and the doors and windows were wooden frames covered with *yaguas* and fastened with wooden hinges. The floor was earth, packed down to make it even.

I had always wanted to own a house. It gave me great peace and satisfaction and I didn't have to worry about paying the rent or being evicted. But that house was very different in every way from the one I have now, so my living habits were different too.

Eloisa was satisfied. For one thing, she had my attention, and for another, she loved to feel that she was, so to speak, the owner of a house. She felt real proud about that. She insisted that I visit her family to let them know she was living a different kind of life. I could tell they thought our marriage was good for her.

Las Yaguas was so big it was divided into three parts—Havana, Guillén, and Matanzas. Havana, entered by the Calzada de Luyanó, was owned by José María Bouza; part of the land was also owned by Catholics who had a school there. Guillén was on higher ground, facing the Havana section. It was owned by a politician named Guillén.[34] The third part, Matanzas, was built along the ditch. It was named after the original settlers, many of whom came from the town of Matanzas.

When I first moved to Las Yaguas, the streets had no names but there were already over 300 houses and some stores scattered throughout the barrio, most of them in the section called Havana. Las Yaguas was very crowded with country people who came to settle in the city. They left the countryside because of the abuses committed against them by the landowners and the Rural Police.[35]

Life in the country was very hard. Food was scarce. The people were plagued with illness. A woman in labor had to get an old neighbor woman or a midwife to help. If the child lived past birth, he was put to work on the land at age four. This exposed him to intestinal parasites that get into the body through the feet, and children living in such remote places had little hope of being treated.

Being an activist, I immediately got in touch with the communists in Las Yaguas to see what the Party could do about the incredible poverty there. That's how I met Juan Carlos Montano, Minerva Ruz, Salomé Ruz, Rodrigo García, and other communists in Las Yaguas. One of them explained to me why the Communist Party wasn't able to develop its doctrine in Cuba. Cuba was a bourgeois country—but not typically capitalist—and its great leaders didn't understand that every man is a human being, not just so much manpower. I studied it and thought about it, realizing that it's a question of developing a conscious concern that comes only with experience.

I was never a member of the Communist Party. I was just an outside activist, though fanatical enough to join Minerva, Juan Carlos, Manolo Menéndez, and Constantino Vidal in swearing a blood oath to support the Revolution. Each of us drew a drop of our own blood and let it drip into a jar that we buried. Then we knelt and swore by our honor, dignity, and good name that we would remain faithful to the purposes of the Revolution.

In Las Yaguas only a few militants like Juan Carlos, Minerva, Quintano, and González actually belonged to the Party. Juan Carlos and Minerva were already known for their work, so they worked openly. The rest of us were advised not to join but to continue working for the cause

34. Ownership of the land on which Las Yaguas was built is also discussed in García Alonso, *Manuela,* pp. 213–14.

35. *Guardia Rural,* a branch of the national police stationed in the rural areas and under the command of the army chief of staff.

unofficially. Whenever we had a chance we joined in the formation of any non-socialist group, but we always did it with the greatest discretion since the Communist Party was being persecuted.

Under the auspices of the Popular Socialist Party,[36] and with the cooperation of Comrade Hilda Velázquez, who lived in *reparto* Marianao, Juan Carlos and Minerva tried to start the first proletarian school. They hoped to teach their students about the capitalist government and the social system of Cuba. The school was persecuted and never got organized because the Catholics didn't want to compete with a proletarian school that would be preferred by the people. We sent our children there because we knew that the first thing the communists teach a person is how to read and write. We also met there secretly to read and discuss some of the books, and we always invited young people interested in such matters to join us. The struggle with the Catholics began right off because they claimed it was a hotbed of communism.

Eloisa was like a new woman after she became mistress of herself and had erased the idea of suicide from her mind. It was then that she began to harp on the difference in our ages. "I'm still young," she'd tell me.

I answered "Sure you're young. When I met you, you were even younger, remember? And how did I find you? Sick, broke, neglected, abandoned. Now that you're in good health and living a decent life, you remember the difference in our ages. You're putting me on my guard because you're going to play a dirty trick on me with the first young man who makes a pass at you."

"No, no, I haven't had any such thoughts!"

"That's what your words mean, whether you know it or not."

She called me old because my habits were different from those of a young man, who will do practically anything to please his wife. If she wants to go to the movies or a dance, he'll say, "All right, let's go." But an older man knows enough to figure out whether he can afford it.

I was a fool to marry Eloisa. I've known men who married prostitutes and everything was wonderful between the couple, but deep inside, a woman of the life is really frigid. Eloisa had known men who were interested only in getting it over with, *pam!* "Here's your money," and that was that. She was a woman with so much experience, yet she didn't know how to excite a man. When I went to bed with a woman, I wasn't satisfied to have her simply lie beside me, stripped to her panties and brassiere. "I want to see you naked, *chica*," I'd tell her. And when she'd

36. The Communist Party changed its name to the Popular Socialist Party (PSP) in 1944, during the World War II period of cooperation with the Batista government. The PSP was dissolved in 1961 and the new Communist Party was formed in 1965. Througout his story, Benedí uses "Communist Party," "Socialist Party," and "PSP" interchangeably.

taken off all her clothes, I'd ask her to walk around and turn this way and that.

What I liked most about Eloisa were her breasts. They were firm and youthful. If a woman's breasts sagged, my desire cooled considerably. The truth is, flabby breasts disgusted me. Out of self-respect I'd go through the sex act but not with much enthusiasm. That's happened to me with a number of women. Some caught on and tried to distract me by talking about something interesting—I've always liked a women who has ideas—and I'd get excited all over again. When a woman has the sense to do that, a man forgets his obsession and his part becomes virile.

It seemed to me that just out of gratitude, Eloisa should have been a little more generous and understanding with me. She didn't want to bear me children. In her simpleminded way she'd say, "What will people think if we have children when you're so old and I so young?"

"Very well, you're absolutely right," I'd reply. "If you don't want children, just see to it that you don't have them." These are sad memories that have faded away.

I don't know what specific technique Eloisa used to prevent a pregnancy; that was her secret. But after we'd been living together awhile, she told me she didn't feel well and I realized that she was pregnant. "Didn't you tell me you didn't want my children because I'm so much older than you?" I reminded her.

When Eloisa's daughter Nidia was born I was suspicious, just as my father had been when I was born. I was almost sure she wasn't mine, even though Eloisa always told her I was her father. For one thing the child was light-skinned while Eloisa and I were black. I decided not to ask any questions, because I didn't feel like facing the whole series of problems that might be raised. What would be the point? It would only bring forth lies and create confusion. Some men become even fonder of a woman when they doubt her fidelity, but I'm not like that. I love only as much as I am loved.

One day Eloisa told me she was ashamed to go out carrying the baby because I was an old man! It was her own remarks about the child and the strange things she did that made me doubt her in the first place. I had trusted her to remember my generous motives in marrying her. I was a good provider, a home-loving man. No matter where I was, my one thought was, "What shall I take home to make Eloisa happy?" It was deeply satisfying to return home to a cheerful, happy wife. If I saw her looking worried or sad, I'd ask first of all, "Do you feel sick?"

"No."

"Then what's wrong with you?"

"Nothing." But then I'd get annoyed. If she wasn't sick and nothing was the matter, what was she sulking about? Once I came home and found her looking very sad and thoughtful. I finally made up my mind. One day I suddenly said, *"Chica,* don't you think it would be better if we separated?"

"Eh? Why? What have I done to you?"

"Nothing. Nothing at all." That's my way. I never like to argue. But if both parties aren't willing, why should one of them live unhappily?

My main motive for wanting to separate was her apathy around the house. If I said to her, "Eloisa, I want something done by 5:00 this afternoon," she would go about it in such an indifferent way! I admit that at first she was diligent, but after a time she didn't care. Frankly, I can't live that way. I'm no slave driver, but I told my wife what I thought was right and expected her to do it. We had a number of quarrels about it.

Eloisa's outlook on life was completely different from mine. For example, one of her habits that made me sick was her gambling. I gambled a little, sure, but it wasn't a vice with me. At one time I had a job at a gambling joint in La Víbora, selling chips and making change. With such a good chance to observe gambling games, and spurred on by my desperate need for money, I learned fast. It wasn't vice that made me gamble but pressing need. Money was scarce and what other way was there of getting it? But I was always careful how I gambled because I didn't want to risk seeing my name in the newspaper connected with scandal, and besides, respect for my mother had always made me act cautiously.

I played *bolita* and *charada.*[37] I started playing poker to amuse myself and then learned its consequences, so it didn't become a habit. Dominoes was my favorite game. I seldom played craps because you have to get down on your knees to play the game, and I have the superstitious idea that if you get money that way, you have to spend it that way too.

For Eloisa the lottery was a habit, and we quarreled about it practically every day. I could see what other people thought of her. A gambling woman is almost as bad as an immoral woman. Even a man has to be darn lucky not to lose everything he owns. A loser can get desperate and a gambling woman is apt to do just about anything. But Eloisa kept on gambling—she didn't believe I was really serious about my objections. That woman is a disagreeable memory to me.

During our last year together Eloisa was employed as a cook in the house of a Polish family. But she didn't have fixed wages and I didn't have a steady job. One day we'd have 50 *pesos,* but the next day we might wake up broke. I didn't have a strict budget or save a fixed amount but I always had a few *centavos* put away as a reserve. Things weren't too bad. In Las Yaguas we didn't need to spend any money on display and every-

37. An illegal lottery and a numbers game.

thing was dirt cheap. But it bothered me to watch Eloisa gamble away our money.

I didn't have to worry too much about medical help because my sister Irene was a midwife. I won the friendship of the grocers so we didn't have to worry about starving. If the grocers needed a bit of carpentry done, I'd do it for them. I had my own tools—a saw, hammer, plane, and whittling knife—and after I'd finished the work they'd ask again, "Well, how much is it?"

"Ah, *chico,* forget it! Some day I may need your help." I built up that credit as my last line of defense. I knew I'd never go hungry. But I never abused the privilege. I only asked for the most necessary things. Neither did I take advantage of their offers to buy myself a lot of clothes. I budgeted our earnings carefully to avoid asking favors from other people.

There was another thing that bothered me about Eloisa. Nothing annoys me more than getting home and not being able to have a conversation with my wife. Everyone has a certain inner vision, a certain spirituality, and I hated having to go to someone else when I wanted to converse intelligently . . . about clouds, for instance. "Look, doll, see the way those clouds are moving? Don't you think it's strange?"

As time went on, I discovered that Eloisa was not bright enough to be interested in conversations like that. I had to tell her, "*Chica,* the reason we don't get along is that we think differently. When I ask you about some things, you simply aren't intelligent enough to answer, understand, or even question me."

The Popular Socialist Party, which should have fought Batista, made a pact with him instead.[38] It wasn't until much later that I saw this action as one of the greatest betrayals of the people who had sacrificed themselves for the Party. At first it seemed the right thing to do. Since Batista was clever enough to give the socialists a place in his government, we said, "Now we have to help him more than ever." We were convinced that when Batista accepted the plans submitted to him by the Communist Party he'd inevitably become a communist, so we put up with his attitude. I reasoned, "Maybe this is a necessary expediency for spreading the socialists' ideas among the masses. If there is no electoral machinery how can we ever have representation in Congress?"

I confess I had also approved of Batista's coup of September 4, 1933. "Batista is a man of the people who is bound to work for their good," I thought. I admired him as a man of humble estate who exuded strength

38. In 1938 the Communist Party agreed to support Batista and his program in exchange for official recognition and the right to reorganize the union movement under its control. During World War II, support of the government in power was part of the Party's "popular front" policy.

and had managed to get control of the Army. If some pompous general had carried it out, I would have realized from the first that the coup d'etat was merely a matter of "get out so I can take your place and enjoy your privileges."

If I'd had an inkling of how matters really stood I would never have applauded Batista. And if I'd even begun to imagine his fight against Guiteras, maybe I wouldn't be alive to tell about it today.[39] I'd have gone to Matanzas with Guiteras and fallen with him. But I believed only the government officials were guilty, not the soldiers. Even though Batista was a colonel and already chief of the Army by the time of the massacre at Mella's funeral on September 29, 1933,[40] I never suspected he'd be like all the rest.

The day of the massacre, I was glad to escape with my life. When the trouble started, I was standing in a crowd along the causeway of La Reina. I ran down Chávez Street, along the side of the export offices. If I'd been carrying a weapon, there's no telling what I might have done. Sometimes one is so blinded by emotion that when somebody says, "They're shooting," you pay no more attention than if he'd said, "They're scattering flowers." I hope I never again feel what I felt during that massacre. I even cried. It was such a criminal attack by the government, and some people resisted so valiantly!

But I didn't know about those things when Batista came to power, and I had hopes that he'd rehabilitate the Republic. I observed not only him but the men around him. And I studied, thought, and analyzed, day by day, the policies they might develop.

One of the first problems we brought up was the elimination of all the slums. There were sixteen of them in Havana. We hoped that by eliminating these barrios of indigents we'd be able to eliminate indigence itself. But the political situation got bad, so bad that if you weren't decidedly for Batista, your life was in danger.

Around that time some people asked me, "What do you think about the problem of Las Yaguas?"

"Well, *chico*, I see a lot of miserable poverty and think we should find a way to pull ourselves out of it."

"Ah, so you're a communist?"

39. Antonio Guiteras Holmes (1906–35), a university student leader of the twenties who briefly served as Minister of the Interior under President Grau San Martín after Batista's 1933 coup. He resigned and, through his political action group, *Joven Cuba*, became a militant opponent of the first Batista dictatorship. Guiteras was killed in Matanzas on May 8, 1935, in a gun battle with Batista forces, while trying to escape to Mexico.

40. Julio Antonio Mella (see n. 32) had been assassinated in Mexico in 1929, but his ashes were not returned to Cuba until after the overthrow of the Machado government in 1933. The interment ceremonies turned into a riot as police, Mella supporters, and other antigovernment groups shot at one another. Six people were killed and twenty-seven wounded. (Thomas, *Cuba: The Pursuit of Freedom*, p. 656. For another version of that day's events see K. S. Karol, *Guerrillas in Power* (New York: Hill and Wang, 1970), p. 79n.)

"If that's being a communist, you're welcome to think I'm one. But it seems to me none of you would want to live with such poverty or discrimination."

My words cost me a blow. Somebody in the group just hauled off and hit me. I had no intention of getting killed, so I let it pass. I just stood there.

"Go on, answer!" they shouted. I didn't say a word, so then they kicked me. Finally one of them said, "Come on, let's leave this queer alone." I ignored that too, thinking, "These people are capable of anything. It's obvious they don't respect anyone." Incidents like that made us act even more cautiously. We were in constant danger; just for being a communist, a comrade of ours was found dead one day in San José Park in Luyanó. But we said, "Let's continue the fight."

We tried to develop a social conscience in the young people, to wake them up to reality. We made no demands, simply offered orientation. Whenever I met a union leader or a worker, I tried to awaken his mind to the problems that existed and to introduce certain ideas. The communists watched the development of the various Cuban youth groups with great interest. We had hopes they'd present a united front when necessary and become the vanguard of all that's happening now.

I was especially interested in the university students. I've always been a romantic in my belief that the independence of Cuba would be born somewhere, and in what better place than a university? My first contact with students was in 1912, when I had a job across the street from the University of Havana. I could see all those kids coming and going, and the protests they organized. I knew little about the Student Directorate[41] but I kept in touch with the students as much as possible. They have always been very reluctant to bring other groups into their movement. Perhaps it was wrong for them to be so exclusive, but I feel they were justified, because, unfortunately, some people turn into stool pigeons if there's a profit in it.

I was closely connected with the Communist Party by the time of the 1935 strike.[42] Not one resident of Las Yaguas was a strikebreaker because a majority of the people were socialists. Besides, there was a strong organization backing the strike, which would have made any strikebreaker's life very difficult.

41. *Directorio Estudiantil,* an organization of student leaders at the University of Havana that functioned essentially as a political action group from 1927 to 1933. The *Directorio Estudiantil,* its successor groups, and student activism in general were important forces in Cuban national politics.

42. The strike was called in March to protest the delay in establishing a constitution following the 1933 coup. A general strike involving many trade unions, government employees, communists, members of *Joven Cuba,* and university students paralyzed Cuba for several days. The strike was broken by the Army, with many killed and thousands jailed. The death of Guiteras, a strike leader, came less than two months later.

I worked with the group of Las Yaguas communists but we didn't go out in the streets because there were so many secret service agents that even a single remark was enough to get you reported to the authorities. I liked to talk and tell people the truth, so naturally I was in trouble. They couldn't pin a more serious charge on me, so they ran me in for talking.

One night I was at home when there was a knock at the door. I opened to the police! "Come along to the station with us."

"All right, let's go." I wasn't going to ask a policeman why he was arresting me. We communists had been instructed that it was better to go quietly. If we resisted or ran away, the police would apply the "law of flight" and shoot us dead for trying to escape.

I had prepared Eloisa beforehand. "If the police ever interfere with us, keep out of it," I told her. "Play innocent. That way they won't arrest you and maybe you can do something to help get me out." I'm sure she must have cried after I left, but she didn't make a scene with the policeman.

The police took us to the station on foot. We were upset because they chose the back way to the station, instead of the causeway where there was heavy traffic. We went through a small park by the river, where it would have been easy to take a shot at us or even have a rope ready to hang us.

In the police station they asked me if I had a job.

"Not a steady job," I answered. "I pick up what I can get."

"We have some information here on you as a member of the Communist Party."

"But sir, I am not a communist. I simply follow the line of a party that defends workers' rights. As for my activities, the only thing I do is talk with other workers about their jobs.

Many Party members would have said yes to their question, "Are you a communist?" But not I! I was taking every precaution in case of a surprise attack. I knew I was endangering myself by my activities and I, having never known fear, was willing to die for the cause if necessary. What I wasn't willing to do was to die passively, with my arms crossed.

After they took down my statement, I was sent to the El Príncipe prison. About ten days later I was tried, not on a political charge, but for violating public-health regulations. I kept a few roosters and hens at home, and according to the police, fowl should not be kept inside the house. What could I say? I was sentenced to forty days in jail.

Juan Marinello[43] was a prisoner in the same place. Everybody sent there, no matter who he was, had to clean and scrub the place. Once

43. A professor of literature at Escuela Normal in Havana, Marinello joined the Communist Party in the 1920s. In 1942 Marinello and Carlos Rafael Rodríguez became ministers in Batista's cabinet, the first communists to serve in any Latin-American government. (Karol, *Guerrillas in Power,* p. 90.) Marinello was president of the PSP throughout the period of Castro's fight against Batista, and as such was spokesman for the PSP policy of

when Juan Marinello had to do the cleaning, the captain asked the sergeants, "How can you make one of the most brilliant intellectuals in Cuba do this work? I don't say this in defense of the Revolution but in defense of this individual." So they didn't make Marinello clean anymore. But the system in that jail was the dirtiest imaginable.

I didn't want anybody outside to intervene so I served out my sentence. They kept me in jail 180 days. During that time Eloisa would bring me condensed milk, oil, and other things they didn't provide for the prisoners. She was the one who brought me the news of my brother Jacinto.

Jacinto drove a car for hire and would often wait at the docks for tourists. A few days before the strike ended, he was waiting for a ship that was to dock at 5:00 in the morning. It was forbidden to be on the street that early and a guard challenged him. Jacinto, who was a bit deaf, apparently didn't hear him. Then a shot rang out, a single shot, and Jacinto's skull was shattered. The guard said he had aimed at one of the car's tires. Maybe so.

I tried to get permission to go to my brother's wake, but I couldn't get it. I resigned myself, thinking, "I must avoid being too conspicuous. I'm not going to try anymore."

While I was in jail some people made a point of looking out for Eloisa, for my sake. Minerva Ruz was one who worried about her and helped her and gave her good advice. When I finally got home I heard different stories about Eloisa's behavior. One neighbor would say, "Your wife behaved perfectly while you were in jail." But another would tell me, "Man, that woman of yours is no wife to you!" Perhaps those who said things like that were simply referring to her past life, thinking I didn't know about it. It was shortly afterward that I told her I wanted to separate. "It's the best thing we can do," I said. So she left.

I haven't seen Eloisa's daughter for a long time. She hasn't become darker with time and I'm told her hair is still straight. According to certain medical theories, a child's appearance may be completely transformed by the age of seven. I waited for such a transformation but my hope was denied. I never found any sign in the girl. However, I always treated her considerately for my own self-respect and because she was innocent.

In 1940, when Las Yaguas was already heavily populated, its landowners suddenly decided they needed their land back and tried to get

nonalignment with the Castro forces. (See his 1958 letter to Herbert L. Matthews explaining PSP policy, in Matthews, *The Cuba Story* (New York: Braziller, 1961), pp. 51–52.) In 1965, when many members of the old Communist Party were being removed from important positions, Marinello was replaced as rector of the University of Havana and sent abroad. He is now a member of the Party's Central Committee and president (and founder) of the Movement for Peace and the Sovereignty of the Peoples.

everybody evicted.[44] But we knew how to work our case and we studied the laws and found out that Cuban landownership laws originated in Greek law. Any piece of land occupied by no less than twenty-five people for at least twenty-five years and not reclaimed by its original owners during that time became the property of the squatters. So we kept on fighting to gain time until the twenty-five years were up, and we won.

Then in 1944, the landowner Bouza made a second attempt to evict us. He went to court to sue us for not paying rent. He tried to bribe a resident of Las Yaguas to sign a paper stating that he had leased his land by contract. When we found out what Bouza was up to, we decided to get outside help. We explained our case to some of the university students and they went to the Municipal Courthouse and found that no one in Las Yaguas could be sued for nonpayment because there weren't any contracts or documents stating that the land had been rented to anybody. We based our case on that, and with the students' influence we won. The land was ours and nobody could evict us.

At that time the people of Las Yaguas lacked the most essential things. Housewives couldn't even buy what they needed at the grocery stores because the food just didn't get there. One day a woman saw another carrying a paper sack of rice. "Could you give me some rice for my children?" she asked.

"No, I can't. This is for my children," the other one answered. Then, in desperation, the first woman snatched the bag of rice. That's how bad things were. I don't mean to say that everybody in Las Yaguas went hungry or had the impulse to take other people's property violently, but it was obvious something had to be done. The incident caused quite a scandal, and the university students asked us if we had objections to their helping us. Objections? Not likely!

A group of us from Las Yaguas—Juan Carlos, Minerva, Gabriel Pérez, Constantino Vidal, Manolo Menéndez, and I—got together. There was also a shopkeeper named Joaquín at the meeting. Even though he had a grocery store in Las Yaguas, he was very interested in helping our cause. He said, "Wherever you go I will go, and if you fall I will fall with you. But I will not desert Las Yaguas."

We discussed the question of distributing supplies to the stores. I was put in charge of raising money and of distribution. I thought a lot about how we could buy and sell things cheaper. I figured that the reason for high prices was just plain profiteering. For instance, lard cost 56 *centavos* a pound in the warehouses but was sold in the grocery stores for 80 *centavos*. And rice cost at least 13 *centavos* a pound, a can of milk 25 *centavos*, and fuel alcohol 25 *centavos* a bottle. It seemed to me that was just too much!

44. An account of this dispute appeared in *Granma*, May 13, 1970, p. 2.

So I talked it over with the people of the FEU[45] and said, "Look, kids, you're working hard for us, but we should do something for ourselves, too. For example, I think we can manage to sell lard for 17 *centavos* less than the stores charge. If we buy these other items at the warehouse, we'll only need to charge 1 or 2 *centavos* more for transportation. That way we can resell them at the minimum price instead of the maximum the stores charge, and save the barrio about 4,000 *pesos* a month.

I also talked it over with the grocery-store owners because I didn't want them deprived either. When they heard my plan they said, "Well, *chico,* if it's done that way, we agree. We'll sell lard for 7 *centavos'* profit a pound; that's 3½ for you people and 3½ for us."

Grau[46] was still in power when the FEU decided to start the food-distribution program in Las Yaguas. The government department in charge of this accepted our movement in the hope that it would cover up all their irregularities, from taking bribes to embezzling funds. They instructed us to make a census and tell them how many residents there were in Havana's sixteen slums. We said, "We're willing to include the residents of all sixteen slums in the census, but we can't be responsible for distributing supplies to all of them." The department accepted this and our distribution program included only the two barrios next to Las Yaguas, Isla de Pinos and Cueva del Humo.

I was called into the police station and questioned, but for the most part the food-distribution program was successful. Often, when we didn't have enough money to pay for the food, the storekeepers helped us. They'd agree among themselves that one would give us the rice, another the milk, another the lard, and so on. But there were times when I left my own home without food in order to fulfill my obligations to my neighbors.

Some people just couldn't understand what we were doing. One night we had a meeting with the students and residents and gave them an account of the money that had been saved in the distribution of food. Then one of the men jumped up and said, "Where's that 1,000 *pesos* Lázaro is talking about? I haven't seen any of it at home!"

A student had to explain. "Add up what you save on each item and multiply it by the number of residents, and you'll see what Lázaro means."

"Oh!" the man said. "I thought he meant that what was left over would be shared among all of us."

"No, no. What's left over is what you didn't have to spend."

Some people are like that. You explain things to them and in their ignorance they're apt to rise up and accuse you of something even when

---

45. *Federación Estudiantil Universitaria* (University Student Federation).
46. Dr. Ramón Grau San Martín, President of Cuba 1933 and 1944–48.

you're going hungry to defend their interests. But we didn't care. We just kept right on the job.

In 1945 the Ministry of Health ordered yellow banners with the words "Infectious Zone" put up all around Las Yaguas. They planned to isolate us from the rest of Cuba. How much lower did they want us to sink? Labeled as an infectious zone, we'd be poorer than ever! With those banners around, anyone from Las Yaguas who asked for a job, or went begging outside the barrio, would be avoided. People would greet us, "What? From Las Yaguas, the infectious zone? No, we can't have you here!"

Finally we decided, "This is some kind of a challenge." So we organized a brigade. We allowed government workers to set up the banners—they were only carrying out orders—but as soon as they were gone we pulled down all sixteen banners and burned them. People began gathering to find out what was happening. Then a lieutenant appeared with some policemen and asked, "What's going on here?"

We'd been expecting the ax to fall. "Nothing, lieutenant. It's just that they set up those banners; if we had left them there, what would have become of us?"

Next a captain showed up with another group of policemen, so we were surrounded. Finally, the *comandante* presented himself arrogantly and called me over. "Come here, you. You look like an agitator."

"I'm no agitator, only a man who hates poverty." I was about to add "and hates to be bullied," but I stopped myself in time, thinking, "These fellows have come here with the worst intentions."

"Well," he said, "the thing to do is close the whole place down."

"Then where would we go?" we argued. "We'd be worse than bums and beggars."

The *comandante* closed all the stores and cut off the water supply, hoping to provoke a riot. We remained calm and waited for reporters to come, especially those of the opposition, so they'd write about how we were being treated. The newspaper *Prensa Libre* took up our cause. Their article called the students' attention to our problems.

We organized a night guard at one of the main entrances because we thought the government might send someone to set fire to the barrio and then accuse us of doing it. We agreed that whenever anybody entered late at night, the guard would tell him to halt and then whistle for the rest of us. One night students came in a garbage truck, followed by a jeep. When the guards stopped them, the truck driver said, "We came to bring milk and have a talk with you people."

We told them what had happened and they were convinced that our stand was reasonable. We got several handcarts and helped them pass out the milk door to door. They promised to return the following day.

Some newspapers said we were communists rebelling against the government. A very prominent newsman, German Pinilla, ended a radio broadcast over station CMQ saying, "Do you know what the people of Las Yaguas are like? There are no virgins there. Mothers make their daughters sit in the doorway while they themselves carry on their business with men."

When we heard that, we decided to go as a group to CMQ during Pinilla's program and take over his hour. Among the group were four señoritas, to see if he dared repeat what he'd said. We planned to kidnap him and drive him to Las Yaguas, but he must have figured out what we were up to because he sent word that he couldn't see us.

We were taken to the police station and questioned. We told them, "That program must have been taped. Get the tape and listen to it. Then you'll understand our attitude." The police did that and said, "You were right to object." Next they asked us a few questions and let us go.

A newspaperman who was a friend of Pinilla's wrote an attack on us. I sent him a letter explaining in detail why we'd rebelled. "Is it our fault that we're poor and live in such miserable conditions? Right now there are 2,335,000 unemployed citizens in Cuba. In a country with a total population of 7,000,000 that means something is wrong with the system."

I think my powers as a *santero* probably helped me in my political work in Las Yaguas. You can make a lot of friends by trying to help others. When people were broke I helped, not with money but with my credit. The storekeepers in the barrio trusted me. Many sick people came to me and I'd say, "Well, let's see what I can do for you."

I can't say exactly when I did my first job of *santería* because it was completely mental. It was one of those cases when you warn somebody, "Get out of there, because if you don't, this is what's going to happen to you." After that I knew that what I told somebody would be accepted. This gave me self-confidence and influenced me a great deal.

Sometimes I got paid for my religious activities, but not much. For example, I was at home one night when someone came to see what I could do for Enrique Santillana. He was unconscious and nobody knew what ailed him. I went to his house and found a group of friends and neighbors from the barrio there. They had four pieces of coconut shells which I asked questions. In this particular case, I asked the coconut, "May I use *romerillo?*"

The coconut answered, "Yes."

Then I mixed some of the herb *romerillo* with some dry wine and honey and gave it to Santillana in three portions. After the patient regained consciousness, I showed my gratitude to the saint by taking a mouthful of *aguardiente*[47] and spraying him with it. I also blew tobacco smoke on him.

47. An alcoholic drink, in Cuba made from sugar cane.

When Santillana's friends asked, "How much do we owe you?" I said, "Let everyone present drop a *centavo* into the vase on the table." It came to 17 *centavos*. I could have said, "What kind of payment is that, 17 *centavos*, for saving somebody's life? Give me 17 *pesos*, or 40 or 50." But people asked me for help precisely because they knew how little I cared for money. I have never charged as much as 20 *pesos* for religious work. If somebody wants to give me a present, that's something else.

I asked for a cup of coffee, and after I drank it I picked up the money and left. I went straight home to my St. Lazarus and told him, "Look, it seems that you influenced this matter. They have given you the exact amount of money for your rattle—17 *centavos*." And I laid the money in front of him.

I helped many people avoid danger. When I lived in Las Yaguas I averaged six or seven consultations a week. The clients always offered me something, 1 *pesos*, 2 *pesos*, or whatever they wanted. There were times, though, when I desperately needed the money but couldn't accept it, not even 1 *centavo*, though I might not have had the money to pay for a cup of *café con leche* for breakfast.

I had learned about curing from my friend Rogelio Díaz, who was a *santero*. I was twenty-odd years of age then, but I didn't act much like a kid. So one day he showed me some religious objects and asked if I'd like to have them. I said I would, very much indeed. Since I was willing to be guided, he was interested in teaching me. He knew that was all the pay I wanted for running errands for him. Most of the time he invited me to dinner at his house and always gave me breakfast in the morning. He would call me over when he did his religious work. So little by little I learned quite a bit about *santería*, and I liked it very much.

I remember the first time I saw a sick man presented to Rogelio as a victim of witchcraft. Rogelio sat down, examined the patient, and said, "It's going to be all right." He laid a hand on the man's forehead, said a prayer, and the man stopped gasping.

Next, Rogelio began chanting a prayer for aid and protection for the sick man. He prayed in Spanish so the patient would understand. Then he sent me out to get some herbs. "Look, the plants I want have these shapes and these qualities, and you have to pick them in a special way. Each herb or twig has a life and an owner, so you must first ask permission of the spirit who owns it. After that, lift one foot and deposit a coin. That is called 'paying for the rights.' Be sure you face the sun when you pick this particular herb. This other herb must be picked with your back to the sun. Some plants should be plucked out by the roots, so they will have enough strength to produce their effect." With this explanation, I was able to gather the twigs and leaves Rogelio needed. He boiled them and gave some to the patient. In a short while he asked the patient, "How are you feeling now?"

"Better already." A little later the patient got up and said, "Now I feel just fine."

Santería cures are different from medical cures. They utilize prayers and certain explanations to calm down the sick person's family. There are medical doctors who will say to a patient, "*Chico*, I can't do anything for you. I don't know what's wrong with you." Even doctors who have some relation to *santería* say that. Or if he writes out a prescription, it takes time for the medicine to be effective. In *Palo Monte*, which I have become more inclined to than Yoruban *santería*, there isn't the experimenting that the doctors do. A practitioner will say, "Here, boil this herb a minute or two." While the preparation is coming to a boil and cooking, he'll say prayers. Then the patient drinks it and immediately feels better.

Ochún[48] is a saint who is depended upon a great deal. I speak from experience, because someone took possession of my foot and Ochún saved me. A man who lived nearby decided to experiment in witchcraft on me. I told him, "Look, *chico*, I'm not the right person. I have my beliefs and I want to go deeply into *santería* and understand it. So pick someone else for your tests."

He said, "Well, all right." But one morning not long afterward, I stumbled on a pebble outside my door. Immediately my foot began to swell so much I thought I would lose it. How was I to guess somebody had placed that pebble there?

That night Ochún appeared to me in a dream, jingling her little bells and singing. She's always happy and smiling. "Don't worry about your foot," she said. Then she told me who had put the curse on me and how to get rid of it. She said I should brew a certain mixture at high noon, when the sun was shining directly into the yard.

After five days, when my foot was almost normal, Ochún appeared again and told me to go down to a river and dip my foot in the water. I was to ring a bell while calling for her. I did this, and when I took my foot out again it was cured. Then Ochún appeared and said, "You see, my remedy worked. That proves I really am Ochún." Three days later she revealed herself in a dream, singing and calling herself by her *Palo* name. She said "*Choa huengue, choa huengue*, I am leaving, I am leaving. *Choa huengue.*"

There's a saint for each part of the body, and for various illnesses too. Obatalá[49] controls the head. She also rules over peace, calm, and harmony. If you call upon a very difficult saint and he refuses to appear,

48. An African goddess identified with the *Virgen de la Caridad*, the "compassionate Virgin" and patron saint of Cuba enshrined in Cobre and Santiago de Cuba. (Jahn, *Muntu*, p. 67.)

49. The Yoruban spirit (*orisha*) of creation who is believed to have modeled man from clay. In Cuba Obatalá is identified with the *Virgen de la Merced*. (Jahn, *Muntu*, p. 68.)

then you call on Obatalá at once. Osain[50] has power over herbs and can cure impotence. After you appeal to him, a remedy is made up to return your sexual powers. Yemayá controls the throat. Ochún controls the chest down to the stomach. St. Lucía controls eyesight. The feet are controlled by St. Lazarus, whose African name is Babalú-ayé. He has great power in the land of Arará, in Africa, because each god is more powerful in his birthplace. Besides the feet, St. Lazarus controls sickness in general. When somebody gets sores or starts to feel pains, it may be that St. Lazarus is punishing him. The only thing the person can do then is pray to St. Lazarus again and again. When he answers and gives his word he'll take the case, then there's no doubt the patient will get well.

Eleguá[51] is the god of many things. As the owner of all paths and roads, it's his mission to serve as an escort for travelers. Suppose you have to go somewhere and don't know the way, but you have faith in Eleguá, so you say to him, "Go with me, guide me to the best way to get there. Remove all dangers from my path and do not let me meet any enemies" and so on. If you see someone you don't want to meet going down the street, Eleguá will make him take another route to keep you out of trouble.

One day Rogelio warned me I'd meet an Eleguá. "How will I recognize him?" I asked.

"You will suddenly notice a stone with an odd shape," he answered.

And that's what happened. I found a stone that was shaped like a face, with a nose and a clearly marked mouth. I picked it up and took it home for my Eleguá. I may touch him because I'm a man, but it's forbidden to women since they go through a period of transition every month and would lessen his strength. That's why I never let my wives touch Eleguá.

For the more than forty years since I found my Eleguá, I've greeted him every morning and asked him whether I should go out or not. He has always answered me, and I've always regretted the times I didn't take his advice.

One day I was so broke I couldn't even afford to buy 1 *centavo*'s worth of sugar. That morning Eleguá told me to stay home, but I was disgusted and replied, "I beg your pardon, but I have to go out. I can't just sit here waiting for something to materialize out of thin air, and I don't like to beg either." So I walked all the way from Las Yaguas to El Unico market. There I ran into a friend who always invited me to have a cup of coffee with him, unless I invited him first. Naturally I couldn't invite him that

50. Osain is identified with the Roman Catholic St. Joseph and is the god of drugs, herbs, and medicinal preparations. (Romulo Lachatañere, *Manual de Santería* (Havana: Editorial Caribe, 1942), p. 22.)
51. Regarded as the mediator between the gods and human beings; the Catholic saint identified with Eleguá is St. Anthony. (*Ibid.*, Appendix, Table 1.)

day, and you know what? He didn't invite me either! And I didn't even have the bus fare to Las Yaguas, so I had to walk back again.

When I got home, I found a fellow there who'd been waiting for me all morning with some money for a certain transaction. I was disgusted with myself, thinking, "If I hadn't been such a fool and disobeyed the saint's orders I'd have had plenty of money for a good breakfast simply by staying home."

If you need something, like an herb from the drugstore or grocery, the first thing you do is consult Eleguá. He will get it for you from the grocery, drugstore, or anywhere. Spiritually, not materially. How does he do it? Well, while you were wondering who to send, a boy or an older person might turn up just in the nick of time. Probably this person was sent by Eleguá. That's why Eleguá is adored and respected as the messenger.

Rogelio told me, "Whatever you see that compels your attention, give it to your Eleguá." So through the years I've put a number of ornaments around my Eleguá. There I also keep four coconut husks that Rogelio gave for my consultation. I built Eleguá a good house in a bookcase in the living room. Eleguá controls and builds all houses, so the better the house we build for him, the better ours will be, since he returns our courtesy.

Other religious objects I've given to Eleguá are some sickles, which represent the long road. These sickles have their own special power and are indispensable in certain religious rituals. I also gave Eleguá a little drum to amuse himself with. I've heard him playing it, even though he doesn't have hands. And I've heard him talk, too.

Besides ornaments, I offer him *aguardiente*, food, and tobacco. Saints have their physical side, so naturally they get really desperate for a smoke sometimes. Now you may be wondering, "How can a stone and some bits of iron smoke?" Well, believe me they do, and it's not just my imagination. I've lit cigars and left them on Eleguá's altar when there wasn't any human being around to smoke them, and I've seen them burn down to a small stub.

Nature has granted objects certain religious powers because men have no other means of defense. That's why we keep these images in our homes. For instance, I keep a representation of Ogún's[52] cooking pot as a means of defense against my enemies. Ogún is king of iron and the mountains, and he prepares his defense in accordance with these attributes. He has a system of his own. Ogún is also connected with agriculture and knows all about plants. That's why agricultural tools are spiritual

52. The Yoruban *orisha* of iron and fire. Worshippers of Ogún place on their altars miniature machetes, pickaxes, hammers, and also now, in Cuba, tanks, planes, trains, and cars. (Jahn, *Muntu*, pp. 44, 65.)

powers for defense. For that reason I keep a spade, a pick, and a machete on my altar.

Some people can't get help from any saint because their faith is too unreliable and the saints don't like that. When an appeal is made by or for such a person, every saint will try to slough him off on another one: "You take that case.... No, you.... How about you? Not me, let someone else do it."

People also call upon specific saints for special needs. A saint is like a lawyer for a person. There have been cases of people who have been sentenced to eight years in jail. By the influence of the saints this can be diminished to about four. I've observed all these things and have come to the conclusion that anything is possible. How can people say this is a myth and that its followers are a bunch of fanatics, when the effects benefit people physically?

Although the African religious beliefs originated where there were no schools, universities, or academies, they have a very profound logic and philosophy all their own. There are two positive aspects in the African religion—supplication and divination. Divination means the ability to see a person's situation and to consult him as to his future. Supplication means if someone wanted something to happen, he'd make a petition based on his faith. If you say, "I wish this would happen," and it does, that's a coincidence, mere chance. But supplicants ask for and obtain material remedies—a stone, some grass, a leaf. These religious remedies are based on peoples' knowledge of the virtues of plants. Some ignorant people don't realize how important plants are, but anybody who studies the matter must come to the conclusion that they're living bodies with powers of their own.

One way of finding out about the future is to ask a *babalawo*.[53] The *babalawo* is a man of flesh and bone but who has special powers to tell what's going to happen. I've seen these diviners go into convulsions before beginning a consultation. They will tell the person, "In your home a certain situation has existed for so many years." And very often the person says, "Yes, that's right." After seeing things like that happen, I couldn't have doubts. However, I didn't discard the scientific point of view, because it often coincided with that of the African religion. Besides, believers weren't being exploited, and nobody made a living from divining or giving remedies.

There are various objects that are important in divination. The coconut is almost as powerful as the saint since you can't work the saint without the coconut. The seashell is also important in divination. Some

---

53. A specialist in *santería* divination with high status but no generalized authority. According to one estimate, there were about 300 *babalawos* in Cuba in 1969. (Booth, "Neighbourhood Committees and Popular Courts," pp. 260, 125n.)

people can pick up a shell and tell you things you wouldn't believe anyone could possibly know about your life. It's plain to see, nature has given man these spiritual powers to discover such information.

In matters of divination many people try to exploit the credulity and fanaticism of others even though it's forbidden by the religion. But most of the *santos* involved do let people charge something—a *peso*, half a *peso*, or even only a *peseta*. Of course, if an egg or anything like that is necessary for the cure, the person to be cured should pay for it.

Rogelio loved money and it annoyed him that when the saint came down and performed a job, he didn't let Rogelio charge anything. When that happened, Rogelio would curse and rave. He was an older man but he had a lively spirit. People used to marvel at the things Changó[54] did when he came down. Finally Rogelio said, "Changó, I won't put up with your dirty tricks. I don't want you coming down over my head anymore." So he dug a hole under a bush and buried Changó there. Changó got even; he swore that the next time he came down, he'd take Rogelio with him. He put his curse on Rogelio. Rogelio would pay a call on someone and the first thing you knew, he'd doze off right in the middle of a conversation.

Changó kept Rogelio in that condition for twenty-one years, and Rogelio was convinced that he would never get well again. Finally he started to get fevers. His daughter called a doctor who sent him medicine. We were gathered around Rogelio's bed when a youth suddenly came down, with Changó mounted on his shoulders. "Rogelio, Rogelio, look who's here!" his daughter exclaimed. "Look, it's Changó!"

Rogelio tried to greet Changó, but Changó turned his back on him and went out to the yard and climbed a palm tree. We tried to make Changó get down to help Rogelio, but nothing would move him. We finally gave up and went into the house. No sooner had we turned our backs on him when Changó slipped down and left.

Then *pam!* Rogelio closed his eyes. Everybody began to weep and wail, "Rogelio is gone. Rogelio!" The doctor was sent for and he certified that Rogelio was dead.

You can't play with the *santos*. We all knew the history of Rogelio's burying Changó. Rogelio wanted to exploit his powers and the saints won't stand for that. The supernatural agent warns you that you must not charge for your cures, or they tell you how much you may charge. But if you're called by somebody who doesn't have the money and the saint is urging you to do the job, you should do it for free because saving the person's life is the most important thing. But your true rewards are

---

54. A son of Yemayá and husband of Ochún, Changó is worshipped as the *orisha* of war and of masculinity. (Jahn, *Muntu*, pp. 65–66.) In Cuba Changó is identified with St. Barbara.

the grace of the spirit who helps you and the satisfaction of doing good for other human beings. Some say, "That's all very well, but how am I supposed to eat?" Well, a man doesn't need money to live. He needs to eat, yes, but nobody is going to deny a plate of food to someone who heals him. You will have whatever food and money you need if you live according to the rules of the religion.

The religion I now believe in and practice is *Abacuá,* although I respect the other two religious orders, especially *Mayombé* because of its violence. They are both very powerful orders. The *santeros* have cured many people that doctors couldn't help. Nature has given the *mayombero* the same powers as the *santero*—a straw hat and a cigar, and they can destroy the world. That's the way they are. Among other things, Duvalier of Haiti has been accused of being a *brujero,*[55] and now they say he killed Eisenhower with his magic spells.

I prefer *Abacuá* because of the way it's structured. I like the fact that only men are admitted, because it seems to me that the purpose of religion is to unite men. Women are allowed to participate in some aspects of the *Abacuá* religion, but it's forbidden for them to belong to the order because they're unable to keep secrets. It's been proven that in every aspect of life women are much less discreet than men. Just say something mysterious to a woman and she'll go straight to some other person, not only to tell them the whole thing but to add a few touches of her own.

There have been cases of men who asked to be initiated and were also refused because they had certain faults. I can be friends with anybody, even a queer, as long as he behaves decently toward me. After all, I've been told that a man with this weakness doesn't necessarily want to be that way; it can happen because of the development of certain glands. But I'd never tell a homosexual, "Look, in our religion we have such-and-such secrets."

There is a saying, "Friendship has its place and the *ñáñigo*'s[56] place is apart from it." The saying means that friendship is one thing and religion is another. You have to be just as discreet with your friends as with anybody else about the mysteries of religion.

An *Abacuá* must obey the rule of secrecy until death. It's as binding as any other oath. I've made a firm decision and sworn to be faithful to this cause with all my heart. All I can tell you is that all religions have an animal as a symbol, and the *Abacuá* symbol is the goat. That's why we eat goat meat and roosters. Drums are usually made with goatskin, you know, and we have a saying, "The goat who breaks a drum pays for it with his own skin." As to the rest of the mysteries involved in the *Abacuá* society, I must remain silent.

55. A sorcerer.
56. A member of the *Abacuá* (see n. 10).

Chapter Four

I'm a Man of Flesh and Blood

I MET MY THIRD WIFE, Perpetua, during the Christmas season of 1942. She was staying at Minerva Ruz's house at that time. On Christmas Eve I offered to pour her a glass of wine and then I suggested, "Let's change glasses. You take a sip from mine and I'll take a sip from yours." So we did. Then she offered me a piece of meat she was frying. I took just one little bite and gave it back to her. I could see that she took it well, so I started courting her. At suppertime we continued taking sips from each other's glasses and feeding each other tidbits from our plates.

The next day we talked more seriously and I proposed to her. I put it quite bluntly. "I'm all alone. If you like, we can be man and wife from this very moment."

And she said, "All right, I'll think about it."

On New Year's Day we went out drinking together, and on January 5 Perpetua asked, "Have you asked the Three Kings for anything?"

"Well," I said, "I wrote my letter to them last month but I still don't know whether they'll give me what I asked for."

"What did you ask for?"

"That's my secret. I'll just wait and see if I get my gift tomorrow."

She caught on all right, because next morning, the Day of the Three Kings, she came knocking on my door. When I opened she asked me with a straight face, "Have the Three Kings been here?"

"No," I said.

"But I sent them!"

"Then come in, come in," I said, laughing. "Maybe *you* are the gift they sent me!" So we laughed and kissed and celebrated the Day of the Three Kings.

"What shall I do with the gift the Three Kings brought? Shall I throw it away?" I teased.

"That's up to you," she answered.

"Then I think I'll keep it, because one shouldn't just toss away what the Three Kings bring." So we stayed together for the next two years.

I think we were about as happy as any married couple can be, mainly because of Perpetua's frankness. From the very first she confessed that she'd been a prostitute in Palmira, where she came from. "*Chico,* I'm telling you this in case some old friends from Palmira happen to come here and I have a drink or a beer with them out of politeness. I don't want you to think they have any special interest in me. It's just that they've known me a long time and know I was no homebody but a woman who had the misfortune to be a prostitute."

In Palmira, as in every country place, women were no better than slaves. Perpetua had tried other kinds of work, even cutting cane. But prostitution was the only way a lone woman could survive in the country. And even so they had to give the Rural Police a cut in order to carry on their business.

I didn't doubt that Perpetua was faithful to me, because she had gone into the life out of need, not from choice. "The truth is, I didn't like it," she said. "I hated to exhibit my body to strange men, even though I do need a man."

I don't know whether she said that just to please me, but I believed her affection for me was sincere. She respected me, and being older than Eloisa she realized what it meant to be expressive in bed. She wasn't frigid; in fact, Perpetua was all warmth. Another thing she spelled out for me was that she liked to drink. She didn't do any hard drinking, but sometimes she'd have a few too many and then we'd have problems.

I was working on my own as a carpenter, and Perpetua got a job in a laundry which paid 5 or 6 *pesos* a week. Her son, Esteban, who was nineteen when we got together, came to live with us. A lot of the boys in Las Yaguas gathered rags, empty bottles, and things like that to sell, and one day Esteban said to me, "I'm going to work, like the rest of the kids here. I'm no deadbeat, I want to help you out." So Esteban worked, as best he could. He and I were always on good terms.

Perpetua was a good woman but completely illiterate, and that's a defect I find hard to put up with. It was her ignorance that made her jealous—if she so much as saw a leaf stirring, she thought I had another woman. That kind of thing makes me sick. I'm a man of flesh and blood like everybody else but I've always been very respectful of my home life. Perpetua's constant suspicion irritated and bored me, but her illiteracy caused our separation.

I've always had the misfortune to choose illiterate wives because they were the only kind I could get. The mere fact that a woman has some culture or even a smattering of knowledge indicates she's not going to be content with poverty, and I've never been so well off that I dared ask one to live with me. But there's no substitute for having a woman in your own home, so I kept taking the plunge with my eyes shut, like a fisherman casting his nets into the deep. If I caught a crab I kept it, and if I caught a shark I kept it too.

If a man and woman have the same degree of schooling they get along with each other; the same holds true if they agree in politics. You're always in danger when you're involved in a political movement, so you have to be careful about the kind of woman you take up with. When the police come knocking on your door, you don't want a wife who tells them, "No, he isn't here. He went that way."

Besides, it's difficult to live with a woman who doesn't understand politics since you can't talk to her about what's happening. I like to talk about why this policy is good and that one isn't, or why things should be done in such-and-such a way. But if she keeps interrupting to say, "Wasn't last night's dance fun?" I can see that she isn't interested in what I'm saying.

I often tried to explain things to Perpetua because she was so ignorant. Finally I came right out and told her, "You can't read or write so you see everything in the light of your own opinions. They aren't necessarily wrong but you don't know how to size things up. You even lack the most elementary knowledge of what virtue is."

She was hurt. "No matter what you say," she told me, "I've been faithful to you and I love you."

"I believe you, but I'm talking about something else. If a woman's too stupid to know how to make a man happy, marriage is a rough path."

That made her very angry. She brooded over it until one day she said, "I'm leaving."

"What do you mean, you're leaving?"

"I'm going back to my hometown."

"Well, you've already decided so what can I say? I'm really sorry, because I know you're a sincere woman, but if that's what you want. . . ."

So one morning she got up earlier than usual, picked up her bundle of clothes, and said, "I'm leaving now."

"Well, what can I do? I'll be seeing you."

"No you won't. I'll never come back to Havana, *chico*. And if I do, I'll be very careful to stay out of your way."

Then I answered, "If you bear me a grudge, all right. But if you ever want to be friends with me, I'm willing. I feel no resentment toward you."

And so she left with her son. Later on she wrote me, saying she was sorry for the way things had turned out. I haven't seen her since she left. I don't even know where she lives.

I got together with my fourth wife, Digna Deveaux, in 1947. She was fourteen years younger than I, and had a job washing and ironing in a house right in the *reparto*. Digna didn't have any schooling and wasn't very intelligent. In my opinion, the more intelligent a woman is, the more she wants to be out doing things all the time. There wasn't a trace of that in Digna. At 7:00 in the morning she was already at her job. After it got dark and the children had their dinner, she shut the door and nobody saw her until the following day.

From what little I saw of Digna, I liked her. I liked her modesty and her way of life. Here was a decent, virtuous woman who needed help and deserved to get it. Since she was a neighbor, it was only natural for me to ask her if she needed help from our food-distribution program.

"Of course I do, I have three children," she said.

My question had nothing to do with the fact that I was interested in her as a woman, though I did need someone to look after my house and she seemed very suitable. We became sweethearts right away, and I told her, "Don't worry. You and I are going to get married, so it's only right that I should help you." I didn't have a steady job then but I knew more than one trade and always found some kind of work. And I always knew how to make my money last.

Later, when Digna and I started living together, I got a job at the Zequeira workshop. We were paid on a piecework basis. If the owner contracted to deliver 100 chairs, he paid us 1 *peseta* for each chair. We'd work fast, and if we finished the chairs in three days, we'd earn 20 *pesos* for three days of work. When one job was done there was another one waiting. That way, in six days I'd earn 40 or 50 *pesos*—good money in those times. So I didn't have any serious financial worries.

Digna helped us in our political work in spite of her little schooling. I'd tell her, "Look, here are our plans and we must do these things." She was very obedient. She'd always answer, "Well, *chico,* if we have to do it, we'll do it." She was so dedicated that when we got a shipment of food to distribute, she wouldn't even light the stove at home that day. She'd say, "Let's get busy and take care of everybody. If there's time later on, I'll cook something for us." Her community spirit and concern for others impressed me. Seeing how Comrade Digna was developing into a revolutionary, I was glad we had gotten together. I needed to confide in somebody near me who was discreet and willing.

Digna Deveaux:

When Lázaro first started to court me, I told him, "I have to think it over because I've certainly had bad luck with men in the past. All the men I've had anything to do with have been jealous, but since you're older, maybe you won't wear my life out with jealousy. That's something I don't want to happen again."

Men are the ruination of women. My father was a very jealous man. He didn't like visitors in the house and didn't want my mother to go out or anything like that. She used to cry all the time. I'm just the opposite; I never cry over men. There are lots of fish in the sea.

It upset me to see my mother suffer, but I respected my father more than her. I have to admit I never talked much with him because of his rough disposition. Of course I loved *mamá* more than I loved *papá*. She used to pamper and kiss me a lot. But when I gave her cause, she'd beat me hard, on the behind, just the way I spank my children with a stick or a strap, or whatever happens to be around.

I have nothing but good to say about my mother's treatment of me; maybe that's because I was her favorite. She supported us by taking in laundry and she also did healing. She would cure children by the passing of hands. During healing, she always had a basket of herbs and would sprinkle rice about. Later, when I grew up, I did healings also.

At fifteen I began to want to get free, to test my independence. I loved to flirt and all that, but I didn't have a sweetheart. Maybe if I'd gone through the experience of having a boyfriend like the tots of seven today, I wouldn't have married so young. Now a girl thinks it over a long time before she goes off with a man, but my family never took me anywhere and I wanted to get free.

The truth is I wanted a husband and I wanted to get laid. I'm a frank person, I tell the truth and that's that. When this little baby itches, she wants to be scratched. To be honest, the only thing I'm not willing to do is make it with another woman. And if the man isn't up to satisfying me, it's, "Well, son, I really like you a lot but frankly you can't make me happy in this department and I want someone who does."

The thing is I'm hot-blooded. Even now I'm a pretty hot number and I feel the urge because I still have my cycle. But I don't want to get involved at the moment; I'm sick and I'm not in the market. It's not like the good old days, if you know what I mean.

My first husband, Tulio, and I had three children, but one of them died before we had a chance to name him. Leaving Tulio really hit me hard, but I was still just a child, wet behind the ears. Later I realized men are so perverse that they aren't worth moaning over. When a man starts to play around, the only thing to do is leave him. That's why I've never married legally, so when things don't suit me I can just leave. I don't put up with nonsense from anybody.

I left Tulio in 1939. It wasn't until 1942 that I took Vicente, my second husband. He was a kitchen helper and earned 150 *pesos* a month. I got along mighty well with him. But one day he lost his job and we couldn't pay the rent for three months and were evicted. Then we moved to Las Yaguas, where they sold little shacks for 10 or 20 *pesos*, or rather you'd buy the land or the mayor would give it to you and you'd build your own house.

"Dear Lord," I said, "you never know what's coming next." I'd seen all this in the movies and had felt sorry for the people living there, and lo and behold, I end up in Las Yaguas myself. That first morning I was shocked. "Just a minute," I said, "where's the bathroom?"

"There's no bathroom here," he answered. "What they have here is a ditch."

A ditch, imagine! I'd lived in the country and we had privies and houses made of plywood and palm thatch. But our house in Las Yaguas was made of *yaguas* and tin bound together with iron bands. "This kind of thing still existing right in the midst of Havana!"

Vincente said, "Now don't get mad. This will only be a matter of a few months."

I finally had to leave Vincente because his jealousy got to be too much. He was always after me, telling me not to go to the grocery and giving some boy a few cents to do the shopping for me. He wanted me to buy water for a nickel a can so I wouldn't have to go to the public water tap. He also got upset whenever he saw me using makeup.

I went to Santiago de Cuba and Vincente's mother took my little boy, Juan. Since she was living alone, she said she'd like me to give her Vincente's child. Well, it didn't make any difference to me and he was her only grandson, so I let her bring him up.

I went to live with Lázaro just after I separated from Vincente. Lázaro was forty-some years old then. I was washing and ironing in Señora Argelia's house and one day he came up to me and said, "Señora, every time I pass by here, I see you here busy as a bee." He said he liked my way and he began to court me. Imagine that!

A lot of men were in love with me at the time but I didn't care for any of them. I always said that when I looked around, I'd search for an older man who would help me raise my children. I wasn't out for romance because the chances were they'd get me pregnant and leave me. Lázaro never appealed to me as a man. That would have been impossible, just impossible. He was so homely and I was very good-looking at the time.

I took up with him for the sake of security, because he was a good man. He was jealous but, well, more controlled than my first two husbands, and he wasn't always after me with sermons, saying I shouldn't go out anywhere or any of that stuff. But of course I didn't give him any reason to. I have no complaints to make about him. He was always good to me and my children. He gave me all I needed and I didn't have to work at all.

Lázaro was decent and sensible. He wasn't the kind to spend his time running around, and I never suffered when I was with him. He was a good father, a man who finished his work, came home, bathed, had his dinner, and then sat down to read. He was really sharp, a real intellectual. He used to read an awful lot. He had a whole collection of books.

It was hard to quarrel with Lázaro because you'd try to start a fight with him and he would get everything onto the plane of reasoning and convince you. That's the way he is, he doesn't argue. For that reason we led a very peaceful life. He used to soft-soap me and he still does. He tells me, "If it weren't for that temper of yours, any man would live happily with you."

But to tell the truth, in some ways Lázaro isn't a man. Practically anybody might say "shit" from time to time, but he doesn't. I say it when I'm really upset. There's no denying it, I get foul-mouthed. "Don't fuck around with me," I say. It's true. And when I'm in a hurry, sending someone out on an errand, I yell, "*Maricón*[57] and motherfucker, the grocery's going to be closed!"

I went to bed with Lázaro after two months of flirting around with him. It was like nothing and I went to sleep right off. We'd sleep together at my house, because with me the man has to come and go from my house. When I'm at home I like to know I'm in my own house. When he feels like it, my man can come over, but the house is mine. Otherwise, before you knew it, he'd decide to throw me out and I'd have no place to go. And the same goes with this house in Bolívar that Fidel gave me. I'm taking no chances. A man can stay here all he likes but I don't put him on the ration book. When I die my children will have this house. But if I go around putting a man on the ration book, he might take it into his head to kill one of the children to get the house.

Lázaro never brought anybody to my house. With my disposition, he was probably afraid I'd embarrass him in front of people. I know he was very active in politics in Las Yaguas, but he had his own house and his political activities were all taken care of there. He never talked about them to me; I don't know a thing about politics. I was registered but I never even voted. Maybe it's because I only went through second grade, but politics just don't interest me. I'm satisfied with any government that's in as long as I don't have a hard time. I'm interested in having a pair of shoes, a dress, and enough to eat. Beyond that I couldn't care less.

I've never been the type of woman who goes around getting things free. I've worked and have been able to support my five children by myself. For example, the Purísima truck used to come around and give out bread and other food, but my children and I never went. I was poor, all right, but I didn't go begging my bit of bread. And I

57. Slang term for homosexual.

never got anything from the Home Relief, either. They gave food and clothing but I never cared for begging. Lázaro was always against it too.

Not too long after I went with Lázaro, I found myself pregnant again. When my period didn't come, I told him I thought I was going to have a baby. "Now don't go taking medicines and things," he said, "just because I'm old and you don't want to breed with an old man."

But really, I wanted to have the child. I'm not much of a breeder, but I've never tried to keep from having a child in my entire life. Let them come when they want to. Why should I stop them? You can't get a baby from a slot machine and you can't have one just because you have a mind to. No, it's nature and God's will.

Lázaro pampered me a lot when I was pregnant. If I felt like eating chicken, he'd go out and bring it to me, no matter how much it cost. He used to bring me candy apples from the Hijas de Galicia too. And did I eat when I was pregnant! I ate all my regular meals and anything else I had a yen for. At that time *maltina*[58] was easy to get so I had a liter of it in the morning and another at night. I got as fat as a pig. When I went to see the doctor he said, "What you have here isn't a baby, it's a monster, and when you go into labor we're going to have to do a cesarean."

Yara was born on October 10, 1948. I was attended by a midwife from the emergency clinic, a friend of mine. If you like you can pay, but the clinic itself doesn't charge anything. I've never had a child in the hospital. I've always been at home with midwives and they were all easy births. Yara's was the most difficult birth I had. He weighed almost 10½ pounds. I nursed him for three years.

Lázaro was as happy as could be. My baby had everything a poor child could have, and Lázaro bought the layette things himself. He was so excited that by the time Yara was born we already had his high chair, cradle, his comforter, and his little chest. Lázaro was out of his mind over the baby, and as for me, you can imagine. Yara was darling.

When the students came around to see the baby, they began to tease me. "Wow! That's a good hunk of nigger you've got there, girl. Where were you keeping all that?" They asked me what I was going to name him.

"Joaquín," I answered.

"No, no," they said, "not Joaquín, not when he was born on the anniversary of the beginning of the War of 1868. Why don't you name him Yara?" And sure enough, everybody calls him Yara, even though his birth certificate says Francisco. Yara is the name he goes by—on the ration book and everywhere else.

58. A bottled drink made of malt and other grains.

I lived with Lázaro for four years—until 1950. When I left him I had been thinking about it for some time, about how our characters clashed. Finally I told him we shouldn't continue and that he should pick up the few things he had and leave. He said OK.

I don't know why I finally got tired of living with Lázaro. He never gave me any cause for complaint, never laid a finger on me or mistreated my children. In fact, he was very sweet with the children.

BENEDÍ:

In spite of the fact that Digna had borne children before, she knew as much about pregnancy as an animal. She thought she was sick until I told her, "Well, *chica*, it seems to me you'd better see a midwife." She did and the midwife said, "You aren't sick, *chica*, you're pregnant."

Digna had a happy, healthy pregnancy because I was careful not to let her overwork. As her pregnancy progressed, I eliminated more and more of her work. Finally, the only thing I allowed her to do was to go out to do an errand. Even then I'd tell her, "Don't walk too fast."

It was a great satisfaction and happiness to me when I learned that Digna was pregnant. A man always feels that way when he's the real father. I was even happier when Yara was born on the anniversary of the declaration of Yara, the first cry of independence. I was so in love with Cuba's independence I insisted on naming him Yara. It seemed to me my son was born a patriot. The day I went to register his birth, the secretary said, "That isn't an appropriate name to register him under. What day was he born? October 10? That's San Francisco de Borja's day. Suppose we register him as Francisco Yara." I agreed and that's the way his name appears in the registry.

I had such hopes for Yara! Yet what a muddle-head he turned out to be. He's been in jail twice and he even ran away from the prison farm.

When Yara was a child I argued a lot with his mother because she didn't send him to school. Digna had so little schooling herself she could just barely read and write! I told her, "Look, I'm going to get a primer. You should at least know the alphabet so you can teach it to the children in your spare time. It's very important for them to have an education." But it was no use, Digna didn't understand.

Once, when Yara was seven and going to the priests' school in the *reparto*, he said to me, "Lazarito, I bet I know something you don't know."

"What is it? Tell me."

Then he started spouting a lot of prayers: *Ave María*, the *Credo*, and all the rest.

"Now let's see you write your name," I said.

"Oh, they haven't taught me that yet."

His mother was standing there. She was the one who sent him to that school. I had a violent quarrel with her because of that. "Now you see the kind of teaching they do. Indoctrination, that's all it is! That's the way they keep control of ignorant families." From then on we started to drift apart.

Besides being ignorant, Digna was kind of jealous. In the course of my political activities I have to deal with many people, and many of them are women. But I swear, when I'm working with a woman comrade I don't even notice whether or not she's pretty. My only interest in her is political. Digna began to nag me. I've never been able to put up with that kind of thing. It seems to me that jealousy, whether from the man or the woman, does great harm to a marriage. That's why Digna and I separated and never got back together, though sometimes I visit her.

Around 1950 I was involved in the Revolutionary Socialist Movement.[59] There was a meeting in Oriente that I went to. Our aim then was to build a strong organization. But there's a big difference between resolving a revolutionary problem out in the street and centralizing it someplace. It was a matter of establishing contacts and organizing the movement better. There were deep differences of opinion on how to go about it, and it ended in a power struggle. A lot of the people were trying to get rid of someone so they could take his place. And all this was going on to the tune of how we should be willing to "sacrifice ourselves on the altar of the fatherland." Some of those people thought *they* were the fatherland.

At that time my comrades and I were deeply involved in the Cayo Confites expedition[60] to liberate Santo Domingo. Fidel was among those who took part in this movement. We said, "Let's organize the Army for the Liberation of the Americas. If we have to die, we die. If we have the good fortune to win in Santo Domingo, we'll go ahead, because from that point on nobody can stop us."

59. The *Movimiento Socialista Revolucionaria* (MSR) was founded by Rolando Masferrer in 1944 as an anticommunist action group. It had about 300 members. Before that, Masferrer had been a leader of a militant communist university student group and had fought against Franco in Spain. However, he later reversed his position and backed Batista's second dictatorship. (Thomas, *Cuba: The Pursuit of Freedom,* p. 741.)

60. In 1947 José Manuel Alemán, Minister of Education and intimate friend of Grau, sponsored an expedition against Trujillo and the Dominican Republic. Juan Bosch and many Dominican exiles who were living in Havana were involved. The plan was to land 1,200 armed men in the Dominican Republic in advance of a liberating army. Supporting Grau, the leading Cubans in this expedition were Manolo Castro and Masferrer of the MSR, Eufemio Fernández of the ARG (*Acción Revolucionaria Guiteras*), and Fidel Castro representing the UIR (*Unión Insurreccional Revolucionaria*). They moved their men and arms to an island, Cayo Confites, off the coast of Camaguey Province, but Grau declared the group a danger to the state and ordered it to disband. Disregarding Grau's orders, part of the group set sail under Bosch's command, but most were later arrested. Fidel Castro escaped by swimming through the shark-infested waters of the Bay of Nipe. (Thomas, *Cuba: The Pursuit of Freedom,* pp. 755–56, 812.)

I was given the responsibility of doing liaison work for the expedition in the three poor barrios, Las Yaguas, Isla de Pinos, and Cueva del Humo. We distributed propaganda and a lot of people joined up. About 120 residents of Las Yaguas and more than 40 from the other barrios participated in the expedition. Most of them were young. They didn't go in the hope of being paid or having it soft because we warned them that the life of a revolutionary was a hard one. They said, "That doesn't matter. We want to go."

But when they got to Cayo Confites differences sprang up, and that business of detaining the ships occurred. So their enthusiasm cooled off and people began to break away from the movement. I myself drifted away from it because I couldn't agree with many things. I thought too much emphasis was given to money. Some people had joined only because they were ambitious, and those of us whose minds didn't work that way distrusted them. We thought, "What good can they be to us? If they're thinking of money now, what will they be like when they get power?" So there wasn't any real unity among us.

Greed was always a serious problem in Cuban politics. Penniless men would rise to power, but as soon as they got some money they'd forget the poverty behind them. Many revolutionaries left us to seek the comforts of life. Take the case of Prío.[61] He was a revolutionary until he began to get rich. That was the end of his revolutionary fervor. The same thing happened with Grau. He kept preaching honesty, then it turned out that he was one of the presidents who took the greatest advantage of his post.

Prío was overthrown by Batista's second coup, on March 10, 1952. Prío was rich already and was either in agreement with Batista, or afraid or indifferent. His only instructions at the time of the coup were "communicate with Matanzas to see what's going on." All he did was phone one place, then visit another. We realized he had no intention of counteracting Batista. We were rather bitter about Batista by then because we'd had a chance to gauge his self-interest. He worked for himself and for the colonels and generals around him, not for the people. I didn't exactly go out and protest Batista's coup, but I went to the Palace with Juan Carlos Montano and found out what Prío's instructions were. Then we went to the University to see about the students' reactions. We contacted a student called Jorge. He said they were waiting for Prío's decision.

We could already see what Batista was aiming at. There was a lot of violent talk against Las Yaguas. "They're going to burn Las Yaguas because the people there have always been in favor of Grau . . . they've been against so many things . . . they're communists. . . ." We were willing

61. Carlos Prío Socorrás, President of Cuba 1948–52.

to confront Batista, but what could we do in a situation like that? So we decided to go back to Las Yaguas and wait for something to develop. In the end we couldn't do anything, because the force we were hoping would join us disappeared.

I continued to be deeply involved in all the important political movements in Las Yaguas. But in spite of that, I never wanted a political position. People used to look upon me as the mayor, because when they had to get something done many of them would come to me, and I solved their problems. But I was never mayor of Las Yaguas, oh no! The mayor of Las Yaguas had to take orders from the police and that's not right.

The mayor of Las Yaguas was old Alfredo Barrera,[62] an honest but conservative man. He had no racial prejudice and got along with everybody. He often consulted me. I was more than willing to help him since he was noble-hearted, although he was ignorant about some things. He didn't know enough to direct a mass of people like that without help, but I never criticized him the way some people did. Barrera spent all his time drinking in a grocery store, so he couldn't expect people to take him seriously. Being mayor is just like bringing up children: before you can make any demands, you must set a good example.

Before the Revolution every administration was dead set against communism, so a communist couldn't do anything toward solving certain problems. I'd say to Barrera, "*Chico,* I have a friend with a problem. Let's see what we can do about it." Barrera was on such good terms with the police that usually all he had to do was call them to settle the affair. Naturally the person we'd helped would be grateful, so he'd join my movement. But I'd always warn Barrera, "Don't tell anybody you're working with the communists, or do anything conspicuous which would make people connect you with us. Just say that you're doing a favor for a friend."

The government made some attempts to improve the situation by organizing the National Housing Commission. But instead of offering funds for constructing new houses, they began to destroy the *repartos* where the poor lived. They told the residents, "If you rent a house and land elsewhere, we'll give you 200 *pesos.*

I was opposed to the plan. A tiny room cost 30 *pesos* a month, so how long would 200 *pesos* last, especially for somebody who'd never before paid rent? Besides, give that much money to a family with four or five starving, naked children and what are the first things they'd spend it on? On satisfying the kids' hunger and buying them some decent clothes. The money would be spent before the rent was due. If they had to pay

---

62. The father of the Alfredo Barrera whose story appears in Part II of this volume.

rent every month, how were they to solve the problems they were unable to solve when they didn't pay rent?

Some people understood my objections to the plan but others didn't. One woman cursed me with every possible curse. "May evil lightning split that black!" she burst out. "What business is it of his anyway?"

I was persecuted for opposing it, but what else could I do? By that time I'd rather have died than go on living in such miserable conditions, and seeing others living that way too. Later people came to see that I was right. I told them, "We hope they'll build new houses, find us work, and put an end to this system so we can have the rights of citizens. But they'll never achieve those things by handing us 200 *pesos* and telling us to get out of Las Yaguas."

I wrote several articles about our economic situation. In one interview for a newspaper, I told about a man who worked in City Hall. He had a wife and five children and he only earned 37 *pesos* a month. He was classified as an indigent since he was living in Las Yaguas. But as I told the reporter, if that man left Las Yaguas, he'd really be an indigent because on his income he couldn't possibly support such a large family and pay rent as well.

What the people of Las Yaguas needed was work. Many families had low, unsteady incomes or none at all, and they disintegrated because the woman would say, "I won't let my children starve as long as I can get a man to support them." Lots of men living in Las Yaguas had two wives and two separate households. It was practically a custom, not because it was approved, but because so many men were apt to find themselves in a situation where they couldn't do anything else.

Sometimes while a woman's husband was collecting rags and empty bottles, she would walk the streets. Finally the husband would say, "All right, *chica,* you go your way and I'll go mine." How can a man make certain demands on his wife when she and their children are going hungry? He has to leave her at liberty to find a way to survive. That was one cause of the prostitution problem in Las Yaguas.

One of the things Minerva Ruz fought against was discrimination toward the women of Las Yaguas who tried to find regular jobs. She made friends at La Corona cigar factory, and whenever she could, she'd get the women jobs there. Naturally she couldn't tell the factory management, "Fire every woman who isn't from Las Yaguas," but she managed to get quite a lot of jobs for members of her family, as well as for women not related to her. She was unfairly criticized for that. Poverty can twist a person's mind. That's one reason why we should fight against it.

The youth in Las Yaguas were entirely discredited. Why? Because when Sunday came it was only a minority who could afford to wear a new shirt and pants. The rest stood around on street corners, shabby and sad. They had the soul and the feelings of youth but couldn't take part in their activities and were depressed.

Around 1950 construction was begun on the airport of La Cayuga,[63] in San Antonio de los Baños. We hoped this project would offer a new source of jobs for the youth of Las Yaguas. One day we had a conference about it. After discussing the unfair reputation of our young people and our desire to find work for them, we decided to send a group to La Cayuga to apply for jobs.

When the police saw such a large number of young men leave Las Yaguas together, they were startled. They called it "an invasion of delinquents," which was unfair. Those boys wanted to work but they hadn't been given an education or any kind of training. Nobody had ever tried to ease their sorrow or relieve their hunger. I told the policeman, "If you want to know what those boys are up to, why don't you take a little trip to La Cayuga? And go on foot as they did. A delinquent wouldn't take the trouble to walk that far."

There was always somebody ready to exploit our youth. The police would see those sad-looking boys out in the street and say, "What are you doing here?"

"Me? Nothing."

"Well, how would you like to earn some money? You could earn 4 *pesos* a day, easy."

Of course the boy would jump at the chance. "Sure. What do I have to do?"

"No heavy work or anything like that. Why don't you sell marijuana?"

"But I'll go to jail."

"No, *muchacho,* don't worry about that. I'll bring you the stuff myself and I'll protect you." And many of those boys didn't have the spirit to say no, any more than they'd have had the spirit to think of peddling marijuana in the first place.

The police did this because they had to bring money to their captain. They got 35 *pesos* a week just from the businesses in Las Yaguas! And the police from the Bureau of Investigation who dealt with robbery, drugs, and so on had to have their cut, and so did the vigilante assigned to Las Yaguas. The marijuana peddlers had to give money to all those guys!

I saw the problem, and I raged, "This is criminal! Criminal! It's destroying our young people!" I talked about it often with Juan Carlos, but what could I do, all by myself?

We even have a martyr to this sort of police corruption. His name was Osvaldo Morante. Some policemen belonging to the anti-drug squad talked Osvaldo into peddling drugs.

63. A U.S. Army airfield.

I was a pretty good friend of the boy, so I gave him a lot of advice. "I'll get you a room," I promised, "if you stop smoking and peddling marijuana, because we want you to be representative of communist youth." I had to make Osvaldo promise to quit before I could help him, since the communists consider marijuana a vice and don't want to be associated with it in any way.

Osvaldo told the police, "I want to marry my girl so I'm going to quit this and sell newspapers instead." But the police had to pay those higher up, so they kept coming around to collect the money. "There's no way you can quit," they'd say. "We'll be around again on Monday."

Monday came, and when Osvaldo got home from selling newspapers his friends told him, "The police are after you." Osvaldo ran, dodging in and out of alleys until he got to the part of Las Yaguas called Matanzas, where it was easy for the police to surround him. He disregarded their order to halt and they shot him dead.

Osvaldo was buried at the Colón cemetery. I agreed to deliver the funeral oration, and of course I had to tell the truth. Among other things I said, "Let this corpse be our emblem. Let him raise his hand from the tomb and point to those who are guilty of murdering him, because this is only one of their crimes."

The grave was surrounded by Osvaldo's relations, but behind them were several people we didn't know. Minerva Ruz, who was standing next to me, whispered, "Don't leave in the car you came in and don't take the bus or you'll never get to Las Yaguas. We have a car for you outside."

After the funeral we drove around a bit. Minerva said, "Whatever you do, don't let yourself be seen in Las Yaguas tonight," so we headed for Guanabacoa.

During the 1958 elections the situation in Las Yaguas was a tough one. There were enough votes in the *reparto* to elect a representative, so we were constantly threatened by mean-spirited rascals who were interested in the position. Participating in the elections were the *Auténtico* Party, the Democrats, and the *Accíon Progresista*. If I remember correctly, the *Ortodoxo* Party didn't take part in the 1958 elections and they were the only ones we trusted, to a certain extent. We trusted Chibás,[64] but we couldn't count on his followers.

The politicians would go down to Las Yaguas and tell us, "You must join the Democratic Party," or whatever party they represented. Those who didn't join risked being dragged out of their houses at night. And the next day when his friends asked, "Where's so-and-so?," nobody

64. Raúl Chibás was the brother of Eduardo Chibás (d. 1951), who founded the *Ortodoxos* (Cuban People's Party) in 1947 with dissident members of Grau's *Auténticos* (Authentic Revolutionary Movement). Raúl, himself a former head of the *Ortodoxos*, had by this time left the party to align himself publicly with Castro and the Twenty-sixth of July Movement. An anticommunist, Chibás is now in exile.

knew. Some of those who disappeared were never seen again. My comrades and I weren't afraid of death, but a man is more useful alive than
dead, so we tried to be discreet, for the sake of our beliefs.

We couldn't openly support the Communist Party, so we asked ourselves, "Which parties are active? Which threaten the people? Which
party advised the communists to work for it?" We hoped to see a candidate elected who was concerned about our problems.

In the 1958 elections the *Auténtico* Party was the most sympathetic to
us. The Communist Party didn't directly or publicly instruct its followers
to cooperate with the *Auténtico* Party, but in Las Yaguas we were in
contact with Osvaldo Sánchez,[65] who represented the Communist Party
in Luyanó, and he said to us, "Look around before you decide what to
do. The party nearest to us ideologically is the *Auténtico*." When the time
for decision came, opinions were divided. Some of us went to the *Auténtico* Party, but others argued that there wasn't any point in it, since the
election results would be altered anyway. I was among those who decided to put up the best fight we could for the *Auténticos*.

We didn't dare work openly, but that doesn't mean we weren't active.
We spread propaganda by approaching individuals and explaining,
"Look, *chico*, we need your vote for this man." We had to be cautious so
we never insisted. After all, if someone didn't see eye to eye with us it
might have cost us our lives. But all our work was in vain. Instead of
taking the ballot boxes to the provincial *junta*, they took them to a private
house and counted them secretly. We knew how we'd voted, and when
we heard the count we knew they'd changed the ballots.

65. Osvaldo Sánchez Cabrera, who served as a go-between for the old Communist Party
and the Castro forces in the Sierra Maestra in 1958. Sánchez was killed in an air crash in
1961. (Theodore Draper, *Castroism: Theory and Practice* (New York: Praeger, 1965), p. 31.)

Chapter Five

Casting off the Yoke

IN THE BEGINNING, I had my doubts about the outcome of the Revolution and about some of the people involved in it. How could we have known then that Fidel was to be trusted? He was an upright man, but in a capitalist country a lawyer today would probably be a millionaire tomorrow. Since Fidel could carve out any kind of future he wanted, how could we imagine he wanted above everything to make the Cuban people independent?

Of course there'd been certain rich men, like Ignacio Agramonte, who joined wholeheartedly in the Cuban Revolution.[66] Carlos Manuel de Céspedes had also been a man of wealth—a professional, a sugar-mill owner, and a slaveholder—yet he gave his whole life to the task of fighting for Cuban independence and freeing the slaves.[67] But there were more cases of corrupt men who were in politics just for the money. They and many others born here were not Cuban in their feelings. We never lacked politicians who made splendid promises, but who were they? Not workingmen. Poor workers were in no position to promise anything. Who would have believed them?

As the Revolution developed, we realized this time it wasn't just another false hope. We felt sure, because we'd been following its progress closely. Our suspicions of Fidel were quickly lifted, because we figured if the Revolution wasn't honest, nobody could persuade the University to participate. After all, Fidel's Movement originated with the students. In fact, he became a leader after the Movement developed. Besides that, none of our previous leaders even admitted they might make mistakes. But Fidel told us, "In the beginning, probably we'll do all the wrong things."

66. Ignacio Agramonte y Loynaz, a cattle rancher who led guerrilla fighters in Camaguey Province during the War of Independence, was killed by the Spaniards in 1873.

67. Carlos Manuel de Céspedes was from a family of landowners and slaveholders. Educated in Spain, he became a leader of the Cuban insurrectionists and President of the Rebel Republic. He was killed by the Spaniards in 1874.

On January 1, 1959, Batista and his guests were sitting at his table, ready to welcome in the New Year, when they got the news, "Those people are already in Las Villas." As you can imagine, Batista and his friends left in a hurry.

I was at a New Year's Eve party when we heard how things were going. Naturally we celebrated, in our own way, but we'd made up our minds not to give way to emotion until we were sure the Revolution had triumphed. There had been many false announcements of Fidel's entry, and when people rushed out to see him, they were received with machine-gun bullets. We weren't sure the Revolution was victorious until January 2, when Camilo[68] and Fidel led the grand entry into Havana.

The Cuban people's feelings were mixed when Fidel entered Havana. Until then the press had been saying, "Those so-called revolutionaries fighting in the mountains were nothing but ordinary troublemakers who were only thinking of the day when they would have the power to steal public funds." And it's true, many Cubans didn't believe that the ideals of the Revolution could be put into practice. But we had our 20,000 dead to answer for, and since the Revolution was the product of their effort and sacrifice, we were bound to be faithful to their principles. Our trust proved to be justified. It became obvious to us that Fidel and several other leaders of the Party would continue to make great personal sacrifices. They weren't just sitting down in some government office and giving orders; they were facing the situation. To them we owe endless respect and consideration.

Even though we supported the Revolution, the people of Las Yaguas were under suspicion immediately. On February 10, 1959, some revolutionaries came to Las Yaguas at midnight, accusing us of bearing arms against the Revolution. We were herded into trucks and taken to police station 13. Ameijeiras, the chief of police,[69] sent one of the vigilantes to tell us to appoint a committee to talk with him. We did as he said, but before we got down to discussing anything with him, a vigilante walked in with a package of marijuana. "Look what we found in Las Yaguas, and they even have radios there in spite of all their poverty."

I asked for permission to speak. Then I said, "I'll tell you why you found marijuana in Las Yaguas—the police forced it on us. They even killed a young fellow because he refused to sell it. As for the question of radios, I myself would have told you which houses have radios and what

68. Comandante Camilo Cienfuegos Gorriaran, who, with Ernesto "Che" Guevara, led the Rebel Army's Las Villas Front. Next to Fidel Castro the most popular hero of the Revolution, Cienfuegos died when his plane was lost at sea in October, 1959.

69. Efigenio Ameijeiras, a veteran of the Sierra del Cristal campaign, was Castro's first chief of police. He later became Vice-Minister of the Armed Forces, but in 1966, as part of a drive against corruption, he was removed from the Communist Party's Central Committee and imprisoned for "moral offenses."

kind of radios they are. They're all homemade. A guy takes a loudspeaker and other parts and puts a radio together, and it works."

After he heard my explanation, Ameijeiras said, "Well, we have to clean out Las Yaguas anyway. We have to find out whether there are any escaped convicts, or anybody waiting for trial."

I spoke up, "Comandante, I don't know who may have escaped, but on January 1 there was a man whose attitude seemed to be that of a true revolutionary. Do you know what he did? He flung open the doors of the jail, saying, 'I bring word of freedom.'"

Ameijeiras smiled, because he was the man who'd done that. Then he said, "All right, anyone who wants to may go."

But I said, "No, first we have to repudiate the charges against us. We'd be infinitely grateful if you'd come down to Las Yaguas with us."

Standing on the stairway, he asked, "Is it very far?"

A guard was already opening the doors. I said, "No, but come with us because you'll be better protected than you have been on other occasions."

When we got to Las Yaguas, a crowd gathered around us. Seeing it, Ameijeiras said, "Let's organize a committee here so we can help the Revolution together."

A voice called out from the audience, "More than we have already?"

"Yes, we must keep making the Revolution stronger. Do you agree to name the group from Las Yaguas the Committee Thirteen, after the station?" Applause. "Well then, you people will organize a committee and select the officers."

Naturally, since we were innocent of any conspiracy against the Revolution, we were freed and the charges against us were repudiated.

In general, I felt the Revolutionary Tribunals were too merciful. When Sosa Blanco[70] was tried at the Stadium, I didn't think he should have been given any chance to talk. They should have turned him over to all the mothers who were eager to pass judgment upon him and let them decide what was to be done with him. I'm pretty sure they wouldn't have sent him before the firing squad. For criminals like him, the firing squad is too mild.

I suggested to somebody, "Get yourself a sharp, dirty knife and jab him every now and then. And with every jab tell him, 'This is in memory of my son. This is in memory of so-and-so's son. . . .' And for every son that was lost, give him fifty, sixty, or seventy jabs." He deserved to suffer a long-drawn-out physical punishment, because his conscience never

70. Jesús Sosa Blanco, an officer in Batista's army accused of crimes against the people of Oriente Province, was tried and condemned to death in the first public war trial under the Castro government (January, 1959).

bothered him and he didn't feel even the slightest part of the sorrow suffered by so many Cuban families.

Also I would have judged the case of Hubert Matos[71] differently. Aside from the movement Matos started against the Revolution, we can't be sure he didn't play some part in the death of Camilo Cienfuegos. It was a strange thing. Camilo flew out to Camaguey Province in his plane one day and was never seen again. Matos was chief of the province, so to my way of thinking he must have known something about it, because what movement could take place there without his knowledge?

I wouldn't have let Matos off with a prison sentence just because he'd been a *comandante* in the Revolution. Show clemency to such people? Not me! I'd make him die in such a way that his suffering would be greater than that with which he has pierced the hearts of so many Cubans.

I was deeply moved by the reaction of the people of Las Yaguas when Fidel declared himself a communist. We believed that a communist was faithful to his ideals and not corrupted by self-interest. When Fidel went to the United States[72] they offered him 100 million dollars. He answered, "I didn't come here to get money; I came to talk to the people." We could see he had a conscience and we began to trust him. But others criticized him harshly, saying, "If the United States wants to help Fidel, why does he reject them for no reason at all?"

The United States also tried to bribe El Che. They'd heard about his political drawing power and his obstinacy, so they offered him about 10 million *pesos* to abandon the struggle. Many Cubans were already trying to figure out how much each would get if you divided 10 million *pesos* among a population of 7 million people. They were capable of selling the honor and prestige of their families. Yet there were others who said, "No, we must fight to the last. And if we must die, we die."

In 1959, when Fidel offered to resign, the people of Havana trembled.[73] "Why?" we asked one another. "Has somebody opposed him in the midst of our difficulties?" We all felt blind love for Fidel by then and we were ready to tear the head off anyone who dared tell him to resign!

71. Hubert Matos resigned as military governor of Camaguey in 1959, protesting the appointment of Raúl Castro as Minister of Defense. Fourteen officers from his command resigned with him. Camilo Cienfuegos replaced Matos as military governor. Matos charged that Raúl was directing (behind Fidel's back) a conspiracy to infiltrate the revolutionary leadership with communists. Matos was tried by tribunal in Havana in December, 1959, on the charge of "uncertain, anti-patriotic and anti-revolutionary conduct." He received a twenty-year sentence and was still imprisoned in La Cabaña in 1974. (Thomas, *Cuba: The Pursuit of Freedom*, pp. 1244–56.)

72. April, 1959.

73. Castro's resignation as Prime Minister came in July, 1959, climaxing a dispute with President Manuel Urrutia Lleó over the new Agrarian Reform Law and the growing influence of communists in the new government. Unable to hold a government together without Castro, Urrutia resigned (for the fourth time) and was immediately replaced by Dr. Osvaldo Dorticós Torrado. The Castro resignation was not accepted and he returned to the office of Prime Minister.

One of the Revolution's first steps toward reorganizing the economy was the Law of Agrarian Reform.[74] Rich owners had always kept large tracts of land fallow, leaving the peasant without work or food. Now all that idle land is being used, and Cuba produces enough food for her population. We can even maintain commercial treaties with our agricultural production.

At the time of the Agrarian Reform Law, Pedro Seguret, a newspaperman in the Movement and one of Camilo Cienfuegos's guards, said, "*Chico,* we're going to have demonstrations here to show that we support the Revolution. We all have plenty of farm implements—hoes, machetes and all—so let's put them at the service of the Revolution."

We gathered a large quantity of implements in the barrio. Some people even gave their only pair of shoes to the Revolution—at a time when to be able to say "I have a pair of shoes" meant you were practically a millionaire. The poor people from the country cried like babies when they saw that this Revolution was no game.

At the time of the Triumph, I was already living with Diana María Rivera, my university-trained wife. She was twenty-five or twenty-six years old when we met and I was her second husband. She'd met her first husband, Anacleto, when she was a student. He was an unemployed bricklayer who was helping out with a car-rental agency. She had to pass by him after class every day and he always got into conversation with her. Being a man without morals, he was incapable of appreciating Diana María's moral stature. He was clever with words and so persistent that he managed to talk her into letting him have his way with her. They became sweethearts.

When her parents objected, Diana María quit her studies and took off with him. After that her life changed completely. Her relatives cut her off. She often tried to visit them but her mother told her they never wanted to see her again. Then something stirred Diana María's conscience and she broke up with the man, but her family refused to take her back. She had to sleep in alleys with her children.

One day Diana María's aunt went to Las Yaguas to visit her *comadre,*

74. The first Agrarian Reform Law, adopted May 17, 1959, prohibited private farms larger than 400 hectares (approximately 988 acres). The expropriated lands were to be distributed among former tenant farmers and sharecroppers, but during 1961 and 1962 most of the land was organized into state farms (*granjas*). The second reform law, enacted in October, 1963, prohibited private farms larger than 67 hectares (about 5 *caballerías,* or 167 acres). The remaining privately owned farms were incorporated into the National Association of Small Farmers (*Asociación Nacional de Agricultores Pequeños,* or ANAP) under the National Institute of Agrarian Reform (*Instituto Nacional de Reforma Agraria,* or INRA). INRA has been responsible for all major agricultural and marketing functions since its establishment in 1959. (Carmelo Mesa-Lago, "Economic Policies and Growth," in Mesa-Lago, ed., *Revolutionary Change in Cuba* (Pittsburgh: University of Pittsburgh Press, 1971), pp. 282–83.)

Sofía Bernal. "*Chica,*" she said, "I'm going to send the girl to you, to see if you can help her find a room."

Sofía consulted me and I said, "Well, let's see what can be done." I had a certain amount of influence in Las Yaguas and I managed to get a room for her. One day Diana María told me she had never met a man who understood her. After that we talked together often, until I asked her, "Do you think perhaps I could understand you?"

"Maybe," she said.

"Good, I'll do my best," I told her. "But you'll have to try to understand me too. And you must change your way of life completely. I have some student friends who might help you get back into the University to finish your education. I'll use my influence with them."

It was very important to me that she should complete her studies and have a career. I wanted to erase her sad past, especially if she was to have more children.

I introduced her to a lot of my comrades and we got her involved with some of the revolutionary groups we were organizing. She was a good worker, and working together, we got to understand each other very well. One day I said to her, "Look, *chica,* you're welcome to move in with me if you like."

"It's about time you asked," she said. "I've been waiting for that." And so we started living together.

Diana María and I were both jealous but we didn't carry it to extremes. For instance, sometimes she had a problem at school or at work and said to me, "They've come to get me, I'm going." I wasn't going to ask her, "Who came to get you? Where are you going? What are you going to do?" That's not my way.

I tried to help her mature, and could see that she was really eager to complete her studies. But she wasn't able to stay in school long enough to graduate because we couldn't afford it. At that time you still had to have money if you wanted to study at the University. Batista's system closed all doors to young people and to children. Even so, Diana María kept on getting books here and there. Education has always been one of my chief concerns, since I believe that's where our hopes for the future lie. So we established a small school where Diana María could teach the neighborhood children.

DIANA MARÍA RIVERA:

My family had never approved of my first marriage because Anacleto didn't earn much money and had only finished third grade. My aunts on my father's side were teachers, and my parents went to a lot of trouble to have their children educated. My mother finished the sixth grade, my father went only to the fourth. He was a Mason and married my mother in the Lodge, as well as in a civil ceremony. We lived in a tenement, but we never wanted for anything because my father was a stevedore earning good money and my mother worked in the stores as a dressmaker.

My brother, sister, and I all went through grade school. My sister entered the Normal School but never completed her teaching course. My brother studied bookkeeping and now works on the docks. I went to the School for Homemakers[75] but left in my second year because I fell in love with Anacleto.

My father finally accepted Anacleto but my mother never did. When I first started living with him, she told my aunt that I shouldn't "count on her for anything." When I heard that, I cried for several days. *Mamá* liked to be connected with people who were better off than we were. She always rejected my poorer girl friends. I wasn't like that. I made friends with all kinds of people. My mother wanted something better for us.

Anacleto drank and didn't pay the rent, and when I found out we were to be evicted and my furniture thrown into the street, I decided to leave him, even though I was pregnant. I've always thought for myself and my thinking hasn't been up in the clouds, so I took the children and went to my Aunt Serafina. She knew the Las Yaguas section and thought she could find a place for me there. It was a slum and I really didn't like it. I felt afraid.

"Oh, Auntie, I've heard that the people are very bad here," I said.

"There are all sorts here, good and bad," she replied. "Some people are here because of necessity, others because they enjoy it. They like the atmosphere. If you live a decent life, nobody will bother you. What you have to do is adjust." She knew Lázaro and decided to take me to his house. "You'll see," she said. "He's going to be your friend and will help you. He's very well known and respected around here, so the people here will respect you too."

Lázaro's house was one of the best in the neighborhood. It was quite well constructed of wood and palm thatch. It had a living room, two bedrooms, and a small kitchen. The floors were of cement except for one bedroom, which had a dirt floor. One of the rooms had a bed with a mattress and a sort of clothes rack. The other had a wardrobe and an altar. In the living room was a sofa, an armchair, another chair, and a large table that he used as a carpenter's workbench. There was a table and a chair in the kitchen, too.

The house was very disorderly. Many books and papers were strewn around. "He likes to read a lot," my aunt said, "because he's very intellectual."

75. In 1958 there were in Cuba fourteen private schools for the study of home economics; pupils could enter after graduation from primary school. (Cuban Economic Research Project, *A Study on Cuba* (Coral Gables: University of Miami Press, 1965), p. 427.)

Lázaro received me well. He remembered me as a child, when I used to go there with my aunt, but I didn't remember him. My aunt explained my situation to him and he said I could sleep with the children in one of his bedrooms and he'd sleep in the other.

That night I was very frightened. I heard some shots outside so I huddled into a corner with my two children and began to cry. Lázaro heard me crying and said, "Don't be afraid. The police are probably after some marijuana pusher. Nothing's going to happen to you." I lay down beside the children and covered myself from head to foot, and put the pillow over my head so I couldn't hear.

After I'd been there two days, I began to clean the house. There were a lot of papers and empty cigarette and match boxes in the living room. When he got home, Lázaro spoke sharply to me and said I should have asked him before throwing out his papers. I answered that I'd left those that I thought would interest him. He wouldn't let me continue cleaning. The next day after he left I went on with my work. When he came back he said, "My, how stubborn you are. If I'd known this, I'd have returned you to your aunt." But I didn't pay any attention because I found him agreeable and I trusted him.

A few days later I began to cook and sweep. He had a lot of dirty clothes. I washed about thirteen shirts, a great pile of undershirts, and some shorts. He certainly wasn't fastidious. The neighbors told me he went days without bathing, so I made him bathe and wear clean clothes. I also got him to shave and cut his hair, though he'd made a vow not to.

Lázaro slept in the room with the *santos'* shrine. He said he had to because the saints were there. One day he told me, "You can go in if you like." There was no door but he had a curtain that he'd close when he went to bed.

Lázaro was a devotee of the *Virgen de Regla*. He made his own protective charms and gave them to the people who came to consult him. Sometimes he charged for his consultations but other times he didn't because the *santo* told him not to.

After I'd been living in Las Yaguas for about twenty days, my third child was born. I went on living at Lázaro's for two months and he always respected me. He seemed like a relative and I began to feel affection for him. I was much younger than he. I was born in 1934, which makes me thirty-five years old. He supported me as though I were his daughter or his wife. He didn't let me work, except to do the housework. Anacleto also helped me. When he learned that I'd given birth, he came over to see the baby. He began to visit me from time to time to see the children, and he brought me some money.

I bought a room for 18 *pesos* and moved in the things my aunt had been keeping for me. After I had my own apartment, I began to go to my mother's house again. My brother and sister came to Las Yaguas once but never returned. They were disgusted with my decision to live in such a place. I told them I wanted to live alone even if it were in a hovel. That's the way I am.

I rented the room for five months, but I spent little time there because I was nervous at night. Often I'd hear street fights and sometimes shots. The children and I almost always stayed at Lázaro's until late. Then he'd take us to the room. Little by little we began to stay overnight again at his house.

That was when Lázaro began to court me. He had a very nice lip. I mean, he could converse very nicely. He'd compliment me and give me advice. He told me to be careful not to get involved with some man who'd lead me into evil ways. He complained that he'd never had luck with women, that he needed a woman at his side.

Once he wrote me a letter, a very beautiful letter. I still have it. It had some lovely phrases in it. I think that was what made me decide to love him. One night he said to me, "Let's put the children in the other room because I'm going to sleep here with you." And I answered, "No, no, not with me." But I had such trust in him that I lay down in the bed beside him. I always thought that at his age he must be a little on the weak side. And he was, which disappointed me, but I felt embarrassed to say anything. He caressed me and kissed me, and told me that he felt happy, and asked me to accept him. He ended up falling in love with me, deeply in love, and wanted me to become his. He was a very good husband, a good man, and struggled a lot for me.

Lázaro was, to put it vulgarly, top dog in Las Yaguas, and when I began to live with him everybody respected me. But all the neighbors remarked on our marriage. "Look who Lázaro's living with! Isn't he ashamed to live with that young girl!" Some people even told me, "You're crazy. Why do you want to live with a man who could be your grandfather?" But what I felt for Lázaro was the kind of affection you feel for a father, nothing more.

My life became very quiet, very methodical. Before 7:00 A.M., when the ice cart reached the neighborhood, I'd have already gotten the water. I'd go to the water tap early to avoid the quarrels that sometimes arose there. After buying the ice, I'd wait for the milk wagon and buy two liters of milk. Then I'd make breakfast and wake up Lázaro and the children. The first thing he'd do was throw water into the street,[76] then he'd go into his room to speak to the *santos*. He used a language with them that I didn't understand. After that he'd have his *café con leche*.

---

76. The practice of throwing water out of the house stems from a folk belief in the power of water to cleanse the house of evil and protect it from harm.

My children and I never went hungry when we lived with Lázaro. He gave me money for the groceries every day, and I'd buy 2 or 3 pounds of rice and some meat or chicken. We always ate with the children, even when they were little, and when Lázaro was late they waited for him. He made a high chair for the baby and we put it right beside us.

Lázaro advised me to finish my studies but I didn't want to. I was used to staying at home. As I got to know people in the neighborhood, I began to give classes for the children. They came to my house and I read them stories and taught them to bathe every afternoon and wear shoes. I and another girl who had also studied to be a teacher set up a little school in a house we found in the neighborhood. But after a short time the place was taken away from us.

Lázaro has his own religion, which I didn't participate in. He believes in *santería*. This bothered me because my family is Catholic. My brother, sister, and I were baptized and made our First Communion, although we're not very regular churchgoers. While I was with Lázaro I sent my older children to catechism and he didn't say anything. At first I was afraid of him because I thought he was possessed by a spirit and had power, but then he told me it wasn't that way and I shouldn't be afraid. Later on I got used to it and helped him clean the stones, the jugs containing water, and other such things.

I never believed in Lázaro's religion and I always told him that they were just stones in water and stones with strings of beads. Sometimes my children would play with them. At first this made him angry but later it didn't. He said, "Don't throw them out, but put them back in the same place." Sometimes when he put out candy or some other food for the *santos* my children ate it, although he told them, "Don't eat them because they'll make you sick. You'll be punished."

I'd always ask, "Oh, what punishment? Those are only stones." When he put bananas there I'd eat them myself. He'd scold me and say, "You don't want to believe but you're in line for some sort of punishment and you'll see how you get to believe in this."

I answered, "All right, let them give me some sort of proof and I'll believe."

Lázaro never explained anything to me—quite the opposite. When he was going to perform a religious work, he sent me away with the children. But if I watched, he did explain what he was doing. Sometimes he'd throw the coconut shells and tell me what they meant. But I'd say, "I don't understand, I don't understand. Let me have a little bit of coconut." And I'd eat it.

Lázaro was a carpenter and did private jobs so he seldom left the neighborhood. He had lots of friends and acquaintances nearby and he liked to stay at home. We didn't go out much to movies or parties.

At Christmastime we'd eat dinner together and then go to the neighborhood parties. We danced there, and a lot of people got drunk, but not Lázaro. He never appeared to care for drink, although I've heard that these days he sometimes does.

Lázaro was interested in politics and, from what he says, he was involved in the Cayo Confites conspiracy. In 1958 he was on an electoral board. That was the only time I saw him talking with a large group of people. But I was never interested enough to find out what political party he belonged to. All I know is that on two or three occasions he spoke in favor of tearing down the slum. I never had anything to do with politics. I don't care for it. I didn't even register to vote in the elections. Anyway, nobody asked me to.

About five months after I began to live with Lázaro, Anacleto, the father of my children, began to make overtures to me. He suspected that I slept with Lázaro and he'd tell me, "You're soft in the head. Why do you want to live with that old man?"

Lázaro didn't much like Anacleto coming to the house to see the children. He didn't say anything, but I could tell by the way he looked at him. Finally Anacleto stopped coming and I took the children to his house. My visits weren't frequent, and I always told Lázaro I was going to visit my Aunt Serafina. Then Anacleto and I began to have relations again. I'd have felt remorse because of the affection Lázaro had given me, except he never satisfied me . . . though I never let on I was unhappy.

Anacleto had always appealed to me as a man, but I wouldn't agree to return to him as he was still drinking and I couldn't leave Lázaro. Pretty soon I became pregnant with Antonio. I knew Antonio was Anacleto's son. Women always know such things, but Lázaro believed it was his son. Antonio was born at home, on February 23. Lázaro was overjoyed and loved him very much.

The day before the counterrevolutionaries attacked at Playa Girón, they bombed the FAR airport.[77] I'd heard the bombing that morning and I wanted all my children with me, so I went through a lot of red tape to get my son Tonio, who was in the hospital. When I got home Lázaro said, "Sit down here because I want to talk to you." He seemed suspicious. I thought it was because I was pregnant again, but it turned out he was jealous of a neighbor boy named José. It's true, José and I were always conversing, but he was just a young boy. I said, "José is just a child, and besides, he's the son of your *comadre*. What possible

77. On April 15, 1961, two days before the Bay of Pigs invasion at Playa Girón, Cuban-marked American planes bombed the airport of the *Fuerzas Armadas Revolucionarias* (Revolutionary Armed Forces) on the outskirts of Havana. Playa Girón is the beach in southern Las Villas Province where the invading force came ashore.

interest could I have in him?" Then I added, "If I were to have such interests, I'd be likely to be thinking of the father of my children. After all, he is their father."

Lázaro asked me, "Do you still care for him?"

I answered, "Well, he'd interest me more than anyone else. You already know that I took a liking to you, or if not to you, at least to your ways . . . but today they don't appeal to me because you're treating me as though I've been a loose woman. Your words hurt my feelings."

He said, "Well, God knows you must be pinning the horns on me some place around here, because you're giving me a name for being more potent than I am."

"Well, if you think you're not so potent, if you think you're played out as a man, why are you living with me?" Then I added, "I'm leaving."

"Why? Do you want to go with someone else?"

So I told him, "Well, yes, *chico,* I'm going to live with the father of my children again. I'm going to remarry him."

Then he threw me out. At the very hour of the second bombing, Lázaro threw me and the children out, with my little boy sick. I was crying because I was afraid of the bombing, but he'd made up his mind that I should leave. That's the only thing I can hold against him. We'd lived together for four years and he'd always been good to me and my children. I know I hadn't treated him right and that I really was pinning the horns on him, but it hurt me that he should put us out.

The children and I went to my *comadre* Casilda's house. A few days later I heard that Lázaro wasn't feeling well. I thought that it was because of having gotten upset, so I went to see him. He told me no, that it was rheumatism, that it was this, that, and the other thing. We remained friends as we had always been.

Casilda gave me advice. "Either you go to live with the children's father or you leave him for good." Anacleto was losing interest and we hardly ever saw each other, so I decided to separate. I never returned to him. I stayed in Las Yaguas with Casilda from April until June. They were already tearing down Las Yaguas. I was helping the Ministry of Social Welfare activate the blocks in the neighborhood and count the families.

In June, 1961, I moved to where I'm living now, and I began to live with Ulises. I'd met him while I was still in Las Yaguas. He sometimes worked as a barber and came to the house to cut the children's hair, but he always respected me. I've had four children by him. My first four children are recognized by Anacleto. Lázaro suspected that An-

tonio wasn't his son and it hurt him, but we've never spoken about that
problem.

Though I've never understood politics, for me the triumph of the
Revolution was natural. To me it was just another kind of politics.
Shortly after this regime began, some girls invited the women in my
CDR sectional to participate in the militia. The way they talked appealed to me, so I entered the militia. They taught me to load and
unload a rifle, and little by little I learned everything. Later I asked for
a discharge because I have a little arthritis in my legs. They only gave
me a leave, but I don't have to do guard duty.

Then I joined the Federation of Cuban Women[78] and went to work
in the country as a volunteer. When they said they needed regular
paid workers, I convinced my husband to let me go. I liked it very
much. The first thing I did was fill plastic bags with dirt for planting.
Later I worked in the orchards. Ulises doesn't like me to work and is
always after me. He wants to go with me but I tell him, "You stay here.
Let me go by myself." At times Ulises's jealousy embarrasses me before
the *compañeras* of the Federation. We're all women but their husbands
trust them.

I have to work because Ulises earns very little. He's a policeman now
and earns 110 *pesos* a month, and we're a family of eleven. The children are worse off than ever because they always had a lot of clothes
and shoes and all. I like to dress well too, because my mother always
dressed us nicely. Even with both our salaries, I'm still on a tight
budget.

I've kept my friendship with Lázaro. I still have a great admiration
for him. He's always been a very intelligent and realistic man in his
affairs, but these days his mind isn't as sharp as it was. Sometimes
when I speak to him, he doesn't pay much attention and makes vague
answers. It's true he's seventy years old now, but some people are
still strong at that age. He's all worn out. I don't know the reason for
his being so exhausted. He wasn't ever a man of vice, nor a drinker or
smoker or dancer. A ladies' man yes, although I don't think he had
any other women while he was living with me. But he'd been a real
ladies' man in his youth. And I can tell you that when he liked a

78. *Federación de Mujeres Cubanas* (FMC), a mass organization founded August 23, 1960,
was open to all women fifteen years of age and older. Headed by Vilma Espín, veteran of the
Sierra del Cristal campaign and a member of the Central Committee, the FMC had
1,192,843 members in 1969 (46 percent of all women between fifteen and sixty-five).
(*Granma Weekly Review*, Jan. 25, 1970, p. 5.) By 1975, 77 percent of all women fourteen and
older (the admission age was apparently lowered by one year to match that of the Committees for Defense of the Revolution) were members of the Federation. (*Ibid.*, Aug. 31, 1975,
p. 6.)

woman and was bent on courting her, he had an agreeable way of doing it. I knew two of his wives, Digna and Perpetua. I never new María del Carmen, though he used to talk of her and her children.

BENEDÍ:

Diana María left me precisely on the day of the invasion at Playa Girón, in the year 1961. She and I had lived together for five years. I separated from her because of her light-mindedness. I've never liked to keep telling a woman the same thing over and over. If she adapts to my ways, fine, otherwise she has to go. I also realized from the very beginning that our age difference would bring problems, so I waited and watched for an opportunity to set her free.

When I learned she was having an affair with a son of my *comadre*, Bernarda Naranjo, I told them, "Look, the best thing both of you can do is leave. You won't find any sympathy here. On the contrary, a lot of people will come to me with gossip and I might lose control of myself. I don't want to be led by pride, but I don't want to lose prestige."

Diana María wept and protested I was imagining things. "Very well," I told her. "I'm imagining things. But my decision is made, we can't keep on this way." Then she said, "If we ever separate, please keep on being my friend. I'd like to keep seeing you."

"I won't deny you my friendship," I answered, "but we cannot keep on living under one roof."

After that Diana María moved to a room that Ulises Campos got for her. I've kept on visiting her and she visits me.

Chapter Six

Life in Bolívar

THE EXODUS FROM LAS YAGUAS began in 1961, when the new *repartos* were built. I was in the third group to leave. Seven housing projects, including mine and Buena Ventura, were submitted for our approval. The government gave us the materials and we did the work. There was no talk of wages. Finally a young fellow from Guillén complained because we weren't being paid, so the Social Welfare office went to the different ministries and collected a sum of money to pay us.[79]

That Christmas Eve, the Feminine Brigade, a group of women who were learning about the Revolution, visited us to see what our situation was. The first thing they did was to invite us to a Christmas Eve party. We told them that it was unlikely everybody could go because we simply didn't have the proper clothes to wear.

"You're right," one of them answered. "We'll get supplies of food and distribute them fairly, house to house."

There was a meeting of the people in the barrio and the comrades from the Feminine Brigade. Those who attended—and many did—agreed to the plan. As Christmas Eve approached, I felt a profound satisfaction in seeing how happy everybody was about it. One man said, "*Ay*, dear God, if you hadn't brought us this food, my children would have gone to bed hungry on Christmas Eve. May God and *La Caridad del Cobre* bless you!" He lifted his head and tears started to his eyes. I said to him, "How happy I feel now!"

But when a sergeant saw what we were distributing, he said, "What's this garbage you're bringing me?"

"Listen, *compadre*," I answered. "I've come up against some pretty hard people in my life and I've never held my tongue. Your attitude makes

79. The new housing for former slum dwellers was constructed under the Self-Help Mutual Aid program (*Esfuerzo Propio y Ayuda Mutua*), which provided "financial assistance to families who did the construction work themselves (all members of a family could participate with a minimum commitment of 24 hours per week)." Under this program alone, 3,400 homes were built in 1959–61. (*Cuba Review*, Mar., 1975, p. 6.)

me sick." I felt like cutting up the bastard, him and everyone else who didn't have the feelings to appreciate the value of our sacrifices. "Look," I told him, "these things were collected to help out the neediest ones here, and believe me, it wasn't easy."

I'm telling you, if he had been able to see through my skin, which is as black as black can be, he would have seen the blood rush to my face.

While we were working on the housing projects, I saw Che Guevara. To our profound satisfaction, he participated directly in the construction of one of the *repartos*. As soon as people heard that El Che was working on projects for the so-called indigents, they sent him a tray with a pitcher of ice water, a thermos of hot coffee, cigars, and all sorts of things, thinking Che would accept their servile flattery. But he stood up and asked us workers whether those people sent us goodies when he wasn't there. "No, no, no!" we answered. Then he refused to accept the refreshments. He said he'd drink water where the most humble of us workers did, and the coffee our women comrades from Las Yaguas made for us. As for the tobacco, he said, "I have some given to me by the comrades here. I want no special treatment for myself."

Just then one of his guards passed by, pushing a heavy wheelbarrow full of cement, and El Che made a remark we admired greatly. He called the man over and asked him, "What are you doing?"

"Carrying cement."

"Leave that," said El Che. "That's women's work."

There was no denying El Che's open, unassuming temperament. His wife, Aleida March, was also working there. She wasn't the least bit uppity and was really working, like any of the poor women from the *repartos*. Seeing people of their caliber working like laborers showed us what a revolution signified. We realized that a true revolutionary thinks more of the people than of his own personal problems. We loved El Che for the way he acted there. When he said goodbye, he left a radio that I've been told is still there.

I saw El Che again around 1964, when he visited a cane field I was working in. We all stopped working to look at him, and he, modest as ever, said, "Nobody has come here worth stopping work for. On the contrary, it gives me great satisfaction to see men and women working hard to fulfill their duty to the fatherland."

Now that they're out of Las Yaguas, some people think they're aristocrats or something. They won't admit they remember anything about their past lives. But I'm glad they feel that way because they act more responsibly, and they respect each other a lot more than they used to. Unfortunately, the feeling of community we had in Las Yaguas has broken down. I really believe that these poor people have come to feel superior simply because they have better housing and more independence.

In Las Yaguas, suppose you told somebody, "Juanita's house is on fire; come help put it out," and the other person answered, "Why should I? Juanita and I haven't been on speaking terms for ages." All you'd have to do was remind her, "Look, *chica,* if we don't put out that blaze, your house can catch fire too." At a time like that, people forgot their quarrels. They might even make up and be friends again.

Here in Bolívar, people are more independent of each other, more indifferent. If somebody else's house should catch on fire, they'd think, "My house is safe because it's made of concrete."

Some people have forgotten so much about Las Yaguas, they even say such things as, "If I'd known how things would be here, I'd have stayed in Las Yaguas."

So we remind them, "But look, *chico,* don't you remember all the problems we had in Las Yaguas? Remember how we used to send the kids to stand in line for water and how we used tin cans for toilets and then threw them away in a ditch? Now we get water from a tap in our own homes, and our bathrooms even have certain fixtures for women. Don't you realize all that? Think of the comfort we have now! And it isn't only the bathrooms. Every resident here has a kerosene stove in his kitchen and furniture of his own.

"We're in a much better situation, socially speaking. In Las Yaguas you couldn't even clean your house because every time you bore down on the broom, you gouged out a hole in the dirt floor. When visitors came, you had to take them into the kitchen and wash a cup and saucer right in front of them before you could offer them some coffee. That looks bad, very bad. Here you can have your dishes washed ahead of time and serve visitors as soon as they arrive. Don't you know what it means, socially speaking, to have our guests accept food and drink, knowing the place is clean? Think of that, *chico.* All those things benefit your family.

"Even the terrain is better. In Las Yaguas there was a ditch by Tres Palacios and another one where the drains of the tuberculosis hospital emptied. Water was so scarce our kids used the contaminated ditch as a "beach" to go swimming. Sometimes our women bathed there at 11:00 or 12:00 at night. Often women washed the clothes there and spread them out beside the ditch to dry in the sun. Those clothes, still full of germs, were then starched and ironed and we all wore them.

"And what about the food we bought in Las Yaguas? We had to wait till it came. Some people even gathered up the canned food that the Ministry of Health ordered thrown into Cayo Cruz, and we made small punctures in the cans to let out the gases of decay, flattened them a bit, and sold them cheap. We were lucky that nobody got sick from that.

Taking all those things into account, how can you possibly say that you'd be better off if you'd stayed in Las Yaguas?"

The Committees for Defense of the Revolution[80] were founded before we moved to Bolívar. Osvaldo Sánchez, our beloved, unforgettable comrade, organized them in Las Yaguas with the help of several members of the Communist Party—Juan Carlos, Manolo Menéndez, Minerva Ruz, and others. Before the CDRs were formed, we had vigilante committees for each of the sixteen streets in Las Yaguas. We needed them to protect ourselves from a small group of people called the "Black Jackets" who went around doing horrible things.[81] The CDRs were formed from these vigilante committees. We were known by our blocks, like my Block 13 Committee, and about 80 percent of the neighbors cooperated.

Education was the first front I was in charge of.[82] I decided to restructure the Committee because some people were dissatisfied. I didn't discuss my position or anything. I just said, "Anyone here can be president and anyone can be organizer. We must centralize our work and try to maintain a higher morale than we now have in Las Yaguas." With all their poverty and lack of understanding, the individuals belonging to the Committee at that time were in no position to understand the Revolution, and the way I saw it, we had to start somewhere.

When we moved into the 100 new houses built in Bolívar, we managed to organize a Committee for each of the ten blocks. When the demand for volunteer workers came, our Committee sent more volunteers than any other in our district. I was put in charge of getting together a group every Sunday. We couldn't send the same people all the time, but even

80. The *Comités de Defensa de la Revolución* were founded September 28, 1960, and later organized, in urban areas, at the city block level. The CDRs, or Committees, are active in a broad range of programs including public health, education, political education, urban reform, sports and recreation, local administration, as well as in surveillance work against counterrevolutionary activities. The Committees' activities (organized as *frentes*, or fronts) include recruiting volunteers to work in agriculture, standing guard duty to prevent neighborhood vandalism as well as sabotage, administering vaccines and other injections, encouraging adult education, organizing study groups, and calling meetings to deal with problems that arise at the block level (e.g., noisy or disorderly conduct by residents, neighborhood clean-up, school attendance, organizing support for national campaigns, etc.). Membership in the CDR is open to all Cubans fourteen and older who are "willing to defend the Revolution."

81. *New York Times* correspondent Ruby Hart Phillips was still living in Havana when the city was menaced by youth gangs such as the "Black Jackets," "Red Wings," and "Rock 'n' Rollers." She said they "wore distinctive jackets, hats and even gloves. They fought each other, broke up dances, attacked people leaving motion-picture shows, cocktail parties, and fiestas. They insulted girls on the street and sometimes tore their clothing." (*The Cuban Dilemma* (New York: Ivan Obolensky, 1962), p. 127.)

82. *Frente* is the term used to designate the various areas of responsibility with which the CDR concerns itself. "Front," as opposed to "committee," for instance, suggests militant action, as in its meaning: "line of battle."

dividing things up among the households on our block, the least number of volunteers we ever sent was twenty.

Now there are fewer households contributing volunteers, because brigades are organized in work centers to work ten or twelve hours a day for special periods like the *Jornada de Girón*.[83] Where I work there are two brigades, so the work goes on twenty-four hours a day. People who work twelve hours a day during the week need to rest on Sunday, their only free day. You can't expect them to spend it doing volunteer work in the country.

A lot of people have lost interest in the Committees. I don't know where they've packed away their consciences, but we've had to abolish the original ten Committees and substitute them with only two. So once again we have consolidated our forces to keep the place from getting run-down or dirty. The people seem to have forgotten what Cuba was like before the Revolution. I tell them, "You have no idea how valuable our revolutionary government is. Don't you remember how we struggled and were ready to do anything for the Revolution? Well, now that it is in power, every resident here should join one of the Committees." At present, I'm in charge of the Front for Solidarity with the Peoples.

We still have various housing problems in Bolívar. There was a hurricane and rains, and so on, and we sheltered a dozen extra families here. It's been seven months now since all that began, and the last two families have been told they'll have to leave Bolívar. I've heard some comrades in the Party say, "If somebody doesn't have a place to sleep, let him look for one." In contrast, Fidel said, "If somebody doesn't have a place to sleep, we must get him one." To see people sleeping in alleys is a stain on the Revolution and I don't understand who lets this happen or why.

Many things are still being done wrong here. When they cleared the land on May 19 of this year, they destroyed all the residents' vegetable plantings in order to plant flowers. It was disheartening to see our work destroyed after we'd cooperated and got up at 2:00 and 3:00 on Sunday mornings to plant those vegetables. I cannot under any circumstances

83. The *Jornada* is one of four annual worker-emulation periods established by the Historic Dates Emulation program to observe the anniversaries of important events in the Revolution. *Jornada de Girón* commemorates the Cuban victory at Playa Girón (Bay of Pigs) in April, 1961. During each fifteen-day emulation period, workers in the same enterprise (or teams of workers in other production units) compete to fulfill or surpass work quotas, do voluntary work, raise political consciousness, participate in civic activities, etc. Reports on all workers' efforts are placed in their labor files in the Ministry of Labor. In 1966 the policy of giving material rewards (cash, vacations, consumer goods) to the most productive was abolished in favor of moral rewards, such as banners, flags, and honorary titles (e.g., "National Work Hero"). (Roberto E. Hernández and Carmelo Mesa-Lago, "Labor Organization and Wages," in Mesa Lago, ed., *Revolutionary Change in Cuba*, pp. 235–38.) Since 1970 the trend has shifted back to material rewards.

condone this, but it's up to the right authorities to investigate the matter and find out who's responsible for it. It seems to me that isn't the kind of decision a Marxist Party should make.

Wherever there's a free plot of land, the INRA[84] takes it over to plant fruit trees. One day someone decided to tear down some new trees the INRA had just planted. I was away at the time so another person tried to stop him, but the man insisted he'd been given those orders by someone at the *Cordón de la Habana*.[85] Then he asked to speak to a member of the Committee and was told that there weren't any members around. So he began cutting down trees.

I think those trees were cut down without proper authority. I don't believe an administrator would make that kind of mistake. A *guajiro*[86] fresh from the country might have, but the man in charge of the program was a student in his third year of medicine. Besides, I think the Party must have had a detailed program that wouldn't include cutting down newly planted trees.

A lot of people are still so uneducated that they're easily impressed when someone tells them, "I'm a Party member and the Party gives the orders around here." But now we realize we should check a person's credentials before we let them do anything, because some bureaucrats here are kind of harsh. I've told many people, "When somebody tries to throw his weight around, claiming to be a Party member, ask for his identification. I can't be here to defend you all day long, so you'll have to learn to take care of yourselves."

Now if someone plants a plot of land and fences it in, and another person wants to take it over, he must have written orders. They can't just say, "Here I am, I'm going to do thus-and-so." If they do that, how can we convince the people that the Revolution is good?

When a brigade of us went to pick tomatoes, we ran into a guy who thought he could boss people around just because he was a Party member. He tried to tell us we couldn't pick the tomatoes, but I answered, "We were sent here by the CDR regional to pick these tomatoes."

"The Party . . . ," he began.

"Look here, comrade," I broke in, "you're not the only Party member here. Any of us, poor and humble as we look, might be Party members. The Party doesn't give you the power to commit abuses or to impose. On the contrary, the Party offers orientation. If you don't understand their advice, they'll discuss it and make everything clear. At the moment, there are no tomatoes to sell in Havana and yet tomatoes are rotting on the

84. *Instituto Nacional de Reforma Agraria* (see n. 74).
85. The cultivated greenbelt encircling Havana.
86. Cuban peasant, sometimes used derogatorily to mean a rustic.

vines here. How dare you say that we can't touch them? Come on, gentlemen, let's pick tomatoes!" So everybody got busy and picked them.

As soon as I returned home, the first thing I did was write a report to the INRA. I don't know how it all turned out because I didn't follow it up, but after that there were plenty of tomatoes in Havana.

We've had several small difficulties with government bureaucracy. For instance, the Regional Committee for Handicrafts stored more than 2,000 coconuts near here for some time, and we began to worry because coconuts rot and they could start an epidemic, especially among the children. When we went to the Regional Committee for Handicrafts to find out about it, they told us, "Leave them. They're for handicrafts."

"Well, they should have been put to use long ago," we answered. "The meat is good for sweets, the oil for medicine, and the husk can be used for handicrafts. But instead they're just rotting there."

Finally, when children started getting sick, people said, "We're going to scatter those coconuts all over the street to provoke some kind of action."

I told them, "No, no, don't do that, that's not going to help. Let's take all the necessary steps." But they paid no attention.[87]

Another problem is our inability to prevent delinquency. Only last night a group snatched a girl's transistor radio as she walked down the street. Then they scattered in different directions and got away.

Juvenile delinquency has always been one of my greatest preoccupations. The Revolution took some steps to prevent it, but a lot of kids still go wrong and I blame the parents. What hurts me most about poverty is what it does to children. Children are not born bad. They become bad because of lack of guidance and the wrong kind of upbringing. Once I dared to write President Grau, saying that if he gave me the opportunity and put several million *pesos* at my disposal, I'd buy some land and build a community exclusively for children.

Illiteracy is at the bottom of juvenile delinquency because illiterate parents don't understand the development of the Cuban Revolution. I've always been an enemy of slavery and illiteracy. I uphold Martí's saying, "Knowing how to read is like knowing how to talk." A person who can't read and write can't find his spiritual liberation. So he lives in a kind of slavery because of his own ignorance. My dearest wish is that every person, not only in Cuba but in the whole world, should know how to write his own name.

The Literacy Campaign showed that over 70 percent of the people in

---

87. It was later learned, in an interview with another Bolívar resident, that after taking their request to the Regional Committee for Handicrafts, residents of Bolívar received eight bags of coconuts. The rest were left in storage for use in handicrafts.

the rural zones were illiterates.[88] That's why even now, you find that more than 60 percent of the people in Bolívar still don't really understand the Revolution. Is it any wonder that their kids become juvenile delinquents? Cuba hasn't made enough progress in this direction because of our economic problems. Even though there are opportunities that didn't exist before to send children to school, as soon as a child is twelve or fourteen, he begins to think of dropping out. There's no future for those children.

I never wanted to be anything more than a man of the people, but if I'd had the opportunities to develop my ideas, I'd have worked hard to establish all kinds of schools. The first thing I did with my wages after the triumph of the Revolution was to start savings accounts in Las Yaguas for school children who were promoted. Kids love that. Besides, one child would tease the others and say, "Look, because I study my lessons, I have a savings account and you don't." So it was a stimulus for the other children. On my first payday, I got 38 *pesos*—and thirty-eight children came to tell me they had been promoted. I let those 38 *pesos* go as if they were nothing. In this way I fought against poverty, illiteracy, and juvenile delinquency.

Later, when the banks required a minimum deposit of 5 *pesos* to start a savings account, I always managed to keep a reserve of 40, 50, or 100 *pesos* for that purpose. I helped several children in Las Yaguas, including my grandchildren. I kept it up as long as I could, but of course more children kept getting born, and after a while I had to stop. But the example had been given.

Now I tell the children that every time they pass and show me their diploma, I'll make them a gift. Often it takes the form of a street party with a treasure hunt, the hidden treasure being books.

Drastic measures are needed to fight delinquency. First, I'd give a juvenile delinquent good advice. Second, if that didn't help, I'd suggest going to the work farms, along with study. That way I'd gradually try to perfect the individual's feelings and conscience. And finally, if the first two measures brought no improvement, I'd send him before the firing squad. Or maybe I'd advise Fidel to have an incinerator dug about 40 or

88. The year 1961, declared by Castro as the Year of Education, saw a massive campaign to stamp out illiteracy in Cuba. Schools were closed in April and 100,000 students from junior high through college level were mobilized as *brigadistas*, trained, and sent into rural areas to teach reading and writing. Teachers called *alfabetizadores* taught illiterates in the cities. The Campaign was reported successful in reducing the illiteracy rate from 23 percent to approximately 3 percent. (Lee Lockwood, *Castro's Cuba, Cuba's Fidel* (New York: Vintage, 1969), p. 126.) A Cuban government publication set the illiteracy rate at 3.9 percent in the mid-1960s, stating this figure included 25,000 Haitian residents who did not speak Spanish and people who were mentally retarded or "too old to learn to read and write." This pamphlet estimated the total number of volunteer teachers during the Campaign at 271,000. (*Cuba: A Giant School* (Havana: Ministry of Foreign Affairs, n.d.))

50 meters deep, and every time one of those obstinate cases came up, to drop the culprit in the incinerator, douse him with gasoline, and set him on fire. The incorrigible delinquent is a blot that can't be washed out. If he's allowed to go on living in our society, his influence will carry into the future. So it's best to make an example of him for future generations.

I've had little luck with my children. My eldest son, Octavio, was kind of wild as a boy. As soon as he was five I said, "Time to start him in school." But mothers! Sometimes I can't understand how their minds work. María was afraid that if Octavio was away part of the day he'd lose his fondness for her. She was semiliterate and must have gone about as far as the second grade, so school wasn't important to her. I gave her many examples to justify my arguments. An ignorant person doesn't know what troubles he may meet in life, I told her. Finally she gave in, grudgingly.

Octavio went to school, but he began to work at the age of fifteen. His *mamá*'s character is like my *mamá*'s and he had to share his earnings with her. She'd tell him, "Get used to earning money and learn to manage it so in the future you and your wife won't lack the essentials."

At least Octavio learned a trade. A friend of mine who is a mechanic and a housepainter had a workshop, and I talked to him about my son. "*Chico*, I need your help," I said. "I'd like you to take on my boy. Don't pay him anything in the beginning. I want him to learn, that's all."

Octavio fell in love at the age of seventeen, while we were still living in Las Yaguas. People would say to me, "I saw your son kissing a girl in an alley." When he got home I'd say to him, "Octavio, someone told me what you were doing in that alley. Don't you realize that besides being a great immorality, your behavior is downright stupid? You're a young fellow with your way to make."

"She's a good girl," he told me.

"All right," I answered. "What are your intentions?" To put it in good Castilian, he knew I wouldn't stand for his playing dirty tricks on any woman.

I was in jail because of a strike when they told me that Octavio had been arrested for kidnapping a girl. I had to wait until they had tried and judged my case, but as soon as I was free, I went to see Octavio. He told me what had happened—that he'd persuaded the girl to take off with him and her mother had accused him of kidnapping.

My sister was alive at that time and she had done some favors as a midwife for the mistress of a captain in Luyanó. In return, the captain was ready to help with my son's problem. He said, "That can be fixed, it just takes time. Let Octavio formalize his relationship with this girl and then let them begin to have children."

Octavio has eight children now. I haven't seen them for about three years. I'm disgusted with them because they've become Jehovah's Witnesses. I found out when Octavio sent for me to go to court to legally change his surname. It mistakenly appears in the register as Octavio Méndez Benedí, and he wanted it to be Octavio Benedí Méndez. I asked him why he wanted to change it after all these years, and he told me he planned to get married again and had to sign papers and that's the name he wanted.

I was ready to do it, but when I found out he planned to get married in the church of the Jehovah's Witnesses, I said to his mother, María, "Tell him not to count on me. I'm not an enemy of the Jehovah's Witnesses but I know what hypocrites they are." I have no idea why Octavio is so involved with Jehovah's Witnesses. Anyway, I didn't help him because I don't want that kind of split in the family. But it didn't stop him.

So now my grandchildren don't go to my house and I don't go to Octavio's house either. When he realizes the error of his ways, then let him come to me. It isn't up to me to go there and make a pretense to feelings I don't have. I love my grandchildren and I've always tried to get along with Octavio's third wife. I think she's an outstanding housewife, which is more than I can say for his other wives. But I feel that both Octavio and his wife should have enough sense and feeling to tell the kids, "That's your grandfather."

Octavio doesn't want his children to take the same road he took, so he encourages them to go to school. His eldest daughter is a teacher. He has one son in the university-preparatory course, three in second year, and the youngest is now in the sixth grade.

Some day, when Octavio has a day off and his kids are on vacation, I'm going to visit him so I can say, "Now that your kids are studying, what do you say? You had to pay attention to my advice in the end, didn't you?"

Yara turned out even worse than Octavio. When Yara was still very small his mother asked me what she should do about him. I told her, "Don't worry. Just let me raise Yara and some day you'll be proud of him. The trouble is you treat your children too tenderly. Everyone loves his children and feels sorry for them but those things should be kept to one's self and never be known to them."

But Yara's mother wouldn't let me take care of him, so instead of working or studying, he went around with a gang of delinquents. Then, while the boys were being rehabilitated, they committed several armed robberies.

They had quite a little gang. Altogether there were seven boys, and among them they owned three revolvers. First they threatened their victims, and if that didn't work they shot them. There were more than ten accusations against them. Among their victims were three Chinese. One of them looked like a refugee from the grave because of the beating those boys had given him. Imagine that, twelve-year-old boys! What a beginning!

When Yara was older he was involved in other things. I had my suspicions but I decided, "Let's not jump to conclusions, maybe I'm mistaken." I didn't visit him in jail because I knew he wouldn't tell me the truth. I thought, "I'd better go to the trial. There I'll find out what he's been up to." I went to one trial and found out all right. My suspicions were correct. Even before the prosecuting attorney finished speaking, I'd mentally dictated my sentence. I'd have taken the whole bunch, including my own son, into the courtyard and shot them. That would have put an end to the problem.

I've seen cases of neglected children and I know how they turn out—they do as they please. Well, if a mother neglects her children and lets them be brought up by just anybody, what else can be expected? Children should be raised the way my mother raised hers. We were good children because if we weren't, we'd get blows from her—and what blows! But after we grew up we realized that *mamá* was like that because she loved us and was ambitious for us.

DIGNA DEVEAUX:

Lázaro always wanted Yara to study, but Yara wasn't born for it. We tried to send him to school, but he only finished the fourth grade. If a child doesn't like studying, his parents can spend everything they've got on his education but he won't end up having a career. Yara never gave any time to his school work, never picked up a book. His father will buy a newspaper and get all interested in what it says and go about explaining this and that, but Yara isn't interested. He isn't like his father in any way. If only he had his father's brains.

Of all my children, Yara turned out the worst. He has bad nerves and acts like a madman. He couldn't ever stay in the same place. He even has papers from the doctor about it. That boy had bad blood in his veins. Lázaro spanked him when he was little, but Yara was more afraid of me because I gave it to him real hard. Lázaro was more for scolding and making the children do penance. He didn't believe in beating. He would make Yara stay on his knees or take off his pants, but he didn't like to go around beating people.

From the time Yara was a child he was crazy about riding horses. That's what got him into trouble in the first place. When he was sixteen he was put in prison because he borrowed a horse from a friend and let it get away from him. Then, when he didn't have it, they said he'd killed it, so he was put in jail for unauthorized slaughter.[89]

They kept Yara on a prison farm for almost three years, taking their own sweet time, without holding a trial or anything. I can swear to that. Then, at the end of two years and nine months they sent him a

89. Under a law passed in 1963, the unauthorized slaughter of any animal for sale or consumption was made punishable by up to five years in prison.

summons to my home. I took it and went to court. I waited until they called his name and presented myself. "Your honor," I said, "the minor Yara is not present. I am his guardian here representing him."

"Are you his mother?"

"Yes."

"All right, but where is he?"

"He's been shut up now for three years less three months, without trial or anything."

"Look at that!" he said. "Here's one of those cases of men in prison and no record. This minor doesn't appear here as a prisoner but as being at liberty!"

The next week they sent me a telegram to appear again and Yara was set free.

Lázaro never went to see Yara in prison because he said he didn't approve of such things and that my son was a nut to have borrowed the horse in the first place. The only familiar face Yara ever saw in prison was his mother's. Many times Lázaro told me, "You shouldn't go out there taking him packages. He's the way he is because every time he ends up in jail, you go taking him bags of stuff." But I answered, "I have to because I'm his mother. After all, you're only his father and anyone might be a father. If it weren't you, it would be someone else."

Lázaro must have suffered over Yara, because he had such great hopes when the boy was born. He wanted his son to be the greatest man in the world. But as I've said, everybody comes into the world with his destiny set out for him.

If Lázaro cares for his son, he doesn't show it. In fact, he doesn't pay any attention to him. Hell, I wish he'd take some interest in guiding him, and sit down and talk with him as a father should. "Look here, son, you have to work in this life and you have to help you mother." Lázaro used to tell me, "If I get hold of your son, I'll kill him," but he never did a thing. And I'd tell him, "If you kill him, you'll go to jail. Go peddle your potatoes, because I was the one who gave birth to the boy."

Yara was picked up again for slaughtering a pig. Or maybe he just bought the meat and they caught him with it in his car. Anyway, he was sent to prison again and spent two more years working on the prison farm. He got out last December. He's rehabilitated now. He began to work as a carpenter when he was sixteen and has all his tools. He worked on all those new houses over there on the prison farm.

While Yara was there he had a pass every weekend, and it was during one of these visits that his girl friend got pregnant. One day last year he came to me and said, "You know, I'm going to have a child."

"Who with?" I said.

"With a black girl I have in Cayamas," he answered. That was the first I'd heard of his having a woman. I think she's just a bird of passage. But Yara's father isn't a skirt-chaser, so maybe he isn't either.

When Lázaro heard about the baby, he asked me, "Digna, what do you think?"

"Nothing," I said. "It's his baby but it will have to stay with the mother because I'm not raising any more children."

"Always the same," said Lázaro, "balky as usual."

"That's right," I said, "I'm no pushover."

Yara took his baby girl to see Lázaro, who was pleased as he could be. But he doesn't trouble himself about the baby either. Since I moved to Bolívar, Lázaro visits me from time to time to talk about Yara. He asks whether I've seen him and how he is, but Lázaro never goes to see him himself.

As far as I know, Octavio and Yara are Lázaro's only sons. I haven't seen Octavio lately but Yara visits him every so often. Octavio is forty-some years old now. He's a good youngster and a real family man. He's like his father in every way, really decent and serious, and he keeps a good home for his wife and children. The children are even going to high school.

I met María del Carmen through Octavio. We got along very well and she began to visit me and my little boy. She was very good-looking, a tall dark girl with fine features, lots of hair, and a charming personality. People say she was a beauty when she was young. But I haven't seen her for years now and they say she's gotten very thin. She and Lázaro always got along very well after they separated.

Yara isn't living with me but with my other sons. He comes to visit me every day though. Until recently he was planting coffee, hoeing and weeding in the *Cordón de la Habana,* but he was told to wait for a letter of referral for a new job. He's twenty-two now. You have no idea how I wish he would study—he has only a fourth-grade level—but he says he wants to work.

My other son, Floriano, is awfully good to me too, poor boy, but he's in prison now and half out of his mind. I visit his wife and she brings the five children here to see me. People say that the children of prisoners get scholarships, but they haven't given Floriano's children anything so far.

It was on account of his children that Floriano got into trouble. They didn't have anywhere to sleep so he went into a sealed house and took out a mattress and bed frame. He was tried and given a four-year sentence. Now he's in a prison in Las Villas where the prisoners can't even get out to get a little sun. I visit him every month and a half.

I'm very happy with my children. No matter how many faults they may have, for me they don't have any. My sons, Floriano and Juan, favor me, but I've always been crazy about Zoé, my only daughter. I love her deeply and she's awfully good to me. Lázaro used to tell me that she had a very quick mind and should study for a profession. He always wanted his children to study. But I told him, "I don't want my daughter on a scholarship because I want her by my side." Now I'm sorry I took that line.

I always wished that all my children would be girls. I didn't care for boys, but now I have them and what am I going to do? I just love girls! With a little girl you can make a dress out of any old patch, and it changes her completely. And no matter how bad a girl may be, she always favors her mother. Women suffer more than men, but a woman has only two roads, good or bad, while a man has many choices. And so a mother who gives birth to a son suffers more because she doesn't know which road he will choose.

One of the best things Fidel has done is give women lots of work and opportunities. If I were young I'd be studying, and even with forty-nine years behind me, if I got a scholarship I'd study. It's true that I married very young, but since then I've developed a lot of good sense. Nowadays when young people get married, it's because they really want to. A young girl can study to be a nurse or anything she likes. If she's interested in fishing, she can even study that. Everything's available and out in the open for everybody.

Now, even with my bad economic situation, I think I live better than I used to. At least I live in a decent, comfortable house. They gave me a living-room and dining-room set, and a cane bedroom set with a frame bed and two night tables. Then there's a bunk bed and an extra cane cot. They've all come apart now because I took them outside. The mattresses were thin and they're all in pieces. No matter how you plump them up, you don't have much more than the covering. The frames are broken-down too, but I've fixed them up with cardboard from milk cartons.

Compared with Las Yaguas, relations between neighbors here in Bolívar are better. It's hard to say, though, because people keep more or less to themselves. I was never given to neighborhood life. Here at least I can live in peace without worrying whether a fire may break out at night while I'm sleeping. I hang my wash out in the patio and never lose anything. Right now I don't have a lock on the door because I sent it off to have a key made, but I leave the door unlocked and there's never any problem. No robberies around here.

One thing, though, there's no light on the street. When Hurricane

Inés hit here,[90] most of the streetlights in this neighborhood were broken and they haven't gotten around to fixing them. So this street only has two small lights and the whole subdivision is dark. They've come to ask me to stand guard, but I said I wouldn't stand in the dark. With all the blessed trees around, you can't see who's coming toward you. I'm not interested in being bopped on the head. You lose your life and nothing can replace that, if you see what I mean. I told them that when the neighborhood is well lighted as it was before, I'd be glad to do guard duty any time.

I belong to the Federation and the Committee but I never go to any of the meetings because I don't like gatherings. A neighbor comes to collect my dues for the Federation. "How much?" I ask. I pay her and that's all.

There are two Defense Committees here in the neighborhood. I've seen the street games and activities they've organized, and they do very prompt work with polio vaccine, too. But I don't do voluntary work or anything. I do have a sister married to a Party member, but I never see her. My family keeps away from me because I'm the worst off.

I like this neighborhood and its peaceful atmosphere. I've never considered leaving Cuba, not for my life. Why would I do a thing like that? I was born here and here I die. I live well. I know the law isn't going to bother me. I have my hardships, it's true, but you have to learn to adapt to everything. Here if you have a rag on your back and enough to eat, why worry about the rest?

90. September, 1966.

Chapter Seven

I Marry a Daughter of Ochún

IN 1965 A COMRADE FROM THE CDR sectional offered me a job as night watchman in a lumberyard, and I started working there for 48 *centavos* an hour. Many family men worked there, and if it had been sabotaged, which could have happened any time, God knows what they would have done. So I spent my nights there, standing guard from 11:00 P.M. until 7:00 the next morning. Later it was decided to eliminate the night watchman and have militiamen stand guard instead, so I registered for another job.

I was assigned to a woodworking shop, but then I had a problem that depressed me very much. I accidentally bumped my head one day and I asked the boss if I could see the doctor. "Sure, man, go ahead," he answered, and he gave me a note for the doctor. They made a general examination and found a deficiency in my heart. I was under medical care for three months and was told not to exert myself. The manager, the head of Personnel, and the head of Production discussed the problem. "Let's send him to our farm," one of them suggested.

"No, *chico,*" another objected. "We know Lázaro is not a man to be idle when there's work to be done. If we send him to the farm, he'll be wanting to take up the hoe, the pick, or the plow, and that's just the kind of work he shouldn't be doing. Let's keep him here in the workshop, doing light work."

I was willing and that's how I happened to get a job on the maintenance brigade, which repaired things and helped start new workshops. It was organized when a number of retired comrades offered to form a work brigade so they could continue doing their duty to the Revolution. Appreciating the spontaneity of their offer and not wanting to frustrate them, the government accepted. Recently all the different workshops were combined under the Ministry of Light Industry.

Around that time, over two years ago, I met my present wife, Amalia. She was forty-four then and I was sixty-seven. We are man and wife because circumstances brought us together, but love is something that builds up gradually, takes root, and, no matter how old one is, it comes into being.

I saw that Amalia was always alone, so one day I asked her, "Tell me, don't you have a husband?"

"Why do you want to know?"

"Because I have no wife, and if you are alone too, we might give some thought to the matter. The truth is, I feel lonely and need a woman in my home."

"And what makes you think I'm a piece of goods on the counter that you should come and propose to me like that?"

I passed that off as a joke because I knew she was really listening to what I said. In fact she told somebody, "I like to talk with that man because I can understand everything he says." Naturally, after I heard that remark I liked her even more. Those little things get under one's skin, you know.

One day I said to her, "Well, *chica,* there's only one problem between us—you say no and I say yes."

"Oh, so you're trying to force me?"

"Yes. It's a force I can't resist. I'm quite capable of grabbing you right here in the street, carrying you off to my house, and locking you in!"

She burst out laughing. "Don't laugh," I said. "I just might do it!"

Not that Amalia had much occasion to laugh then. Most of the time she cried. She was staying at her son's house and her daughter-in-law was terribly mean to her. Nobody who sees how lively Amalia is now could imagine what she was like then. She spent her whole day finishing one task only to begin a new one, with no break in between. When I visited her in the morning, I'd find her hard at work cleaning the kitchen. As soon as she got through with that, she'd bathe the children.

The only time we could talk was at 11:00 at night, just before I went to work, because I was a night watchman. I'd notice her nervously glancing here and there to see if she'd left anything undone. She was being treated unjustly, and one day I said, "Look, Amalia, I won't visit you here anymore and I don't think I'll make much effort to keep up our friendship either. I don't like people who are too submissive. When one has rights, one should claim them, cost what it may." My words disturbed her, so I said, "Look, *chica,* you have no peace of mind here. If you like, you can live with me."

"I'll think it over," she said.

"Well, don't be long about it. I can't wait. I need a woman at home." And it was true. A man living alone has a lot of problems. I often ate out because I didn't have time for cooking, and when I went to look for something to eat at home, I'd find it spoiled.

Amalia and I were sweethearts for about three months. Old as we were, we talked, kissed each other, and did as any other sweethearts do. I could see Amalia's virtues and thought she must be easy to get along with. Was I mistaken! She's turned out to be worse than a panther, but I put up with her because, after all, I am the son of a woman. But if I didn't love Amalia she wouldn't be with me now.

AMALIA CARRANZA:

Lázaro and I met, fell in love, and started living together. There's nothing unusual in that. Mainly what brought us together was my need to have a home of my own and his need to have a woman.

Three years ago my husband, Julio, and my mother both died and my nerves were shot. Then I went to pick coffee in the country and got the rot in my feet. Honest, they really rotted. On top of that, I had gall-bladder trouble and allergies. Finally, I went to live with my son in Bolívar because I was sick and lonely and wanted a new life.

There's where I met Lázaro. At first he came to visit my son, but then he began coming to court me. My son was very good to me, but it's hard living in someone else's home. Besides, he had enough responsibility supporting his three children. So I was happy when Lázaro started courting me. He isn't handsome but he has charm. It was his manner that attracted me. He said he was an old man and needed a wife. He looked fairly young to me, but compared to me I guess he was old. He looked so neglected, I could tell he needed a wife to take care of him. And I needed a man to support me. That's what brought us together.

One day I had a quarrel with my son and Lázaro was there and took my part. "Come on up to my house," he said.

"All right, let's go."

When we got there he said, "You know why I brought you here? Because you aren't going back to live at that house ever again. From this day on, you will have a home with me. Here's a key to the front door. It's yours, as mistress of this house."

I accepted the key. He was very affectionate. We hugged and kissed, then we took a bath and lay down. We didn't do anything more that first night. I hadn't had relations with Lázaro before I went to live with him. I feel it's wrong to sleep with a man until one has a permanent relationship with him. I've never been the kind of woman who sleeps with a man and then forgets she ever knew him. My husbands are the only men I've ever known.

After we got together, Lázaro and I planned to go to the country so he could meet *papá* and we'd get married. But then *papá* sent word that he was sick and we had to postpone the wedding. The upshot of it is that we've been living together since April 10, 1967, more than two years, and we haven't married yet.

BENEDÍ:

I never had a wife who was a virgin when I met her. But frankly, it made no difference to me. To my way of thinking, that's a waste of time. A virgin has to be re-educated to a man's good or bad habits, which amounts to setting up a school just for her. And after you've gone through all that, she has to take her time to think deeply about whether or not it's best for her to accept you. Give me experienced and thoughtful young women every time, women who are able to reason.

Incidentally, women who smoke are less dangerous than those who don't. Practically all of my women have smoked. I have urged them to and explained why. While a woman smokes she's thinking constructively. After the man leaves, while she smokes, she's weighing his worth and pondering his qualities. All those reflections are given to her by the cigarette. A woman who doesn't smoke has nothing to distract her so she takes violent action, imagining that the man is her enemy and that some other woman is after him.

I can't tell whether I'm really jealous and demanding or not. They say that if you're jealous it means you love. I'm demanding when I'm in love, but I don't demand love in return, only that the woman should react to things as I do. I guess I'm a bit selfish. If I show a woman just so much love as will cover the head of a pin, I expect her to correspond in equal measure. I don't claim to be the best but I do like to be in the right.

In my time, I liked to have a drink now and then, to go to parties and to dance. I was a lively young fellow. And I danced like a top—*danzones, sones,* rumbas, and all that. I also liked to have my little adventures with women, as was only proper. Any Cuban fellow who didn't have them wasn't considered a man. But I don't think it's right that just because a man has amorous adventures, a woman should have them too. No indeed! I always kept my steady women at home. Only a quiet and virtuous woman could do as she pleased, because that kind of woman wouldn't cheat on her husband.

I guess I'm jealous in my own way. You have to keep an eye on women. I've treated all my wives the same—even Amalia. Every few minutes I ask her, "Where were you? Where did you go?" I do that because she's flesh and blood. She's no spring chicken, that's true, and it would take a blind man to fall for her, but she just might meet someone blind enough!

I've always had my own thoughts about women who go shopping all by themselves. And another thing, if my wife should go to the doctor every day—or even every week—I'd be certain something was going on. Of course I don't approve of having a woman kept as a slave, as they used to be here. A woman who is shut up in her house all day long, sitting in front of a mirror, experimenting with lipstick and eye shadow all day long, has too much time to think of things she shouldn't. All that coquetry is not intended to please her husband but to impress other men. I like to have my wife use makeup like other women, but I'm selfish enough to want her to use it for me. After all, I'm the one who pays for it.

I like women to be as modest and demure as possible, because whatever is hidden and unknown is more exciting. I'm against short skirts. They hide nothing, and now men have hardly anything to wonder about. That kind of thing disenchants a man. In my time women took good care to walk so as not to provoke the kind of rude compliments that are often heard in the streets these days.

Nowadays women do have freedom. They work just like men and pay their part of household expenses as men do. Rather than a marriage, a kind of comradeship exists, with both comrades having the right to do the same things. With regard to morals, a woman has a right to make the same demands on the man that he makes on her. Since the Revolution has molded women's minds, we see very few cases of adultery. Sure, a woman may have a career nowadays, but nobody can concentrate on work all the time, so she tries by every means to find some pleasure in life. Then she marries and has children and concentrates her energies on them. After all, a woman's children make her life.

A lot of Cuban women have more children than their share. Ask girls of eighteen or nineteen, "How many children do you have?" Many will answer, "Six." Now, any woman in Cuba can use a ring. So when a woman gets pregnant every year, people say, "That woman should wear an IUD." And she gets one inserted. I'm absolutely against that. To limit the number of children would be to fight against nature. If it's a woman's nature to have a child every year, an IUD interferes with her natural functions.

There are certain things that aren't true that one doesn't contradict publicly because people would say you were contradicting scientific conclusions. The supposed safety of the IUDs is one example. Another is the belief that a woman can get pregnant against her will. I don't think that's true. Although we men are necessary, it's the woman who provokes and produces her own pregnancy. Let me speak freely. If I should want to have a child with a woman, she'd have to be in the right condition to get pregnant. I'm not talking about physical condition. I'm talking about such incompatibilities as differences in schooling, which at first glance would seem to have nothing to do with the case. Of course even when these conditions are met, the woman can't get pregnant by herself. So she gets together with her man in whatever position pleases her best, and sure enough, she gets pregnant. Of course this is outside the techniques of scientific study, but there have been many cases that demonstrate this. I'm not trying to belittle science, but these cases should be given consideration. There's a Spanish author who says, "In this deceitful world, nothing is false . . . or true. It all depends on the color of the glass you're looking through."

AMALIA CARRANZA:

Lázaro is very pleasant to friends and acquaintances but he's different at home. A man should be kind to his wife and she to him— that's what marriage is all about—but Lázaro isn't understanding the way some men are. He used to kiss me when he left for work or came back home, but that only lasted for the first few months. He never kisses me anymore.

It's not that Lázaro isn't good. I don't say that, but he has one defect—he disapproves of everything. Everything I do is bad or ugly. I admit I have a temper when I'm provoked, but Lázaro wakes up in a good mood one day and an angry mood the next. You never know where you stand with a moody person like him. When I'm feeling secure and everything's going well, he's apt to let loose one of his outbursts and spoil it all.

At first I excused him, thinking that illness and old age made him the way he is. Now I've begun to analyze things and realize he must have been like that all his life. He had so many wives and mistresses and none of them lasted long. He's never lived with any woman ten, twelve, fifteen years. There must be some flaw in his character that prevents him from getting along well in an intimate relationship and I've told him so. After all, women come in all sorts of temperaments—calm, rude, violent, or whatever—and if the defect weren't in Lázaro, I figure he could have made a go of it with at least one of his wives.

Suffering ages people and I've suffered a lot with Lázaro. I look about ten years older than I did when I first came to live with him. Ordinarily I'm a very happy person who loves to laugh, but in the past two years I've turned sour. A man and woman marry looking for understanding and harmony, but that's just what's lacking in this goddamned house.

One problem is, Lázaro won't talk to me anymore. He can talk well on any subject and I've always liked people who talk well, because I'm illiterate and I can learn a lot by listening to them. But whenever I start to talk about something, Lázaro changes the subject. He talks backwards and forwards and is apt to say no to something that he's said yes to before. I don't know why he's like that, but it really upsets me. He says he talks to me that way because I never read and don't understand anything. Well, I admit I'm stupid and ignorant, but I can figure out some things. It just happens I understand them differently than he does.

Actually, there still are times when we sit and talk and he's willing to answer my questions. He used to love explaining things to me. He's a quiet man, affectionate when he's in the mood, and really worthy of love, but he gets on my nerves all the same.

Lázaro has his ways and I have mine. A few days ago we had some visitors from the University and I said to them, "Please execuse me for not offering you a soft drink. All I have is coffee, would you like some?" After they left, Lázaro told me, "What you did was wrong. It looked very bad. You didn't have to come right out and say you had no soft drinks. You should never say to anybody, 'Excuse me for not having this or that.' That shows vanity."

Is that vanity, I ask you? To my limited understanding, offering refreshments to our visitors has nothing to do with being vain. We don't have to stand on formality with those people. Why shouldn't I offer them what I have on hand? It would be worse not to offer anything and not even make an excuse.

Here's another example. Suppose we're having our supper when a friend comes in. Naturally I'd ask him to sit down and eat with us. Then he'd excuse himself, saying, "Oh, but I've already eaten."

"Eat again then, if you see anything here you like," I'd urge, and I'd set a plate before him. To me this is only plain ordinary politeness but Lázaro claims it looks bad.

Everything I do rubs him the wrong way. If I fix up the house, it must be that I'm expecting some very intimate friend. I like to keep the house looking nice in case anybody comes, and I enjoy changing the furniture around to make the place look prettier. He wants to have the house clean, yes, but he doesn't care about having it neat too. He drops his things anyplace.

The first night I came to stay, the place was a pigsty. Clothes were piled up on the bed and the table was heaped so high with papers there was no telling what was underneath. Even now, after all this time, I haven't been able to really get it straight. Lázaro gets mad if I so much as shove a piece of paper aside, because he claims he needs it.

"I know why you get so fancy," he says. "You want to have the house spotless in case some of your friends drop in." Well, that's reasonable, isn't it? A house should always be in order. I like to have it painted as soon as the old paint doesn't look fresh anymore. Well, now there's no paint to be had, but water costs nothing and a clean house looks nice. But he claims I fuss too much and says there's no point in having ornaments in the house.

"It isn't a necessity of life," he tells me.

He thinks people don't need lots of clothes to go visit friends or amuse themselves or anything like that. "What one needs to live one's life is to read a lot, to be very studious and know a lot of things." Oh well, those are an old man's quirks.

Another thing that causes trouble between us is that Lázaro won't bother to bathe. We quarrel about it often because I can't stand dirty people. Cleanliness is beautiful in a man as well as in a woman. I put myself out to keep all his things clean, especially his towel and his underclothes, to feed him well and on time, and to keep his clothes clean and pressed. In that, nobody could do better than I. Of course his shorts and pants get dirty at work, but he should bathe and change into clean clothes as soon as he gets home.

Lázaro's just plain sloppy. He won't even wear pajamas at night. It's very unpleasant to sleep next to somebody who, on top of not having bathed, doesn't even change his underclothes. I nag him and nag him to keep clean, not just for my sake but because he meets so many people. I ask him, "Aren't you ashamed to be in such a condition when people come to see you or when you go out with them?"

"Not a bit," says he.

"All right then, that's your business. As for me, I'm going to keep on bathing every day."

And do you know what he says? That the only thing that matters is having a clean heart. I tell him that isn't the only thing. Then he answers that I'm illiterate, self-centered, and vain. This has nothing to do with vanity—dirt is bad for your health.

Lázaro is so cranky and domineering. I suppose that's why most of his women have left him. His word is law. The first day I came here he told me how he expected me to behave. "Look," he said, "I don't want my wife gadding around the neighborhood, chatting with everybody. I want you to dress well and fix your hair, but stay at home."

I agreed with everything he said, but secretly I thought, "I'll do as I please. If I feel like being naked all day long, I'll close the door and walk around naked."

Lazarito used to complain all the time about the way I dressed. He objected to my wearing short skirts, low necklines, or tight dresses even if they were in fashion. I never wanted to wear my dresses too short because that's for young girls. I wouldn't wear them too close-fitting either because I'm so thin they don't look good on me. I like to dress fashionably, within reason, taking my age and figure into account. But no, he won't let me.

I need to have some dental work done but Lázaro refuses to pay for it. At the polyclinic they only pull teeth for free.[91] I need to have a bridge

91. Cuba has a massive public-health program founded on the principle that medical care is a biological right and should therefore be made available to everyone at no direct cost. The country is divided into thirty-eight health regions that are subdivided into public-health areas, each having at least one polyclinic. Urban polyclinics are designed for out-patient treatment (rural polyclinics also offer in-patient treatment) and are required to have on duty a gynecologist, dentist, pediatrician, epidemiologist, internist, and

made, and that'll cost. But Lázaro will neither give me the money for fixing my teeth nor allow me to earn it. He says that if I fix my teeth it will improve my appearance and then I'll change.

I feel hurt by this attitude. Really, a husband should allow his wife to improve her appearance. Thanks to Lázaro's jealous nature, I spend my whole life stuck in this house. I like to go out now and then, to take in a movie or to go dancing. I haven't danced in years! Sometimes he takes me out to eat, but not often. And I love the movies but I don't even feel like going anymore. In all the time I've lived with Lázaro he's taken me only once, when we went to see *Lucía* with a friend of his. He didn't like the picture because there were swear words in it. I haven't been to the movies since.

There are lots of places where I could go, because I have many friends in spite of the lonely life I lead. Lazarito has lots of friends too, but when I suggest we go visit somebody, he says he's too tired. I understand that he must really feel tired and worn out, but if he doesn't go, I don't either.

He says, "Your duties and obligations"—those are his very words— "lie inside the four walls of this house." I ask him, "But why?" And he says, "Because it's your obligation to look after me. A woman belongs in the home, not wandering all over the place. When you're out, how do I know who you're with?"

When I go out alone Lázaro makes such a fuss. He starts asking, "Did you go alone or with your son?" And he keeps on and on till I wish I'd stayed home. When he goes out by himself I receive him pleasantly when he comes home. I think I should be able to go out alone too.

When I wake up feeling I just have to get out of the house, I wait till he goes to work, then I go out. I have to visit my friends now and then, because if I didn't, they wouldn't visit me. I'm not a shut-in by nature. I like to be friendly because that way one learns how to behave socially. I'm very unhappy and I cry a great deal, remembering my past life. I suffer, oh how I suffer, living the way I do!

I still long to find a man to the measure of my desires. Not one younger than me but not too much older, either—somebody suitable in age, a man who enjoys cleanliness. For me, an ideal husband is one who comes home from work, bathes, changes his clothes, and takes me out somewhere. To pay a call, to walk around—anything. Home life comes first of course, but one should be able to gratify other wishes too.

The main thing I want is a man who loves me and my grandchildren. If *mamá* were alive I'd say, "One who loves my *mamá,* too," but she's

nurses. Health workers are also assigned to polyclinics to teach basic hygiene practices. Greater Havana had over fifty polyclinics in 1970. (Richard Leyva, "Health and Revolution in Cuba," in Rolando E. Bonachea and Nelson P. Valdés, eds., *Cuba in Revolution* (New York: Anchor Books, 1972), pp. 476–77.)

gone. That's the main thing a woman seeks in a man, that he be fond of her family. Next to that I put mutual understanding.

It isn't easy to find a man like that but I haven't lost hope. That's what keeps me going and makes me snap out of my gloomy moods when I feel I might as well die. Heck no, I'll keep on living. Maybe tomorrow I'll find the man of my dreams. But how? If I worked outside, I might find a comrade I could love and who would love me, a man I could marry and be happy with. But locked up in this house? No. The only thing I can find here is what's here already.

Lázaro never asked for a great deal in the way of sex, probably because of his age. He wasn't after me every single day. As he says, one can't be doing that all the time. It's been several months now since we've had relations.

While we still had a sex life he did everything very normally. There were always variations, of course, but very normal ones. The trouble was that he was always grumpy afterward. At first he used to have erections, but only weak ones. Now he doesn't have any at all. He gets mad when I tell him, "It isn't my fault you can't get an erection, Lázaro. At your age that's natural." A man like him, who's had a lot of women, is worn out physically by the time he reaches a certain age.

Still, I feel very upset, very hurt, when he starts making love and nothing happens. When a woman gets all fired up and there's nothing to slake her, she's bound to feel bad.

He says to me, "You must realize that I'm very old."

"All right then, be old!" I tell him. "But don't try to get me in bed, because when you do, I'm upset the next day."

"You're no help at all," he complains.

Well, I'll soon be forty-seven years old—I'm no spring chicken. One's body calls out for it at any age, but when one is older one can adapt, and I've adapted myself to my circumstances. What else can I do? He can no longer act like a complete man so I have to put up with it.

Lazarito never talks to me about these problems or offers any explanations. Maybe he's embarrassed. I used to tell him, "Go see a doctor, he can tell you what's the matter." But he refused.

He can tell I'm disappointed and that convinces him all the more that I'm unfaithful. "You don't react to me because of the other men you have," he says. That's what's at the bottom of his jealousy, knowing he's too old to satisfy a woman.

He's wrong to be jealous. I wouldn't leave him for another man because that would kill him. No, thinking it over, I would do no such thing. Lázaro is a sick man, and he'd drop dead of sorrow. I can wait. I've known women to marry as late as sixty or seventy.

Lázaro has told me about some of the women he had before me, especially about María del Carmen. She was the only woman he loved passionately. He was even more jealous of her than he is of me! He left her just because she went to a dance he didn't want her to go to. I've never met her even though I know her son Octavio. Lázaro says María's a very good woman and a good mother.

He's also told me about Diana María. She was a young girl, nineteen or twenty at most, when she lived with him. She was very studious, active, and clever. I don't know whether she walked out on him or was unfaithful or what. As I've said to him, "You got what was coming to you. Why should such a young girl stick to an old man?" I'm acquainted with Diana María but we haven't talked about her life with Lázaro.

Another of his women I've met is Digna. She lives her with her son Yara. They aren't on particularly friendly terms with me. When I first came here, Digna used to visit and chat. She'd talk about being over-weight, about her children, and so on but never about Lázaro—we weren't close enough for that. We also talked about the house. Digna used to say, "*Ay*, Amalia, you've certainly improved this place!" We had many pleasant chats. Then one day we met in the street and she didn't return my greeting. Neither she nor her son has spoken to me since.

When Lázaro gets angry he stays angry. He doesn't curse or use dirty words. He hates it when I say *coño* or "shit-eater" or "don't screw me up!" He doesn't mind *carajo*. Sometimes I say something like "Stop screwing around, you ugly old man, *coño!*"

Then he tells me, "Don't use such language, Amalia. It's very ugly."

Lázaro does so many strange things. He worries about his possessions and marks them so he can tell if someone has handled them. He keeps the radio tied up—not only so it won't be stolen, but so I won't use it. He thinks I might show it to somebody who'd steal it later. I can understand that he doesn't want the radio going all the time, but tying it up? That hurts.

But in spite of his grouchiness and peculiar ways he's a good man. The truth is, I've become very fond of Lázaro. I don't admire him but I feel sorry for him because he's utterly alone. He has no father, mother, or sisters. One of his brothers works in the country and can only come to see him every week or two. He never sees the other one. Lazarito isn't on friendly terms with any of his sons, not even the eldest, Octavio, whom he used to be crazy about.

I don't like to see him not getting along with his children but maybe I shouldn't criticize so much—my own parents didn't lead a terribly nor-mal life either. They had seven kids together, but I was the youngest and they separated before I was born. Still, they gave a lot more thought to their children than Lázaro does to his.

BENEDÍ:
The way I see it, Amalia's life and personality make it very clear she's a daughter of Ochún. I have a great respect for Ochún; they say she's a

very protective mother. Many aspects of Ochún are not at all what they first seem to be. She's always smiling and friendly, but take care! She smiles a lot at her enemies to fool them. Then, the next day, the person she smiled at is found dead and nobody knows why. Ochún's no softy. She can tear a person limb from limb and laugh while she's doing it. She has no pity; she'll take anybody's child away from him.

Amalia may seem like a very soft and mild person, but with me she's as inconsistent as Ochún. Of course, she's not as bad as some of the daughters of Ochún. They bear a grudge a long time, but hide their anger and lead the offender wherever they want. Ochún's daughters hate to tell anybody that they need anything, no matter what it is. They won't communicate such things in words but others can see it by their sadness.

As a daughter of Ochún, Amalia is faced with many problems other women don't have. For one thing, she's in constant danger of betrayal. We have argued that point often. I tell her, *"Chica,* I've lived many years and gone to many places. Besides. I know about *santería* and I've seen that you daughters of Ochún are too trusting. If anybody smiles at you, you immediately think, 'She's my friend.' It never occurs to you that somebody pleasant might want to harm you."

Amalia has the generous openhanded ways of Ochún's daughters. If there are leftovers, she will immediately think of somebody that needs it. She waits till I'm out of the house to slip over to that person and say, "Here, take it." It's not that I'm hardhearted, but frequently Amalia gives away things we could use and her kindness isn't even appreciated. People think that since Ochún is the mistress of gold, her daughters are wealthy. This just isn't true. But this false belief causes a lot of trouble, because instead of being grateful, people think a daughter of Ochún should help them even more.

Another reason why daughters of Ochún are in constant danger is that they have a certain unstudied attractiveness about them. Even though they may not be beautiful or wear elegant clothes, they have a natural grace that makes anything they wear look good on them. A cheap pair of shoes, a simple little dress, a pair of earrings, an attractive hair style—everything becomes them.

Amalia has this natural grace. She isn't pretty and she doesn't have a figure—she doesn't even have any sparkle because she's rather reserved. But when she walks into a crowded room there are more eyes on her than if she were a millionaire. That kind of thing makes the daughters of Ochún victims of other women's envy. Yet Ochún's daughters are so simple and openhearted it never occurs to them that anybody might envy them.

Often when one woman refers to another as a "daughter of Ochún" she really means she's a whore. That's because Ochún managed to make Ogún come out of hiding. Ogún is a strong black, a laborer in fields and mountains, who knows all about plants. Many had tried to bring him out of hiding with no success. But with a little bit of honey and a smile, Ochún found him and gradually charmed him out of the mountain. What other woman could have made such a conquest? That's why people sometimes say Ochún is a whore.

I'm a son of Yemayá, but when Yemayá can't help me, Ochún does. In return, when Ochún can't come out, Yemayá takes care of whoever called for Ochún. There are many legends about this, but only someone completely involved in the religion can understand how it works.

Sometimes the marriage between a daughter of Ochún and a son of Yemayá lasts in a way that is impossible for an outsider to understand. A lot of times I foresee some danger in Amalia's life and am impelled by Yemayá to warn her. "Listen," I say, "one must use a bit of psychology in dealing with people. Keep your troubles to yourself. If you don't want to tell me about them, don't tell anybody, unless you want people to laugh at you."

Unfortunately, Amalia seldom listens to me. It's a rare daughter of Ochún who escapes having the dagger of treason plunged into her back, but just try to tell them so! They are very obstinate on that point and protest, "Who, me? Oh no! The person hasn't been born who can play any dirty tricks on me!"

Most of the time Amalia is easy to get along with, but all I have to say is, "Now look, Amalia, this is thus-and-so," and she gets huffy and refuses to listen. It isn't that Ochún doesn't pay attention to Yemayá. It's Amalia who doesn't pay attention to Lázaro. I say to her, "You must realize what your situation is, not as a *santera* but as a daughter of Ochún. Also, you don't know your guardian angel. If you did, you'd admit that lots of times I'm right when I warn you about things."

But Amalia is blind to evil. And she's too proud to ever admit that I was right. She answers my warnings, saying, "I'm a daughter of Ochún and we are the way we are."

Whenever I'm mistaken about anything, Amalia throws it back to me, saying, "Look at that—an illiterate like me has to teach a wise man like you!"

"Anyone can make a mistake, but don't you go believing that the illiterate can teach the wise," I answer. "An illiterate has nothing but his natural wits."

Then she laughs disagreeably, "And you think I'm the stupid one!" But I forgive her because she has little knowledge of the philosophy of life.

I've done a lot to help Amalia in her spiritual progress. For instance, when she was presented to the *santo*[92] she was 100 *pesos* short of the sum she needed to get her things, so I gave her the money. Amalia had to go

92. See n. 12.

through that ceremony to be a complete member of her religion. Until she did she was like an unborn child as far as her religion was concerned. So the money I gave her was very important to her religious development.

During the ceremony to become a *santero* certain people tear herbs and say words over them. These herbs are living bodies with powers of their own. The amount of time it takes to become a *santero* depends on how rapidly the person feels the effect of the ceremonies. It's just like medicine. A doctor may prescribe the same pill to two patients and one might get well with the first pill while the other doesn't.

Following the ceremony, the *santeros* must dress in white for a full year, because white is Obatalá's color and it symbolizes the peace that people seek when they make themselves *santeros*. A woman who has completed the whole ritual is called a *yabó*.

In spite of the fact that I gave Amalia the money to complete this ceremony, she fails to be appreciative. If only she had the philosophy of life to understand what this means! I wish she had a bit more education. Not that I want a woman who's done too much studying, but I'd like more than a *guajirita*, an ignorant country girl.

AMALIA CARRANZA:
    Lazarito and I argue a lot about religion because our beliefs are different. And yet, all religions are the same in a way, like different paths leading to the same place. When Lazarito looks down on me from his superior knowledge, I feel he's belittling me. He speaks in tongues and knows many aspects of the saints that I know nothing about. But I have faith and love for the saints, too.

Lazarito used to practice the religion when he lived in Las Yaguas. I've been told that many people went to his house for consultations and he was very good at it. Lazarito has given up all that consultation business, so far as I know. I've never seen him throw the shells, in fact he doesn't keep any at home, but he knows how to do it. I've seen him consult coconut shells though. Sometimes when I get home I find him busy at those things, but I never ask him what he's doing because he wouldn't tell me. He's a strange man.

Lázaro's guardian angel is in *El Palo*, mine is in *Regla Ocha*. Actually, Lazarito has never told me that he's a *palero*. I found out by his warnings not to touch this or that. I've asked him more than once if he ever was an *Abacuá*. He answers with a question, "Why do you want to know?"

"Never mind," I tell him. "The day you die, I'll find out."

If Lázaro had told me he belonged to *Abacuá*, I'd never have married him. Well, maybe I would have, considering the way I felt and the situation I was in, but at least I would have known what I was getting into.

I've never known Lazarito to do anything bad with his religion, but I'm terrified of the *paleros*. I've heard that the people in that religion are terribly impulsive and if they get annoyed at any little thing they're apt to kill. Actually, I'm not so much afraid as I am wary. I keep my distance, not that I believe all those stories. After all, if the *paleros* were as violent as they say, wouldn't untold numbers of people have disappeared?

Lázaro despises women because of *Palo Monte*. There are women in *El Palo*, sure, but when a woman is menstruating, she's not allowed even to look in the door where they're gathered. I never touch Lazarito when I'm menstruating, not because he forbids it but because I'm cautious. I know it weakens a man if he touches a woman then.

I know that Lazarito hasn't called down a *santo*, because a number of people have told me they were waiting to do it together with him. He has such deep knowledge of the religion that they wanted him to be their *padrino*.[93] But they say he dropped his religious activities after the Revolution.

My religion is very different from *Palo Monte*. But it's very powerful and worthy of respect because it also knows how to make itself felt. I can't understand why Lázaro, who is such an intellectual, belongs to *Palo Monte* instead of to *Regla Ocha*, which has more instruction and is more intellectual. I guess it must be because of his guardian angel and because he has learned more about *Palo Monte*.

I joined the religion for a number of reasons. I was very ill and consulted several doctors but they prescribed remedies that made me unconscious. I met a man who told me I needed to be presented to a *santo*. No one in my family ever went in for that kind of thing, not even *mamá*, and I was scared. But since it was a matter of my health, all my folks, especially my son, agreed that I should give *santería* a try. In 1953 I started going to places where it's practiced. I called down a *santo* in 1965 and right away I felt like a different person.

Practically nobody who's integrated belongs to the religion, because the Revolution forbids it. So Lazarito doesn't want me to practice it. He shows his opposition by forbidding me to go where the religion is practiced. But it isn't my religion Lázaro objects to, only my going out. If he goes out in the morning, I can leave the house, so long as I come back that same day before dark.

One can't keep up with the religion if one has to get home too early. Suppose somebody is calling down a *santo*—the ritual could go on all night. According to the rules it should last three days, but I never stay that long so as not to provoke Lázaro. Whenever I go, I come back

93. Godfather.

home the first day. If I have a chance, I go back the second day, but I never stay through the night.

I go to those *santo* ceremonies when friends of mine are in them. This is an act of friendship, because the ritual can't be carried out with only the one person. Several people are needed to carry out different tasks. For instance, on the day of the washing, seven basins of water are used and seven persons must sit there to perform different parts of the ritual. They have to pray while they crush certain aromatic herbs and so on, then the person who is to be the *santero* goes into a separate room to have the bath. Not everybody is allowed to witness the bath. There may be as many as fifteen *santeros* present at this part of the ritual, but they must be complete *santeros* before they can lay hands or look on.

When I decided to become a *santera,* Lazarito told me to go ahead and do it if I wanted to, but not at home. I didn't argue. Our house is too small and the water goes off now and then, so taking all things into account, I did it at my godfather's house.

I waited almost five years before doing it. I'm not sure exactly how long the ceremony took. When one is in a fiesta, the hours fly and one can't keep track of them. I left home around 9:00 at night on the 28th and returned two and a half days later, on the afternoon of the 31st.

For a full year afterward I dressed in white. They cut my hair off completely. It cost me a lot of trouble to get all the things necessary for the fiesta because I wasn't allowed to keep animals where I lived. The goat and the sheep were the most difficult to get. The fowl were no problem because I was allowed to raise those and I already had pigeons and hens.

I needed money for the ceremony so I asked Lázaro's permission to go work in *El Cordón.* He refused because it's bad for my health to work on the land. So I had to ask him to lend me the money. The trouble I had before I got him to agree! I wept tears for that money. He wouldn't give it to me all at once. I had to get it in installments. For instance, I'd buy an animal, and when it was delivered I'd say to him, "Here, give the 60 *pesos* I owe for it." So he'd fork out the dough because he couldn't help it. That way I finally got together all the things I needed.

As soon as I returned from the ceremony he said, "All right, now pay me back my money."

"I can't," said I. "You know I didn't go there to get paid." We quarreled about that.

He knew I still had 50 *pesos* in my bank account and he wanted me to give them to him right away. I argued until I got so mad I was on the point of leaving him for good. His attitude disgusted me, and to top it off, he said what he always says, "Naturally you have to be stupid, you're illiterate."

"All right," I said, "I agree. But I can go further on my stupidity than you can with all your knowledge and wisdom. Illiterate as I am, I have to explain to you things that should be clear to anybody. Knowing where I just came from, you shouldn't ask me to go straight to the bank and get you the 50 *pesos*. It takes an awfully stupid person to say that, especially considering that it was almost 8:00 at night when I got home."

It wasn't as if he were putting obstacles in my way because he didn't want me to become a *santera*. He said he wanted me to. But he didn't want to fork out even one miserable little *kilo*[94] to pay for it. He's stingy—that's the whole problem.

Lázaro didn't need the money—he has a bank account, and for all I know he may have money right here in the house. I have no idea what his bank balance is. If I wanted to pry I could find out in a minute by getting hold of his bankbook. But what good would that do me? Anyway, it's his money and I don't need it or want it. Whatever money Lázaro lends me, I have to pay back. He loaned me almost 300 *pesos* for my *santo* and I still owe him a bit over 130. I don't know just when I'll pay that back but I will, I will.

BENEDÍ:

The fact that I'm religious has not done me the slightest harm with the Revolution or in any other way. After all, if the Revolution didn't recognize the effectiveness of *santería,* it would have suspended all our religious festivities long ago. On the contrary, it leaves us totally free to belong to any religion as long as it doesn't interfere with politics.

I went to the museum of the African religion established by Fidel and was impressed. I'd never imagined there could be a museum dedicated wholly to religion! I still think that the African religion will disappear completely, but I once heard Fidel say that he wished they would build a temple to that religion, just as the Masons and the Catholics have their temples.

I've had many arguments with Catholics and with believers in the African religion, and have never been able to come to an agreement with any of them. There are those who say that African religion is a myth, a dream, a means of exploiting the ignorance of others, a web of deceit. But I, and all believers, have faith because we've had proof. It's exactly the same in the case of Catholicism. Men pick and choose among its teachings, and in the end each does what is most convenient for him.

94. One *centavo*.

Christianity teaches that all men are equal, yet who invented the Inquisition? Christians!

Each person must figure out whether he can reconcile his politics and his religion. We all know cases of Catholics involved in politics. Take Father Sardiñas,[95] priest of the Rebel Army here in Cuba. And there were Catholics in the Sierra Maestra who said their prayers at the same time they were fighting in the insurrection because they felt that prayers could help them. On the other hand, there was a Catholic church in Las Yaguas that campaigned against the Revolution in 1959. They went so far as to organize a parade of people waving empty frying pans and chanting, "We're hungry, hungry, hungry!" When we found out about it we said, "This has to stop." Of course, some *santeros* are counter-revolutionaries too. I don't argue with them because that would be going outside of religion and meddling in politics.

We cannot allow the confusion of politics and religion. There are people who claim that Christianity is a religion that helps mankind. But at the same time, Christians are manufacturing explosives to make the human race disappear. They must know that Christ wasn't like that. Christ tried to redeem mankind. The way I figure it, the motives for this contradiction are political.

A man creates his own faith as he goes along. I believe in the African religion, but I've had faith in other things too. I believe the Revolution triumphed because of all the people who concentrated their faith on Martí's ideas. When I find myself in difficult situations I concentrate on my faith, saying, "I do what I'm doing to save a part of mankind and I trust this will help me."

95. Father Guillermo Sardiñas joined the Rebel Army in the Sierra Maestra in 1957, the first of six priests to do so.

Chapter Eight

I'm in Love with the Revolution

A LOT OF PEOPLE KEPT asking me, "Lazarito, why don't you retire?" Well, why should I? For all my years, I don't feel old. There's a regulation now that says nobody shall be retired because of age but only because of disabling illness. Actually, I don't call what I have an illness. If a man has enough spirit, nothing can get him down. My body is still sound and I like to work. I've suffered only because I'm egotistical enough to believe that if I don't participate in the struggle for the good of humanity, it won't succeed. Besides, I promised my departed father that as long as there was strength in my body, I'd help destroy the system of slavery we used to have in Cuba. I can't sit back and take it easy, I just can't. I'll keep on working until I drop dead. Something in me drives me on.

Well, time passed and finally I had to give in. About a month ago I began to take steps to retire. I earn 63 *centavos* an hour and work eighty-eight hours every fifteen-day period, which is only eleven workdays. Nine and nine-tenths percent of my salary is discounted for social security, vacations, and illness.[96] So it alternates, 44 *pesos* one fifteen-day period and 56 *pesos* the next. I haven't tried to figure it out exactly because I trust the administration. I'm still receiving full wages because it hasn't been decided yet whether, since I'm retiring because of illness, I'm entitled to 100 percent, 50 percent, or 35 percent of my salary.

AMALIA CARRANZA:
   I try to get Lázaro to take care of his health but he won't pay any attention. He thinks he's in fine shape but that's very, very far from the truth. The doctor told me Lázaro has some kind of heart condition. I forget the name of it, but his heart doesn't function the way it should. He might be sitting quietly at the table one minute and drop dead the next. He'll get desperate all of a sudden and start rubbing his

96. The 9.9 percent also includes withholdings of 1 percent for union dues and 2 or 3 percent "voluntary" deductions for aiding disaster victims, financing national campaigns, building monuments, and so forth.

chest and gasping for air. He doesn't suspect that he might die when that happens.

The doctor told Lázaro that he shouldn't exert himself too much, lift or push anything heavy, or climb stairs. He also prescribed two kinds of pills to relieve the pain. Lázaro doesn't have any special diet, but his food must be prepared with very little salt. The doctor never told him the danger he's in. He told *me* instead.

The doctor sent a letter to Lázaro's place of work and I talked with the person who got him the job. "Any day Lázaro is going to die on you."

"Oh, don't say that!" he said.

"Yes, the doctor wants him to quit but Lázaro's got a psychosis about work."

"Well, at least we can give him the lightest kind of job, like sweeping," the man promised.

Lázaro's friend Amanda, a woman doctor at the National Hospital, gave him a checkup. She warned me that he shouldn't even sweep.

"And how is anyone to tell him so?" I asked.

All I can do is wait and try not to shock him in any way.

BENEDÍ:
I've never thrown money away. I believe in taking care of what I have. If a group of us get together to go to a pizzeria, I never say, "The bill's on me." But if I specifically invite a family, I pay. When they invite, they pay. That way things are even. I don't want to be destitute when I'm old, so whenever I can save a few *pesetas,* I do.

With all my careful management, I have 556.37 *pesos* in my savings account, which I started in March, 1967. At that time I lived alone so I only spent what was necessary. I also played the lottery and was lucky enough to win 200 *pesos* in the last drawing before the lottery was abolished.[97] I held on tight to that money. Once I loaned 300 *pesos* to a newsboys' club that was being organized. They had asked me, "*Chico,* how can we get 300 *pesos* to buy uniforms for the baseball team?"

"I can lend you the money," I said.

That surprised them because I had never boasted of having that much money. They accepted my offer and went to the bank with me. When they paid me back in December as agreed, I thought, "This money isn't

97. Gambling, especially through purchase of lottery tickets, was a widespread practice in Cuba. The Castro government allowed the lottery to continue for approximately a year and a half before abolishing it, using the revenue to finance housing construction. The lottery tickets "were sold as bonds, recoverable after five years at 110 percent of cost with annual interest reaching 4 percent after seven years." (*Cuba Review,* Mar., 1975, p. 5.) According to Ruby Hart Phillips, Cubans would not buy the bonds because the few prizes (one of 100,000 *pesos* and others of 100 *pesos* each) were not attractive enough, nor were people interested in savings. (*The Cuban Dilemma,* p. 53.)

going to do me any good loose in my pocket." So I put it right back in the bank.

I feel I have quite enough money for my needs now. Oh, sometimes Amalia and I will get into an argument about it, but we all know women. Give them 100 *pesos* with careful instructions on how to spend them and they will undoubtedly spend them on something else. I'll tell Amalia specifically, "Buy yourself a pair of shoes, and if you see shirts my size, buy me one." But if she sees a basket of flowers or an ornamental doll that catches her fancy, she's sure to buy it.

I have a system now. First, the food money must be set aside so it's available when our food quota falls due. Though there are only two of us, it's a pretty tight squeeze sometimes as we try to trim expenses without actually having to go hungry. I try to cover Amalia's expenses with the money left over.

I give Amalia about 60 *pesos* a month for her personal expenses, which leaves me a bit over 40 *pesos* for household expenses. I only spend money on necessary things, like the 2 *pesos* a month for the furniture I bought on the installment plan, or the 25 *pesos* I contributed to the sectional library. There have also been cases of families needing money for an emergency: "Lázaro, can you lend me 10 or 20 *pesos* for my groceries?" In a case like that, I hand over the money, though half the time they forget to repay me.

I pay the electric bill directly so it doesn't come out of the household budget. It's usually between 70 and 80 *centavos* a month. That's another of my economies. Suppose a light has to be turned on in the bathroom; it lights the kitchen too, so the kitchen light can be turned off. Sometimes the bedroom and living room can be lit from just one light. The only extra bit of electrical equipment we have is the electric iron. I don't count the radio because that doesn't use up much electricity.

Smoking costs me a bit of money since I smoke one or two packs a day,[98] and then too, I have to buy the matches. But that's all I buy for myself. I don't even buy clothes. The husband of a comrade died and she said to me in a kind of embarrassed way, "Look, Lázaro, I have some clothes of Gabriel's which you may have if you like. It isn't charity or anything like that, but I have to either throw them away or give them to somebody, so it might as well be you." I accepted her gift and saved myself about 100 *pesos*.

AMALIA CARRANZA:

I have no idea how much Lázaro earns. He's never told me. That's his way, and why should I care? He gives me the money I need and that's all I need to know. People usually get paid on the 1st and 15th of

98. In 1969 cigarettes were 20 *centavos* per package of twenty.

each month, so I guess that's when he gets paid, but I don't know for sure. According to him he doesn't earn much and I'd spend it all if he left it with me. Sure I'd spend it, but only on things we need. I'd like to fix up the house and make it look nicer but . . . oh well.

I don't keep track of how much Lázaro gives me for household expenses. I just ask for whatever I need. He doesn't give me a lump sum but a bit now and a·bit later, as things arrive at the shops. I used to write down all the household expenditures in a notebook, but I stopped. It didn't do a bit of good and it was a headache. What's the point of keeping track of every *kilo* you spend? Spend a *peseta,* write it down. Heck no! I haven't the patience.

Expenses aren't exactly the same for every fifteen-day period, because different things come to the grocery store every day. Sometimes you can get by on 20 *pesos,* other times it takes 30 or more. Lazarito simply doesn't understand that. He expects me to get through the fifteen days on 15 *pesos,* which just isn't enough. That's another reason why we quarrel. He won't leave me any extra money.

I never know for sure how much the electricity bill is going to be. Sometimes it's a bit over 1 *peso,* other times it's 3 *pesos,* and only two months ago it was 8 *pesos.* When the man comes to collect the payments, I say to Lázaro, "Hey, give me the money for the electricity," and he gives me whatever it is. Afterward I repay him out of my own money.

We don't start making payments on the house until 1975. We're paying 2 *pesos* a month for our furniture. I make the payments myself at the bank. We're caught up on the furniture payments now, but the last time I went to the bank with the book of payments, we owed a terrific amount. I had to pay for practically every card in the book. In December I'll have to get another book for next year's payments.

I pay the Committee 25 *centavos* a month for the little dues stamps. Lazaro gives me the money, or if I have some of my own, I use that. Sometimes Lázaro gives me money for my personal expenses. When we first got together he gave me 40 *pesos* and I bought a number of things. Then, one year and four months ago, he gave me 140 *pesos.* That's all. One hundred and forty *pesos* for a whole year, knowing that it would be spent in one second if I bought all the things I wanted!

My son gives me some money twice a month for my personal expenses. Sometimes it's 10 *pesos,* sometimes 15, 20, 30. It depends on what he has to spend at home. After all, he has a family to support. He's made it a kind of duty because I'm his mother, but he really doesn't have any obligation to give me anything. I save whatever he gives me, then if I have to go somewhere in connection with my religion, or if I want to buy a picture or a little ornament for the house, I have some spending money, or if one of my sisters has a birthday, I can give her a present. Nowadays it's practically impossible to buy anything, so I give them a couple of *pesos*. They do the same for my birthday.

I never tell Lázaro how much money I have. If he knew, he'd want me to use it for daily expenses, and there's no reason for that because he never spends all he earns between one payday and the next.

When I first came to live with Lázaro he said to me, "There's always money in that little box." And he always left 60, 70 *pesos* there. I only used what I needed. But one day when Lázaro was out, I loaned my nephew 10 *pesos* from it. I said to him, "Look, sonny, I'll lend it to you, but this is Lázaro's money, not mine." But when I told Lázaro, he didn't like it. "Why didn't you wait till I got home so you could ask me?"

"How could I? The boy needed money right away—he had a problem." Then we quarreled about it. "All right, I'll never touch your money again," I told him. So he started leaving less and less until now he doesn't leave anything. Sometimes I search all over the place for a bit of money but I never find any.

I've made up my mind to be satisfied with whatever Lázaro gives me. If there's money, fine; if there isn't, why quarrel about it? He knows it's needed but he's made up his mind to keep me short. So I never quarrel or cry about money anymore.

I won't say that I ate any better before the Revolution, but I didn't eat badly in those days. A good manager used to be able to go to the marketplace with 5 or 6 *pesos* and do all right. You could vary your meals then because the grocery store was always kept open and it was well stocked with tinned sardines, Spanish sausage, fatback bacon, and all sorts of things. Also, the butcher was open every day and you could buy any amount of meat you wanted. Now I just buy whatever food we have in the ration book. If we don't like it, we eat it anyway. There are lots of things the grocery store gets that we aren't allowed to buy because they're only for children.

The meat is delivered to the butcher shop once a week. I spend 1 *peso* a week for the 1½ pounds of meat allowed us. Some weeks a lot of that is bone. If I only had to plan for the two of us, I could make our meat rations last out the week. But as it is I have to consider my son and grandchildren, who eat with us. Anyway, I have no way of keeping food cold so I never try to make it last more than two days.

We get thirty eggs, which I usually buy in two batches each month because it's better that way. This week I bought the whole amount, 1.20 *pesos'* worth. How long the egg ration lasts depends on lots of things. If we have meat we don't eat eggs, but when I make rice I cook eggs to go with it.

Lazarito has a brooder hen, and if the chicks live I plan to raise a flock. I got the hen when I was buying the animals for the *santero* ceremony. A man who had exchanged houses was selling his fowl before moving and I bought two hens, a rooster, and a chick from him. The whole lot cost me 60 *pesos*.

Lazarito likes fish but it doesn't agree with me so I don't buy it very often. This month I haven't bought any at all because the only thing they have is fresh sardines, which are full of sharp little bones.

We're allowed 3 ounces of coffee for 18 *kilos*. It's sold on Fridays and on that day I make it real strong to kill my craving for it. My daughter-in-law sends me my son's weekly ration of 1½ ounces and I manage to stretch it out until the following Friday. Some of our visitors are real coffee drinkers and I make them some because I'm a coffee drinker myself and I know how one can crave it. When that happens, there's less left for us. In fact, we may wake up the next morning without a drop of coffee in the house.

We buy only condensed milk—three cans a month for me and six for Lázaro. He gets more because of his age.[99] How long the milk lasts depends on a lot of things. We always use it in our breakfast coffee. Sometimes, when there isn't much for dinner, Lázaro drinks milk because he has a big appetite. Then, my son and my grandchildren eat with us, so I prepare some for them. When I prepare it for the children three times, a whole can goes in one day.

Around the 20th of the month I start running out of one thing and another, but I can always manage somehow until the end of the month. If I run out of food, I go to my daughter-in-law and tell her, "Your husband and children eat at my house, so give me their food."

She hasn't sent me anything lately, except rice and meat. I've spoken to my son about it, because everybody is entitled to a certain ration. Why shouldn't she send me my son's entire quota since he eats with us? I understand she keeps some back in case her children visit her. But she has rations for eight and one of the girls eats at school, two of the children are away, and she herself is hardly ever at home.

With three extra mouths to feed I have to have more food. And my grandchildren really eat! I have to turn into a real artist when they come to dinner. We always have breakfast and one other meal, usually with more than one dish. One can always think something up.

So far, I don't have any other way to get extra food. My relatives in the country never send me anything. One of my sisters lives in town and she gives me sweets and such, but not vegetables.

When I get very short of food I go to my sister or to a lady friend of

99. Adults over sixty-five years of age were allotted six cans of milk every thirty-four days as opposed to three cans for those between the ages of fourteen and sixty-five.

Lazarito's and borrow some to pay back later. I never borrow food from anybody else. Lázaro's friend mostly borrows alcohol or kerosene from me. I cook with both. I often exchange alcohol for kerosene from people who cook only with alcohol. That's barter—you give me something, I give you something in return, and that's all. I don't barter food because I never have enough left over. Besides, Lázaro doesn't approve.

I've never gone really hungry since I started to live with Lázaro because I know how to make use of what I have. This month I only served a skimpy meal once and it wasn't all that bad because that day I had bread and eggs besides coffee and milk. If there's only enough of something for one person, I leave it for Lázaro because he has to work. I can manage on a little milk and a little sugar water to deaden the hunger pangs, though it doesn't always work for me. They do say sugar water is good for your blood pressure and for gaining weight, but Lázaro couldn't get along on just that, even though he always gets coffee and a snack at his work center.

I clip recipes from magazines and use them when I have what they call for. I make desserts often because Lázaro has a sweet tooth. Sometimes I ask Lázaro to get me some bread from the factory cafeteria so I can make pudding. I also buy cake in the pastry shop.

I don't stand in line unless I really want something and the line is short. Otherwise, I wait until all the turns are gone and buy whatever is available without a ration book. I've always hated waiting in line, and after all, it's not necessary. It's the people themselves who are responsible for those long lines, because when something is due to arrive at the store they think that unless they sleep in the line the night before, there won't be anything left for them in the morning.

That's silly, because when the store gets something they get enough for everybody. If it runs out before everybody gets his share, they'll bring more of the same tomorrow. There's no point mobbing the place. In the grocery, for example, whether you go at 8:00, at 9:00, or at any later hour, your month's supply of rice and beans is waiting for you. Even if you don't buy them the day they're released, they'll be kept for you till the end of the month if need be. So what's the point of lining up at 10:00 the night before? I really hate those disorderly crowds, so I go when the least number of people are there, usually after 11:00 A.M.[100]

---

100. In 1970 the government began an experimental food-distribution system to reduce the time Cubans spent shopping. The *plan jaba*, or shopping-bag plan, allowed families in which the adults were working and/or studying to have their shopping done by the employees of the grocery store where they were registered. Workers could leave their empty

The clothes shortage is as much of a problem as the food shortage. It gets boring to wear the same old dress every single day. Besides, if you can't change clothes often, they wear out because it's wash, wash, wash, scrub, scrub, scrub, until the cloth tears and then you're naked. I manage because I'm short and skinny and can get two dresses out of the 3½ meters' ration of cloth. At least it's plenty for a blouse and skirt. Fatties aren't as lucky because they have to use the full ration for just one dress.

I never buy secondhand clothes, only new clothes listed in my ration book. I won't say I have heaps of dresses but I have enough to get by. Some I buy ready-made and some my sister sews for me. She has lots of ideas and can get the most out of a piece of cloth. She doesn't charge for making my clothes but I always give her something. Last time she made me a skirt and two dresses and I gave her 5 *pesos*, though she insisted she didn't want payment.

Everything I have today I owe to the Revolution. Before, I had to worry that if I didn't have a job, I wouldn't have anything. Not that I didn't work hard—I really worked at bringing up my son. I quit my job because my husband, Julio, was a good provider and I was better off working in my own home than in somebody else's. Besides, I took in laundry. Of course we never had very much money because Julio had to pay rent, but we knew exactly how much to set aside for that each month. We helped each other. Each of us would contribute to the household expenses, according to what we had and what was needed.

I lived well enough, but I kept worrying about the way things were going. I didn't think everything was fine just because I could eat every day, not while there were about 40,000 others who never had a decent meal. But I didn't work against Batista. I was too ignorant to know what was going on. Ignorance, that was my trouble.

On January 1, 1959, I happened to turn on the radio when they were giving the joyful news. Fidel's coming filled me with happiness. So many had been killed! Every time you picked up a newspaper or turned on the radio or even heard people speak, it was all about bombings and killings. People like me, who didn't have much book-learning, who didn't know what it was all about, we felt for all those people, strangers to us, who had those terrible things happen to them. Often people went out of their houses and never came back. What their mothers must have suffered! One of my nephews was actually on

---

shopping bags and ration books at the store in the morning and pick them up, the bags filled with groceries, on their way home in the evening. The system went into effect across the island in 1972.

the police "gift list" for January 6, the Day of the Three Kings. Do you know what the "gift" was? To be arrested and killed!

There's been real progress under the Revolution. Today's children have a future, because they learn things we never knew and participate in more activities. There wasn't anything like the Pioneers[101] when I was in school. In those days things were easy for whites, but a colored child didn't have a chance, no matter how good a student he was. If he wanted to learn more and make something of himself, he had to go to night school. It used to be that a black couldn't set foot in places that were for whites. Now, where a white can go, a black can too. Colored people are much better off then before.

To me, Fidel is a great leader. He has the patience to deal not only with Cubans but with other peoples too. If it weren't for his great patience he would have died of a heart attack or quit in despair, because in the beginning practically nobody agreed with him. Those people have left already or will leave. Fidel must keep up the hope and patience of those who remain.

Before I went to live with Lázaro, my sister and my daughter-in-law told me he had a very good reputation as a political worker and everyone relied on him. If a committee was to be formed or anything was to be done, people always consulted him. They wanted his opinion, no less! He was quite active in the *reparto* before the Revolution triumphed, but secretly, of course. Many people have said, "If we have a house it's thanks to Lázaro, because he always took a firm stand, even when many people were against the Revolution." But my daughter-in-law told me that others criticized him for playing politics.

I was already living with Lázaro when he was made CDR organizer. In fact I was present at that meeting. They announced that several comrades of the barrio would be elected. We went to the meetings but we had no idea they were considering him. A group there nominated him and he was accepted as organizer for the sectional.

Then, at one meeting, certain comrades said that several people had to be removed from their posts because their work schedules didn't allow them to give enough time to the sectional. They said Lázaro was one of them. It was true; he worked the morning shift one week, the afternoon shift the next, and so on. He was working on the night shift then, so he couldn't attend the meetings. Lázaro was very hurt not to have been told what was brewing, but he agreed that he should be

101. The *Unión de Pioneros* is an adjunct of the Union of Young Communists open to all children seven to fourteen years of age. Many Pioneer activities are incorporated into school curricula although there are also extracurricular activities, including group outings and productive labor.

removed. I was hurt too, because they didn't call a mass meeting to explain why he could no longer be organizer.

Nobody criticized him. On the contrary, the people of the sectional still come to consult him. They rely on him for certain things which he knows more about than the present organizers. He has no post in the sectional now but he does do some kind of volunteer work in the block Committee, I think.

Between his work and his political activities, my husband really can't spend many hours a day at home. Sometimes Lázaro has to leave for a Committee meeting or some other political activity almost as soon as he returns from work. I don't mind him spending so much time on politics as long as his activities produce results. Nowadays a man should be aware of problems outside the home.

Lázaro never quarrels about my going to do volunteer work on the farms. In fact, he wants me to go every Sunday. He wants his wife to be politically active.

I enjoy doing productive work because you meet a lot of people from different barrios and make new friends. In the bus, on the way over, I can laugh and joke and be happy in all the gaiety I never have at home. Sometimes Lázaro goes along with me, other times not. We go to different places—Güira de Melena, *El Cordón,* and Nueva Palma, near Matanzas. A few months ago I went to Artemisa, but the fine dust gave me such a sore throat I've never gone back.

Lázaro never objects when I go out to Committee meetings. If we meet at night, he always accompanies me. He won't let me go alone. I'm the finance officer and I collect the contributions from the members, so naturally I go to all the meetings. I'm also a member of the Public Health Front. My activities on behalf of that consist of distributing vaccines, results of cytological tests, and so on. Lázaro always reminds me to do those things on time and he helps me too, if need be.

I first joined the Committee and the Women's Federation when I lived with Julio. As a Federation member I was number one in my block, because at the time I was the only member they had there and the Federation had a lot of activities. When they set up the Defense Committee they made my house its headquarters. Nobody wanted it in his house and Julio said to me, "Amalia, do you think we could let the Committee set up its offices here?"

"I don't know the first thing about it," I told him. "But if you think it's all right, I'd just as soon."

They called our Committee the Camilo Cienfuegos Committee in my honor, because I was the only woman who'd offered her house and I was a great admirer of Camilo Cienfuegos.

At first people gave me a hard time for letting the Committee set up headquarters in my house. In those days, a woman who did that was called *chiva*[102] and all sorts of horrible names. Children would throw stones at me because their parents told them to. They'd shout at Julio, "Curse your whoring mother!" People avoided me and called me "the Jesuit." None of this mattered to me because I was taking night courses at the time so only Julio was home when the Committee met.

Julio and I worked hard for the Committee. In those days the broad avenue leading to our neighborhood was nothing but stone and earth. When it rained it was mainly mud. Nothing, not even trucks, could get through. Julio and I put up quite a fight to get the streets fixed, and they were finally paved. We also fought to renovate the houses, but so far that hasn't been done.

Whenever I tell Lázaro, "Next Sunday I'm going to do volunteer work," he's delighted. But when I asked his permission to look for a paying job, he said, "Wait a bit, wait a bit."

"But I've already filled in the blanks. And I really need a job."

But it was no use. "Wait anyway," he told me. He suggested that I step straight into a job at the place where he works.

"Don't ask me to work where there's a noise from machinery all the time," I told him. "Noise drives me clear out of my head. It's sheer torture. But there are lots of other jobs I could take."

"Sure, sure," he answered, "but wait a bit."

I've been waiting over a year. I haven't worried too much about getting a job, though, because I don't actually need one. But I know that's a bad attitude because we're all needed. Whatever work I did would help the Revolution just a little, no?

Lázaro tells me, "Being my wife you should be able to qualify for a management post or whatever else you please."

"Look, my son," I answer. "I would never qualify as manager of anything because a manager must know how to manage people. That's simply not my line. But no matter where one works nowadays one is sure to rise, because every worker is entitled to one hour off a day to study."

I never completed the third grade. I could take a placement test but I'm afraid I might not even test as high as second grade. Still, I qualify for all sorts of jobs—like farm work, which I enjoy—and I could make a transfer to a higher-paying job later, after I've furthered my schooling.

Lázaro keeps telling me to read, but I don't have the time. It isn't necessary to read books to know what progress we're making. Some things you know without having to bury your nose in a book. Lázaro spends his life reading. He knows so much, he can talk about anything

102. Colloquial term for an informer or a troublemaker.

to anybody and he explains things so intelligently. He doesn't talk to me much about politics, though, because I don't understand it too well. Rather than say something foolish, I keep my mouth shut.

Lázaro says if I want to be of real help to the Revolution, I should study. Trouble is, I don't have the brains for it. I don't know whether it's because of my age or my worries and unhappiness or what, but nothing sticks in my mind. Nothing, nothing, nothing. I tell him, "What's the point of going back to school if I don't get anything out of it?" So I stay home and time slips by. I write a little and read well enough to read the newspapers, but I'm ignorant. I may not know much about politics or Cuban history, but from what I've seen so far, the Revolution seems perfect.

BENEDÍ:
Since the Revolution, the course of Cuban history has undergone great transformation—in our government, in the rights of its people, and in their independence. I wasn't interested in the other administrations' form of government because they never did anything about workers' problems. But I have a real interest in this one—first, because of its recognition of human rights and freedom, and second, because trades are classified by the skill they require and are paid accordingly.

Of all the governments I've lived under, this one is the best in every way. Materially speaking, I'm better off now than ever, and I have the spiritual freedom I've always wanted. My soul feels a deep satisfaction I never felt before. When I shout, "Long live the Revolution!" it isn't an individual satisfaction I feel, it's a collective satisfaction.

From the day I discovered Fidel, with his sincere love of liberty, I recognized Martí's inspiration in his political ideals. Martí once said that tyranny does not corrupt a people, it prepares them. In Cuba we lived under barbarous oppression until we were ready for Fidel and the Revolution. Fidel convinced the Cuban people to break the yoke of slavery forever, and from that day on I was ready to follow him wherever he led me. We might say, meaning no disrespect to Lenin, that Fidel Castro is the Lenin of the Americas. He is internationally recognized as one of the great heroes of the world.

I'm not afraid to say that even now some people in the Party, for example Carlos Rafael Rodríguez,[103] who came from the masses, speak with more style than Fidel. But Fidel is a real statesman. He can discuss anything, even science, like an expert. He also knows about the workers'

103. A leader of the old Cuban Communist Party (PSP) and former Minister for Economic, Technical, and Scientific Coordination, Rodríguez is now a member of the Party's Political Bureau and Deputy Prime Minister for Foreign Affairs.

real problems, so that one thinks, "He might have been born a carpenter, a mason, or in any other trade."

Fidel's parents were landowners and he was brought up as a Catholic. But none of those things matter. After all, the Christian religion has communist roots. The Bible and all Catholic books present Christ as a redeemer of humanity, and communism is a way of redeeming humanity. Nothing could be clearer. Communism takes no account of differences in color or creed, only in the development of work. What can we think except that communists are the true representatives of Christianity?

The Revolution has overcome the problem of racial discrimination. Martí said, "More than white, or black or mulatto, a man is a man." Even as a child I realized the truth in this saying. So I've always comforted myself with the symbol for Cuban independence, which is two clasped hands, the white hand of Martí and the black one of Maceo. I'm in love with the Revolution for its stand on racial discrimination. It moves me to see a white man joined together honestly with a black woman or a black man with a white woman, because I'm thinking of the future of my fatherland. We've overcome the problem of racism, probably because we've eliminated class distinctions and social prejudice.

I've never measured men by the color of their skins because I've known too many blacks who were sons-of-bitches. And look at Guiteras, a white man who never discriminated against blacks. He, like Mella, understood that all men are equal. As I see it, if a man is invested with right and reason, then he should have the courage to speak up and say what must be said.

Once I met a man who said to me, "You don't want the Americans here because you're a black!"

I just answered, "Well, maybe that's the reason," because I figured he was a hopeless case. Actually, I think that right now the blacks in the United States have the best opportunities they've ever had to solve their problems. And according to what I've read in the papers, they're making good use of it. Of course the United States hasn't overcome all of its racial problems. I've read about a number of incidents showing race prejudice in the United States, such as the time a busload of white and black women stopped at some public restrooms with a sign that said, "Whites Only." Black women had to relieve themselves outdoors in the middle of a park.

That sort of thing disgusts me. I can imagine how terrible it would be if in my own native land I couldn't sit down in a restaurant. Discrimination is something I just can't stand. I don't believe a black is inferior to anybody; at least, I've never in my life seen a white man any better than I am.

The Revolution has had its problems. When the Americans announced they were eliminating our sugar quota in 1960, they thought that they'd make us Cubans hungrier and poorer than ever. But what happened? Our government said, "All right, we'll take care of that," and they took over the sugar mills. I was glad because that little American game of paying what they pleased had come to an end. And when the Americans said they wouldn't refine Soviet petroleum, the government intervened and took over the refineries too. I was very happy about that because it gave us more opportunity to develop our industries.[104]

When we broke relations with the United States I felt great satisfaction, but also great nervous tension.[105] Martí had said we should have relationships not with only one country but with all the countries of the world. So I was worried. "What will happen to us now?" I wondered. "If we break off commercial relations with the United States, where are we going to get commodities? With the influence they have over Latin America, what country will trade with us?" Our agriculture was so poor I feared we'd go hungry.

Then the Yankees said, "Let's pressure all the European countries into blockading Cuba." And they used their organization, NATO, to do it. But trade is something else again. When the English wanted to sell us the Leylands[106] and the Yankees opposed any trade with Cuba, the English said, "We'll sell to anybody who wants to buy from us."

The Yankees are used to saying, "We give the orders and you shut up and obey." But it doesn't work; you can't pressure people too much. I saw every door open to us when we resumed diplomatic relations with the Soviet Union. They offered to buy all the sugar we could produce. Sugar is our main source of income so with that offer we could look forward to our country's progress.

The October crisis, when the Americans demanded that Russia take back the missiles she'd placed here, was one more instance of the pressure America continues to exert on us. I wondered why Russia had sent them in the first place. But now I ask myself whether all those missiles were really taken away? Since we know we're surrounded by enemies, how could we be so careless as to strip ourselves of all our defenses? And

104. In June, 1960, Castro nationalized U.S.-owned refineries after they refused his order to refine petroleum from the Soviet Union. This order came after the U.S. Congress approved an administration-backed bill authorizing President Eisenhower to cut or eliminate the quota on sugar imported from Cuba. In July Eisenhower signed the sugar-quota bill and issued an order refusing purchase of the 700,000 tons of sugar remaining in the 1960 sugar quota. In August Castro began nationalizing U.S.-owned sugar mills. The United States increased its economic sanctions by imposing a partial embargo on trade with Cuba in October, 1960, and a total embargo in April, 1961.

105. On January 3, 1961, the *United States* broke off relations.

106. A British-made bus. Cuba bought approximately 1,000 of these buses between 1959 and 1969.

if we'd kept some, would we say so? Maybe, when the moment comes, we'll say, "Let's take them by surprise," and we'll push a button to lift up a piece of land with houses on it, revealing the threatening mouths of our weapons. We took exactly the right attitude during the crisis to prevent a world war, but we must keep our defenses ready at all times. We're living on a volcano, and when a volcano erupts, the lava flows on every side.

When Kennedy was elected, many Cubans hoped that the United States' aggression was at an end. We saw Kennedy as a President who was concerned with the problems of Latin America as well as those of his own country. He believed it was better to have good relations with other countries than to subjugate them. But his attitude didn't coincide with the capitalists' interests so they said, "Let's eliminate him to put an end to his policies."

Kennedy's death is still speculated about in Cuba. How can anybody believe that a President, surrounded by bodyguards, could have been killed without anybody knowing who did it? After all, very few Presidents of the United States have been assassinated. That's because they're elected by the majority of the people. They're liked by most of the people and they give them hope of better things. So Kennedy's murder was a political conspiracy because there are people who put self-interest above the interests of their fatherland.

The men responsible blamed Lee Harvey Oswald because he'd been seen up on a roof, shooting. Then, to keep all the rest in the dark, they eliminated him. Ruby said he shot Oswald because he was sentimental and felt great affection for Kennedy. But it turned out Ruby was Oswald's accomplice, so then they killed Ruby. Strangely enough, he fell ill of cancer and a few days later disappeared without making any further statements. And that was the end of the Kennedy case.

That sort of thing will never happen to Fidel, though he's been watched and followed by men waiting for an opportunity to kill him. Anyone who does that will be living on borrowed time unless he can disguise himself as an invisible man at the moment of the assassination.

I don't know whether I'm right or not, but I blame the United States and other capitalist countries for the discord between Russia and China. It is U.S. policy to weaken the socialist countries by provoking clashes between them. Even Cuba had a crisis with the Chinese, and when we made a detailed study to find out where and why the problem arose, we discovered that the United States was responsible.

Just look at the way America is hovering over Asia, trying to do away with its great potential by destroying all of Asia's socialist movements and sowing discord between India and China. The only reason the United States wants to take over Vietnam is to destroy the socialist advance in Asia. I don't know whether the United States has always been this way, but at the moment it's run by a mere twenty-seven families. The moral and political stature of its average citizens goes unrecognized. American mothers protested against having their sons killed in Vietnam, and senators have also protested, but the American government won't listen, so the rest of us must do what we can to avoid a third world war.

I figure by now, 1970, we should be developing our ideas for the sake of the collective purpose. Then we can feel happy. We've made great strides toward solving the housing problem. But the process is slow because we're backward, very backward, especially regarding education. Why? Because the government gives priority to the production of the 10 million.

I can't get the sugar-cane problem out of my head. I'm old, but I want to cut at least one stalk of cane and say, "I cut this myself. Now I've earned the right to drink a glass of water with sugar in it." I'm kidding of course, but the truth is, I'd like to help.

It was a sad day when Fidel told us we wouldn't make the 10 million.[107] It didn't take a psychologist to notice he was tense and nervous. The words came like a cry from his heart. He hated to discourage the people and give them cause to mistrust him. At first I thought it was a ruse to confuse the United States because he feared they'd never allow us to achieve our goal. They might increase their sabotage—or even declare war. I wished I could turn into a helicopter with a couple of machine guns on board, so I could kill all our enemies.

After all the trouble the Cuban people went to, to harvest those 10 million, the news really depressed me. Even Fidel had spent a month cutting cane, sacrificing himself, thinking of his family, and so on. How many mothers have left their children, a piece of their hearts, so that they could help attain the goal? They were so happy when they came back, talking of all they had done! And how many fathers left their families to contribute to the harvest? There were no institutions, no work centers, that didn't mobilize.

How can we explain the harvest failure to the children? I've heard some of them ask, "Why don't they shoot or hang the people in charge of this?" But I've heard others say, "*Papá* said we couldn't make it no matter how many people kept saying '*Van, van, van!*'"[108] Imagine school children hearing their own fathers say such a thing! Because of his father's attitude, that child will go through life with a negative idea in his very bloodstream!

Right after Fidel's speech, I could have filled a bucket with my tears. But then I thought about it. "He must be kidding," I decided. "He's

107. The announcement was made by Castro in a speech on May 19, 1970.
108. In this context *van* means "We will make it!" (that is, the 10-million-ton sugar-harvest goal).

simply trying to rouse us to greater efforts, to make the people shout back to him, *"Van, van, van!"*

Maybe it's all an illusion or a fantasy I've created for myself. But after having heard certain explanations, I still say we'll harvest those 10 million tons in spite of everything. The way I see it, solving the problem of the sugar harvest will mean the termination of the slavery system imposed on the whole world. If we struggle for the sake of our family, we're doing it for the sake of every family in Cuba. We're defending the fatherland. You can't work only for a part and forget the whole.

Not long ago the government decided since we wouldn't solve our problems on the basis of a monoculture, we must diversify our agriculture and work with coffee, tobacco, and citrus fruits too. We must also speed up our industrial development so we can feel entirely responsible for our economy. If Cuba wasn't such an underdeveloped country, we could be producing all sorts of things instead of importing them. But we need to import machines to develop industrially, and the price of acquiring those is the contract for sugar. At the moment, sugar is all we have to pay for our imports.

When the government first decided to make a 4 percent discount in wages to help finance the construction of certain buildings and work centers,[109] some people didn't think that was right. "What, take 4 percent out of my wages as long as I live? How am I going to manage?" They simply didn't understand. Study circles were started to explain things like that.[110] But then those people stayed away from work and excused themselves, saying, "But I'm studying. I can't be expected to study and work at the same time!"

Other people claim that money is being lost because of the hours spent doing volunteer work. Can't they see they're enjoying things now that they never had before? Haven't they noticed the workers' cafeterias where for 50 *centavos* they can get a nourishing meal? Aren't they proud to see their children being educated and even fed in many schools? Can't those people remember the time when many children were unable to go to school because their parents couldn't afford to pay 10 *pesos* for clothes

109. The Four Percent Voluntary Contribution for Industrialization was enacted into law on March 18, 1960. This amount was withheld from the wages and salaries of workers who did not refuse, in writing, to participate. According to the Cuban Economic Research Project: "The contribution was considered a loan or an investment on the part of the worker," and at the end of each year he or she was to receive a "People's Saving Certificate." (*A Study on Cuba,* pp. 688–89.) In reality, of course, the deduction was the same as a tax on earnings.

110. Study circles are organized by the Political Education Fronts of the Committees for Defense of the Revolution, which have official responsibility for the Marxist education of the public. These study circles often are led by CDR cadre trained at the Party's Schools for Revolutionary Instruction.

and shoes? Now children wear uniforms and are decently clothed, as well as being educated and fed.

And how about medicines? In the old days you had to pay 3 or 4 *pesos* just for an X-ray and then you had to pay for the medicines and all sorts of other things. Now, at a polyclinic they examine you thoroughly for free. What more could people want? And what makes all those benefits possible if not the efforts of the Cuban workers? But they don't understand. That's their trouble, ignorance.

Of course things have been bad. We're living through a bitter time here in Cuba. But we don't care how little we eat because we're ready for anything. Life is sweet, yes, but it's even sweeter if you really live it. It's better to stand up for what you believe in than to have mere comfort at the cost of fear and anxiety.

Workers are better off now even if some people don't want to admit it. It's true that formerly some workers had weeks when they earned 100 or 200 *pesos* but they had to work much harder and in much worse conditions. Besides, money's worth more now because prices are regulated.

I don't mind using a ration book. After all, I was one of the pioneers in protesting profiteering and private enterprise. As soon as there's an abundance of things and the people are politically educated, we can end rationing. Right now, if we were free to buy all we wanted, the counter-revolutionaries would deliberately buy up everything they could. And the results would be disastrous! The workers who really need those products wouldn't be able to get them. Besides, we must consider the effect the Cuban Revolution is having on imperialist countries, and the example we're setting for the world.

It can't be said that everybody in Havana is a revolutionary, as it can't be said that all those against the Revolution are actively fighting it. Some of them are efficient workers even though they disagree with the system. But that's why Cuba is not ready to end rationing or to hold elections.

It's true other socialist countries have elections, but Cuba can't at present because we're in the midst of a revolutionary process.[111] Frankly, until Cuba becomes mature as a country and develops a true revolutionary conscience, until the Cuban people understand the causes of the Revolution and why so many sacrifices have been made, we must trust in our leaders.

111. Cuba's first elections in fifteen years were held in Matanzas Province in 1974, as the preliminary stage in implementing *Poder Popular* (People's Power), a new system of administrative-legislative assemblies. All citizens sixteen years of age and older, with the exception of prisoners, applicants for emigration, and candidates in the 1958 elections, were eligible to vote. One candidate for the post of delegate to district-level representative assemblies was nominated in meetings held in each base area, or neighborhood, in an electoral district. In Matanzas, 1,079 delegates were elected by secret ballot from among 4,712 candidates. The delegates to the district assemblies then chose from among themselves delegates to regional and provincial assemblies. (*Cuba Review*, Dec., 1974, pp. 10–15.)

Before we draw up a constitution, our study circles must teach people the value and duties of each individual.[112] When every Cuban knows these things and is able to evaluate our economic system, the study circles should make a list of what they consider beneficial to the Revolution and present it to the leader of the Party. That way all of Cuba can reach an understanding and we'll be ready to draw up a constitution and hold elections. And whom shall we elect? Only the best. There'll be no cheap politics for us!

Don't get the idea that I want to force anybody to love the Revolution. I believe everyone has a right to his own opinion. If a guy says, "I don't like it," I figure it's his problem.

As for me, I'm completely in love with this Revolution. In love, in love, in love! I'd do anything for it. *Viva la Revolución!*

112. A commission was appointed in late 1974 to draft a new constitution for the Republic. The draft was finished in February, 1975, and the full text, in English, appeared in *Granma Weekly Review,* Apr. 20, 1975, pp. 7–10. The new Constitution received overwhelming endorsement (97.7 percent, 5,473,534 of 5,602,973 votes cast) in a referendum held on February 15, 1976. (*Granma Weekly Review,* Feb. 29, 1976, p. 1.)

PART II

Alfredo Barrera Lordi

Chapter One

Practically an Outcast

MY CHILDHOOD WAS FULL of vicissitudes. All *papá*'s effort and care were for us, but he could barely stretch his money to cover our needs. With eight children to feed he could never manage to keep his head above water. We ate—there was always something, if only soup with rice and a bit of meat—but *mamá* practiced the strictest economy and we children had to share whatever there was. We were clean, too, although it was quite an undertaking to bathe. *Mamá* was a stickler for cleanliness and was forever mending, washing, and ironing our scanty supply of clothing so we'd look neat and respectable. We didn't, though, because most of the time we played barefoot in the streets.

When I was about seven I had a serious accident. Near our house in Las Yaguas there was a stone quarry where I used to play with a group of kids. We each had a sled made of the *yaguas* that *papá* sold, and we would slide on them down the slopes around the quarry.

One day, as the other kids watched, they saw me disappear over the edge of the quarry. They ran home yelling, "He's dead, he's dead. Alfredo got killed." I wasn't dead, but *mamá* didn't expect me to live, and she suffered terribly during the twenty-nine days that I lay unconscious. They called me the "living corpse." According to *mamá*, if the doctor hadn't gone to endless trouble to extract a blood clot from my brain, I would have died. What a thing to happen to a seven-year-old boy! And then all that time I had to spend in a hospital. . . . The truth is that my childhood memories are bitter, far too bitter.

Alfredo Barrera was interviewed seven times by Oscar Lewis and twice by the Cuban assistant Enrique Vignier Mesa, totaling 779 transcribed pages. There were 185 additional pages from seven interviews by Lewis with Barrera's mother, two sisters, and one half-sister. Excerpts from his mother's and elder half-sister's material appear in Barrera's story. Also interviewed by Oscar Lewis and Maida Donate were the grandfather of Barrera's first wife, a brother-in-law, a niece, and his mother's first husband. Barrera's Aunt Constancia was interviewed three times by Oscar Lewis and Enrique Vignier, and his second wife, Esperanza Llera, was briefly interviewed by Nisia Aguero Benítez.

The *reparto* Las Yaguas, where we lived, was a real slum. Our house had a dirt floor and was one of a whole row of connecting houses. Nearly everyone in Las Yaguas was very poor and people lived as many as nine or ten in one house. Some families were downright filthy. It's disgusting really. Many houses were infected with bedbugs because the house walls were built one against another. The bedbugs would travel from the dirty houses to the clean ones. To be frank, bedbugs were the most common insect in Las Yaguas.

Later *papá* had a house with cement floors. There he had a set of living-room furniture consisting of a table, four stools, and two cane rockers. We also had a cabinet for the china and glasses, with an altar on top where *mamá* burned candles before saints' images. She had a special devotion to the *Virgen de la Caridad del Cobre* and to St. Lazarus. Lots of pretty pictures hung in the parlor and there were a few plaster ornaments set around, too.

The first bedroom belonged to us boys. It had three beds, each with its own mattress. It also had a large chest of drawers, a small wardrobe, and two small tables. In the old lady's room there was an old-fashioned bed trimmed with bronze balls, a big wardrobe, a chifforobe, a large mirror, and a night stand where *mamá* kept photographs of dead relatives.

There was very little in the kitchen—just a rustic table that the old man had made to hold the charcoal stove and the clay casseroles used for cooking. There was no refrigerator, only a small icebox, but Pedro, the iceman, came by every day so we had plenty of ice. We had electricity; we used kerosene lamps only when the electricity failed during hurricanes.

Papá was a hard worker and was always on the go, finding work to do. In Las Yaguas he had a small business selling housebuilding materials. He sold *yaguas* at the rate of 6 *centavos* per dozen for the short ones and 12 *centavos* for long ones. *Papá* did quite well because he never had to pay for the *yaguas*. They were used to wrap the bundles of tobacco that came from La Corona cigar factory and he was paid to cart them away. All those discards he later sold. He had a monopoly because he was the only one who had a cart to transport them from the factory. He also sold sheaves of forty or fifty 1½-inch laths that he got from the Díaz brothers, who owned a lumberyard. *Papá* was well acquainted with them and they gave him the laths and hooks and all sorts of discards. Then, too, he collected 5-gallon oil cans that he cut open, flattened, and sold for roofing.

Papá was elected mayor of Las Yaguas by the few, the very few, honest people there. They wanted him because he provided practically all the housebuilding materials used in the *reparto*. Now I want to make it clear that when he was mayor he never took bribes, from either the businessmen or the government. Not even the police could give him orders.

If they asked him for somebody's address, he'd give it to them because he knew the place, all the street numbers and everything, but he never received any monetary help for his services.

As mayor, *papá* had a lot of problems trying to deal with unsavory characters. There were some to whom he simply turned a blind eye, but there were others he couldn't cover up under any circumstances. His biggest problem was with the police. Now *papá* was usually on good terms with the police department—one of his good friends was a policeman named Aranal—but there were González and two other men *papá* had crossed, and that was his undoing.

These three policemen wanted to unjustly accuse two of our neighbors of selling marijuana. One of those accused gentlemen, Lino Jiménez, was a captain and a veteran of the War of Independence. I knew him personally and I can testify that he hardly went out of his house at all and didn't mix with corrupt characters. The other man they accused was Ciro Flores. He owned a small stand at the crossroads in front of Joaquín's grocery store. The police accused him of having set up the stand as a cover for his dealings in marijuana. There wasn't one word of truth in the accusation. For one thing, marijuana wasn't popular then as it is now, and it was practically unheard of in the *reparto*.

But Flores was a minister of the Jehovah's Witnesses and the police didn't want anything like that around there. They asked *papá* to plant some marijuana cigarettes in Ciro's and Lino's homes, that is, they wanted to use him as a stooge and have him plant false evidence so they could kick those two honorable men out of the neighborhood. How could anybody play a dirty trick like that?

Papá refused to fall in with the plans. He said it was unjust and abusive, and he was too much of a man to take part in it. He told the three of them, "First and foremost, I'm here to serve this neighborhood. I don't have to turn anybody over to the police nor get involved in such twisted and tangled doings."

The next night the policeman González sent a boy to *papá*'s house with the message that *papá* was to meet him at the iron bridge. My old man had more courage than brains so he went, thinking he would meet only González. But González had brought the two other men along and they beat up *papá* so brutally they practically killed him.

My father was never a boxer and he looked rather weak. He was more or less my height and skinny like me, but he had great strength in his hands. If there had been only one that night, the attacker wouldn't have lived to tell the story.

As long as *papá* was laid up *mamá* took in laundry, and my aunts sent a large box of groceries every week. Everything we ate during *papá*'s illness came from my aunt's house. As soon as he was up and about, *papá* got a job as a driver in a trucking agency. He was paid by the job and worked only when he had a load of furniture to move. He didn't earn much, 4 or 5 *pesos* for each trip, but he couldn't get any other job.

My *papá*, Alfredo Barrera, whom I was named after, was my mother's second husband. She was married first to Rafael Valverde and bore him a daughter, my sister Anita. *Mamá* met Rafael because he used to visit her parents when they lived on a farm near San José de las Lajas outside Havana.

Mamá has never told me much about her parents, which is strange considering how little reserve she has shown over things she'd have done better to have been silent about. Her father, Leonardo, was born in Sicily but he immigrated to New York when he was quite young. He had brothers there who owned a jewelry business. *Mamá*'s mother's family lived in New York and was very well off. My grandparents met and fell in love and decided to get married. Then they came to Cuba and settled in Havana.

Grandfather was a sculptor and an engineer. He worked in Havana and in the central region and also on the model penitentiary on the Isle of Pines. My mother says that her father was just a plasterer. Well, it's not that I want to boast of great connections. Why should I boast about Grandfather Leonardo? He never did anything for me. But as I see it, anyone who takes a bit of plaster and molds it into an ornament for a building deserves to be called a sculptor. And he was well paid. I've seen many of his works—very pretty they were—but they have all disappeared, like his good tools. That's one thing I wanted, his set of tools, but I couldn't manage to get them. He also had a phenomenal set of paintbrushes, big ones, because between jobs he did housepainting for the rich.

Once, when Grandfather worked on La Purísima Concepción Hospital, he offered my *papá* Alfredo a job as his helper, but that brought a lot of problems. My grandfather had hired one of his sons, Uncle Genaro, to work on the same job, and when it came to getting paid, Grandfather gave all the credit to Genaro and cheated *papá* out of his pay. That caused a lot of bitterness in my family. I was only a boy then, but I saw clearly from the first that when you do business with a relative you always come out the loser. And I was right.

Alfredo Carlos, a son of *papá*'s first marriage, beat up Genaro and smashed his face in with some cans of condensed milk, but it made no difference—my *papá* was still the loser. He got only 65 *pesos* from Leonardo, and by that time *papá* owed practically all of it in debts he had accumulated. Afterward he admitted to me, "You were right about working for relatives."

I had problems with Leonardo myself. He was always boasting and I never could stand a braggart. One day he was in the grocery store, drinking with a bunch of his Sicilian friends. I had learned a few words of Italian from my *mamá* and I was standing there, listening quietly, smoking a cigar. I was seventeen or eighteen at the time and had been on my own for years. The old man was old-fashioned in his ways and thought no youth should smoke in front of his elders, and he had the gall to slap the cigar from my lips. "Hey, snotnose," he said, "how dare you smoke in front of your grandfather!"

That's when the trouble started, because I was no longer a child. What right had a man to whom I owed not so much as one can of milk to take such liberties with me? He simply wanted to show off before his friends by that bit of rudeness. So when he slapped me I slapped him back. "You're no grandfather of mine," I said. "From the day of my birth to this, you have done nothing for me. All your life you have spent your money on drink."

Those were my very words. In my opinion he didn't care for me, his grandson, and furthermore, he didn't love his wife and children either. All I know about my departed grandfather is bad. He was, as we say, "the light in the street and the darkness at home."

At one point Grandfather's economic position was quite good. He got to own houses in Havana and was comfortably well off. *Mamá* now says that Grandfather never earned more than 4 to 6 *pesos* a day, but it was she who made up that story about her father being rich, not me. She was the one who wanted to put on airs. *I* know I come from poor folk. If anybody has delusions of grandeur, it's my old lady.

Well, whether he was rich or not, Grandfather was a gambler and a drunkard. His way of life was such that he had to fail, because when you earn 100 *pesos* you can't go ahead and squander 200. Eventually he ruined himself. He fell into a bad spell and couldn't find work. There was a lot of unemployment in those days. Finally, Grandfather was evicted from his house in San José de las Lajas and he moved to Las Yaguas. What irony that a man of my grandfather's accomplishments should have wound up in such a place! It was he who showed my *mamá* the way there. My grandmother Angela had to take in laundry to support the family, and *mamá* had to work too.

Mamá was sixteen or seventeen and Rafael Valverde about twenty-three when they met and fell in love. They were married by a judge, not in a church. Analyzing that "love" after all these years, I believe *mamá* accepted Rafael because of her family's poverty and my grandfather's waywardness. *Mamá* worked very hard as a girl and you know the saying, "Necessity makes you bear twins." But as it turned out, *mamá* was a lot worse off with her husband.

Rafael worked as a farmhand in San José de las Lajas, on a farm called La Roca. He was in charge of the cows and *mamá* looked after the hogs and chickens. Every morning she helped milk the cows, then he sold the milk, pulling it in a little two-wheeled cart called a "spider." He didn't bring in much money so *mamá* took in laundry to help out.

Mamá and Rafael didn't get along well and the fights between them were just terrible. *Mamá* always told my sisters, "Hunger and poverty a woman can put up with, but blows never!" If a man is badly off it's quite right that his wife should help him out by taking in laundry or doing any honest kind of work, but if on top of that her husband should beat her . . . that's not right.

I think the main source of the trouble was that Rafael had another woman. I have an idea that when he fell for this woman, *mamá* became an obstacle to him. *Mamá* was pregnant and one day when they were fighting Rafael kicked her. She had to have a cesarean section and her child was born dead. That was the immediate cause of their separation. *Mamá* took my sister Anita, who was just eight months old, and went back home to my grandparents.

Rafael stayed on in San José de las Lajas for many years and there never was any contact between us. The one time I saw him I was almost eleven. I was with Anita, who was by then a well-grown girl of thirteen or fourteen, when a strange man went up to her and started talking to her. He was tall, dark, and heavily built. I saw him kiss her and she already a señorita! "Anita, who was that man who kissed you?" I asked.

"Why, that's *papá*," she answered. I think he still goes to visit her, but I never saw him again.

Mamá stayed with my grandparents for six or seven months. Then, after they moved to Las Yaguas, she met my *papá*, Alfredo Barrera, and they got together. His parents were both dead by then. All I know about them is that his father and his brothers worked at the slaughterhouse at the old junction of the roads to Regla and San José de las Lajas.

Alfredo's first wife was a *mulata* called Sara Ubeda. According to him, they broke up because Sara got too involved in spiritist rites and all that stuff. Alfredo was an atheist and had no patience with any kind of religion. "The life of the living, that's what's real and vital. That's the only thing that interests me," he always said. "All I care about is what I can do and produce. That's the only truth. All the rest is fantasy."

He left his wife because one day she cut off a lock of his hair, wrapped it in colored thread, sprinkled it with a red powder, and wished evil on him through her witchcraft. It must have scared *papá* because he began to suffer from strange afflictions. For instance, he'd get terrible headaches that would start exactly at noon.

Finally, one day he said, "I'll show you how I'm going to break that woman's curse." He went to her house and smashed a lot of saints' images and bits of wood and iron she kept in an iron pot. After that his headaches stopped, but it seems to me that it was his obsession with the whole thing that gave him the headaches in the first place.

My mother's father disapproved of Alfredo because he was a mulatto. He had what we call "good" hair, because it's straight, but my grandfather didn't like his daughter taking up with a half-breed. That was the long and short of it. That explains why he never helped *mamá* or us, his grandchildren, even after his economic position improved. If a man has thousands of *pesos* put away in a bank, what is his duty as a father? As I see it, it is to give the best he has to his children. He saw how my mother went through twenty vicissitudes and suffered twenty needs in order to raise us, but he didn't help her. If a man owns several cottages and disapproves of the place where his daughter lives, his duty as a father is to say, "Well, since I don't want to see my daughter living in Las Yaguas, I'll fix up one of my cottages and give it to her." But he didn't. Not he! He rented it out and never gave a thing to his children.

I was born on September 9, 1932. After me, *mamá* had seven more children: Adela, Angela, Berta, Andrés, José, Manuela, and Celia. Then she bore another one, Susana, who has another father. So that's the way it is.

Mamá never gave me much affection. For a long while my sister Anita got the most warmth and affection from *mamá*. Then when my brother Andrés was born, he became the child of her eyes. After he grew up he still remained the favorite, probably because he let *mamá* rule him. *Mamá* and I have always fought because she could never dominate me. She saw things her way and I saw them my way. After Andrés, *mamá*'s favorites were Berta and José. It was natural she should spoil them more because they were the youngest. I wasn't jealous. I was awfully fond of them myself, but I felt practically an outcast at home.

When I was about eleven I had this quarrel with *mamá* about my birth. *Mamá* claims that at the time I was born she was living in Las Yaguas with my *papá,* Alfredo Barrera, and it's true that in the registry of births I appear as having been born there. But after this quarrel I stopped believing it.

It was the Day of the Three Kings and all my brothers and sisters received toys, but as I was the eldest I got nothing. I asked *mamá* why the others had presents and I didn't; wasn't I her son too?

She said, "No, you aren't my son nor his."

Said I, "Then I guess you must have picked me out of the garbage?"

"That's right," she said. "I picked you out of the garbage can."

I don't know whether she was joking or telling the truth, or if she just wanted to hurt me, but I've never forgotten her words and never will. Because after that, I, being an ignorant boy, believed I wasn't Alfredo's son. God only knows what she meant but she killed a lot of the love in my heart for her. For a long while I wouldn't even look her in the face. I swallowed that bitter pill and kept my sorrow locked inside me. The hurt festered, but even if it killed me I couldn't ask her to explain why she said that. I'll have to die feeling all the bitterness without ever knowing whether Alfredo Barrera was really my father or not. I never dared ask him or my *mamá* if they were my true parents. It would have shown a terrible lack of respect.

My sister Angelita told me that *mamá* said it only because she was annoyed with me and that I should never have taken it seriously. Well, maybe so, but the way *mamá* treated me was no passing annoyance. There were other things she said to make me doubt that Alfredo was my father. *Mamá* used to say that Anita and I were blood brother and sister. Well, what was I supposed to make of that? Didn't it mean that Anita's father was my father also?

If I have a problem it's *mamá*'s fault. She created it for me. I began to feel estranged from Alfredo. I noticed how different I looked from him in the nose, the eyebrows, the eyes. His eyes were black, mine were gray. His nose was rather thin, but there was something about his features that showed his colored ancestry. His hair was straight but it was bad because it was coarse. I'd look at Alfredo Barrera and think, "From his color I can tell he's no kin of mine. I'm more like Rafael Valverde than like Alfredo."

I have only seen Rafael once in my whole life but I know that I resemble him in everything, not only physically but also in personality, except for his stinginess. I began to believe that Rafael Valverde was my true father and that I was born before *mamá* left him. The census which records my birth in Las Yaguas was taken when I was a few years old so it could, in fact, be possible that I was born in San José de las Lajas before *mamá* met Alfredo Barrera. After I'd analyzed all the possibilities I began to suspect that *mamá* had lied because she was trying to hide something. I don't want to gossip about *mamá* but the truth is she has behaved shamefully ever since she was a young girl.

Let me speak plainly. When a hero has a shady past, he tries his best to pretend he's some kind of saint. How? By talking a lot about his good deeds and hiding the bad. *Mamá* is always saying such things about herself which any one of her children can contradict, so I'm convinced that she must be trying to hide something pretty awful. I talked the whole thing over with my sisters years ago. They have doubts about *mamá* too, but unless she opens her heart to us we'll never know what's true and what isn't. Maybe on her deathbed she'll set things straight.

In spite of all my doubts about my birth, I loved Alfredo Barrera with a son's love. I never rejected him as a father and Alfredo was very attached to me. I had seen how some of my friends were mistreated by their stepfathers and made to work hard, but Alfredo Barrera didn't treat me roughly or exploit me. On the contrary, whatever he got was for me. He was always good to me and I never lacked affection from him. I was puzzled by the contradiction and would wonder, "If I'm not his son, why is he so fond of me?"

SEÑORA LORDI:

Alfredo is my eldest son. He was named after his father, but we call him Fredo for short.

Fredo had an accident when he was five years old. I told him not to slide from the top of the hill, and what did he do? He went right to the top of the hill and slid down on a palm leaf and fell into the stone quarry which was behind my house. I saw him hurtling down and tried to run and catch hold of him but I couldn't, so I stood out in the middle of the street and prayed, "*Ay*, my Mother of Regla, shelter him with your cloak so he won't get killed!" And would you believe it? He didn't fracture even one little rib after falling from such a height onto stones *this* big!

After Fredo got out of the hospital, I took him to the church at Regla and presented him to the Virgin there. Then I had a vigil at my house with soft drinks and candy for the kids. Fredo hasn't had a serious illness since. I don't know whether he's a son of Yemayá; all I can say is that she heard my plea and saved him. He's been half crazy ever since, but at least he lived.

Fredo will tell you one thing today and exactly the opposite tomorrow. He isn't all there. He's always jittery, and, frankly, he's crazy. I've been told he's convinced that he's the son of my first husband, Rafael Valverde, and that he was born in the same hospital as Anita. Imagine!

My *papá* was a mason and a plasterer. He worked well and did some very pretty facade work. He earned 4 *pesos* a day as a mason and on plastering jobs he earned 6 *pesos* a day. But *papá* was a drinker and money slipped through his fingers, so *mamá* had to help out by sewing in a factory. Most of my childhood memories are of helping *mamá*. She sewed shirts and I made the buttonholes and sewed on the buttons.

I don't remember ever seeing my parents quarrel. There was no suffering in *mamá*'s life. What was there to make her unhappy? Only *papá* could have done that, by making a fool of himself over another woman, because that's the kind of thing that really makes a woman suffer. But *papá* was always home and all he ever earned was for his family. *Mamá* didn't have a taste for fiestas and dances, she was a real homebody, but there was nothing dour about her, she was always gay and happy. She never complained. She was a kind, simple woman, a "soul of God" as we say, and a loving mother to me. She was a good, good woman.

Mamá raised me modestly, as she'd been raised. I went to a private school that I liked real well. When I was eleven I was sent to a public school, where I studied until I was thirteen. My evenings were spent at home, helping with the housework, sewing, embroidering.

I went to church on Sundays and to catechism classes on Saturdays. And I made my First Communion at a little church in Suárez. *Mamá* didn't inculcate her religion in me, I simply saw what she did and followed her example. She always went to church and had a large St. Lazarus who was the saint of her devotion. In her generation everybody believed in those things. Most people still believe today.

My *papá* was not a believer. I mean, he never spoke of religion for good or ill, but he didn't interfere with *mamá*'s lighting candles or setting flowers before her saints.

When Rafael and I were sweethearts, our courtship was spent beside *mamá*, she busy at her sewing machine and I attaching buttons. Rafael had permission to visit me on Sundays and he'd sit beside us as we worked. *Papá* was a very strict man. He never allowed us to speak to each other alone or to sneak around behind his back.

Rafael went alone to ask for my hand in marriage. *Papá* gave his consent and we were married by the justice of the peace in Regla when I was fifteen. After the ceremony we returned home. We didn't have a wedding fiesta. Who could afford fiestas in those days?

Rafael went to work at the farm in the morning and returned home in the evening. At the farm he cleaned and weeded, looked after the cows, and helped bottle the milk. If I remember right, he earned 20 *pesos* a month, but they also gave him breakfast, lunch, and dinner. He wouldn't allow me to get a job.

New brooms sweep clean. At first everything was fine with us, but eight months after our daughter, Anita, was born, I had to leave Rafael. I learned that he had taken up with a little tramp. When I threw it up to him, he got mad. "It's a lie!" he swore. "I'm going to beat you up for that!"

"Don't you dare!" I yelled at him. "My father himself has never hit me, and if you dare lay a hand on me, I swear I'll kill you!" That's when I packed my things and left.

I left Rafael forty-two years ago and I haven't seen him since. We never got a divorce and I never asked him for 1 *centavo* for Anita or anything else. That's the way I am. I'll go so far and no further. After I break with somebody, I stay on my side of the fence and he on his. As long as he doesn't bother me, I don't bother him either.

I got a job at a drugstore in La Fernanda, cleaning, washing bottles, and so on. Times were hard then and my parents were forced to move. They couldn't pay rent for two months and the landlord filed a complaint against them. So we talked with a man who was giving away land in Las Yaguas. He gave us some and we built our little shack here in 1929. We covered the walls with *yaguas* that Alfredo gave us and thatched the roof with palm leaves. Most of the shacks in Las Yaguas were built like that.

When Alfredo told *mamá* he wanted me for a wife, she answered, "Argentina is a grown woman. It's up to her." So Alfredo and I got engaged. Six or seven months later, he bought a little house and several other things for me, and we lived together for almost twenty-five years, until he died. We never got married.

I bore thirteen children, twelve of them in Las Yaguas. Of the ten that lived, eight were Alfredo's. Besides my own children, I raised Lando, my *comadre*'s son, from the time he was twelve years old until he got married. In the old times one counted on one's *comadre* to raise one's children in case one died.

I liked having children and bore all that God sent me. I never had an abortion. I never had problems with my pregnancies, thank God. I ate lots of tubers, which are my favorites, so all my babies were born big and plump. When my pains started, I'd phone the emergency clinic and they'd send a car to my door. I already had the baby clothes out, water put on to boil, and everything ready. They'd stay with me until the baby was born, then they'd cut the umbilical cord and go. Three days later I'd take the baby to them to have his navel treated and a band put around his belly and that was that.

Two of my babies died of vomiting and diarrhea. Except for Adela, who got whooping cough as a result of asthma, the rest were healthy. Another baby died in the cyclone of 1944, when our house was blown down. My sister-in-law Dalia asked me to stay with her, but I said, "With so many kids, I'm not moving in on anyone." I made a kind of roof with what was left of the beds and covered it with canvas. At night we'd creep underneath to sleep. My other sister-in-law, Constancia, brought us food at night, and bread and milk for the children. And so we lived until we managed to rebuild the house.

My husband, Alfredo Barrera, was nicer than bread, softer than cotton—I never expect to see a better man anywhere as long as I live. He never mistreated me, never let me go hungry, gave me everything he could, and really looked after me. He was a poor man but a good one. He earned his living by moving people's things, cleaning the cigar factory, and when he had a chance to pour concrete for a building, he did that too. He had an agreement with the people at the cigar factory that he could keep anything he found while cleaning. So he'd pick up the *yaguas* they left on the floor, trim the leaves off the central stems, and sell them at 3 *kilos* a dozen. We both worked hard and we managed. I earned a little money by sewing and mending. Sometimes people gave me their old clothes and I'd cut them down to fit the kids.

Alfredo was the mayor of Las Yaguas and a good one, too. As mayor, he helped people whenever they had problems. If they had no money to move, he'd cart their furniture free. If somebody's roof leaked, he'd give them the *yaguas*. If somebody couldn't afford to buy milk for their baby, he'd get a can somewhere and give it to them. He got along well with our neighbors—we both did. I respected them and they respected me.

Alfredo was a mulatto. His sisters Dalia and Constancia, who are both little old women now, were darker. I like both of them. They were a big help to me with the younger children.

After I married Alfredo, *mamá*'s folks treated me distantly because they didn't like me living with a colored man. But *mamá* was no racist; she got along with everybody. My father, too, always liked Alfredo; they never had a quarrel. As for *mamá*'s family, they never set foot in my house after I married him. I haven't seen their faces since *mamá* died in 1934.

What a woman looks for in a husband is love, kindness, and support. Rafael, my white husband, didn't give me those. Alfredo Barrera, the black man, gave them in abundance. How could I help preferring Negroes to whites?

BARRERA:
You might say I had two mothers. One mother is the one who brought me into the world, and I must bear that in mind and love her always, but I owe even more love to the other, my Aunt Dalia, who is *papá*'s sister. Whenever we were hard up Dalia was the one we went to. She was our consolation, our "crying towel," in all our troubles. She never had a child so she was very fond of us, her brother's children. Aunt Dalia was more gentle and affectionate than *mamá*. She took endless trouble over me and gave me love and warmth. She played with me, worried about my problems, and didn't try to dominate me. If I did something wrong she would take me aside to reprove me; she understood that I hated to be scolded in front of other people.

Mamá had less polish. She was harsher, yet it would have been natural for *mamá*, a woman who had borne children, to be sweeter than my aunt. My aunt couldn't say, "This is a child of my womb," so she had every right to be bitter, but she had a better knowledge of life than *mamá*. She lived the reality of life, the good and the bad, not just her own fantasies. She had a kind of insensitivity though, and sometimes she'd get stubborn and not believe what anybody told her. She didn't use rude or obscene words, and unless you were very clearheaded you didn't even notice she had offended you, but she said offensive things all the same.

I'll tell you sincerely, because one must lay aside one's mask in order to tell the truth about some things, that my aunt and *mamá* didn't like each other any too well. You see, *mamá* would come to you with a knotted handkerchief full of money nestling between her tits, and say that unless you gave her a *peso* the kids would starve. When we were older she'd go to my aunts complaining that not one of her children condescended to help her. "I have to beg my bread from strangers because I dare not ask my own sons and daughters," she would say. "If I go to them, they slam the door in my face and refuse to help me."

She'd carry on, sniveling and begging. And if you gave her something, she was the kind who would go and slander you anyway. She spent her time criticizing. She was a real "ball of smoke," as we say.

My aunts had *mamá*'s number though; she couldn't go playing her little games with them. They'd set aside 10 or 12 *pesos* for her but never hand her the cash. Instead they'd spend the money on meat, rice, bread and such, and give her that, plus carfare. Aunt Dalia said, "If I give Tina a *peso*, she'll simply hide it and come around again, claiming she has nothing." That was *mamá*'s favorite ploy.

All that annoyed Aunt Dalia. So partly because of that and partly because Aunt Dalia was so fond of me, they didn't hit it off. There was a quarrel once, soon after my accident in the quarry, because I went to Aunt Dalia's house without permission. I just walked off without a word to *mamá* and she had to come and fetch me back.

Another conflict arose between my aunt and my mother when my *papá*, old Alfredo, started drinking. Originally he wasn't a heavy drinker—he only had a few drinks now and then with his friends, to be sociable, but then it happened that he got insomnia, especially during the rainy season. He had to get up and go to work at 4:00 A.M., but he couldn't fall asleep until it was almost time to get up. Then someone told him that four drinks of *aguardiente* would put him to sleep right away. Alfredo followed that advice but it didn't help. It only made his situation worse because he got into the habit of drinking. My aunts didn't know why their brother started drinking all of a sudden so they blamed *mamá* for it.

At my aunt's house the customs were different from those I was used to at home. At my aunt's we'd all sit in the parlor to listen to the radio in the evening. They would take their coffee and we'd exchange a few remarks. Often Uncle Armando would go out to play dominoes or see a ball game and he'd take me. Now and then he'd take me to a movie, too. I think it was a special privilege for me because he never took my cousins Basilio and Narciso.

Narciso was the son of *papá*'s other sister, Constancia, who lived with Aunt Dalia and Armando. My cousin Ursula and her son Basilio also lived with them. Narciso was two years older than I, Basilio was three years younger. Whenever I visited my aunts I couldn't help noticing how much better off my cousins were than me and my brothers and sisters. They had twenty times the comfort we had at home. They had good beds and there was a bathroom and a shower so they could live cleaner, more decorous lives. In Havana it's taken for granted that you should shower, put on clean clothes, and wear shoes, but it was very different out in Las Yaguas. There you were allowed to run around barefoot and dirty, rarely taking a bath unless you happened to have an unusually strict mother.

At my aunt's house I ate better than I ever did at home. I had three good meals a day there, and if I didn't feel like eating meat at dinner, my aunt would cook some fish or an egg. She spoiled me. For breakfast I always had some kind of fruit juice—mango, orange, whatever was available. Then there was bread and butter and *café con leche*. But after every meal Aunt Dalia would force a tablespoonful of Scott's Emulsion down my throat. I remember the name because of the picture on the label of a man with a codfish. It was tremendously nourishing and it cleaned out the organism because it had loads of calcium.

I got used to a good life at my aunt's house and after that I didn't get along so well at home. I was choosy about my food and I'd often not eat because I couldn't force down the messes *mamá* cooked. Aunt Dalia indulged my whims but *mamá* would let me go hungry rather than cook something different for me. She served what she called *isleño*[1] food, plain peas with no trimmings or kidney beans with macaroni, but I never touched such crap. She *knew* I didn't like it and I'd think, "*Concho,* the woman serves this stuff on purpose, so I won't eat."

At my aunt's house I could have a snack whenever I wanted to—bananas, cookies, candy. All day long I amused myself picking at this or that. But at *mamá*'s house that simply was not possible. I quite understand that *mamá* couldn't afford to be as lavish as my aunt, but she did prepare sweets and my brothers and sisters could take as many as they wanted. I'd hardly get any at all even if they'd remembered to leave some for me, so I always fought to be first in everything and to have the biggest and the best.

One day *papá* came home with a big chunk of coconut candy in a bag. I wanted the whole piece and I started to cry and protest because he was breaking it up to distribute among us kids. *Papá* said there wouldn't be enough to go around unless he broke it into pieces, but I insisted that he satisfy my whim. Finally he got so angry he said, "You want candy, *cabrón?* All right, take the candy!" And *bam!* he smashed the entire bagful on top of my head. What a scene that was! I remember it because at the time my hair was infested with lice and they had shaved my head.

I'm convinced that *mamá* did things deliberately to annoy me. For instance, I've never liked to have my clothes dumped in to be washed with my brothers' and sisters' clothing. Not because I thought they were dirty or anything like that, but just because it's something I was born with. So *mamá* would take care of their clothes and I'd see the others clean and neat while my things were still unwashed. "Oh, I didn't get around to washing your clothes," she'd say, and that was that. These are little things, but added all together they were more than just a passing annoyance.

1. The word *isleño* (islander) is used in Cuba to refer to people, or things, from the Canary Islands.

My Aunt Dalia was comfortably off because both she and my Uncle Armando worked. Armando was a master cigar-maker and worked as a foreman at the Partagás cigar factory. He earned very good money there, about 5,000 or 10,000 *pesos* a year. He had money in the bank. Aunt Dalia ran a business providing meals for the workers at La Corona. She used to work there herself as a tobacco stripper. She and the other women workers had to eat lunch in cheap restaurants and they continually suffered from stomach upsets. My aunt saw there was a market for good lunches and that's what inspired her to start her business. She and Aunt Constancia cooked the food at home and sent out meals at midday.

My aunts made quite a name for themselves and were asked to cook for various government officials, including a prosecutor for the Court of Havana. They never earned more money working for the big shots, though. Those rich people were stingy, not only about paying wages but about the amount they spent on food. Aunt Dalia charged only 45 *centavos* for each lunch. It wasn't much but some of the customers were very slow to pay. Some tobacco workers earned 120 or 130 *pesos* a week, working only Monday through Friday. Even so, I beat my brains to collect. Truly, I can't conceive how someone earning over 300 *pesos* a month could begrudge paying 45 *centavos* for a meal. But those people wanted to own this, that, and the other thing. They wanted to have more than anybody else. They borrowed from the loan sharks, who drove them crazy demanding payments, and they'd get into debt to eleven thousand virgins.

When I was older I tried to convince my aunt that a sixty-five-year-old woman shouldn't be on the go all the time, getting up at 4:00 A.M. to do the marketing, cooking all morning, and not resting one moment during the day. But she kept up her business for an endless number of years.

Papá had another sister, Silvia, who was really well off. Silvia's husband owned a business and had a lottery-ticket agency. They had money and could spare lots of clothes that their only daughter, Febe, had outgrown. On the Day of the Three Kings, Silvia would give Febe's old shoes and dresses to Aunt Constancia, who would make them up into a parcel to send home for my sisters. But I remember how she'd set aside the best things to give to the daughters of some friends of hers. I hated her for that. It wasn't right that she should give the best things to someone else.

I started school in Las Yaguas when I was eight. There was a janitor there who mistreated children. One day he hit out at a boy with a metal-edged ruler and scratched my eye instead. I had to be taken to the emergency clinic and the janitor stood trial and paid a fine.

After that I was afraid to go to the school so I was taken to a nun's school. There I was an outstanding student because those nuns were sweet and kind. Everything they taught me I learned quickly and well. I won lots of prizes for my work. They would reward us by taking us to the theater in the Colegio de Belén. I could have had a scholarship to that school, but I refused it. There was one nun called Sister María who, if I didn't learn my lesson well, would pinch me and say, "Look, my child, you should have done thus-and-so." I wouldn't have minded, but to be criticized in front of the others hurts a child's feelings and shames him. Analyzing this years later, I realized that being punished for not learning a lesson only makes a child look upon his teacher as an enemy and keeps him from learning altogether.

Every evening we used to play ball on the hill behind the school. Quite often the ball would fall inside the convent gardens and we'd have to climb up over the wall to get it. The convent gave classes at night for girls, and once, as I climbed the wall, I caught one of the priests pawing over a girl. Later I met a lady who had three daughters studying there, and the same priest "ate" all three of them.

When I saw the priests' goings-on I thought, "Why, what sons-of-bitches! And then they stand up in the pulpit and tell us that's a sin!" I thought all priests were shameless layabouts. That's why, even though I went to a nun's school, I grew up without a religion.

My folks were all Catholics and believed in God, and for all I know, God may have existed through all the centuries, but since I never saw Him, how can I believe? Some people say that one's spirit lives on when one dies. Well, I think that once the worms have eaten you, no spirit or anything else comes out of your body. If that sort of thing had been going on since the beginning of the world, we couldn't go down the street now without colliding with ghosts. What encounters! See what I mean? My own personal belief is that it is nature that gives me all I have and nature eventually takes it all away. Of course I respect people's right to have a different belief, but for myself I think there's nothing in the world like science, and cults are only cults.

I left the nun's school after first grade and went to the school in Las Yaguas. We went in two shifts, the girls in the morning, from 8:00 to 12:00, and the boys in the afternoon, from 12:00 to 4:00.

I began working for my aunt, delivering meals to her customers, when I was twelve years old. Every day I'd carry lunches to the canteen at La Corona factory. I made two trips, and each time I carried twenty-four pails slung from a long pole that I carried over my shoulder. I was on the go all the time, rising early so I could have breakfast with Aunt Dalia and go with her to the market. I washed empty lunch pails and ran errands for her so she spoiled me even more. But what was the result? My cousins Narciso and Basilio were jealous because I ate breakfast twice. I ate again with them at 9:00, see? As for me, I resented working the hardest and yet being the worst off.

I fought a lot with Narciso, but Basilio and I got along well. We went to school together and shared everything 50/50. Basilio was the princeling of my aunt's house, the spoiled darling, the favorite. The best of everything was for him. I never envied him though. On the contrary, the more he got, the more pleased I was, for his sake. I'd get mad sometimes, though, when they bought him something they had refused to buy for me. Then I'd go home to the *reparto* and stay there for months. I was never able to buy things for myself or give any money to *mamá* or my brothers and sisters. I felt helpless. I could neither solve my problems nor help my folks with theirs. I felt suffocated.

Basilio's father had died of lung sickness and Ursula was always afraid Basilio might catch it too. She seemed to be jealous of Narciso and me because we never got sick. Basilio did have a fragile constitution and build, but I never knew him to really be sick. Even so, Ursula coddled and fussed over him and I honestly think he pretended to be sick in order to get all those privileges.

Another thing I disliked about Basilio was the mushy way he acted with his mother. There's such a thing as a son's being *too* affectionate with his *mamá*. Maybe a mother will kiss her son once or twice to say goodbye when he sets off on a trip for several months or to a faraway country, but she won't slobber over him. It was disgusting, the way Basilio and Ursula pawed each other. I slept in his room and every single morning, before he was out of bed, his *mamá* would sit on top of him— even when he was a young man. He was bound to get an erection and she to get hot, there are no two ways about it.

I spoke up more than once and told them what I thought of their doings, but they'd just answer, "You're crazy!"

"Crazy I may be," I'd tell him, "but not that way. When I want to get hot about a woman, I go find one out in the street. I'd never allow my mother or sisters to sit on me first thing in the morning because at that time a man's always hard. It's brazen of you, Basilio, to allow your mother to do that."

It made me sick to see them. Those two acted like husband and wife, not like mother and son. Every time Basilio began to speak of liking a girl, his *mamá* would cut him short. Honestly, I suspected Ursula was in love with her own son!

As I said, I didn't get along so well with Narciso. He was mean and aggressive to his mother and mistreated her in word and deed. Oh sure, my cousin was a good guy as far as his friends and acquaintances were concerned, but he was "the light in the street and the darkness at home."

Narciso was my Aunt Constancia's only child and she brought him up alone. His father, Jorge Montoya, was no good. It seems that when Jorge met my aunt, he took her by surprise and dazzled her, and my aunt, being an ignorant woman, will eat any shit life sets before her. Jorge really screwed her up for good. He lived with her, got her pregnant, and left her. She never remarried and devoted herself to bringing up her son.

Constancia was in the habit of spending the last weekend of every month at her sister's house. She'd sleep there on Sunday and return home Monday. One time she returned to find her house empty. Jorge had stolen everything! It was no problem for him to turn it all into money, because before the Revolution people didn't need documents to sell furniture. It wouldn't be easy now.

Jorge was the aggressive, adventurous type who didn't care what kind of life he led. All he ever cared about was money. Once he was jailed in El Príncipe for forging some documents, like checks and money orders. You really had to take care when you saw that guy with pen in hand!

Juana Elena, Jorge's sister, brought him food when he was in jail. One day I went to visit her and she said, "I can't take Jorge his food, I feel too sick. Would you take it?" I went because I was fond of Juana Elena and saw what sacrifices she made for her brother. Besides, I was obliged to her for the many times she had washed and ironed a shirt for me when I wanted it in a hurry.

I got to El Príncipe and was allowed to go in. It was the first time in my life I'd set foot in such a place. I asked for Jorge Montoya. "There's your man," said the guard scornfully. "He's sitting there, bold as ever. That one's an original piece of barefaced brazenness!" It was the guy all right! Knowing Jorge's gall, I was really scared just talking to him.

Narciso was three or four years old when his parents separated. He grew up to be like his father and they were like cat and dog together. Everyone had called his father "the Prick" on account of his goings-on, and Narciso was known as "Little Prick." He took from his mamá whatever she had and spent it for his own enjoyment.

I tried to reason with him. "Look, chico," I'd say, "if you gave your mamá 10 pesos last payday and then, because of your generous gift, you ask her for 20 pesos, just how much do you think you've given her? In the eyes of everybody else you help your mamá, but surely you can see that she's 10 pesos out of pocket on account of you."

I'd tell him, "Listen, I know that mask of nobility you wear hides a lot of perversity and I won't part with so much as one copper kilo for you." But in spite of these words, when Narciso got a job at a garage I loaned him money to get a chauffeur's license. Not that I minded—I forget how much a license cost but it was cheap—besides, he paid me back, which is more than I can say for my cousin Basilio.

It was hard for me to go on living at Aunt Dalia's because my cousins often picked on me. Finally I thought, "The best thing I can do is get out of here and strike out on my own." So I left and stayed away for one year. I never told my old man why.

I stopped working for my aunt when I was thirteen and began to work for Joaquín Gómez, who owned a little grocery store in Las Yaguas. I worked from 7:00 A.M. to 7:00 P.M., with a few hours off each afternoon to go to school. I played ball for one hour after school and didn't report back to work until 5:00 P.M., but Joaquín didn't dock my wages for it.

That little grocery store did 300 or 400 *pesos*' worth of business a day. Customers flocked to Joaquín because of the courteous treatment they received and because they could count on him for help when they needed it. He sold on credit to anybody who asked for it, though he was a practical man. He explained, "If someone gives me a song and a dance about why they need to buy a pound of rice on credit, I know they aren't going to pay for it. But if someone asks abruptly and takes me by surprise, he does mean to pay." And he was right, it worked every time!

I liked working for Joaquín and I did my work well. He liked me, too, because I had a great sense of responsibility and I was a whiz at arithmetic and never made a mistake counting money or giving change. Joaquín wanted me to always keep on working with him. I made good money there, 12 *pesos* a week.

My brother Andrés was a big boy by then and he was earning a little money too, selling newspapers and cleaning drains. Whatever my brother and I earned, *mamá* wanted. She took all she wanted from him but I damn well wasn't going to let her dominate me and I hid my money. I had to, because if I had 5 *pesos*, *mamá* would take 4 and leave me 1, or even only 50 *kilos*. Once I gave her some money to save for me, and she either spent it or had the gall to give it away. That's the sort of thing I had to put up with! I was so angry that day, I looked her up and down and said, "What a pity you should be my mother! I'd give all I have and more to make it not so!" After that, I began to hide whatever I earned.

When I was fifteen or sixteen, things came to a head between *mamá* and me. I had quit school because I'd flunked the third grade twice and wasn't promoted to the fourth grade until I was fifteen. I was working on Saturdays selling soft drinks in the canteen at the bus station. One Saturday there was a fiesta in Havana, and in the evening the owner of the canteen said to me, "Let's go there."

"I must get *mamá*'s permission first," I said. We were allowed to wander around all day long but at night we had to be home. My friend phoned and got *mamá*'s permission for me to go so I went with him. The fiesta didn't end until about 4:00 in the morning. When I got home *mamá* was waiting for me. It seems she had never given her permission. I explained that my friend told me he'd called her but she gave me a beating anyway.

Once *mamá* sent me to buy a liter of milk from a *gallega* called Hermilda, who lived up the hill. Doña Hermilda had a whole flock of chickens, and she gave me ten or twelve eggs to take home with the milk. I arrived with the gift and said to my mother, "Look, *mima*, Hermilda sent you these."

My old lady didn't believe me. She thought I'd stolen the eggs and gave me a terrible beating, right in front of her *comadre* Celia, who was there. Then *mamá* took the eggs back to Hermilda, who explained that she'd really given them to me. Much good it did me! There was no taking back the blows I'd received. It hurt my feelings terribly that *mamá* should humiliate me in front of her *comadre*. I was so mad I told her, "You go to hell!" Then I piled all my clothes in front of the house, soaked them in alcohol, and set fire to them right before *mamá*'s eyes.

"Aha!" she said. "Now you have nothing to wear!"

"Is that so?" I said. I didn't have many clothes at home, just two or three undershorts, three pairs of pants, three shirts . . . the rest were at my aunt's house. "You know I always come out on top," I told her. "God may choke me but I always float to the surface."

Those were little things that happened, but it got to the point where I couldn't control my rage anymore. After I burned my clothes I left *mamá*'s home and never went back to live there again. For three or four days I slept in buses and doorways. I didn't go to Havana but wandered around Luyanó. There I met Evaristo, who had a tumbledown mechanics workshop on Herrera Street. He'd never seen me before but he liked me right away, and I began to work as a mechanic's assistant. He taught me the trade. He didn't pay me while I was an apprentice so I was broke all the time. I slept in a bus at the shop and he brought me food from a cheap restaurant nearby. After a while he started to pay me, not much at first, but later on he paid me over 30 *pesos* a week.

I had a hard time with Evaristo because, like every worker, I expected to get paid punctually on Friday, but instead I had to wait until Saturday or Sunday, until he sobered up, and even then sometimes he didn't pay me. He'd have some sort of story: "Wait till so-and-so brings me the money and then I can pay you." If it wasn't that, it was something else.

Finally I said, "I'm fed up with being a mechanic, bashing my fingers with the hammer and working as a handyman, painter, and everything else. I'm going to get myself another job." I found work helping a driver of a truck belonging to the Blue Line. They carried bales of paper to the warehouse at Correa. I still didn't go back home but lived at my aunt's house on Pasaje de Córdoba.

SEÑORA LORDI:

Fredo has always had a temper. He was a bit disobedient to his father, refusing to run errands, and every little while they'd get into an argument, but I would smooth things out between them. My husband wasn't in the habit of spanking his children. If he had to, he'd flick them with a palm leaf, that's all.

Fredo was a little jealous of his brothers and sisters. He always wanted to be first. When dinner was ready, he wanted to be served before anyone else. When clothes were to be washed, he wanted his washed first of all. He'd get angry because there were many children and everybody had to wait his turn.

Fredo started school at the age of six but he kept flunking the third grade. I don't know what was the matter with him—it wasn't for lack of scolding. I really kept after that boy. He was about fourteen when he dropped out of third grade. He refused to go to school any longer because he didn't want to study with the nuns who were teaching in the barrio. He never went to public school, just to that school there in Las Yaguas. It's still standing, though it's been renamed. All of my children were taught there.

When Alfredo was fifteen or sixteen and old enough to belt his pants, he went to live with his aunts and help them deliver the meals they cooked for customers. He had his little girl friends while he was there and he stayed until he got engaged.

BARRERA:

There are times in one's life that are sad and hard to bear. In my early youth, I used to look around at all the other boys who had sweethearts while I, who was fully seventeen years old, had none. I felt stupid when one of the boys said, "*Caramba,* I'll have to court a girl for you. We're all going to the movies and you're the only one who hasn't got a girl."

I was awfully shy with girls. Whenever I got up the courage to pay a girl a compliment, I was paralyzed with fear if she happened to respond. I couldn't analyze what was happening to me, and I was saddened and disconcerted because my youth was going to waste. I said to myself, "I must stop being so awkward with girls." Much good that did me!

The first woman I made love to was a married woman named Maya. I was living with my aunt in apartment D and Maya lived across the hall in apartment A. Maya was a young woman and it seems her husband didn't satisfy her. She chased me indirectly, giving me lots of chances with her. Oh, her intentions were clear enough. Whenever anything broke down in her place she'd ask me to fix it. She knew that having me in the house so often, sooner or later something was bound to happen. But I respected the fact that she was a married woman and that if her husband came in and caught us together he just might kill me.

One day she called me over to tell me all her lights were out and would I fix them. Well, I found not a single light was out so I caught her meaning right away. I walked into the bedroom with the ladder and there she was stretched out on the bed, wearing a housecoat and nothing underneath, with her tits hanging out. I looked at her naked body from head to foot and she said to me, "What do you think of this, baby?"

"Looks fine to me," I said and walked out.

Next day she called me over again to fix the dividing door in the parlor. Same thing again. There she was, in nothing but her housecoat, piling provocation on provocation. All of a sudden she threw her arms around me and said, "What's the matter, stupid? Don't you know the facts of life?" I did, and I showed her. After that, Maya called me in every day. It was a way of relieving my needs and it was a delight. Every time I thought of it, no matter where I was, even in the bus, *bang!* my organ would get stiff.

I painted Maya's place and charged 120 *pesos* for the job. I paid my brother 40 *pesos* for helping me, although he couldn't do anything except hold the ladder and scrape away some of the old paint. I finished the job in a week and both Maya and her husband were quite satisfied. Yet when she paid me I noticed that her husband seemed to be distrustful. Then Juan, the janitor, said to me, "Look, kid, don't go too often to Maya's house. Somebody is jealous of you." I didn't want to get into trouble so I told him, "All right, when she calls for me tell her I'm out." That way, I left her little by little.

After I'd finished with Maya, I began to visit Estela. She lived just across the street from my aunt, in no. 2. She was about my age, sixteen or seventeen, and she was a virgin. I was the first to stick the machete into her but she was the one who started the whole thing. She gave me the chance and I took it, so I never spoke to her of marriage. We quarreled then, because she'd lost her head over me and wanted to be my legally married wife.

I said to her, "Look, I don't mean to get married, at least not now. If I ever do, it will be because I'm earning enough money to support a family and that won't be soon." The truth was, I had never even thought of marrying her. As far as I was concerned she was just another meal and one that someone else would chew on soon enough.

Just around that time, I started seeing a girl called Zenaida. We weren't serious, but I liked her and was thinking of asking her to be my sweetheart. Then one day we met at our usual meeting place and she asked me if I knew Sara Ubeda, who was my father's first wife. I answered yes, I did. I had never met Sara but I knew her name and what old Alfredo had told me.

Zenaida didn't explain straight off, then finally she told me. We were brother and sister! She had recognized me from a photograph *papá* Alfredo had shown her. I was so shocked the wings of my heart drooped. My legs trembled. The girl stared at me and I stared back at her. The only thing I could think was that the hour of my death had come. I was desperate to break loose from that tie, because how was it possible to have such a relationship with one's own sister?

Then Zenaida took me to her mother. Sara Ubeda was a slender woman, very pleasant in her manner. She lived with Zenaida and my half-brother, Alfredo Carlos, in a tenement on Santa Beatríz Street in Bella Vista. After our first meeting I went there every two weeks to get my hair cut by Alfredo Carlos, although he charged me more than the barbershop in Las Yaguas.

I lost touch with Sara about six years ago, but I still see Zenaida. It's very difficult to get to see Alfredo Carlos because he works for military intelligence. His two sons are in the Army too.

My first real sweetheart was Rosita. She was plump and light-skinned. She worked as a housemaid for a man called Lope, who was a big executive with Standard Oil. He lived in *reparto* Santos Suárez, and when I went to work I always passed by the alley at the foot of the hill where his house was. Every morning I'd see Rosita, because she was on the hill emptying the chamber pots.

Sometimes after work I'd walk by the house, and whenever I passed Rosita would fling some remark at me. There was a small bench nearby where I always sat down to rest. We'd talk and look at each other a lot and kid around, but I couldn't make up my mind to ask her to be my sweetheart for fear she might say no. Besides, I would think, "If I court the girl I might have to marry her, and how would I support a wife?"

What with shyness and fears, I put off taking the plunge, until one day Rosita herself took the initiative. She said, "Hey, kid, what's wrong with you? Are you a queer or don't you understand the meaning of a woman's glances?" No sooner had she shown her preference for me when I said to her, "Look, kid, you're a little tramp and the truth is I'm attracted to you, so stop calling me a queer unless you want me to kick you good. Did you think that up because I've never made a pass at you? If that's the case, I'll tell you right now that I like you and would like to get together with you."

"That's what I wanted you to say," she admitted. "We've been kidding around so long without ever coming to anything." She was right, too—we had wasted a year and a half on that shit-eating foolishness—but that very night we were hugging each other in Fábrica Park. I thought, "This girl is easy, not somebody to take seriously." Hell, she wasn't the kind of girl to get tied down with, what with her character and upbringing. I've always been serious-minded and that girl was forever kidding and laughing. She wasn't the kind I approved of. We became sweethearts but I never considered marrying her.

I've always thought that whatever begins in joy is bound to end in sorrow and pain. Rosita is the only woman who ever left me. The others I have left, without argument or explanation. I just picked up my feet and went. But Rosita gave me my walking papers because she thought I had T.B. I was working as a cook at the Luyanó Popular restaurant for three years, off and on, and I liked the place and the way they treated me. The work was pretty hard though. At first I worked part-time, but then I started at 6:00 A.M. and was still there at 10:00 A.M., preparing the next day's dishes. The chief chef, José Martínez, taught me to cook. He was a Spaniard from Barcelona.

At the restaurant we cooked with hard coal and petroleum gas, and after three years of working in the steam and fumes my liver was affected. I turned yellow, and my right side, just above the liver, swelled. People kept telling me my face looked yellow, and I wondered, "Why do I look so sick?" I ate well and lived a healthy life. I weighed 113 pounds, and though I was small and skinny I was strong and had a lot of blood in my system. I had so much blood that sometimes when I exercised a lot or got hot, it would spurt out of my nose and mouth. So I often went to get a bloodletting.

I didn't think there was anything wrong with my lungs until Rosita put the idea into my head. She told me that anybody who spat blood had the lung sickness, and when one got yellow it meant both lungs were shot. She said, "I'm through with you because that yellowness of yours can only mean one thing. You've got T.B."

It bothered me, seeing everyone else with their own natural color and me yellow for no reason at all. My grandfather was an intimate friend of the director of La Purísima Concepción Hospital, so he arranged for me to have some tests right away. I had about seventeen X-rays and blood tests and the doctors forbade me to eat meat, fish, or eggs. But I acted like an *isleño*, and as soon as I returned to the restaurant, I fried myself six eggs and ate them, with bicarbonate of soda as a chaser. I didn't believe I was really sick. How could anyone imagine a strong young fellow like me had the lung sickness? I had always been strong and healthy from childhood.

My yellow tinge didn't go away. I took so many medicines and went so often to doctors, I was fed up. I bought Dr. Rosa's brand pills, wrote two letters in case I died, then sat down in the emergency clinic at Luyanó and swallowed fourteen or fifteen of the pills. "Either this cures me or it finishes me," I thought.

At the clinic there was a little old pharmacist who knew my parents. He took one look at me as I sat there and asked, "What's wrong, Alfredo? Why are you shivering so?"

"Nothing, I'm all right," I said. Be he saw the two letters sticking out of my pocket so he took them and started to read one. He didn't wait to finish it. Right away he called a doctor. I was losing consciousness fast but I remember a doctor listening to my heart with that gadget doctors carry and then he gave me a shot. *Mamá* had arrived there somehow and I remember the doctor saying to her, "Take him home now, Tina, and bring him back tomorrow for another shot. He's out of danger now." That crazy trick had almost cost me my life. I didn't want to die then, hell no!

After that little episode, I began to get better fast. I stopped working in the restaurant and the yellowness went away. When Rosita saw me in sound health again she tried to make up with me, but I told her, "Oh no, I wouldn't make you live with a guy who has T.B.!"

Rosita was my first youthful love. It hurt me when she left me but I thought, "Well, if she doesn't love me, maybe it's better that way. Let her get herself another fellow; I'll get another girl." So I never went back to her. I have a lot of willpower. I'm a man who loves deeply . . . and forgets completely. Besides, by that time I had met Ida.

Ida was a minor but she was already a prostitute. She'd made a slip with her sweetheart, who had abandoned her. I met her at the restaurant, and again at *"la piecesita,"* where one went to "clean one's gun," as we say. She and I fell in love but I never wanted to set up a home with her. She lived in her home and I in mine, and when she wanted to satisfy her whim, fine, she came to me, or when I wanted to satisfy mine, I'd go to her, and that was all there was to it.

Ida and I went together for about a year. I was very careful that she didn't get a big belly because she was still a minor. I would have been really screwed up with the law if she'd become pregnant. You see, if a fellow "ate" a girl before she was sixteen—even if it was the day before her sixteenth birthday—and she became pregnant, then the full force of the law applied and she could make him marry her. But once a girl was sixteen, if she got pregnant, there'd be nothing she could do. At that time I couldn't afford to marry. I had to consider the needs of my family and help them out. I was never engaged to her and she never expected me to support her or give her any money. I never had to pay for having sex with a woman. I was just lucky that way.

Ida chased after me all the time and cried if I didn't go to see her. I was working in another restaurant and one day she came there and threatened me. "You'd better go to my place tonight, because if you don't I'll make a row out in the street and you'll get arrested." Well, work wasn't easy to find then, and if she had created a scandal I could easily have lost my job. So I told her, "Look, kid, I don't like women who chase me. Besides, you're doing me harm by coming to call on me here at work. So don't bother me anymore."

There was a much older man who was after Ida, and since I gave her nothing, she went to bed with him. He was the one who bought her clothes and gave her money to buy food. Actually, it turned out to be convenient for me. The old man was looking for an apprentice plasterer and he hired me because I wanted to learn the trade. I didn't work for the old guy very long but I got my start as a professional plasterer.

I tried to persuade Ida to leave that life. I said, "Look, kid, get yourself some honest work cleaning house for somebody for 15 or 20 *pesos* a month. That's better than having to take on old guys who dribble all over you. Those were my very words, but she chose to disregard my advice. She could have had a happy life if she'd stopped to think instead of taking the easy way out and selling her body for 4 *pesos* a throw. She became a real tramp later.

It's true that I was lucky with women, but you know the saying, "Never look a gift horse in the mouth." Well, I'm leery of gift horses—they're apt to be the most expensive in the long run. Offer me something for nothing and I'll refuse it every time. I like things I have to work hard for and it's the same with women. The easy ones are worthless and there are no two ways about it.

Chapter Two

I Never Gave My Address

To THOSE WHO DIDN'T LIVE there everybody in Las Yaguas was a tramp, a marijuana smoker, a thief, and a pickpocket. You could be honest as the day is long but to outsiders you were some kind of criminal. I never gave my address to anybody when I was job-hunting. I knew I'd better not say I lived in Las Yaguas because I'd have little chance of being hired. When I had a sweetheart and wanted visiting rights, if I'd said I was from Las Yaguas the girl would have been forbidden to see me. If a fellow had friends who could be useful to him he couldn't go around confessing he lived in such a place. Unless, of course, they happened to run into you there when you were walking barefoot. Were my friends ever surprised when they saw me there!

Las Yaguas was full of shady characters. It had its share of pimps and prostitutes, and I was one of the pimps. The girls fell for me because I was a classy dresser and was clean, and I always had 4 *pesos* to take them to the movies or buy them some little gift. Once they fell for me they worked for me, and there I was, in business.

There were married women of thirty-five or forty in Las Yaguas whose husbands didn't satisfy them. Those middle-aged women were driven by their husband's inadequacy or maybe by some sickness of the ovaries that made them hard to satisfy. They'd find themselves a discreet young boy and buy him clothes and pay him for the pleasure he gave them. Many young fellows had that kind of connection and I was one of them. My mistress, Delia, gave me everything. After we broke up, she was killed in a railway accident on the way to Santa Clara.

There were three *posadas* in Las Yaguas.[2] Miguelito's was near the hill, at Rijol. Another one belonged to José Fish Head and was near the bend of Four Corners. The third one was built on the hill, near the rear entrance of the *reparto*. They were all the same. The owners usually charged 50 *kilos* for a room, but if you were a stranger he'd charge 1 *peso*.

2. A *posada* is a lodging house where rooms are rented by the hour.

There were only three mean little rooms, each furnished with a bed and nothing else. You went there, spewed it out, and left.

A lot of blacks lived in Las Yaguas and racial prejudice was strong. For example, we white fellows laid black girls oftener than white girls because the poor things weren't so well looked after by their parents. The daughters of black families were always getting knocked up. If people saw a black girl with a white boy, right away they'd begin to criticize her. They'd say, "You're a slut and a fool. That white boy is going to break your pussy and then leave you with a big belly." And they were right, that's what happened. Every time I had a chance with one of those girls, I'd stick my machete into her, and afterward, let the sun rise where it may. What did I care? If a girl's father tried to call me to account, I'd say to him, "What do you expect? I'm a man. It's up to you to keep your daughter home."

The blacks weren't as well off as the whites. Some blacks owned cars but they never took them into Las Yaguas. Lamberto had a 1952 Ford that he won in a raffle. Another car-owner was Nilo, the mechanic. A black on the hill owned a truck and one down below also owned a car. Three of the grocery stores were owned by blacks, but they didn't prosper like the five white grocers because they gambled.

In a way, people like that lived better before the Revolution because they made their living in the underworld. But in another way they were not so well off because they spent their lives in gambling dens, where they lost all their profits. They got into debt and borrowed from the loan sharks, who made their lives a misery. There were three black loan sharks and one white, a guy named One-Eyed Felo, who loaned only to other whites. He was considered quite a monopolist. The three blacks loaned to the blacks. There were no pawnshops in Las Yaguas, only these four moneylenders.

People were poor in Las Yaguas but you could live quite well if you chose to. Anybody who really wanted to work could earn an honest living, although it's true there was unemployment. But people collected and sold empty bottles, hawked candy or newspapers, shined shoes, or poured concrete. Doing odd jobs like that you could save for the days when you didn't find work. I always had at least two or three jobs going at the same time. Even when I was a plasterer, I kept my shoeshine chair open for business and I sold newspapers.

There were, of course, some people in Las Yaguas who had nothing. They'd pawn or sell their possessions to buy food. Their need was so great they were always being exploited. You'd find one of them trying to sell a watch worth 50 *pesos*, then someone would come along and say, "I'll give you 15 for it," and the seller would have to take it. There were others in the *reparto* who owned a TV or a refrigerator and some rich man would make a profit on it.

Still, I don't know of a single case where somebody starved to death. In my home I remember no scarcity of food. We always had milk and bread or crackers for breakfast. All day long we ate candy, cookies, caramels. We ate lots of fried eggs, too. In Las Yaguas if a mother couldn't afford to make lunch at home for her children, she could go to an eating place called The Twin, and for 1 *real*[3] she could get a panful of cooked yucca with spicy *mojo* sauce or *gandinga,* a stew made of liver, heart, and kidneys. For supper she could buy 1 *peseta*'s worth of ground meat, and for 2 *pesetas* more she could get a half-pound of lard, a pound of rice, and a couple of plantains. Hogmilt, tripe, jerked beef, canned sardines—all good nourishing food—sold very cheaply.

Meat sold at low prices because the butchers in Las Yaguas got it cheaply. It's not that they sold spoiled meat, but suppose a machine in a meat factory slipped and mangled a leg of pork. It couldn't be sold on the regular market so it was sent to Las Yaguas. There you could buy a half-pound of fatback bacon for 1 *peseta,* and with a *real*'s worth of beef you'd get a bagful of bones. You could put all that together with some beans and you had a good nourishing meal. A quarter of a chicken cost only 15 *centavos,* and a bag of chicken livers, gizzards, and necks cost 2 *centavos.* Who couldn't afford to buy it at that price? Besides, many families raised pigs and chickens for their own tables.

There were more than enough beans to eat all year round. Black beans sold in Las Yaguas for 9 *centavos* a pound, although in downtown Havana the price was 13 or 14 *centavos.* We got them cheap in Las Yaguas because the grocer bought them at a discount from the warehouse. You see, the people who worked in the Health Ministry had a racket going. The beans were stored in a warehouse, and when the owner refused to bribe the public-health inspectors, a Health Ministry truck would be sent to fumigate the warehouse. They'd pollute the top sacks with the fumes and the beans would spoil. But some guys would set aside a few good sacks from the bottom, and these were sold cheaply to the retailers in Las Yaguas.

The wholesalers played the same game selling codfish. They'd bribe the government agents so they could sell confiscated fish cheaply to the fish peddlers in Las Yaguas. Any kind of food you can think of was available in Las Yaguas. So if anybody in Las Yaguas starved he must have lacked the spirit to go out and earn an honest *peseta,* or he was too stingy to spend it. I mean, anybody who starved to death let himself die of his own neglect, that's all.

You only needed a little money to live well. If a man earned 3 *pesos* a day as a construction worker, he could still manage to save money and indulge himself. If he was a heavy drinker he'd go to Joaquín's place and

3. Ten *centavos.*

buy a couple of shots of *aguardiente* for 1 *real*. The glasses were pretty big, the kind we call *cañitas,* and after downing one *aguardiente* you'd already be singing "The Peanut Vendor."[4]

There were four cheap restaurants in Las Yaguas, and at any one of them 25 *kilos* would get you a complete meal of rice, soup, meat, and fried plantains, and your plate would be so heaped with food, you couldn't eat it all. I myself would buy only half a *peseta* of white cheese with guava paste, wash it down with a Pepsi-Cola or a Spur-Cola, and I'd have had my meal. I'd go on to a café, drink a cup of coffee, and smoke a cigar. A small cup of coffee used to cost 1 *centavo,* and if you didn't have a *centavo* anybody would give you a cup of coffee or cornstarch pudding or whatever. A cup of hot chocolate cost only 2 *centavos.*

Even the vices were cheaper. A pack of cigarettes cost only 10 *centavos,* now it costs 20. Beer was 15 *centavos,* now it's 40. If you wanted to gamble and smoke marijuana and had no income, poverty was no obstacle. You simply pawned or sold your clothes. Oh, there were ways and means of getting what you wanted.

Clothes were cheap before the Revolution. Anyone who went barefoot in Las Yaguas did so because he wanted to. A woman with three or four kids could go begging and almost always someone would give her a pair of old shoes. Of course no man or woman of spirit would beg, because there were many other ways to earn a living. A woman with no husband, no help from anyone, and no training for a job would go to the marketplace, pick up the plantains that fell from the trucks, and sell them for 1 *real* a bunch.

Some people in the *reparto* never went to the stores to buy clothes. They'd wait until someone came around selling secondhand clothes and then they'd get a dress for 1 *real* and a pair of shoes for 25 *kilos.* If they were going to celebrate a girl's fifteenth birthday, they might buy at a department store like El Encanto. But even the clothes sold in the stores were cheap.

Papá had eight children, and before the Revolution he could walk into a store with 30 *pesos* and get them everything they needed in the way of clothing. A pair of pants for 3.99 *pesos* were of such good quality they'd last you ten years, and when you bought them you'd get a belt or a pair of socks free. Handkerchiefs and socks were seven for 1 *peso,* a shirt, 59 *kilos,* girl's bloomers, seven for 1 *peso.* Now you have to pay 1 *peso* for one bloomer. There were good-quality American shoes on the market that sold for 2.99 *pesos,* and again, they'd throw in a pair of socks or a belt. The most expensive pair of custom-made Cuban shoes cost no more than 20 or 25 *pesos.*

---

4. "Singing 'The Peanut Vendor'" is a popular Cuban expression used to suggest an imminent death.

One day I went to buy the week's supply of food at the marketplace, and on the floor beside a booth I found a roll of bills. I counted them— 1,800 *pesos!* "Well, well!" I said. "The heck with buying food! I've as good as hit it in the lottery!"

My sisters had no decent clothes to wear to parties, and since it was Christmas, I ran here and there buying everything the girls needed— shoes, brassieres, panties, skirts, dresses. My fourteen-year-old cousin, Tatiana, who had lived with us since she was five, was even worse off than my sisters and had been getting along on their cast-off clothes, so whatever I bought for them I bought for her too.

When the girl saw all those gifts she thought I must be in love with her. It was common in the poor barrios for women to read a lot of meaning into a gift of a pair of shoes or a length of cloth for a dress if it came from a man. But Tatiana was wrong about me. I had a sweetheart at the time, and for another thing, Tatiana and I were first cousins. I've always disapproved of sexual relationships between relatives. I know several cases of first cousins who have married and their children turn out to be paralyzed or undersized or something. What with one thing and another, there wasn't a chance in the world that I would be attracted to Tatiana.

For one thing, there was never any love lost between me and Tatiana's father, my Uncle Genaro. I always had a low opinion of him. *Mamá* says he was the brother who had helped her the most, but the truth is he's a sneak-thief who robbed his own relatives. Once he took 30 *pesos mamá* had put away in a plastic bag in the closet. I hate a man who takes advantage of other people. He was the kind of guy who didn't care whether the sunrise caught him outdoors or in. He used to work as a chauffeur, and after six months, when he had saved up 1,000 or 2,000 *pesos,* he'd quit his job and do nothing but loaf and spend. He wasn't to be trusted by his employers. Once a Chinese fellow gave him a job at his booth in the marketplace and Genaro ransacked his home.

Genaro's wife, Elena, died of lung sickness, though we always thought it was his beatings that killed her. Genaro had to care for their two girls, but he was a bad father and never cared properly for them. His daughter Antonia died of the lung sickness soon after her mother, and the other one, Tatiana, came to stay with us. Thanks to us she ate three meals a day and had plenty of clothes to wear. She lived with us for nine years. Yet Genaro was ungrateful. He always hated me for some reason and was out to harm me.

So when Tatiana fell in love with me, I told *mamá* to ask Genaro to take her back because that situation couldn't continue. My uncle came one night at 1:00 A.M. and said to me, "You know what I want to talk about, but let me tell you first that I'd like to kill you like a dog."

"Listen," I answered, "you don't have the balls to kill me. I may be skinny and weak but I'm not scared even of a dead man. I warn you, I carry a gun and I'm man enough to press the trigger. Take Tatiana back home with you. Such shameful affairs between relatives don't happen in my family and Tatiana is harming me after I've shown her nothing but kindness." He took her away that very night.

Genaro caught the lung sickness and some people said it was Elena's spirit that hounded him to death in revenge for his ill treatment. That's how it looked—every one of his symptoms was a symptom she'd had. He coughed and coughed and finally choked to death. It was her spirit persecuting him.

I continued to work and struggle, with the sole object of getting my old lady and my brothers and sisters out of Las Yaguas. I felt humiliated that my family had to live there. In Las Yaguas a boy was exposed to many bad influences, his own friends being among the worst. I had pals who suggested all sorts of things to me, even inviting me to steal. They'd say, "Ah, come on, kid, nobody's going to find out. Your *mamá* will never know." I never did those things though. Many of the other boys did and landed in the Torrens Reformatory. But my brothers and I never even once had a problem with the police. My youngest brother, José, used to hang out with a gang of young hoodlums, rotten through and through, who'd bum around and waste their time. José had two or three jobs and quit them all. Three or four times when I found him hanging around with that bunch, I slapped him hard in front of them and every time I'd tell him, "I'm doing this to make you kill me or fight me, and I'll do it again whenever I catch you here." I had the right and moral duty to do it. I had to knock some decency into him and make him see he shouldn't hang around with those fellows.

My brother Andrés bore all the stigma of poverty. He had a rougher childhood than I did because, well, if I put on a new pair of pants, he couldn't, because he'd have to wear pants that I'd outgrown. He hardly ever went out of the *reparto,* so he was always poorly dressed. From the time he was a young boy, Andrés was a drifter. He'd steal all our things and was a hard drinker. I don't know from what ancestor he inherited that failing, because at home no one else—at least none of my brothers— ever drank like that.

Andrés didn't like to work, not he! He wanted to have everything given to him as if he were a rich man. He loved to lie in bed till noon and have his women bring home the money. Pimping, that was his line. He always had five or six little tramps hanging around him and involving him in arguments. He was a real, honest-to-goodness pimp who wouldn't put in a good day's work. Well—actually he wasn't a real, full-time pimp because now and then he did show enough gumption to go find himself some easy job and earn a bit of money. But generally he had a flock of black girls for whom he found employment and then he lived off them. Think of it! A little black girl with a white man was quite a show. So they made a good match.

That was Andrés's life. I never knew him to have a *centavo*. He was a nice guy—his only defect was that foolishness of liking loose women and preferring to pimp rather than work. But after all, who can blame him? Heck, the women threw themselves at him. At one point he worked in Joaquín's grocery store and told the women he was a property-owner, that he'd be sole owner of the store when Joaquín died. The women really flocked to him then. After he got the job there he became a pimp on a really large scale.

He fell for one of those little tramps, but I put my foot down. We even fought about it. That tramp, María, had a husband and four or five kids, but Andrés was supporting them all while the "lord," her husband, who they called Maldonado, lived a life of idleness. *Mamá* was worried that when Maldonado found out, he would stab or shoot Andrés.

I spoke to my brother four or five times about getting mixed up with a woman who had so many children. "Why should you be hungry for such a woman?" I asked. "You can get any woman you want. All those little *negritas* of yours have to pay you well for your milk because that isn't something to give away for free."

That offended him. We started shouting at each other and ended up fighting with our fists. About a week later he apologized. "Forgive me, brother, you were right. I broke up with that woman. I realized the whole thing was a mistake."

SEÑORA LORDI:

I never spanked any of my children, not so much as a slap on the bottom. I just put bars and a bolt on the door to keep them inside. That's the way I raised them. Nobody ever caught *my* kids running around in the streets. I should say not! When they were of school age I sent them to school. And when Alfredo was a big boy there was a time when we were short of money so we let him sell newspapers. But as for the horde of little ones, they stayed home.

But you can't keep men home. All of my sons went to live with their Aunt Dalia as soon as they were old enough to make their own decisions. They wanted to get out of Las Yaguas because all sorts of things happened there and the police were always sneaking around.

One time the police beat up my husband because they wanted to make him talk about things he knew nothing about. But that was the worst problem we had. In fact, the police trusted me so much that often when they had a summons for somebody they'd leave it with me and I'd give it to the person. My sons never got involved in any problems in the barrio. We never had arms of any kind in the house, unless you count a kitchen knife. Neither my husband nor my sons were the kind to go around picking fights.

Andrés is my second son. His mind is much, much clearer than Fredo's. But if Alfredo disliked school, Andrés disliked it even more. I don't think he even finished the first grade. He went to school two or three times, then he told me, "I'm going to go live with Aunt Dalia." That was the end of his schooling.

José never liked school either. I had to keep after him to make him go. Two of the girls, Angelita and Manuelita, liked school. They used to go at night. The other girls didn't like school any more than the boys did. All of them had to be pushed into going.

BARRERA:

I wanted my sisters to grow up to be good women. They had no need to marry in a hurry; they didn't have to accept the first man who came along. They had everything they needed at home, but they wanted to be independent and have homes of their own. If their marriages failed, it was not for lack of good advice but because of their own wrongheadedness. They all went ahead and married whom they pleased. Their pussies got hot, to put it crudely, and they went and ruined their lives. *Mamá,* of course, is satisfied with her daughters' husbands because she practically handpicked every one of them.

Both Celia and Angelita picked men who'd had another woman first. I can't understand it. Why should sheltered stay-at-home girls get involved with such men?

Celia was only fourteen and Baltasar over forty when they took off together. I don't know how they managed to get away with it. It all happened very suddenly. *Mamá* and Baltasar were as close as fingernail and flesh because whenever she asked him for money he'd give it to her. Why, I really believe *mamá* actually maneuvered my sister into marrying him.

As the elder brother I never approved of their relationship because Baltasar was an older man who already had children with his first wife. They had been separated for three or four years when he fell in love with Celia. He hadn't set foot in his wife's house since they'd been separated, but she thought he had abandoned her for Celia and she blamed my sister. All this could make enmity in the future.

For three years after Celia and Baltasar were married, I didn't visit them because I resented the fact that a forty-year-old man should want to marry a fourteen-year-old girl. How can such a thing be possible? After a time, I felt more understanding about the whole thing and thought, "Oh well, such is life and there's nothing one can do about it.

What's done is done." So Baltasar and I became friends. He turned out to be a good guy after all. But suppose he hadn't? He could just as easily have been a vicious character.

Of course Celia can no longer dream of having a civil ceremony, as every young girl does, nor of having a husband whose age matches hers. Celia is in her twenties now and Baltasar in his fifties. The child is still young and her husband is a fallen tree. Her woman's nature craves what he can no longer give her. How long can she be expected to control herself in such circumstances? Someday someone will tell her, "Your husband has been very good, yes, but you're sacrificing your own nature and your whole life, and you'll go on being deprived as long as you stay by his side."

Angelita was first married to a black named Junípero whom she met in Las Yaguas. That man was much lower, morally speaking, than she was. He was a thief, a drug pusher, and a hardened marijuana smoker.

I caught her with him one night by coincidence when I was driving along the Via Blanca through a bad barrio called La Cueva del Humo. I saw two people in the dark and thought, "*Coño*, that looks like my sister Angelita!" I slowed down and got out and slapped her good. "Look," I told her, "this man is nothing but a shit-eater. Why don't you take up with a decent, honest man?" It was a waste of time beating her and telling her this and that. She took off with the fellow precisely because I tried to separate them, and she went to live with him over in La Cueva del Humo.

Angelita was a virgin and had no reason to take up with a man who wasn't going to marry her, yet *bam!* she threw herself into that adventure. The result of my sister's adventure was that she bore the man's two children but never got along with him, and after a while they separated and she went home to *mamá*.

SEÑORA LORDI:

I never objected to my daughters having sweethearts and marrying young, as long as they behaved as señoritas should until their wedding day. I raised my daughters modestly, as my mother raised me. I didn't go to fiestas or dances. I've never been to the movies. Never, never in my life have I so much as stood by the entrance to a movie or been to a dance. Now that the children are all grown, I sometimes think of going out. But all of a sudden I lose interest and go back to my housework. That's what I was brought up to do and that's what I do to this day. What can people think of me when I confess that? My only outings have been taking a sick child to the hospital, to the emergency clinic, or to the doctor's office. Those have been my outings and my fiestas and I brought up my girls the same way.

But Angelita was a handful. She was born bad-tempered and there wasn't a thing I could do about it. I tried to tame her by forbidding her to go out. Afternoons or Sundays when she suggested, "Let's take a turn around," I would say, "I should say not! Nobody's leaving this house today."

Angelita was always a loudmouth. Once she called Fredo a *maricón* or something, the kind of thing that slips out when one gets mad, and Fredo socked her real hard. He said, "I'll make you respect me!" She didn't say one word, she just sat there. That was the only time Fredo had a set-to with any of his sisters.

Fredo was always jealous of Anita as a child because I kept telling the boys, "Girls are girls, and should be treated with special consideration." When he heard she'd taken off with her sweetheart, Echegarrúa, he didn't interfere. "The spoon you pick up is the one you eat with," was all he said.

Anita's luck with Echegarrúa was no better than the luck I'd had with her father. She had to leave him when their son, Alfredito, was about one year old. Echegarrúa quarreled with my husband and tried to attack him with a razor, but Fuentes, the watchman, stopped him. Later, Fuentes brought Echegarrúa to trial over the incident.

BARRERA:

Anita's first husband, a boy called Echegarrúa, was not a proper match for her. He would hang around with fellows who were always getting into trouble with the law. God only knows what they did. Maybe they were thieves or drug addicts or something of the kind since all those types were to be found in the *reparto*. We were all against him, and one day *papá* told him we didn't approve of him as my sister's sweetheart. "If you don't stop seeing her, you'll be in trouble," he warned the boy. At that, the fellow pulled out a razor and attacked *papá* but only managed to slit his shirt down the back.

They were brought to trial and Anita testified that it was old Alfredo who had pulled a razor on her sweetheart, instead of the other way around. Both *papá* and Echegarrúa were fined. That was all wrong. That fellow deserved to be locked up, but he got off lightly because he had an uncle who was a judge and, as we say, "he who has a godfather gets baptized."

My sister treated her stepfather very badly. She didn't return the great affection old Alfredo showed her. I upbraided her and said, "How could you take sides against your own father for the sake of a fellow not worth 2 *centavos*?" That soured the friendship between us.

Papá still tried to persuade Anita to give up Echegarrúa, but she faced up to all of us and said if she couldn't marry him she'd kill herself. I told her, "Don't be such a shit-eater and stop jawing. People who really intend to kill themselves don't advertise their intentions. If you really mean it, I'll make it easy for you." I went out and bought two bottles of sulfuric acid and locked myself up in a room with her. She threw a shoe at me so I took a stick to her and beat her good, as I had a perfect right to do, being her brother. I did it for her own good, but it seems that, without meaning to, I hit her on her breast. She fell down like a pigeon.

They took her to the emergency clinic and then we discovered she was pregnant. We had to go to trial and the judge made me pay a 10-*peso* fine, which was abusive because I was a minor at the time and the law shouldn't persecute minors. As for Anita, it wasn't long before Echegarrúa took off and left her with his child.

Whenever we start to reminisce about the past, I upbraid Anita again for her behavior. "Well, you took off with your sweetheart against our will, so if you failed it's your own fault."

We were able to forgive Anita for her mistake because we all grew to love her baby, especially the old man. She brought Alfredito home and we raised him. Old Alfredo nicknamed him "Balls" because he had such big balls. The boy is twenty years old now.

ANITA VALVERDE:

I was sixteen when I got married for the first time. My husband, Crispo Echegarrúa, was seventeen. He worked at a carpentry shop in Cueto Street, near Inés's hairdressing place, where I worked. I saw him around all the time. Then he began to court me and I took a liking to him. We met in the street to talk and sometimes we went to the movies.

When I told *mamá* he was my sweetheart she was dead set against him. "He's just a kid, he can't do anything for you," she said. "You need an older man, somebody who can carry some weight." Mothers! You know what they're like!

I was tired of working and bored to death, because as we children grew up and started to work we all helped our *mamá* with this or that. That is, all but Fredo. When he started selling newspapers, old Alfredo told him to give the money to *mamá* and he refused. He'd give her a *medio* or 3 *kilos,* which was no help at all. Poor *mamá,* she struggled along without him. My stepfather was very loving with *mamá* and his children. He was just as sweet and loving to Fredo as to all the rest, but Fredo was a real son-of-a-bitch. He and *mamá* argued a lot. When he was fourteen he left home and went to live at our aunts' house.

I wanted to leave home too, so when Echegarrúa asked me to go off with him I said yes. I was very much in love, too. We'd been sweethearts for almost a year.

We went to live with his *mamá* in Las Yaguas. Crispo wanted to marry me and rent a room just for the two of us, but that old mother-in-law of mine wouldn't hear of it. She ruled Crispo even after he was a married man, because he was the one who put his hand in his pocket to help her out, see, and she didn't want him spending money on me. She was always interfering, insisting I should stay shut up at home while he went out and enjoyed himself.

Once he refused to take me to the carnival because the old lady objected, so I packed up my things and left. I was fed up. I didn't quarrel or anything—I never quarreled with him in the six months we were together—I just packed up and went back home to *mamá*.

I went to speak to my stepfather, Alfredo Barrera, first, because *mamá* was still mad at me. He said of course I'd be welcome, that was my home. He told *mamá* she had no call to quarrel with me because what was done was done and mothers should be on good terms with their daughters. It was because of him that *mamá* started to speak to me again. She got over it completely when I told her I was going to have a baby. She was overjoyed that she'd soon be having a grandchild.

I went back to work at Inés's beauty parlor until my stepfather told me to quit. He said with what he earned he could feed all of us and buy everything the baby would need too.

Mamá was awfully happy about her first grandchild, especially since he was a boy and born on Alfredo's saint's day. Everybody at home was happy about my baby's birth; they all loved him. And they took good care of me, too. I had nothing to cry about. I had plenty of milk, enough to suckle my baby until he was almost two. I enjoyed it. I've given the breast to all my children until they were at least one year old. But I've had enough big bellies and I don't intend to get pregnant ever again. I'm wearing the ring now. No more babies for me. I should say not!

After Alfredito was born, I kept on working and *mamá* took care of him for me. In the evening I'd bring her the food they served me at work. That way, I kept on helping out at home.

I met my second husband, Julio Marquéz, out in the street, on Calzada de Luyanó. He began courting me but I told him he needn't bother unless he would set me up in a home of my own. I was tired of living with other people. He said he would and he kept his promise. In 1948 he got me a place on San Luis.

BARRERA:

For five years we tried to set *mamá* up in a house outside of Las Yaguas, but every time we did, she'd sell it, pocket the takings, and return to the *reparto*. With 300 or 400 *pesos* tied up in her tit, she'd talk poor-mouth to scrounge a *peseta* to build another house. She had three houses that she abandoned before she finally moved out of Las Yaguas for good.

We first persuaded *mamá* to leave in 1949, to move to the *reparto*

Cuatro Caminos. I gave her 20 *pesos*, and with the help of a man called Lalo, and some friends, we got enough money together to buy a plot of land and build a small house. After all our efforts, it turned out that *mamá* didn't want the house after all. She sold it without letting anybody know and she kept all the money herself. We never found out how much she got for it. All those people who had helped her thought she'd deliberately tricked them into giving her money for a house so she could make a few hundred easy *pesos*. But they all took it calmly.

The second time *mamá* left Las Yaguas, she moved into a house with two bedrooms and a kitchen that my aunts, Dalia and Constancia, helped her pay for. She bought it for 245 *pesos*. Then, in 1951, again the whim took her and *bam!* the house was gone! She sold it without telling us and moved back to Las Yaguas. I said to her, "Very well, if you want to keep on living in the midst of all this rottenness, go ahead!"

Six or seven months later *mamá* decided to get out again. She kept making trips to Havana, and every time she made one of those trips she'd collect 50 or 60 *pesos*, but she never told us, "So-and-so gave me money." She just kept the dough tied to her tit. She'd have about 200 *pesos* stashed away, but if one of us needed 8 *kilos* for the bus to go to work, she'd say, "I don't have any. Wait, I'll go see if so-and-so will lend me a *peseta*." That way she avoided taking out the money in front of us, so we wouldn't know she had money saved up.

The third time I helped *mamá* I gave her 70 *pesos*. That was on top of the 20 I had given her for the first house. Eventually, in 1953 she got together enough money to buy a piece of land and a house in *reparto* California. The house was just a wooden shack when we moved in and it was in a terribly run-down condition. I began to work hard, patching it up with scraps of old lumber. I didn't know much about carpentry, but some friends of mine saw how interested I was and they helped me.

We bought some furniture which was more modern and comfortable than our old furniture, and I gave *mamá* a few piglets to raise. Finally, she was settled there with *papá*, my sisters, and my brother. What mattered most to me was that now they lived outside of Las Yaguas and the change of address meant they had risen in the world.

A few months after *mamá* had moved, Anita's husband, Julio, lost his job and couldn't find another. Economically they were sunk. He asked my old lady if they could move in with her and she said yes, of course. So they moved in with the three children. That made five more mouths to feed, but by working a little harder one can always manage.

Julio wasn't earning anything and he wanted Anita to get a job but she said no. She took in a bit of laundry and as long as she had that she had no need to go outside her home to work. "After all, the children have three sure meals a day at my mother's house and don't lack anything," she argued. They fought about that. They really made life a misery for the rest of us with their constant quarrels and lamentations.

Anita has always been very pretty and shapely. She's gay and vivacious and any man could lose his head over her, but she was an honest woman and a faithful wife. Julio had a jealous nature and a man with that weakness is lost.

Soon after my family moved, *papá* got sick. We kids were all pretty grown-up by then and able to work so we helped as much as we could. But *papá* wouldn't admit he was sick, and being very independent, he didn't want to take anything from anyone. If I offered him a *peso* he would refuse, saying he had plenty of money.

"Take it," I'd insist. "I can see you need it."

"Need, need!" he'd answer. "As far as that goes, everybody in the world needs something, but as long as there's life and spirit in a man he should work, especially when he has a family to support." No matter how much I insisted, he was too stubborn to accept any gift other than cigars.

Papá's sickness didn't have a name or a cure. He went to one doctor who claimed he had cancer, so he went to the hospital, where they took X-rays and gave him a thorough checkup. Every test was negative. They transferred him to the Calixto García Hospital, where they still came up with nothing. Yet he was sick as ever.

Papá's final illness began when he started to complain of swelling on his left side. *Mamá* put hot compresses on it and it went down so she didn't attach any importance to it. She never thought to tell the doctor about it. Later on we had a lot to say to her for her lack of common sense. *Papá* never told us about the chest pains he had. His heart wasn't functioning and the doctors never realized it. He died in the hospital in March, 1954, when he was just over sixty years old. The expenses of that last illness were paid by me and my half-brother, Alfredo Carlos.

All the family went to *papá*'s funeral because everybody loved him. How could they not? A better man I never hope to see. Most people held their wakes at home but we watched over *papá* at the Rodrigo Ponce Funeral Parlor. We provided plenty of coffee, chocolate, and cigarettes for those who kept vigil. At nearly every wake there were people who came to guzzle a pitcherful of chocolate, then sneak out. Others would settle down in an armchair and start to snore, until the kids sprinkled salt into their open mouths or tied them to the chair, though nobody would dare do that at a respectable place. Nothing like that happened at my father's wake. Only serious-minded people came to pay their respects. The funeral cost 160 *pesos* and we had some trouble, but my brothers and I borrowed from friends and managed to raise the money among us. My Aunt Dalia wanted to pay for the whole thing but we wouldn't let her.

Papá left us no money but he left his goodwill and good example. The only thing we argued about were the photos of his children. He had so many and everyone wanted some.

SEÑORA LORDI:

We left Las Yaguas because my husband was getting sicker and sicker. I used to scold him a lot because of his drinking. Sometimes I'd sock him. He'd protest, "No woman is going to rule me!"

"All right," I'd answer. "Keep on drinking, it's your lookout." But I don't like any kind of liquor. Why should anybody drink? It's not necessary. Look at me, I don't drink or smoke. I've seen the effect it has on people and I'm scared of it.

Alfredo had to quit drinking, and when he did he began to hate Las Yaguas. That's when I bought myself the bit of land in California and hired Vicente Quesada to build a little house for me. I bought the house with money I'd saved from taking in laundry. It was all my own money, none of my children contributed anything. I've always earned my own living, washing and ironing, except when I have a man who gives me everything and supports my children.

I'm not one to pester my children into doing things for me, and that Fredo! He has never helped me. Once in *reparto* California we had heavy rains and the place was swamped. There was water inside the room and everything. When I asked Fredo to dig a ditch beside the house to drain off the water, he refused. "No, no, no!" he said. "I won't work here, I'm going to Aunt Dalia's house." Then he up and went to his aunt, leaving me in all that mud. Anita and her husband were staying with me so he dug the trench.

My husband was very ill, but we did very well in California for about a year. He seemed to be in better health and everything, but then he started having bloody diarrhea, so I took him to the doctor and he was hospitalized at Calixto García. He died on March 29, 1954. If God had not taken Alfredo away from me, we'd still be together, as we were for twenty-five years.

After I found myself alone, I sold the house for about 40 *pesos* and returned to Las Yaguas. I married Vicente Quesada sometime around 1955. He was a carpenter by trade. He was a mulatto but his hair was fairly good. He turned out to be a fine husband but he didn't last long. He died of a liver disease in 1957. Our daughter, Susanita, was only eleven months old when he died.

BARRERA:

After *papá*'s death, *mamá* lived on in *reparto* California with Berta and Manuela and José. I was living at my aunt's in Havana and went home on weekends. When my brothers and sisters and I began to make our own way in the world, we'd all go once or twice a week to see our old lady and give her what we were duty-bound to give, but only that and no more.

At that time I was still helping my aunts with the lunch pails. Aunt Dalia paid me 7 *pesos* a week and I would buy a week's supply of groceries every Sunday and take it all the way to California so that *mamá* wouldn't have to go to the grocery store. Little did she know it took all my wages. I sacrificed myself helping her that way for many long years, but she never mentioned it. She thought that weekly box of groceries came as a gift from Aunt Dalia. Not that she ever thanked her for it, either.

In 1954, that same year that *papá* died, I got myself a good job with the Ferrer Construction Company, plastering on high buildings. Heights don't bother me in the least. Oh, when I first climb up I may feel a bit shaky due to some reflex, but I get over that. We'd stand on a wooden platform that was hauled up the side of the scaffolding on ropes and secured with a special figure-eight knot that we called the "fox's tail." But it's very important to work with someone you trust when you're working high up. If you're teamed up with a guy who isn't used to work on a scaffolding, it can be dangerous.

In those days ignorant country boys would come to Havana and take an apprentice's job at the rate of 3.50 *pesos* a day. There used to be a lot of competition from them. Those little *guajiros* loved to show off by leaning way out beyond the scaffolding, and that's when they were apt to get their horns knocked off. Being new at that kind of work, they hadn't acquired the flexibility of a guy like me who had worked for three years. When they leaned out too far, the fox's tail would keep slipping until the knot worked loose, and then the whole platform would be up-ended.

Once I almost broke my neck because of one of those *guajiros*, but I was lucky enough to come out whole. I was working with a very green apprentice on a high-rise apartment building. Well, we were between the seventeenth and eighteenth stories when the kid looks down and sees the heads of tiny people below and gets dizzy. I threw a loop of the rope around him and tied him to secure him to the platform. Then I had to lower the platform by myself. The other guys on nearby platforms helped, but that was one hell of a touchy job maneuvering our platform alone.

When I worked for Ferrer I became a member of the CTC,[5] but I was a member in name only. I carried a card and paid my dues, that's all. We paid according to what we earned. Say a guy earned 200 *pesos*, he'd pay 2 *pesos*, which is 1 percent of his wages. To be frank, I thought they were a greedy lot.

For three years I stuck to that job, working day and night, because the more hours I worked, the more pay I got. I worked sixteen hours one day, seventeen hours the next. There were weeks when I earned as much as 50 or 60 *pesos*. That's over 200 *pesos* a month.

5. *Confederación de Trabajadores de Cuba* (Confederation of Cuban Workers), reorganized after 1959 as *Central de Trabajadores de Cuba* (Central Organization of Cuban Trade Unions).

As I was earning a good wage, *mamá* was always coming to me, pestering me to give her money. From the day I first got paid, she twisted my arm and wheedled all she could get out of me. I was quite willing to give her money when she had none, but she was greedy. If you gave her your eyes, she'd come back for your eyebrows. "Tina Moneybags" I call her, and that's a name she richly deserves.

Do you know how many jobs I've had to leave on account of my *mamá*? One day, when I was working as a cook at Luyanó Popular, *mamá* showed up, wanting me to give her some money because my little sister had a liver disease that was eating up her blood and she needed a transfusion. I borrowed 10 *pesos* from Mercurio, the owner, and right in front of him I handed the money to *mamá*.

Two days later she went to Mercurio and begged him for 2 *pesos* because she said I was a worthless bum who never gave her anything. Mercurio told her to get out. I didn't learn about the incident until later. "Some mother you have, kid!" Mercurio said to me. "Forgive my saying so but she oughtn't to be a mother at all. Sorry if I've offended you."

"No, no, that's all right, don't worry," I said. Then I quit the job.

One day I won the lottery. I can't imagine how *mamá* found out but she did. I wasn't in the habit of playing the lottery, but that day a man was killed in a collision at the corner of Figura and Concepción and five or six others were badly hurt. Later that same morning there was another accident at the other corner, Escobar and Concepción, where two more died. The street fairly ran with blood. I asked a bookie I knew, "Say, Irelio, what number is blood?"

"Blood is no. 84," he told me.

"All right, put me down for 1 *peso* on no. 84 and one on no. 384." Altogether I won over 470 *pesos* on my bets.

A little after 6:00 in the evening *mamá* went to visit my aunts. I knew what she wanted right away. Whenever *mamá* paid a call on my aunts you could be sure she was after something. That day I came in to find *mamá* sitting in my aunt's bedroom. Old Armando was sitting in his usual place by the window in the willow rocker, and I gave her 50 *pesos* right in front of him. About a week later *mamá* showed up to complain about me. "That dirty bum won over 400 *pesos* and didn't give me one measly *peso*," she whined. Good God! How can she go there and say, "Fredo is crazy, Fredo is no good, he never gives me anything." Damn it, how can she say that when I had just given her 50 *pesos*? My aunt and uncle were furious and they defended me. They knew it was a lie and was her way of begging for more money from them. Nobody has to plead for help like that. Why did she have to overplay her part that way?

Analyzing *mamá*, I've come to the conclusion that she's a very complex person. She wants to be some kind of super-person, with a double egotism, always having money stashed away yet living in miserable poverty so she can ask for help.

One weekend when I went home to California, *mamá* and I had a big quarrel. There were many things she did that provoked me beyond endurance. A little while after *papá*'s death, that lazy bum Vicente moved in with her. He did nothing but drink rum and sing tangos. I don't know whether she was in love or if she just lost her head, taking him in like that, but I was disgusted. A mother has a right to have a lover if she likes. After all, you feel an impulse. All right, give in to it all the way, get rid of your craving, but a mother should be discreet about it. She shouldn't take him into her own home so that other people gossip and judge ill of her. But *mamá* fell into that abyss and there's no telling the harm she did to her children. She ought to have known better.

Then it turned out that *mamá* was pregnant. *Papá* died on March 29, 1954, and Susanita was born early in 1955—I forget what month. I suspect that *mamá* got involved with Vicente while *papá* was still alive. It stands to reason that if a woman's husband is too sick to have intercourse with her and only a few months after his death she discovers she's pregnant, there's only one explanation. Nobody can drive the idea out of my head that *mamá* was unfaithful. She hid a lot of things about that matter from us.

Mamá lived with Vicente in free union—or something of the kind. I don't know whether he ever legally recognized Susanita as his daughter. Maybe *mamá*'s present husband, Norberto, did.

I was still bringing a weekly box of groceries to *mamá* while she was with Vicente. Living with my aunt I had nobody to do my laundry. So one day I said to *mamá*, "I'm going to bring over my shirts and a few cakes of soap so you can wash and iron them."

The next time I went to visit her I asked her, "Are my shirts clean?"

"No," she says. "I didn't have any soap or starch or charcoal to heat the iron with." The shirts had been soaking for more than two weeks and were ruined. I said to her, "How is it that you don't have soap or the time to wash my shirts, and yet you can wash and iron the shirts of this fellow Vicente who gobbles up the food I bring you and never does a lick of work? How can you say you don't have soap when I brought you four cakes of soap on Sunday? I don't give you money but I send you groceries every week." Then she knew that it was I who bought the groceries for her.

I told her, "If you want to have a man or a hundred men on the side, that's no business of mine. But I will not permit you to have a man living in this house as long as I'm the one supporting all of you. My father is dead and I refuse to fall to such a low level as to support your lover as if he were your pimp or something." Good God, I didn't even know the man's surname!

Mamá didn't like that and she slapped me. I turned around and left. I went to my Aunt Dalia's home and told her what had happened. She couldn't believe it when I described how *mamá* wanted me to support that man. "It's true," I insisted. "I refuse to go on giving her food. I will not lower myself like that, though I'm sorry for my brother's and sister's sakes." But I kept on sending the groceries each week anyway.

I was in the right. It was that refusal of hers to do my laundry that disgusted me so. I say that any woman, be she my mother or anyone else, who rejects her own son for a man's tail deserves to die. A whole year passed before I went back to see *mamá*. It was during that time that Vicente died.

Mamá found herself alone with my sister Susanita and my brother José. Maybe she felt all her children had abandoned her and she wanted to be nearer Havana, where there was better transportation, because again she was possessed of that madness of wanting to move elsewhere. "I want to get out of here, I want to get out of here, I want to get out of here!" That's all she ever said until *bam!* without asking anybody's advice, she sold all she had and moved back to Las Yaguas. I don't know how much she got for the house but she was certainly fleeced.

In one of those crazy impulses of hers, she sold both the hog and the sow, along with the other things, for a song. She practically gave them away. The hog weighed 180 pounds and she sold it for only 30 *pesos*. I didn't like that one bit, let me tell you. I had bought those hogs, at least I bought the hog and she bought the sow, but I was the one who broke my back carrying pails of slop all the way from the bus stop to her house, and I didn't see 1 *centavo* from the sale.

That was the last time *mamá* moved back to Las Yaguas. After the Revolution triumphed they cleared out the whole place, so she couldn't live there anymore.

After my father's death I felt out of place. I'd lost the one person to whom I could turn. I had always told him all my doings, the good and the bad. Now that I was alone I thought, "My only refuge is gone. I must mend my ways. I must find a way to have a home of my own, and a wife."

I was twenty-two when I had a relationship with a mulatto girl called Melba. Her mother, Ofelia, took a liking to me because I was such a respectable young fellow, and she gave me visiting rights to their home. Ofelia was separated from her husband, Gaspar, and had gone through all sorts of hardship to raise their three children. Besides her regular work, she sold lottery tickets. The poor woman worked so hard she eventually got the lung sickness. I loved Melba and pitied her and her mother because they were so poor. Maybe I'm a bit too sentimental that way . . . oh well!

I was earning about 63 *pesos* a week, so one day I said to Melba, "Look, I can help you and your *mamá* and buy you whatever you need—clothes, shoes, and so on." She accepted, and every week I'd give 5 *pesos* to Ofelia and 10 to Melba.

Melba had an uncle who was an army sergeant, and he opposed my relationship with his niece. I could never understand that man. There was his niece, practically destitute, living on the breadline and on public charity, and not only does he not help her, but when someone else comes along and eases her burden, he interferes and makes trouble for him. I think he must have been jealous. He went and told Melba's father that I was no good, that I'd dishonored his daughter and never intended to marry her. What a stupid lie! Why, I had already bought a set of bedroom furniture. It was plain furniture but not bad for a poor man like me, and it was all paid for.

Gaspar and I had a big argument. He accused me of deflowering his daughter, which was a lie. I hadn't touched her. We'd done nothing except kiss. Gaspar didn't scare me and I still intended to marry Melba. When she had her fifteenth birthday we had everything ready for the wedding. I gave her the money for her party but I told her I wasn't going. I expected that there'd be trouble and I didn't want to be blamed for it. It's well that I didn't go because there was a phenomenal fight.

Soon after that, I ran into Gaspar on Santa Ana Avenue. He pulled out a knife and said to me, "Did you ever see a man bark like a dog at noon? Well you will, because that's what I aim to make you do."

"No kidding!" I said. "And did you ever see a Negro crow like a cock at midnight? Because that's what I aim to make you do!"

I well knew Gaspar was a *brujero,* and sure enough, soon I began to feel pretty darn funny, and I remembered his threats. I explained my symptoms to *mamá.* She advised me to consult a certain spiritist she knew. I objected, "Oh no, wherever I go it's going to cost money. I'd rather let it slide." But I couldn't just forget it.

Frankly, I don't believe I can overcome someone else with some kind of powder or with a glass of water, and I'm not afraid that an evil spirit can do me any harm, because I'm a material being and I lead a material life. People tell me that the dead give me things, but I say, "No sir, no dead person has ever given me anything and I don't know about such things."

I may seem to be contradicting myself, but I *do* see a great many things myself. The truth is, I see some people at night who have a glow around them. I really *do.* To me, that's evidence of some kind of power they've been given.

Once when I was sixteen or seventeen I had a revelation. I was lying half asleep when I heard someone call to me, "Galileo." Then I saw a fairly strong man, copper-skinned and round-faced. "I am Lucifer," he said. And he really did have something that shined like a star on his forehead. Maybe it was a medallion stuck to his cap or something.

I believe Lucifer has helped me many times in my life, when I've been caught in a difficult situation, when I felt I was drowning, and somehow I came out all right. Then he always asks me to offer something in his name. The most I've ever given that man is a flower called Black Prince. I left it out for one or two days, then took it away.

There was a time when I couldn't sleep and strange things happened to me. I would have strange dreams about my friends. I foresaw things that happened to them and to myself, too. One girl used to come to me and say, "Ah, come on, Alfredo, tell me what will happen to me."

"How can I tell you?" I would answer. "I'm no *santero.*" Yet afterward I would dream about the girl, and the next day I'd tell her, "Look, *chica,* last night I dreamed this about you."

Then she'd say, "Man, that's just exactly what happened!"

I didn't take Gaspar's threats lightly. One day I went to his house where he had a big iron pot, and if the saints really exist as people claim, may they forgive me, because I smashed that pot and all the rubbish in it. Amid the junk I found a photograph of myself, so there's no doubt Gaspar tried something on me. After that my symptoms disappeared. Later I came to believe that being a man of nervous temperament, my symptoms were not due to the sorcery but to the impression his threats made on me. Also, it occurred to me that if the man really had such powers, wouldn't he be living decently instead of being down and out? If *I* had such powers I'd be living like the king of India!

After that, Gaspar was on the lookout for me, but then—I guess his sorcery must have boomeranged—he was badly hurt at work. He worked in the warehouse of the Pasiega noodle factory and one day a heap of flour sacks tumbled down on top of him. He sent word for me from the hospital so I went. He told me he'd pay for the wedding fiesta when I married his daughter.

"Marry your daughter!" I said. "I wouldn't even marry your whoring mother if she came out of her grave and asked me!" By then I'd broken with Melba. I was sick to death of all the trouble and scenes her father and uncle had made and I wanted no more of it. So I left her.

We'd been sweethearts for one year and seven months and in all that time I hadn't laid her once. I wouldn't want a man to dishonor my sister and I treated her as I would have wished my sisters to be treated. I left her intact. After that experience I decided, "No more engagements for me. I won't visit any girl in her home or get seriously involved again." And so it was—for a while, anyway.

Chapter Three

Defeating Ourselves?

IN THOSE EARLY DAYS before the Revolution, I never thought of myself as a rebel and I kept away from politics. I always said that politics was for people who knew about it, not for the workers, at least not until some phenomenal change came over the world. My only interests were my work and my sweetheart. I've always lived for myself alone and tried to help my family as much as I could. I never thought about society as a whole. In my family only my half-brother, Alfredo Carlos, thought about those things and was involved in the revolutionary process from the very beginning.

Still, nobody could point a finger at me and call me a bum or anything, because I spent all my time in discussions or reading. I always had some little pamphlet or other to read. They called me "Old Man" because I'd sit down to talk with older people all the time. When I was working in the restaurant, Luyanó Popular, I learned something about socialism from my friend Juan Carlos Montano, who is now dead. Montano was Minerva Ruz's husband and lived in Las Yaguas. I knew what street he lived on and we got to be very good friends. He used to come into the restaurant and talk with some big shots—you could tell they were important people from the way they dressed—and I learned a lot listening to them. Not that they or Montano influenced me any. Nobody has ever been able to do that, not even the mother who bore me. But I got to read a lot of Montano's books.

One day I said to him, "Hey, Montano, do you have a novel you could lend me?"

"No, but I have a much better book for you," he said. About a week later he brought me a book by . . . was it Hegel? No, it was about, let me see, the science of politics or the politics of a scientist? Anyhow, I read quite a bit of that book and liked the ideas in it. It was about a society where everything evened out, I mean where everybody shared what there was instead of some people having a great deal and others nothing.

I really and truly liked that ideology. After that Montano brought me other books.

I began to see that it was unfair for others to have so much and I so little. People were not equal. What struck me most was that some people had more than they needed while others often had to go to bed hungry. There was so much poverty and sadness in the world yet the rich felt no pity. All they cared about was getting even richer. I thought that if I had some power in the world I would have changed things altogether. How young and inexperienced I was!

We had always been in favor of the Popular Socialist Party, as the Communist Party used to be called. The communists opened our eyes about what might be done to put things right. I knew that in Cuba inequality had something to do with politics and the way the police beat up people. Working in a restaurant, I often saw quarrels start and the police hit people with their sticks to make them quiet down, and then they'd arrest them. I didn't like that kind of thing. Those policemen were like savages. They were entitled by the regulations to carry one short firearm, but they carried a forty-five, a thirty-eight, or a twenty-two, and a commando knife, too, because either they wanted to feel bigger than anyone else or they were bigger cowards.

I used to get my hair cut in Miguel's barbershop. Some of his customers were policemen, and I remember one guy who boasted shamelessly about all the weapons he carried. It was disgusting to hear him talk. I spoke with him only because if a guy starts up a conversation with you, it's good manners to answer him.

In 1952, at the time of Batista's coup, I could have joined the government police force or the Army or the Navy if I'd wanted to. I was the friend of the son of one of Batista's chiefs of police. I knew his son because many's the dinner they got from my aunt. To this day they still owe for quite a number of them.

At that time I was living with my aunts on Pasaje de Córdoba. In my aunt's building there were about twenty apartments, and in eight or ten of these lived communists, practically all of them foreigners—Catalans[6] and Spaniards. Every time there was some incident caused by the boys who were doing sabotage for the Twenty-sixth of July Movement, Batista's police would drag the older men out of Córdoba, sometimes in their undershorts.

Every night I went to one of their houses with Uncle Armando to play dominoes. He was pro-American and a rabid imperialist, but he'd talk politics with those people for hours. They had read all the books and would criticize Batista and his followers and comment on the abuses. I'd

6. People from Catalonia, in northeastern Spain.

read some socialist books but I had no political ideas and was never interested in what they said.

My aunts and my cousin Narciso supported the Revolution secretly from the very beginning. Narciso worked with his father, Jorge Montoya, at the Cóndor garage, where there was a cell of the revolutionary movement. Narciso joined it and took part in the insurrection. He was in the group that attacked Batista's army headquarters in Matanzas.[7] Some were killed but my cousin was spared and returned to Havana. Batista's chief of police, Pilar García,[8] swore that none of the men who participated in the assault would survive. He must have been a clairvoyant because all but one were finally killed. The police began searching for the rebels so my cousin hid in the house of a neighbor.

The late court prosecutor of Havana, a client and friend of my aunt, tried to intervene in Narciso's favor. He got the prosecutor in charge of the case to promise that if the men gave themselves up, their lives would be safe and they would be freed. But then the wanted men made the biggest mistake of their lives. They asked for asylum at the Haitian Embassy. The moment they told me, I remembered García's threat and I thought, "They're as good as dead!"

The Haitian Embassy was the shittiest place! The Embassy got their water from an electric pump, and when the motor broke down, months went by before they repaired it. During that time Narciso's aunt, Juana Elena, brought meals and huge bottles of water to him and the other fugitives. A movie camera photographed people going in and out of the Embassy carrying the food in an enormous lunch pail. Some evenings my Uncle Armando went to play dominoes with them. Meanwhile, the police were observing everything and taking reels of movies.

So life went on as the fugitives tried to get a safe-conduct to leave Cuba. The authorities stalled by making difficulties with the visas. There were a lot of promises—"No, not today—tomorrow. No, the day after tomorrow . . . ," and no action. Once Narciso got an opportunity to leave

---

7. The attack on the Goicuría military garrison in Matanzas in April, 1956, was not organized by the Twenty-sixth of July Movement. It was apparently planned by Reynoldo García, an *Auténtico* previously affiliated with Aureliano Sánchez Arango. The garrison troops had been forewarned and the attack was crushed at the outset. Ten of the rebels were killed and many more were wounded. At least one, but probably more, were killed after they were captured. A small number of those who escaped sought refuge in the Haitian Embassy in the Havana suburb of Miramar. (Robert Taber, *M-26: The Biography of a Revolution* (New York: Lyle Stuart, 1961), pp. 78–80. A shorter and somewhat conflicting version of the Goicuría attack can be found in Thomas, *Cuba: The Pursuit of Freedom*, pp. 885–86. Photographs taken just after the rebels' defeat were published in *Life*, May 21, 1956, p. 55.)

8. Colonel Pilar García, provincial military commander and commandant at Goicuría. He did not become chief of the national police until 1958.

but he refused because two or three of his friends were still there. Two of those were able to go to Costa Rica and they left.[9]

Then one day Blanco Rico[10] was killed and Brigadier Salas Cañizares had the Haitian Embassy surrounded.[11] Everybody said Cañizares had killed him, but it seems no man had big enough balls to dare arrest the head of the Cuban police. So he was free, and there were those who were trying to liquidate him to avenge Blanco Rico's death. Well, they succeeded. Salas Cañizares was shot but the refugees at the Haitian Embassy were accused of having done it! Accusing them was simply a trick to liquidate them. One day it will be definitely proved that nobody from the Embassy shot Cañizares.

For one thing, there were no firearms in the Embassy except a small 32-caliber pistol loaded with only two bullets, neither of which worked. Another thing is that Salas's death wounds were in the lower abdomen, and since the only way to drive a bullet into him was to shoot from below, because he always wore a bullet-proof vest, he couldn't have been shot at from a building. Salas Cañizares must have been shot by one of his men.[12]

The very day of the trouble, Narciso called us. He spoke to Juana Elena and told her that dogs had been set loose around the Embassy and the building was surrounded. At 11:00 that morning and later on at 1:00 P.M., Juana Elena tried to phone the Embassy. Then she tried by every possible means to see the ambassador, but the Embassy was indeed surrounded. The whole thing had been planned down to the last detail. They were bent on killing everybody there and decided that not even a cat would be allowed to leave the Embassy alive. That was the day my cousin died.

My cousin Narciso had a noble-looking face, and now my aunts want to build him up into a hero. Well, frankly, for me Narciso is no hero. Only a person who is morally clean can be said to be a hero, and that he was not. But it was natural for the loss of her son to affect Constancia

9. Some of the Goicuría rebels fled to Mexico after the attack. We found no reports that those rebels who sought asylum in the Embassy were able to negotiate with the government for permission to leave the country.

10. Colonel Antonio Blanco Rico, Batista's chief of military intelligence, was fatally shot on October 28, 1956, as he left the Montmarte Club in Vedado with a group of police and army officers. The assailants were students, among them Juan Pedro Carbó Servia and José Machado Rodríguez, who escaped. (Hugh Thomas names Rolando Cubela, who later became a counterrevolutionary, as one of the assailants. See *Cuba: The Pursuit of Freedom*, pp. 889–90.)

11. Rafael Salas Cañizares, an army officer instrumental in the success of Batista's second coup, was head of the Cuban national police. The police search for the two students took Salas Cañizares to the Haitian Embassy, possibly because he believed Carbó and Machado would be found there, or perhaps as an excuse to attack other Cubans taking refuge there. Ten Cubans were killed at the Haitian Embassy and Carbó and Machado were shot down by police six months later (April, 1957), after they had participated in the attack on the Presidential Palace in Havana.

12. Salas Cañizares died October 31, 1956, two days after being shot in the Embassy siege.

deeply. Yet what contrasts life presents to us! Here's a woman who had good reason to feel bitter and turn against the Revolution but Constancia is as revolutionary as ever. Narciso's death for the Revolution has not made her slacken. On the contrary, it has strengthened her support. She belongs to the Federation of Cuban Women and to the Committee for Defense of the Revolution, works hard for them, and continues to be a fighter.

The only one of my relatives who was never involved in the Revolution is my cousin Basilio, Cousin Ursula's son. He's the world's worst bastard. I never got along with him and never thought he had any of the qualities you look for in a man. Even after he grew up, Basilio was always indebted to his mother for all his clothes and shoes. In 1957 or '58 he worked as a radio technician for a station owned by a man called Ramos. Basilio earned over 100 *pesos* a month then, to say nothing of a little business on the side that gave him 200 or 300 more. But believe it or not, that guy never had 1 *peso* in his pocket. On payday he'd sneak off to the dog races and pour his money out on bets. After he lost it all, he'd play up to his mother and aunt and ask them for money for carfare and things. Then he'd borrow money from the loan sharks to bet at the races. He kept piling up debts until he owed more than he could handle. I never could stand that guy!

Eventually Basilio lost every last *centavo* he had. Two or three loan sharks were after him so he didn't leave the house for about a month. He pretended insanity; he wouldn't sit in front of a mirror unless it was covered up with soapsuds or a sheet, because he claimed he couldn't stand to look at his reflection. Somebody else had to shave him.

One afternoon my aunt's sister-in-law, Juana Elena, who was a spiritist, went to visit him. She brought stuff the *santeros* use, including a dead rooster, and said she was going to cure Basilio of the spirit that was plaguing him. I've never believed in any of that stuff. In fact, I don't even believe there are superior beings. A man of flesh and blood, here on earth, may be superior because he's more intelligent, or has studied more, but what you call superior beings—spirits and so on—I don't believe in.

Armando, Aunt Dalia's husband, had no idea they had called a spiritist—they had kept it from him because he has no religion, just like me. When he saw Juana Elena there he asked me, "What's wrong with Basilio?"

I told him everything I knew. I'd done a bit of detective work on my own and had found out about Basilio's debts. "Well," I explained, "there's a certain Café San Miguel where he owes about 800 *pesos*. He hocked his ring and watch that were gifts from his mother, but he's still in debt. That's why he doesn't dare even walk along that street."

The following day Uncle Armando quit early, around 3:00 P.M., and we went and talked with the man at the San Miguel. Basilio owed him 890 *pesos*. Old Armando paid the debt with his savings and got the watch and ring out of hock and we went home. In a mischievous mood, he slyly put the watch and ring on a table where Basilio couldn't miss them. When he found them, he must have thought that all natural laws had been broken and that Juana Elena's witchcraft had worked. Sure enough, the next morning he woke up sane.

When Basilio married his first cousin, Dolores, I thought, "Married to his first cousin? Disgusting!" It was a marriage of convenience. Dolores's father used to own a glass factory and he'd left the country. Basilio married Dolores believing he could get hold of her old man's bank account. She was in love with him but he didn't give a damn about her. I suspect he's stuck to her all these years for the sake of the children. That Basilio is a real hypocrite.

Not long after my cousin Narciso's death, I became more involved and took a stand against Batista's regime. I began to understand a little about politics and in 1956 joined the Popular Socialist Party, which used to have its headquarters on the Calzada de Luyanó. The Party built it with funds they raised. They kept giving fiestas until the workers had contributed 4,000 *pesos*—and that was real money then, let me tell you. But no one ever complained about all the money it cost to set up the headquarters, nor about the workers' sacrifices to raise it just so the eight or ten principal Party leaders could enjoy it.

There's a curious fact about that place. You see, the communists once supported Batista. They made an alliance with him and got him elected President. Sure, Minerva Ruz says she used to be for Batista "in her own way," like now she's for Fidel "in her own way." It wasn't just Minerva, it was all communists. And then, when Batista carried out his coup on March 10, he put a funeral parlor on Calzada Street where Party headquarters had been.

I liked the Party a lot. They had a fiesta every month and when you went to them you paid dues. I had a Party card, but it wasn't the Popular Socialist Party that brought me into contact with the Revolution.

I helped the Revolution because a friend of mine, Orlando Pardo, was a member of the Thirteenth of March Movement. I'd been working for the Ferrer Construction Company since 1954 and was also still delivering lunch pails for my aunt. Orlando worked in La Corona factory and that's how I met him. He was part of a small revolutionary group that met in a garage on Esperanza Street. They used the place as an arsenal and a lot of things came out of there. Orlando explained to me what it was all about and I joined too. I helped in every way I could—fixing cars, getting gasoline, changing a tire. . . . I also got them bombs, pistols, bullets, money, food, medicines, and things like that.

There was a colonel called Betancourt who had a very pretty daughter. To tell the truth, I ate a lot of her cornballs and I could get anything I wanted from that kid. I really had her eating out of my hand. I'd say to her, "I need a pistol," and she'd say, "I can't get you one today or tomorrow either, but one way or another I'll get one." I never found out how she managed it, but little by little I helped increase the arsenal. Many's the blow I received because of that, too.

It was nothing of great importance and it's all in the past so I'm not boasting about it, but I was called to the Bureau of Military Intelligence and was also taken to the Fifth Precinct as a prisoner. They suspected my friend Orlando and his group and they suspected me too, but they didn't know for sure. Actually, I was and I wasn't. Nobody knew whether I belonged or not. Only I and those I helped knew. Even so, I was taken in for questioning and beaten up about five times.

The first time they came for me at Aunt Dalia's. I had a friend, Angel Castañeda, who wrote for the rebel newspaper, *Juventud Rebelde*. He was a revolutionary and had been in the Escambray Mountains. The military knew about him, and one day, when we were sitting drinking coffee, a two-toned car with an American license plate drove up to the house. "Look, Angelito, go quickly out the back way because they've come for you and my brother," I said, and he disappeared.

I had no reason to run away. The things I kept in the house—the supplies and arms from the garage—were well hidden. There wasn't a chance they'd find any evidence. I slipped into the shower but they dragged me out, still soapy, and took me to the Bureau. I was taken to a room where four or five men gave me a working-over. One dark-skinned little fellow kicked me in the belly, then the rest beat me up until I lost consciousness. Well, it was terrible. When I came to, I was in a cell, covered in blood.

Then this colonel says, "We found the keys to ninety-six cars in your house. How is it you have so many keys when you're not a parking-lot attendant or a garage mechanic?"

"I found them and I was going to sell them to a locksmith." I was lying, but I was lucky. They let me go after three days.

During our struggle against Batista, I and my comrades owed a great debt of gratitude to our friend the court prosecutor, may God have him wherever it pleases God to have him. That gentleman really did a lot to help the revolutionaries, especially the ones engaged in sabotage in Havana. As a magistrate he was able to free many of us. Finally, the authorities prepared a file on the judge himself and those papers were as good as the hangman's rope if they'd ever wanted to use them.

Orlando had a plan for me to go to the Sierra with Mario and Pepito, both comrades in the Movement. They were taking three passengers a week, but the week we volunteered they had room for only two people.

So we tossed a coin and Mario and Pepito won. They were captured in the foothills of Guantánamo after a terrible struggle.

The Revolution was mostly a youth movement. Batista's government knew this and they recruited lots of young men into what we called Batista's *casquito* army.[13] They were paid to infiltrate the Revolutionary Army and spy on their movements. The few boys in Las Yaguas who became *casquitos* were mostly bums who joined to earn an easy living. They didn't have the guts to push a wheelbarrow of sweet potatoes in the street to sell at five for a *peseta*. They preferred a soldier's career because they thought they'd be drawing a salary without working. Sure, a soldier wears clean, well-pressed uniforms and eats well—that was the good life to them. Those pimps liked to swagger around, showing off their little pistols, so they fell for it.

They joined up toward the end and many lived to regret it, but by then it was too late. They were already caught—toy soldiers to the last. The longest any of them had been in the *casquito* army before they had to fight was three months. What can a man learn in that time? Barely to shoot a gun. It takes at least a year or two to learn something of the fundamentals of fighting. When they were sent to Santa Clara to fight the Rebels, many of the *casquitos* never got there. Some were in the armored train that was derailed by Che, others turned back and sold or gave away their arms to the Rebels.[14]

I was pretty expert by that time and was often called upon to psychologize many of the comrades who claimed to be with us but who really belonged to the *casquito* army and the intelligence corps. In my old lady's house I have a box full of papers with accounts of the many traitors who deceived us into believing they were on our side.

Those "comrades" joined pretending to feel great patriotic fervor and then they stuck a knife in our backs. They'd steal the codes and plans and the lists of names and take them to the Fifth Precinct. Then someone would be found dead at El Laguito and someone else at Marianao. And who did it? Why those same infiltrators! But in spite of them, the Movement began to burn here and break there and make a big noise all over the Republic.

I was arrested again just before the triumph of the Revolution. A man in Cayo Cruz who collected scrap metal found two pistols, each with 115

---

13. *Casquitos*, or "little caps," is a derogatory term of reference popularly used in Cuba for the men specially recruited by Batista's army to fight the Rebels. The nickname came from the type of military hat they wore.

14. In December, 1958, General José Eleuterio Pedraza sent an armored train with 400 soldiers to Santa Clara, Las Villas, to stop the Rebels' Ciro Redondo invasion column under Che Guevara's command. On December 30 the train was derailed and Batista's soldiers surrendered to the Rebel Army.

shots. I bought them from him for 90 *pesos* and sold them to a comrade in the Movement. Well, in Cayo Cruz they found out who took the pistols, and one fine day a captain shows up at the scrap dealer's house and takes him to the station for questioning. There he tells them that he'd sold the arms to me. Imagine! He really put me on the spot. I wasn't exactly on friendly terms with the police to begin with. For the past few days I'd been preparing small bombs, so I did a disappearing act. The police looked for me all over the place. The day they caught me I was in Las Yaguas. One of the vigilantes from the Bureau lived in Las Yaguas and he liked me. If not, he wouldn't have risked warning me. "Look, Fredito, clear out of here quickly. There are six men looking for you."

I was off like a shot. I ran up the hill behind Las Yaguas and down by way of Jorge González's. Then I went to my sister's house, where they caught me. The lieutenant who came to arrest me said, "Look, kid, you bought those pistols and resold them to the group connected with the church!"

"What church?" said I. "I never go to church. I don't even *pass* in front of a church except on the bus. Besides, church is for women—especially old women, bah!" Those were my very words. I denied everything. "No, I didn't keep them, I threw them in the river and there they are." It was a good alibi under the circumstances. But they took me to the station and began to pressure me. I stuck to my story; they would have had to kill me before I'd tell them who I sold the pistols to. I'd have been betraying him and myself too. Besides, if I'd told them they'd have arrested him, and in those days my corpse might have been found at dawn blown up by a bomb or with four bullets in my brain. That's the way things were in Havana then.

Since I didn't confess, they had no way of proving I had sold the pistols. Even though the scrap dealer fingered me, I got three witnesses to establish my alibi for the day and hour he said he sold the stuff to me. One of them was a sailor, another a soldier, and the third, Lino Jiménez, had been a captain in the army that fought against Spain. It was the word of four people, two of whom were part of Batista's regime, against the word of the scrap dealer. The court decided he was a liar and gave him seventy-two hours to produce the arms in question. The only thing that saved him was the triumph of the Revolution before the seventy-two hours were up.

Two days after peace had been re-established, the revolutionaries rounded up all the men in Las Yaguas. They wanted to investigate to see who'd been involved in the Revolution and who had not. Because of the roundup, there were no men to be seen. Only the women remained, and many of them were out looking for their husbands. I was hiding from certain acquaintances of mine who didn't know I lived in Las Yaguas.

They would never have imagined it! There were several lieutenants and captains who knew me, and when they found me in the *reparto* they sent me to the Thirteenth Precinct.

I waited on the stairs in the courtyard with the other detainees, until finally the revolutionary lieutenant in charge, who knew I lived in Las Yaguas, saw me. He'd done sabotage in Havana and I had helped them with arms. He had me brought inside the station and there he told me, "All right, you can go."

I am by no means a revolutionary. I'm a good worker, a man who does his duty, but to me a revolutionary is one who either was in the Sierra or else really made sacrifices for the cause during the early years of the Revolution. I was not one of those, so why should I, after so many years, be such a hypocrite as to proclaim myself more revolutionary than Fidel himself? I don't play such tricks. That's not to say I don't like Fidel or wish he were not in power. But the men who fought in the Sierra expected one thing from Fidel and got another. When Fidel was in the Sierra he was not communist, and the men there with him weren't members of the Popular Socialist Party. Then, when the Revolution triumphed, circumstances made Fidel fall back on communism. You may be sure that if those men had known in the beginning that Fidel was going to make Cuba communist, they would have hanged him. You can bet on that. I don't mean the Cuban people in general, either; I mean the very men who were up there in the Sierra fighting with him.

Many of them are eating rope now. They earn 100 *pesos* or so—a miserable pittance, and that has changed their feelings toward Fidel. They think, "We spend three years fighting in the Sierra, going hungry, suffering twenty troubles, and when it's over, we're even worse off."

Although people complain about the new system, one should realize there are the good things as well as the bad. So we're short of food—that's something you can't cover up with one finger—but there are schools, jobs, and new houses. Fifty thousand Cubans have benefited from the Revolution, not that they deserve it, because they do nothing but criticize and put down the new government. But I think the government has asked too much of the people. It was El Che who said that a good communist is one who wants the best for his country. Well, as I see it, to be a good communist means to be better than others in everything relating to your conduct at work and at home. In other words, to be perfect. I don't doubt that those things are possible—you can't doubt anything in life—but I think it's very difficult for a man to be perfect. That's asking too much.

I'm firmly convinced that communism cannot exist without capitalism. What I call a capitalist is a man who goes to a country and invests, say, 20 million *pesos* over a long period of time, in building houses, taking all the risks, and making a profit of 10 percent. Who would benefit from that? Why, the nation, to which he makes such a luxury available.

I didn't agree with the way Fidel appropriated people's capital, and took away the property of a man who had made twenty sacrifices to establish a neighborhood grocery store. I would have let that man keep his store. The Revolution could just as easily have progressed and allowed those people to progress, too. In Czechoslovakia, for instance, you find state enterprise and private enterprise side by side. Even in the Soviet Union there was some private enterprise until fifteen years ago.

It's all right if in a communist state you pass a law putting a ceiling on rents. They can say to him, "All right, the building is yours, but from now on you can't charge more than 50 or 60 percent of what you've been charging." But taking away somebody's property? That's another thing altogether.

As for taking people's savings, well, there were certain generals from Batista's regime who had accumulated fortunes of 15 or 20 million *pesos*. None of that money was inherited, so how did they make so much money? By trickery or outright theft, that's how. Well, I myself would have stripped them of their last penny. That was all right. What I don't like is the way Fidel also took away the money of a man like me.

I don't want to go too far but I'll be frank with you. At the time of Playa Girón, 99 percent of the Cuban people were on Fidel's side, but since then he has lost the people's trust. Their eyes have been opened by his unfulfilled promises. He's been caught in the net of his own lies. Fidel is an honest man, but in the eyes of the nation he's been made to look like a liar.

I say that you should not make a promise you cannot keep. Now I'm not saying that Fidel didn't keep his word. No, I can see that circumstances made it impossible for him to do so, but most people don't see that. All they see is that they were promised one thing and got another. Of course they have to accept the present system because it's a condition of life.

If people don't complain, it's because they're scared. Everyone distrusts everyone else because nobody knows who's in favor of what, and there have been many cases where a mother has betrayed her son, or a man his brother or his friend, and turned them over to the police. That doesn't happen so often now, but just after the Revolution the least criticism of the new government was considered counterrevolutionary. You could say, "The Cola drink is no good," and you'd be clapped into jail. If you were very lucky, you might be tried after only a week, but if not you might have to wait three months, four months, a year . . . the judicial processes were often slow. Then you'd be sent to a prison farm for six months. The truth is, the Cola really wasn't any good, but you were arrested for saying so.

Then, when self-criticism was the order of the day, Che himself said that the Cola was no good, that the matches were no good, that this, that, and the other was no good. At that time, if you rubbed the tip of your finger along the side of a match box, it would come away covered with glass crumbs from the sandpaper. "Why," he asked, "are our products so poor when I, as Minister of Industry, buy only the best raw materials from foreign countries?"

El Che was one of the best-loved leaders. To me, he was a very great man. All he said was sound and true. There you see a contrast with Fidel. Fidel lacks that trait which was so peculiarly El Che's—his power of convincing you he was telling the truth. Martí, too, said, "Truth is not to be hidden but proclaimed. Truth must be told."

And that's another thing that has killed the illusions of many Cubans—the loss of so many of the leaders of the Revolution. Camilo Cienfuegos was well loved and had a large following. There never was a clear account of his accident. Many people were of the opinion that Raúl had had him killed. Those were the rumors, see? That business about Hubert Matos[15] was strange, too. He's still in prison. Manolo Ray, the engineer, was another who was with Fidel in the beginning.[16] He was very popular among his people. He was Minister of Public Works, and from the very beginning he was the greatest source of jobs. Well, he too has gone now.

If it hadn't been for my children, I might have left Cuba after the Revolution triumphed. Between 1962 and 1969 I had plenty of opportunity to go. Every night two or three big launches left from Pinar del Río. Five or six times I could easily have left on one of them, without risking my life, English or no English. What were the odds anyway? I have a lot of Spanish-speaking relatives in New York and Florida.

It's logical that people should want to go. It means a new life for them. One of my friends from Las Yaguas, a real underworld type, a marijuana smoker called Baldy, went to the States. He escaped in a small launch, arrived safely, and now he's a happy man. Most of the Cubans who left with their families were technicians. But many now regret it. And do you know why? Because it hurts a lot to jump the frontiers of the country you were born in and go to live far away. It hurts men no less

---

15. See Benedí, n. 71.

16. Head of the Havana underground (Civic Resistance) from mid-1957 until the Castro victory. A civil engineer, Ray served as Minister of Public Works until November, 1959, when he resigned over the Matos affair. While teaching architecture at the University of Havana, Ray organized the *Movimiento Revolucionario del Pueblo* (MRP). The new group, consisting mostly of former Castro supporters, had as its slogan *"Fidelismo sin Fidel."* In November, 1960, Ray escaped from Cuba to Miami, where he became involved in planning the Bay of Pigs (Playa Girón) invasion. He was, however, regarded by the CIA as leftist and (therefore) unreliable. In 1964 Ray planned a second invasion of Cuba; he sailed from Puerto Rico but terminated the operation in the Bahamas.

than women. That's why those people would be a lot better off right here, food shortage or no food shortage.

For myself, how much could I have earned in the United States? I'm expert at doing construction work high up on scaffoldings, and there you get good pay for that. When I worked for the Ferrer Construction Company I could earn extra for overtime, as well as for working on high buildings. In the early days of the Revolution, the state also paid extra for working up high, but they don't any longer, and they don't pay overtime anymore, either. That means there's no way of earning extra money. You have set wages and you either live within your means or you die. That's why it seems to me that the workers have lost some of their rights since the Revolution. I have enough to live on, but not enough to save. If I were still working for Ferrer, I could have saved at least 10,000 *pesos* in the past seven years without depriving myself and my family. Today I don't have 1 *centavo* in the bank.

Nobody had any idea the Revolution was going to wind up as it did. It was disillusioning, I can tell you. In particular, I don't like Fidel's foreign policy. I've been pro-American all my life—I even feel a bit American myself—and I've seen many things that hurt me deeply. When Fidel made speeches he was very offensive to the United States. It seems to me that in the field of diplomacy there are different ways of expressing your views, and I see no reason why anyone should call the president of another nation a son-of-a-bitch, no matter how bad he is. I don't believe that the United States would have supported the invasion at Playa Girón if our government had not offended the U.S. government in public speeches.

The policy of the press in Cuba is another thing I dislike intensely. As I understand it, in a free press everything, good or bad, is told. But the things we hear in the Cuban press about the Americans in Vietnam! Well, look, I'm no fool. I can't believe that an army can lose 13,000 men in one week. That's a pill I can't swallow and it makes my blood boil. It's a deliberate lie.

The Revolution set itself a difficult task in wanting to industrialize Cuba. We're still extremely underdeveloped and lack the natural resources for industrialization. If you're going to go in for heavy industry, you need petroleum, big furnaces, and big rivers, too. Our largest river is the Cauto and even that doesn't have the strong currents necessary to run a hydroelectric plant. It will take ten or fifteen years of collective labor and a high degree of organization to establish enough industry to satisfy the people's needs.

We're told that while we work to industrialize Cuba we're working to defeat imperialism, but sometimes I think we're defeating ourselves. Before Playa Girón, many different committees of American businessmen came here trying to make plans for certain industries—they don't care what kind of political regime exists as long as they make their profits—but their offers were refused. I think that if at Playa Girón Fidel had negotiated with the United States, the country would have progressed much more—anyway, the Revolution would have endured. Look at Tito—he has industrialized Yugoslavia and has everything he needs right there. But Tito knew how to do things; he wasn't rash. As it is, what with the country's natural disadvantages, with Fidel's policy of anti-imperialism, and with the blockade, we're really screwed up.

Chapter Four

A Home of My Own

THE YEAR BEFORE THE REVOLUTION, in June, 1958, I met my first wife, Martita. I was at a fiesta in the little town of San Antonio de Cabezas in Matanzas, drinking beer with some friends. We were there in the hope of picking up some little *guajirita*. I don't know what happened—the fiesta began well, but after 10:00 o'clock a fight began and it ended in a free-for-all. Then we heard they were having a nice dance over in Bolondrón so we went. There I did meet a country girl—her name was Martita—and I liked her looks.

Martita was slender and pretty, a bit taller than I. Her hair was good considering that she was obviously a *mulata*. Her face was sort of round, with a thinnish nose, a rather narrow forehead, quite thick eyebrows, and brown eyes. Her lips were fairly thin, and her jaw was not sharp but more or less rounded. She wasn't a strong woman but she looked healthy enough.

I started a conversation with her and then she asked for my address and I for hers. She told me her *mamá* was dead and she had never known her *papá*, though she knew he was called El Chino and lived in Agramonte. When I heard that about her *mamá* and *papá*, I thought our relationship wouldn't last long. But we struck up a friendship and agreed to write to each other. She lived in San Antonio de Cabezas with a foster mother, Bernarda Castillo, and her sister Dulce. She had many relatives and some of them were in Batista's army, but she herself didn't like politics.

At that time I had a mistress called Mona Flores. I'd known her for one year. We never lived together.... I had my room at home and she had one in Miguelito's *posada*. She was a woman of the life and had several paying boyfriends. Even so, for some reason she thought she owned me. Mona didn't bear me any children but I had a narrow escape. One month she missed her period so I took her at once to Doctor Valdéz, a physician I knew at the cigar factory. "Look," I told him, "you must do something to make her period come; because no matter what happens

I'm not going to marry a tramp like her." The doctor gave her a shot of crude liver extract and she aborted. There was nothing between Marta and me yet, but Mona got jealous when Marta came to Las Yaguas to visit her uncle.

"I know you two are sweethearts," Mona told me. "If you aren't going to be mine, you won't belong to anyone else either." She wanted to rule my feelings and my doings and was clinging to me like a blood-sucking leech, so then and there I made up my mind to court Marta. When Mona saw that, she let go and got engaged to Miguelito.

I took Martita to meet *mamá* so she'd know my intentions were serious. "*Mima*," I said, "I'm going to bring you my little sweetheart from Matanzas whom I intend to marry. I want you to tell me what you think of her."

Mamá liked Martita. She expressed quite a good opinion of the girl. Later I took Marta to my aunts and they liked her too, and truly she had many womanly virtues. She was a pleasant, affectionate woman. Intoxicating and sweet, almost too sweet. A man who didn't know a bit of psychology might even misjudge her because of that. But *coño*, I'm not the kind who thinks that simply because a woman is overly affectionate she has something to hide.

When I met Marta I was getting along in years, being twenty-six years old. I was tired of being alone in the world, having to go out in search of a woman to spend the night with. I wanted to start a home of my own, to have someone to wash my clothes, cook my meals, and look after me. I'd had lots of woman, so it stands to reason that if I bent my head to the yoke and decided to start a home with Martita, I must have loved her, right?

Marta knew I'd had affairs before we became sweethearts but I wanted to give her no cause to be jealous. It has always been my custom when I get engaged to a woman to tell her the names of my close women friends so she'll have no reason to be jealous of them. Take Alejandra Díaz. We've known each other for years, and whenever we meet after not having seen each other for a long time, we hug and kiss in front of her husband or son or anybody. The same goes for Odelia, who has four kids. Her husband was jealous of me—which goes to show how wrong-headed people can be.

Marta wanted me to drop these people, but why should I drop old friends to satisfy her whim? After all, I'm the good guy, the one who works and earns money, so I deserve to be treated with respect and consideration. I don't mean that simply because I support a woman I'm too proud to treat her with respect and consideration. I do as I would be done by. But the woman hasn't been born who can rule me, not even my own mother. It wouldn't be a bit of use for her to tell me, "Don't drink that, it's poison." I never accept advice. I'm as free as a deer in the forest.

In October or November of 1958, after I'd known her only three months, Marta and I were married in a civil ceremony. I didn't have a home to take her to, but her grandfather, Luis Enríquez, who lived in Las Yaguas, offered us a room in his house. I accepted and went to live there with Martita, planning to get away as soon as I could.

At first old man Luis was very nice to us—new brooms sweep clean, you know. He was a quiet, peaceable man, not much interested in politics or anything aside from his job, but he turned out to be a real opportunist. I didn't like it one bit because the old fox wanted the best of everything. He had a room to himself and was happy to have Marta there to wash and iron and cook for him, but he behaved as if he owed nothing to his granddaughter.

Having us there inconvenienced him, I suppose. He kept complaining to people that what he earned was too little to support both me and his granddaughter and that he didn't know why she'd gone and married me when I couldn't support a wife. He had no right to say that, because it was I who paid the household expenses, not he. All Luis gave Marta was 2 or 3 *pesos* a week and I wish he'd never given her even that, so he'd have had no reason to complain.

Luis and one of his sons were charcoal makers, and the old guy also had a job as night watchman in a place selling secondhand cars. He made good money in that job. He told us he earned 60 *pesos* a month, but I had it on good authority that he made about 120 *pesos*. The old man had a girl friend, Gladys, who managed his money and spent it as she pleased.

In spite of all his foolishness I got kind of fond of Luis. I even bought clothes and a pair of shoes for him. I'd planned to live with him only a short time but we stayed for a little over a year and a half. In all that time our only amusement was going to the movies.

Early in 1959 Marta started to complain of not feeling well, so I took her to Dr. Valdéz. According to the tests and X-rays she had an ovarian cyst. That's a pretty serious condition. She was allergic to medicines, injections, and all that but I made her take everything the doctor ordered. "I paid good money for that stuff," I told her, "and I'm not going to see it wasted."

In the midst of the treatment she got pregnant. She gave me the news when she was about two months gone with child. I felt awfully affectionate, thinking, "*Coño,* I shall have my first child!"

One day we went to see a show over on the Calzada de Luyanó, and to my annoyance she goes and gets her period, right there at the movie. Next day, early in the morning, I told her, "Get up, we're going to Dr. Valdéz."

The doctor prescribed another series of injections for that problem in her ovaries and she got well. About two months later she got pregnant again. I had already bought a lot of baby things—boys' things, because I said to myself, "Naturally, my first child will be male. It couldn't possibly be a girl." And I was right. Manolo was born on my grandfather's birthday. I was delighted with my firstborn son.

As I always say, whatever begins in joy ends in sorrow and pain. For other people anyway, I used to think, because I never believed I could fail as so many others did. But in my relationship with the mother of my children I did run into trouble just like the rest. I wanted to avoid that at all costs because it's the children who wind up paying for the broken plates. But struggle as I might, I was cut adrift without a lifeline and fell into that same abyss I criticized others for falling into.

When the baby was eight months old, Marta comes and says to me, "I want to take him to San Antonio de Cabezas to meet my relatives."

"Very well," I answered, "only I can't go with you. I don't want to miss even one day of work because every day costs me over 7 *pesos.*"

We were still living with Marta's grandfather but I'd saved some money that I kept right there in the house. So I paid for her bus fare to San Antonio de Cabezas and gave her a total of 100 *pesos* to take with her. She told me she'd be away one week. The week passed and she didn't return. I was so desperate to see my son I couldn't sleep at night. I ran into Pablo, one of her cousins, who told me, "I saw Martita in Agramonte. From there she was going to Jovellanos and then to Colón." She had gone to Agramonte to see her uncle without telling me beforehand, and she had relatives in Colón whom she hadn't seen in years.

Twenty-three days passed, a month, and there I was, waiting for my son and for her. At last, I was sitting in the doorway one day when I saw her approaching, carrying the baby. I was anxious to see my son and to see her too, of course, but instead of coming straight home, she walked into the house of her friend Hilda. She stayed there a long time chatting with Hilda and Hilda's husband and daughters while I waited and waited for her to come home.

I went inside, thinking, "*Concho,* how can she call on Hilda before coming home to me?" I was right in being angry. Finally, when she came in, I said, "Let me hold the child." While I held him we started quarreling. I insisted that she should have come home to me first, as was right after such a long absence. And I pointed out that I didn't much like having her stay away as long as she did.

I didn't know what she'd been up to during the twenty-three days she was away but I accepted her explanation. After all, what could be more natural and commonplace than paying a visit to one's relatives? I don't know what Martita's past was—I never asked. I didn't care about the past, it was in the present and future we had to live together. That's all that mattered to me and I trusted her completely. I allowed her to go to the country alone, to see her family—what stronger proof could there be that I trusted her? If I can't trust somebody who lives with me, I'd rather get rid of her and live alone than be tortured by doubt. What bothered me was that she went somewhere else before coming to her own house. It wasn't right and I kept brooding over that point.

Martita got angry and called me a *maricón*. That was the last straw. I never expected her to call me that. I said, "Very well, it's all over between us. You can't get away with that. But don't think I'm going to let you keep the baby. My son stays with me."

"We shall see," she answered. She went to her grandfather, who was at work. The old man came home and tried to patch things up between us, but the harm was done.

I began to think I'd married too hastily. Looking back, I began to see that the years I lived alone were the happiest in my life. I had no responsibilities, I had my own room, and when an opportunity presented itself, I was free to take any woman I liked.

Marta had turned out to be sloppy and lazy, because what waits until tomorrow never gets done. For example, I've never liked to have dirty clothes pile up in the house, but Marta would let them accumulate, and then in one day she'd wash, starch, and iron everything. It took all her time and on that day she'd neglect every other household duty. I'd say to her, "You're overworking yourself because you want to. If you can wash six pieces of clothing today and six tomorrow, isn't that better than waiting until you have a whole heap of them and neglect everything else?"

When I was living at my aunt's I never let even a pair of used undershorts lie around after my bath. On Sundays I'd get up at 4:00 A.M., just as I did on workdays, and wash my clothes. By afternoon I'd have them all ironed. If as a single man my clothes were neat and clean, why, now that I was married, should the dirty things just pile up? I was fed up with Marta.

After our quarrel my wife and I slept in the same bed but for three months I had no intercourse with her. Strange, isn't it? I guess I have a special virtue that very few people have—to be able to sleep in the same bed with the woman I love and not touch her. She'd ask for it and I'd tell her, "I'd rather throw it on the floor or give it to a bitch to eat than give it to you." Those were my very words. I resisted her because I felt hurt and absolutely unsatisfied.

Before Marta had gone away we had had intercourse every night. She never rejected me in bed. In fact, often she was the one who asked for it. In her eighth month of pregnancy we stopped having relations. She'd urge me but I always refused. After the baby's birth we had relations as usual.

I can't imagine why Marta called me a *maricón* that day. I often wonder what could have been in her mind, because I was able to satisfy her— thank God, I've always been able to satisfy all the women I've had. I never left them hungry. It was Marta who didn't satisfy me. She was a woman of high spirits but she wasn't an ardent lover. No, on the contrary, she was rather cold and melancholy and too quickly satisfied. She didn't give me time to finish, she came right away. And when I wanted more, she was already satisfied. That was the problem.

It isn't that I'm a sadist, but the fact is I was harsh with Marta at those times because all that mattered to me was how well she served me. She was emotional but I'm not one for sticky sentimentality or a mushy show of affection. That kind of thing puts me on the defensive, because I always suspect that a woman is trying to flatter me in order to get something out of me.

I had to go to other women because Marta didn't have enough fire to satisfy me. It was I who remained hungry, so I went to get meat outside even though I had meat at home. After all, everyone has bodily needs which must be satisfied. As far as I was concerned, I wasn't being unfaithful to Marta, because what I call being unfaithful is having your supper at home and then going out to eat somebody else's. As long as I lived maritally with Martita I was never unfaithful to her, even after two and a half years. I'm telling the truth when I say I don't do such things. When I undertake to be responsible for a woman, when I share a home with her, I don't take on a mistress.

But later I had as many as four or five women in Las Yaguas while I was married. I had white women, black women, and *mulatas* chasing after me. I wasn't in love with them and it was mainly self-interest on their part, I think, because they knew I earned good money and was always well dressed.

There was one girl who fell for me like a bitch in heat. I don't even remember the kid's name, but she spread the word that she and I were sweethearts. I spoke with her mother and said, "Listen, those rumors spell trouble for me, so please make that kid stop telling stories before my wife hears them. I'm not about to break up my home for that little ball of shit."

When the mother heard that, she beat her daughter half to death, which was a blessed remedy because the girl stopped talking about me. Even so, Marta got wind of her stories and got jealous. After that, she was suspicious of the walls of her own house. Maybe I did give her undue cause for worry because I liked to go out a lot, but that didn't always mean I went to call on some other woman. I'd walk and walk because that's what my body asks for—activity. In Havana I'd go to the Malecón, where I'd sit for hours on end, remembering and analyzing things. Then I'd think, "My wife is going to be jealous, thinking I'm with another woman, and she's bound to be upset when I get home." And so she was.

My friend Alejandra knew the problems I had with Marta's jealousy. Alejandra would tell me, "That wife of yours never will change." Marta was jealous of Alejandra, too. Alejandra was in love with me but I never had an affair with her. At that time Marta was going to Alejandra to get her shots of hepatic extract. Which didn't make sense, you know, because if you're angry and jealous of somebody, why should you go ask her for a favor?

Marta complained to Alejandra that I was indifferent and didn't like to take her out. That's not true. Our neighbors can testify that night after night we'd go to the movies or to parties or, if nowhere else, at least for a walk by the wall of the Malecón. But Marta claimed I was a womanizer. Well, maybe she had some reason to say that, although she never knew for sure that I had a number of mistresses. She had a good head on her shoulders, and when she got jealous she was awfully stubborn, so in order to keep the peace I always denied everything.

Why even my family accused me of being a bohemian, and *mamá* says I've had my share of loose women. But she shouldn't go around saying I had all those affairs. She cannot truthfully say I ever had another woman as long as I was living with Marta. If there's anybody who knows for sure that I wasn't unfaithful to Marta, that person is *mamá*. Where did I sleep nights when I didn't sleep at home? At *mamá*'s house. Where did I go from there? Straight back home to Marta.

When someone I love acts badly toward me just once, my love is dead. I'm like the master who, when his burro falls down, bears it a grudge and won't give it a chance to get up again. He stamps on its head until it's sunk for good! So it was with my love for Marta.

One time I packed up my things and moved in with *mamá*. "Go back to Marta," she advised me. "She's a good woman. Besides, she has borne you a child, how can you abandon her?" I went back and we resumed our lovemaking, but I wasn't the same man I'd been before. There wasn't any joy in me.

There's something very complicated about my personality. Perhaps I was a coward to go back to her, but in order to act according to my own character and not let myself down in my own estimation, I had to give my wife a home. My self-respect as a man didn't allow me to give people a chance to say, "Look at that—he abandoned her and his child!" If I did go back to Marta it was *mamá*'s doing—I mean, aside from the fact that I loved Marta and all that—but I really did it just to provide her with a home. I still intended to leave her.

I knew Marta aspired to have a little house of her own. She was a woman who felt the pull of family ties strongly, so I wanted to take her back to the place where she had lived all her life. I explained to her, "Look, I'm going to buy you a house where you can be near your relatives, because I don't want to abandon you here in Las Yaguas. That way you won't ever be so badly off that you have to sell yourself to a man."

It was 1960, and by then I had saved 2,000 or 3,000 *pesos*. I sent Marta to San Antonio de Cabezas and told her, "Find out if there's a house for sale around there and I'll buy it." She found one and sent me a telegram. I rushed there and learned that a certain Señora Margarita was selling a house and a large lot for 250 *pesos*. The plot wasn't fenced and the little house was very run-down—even the houses in Las Yaguas looked good by comparison—but I gave her 300 for it because, truly, it was a real bargain. Why one could make money from just the avocados and fruit planted there!

I had to completely rebuild the house. The heavy palm-leaf thatch was so rotten that water dripped inside when it rained. I fixed the roof first, then I patched the walls with boards and covered the dirt floor with cement. I have a good head for construction. It was a poor man's house but I made it nice and comfortable. When it was finished, I fenced in the plot and turned it into a small farm, planting some vegetables and buying a few chickens. I furnished the house with a bedroom set and the necessary kitchen utensils, and nearly all my furniture from my room at *mamá*'s house, two couches, a stove, a radio, an iron.

I spent part of my time there repairing the house and the rest of my time working in Havana. While I was in San Antonio de Cabezas I met Timoteo Méndez, who was in charge of some construction in Unión de Reyes. Timoteo said to me, "*Concho,* Alfredo, you know so much about building, and here I am, having problems with that. Could you come work for me?"

"Well, since I may stay here for quite a long time with my wife and son, I will."

That's how I decided to stay on in Matanzas. On the new job I earned 150 *pesos* a month and was paid every two weeks. It was very convenient to have that job. Besides, through Timoteo I was able to get a lot of building materials I needed.

Martita lived with her family until the house was ready. Then we moved in. I began a new life and got to like it very much indeed, not because of my wife, but because of my work and the atmosphere I'd created for myself where everybody loved and respected me. Within my poverty, I lived well and felt at peace. But for all of that, I wasn't happy.

Though I stayed on in Matanzas, the gulf between me and Marta was never crossed. She knew I was unhappy but didn't know how to cure me. She thought maybe she could lure me out of it with sex, but I really wasn't interested, not with her anyway. If I had sex with her, I did it only out of a sense of duty.

One day I suffered another shattering disappointment with Marta. I got home, took a bath, and said to her, "Come on, let's lie in bed awhile." We played in bed for a few minutes, and just when I was most excited, she got up and sat in a chair to read a magazine. That made me angry, but after about half an hour I said to her, "*Chica,* come here, or are you more interested in a magazine than in your husband?" Such a thing would disillusion any sensitive man, no?

After that I resisted my desires. It was very difficult. I was able to because my will is strong, not because my sexual nature is weak. You can't confuse willpower with weakness, at least not in my case. There were times when I'd go to sleep and dream all sorts of shit, and when I woke up my underpants would be all sticky. I found I'd functioned in bed by myself but still I made no demands on Marta. I began to sleep in a separate bed. Many nights Marta would come weeping to my bed, and I felt desire but I never used her. I swear by my children that I'm telling the truth. Once she said to me, "What's wrong with you anyway? Are you studying to be a priest or something?"

"No," I answered. "And if I had a wife who was able to understand me and not kill my illusions, things would be different." That way I gave her a hint of what the trouble was, but she didn't have the brains to analyze things so she never understood what I was trying to tell her. Marta's Uncle Francisco was the only one who knew we slept in separate beds. At first he kept after me: "Make up with Marta." Then, when nothing changed, he called me over one day and said, "I know you're tired of my niece, so why don't you two separate? That would be the best thing."

"Look here, *chico,*" I answered, "I'll separate from her when I'm good and ready, not when someone else decides I should."

Six months later our second son, Omarito, was born. Marta was already pregnant when we left Las Yaguas but she hadn't told me about it. I think she kept it from me because she tried to abort. Omarito is the last living memory of what was once between Marta and me.

For two years I kept on living with Marta in the same way, taking care of her and my two children as best I could. I was mother, husband, wife, everything to Marta. A wife can't find fault with a husband who helps her wash and iron clothes as I do, can she? I've even mended pants. Everybody has some defects, but what right has a woman to criticize a husband as good as I? I was the one who went out and earned the living and provided for her better than anybody else ever had, gave her a house, comforts. . . . I gave her all that was necessary for household expenses and you could almost say she was the one who had the say-so about how it was spent. If I got 70 or 80 *pesos* every two weeks, I'd keep 10 for myself and give her the rest.

Nobody can say of me, "That man is vicious, he's a shameless good-for-nothing." No, they can't say anything of the kind. It was her duty as my wife to do everything to seek a reconciliation with me, but she didn't.

When I analyzed things, I saw how much harm Marta had done me without her even realizing it. Or maybe she was deliberately trying to hurt me. One thing that made trouble between us was that she gave my money to her relatives without asking me. Our house in San Antonio de Cabezas was near that of Marta's foster mother, Bernarda Castillo, and several other relatives. They were a sly bunch, always coming between Marta and me. They'd visit every day asking for this or that or begging her to get me to lend them 5 or 10 *pesos*.

Now there's nothing better than sincerity in marriage. Marta should have come to me and said, "Look, *chico*, such-and-such a relative came to me and needed money for this or that reason, so I let her have it." That way everything is open and aboveboard. But Marta kept it from me. She thought I didn't know what was going on, but nature has given me a prodigious mentality—I mean, I have a powerful memory, so I always knew how much I'd saved and how much I'd taken out. If you put your money away in a drawer and then see some of it's gone, you know someone's taking it. Naturally, I reached my own conclusions about where the money went and I didn't like it a bit.

God has granted me a great gift—I don't know exactly what it is, a kind of foresight that enables me to plan today what I'm going to do tomorrow, to analyze today what is likely to happen tomorrow. Well, I analyzed the situation and thought, "I trust Marta but if she now takes money for her family behind my back, tomorrow she may put the horns on me and the neighbors will find out before I do."

I had my little pile of *centavitos* saved up, but I lost it when the government passed a law in 1961 requiring everyone to deposit all of his old currency in the bank. In exchange, he could withdraw a maximum of 250 *pesos* a month in the new currency. There was a ceiling of 10,000 *pesos* that could be exchanged. Some people had as much as 200,000 *pesos* put away at home and they committed suicide because they couldn't change it.[17]

I had 10,000 "coconuts" that I'd earned, not at my regular job—a workingman doesn't earn that much here—but by some other little transaction I've never spoken of to anyone before. It happened like this. On a trip in 1958, I bought some books of counterfeit 100-dollar American traveler's checks for 50 *pesos* each. That's how I got started. Later, people bought American dollars at the rate of 700, 800, and even 1,000 Cuban *pesos* for 100 dollars. The man who sold me the counterfeit ones thought he could play me for a fool. Little did he know what a clever fellow he was dealing with!

17. Law no. 963, passed August 4, 1961, permitted each Cuban to exchange up to 200 *pesos* in old currency for new money, with all amounts over that sum, up to 10,000 *pesos*, to be deposited in "special accounts" in the National Bank. Any amount in excess of 10,000 *pesos* was confiscated. When the first stage of the exchange ended on August 8, each person was allowed an initial withdrawal of up to 1,000 *pesos* from his account (5,000 for businesses), with succeeding withdrawals not to exceed 200 *pesos* a month. (Cuban Economic Research Project, *A Study on Cuba*, p. 647.)

First, I took the checks to Jackson, a functionary in the place I worked. He was leaving Cuba, and I said, "Look, give me 100 *pesos* for one of these."

After that I sold others. "Give me 200 ... 300. ..." Then I sold a book—there were ten 100-dollar traveler's checks to a book—to a man who paid me 1,000 *pesos* for each check. It was dangerous to sell them, but what was I to do? It would have been even more dangerous to keep them in my house. I had my regular job and this business on the side. One had to be really careful. I was scared the authorities would get on to me, but one just had to take the risk and I did. That's all over with now, it's dead, obsolete, and that man Jackson, the mechanic, is now living comfortably in Buffalo. He still writes me sometimes.

So in 1961 I found myself in that conflict of having over 10,000 *pesos* in my house and being afraid to deposit them in the bank. You see, when you deposited money in the bank, you had to give your correct name and address, then the Ministry of the Interior investigated your means—how you earned it. How could I explain—a workingman like me—having such a large amount of money?

I knew a girl of high rank, Rita de Varona—she was once hot for me and had given me a lot of money—and when she put her money in the bank during the currency change, it was taken away from her because it wasn't honestly come by. So what about mine? If it had been properly earned, no problems, but it wasn't and I couldn't explain how I came to have such an amount. I got scared, that's why I lost it. If I'd kept my head, I'd still have that money.

"I'll play my cards," I thought. "If I get screwed I get screwed, and that's all there is to it."

I went to my aunt and asked her to deposit the money in her account. "But what about me?" she objected. "I have 4,000 *pesos* to deposit myself."

"But it's easier for you to make a deposit in the bank, because you've always had an account. I don't care if my money is in your name. I'd rather have it revert to you than lose it altogether."

"All right," she says. "There's no problem." So I gave her 3,000 *pesos*, which she deposited in her bank account. She didn't withdraw any part of it, simply deposited it. I trusted her—whom should I trust if not the woman who raised me?

I went to Marta and told her about the money. It was the first she'd heard of it and she almost pissed on herself, as we say, because she'd never seen so much money. I said, "Ask your Uncle Francisco if he'll change 300 *pesos* for me, and you change another 300. Then deposit 2,000 in your name. You can do that without getting in trouble. Give your foster brother Paquito some money to change too."

It was an easy thing for Marta's relatives to change money because they had none of their own to deposit. All they had was what they earned working the cane fields. So I gave them some of my money and I never saw it again. Marta changed the 300 *pesos,* but later I found out that the people who changed it had cheated her. We quarreled about that.

Next I went to One-Eyed Felo, the loan shark in Las Yaguas, and said, "Look, Felo, I want you to change these 500 *pesos.*"

"Sure I will," says he.

"I'll be back tomorrow," I told him. "I'm in a hurry now. But first sign this receipt for me." That slip of paper speaks as with a tongue. Felo later came to me with the story that he'd been unable to change the money, but I found out he had.

I set things straight and put the food on the table. I said, "Listen, I know you changed the 500 *pesos,* so let me tell you, either that money appears or. . . ."

"All right, all right, I did change it but don't worry, you'll get it," he said.

"Look, just give me 300 *pesos* and keep the other 200," I said, but no, even then the man didn't hand over the money. Finally he explained, "Look, I lent that money at interest. I'll give you 25 percent once a month on it as long as I'm getting 15 or 20 percent twice a month." Get it? My money was subject to all the ups and downs of the loan business. And I became a loan shark without knowing it. Felo paid me back little by little but I never got the whole amount—only 100 or 200 *pesos.* It came out of nothing and turned back to nothing—oh well, such is life!

Once I went to Havana to exchange my money, and when I returned I found things not as I had left them. Our home had been entered and someone had robbed us. The door of the cupboard was open and all the drawers were scattered over the floor. Every last piece of my clothing had been stolen and I was left practically naked. The only clothes I possessed were the ones I was wearing and some dirty clothes I carried in my bag from Havana. The thieves also stole a gold wristband, a clock, two rings, the children's little chains, some bracelets, and even all of Marta's things. Omarito was only a few months old at that time.

I looked the house over carefully, trying to figure out how somebody might have slipped in. It couldn't have been easy since not one lock had been broken. All the windows were closed and fastened on the inside but the yard gate and the parlor door were wide open.

"You left the living-room door wide open!" I told Marta.

"I went out for a while," she said.

"Why the hurry?" I asked myself. I couldn't understand it. If there was one thing I disliked in Marta more than another it was her slowness, her lack of spirit. That, more than anything else, made me get sick of her.

From what I could observe, whoever robbed us knew the house well. I quarreled with her then. I said, "This case is going to go before the court and it's going to go hard with whoever did this. And do you know why? Because it was a relative of yours who robbed us."

"How dare you say such a thing!" she protested. "There are no thieves in my family!"

"Oh, I'm not saying that there are any mere thieves in your family. I'm saying that there are envious, ungrateful thieves in your family!"

To make a long story short, I spoke with Isidro, a friend of mine who was in charge of the CDR in San Antonio de Cabezas. Isidro said, "Well look, *chico,* I saw your wife's cousin Pablo hurrying off to Havana with a lot of packages."

"If it's Pablo, I'll catch him. I know where he lives, and what places he goes to, and all the contacts he has."

It was as I thought. *Coño!* I found some of the stolen clothes in Agramonte, but the jewelry wasn't there. One of my wife's uncles told me that Pablo was in Havana. I said, "Listen, I know he's here, not in Havana, so you tell Pablo to come out of hiding. He and I have a lot to talk about."

Pablo came out and told me, "I didn't steal your things, Castillo did." Castillo was also a relative of Marta's. He was a soldier and we were told he was staying at Colón.

I got home after 10:00 at night. I dashed a bucket of water over me and Marta asked if I wanted anything to eat. I told her I wasn't hungry and lay down to sleep, but tired as I was, Marta quarreled with me until 3:00 A.M. because I had accused her relatives of theft. I was fed up with her.

Pablo was tried and found guilty of breaking and entering. He was the one who broke the lock of the door and the cupboard. The jewelry never turned up. Neither Castillo nor Pablo ever got the benefit of it.

From the time we first went to live in Matanzas, Marta and I had quarreled on account of her family. She felt a great pull toward them. Her family was everything and her interests were locked tight within their circle. Why, she cared more about them than about her own children!

One day my son Manolito got sick and was running a frightful fever. I took him to the ONDI,[18] which is the same as the emergency clinic in Havana. The doctor said there was nothing seriously wrong with the boy and he'd get well in no time at all, but the doctor was wrong. The next day the kid was no better, so I took him back. The doctor looked at him again, then he said to me, "I'm going to give you a letter to get the child admitted to the hospital in Havana."

He saw the child was very ill, yet he had told me it was nothing serious

18. *Organización Nacional de Dispensarios Infantiles* (National Organization of Children's Clinics), founded in July, 1952.

and had waited a full day before transferring the case to Havana. What a farce! He had deceived me and I was furious. I really made a fuss about it. I told him, "You can take that letter and give it to your whoring mother. I don't need any letter to take the kid to Havana."

I boarded a hack for Havana. It was March 19, I remember. At that time a rebel band was causing problems in that region and I got caught right in the middle of a gun battle on the road. Well, in spite of twenty troubles and twenty obstacles, I managed to reach Havana with my son.

The first thing I did was take him to the hospital. They made the analysis right away. The child had measles. They gave him serum and a blood transfusion directly from my arm, while we were lying side by side on two tables. For three or four days he wouldn't eat. All he had was fruit juice, tea, and such stuff. The kid was wasting away, he was skin and bones—a strong boy like him. Then they told me I could take him home, so I took him to my *mamá*'s house. She was already living in the house given her by the Urban Reform Office. My old lady took care of him the five days he was there.

During that time Marta made no attempt to find out how he was. She claimed she was sick in bed, but her indifference to his illness hurt me more than anything she'd ever done. No matter what quarrels we'd had in the past, it was up to both of us to run around and do whatever was necessary to cure the boy. What do conflicts between man and wife matter when their child is sick? Other people go out of their way to help when one's child is sick. How much more should one expect from his own mother, who brought him into the world?

After that, things between Marta and me went from bad to worse. One night, as I lay between sleep and waking, I saw a coffin with four candles. I saw Marta sick and then dead, and the problems with the kids. I woke up crying. Three or four months later it all happened, exactly as in my dream.

Marta's only sister, Dulce, lived in Artemisa, at the Abraham Lincoln sugar mill. The times Marta had gone to visit her sister at Artemisa, Dulce always remarked that she'd like to come to our house. I opposed her staying with us because she and I didn't get along. Besides, when two people marry and have children they don't want anybody else living with them.

One day Marta said to me, "Dulce wants a room here so she can stay a few months, now that the sugar-cane harvest is over."

"Look, *chica*, to be frank, I don't want her here," I answered. But then I said yes to avoid a quarrel.

Dulce arrived the following day. Then her eyes were opened. Although Marta and I lived in the same house, we slept in separate rooms—the house had two bedrooms, see? I didn't share a room, much less a bed, with her. There was no physical contact of any kind between us.

I explained to Dulce, "Look, *chica,* whatever there was between your sister and me died a long time ago. I'm disillusioned with her. I don't have the slightest feeling for her, understand? She's done many things that she thinks don't mean anything, but to me they do. There's nothing greater or more beautiful in life than the sincerity of one person with another. But your sister has been insincere with me regarding her own family, so what's to keep her from being unfaithful to me any time she feels like it? That's why she and I will never again live together as man and wife."

While Dulce was staying with us, Marta got sick again. She missed her period and was running a fever too, so I said to her, "Why don't you go to the doctor?"

She couldn't go to the doctor because there was nobody to make an appointment for her. She had nieces, cousins, aunts, and uncles—yet no one would go. You see, we lived out in the country and the polyclinic was much nearer the place where her relatives lived. When Marta was sick I was the one who always took care of her. I'd bathe her and remind her, "Old lady, time for your medicine." I'd take her to the hospital; I'd see to her food so she could keep up her strength.

This time, after being sick about two weeks, Marta said to me, "I want to go to Artemisa with Dulce so I can go to the hospital there." It was her own choice. Once she got an idea in her head, she was as stubborn as a mule. It was that stubbornness of hers that brought on her death.

Marta took the children and went to Artemisa with her sister. I left Matanzas and stayed with *mamá* in Havana. Dulce says I abandoned Marta but it's not true, except in the sense that we didn't live as man and wife. Even so, until the day she died I was the only man Marta ever had. The trouble was that the doctors deceived me. I didn't know how sick she was.

Well, such was my situation. She rushed off to Artemisa leaving the ration book with me. So who had to run the errands? I did. I'd buy the groceries and take them to her on Sunday, returning on Monday. Everything I brought her, her relatives would eat. She'd keep asking me to send her money. Every month I sent her a money order for 150 *pesos.* The smallest amount I ever sent was 40 *pesos.* I sacrificed my own needs to send it because the kids were there with her. She didn't care where that money came from though, nor who paid for her rent and the food she ate . . . she didn't care about any of that, see?

One day I got a telegram from Dulce. "Come at once. Marta is hospitalized." When I got there I found both kids sick and Marta about to have an operation for an ovarian cyst and also for appendicitis. She needed a donor to give her 500 grams of blood.

"Look," I said to Dulce. "I'm pretty run-down physically just now, what with so many sleepless nights and all that. In my present state, I wouldn't give one single drop of my blood for anybody except one of my sons. If you find someone who's willing to be a donor, I'll gladly pay whatever he wants but that's as far as I'll go."

Then I went to the hospital and had a talk with the doctor. He said to me, "Look, *chico,* your wife is very ill. She has this cyst and bad appendix, and weak as she is, she may not come through the operation."

"But doctor," I objected, "do you mean to tell me that she could lose her life as a result of such a simple little operation?"

"No . . . the trouble is that she has a spot on her right lung, and we'll have to move her. We aren't equipped for that sort of thing here."

I was surprised to hear she had a bad lung. As long as she'd lived with me, she'd had no lung sickness. I know because she'd had X-rays taken here in Havana and they had all come out negative. I thought it was awfully strange that out of so many X-rays just the last one should have come out positive. Later I found out she had a galloping phthisis, the kind of T.B. where you're perfectly well and all your X-rays are negative, and then all of a sudden, between the night and the morning, you have a lung infected through and through. It was only the right lung; her left lung was in perfect condition. I also discovered that it was hereditary. She had it in her blood, see? If I'd known that from the first, I'd have had her treated to prevent it from developing and maybe she'd have lived a little longer.

Then I began to worry about Manolito and Omarito. I went to see Marta at the hospital and told her, "Look, *chica,* the children can't stay with you. I'm sorry, because you're their mother and all that, but you must understand that with a bad lung you can't be pawing and kissing them. They might get infected, especially Manolito, who now picks up eveything like a little sponge."

She kicked up a fuss and said I couldn't take them. My mind was made up. "Look, push the hair out of your eyes," I told her. "You have a bad lung and I won't let you infect the kids even if they are your sons."

Finally she agreed and asked me, "Where are you going to leave them?"

"I'll take them to my *mamá* and my sister Anita."

I went to *mamá* and dropped my bombshell. "*Mamá,* did you know Marta has been hospitalized in Artemisa?" I explained the problem to her and asked her to look after Omarito. Then I went to my sister Anita to see if she'd keep Manolito for me, but when I looked around her place, I realized there really wasn't room for one more. She and her husband had five kids of their own. Anita's husband didn't want Manolito there, but I told him, "You can put up with him for a few days. It's only until I get Marta out of the hospital."

They moved Marta to a tuberculosis hospital in Havana. She was very sick and every single day I went to see her. Dulce said I never took Marta anything and that isn't true. The other patients there know because she gave away the things I brought her.

While Marta was in the hospital I learned something that proved to me she had tried every means in her power to harm me. It so happened that after we moved to Matanzas they began the transformation of the barrio of Las Yaguas. The *reparto* was to be cleared and all the people were going to be moved into new houses. Some were to build new homes on lots and others were to get houses through Urban Reform. The ones who went to Urban Reform got a better deal because they got houses of people who had left the country, complete with furniture, fully equipped kitchens, frigidaires, television, and all sorts of comforts in them, even clothes and money.

Martita had the right to a house and so did I, because her grandfather had put down her name on the deed. A census was made by Urban Reform and they sent for her. She went to Havana, and then, instead of putting the house in my name, she put it in her grandfather's name. It was a kind of infidelity on her part. I still think it was a dirty low-down trick to play on me, may my words not offend the dead. She should at least have been frank and said, "Look, I'm not putting that house in your name in case someday we separate or something." But no, she didn't even mention the matter to me. By the time I knew about it, it was too late to do anything. Marta died on July 24, 1962. On her deathbed she begged me to forgive her.

"I'm no holy saint to go about forgiving people. Ask God's pardon," I told her. "Tell me anything you want done."

"All I ask you is to take good care of the boys and forgive me for not being able to understand you and for all the harm I've done you," she said. Then, at the moment of her death, she said, "I was the one who had to. . . ." I forget her exact words but she meant that she was the loser.

"I'd rather it had been me," I told her. And then she fell into a coma and died.

I was overcome by a sort of nervous crisis. They gave me a shot and I don't remember anything else that happened. An hour or two later I was in Havana, arranging for the removal of the corpse and planning the funeral. I don't know what happened to the things Marta had in the hospital. I don't know who took them but I do know that her relatives were more interested in her belongings than in her corpse. I sent them all telegrams from Havana but they went to Artemisa, believing that the funeral was there. They claimed that they got telegrams from Artemisa so they assumed Marta had died there. That was a lie. They should have been able to figure out that the death occurred in Havana. God only knows why they made up such a story. Maybe they didn't want to go to the wake or something.

On the day of the death I stayed at the funeral parlor, alone with my

son and *mamá,* until about 5:00 the next morning. Then my sisters and
their families came but nobody else. Of Marta's relatives, only Francisco
and Mango, the black, came. Mango helped me make the arrangements
and gave me 60 *pesos.* I tried to refuse, saying I had enough money, but
he said, "No, take it," and stuck the money in my pocket. They stayed
with me and accompanied me to the graveyard. Aside from them—
nobody.

I buried Marta on July 25 at the Colón cemetery. I did my duty to her
in the eyes of God and man until the very last, in spite of the fact that for
two years we had not lived as man and wife, or even as relatives or
anything. She was the mother of my children, that was all, but it was
enough for me.

I wept a great deal when Marta died and I've never forgotten her.
Dead as she is I love her still, in spite of all I had to put up with—her lack
of understanding, my disappointment in her, the absence of affection. I
swallowed those bitter draughts and suffered in silence. The idea of
separating from her never entered my head. I spoke truly when I said to
her, as I often did, "If one of us has to die, I hope I'm the one, not you.
Children need their mother more than their father. Besides, if I died
you might find a good man who would help you raise the kids and
complete what I started." She never understood those things though.

Perhaps with a little more family cooperation, what happened
wouldn't have happened. No one in either family showed us even a little
bit of understanding. The only one of my sisters who got along with
Marta was Anita. Once I told *mamá* if she and Marta had been closer to
each other, more like family, maybe I wouldn't have had so many troubles in my life. Maybe if both our families had been closer, we might have
lived more peacefully, more happily, and maybe things would have
turned out differently for us. At least it would have helped.

Señora Lordi:

I was fond of Fredo's first wife, Marta. For a long time they lived in
Matanzas, but after a while she didn't want to live there any longer so
they came back here. The Revolution gave them a very good house—
somewhere on the route of bus no. 23, I think. Marta's folks have the
house now.

Fredo worked hard and bought Marta furniture and things. All my
sons are good providers for their wives and children; I can't criticize
them in that respect. But Fredo was always hot after women. He was
running around even while Marta had the lung sickness. And she
must have found out because she used to say to me, "Old lady, I think
Fredo has another woman."

"No, *muchacha,*" I'd assure her. "He doesn't have any woman but
you." What else could I say? I couldn't add fuel to the flames, but I

knew Fredo too well to believe he could be true to any woman. My other sons are just the same, but that's their only defect. Nobody can deny that they are very good husbands otherwise. But it seems Marta found out about Fredo and got sadder and sadder. She died of the lung sickness, but I think her unhappiness over Fredo's unfaithfulness didn't do her any good.

Before Marta died, she asked me to raise her two little children. But Fredo disregarded her last wishes and took the kids with him. He didn't have any reason for doing that, it's just his way.

BARRERA:

Mamá claims she was fond of Marta, but when did she ever care about her? They didn't even know each other. Let her say what she likes but she never went to see Marta except to ask her for food or money. *Mamá* knew *I* wouldn't give her even 3 *kilos* to buy coffee.

As for Marta's family, it's incredible, but because Marta's foster mother didn't come to the funeral, she never met *mamá* nor any of my relatives. To see how Marta was treated by her relatives whose duty it was to love her! Marta's mother should have helped us in those moments when we were most in need. I don't complain about the fact that they felt no affection for me ... but for their daughter! I don't know why they didn't love Marta. Perhaps they were jealous of her. A woman will resent her sister or another relative if she's a bit better off and lives more comfortably. Jealousy between relatives is quite common, at least in Cuba.

Dulce was always jealous of her sister Marta. Perhaps because Marta was a shade lighter-skinned, or maybe because Marta had been lucky enough to get a husband while Dulce had to knock about with one man after another. See how it is? Dulce is a witch and believes in sorcery. When Marta died, Dulce accused me of casting spells on her sister. She said I'd gone to a certain place and paid money for a "job" on Marta.

I told her, "Look, you may rest assured that before I'd waste money on sorcery, I'd take it and burn it. I wouldn't spend 1 *peseta* on such non-sense. I don't believe in it, for one thing, and for another, if I wanted to I could have twenty of those spells for nothing."

I can't understand how those people's minds work. I really went to all sorts of trouble for Marta, yet her family remained set against me. When people see that you're kind to their relative and never hurt her by either word or deed, when you share your life with her and are never unfaithful, what more can they ask of a husband? No woman ever had a better husband than I was. But the nicer I was to Marta's family, the meaner they were to me. Oh, what's the point of going on about that! Talk isn't going to solve any problems. Besides, I won't waste time thinking about those people. They aren't worth it.

When Marta died, I was supposed to inherit the house on Campanario Street she'd been given by Urban Reform. That house was and wasn't mine because, although it was registered in her grandfather's name, it should have rightfully been registered in mine. It really belonged to me and my children, but it was Dulce's ambition to get it. She moved in and said to me, "Remember you have a room here any time you want it. And you can bring the kids, too." I never argued about the house. I resigned myself and let her have it. She kept the house, Marta's clothes, and practically everything else. All I took were my children's clothes and mine. I never wanted to set foot in that place again. Later, when I was assigned to a job that took me through that street, I managed to get myself transferred.

Marta's family tried to coerce me—as if I were ignorant of the law!—by saying they could take the children away from me. One day they summoned me to court and accused me of having abandoned my children when they were at Dulce's in Artemisa. But I showed the judge all the receipts of the money orders I'd sent Martita while they were there.

I have proof that they even tried to get Social Welfare to put the boys into boarding school. I refused. I told them, "I intend to keep my children with me till the day I die. So far they've eaten what I provided, both good and bad, and that's what they'll go on doing. As long as I have life and health and God gives me the strength to work for them, they'll never starve. And you may be sure they'll never ask you for so much as a glass of water to quench their thirst." So far I've kept my word. Never have I asked any of them for so much as 1 *peso*.

If they'd managed to get my two children legally, I would never have allowed Marta's relatives to have them—not alive at any rate. God only knows what demon got into my head, but I thought and thought about that, and I'd rather have taken their lives and mine before agreeing to such a thing. That wasn't just fantasy, either; it was my firm resolution. I would really have done it because I carry out my decisions, no matter how drastic. I won't stand for anything that's wrong. I don't like to harm anybody and I allow nobody to harm me.

I can truly say, no matter how harshly people judge me, that in regard to my children, my conscience is clear before man's law and God's. I kept them with me and for years not one of Marta's relatives came to see them. After about six or seven years, their grandmother, the woman Marta called her foster mother, sent for the boys because she was very ill and didn't want to die without seeing them.

I told Marta's uncle, who brought me the message, "Her conscience woke up pretty late to the fact that she had two grandchildren, didn't it? Now that she's on her deathbed she asks to see them, but before she didn't bother to find out whether they were alive or dead, whether they ate and drank or went hungry and thirsty. She never gave a thought to her two grandsons who needed her affection. Well, now you can tell her for me that she can go ahead and die without seeing them." And so she did.

What right had she to expect the children to be fond of her? No, *hombre,* no! I didn't want to get involved with Marta's family again. All I wanted was to forget them and start a new life.

Chapter Five

A Purely Practical Decision

AFTER MARTA'S DEATH I made my plans. Girl friends I would have, but never again would I take upon myself the responsibility of a home, of having a woman living under one roof with me. But then who would care for my children? Having no home was only part of my problem. Even if I had taken Marta's house on Campanario Street, I'd still have no one to care for my two boys.

I went to *mamá* and told her, "Look at my problem, *mima*. Marta is dead, and I don't want to get involved ever again, as long as I live. I have two children and I don't know how I'm going to manage. All I ask of you is to raise Omarito for me. I'll ask Angelita to raise Manolito. I'll send both of you money for the children's support, and of course I'll come to take them out every Sunday."

She agreed to take Omarito for a while. He was my youngest, not even a year old. Who could take care of him better than my *mamá*? It really was the right and proper decision for me to make about the child. Next I went to my sister Angelita. She gave me a place to sleep and agreed to take care of Manolito, who was still living with Anita. I have no complaints against Angelita. Whatever she had in the house she shared with my son.

I always said that new brooms sweep clean. *Mamá* accepted Omarito, and her husband, Norberto, said they wanted to raise him because Norberto had no child of his own. He would love the kid like a son, he said, but in fact Omarito stayed in *mamá*'s house barely a month and a half. The first thing that happened was that *mamá* asked me if she could put Omarito down in her ration book. I said, "Yes, but not quite yet," because there were some matters I had to settle first with the regional office, in order to have my book changed.[19] I had to notify them that I had moved and so on. She wanted to put Manolito and me in her book

19. Ration books are issued by the Office for Control of Food Distribution (OFICODA), under the Ministry of Domestic Trade (MINCIN).

too. Well, I analyzed the matter. How could I do that if we were eating out of Angelita's rations? It wouldn't be fair to my sister. So I told *mamá* I couldn't do it, that I'd get into trouble and that I couldn't take on such an obligation.

Then I noticed that Omarito wasn't getting along any too well. He wasn't being fed properly and he got a terrible skin infection as a result. His back is still marked with scars. Omarito was used to drinking milk and eating well but *mamá* gave him mostly sugar water and bread, which he had never eaten before. Meat or chicken he never got, because according to *mamá*, if little boys ate chicken or beef it killed them. So the adults ate beef and chicken while Omarito ate bread.

Mamá claimed she couldn't feed him well because the child ate a lot and I gave nothing for his food. That wasn't true. There was one fortnight when I gave *mamá* nothing. During that particular fifteen-day period, I only worked about five or six days and earned only 35 *pesos*. I owed over 50 *pesos* to somebody and over 30 *pesos* to somebody else. I told *mamá*, "Look, I can't give you any money this payday because I have a debt that must be paid to keep the door open in case I need credit again." I had a little money, but it isn't so easy to move from one place to another and to change jobs.

Mamá said it was all right and then went off to tell my friend Alejandra that I was a degenerate, that I didn't give anything for the child and didn't even go to see him, and all sorts of lies. All my life *mamá* has gone around trying to discredit and demoralize me. If I had given Tina Moneybags 50 *pesos* that time, everything would have looked rosy to her, but because I didn't she kept yammering on. She told everybody—I had this from Angelita—that Omarito was too much of a bother and that Norberto couldn't sleep because the child kept crying for me. She rejected my son for the sake of that husband of hers. Besides, maybe it's a father's selfishness, but it seemed to me that Norberto was dominating the boy too much.

Angelita advised me to take Omarito away from *mamá* and I agreed. I went to talk with Alejandra and told her the situation. A neighbor, Esperanza, happened to be there. I'd known her since she was a señorita but I never paid much attention to her. Now she had one child and was expecting another. When she heard me telling my troubles to Alejandra she said, "If you don't mind, I'd like to take care of your baby."

I remember when Esperanza's mother died. They held a Mass in her house in Las Yaguas, in back of ours. At the time, Esperanza was all alone in the world—her mother was dead and her brothers were living out in the country. Then her friend Ana Luisa, who lives on 2nd Street, had gotten Esperanza all worked up over this man the kid liked, by praising him as if he were a god. So, thinking he was something out of this world, Esperanza put her foot into it and made the misstep.

At the Mass that day I told her, "Look, *chica,* this fellow you're running around with isn't going to propose or solve any problems for you. He's just looking for a chance to get his machete into you." I was right. The following Sunday she took off with him and a week later they quarreled and he left. But by then she was pregnant with Marilola. Esperanza did what work she could and bought Marilola's layette. Then she took up with another man and got pregnant with Delmira. That guy left her too, and she was alone.

Because of her circumstances, I thought, "Here's a woman who has failed. Out of what I earn, I can give her such-and-such an amount and keep the rest to spend as I like. My sons will have a roof over their heads and will be safe."

Manolito was still living with my sister Angelita. I would have liked him to stay with her if it hadn't been for the way she treated her children and the way she talked. She'd say a lot of dirty words and curse her children and call them names. I didn't want Manolito to learn all that bad language so I took him away. I asked Esperanza if she'd take him as well as Omarito and she agreed.

I made my decision and went to see *mamá.* I told her to her face, "Now listen, I want you to know that never again can you count on me to do anything for you, because whoever rejects a child of mine for a man's tail, be she my sister or my mother or whoever, deserves to die."

I collected my son's things but most of his clothes, his socks and about twenty other things, were lost. I didn't even ask what had happened to them. I said to myself, "I go, defeated." I took Omarito's jars of baby food I had put away—that was the time when the mercenaries were exchanged for baby food,[20] so I had lots of large and small jars of fruit and vegetables at *mamá*'s—and I gave them all to Esperanza, as well as rice, milk, and everything the boy would need. The very next day I went to Esperanza's to see the child and he was getting along fine. He took to Esperanza right away. He even called her *mamá. Coño,* that was strange!

It was very hard to take what *mamá* did to me in regard to my child. It's still a thorn in my flesh. For two years I kept away from her. She didn't know whether the children and I were alive or dead. Not that she cared . . . she never made the slightest effort to see her grandchildren. In all the nine years of his life, Omarito has never had to be beholden to his grandmother for so much as a teaspoonful of benadryl to relieve a cold.

---

20. In December, 1962, an agreement was concluded between Cuba and the United States for the release of 1,113 prisoners captured during the Playa Girón (Bay of Pigs) invasion in April, 1961. The United States agreed to send to Cuba $23,000,000 in drugs, $14,000,000 in baby foods, $9,000,000 in powdered milk, and $7,000,000 in surgical, dental, and veterinary instruments, plus $2,900,000 cash as ransom for prisoners released by Castro in the spring of 1961. *(Time,* Jan. 4, 1963, p. 14.) Castro has maintained that the United States never fulfilled its part of the agreement. (Lockwood, *Castro's Cuba, Cuba's Fidel,* p. 232.)

That year after Marta's death, I would get so dejected and melancholy that I felt physically unable to do anything. I found no relief. I'd go often to Esperanza's house to visit my children. Esperanza and I got intimate, but at that time there was no question of living with her. I had no interest in her as a woman, only in the help she could give me and my children.

I was alone and I went often to visit my sister Celia. It was there that I met Trinidad. Trini is a seamstress and hairdresser who came to the house. She's integrated in the Revolution and is a fine, upstanding *mulata*. My picture was in my sister's house and Celia had talked to Trini about me. The first time we met we started talking and kidding around. I saw that she liked me but I held back and watched for developments. Trini had a sweetheart with visiting rights and she had already bought her trousseau and everything, but that girl fell for me anyway.

My sister's little place had only three rooms. She lived in one room with her husband and children, a girl named Sara lived in the front room, and an old bag called Francisca lived in the third room. Well, that old bag knew I was a widower and that I had two sons, and she cast aside her husband in the hope of catching me. How wrong she was! Even so, Trini thought I was involved with Francisca, who thought I was involved with Trini. What do you think of that? How a man can be surrounded by gossip and lies and all sorts of complications! People accused me of having not two but three different women in that one little house.

In reality there was nothing between me and any of them! There are women with such capricious hearts! A man must be very careful about getting involved with them. Once when I was married to Martita, I almost broke up my home for such a woman. She was married and had small children, yet for an amorous whim—she called it love—she would have broken up her home. If I'd been an opportunist I could have made a pretty profit because of that woman's position, but I didn't. I'm thoughtful and considerate and I couldn't, out of pure mischief, destroy a home. If my visit to a family is going to cause both trouble and joy, I don't go there.

For two months I hardly ever visited my sister, but then I had an adventure with Trini. On August 12, the day of St. Clare of Assisi, I went back to Celia's house for her daughter's saint's-day party. Trini was there and I was surprised to find that the girl had fallen out with her sweetheart. My brother-in-law told me, "Look, Trini is interested in you, but I haven't mentioned it because if there should be any problem, I don't want to be blamed. I don't want her mother saying I pushed you two into falling in love or something."

Well, I started giving Trini good advice and explaining that I wasn't the right man for her. I said, "Look, Trini, I think you're making a serious mistake. You should analyze the situation and remember you're engaged to be married. What can you expect from a widower with two children? I'm not going to marry you or solve your problems. So forget what you have in mind because you're absolutely mistaken. Be realistic. Follow the natural rules of life. What every woman wants is to get married honorably and have a home of her own." Those were my very words.

"You're the man I like," she said. "I don't care whether I get married or not."

It was clear to me that Trini had lost her maidenhood long before she met me. When a woman's organism reaches such a state of heat that she gets desperate enough to ask a man to take her, then you know she's no virgin.

The next day we went to a hotel. Before we did anything, I told her, "I know you aren't a señorita. I know you're a woman who had her fall with another man. I don't want to get into any trouble because of you. Remember that I'm not legally responsible for anything that happens to you because you're eighteen years old."

She pushed all that aside with the words, "Ah, don't be a dope—forget the past and live in the present!" So, *pam!* I plunged in and took her. And when I got there, it was *vía libre*—the way was wide open. In my analysis of her, I'd plumbed the depths; I was right about her not being a virgin.

Eventually we drifted apart by mutual consent. I thought it was strange that a full-bodied female like Trini didn't get pregnant. Later she went to do productive labor, and there in the work camp she met another young girl and they became man and wife. They were hardened lesbians, both of them! How odd, that having tested a man's organ and having had normal sex relations, a woman should turn around and become a lesbian!

How complicated sexual life is! Especially in tropical countries, where passions are more fiery and less controlled. Some say that in certain European countries sensuality is more developed than in the tropics. Well, maybe people live fuller lives there but they're less passionate. Trini is living proof that people in the tropics have this defect. What is she if not sexually ill? Of course, among a million people you can get some who are alike but no two who are identical. Which goes to show you how wonderful nature is.

Life is funny. How often have you seen a man of whom you say, "That fellow is neither *simpático* nor good-looking. He's not even a snappy dresser with twenty different suits to choose from. Where does he get that power he has over women? Why do they all screw for him?" The answer is that everybody in the world has some good qualities.

In 1963, a year and two months after Marta's death, I started to live with Esperanza. It was a purely practical decision, see? I thought, "I have such-and-such needs. This woman is my only tree and that's the tree I'm going to lean up against." Sometimes one man's needs are another's relief, and that's what happened to me with Esperanza. I never came right out and asked her to live with me, but I knew that her life hadn't been very happy—she'd always had an unfair burden of sorrow—so I said to her, "Look, *chica,* you and I have known each other a long time; the best thing we can do is live together."

My own family couldn't help me or understand me and I couldn't expect much more from Esperanza, but I took up with her because of her circumstances. If it hadn't been for that, I'd never have set up a home again or had any more children. She soon bore first my son Fredito, then Eufrasio, then Angela. With her two, I had seven children in all!

Esperanza is good to me and very fond of my children, too. She's been a mother to them even more than a wife to me. I admire her and feel grateful to her but I can't blind myself to the fact that we're poles apart. Once we almost separated because of a trifle. A trifle I call it, but a guy gets fed up. I'd told her to stop soaking the laundry in the tub in the yard because often she couldn't get around to washing it the next day and it just stayed there. I told her, "Those clothes are going to rot there. I can't afford to waste money like that."

She snapped, "Oh, you're always harping on that and I'm fed up with you," she said.

"You're fed up with me? Good! I'm going."

She paid no attention, so I left. I went back after a week but I was still angry.

Having children is no reason for a man to stay with his wife. Suppose Esperanza was unfaithful to me. Should I stay with her simply because of the children? There are many ways a woman can betray a man right in the home. A faithful wife is not merely one who doesn't put the horns on her husband. If a wife does anything behind her husband's back, her lack of sincerity is a kind of betrayal. For instance, when she lends money to her brothers, isn't it her duty to say, "Look, I gave Macho or Guillermo 20 *pesos.*" But no, she never tells me; *they* do.

Esperanza lived with her two brothers, Macho and Guillermo, and I had to kick them both out of our house. I hate people who try to take advantage of me, and those two treated Esperanza like a slave. They exploited her shamelessly. They thought it was her duty to pick up their worn shirts every time they changed, then rush to wash, starch, and iron them. Esperanza fed them but they gave her nothing for their keep. If the grocery store received a supply of food and Macho and Guillermo had 100 *pesos,* did they spend it on food for the household? Not they! They drank it up in *aguardiente.* Those brothers were a pair of *locos;* they'd work one week, then spend two months loafing.

When I first began to live with Esperanza, they thought they could rule both their sister and me but they were mistaken. I was her husband and the man of the house, so they had to be ruled by me, and of course neither of them approved of me. They did all they could to make trouble. The quarrels we had were all their doing, but I won every battle.

The first time I met Esperanza's eldest brother, Macho, he came home drunk at 2:00 A.M. and banged on the door as if he owned the house. Thinking I was asleep, he asked, "Hey, sister, is that creep your husband?"

I sprang up and said, "A creep is a *maricón* like you. I'm no creep, see? My name is Alfredo. I'm your sister's husband and I don't need to account to you, because she's of age." I opened the door and pushed him out into the yard.

"What's this!" says he.

"This is my house, not yours, and if you dare hit me even once, I'll blow out your brains." When I threatened him, Macho pulled out a small machete, but I'm the kind of guy who hits first. I picked up an iron bar and hit him twice, so hard he didn't come back for a third blow.

Esperanza was angry when I kicked her brother out. In fact she almost left me. Macho is her favorite brother and she felt hurt by our quarrel. About five days later Macho showed up at my house again. He complained to his sister that he was out of a job, and having been missed by the labor census, all doors were closed to him. He's single, so he played up to Esperanza, trying to soften her up. He wanted her to get me to let him stay with us until he could find work.

Esperanza told me about Macho's problem and I said, "Look, *chica,* I don't object to his staying but he has to respect this house. I know it isn't registered in my name but that makes no difference as far as I'm concerned. As long as I'm living with you, your brother must live according to *my* rules." In my house things are done my way because I'm the boss. Esperanza won't so much as move something from one place to another without my consent.

Well, Macho begged my pardon and I said, "All right, all I ask is that the problems you caused before won't be repeated. You can drink here but according to my rules. I don't want any fights or scandals. And everybody must be in bed by midnight because I have to get up at 4:00 A.M." I was working on the construction of a factory then.

I went on, "Listen, *chico,* you earn 100 *pesos* a month and squander it all on drink. I'm not telling you to give your sister this or that amount of money—that's between you and her—but every fifteen days, when you get your pay, why don't you set aside 20 *pesos* for carfare and lunches and give her the rest? Or you could spend it on clothes, for instance. A man who is always clean and neat is respected by others, even if he drinks. Nobody can say of him, 'Look at that dirty drunk!' You'll never get anywhere if you're drunk all the time and go around stinking of sweat." Those were my very words.

It took Macho six months to get his work papers straightened out and all that time he stayed with us. When his papers came through I advised him, "Go work in the cane fields for six months, that will make a man of you." It did, too. I don't know why it is but they come back changed. While working the cane, he sent his sister money orders which I saved. When he got back I returned over 300 *pesos* to him.

After Macho got a job he brought his sister money twice a month. He's been doing that for a long time now. When he can't bring it personally, he sends it.

I had a problem when Esperanza's other brother, Guillermo, moved in with us. I was working outside of Havana and couldn't go home every day. Once I was away for seventeen days, and when I came home I found Guillermo and his wife, Pastora, settled in. They had moved in without a by-your-leave. Well, brother-in-law or not, he has to respect me and ask my permission before taking such a step. After all, I'm the one who brings home the money.

The very day I found them there I woke Guillermo early in the morning and said, "Hey, what's this? Who told you to move in here?"

"Well, look, I had to bring Pastora here because I had no place to stay and no money."

"Sorry, *chico,* if you're broke you're broke, but no matter what, you'll have to pack up your things and go somewhere else with your wife."

"But I *can't* go!"

"Sure you can—and I mean now!" So he left. There was nothing he could do about it.

I had a lot of reasons not to want those two in my home. There we were, Esperanza and I, doing our best to stretch out the food allowed us in our ration book and having a hard enough time without two extra mouths to feed. What did Guillermo expect? That I should sacrifice my children's bellies to keep his and his woman's filled? Especially Pastora's! I don't like to speak ill of anyone but that Pastora is slovenly and speaks dirty to boot, which is something I will not put up with. I told her that she stank and it's the truth.

Pastora's former husband was Ramón Betancourt, an old man who lived in the *reparto*. She bore him three chilren who are grown up now and old enough to be married. Guillermo was in love with Pastora and he took her away from Betancourt. I was on the old man's side and I often told Pastora that she had acted very badly toward her husband. I really told her off. You see, Pastora and Betancourt were both white but she left her husband for Guillermo, a black. That's why I upbraided her.

When I threw Guillermo out of my house, he wanted to get even with me, so the guy goes and calls me a *gusano*[21] and charges me with being a

---

21. Literally "worm," used in Cuba to refer to anyone who does not support the Revolution, from passive opponents to active counterrevolutionaries.

counterrevolutionary. Imagine! Guillermo knew well enough what he was doing. He did it deliberately, in revenge. He thought he had me in a tight spot, caught with his bait, little knowing that I could cut cloth in places he couldn't.

One morning I slipped out to see Captain Alcover in the Ministry of the Interior. My sister worked for him as a cook and he knew me. I told him my problem. "If I'm a counterrevolutionary as this man says, if I was a policeman, if I have the slightest debt to pay in the eyes of the law, let the whole weight of the law fall upon me. On the other hand, if you find nothing against me, let the law deal with my accuser."

"Look, *chico*," the captain said. "How can you expect the lion to fall into a mouse's claws?" They tore up the list of charges against me then and there.

Now that Macho and Guillermo know me, they've become reconciled to the fact that Esperanza is my wife. They used to believe what people told them—that I beat her, and all sorts of lies. Now they realize what a good husband I am, that I'm the one who buys clothes for her and her children.

I've taught those two to be real brothers to Esperanza. I made them understand that as their eldest sister, she's the only mother they have left, and she's the one they should take care of and love. Now they've completely changed, thanks to me and the Revolution. Guillermo has stopped drinking and works in a boarding school for scholarship students on the Isle of Youth.[22] He has a home of his own there, and a wife and daughter.

Macho is also about 99 percent changed. I was a guiding light to him and that's something he'd never found before in anyone. I think it was my kindness that helped him, and Guillermo, too. The truth is, I'm the one who made men of those two.

22. Also known as the Isle of Pines, where cattle, dairy, and citrus farms are worked largely by young volunteers, many still students. The name of the island is to be officially changed to the Isle of Youth when goals for the Isle's development have been achieved.

Chapter Six

Getting My Fair Share

WHEN THE NEW GOVERNMENT first took over, Fidel said something that many people didn't understand at the time but understand well enough now. He said, "There will be money to spare, but not enough goods to buy." And so it is. You see a bum in the street and he turns out to have 200 or 300 *pesos* in his pocket. Stop even the poorest man and say to him, "I have three cans of milk to sell," and he'll answer, "I'll pay 2.50 *pesos* for them." What do you think of that?

Today the worst problem our country faces is the food shortage. You must wait in line for everything, even for a piece of candy. *Hombre,* isn't that absurd? It's unbelievable that in the country of sugar you should have to wait in line to buy half a pound of caramels. Before, there were heaps of all kinds of candies available, whole boxes full of different flavors and colors.

Naturally people react. They say, "This is shit." They aren't happy with the situation, especially when they hear that in Russia, which is supposed to be so advanced, fifty years after the Revolution people are still eating their 2 pounds of bread a day. So they think, "What will happen to us if now, ten years after *our* Revolution, we are so undernourished? Five years from now there won't be one human being left to walk down the streets!" You hear some saying, "Under the old regime they killed 20,000 but under the new one they're killing 500,000." In other words, under Batista many young men were murdered, but in the present regime more people are starving to death.

Well, people say all kinds of foolishness because they haven't stopped to consider their own past. It's true that under the old regime there was plenty of everything. The stores were bursting with goods, but then not everybody had the money to buy them. One had to make many sacrifices and suffer to get things. Maybe one week you could afford meat but then for the next thirteen days you'd go without it altogether. Nowadays you know that certain things are going to be available and that you're going to have enough money to buy them.

At least now people can gèt their fair share of whatever there is. Before the Revolution, what security did they have? Now everything is distributed equally through rationing. There's no question of some having more and some less. Each person listed in your book gets a fixed quota and the price is fixed too.

There are still some inequalities in spite of rationing. The government has thousands of students studying on scholarships that provide them with food. But when the students leave home their names aren't crossed from the family ration book. That means their family gets their quota of food, yet there are brigades of men working in the country day and night who should have extra rations because they work terrifically hard, but they don't get it.

I think the government is doing right in rationing goods. Even so, it's harder for some than for others. For old people living alone, I tell you rationing is a sentence of death on the installment plan. Oh, the state helps widows and old people, but here in Buena Ventura about twenty old people are wasting away from hunger. One of them, old man Fajardo, lived alone and was about ready to kick the bucket anyway. But he was used to a good dinner and supper and lots of between-meal snacks. He had a hard time when rationing started. Things are looking up for him now because his son and daughter-in-law moved in with him and he can get more food. The other little old man across the way, Lino, poor soul, helps other people plant their plots and manages as best he can one way or another. Every now and then they hospitalize him.

Rationing is easier for people who have children. Every married couple has heaps of children; the more the merrier. That's the only way of beating the food shortages. Esperanza and I have seven children— four of them are under seven—but altogether there are twelve people listed in my ration book. Besides us there are Esperanza's two brothers and her sister Inés. Esperanza's brothers eat with us only five to ten times each month and their rations are a lifesaver for us. With their rations we can usually eat two full meals a day, besides breakfast. When we can't manage that much, we grownups skip lunch and Esperanza makes something light for the kids, like cornstarch pudding or boiled tubers.

Thank God, ever since I started a family of my own we've never lacked food at home. I always manage to get just a little bit more than we need. Many people don't manage as well as I do. They keep running out of something and are the kind who borrow from their neighbors. People shouldn't borrow; if they can't plan their rations why should their neighbors suffer for it?

Still, even we don't eat as well now as we did before the Revolution. Some people say the government is deliberately trying to starve us but that's a lie! The truth is, Fidel ran into twenty difficulties because the administrators don't function well. Take vegetables. Every day you hear how people are working on the farms raising crops, yet we still don't see any vegetables. In the old days, before the Agrarian Reform, when the bad guys were running the farms, we produced plantains, *malanga*,[23] sweet potatoes, beets, carrots, eggplant, and all sorts of vegetables. All those things were produced here on a large scale; we even exported them.

Why aren't there any vegetables today? People don't stop to think or try to understand what brought on the shortage. I worked in the country and I know what happened. When the Revolution triumphed, there were too many inexpert people going out in the country and planting things on unsuitable land. So the crops failed. The Party blames it all on bad weather, but I blame the men who planned the agriculture. The people blame Fidel himself. He promised there would be vegetables and there weren't, but you can't blame Fidel. He's only one man and he can't have a finger in every pie. He can't multiply himself and be everywhere at once.

The vegetable ration is divided into different kinds of vegetables; we get more of some than of others.[24] People don't like frozen vegetables and they prefer to wait in long lines to buy fresh vegetables when the rations come in. You can get plenty of dried peas when they come, but there aren't many kidney beans or chick peas. But other beans do come to the stores fairly regularly. This month we did all right because we also got 6 pounds of speckled beans that cost 19 *centavos* a pound.

Beans would help a lot in extending the diet—if only they gave us something to season them with. Beans are no good to anybody if they don't have the right seasonings—small peppers, sausage, tomato, garlic or onions, anything to give them flavor. Otherwise it's like eating tasteless soup. Many people have bags full of dried beans in their larders, because they have no spices left to season them with.

People barter vegetables like everything else. Once I exchanged a pound of black beans for a pound of flour. That's a fair deal because people resell black beans for from 2.50 to 5 *pesos* a pound, and flour at only 2 *pesos*. Cuban kidney beans are popular and some people will pay 6 *pesos* a pound for them.

It would be a big help if tubers were plentiful because you can fill up on them. It's been months since I tasted sweet potatoes. I can't understand it! Sweet potato plants bear a crop every four months, or six at least, yet you never see them anymore. They imported Russian farm machinery to sow the land with sweet potatoes, but it seems wherever Russian iron touches a piece of land, no more sweet potatoes grow on it.

23. A root vegetable favored by Cubans.
24. Some vegetables are available *por la libre*, that is, in unrationed amounts. They are distributed to the stores, in season, as they become available.

Honestly, it's as bad as a Gypsy's curse! I don't believe we really need so much iron here; when we plowed the land with oxen we had everything.

Yucca and apple plantain have both disappeared from the market since the triumph of the Revolution. *Malanga* has been exiled too. It's in the stores once every nine to ten months, but it's allotted only to children and to old people over sixty-five. I grow my own plantains and sometimes I go to the country to buy them.

Fruit is scarce too. In December they distribute small apples but you don't see them the rest of the year. Citrus fruits are in season from November to January or February. During that time you can get oranges and grapefruit fairly regularly at 30 or 40 *centavos* a pound. We spend about 4 *pesos* on fruit every four months.

Papaya you will never taste again unless you plant a tree. The same goes for guava. And you can't find them in jellies or canned in syrup. Before the Revolution there were many factories that made preserves, jellies, or pastes. You could get grated coconut cooked in sugar, preserves of papaya, guava rinds, and much more. There was an infinite variety of brands, too, because the fruit grows wild in Cuba and there was lots of competition. But now that the state owns everything, you can't find any of those sweets. They're in exile. That's another contradiction.

In December the state distributed what they called guava jelly, but it was really *membrillo,* which is garbage. It's made from the seeds of Santo Domingo mamey and that's the truth. Anyone who has ever eaten sweets, especially if they've worked in a food store like me, can tell the difference. People complain because everybody in Cuba, even the poorest, was in the habit of having dessert with their coffee.

Sugar is no problem. Each citizen has an allowance of 6 pounds per month. At home we buy 70-odd pounds of sugar a month at 7 *centavos* a pound. We don't use more than 20 pounds so I experiment with what's left over. I make coffee candy with some of the sugar, but my favorite experiment is making rum. I take sugar, yeast, and *miel de purga,* a kind of molasses which is used to make rum and alcohol. After thirty days, or forty-one at the most, you strain it and distill it secretly and then it's ready. It tastes rotten, but even so, I sell it.

Rum can fetch as much as 15 *pesos* a bottle when it's scarce. The selling price also depends on where you sell it. I used to take it out to the country, where *guajiros* drink liquor to guard them from the damp. I charged them 12 *pesos* a bottle. Now I'd rather barter it. My rates are 10 pounds of rice for a bottle of *aguardiente,* 5 pounds of black beans or red kidney beans for a little bottle of dry wine.

My weekly allotment of coffee is 1 pound 2 ounces.[25] Both Esperanza

25. One and a half ounces per person per week, or 18 ounces for the twelve people on Barrera's ration book.

and I are great coffee drinkers so we keep running out of it. You could get it more cheaply in the old days because there were different qualities and prices; nowadays there's only one. I worked in a small food store then and I'd take a quarter-pound bagful home every night. That way we never ran out of it.

The government treats us well as far as milk is concerned. My children love it and drink lots of it. Manolito, who is ten, drinks milk when he gets up in the morning, and just before going to school he finds room for another glass. At suppertime he eats only if he can wash down the meal with milk. Omarito is a real calf too. That kid should have a cow for his own exclusive use! Those kids take so much milk and bread it spoils their appetite.

I kept count of the number of cans of milk Fredito drank between the ages of seven to nine months, when he was still suckling at his mother's breast, and it came to forty a month! It was all to the good though, because he's strong and full of life. Now that he's four and growing fast, he drinks milk as if it were a sport. Delmira, who is six, and Marilola, who is seven going on eight, hardly drink any milk at all. I scold them to try to make them drink their milk and eat.

We used to get fresh milk. Then Eufrasio, who is two, got very sick and couldn't take standard milk, so I asked the doctor for permission to give evaporated milk a trial. Eufrasio thrived on it—he'd drink forty to forty-five cans a month and it still wasn't enough for him. We had to get extra milk. After that I asked the doctor to prescribe canned milk for all the kids.

The fresh milk was going to waste anyway. It was always full of grainy clots—I don't know whether the pasteurizing machines didn't work right or if it was some chemical defect. It was delivered in the morning after the children had had their breakfast and went to school. Because we have no refrigerator, by evening it was sour. We were spending 24 *pesos* a month on milk and a lot of it had to be thrown away.

When the milk doesn't get to you in time you're entitled to file a complaint. Nobody does though, because the milkman is a good guy. The empty bottles must be picked up before the milkman delivers the daily ration, because there's a shortage of bottles. If you break a bottle you have to turn it in broken and wait until you're assigned a new bottle before you get your milk. Some sluts don't bother to put their empty bottles out, so the milkman has to knock on the door and ask for them. If no one answers, he doesn't leave any milk. Then those people complain.

Now, altogether we get 138 cans of milk a month. My four youngest get one can each, every day. Manolito, Omarito, and Marilola, who are over seven, each get six cans of milk a month. Every thirty-four days we adults get three cans of milk and one liter of fresh milk besides what is assigned to the children.

You can always get more milk than your ration allows for. Among your friends and neighbors there are always people who are willing to sell or exchange milk for something else. But that way it costs from 2 to 2.50 *pesos*. If you buy milk with your ration book, milk costs 21 *centavos* a can. I spend a total of 32.40 *pesos* a month on milk, which I can well afford.

I have to fetch the canned milk from the grocery store on any of the assigned days of the week. It's my habit to go and get sixty cans every two weeks. Sometimes I take a handcart to carry the cans, other times I ride a bicycle.

The bread situation at home has been good since rationing began a few months ago. Now it's no trouble to get it every day since we don't have to stand in line. We're allowed one-fourth of a pound per person. For us that's 3 pounds a day, more than enough for the whole family. We have actually increased our consumption since rationing began. The kids always eat a slice of bread before they drink their morning milk. They also eat it at dinner and supper and sometimes at night before going to bed. Often I fry a few slices in a bit of lard, oil, or butter for them. It's delicious that way.

Our rice ration never lasts the month through. Today nobody gets enough rice. When I think of where the Revolution is leading us, a thing like that confuses me. Before the Revolution, everybody, rich and poor, had plenty of rice. A small family never consumed less than a couple of pounds a day, so you can imagine how much a large family used. Some groceries carried as many as eleven or twelve varieties of rice that cost from 9 to 21 *centavos* a pound. Today rice sells for 19 *centavos* a pound. There's only one price and one quality: that awful Valencia type that turns to soup when you cook it. This is really terribly hard on us because rice is the basis of the Cuban diet. And where did all the rice go? Why, down the same path the vegetables went.

We used to grow lots of rice in Cuba. Before the Revolution, the whole region of lowlands along the coast were planted exclusively with rice. Then the Revolution triumphed and *bang!* Some clown of a manager decided, "What we have to do is to get the bulldozers here and plant the whole thing with sweet potatoes and *malangas*. Everyone had known for years that those lowlands were only good for planting rice; eventually they realized that fact but by then the farms had been destroyed.

We were forced to import rice from China. Then the Chinese played us Cubans for fools; they doublecrossed us in the rice contract because of the problem that came up.[26] So on March 13, 1965, the rice ration was

---

26. The problem Barrera refers to is a diplomatic disagreement between Cuba and China made public in September, 1965, when Castro and President Dorticós formally protested against the Chinese distributing propaganda among Cuban army officers and

cut in half, to 3 pounds per person each month. It stayed at 3 pounds until just recently, when it was increased to 4.[27] Now we get 48 pounds a month but it simply isn't enough. It lasts only eighteen or twenty days. Still, we're better off than some people. We've never gone hungry but others do, especially old people. A little old lady living by herself used to buy, say, half a pound of rice daily. Now each month that same old lady gets 4 pounds of rice, enough for eight days, which means that for the remaining twenty-two days she has to sit looking at the moon.

There are rice plantations within the greenbelt around Havana but they belong to the state. Outside those limits people can grow their own rice, and you'll find people from the city going out to buy it on the black market. I myself keep sending telegrams to the country to buy rice. Those transactions are illegal of course, and the government keeps an eye out for them. Some people try to rob you by asking 3 *pesos* for 1 pound of rice. I'll pay up to 2.50 *pesos* but even that is barefaced robbery. Still, it's better than going without.

The *guajiros* refuse to sell their rice but insist on bartering it instead. I once bartered a pair of work pants worth about 4 *pesos* for 10 pounds of rice worth 30 *pesos*. It was a real bargain. I would have preferred to pay cash for the rice, but the *guajiro* pulled out a roll of money so big a goat couldn't have jumped it. He said, "Look, I have plenty of cash but what good does that do? You can't get anything with it. What I need is shoes, socks, a pair of work pants, shirts, and undershorts." That's the way it is nowadays. Any *guajiro* will have about 1,000 *pesos* in cash but not one decent pair of pants.

Most people don't get enough fat. The ration for lard is only 1½ pounds per person each month, and it's very low-quality, no good at all, and that's the truth. We have plenty at home because I raise pigs in the country with my partner. Every time we slaughter a pig we save the lard and I go out to the country to get it.[28] It's free but it isn't much, and even with the extra we run out of fat sometimes.

It's quite usual for neighbors to exchange rice for fat. We know a family who runs out of lard and oil at the end of the month, so we buy extra lard or oil and barter it for some of their rice. A bottle of oil is

government officials. The action was apparently in retaliation for China's decision to cut rice exports to Cuba, which, according to Castro, resulted in the 1965 decrease in the Cuban monthly rice ration from 6 to 3 pounds per person. Cuba received 250,000 tons of rice from China in 1965, and asked for 285,000 tons in 1966. China promised to deliver only 135,000 tons, citing increased aid to North Vietnam as the principal reason for the decrease. Castro's statement of Cuba's position (appearing in *Granma*, Feb. 6, 1966) was reprinted in its entirety, with editorial comments, in *Peking Review*, Feb. 25, 1966, pp. 13–25. (Also see Ernst Halperin, "Peking and the Latin American Communists," *China Quarterly* (Jan.-Mar., 1967), pp. 148–50.)

27. This was in 1969; in 1970 the ration increased to 6 pounds per person per month.
28. See Benedí, n. 89.

worth 2 pounds of rice. That kind of deal is a touchy problem; you can only bring up the subject with somebody you trust, and then make the deal secretly. Lard is even harder to get in the black market than coffee, even though coffee costs 10, 12, or 15 *pesos* a pound. Isn't that something, though!

We used to buy lard at 16 *centavos* a pound and it tasted good, like pig cracklings. The stuff we get now has no taste at all. It's like tallow; if you pour a bit on top of the rice, the grains stick together in a lump. I don't know what the hell that stuff is, and it costs 24 *centavos* a pound.

Oil is more plentiful than lard. It sells for 30 to 33 *centavos* a pound. Recently they increased the ration by half a pound, so now I get twelve bottles of oil each month. No less. We use up six bottles in eight days because Esperanza fries a lot and the oil is of such poor quality it doesn't last. Esperanza gets desperate with that oil, but anybody who can't get enough oil is out of luck. By the fifteenth of the month they have to cook everything in water.

Before the Revolution, the people in Las Yaguas ate better than many of the rich, even though they did live in huts. In my family we had meat daily and we weren't exceptional. Today we eat beef only three times a week. We get three-fourths of a pound of meat each, or 8½ pounds a week for the whole family. That costs 4.80 *pesos* a week. They really break your neck when they give you that second-class stuff. For instance, I might get 3 pounds of bones in my meat ration. If they gave me 3 pounds of a tough cut instead, we could make meat-and-potato stew or any number of other dishes which would be a lot more helpful. Of course the bone gives substance to whatever you cook, but it can't compare with meat.

Many people speculate with meat. For instance some people buy their full ration, then resell part of it at a higher price. People who need extra meat will pay 3.50 or 4 *pesos* for 1 pound of meat, so if you sell as much as half of your meat ration it pays for itself and more—then there's money left over to buy other things. Lots of people juggle their rations around that way.

Once I went to the grocery to collect the meat ration for a woman who couldn't go herself, so she made a bargain with me. I collected her meat ration and she went halves with me. That woman had no idea how much people were paying for extra meat because she had no contact with others.

I once knew a butcher who gave all his customers short measure. He'd keep back half a pound of meat from one customer, a fourth of a pound from another, and so one. He played that trick on me for a while before I caught on. Esperanza's sister Inés, who is kind of dumb, picked up the meat each week—that's how he got away with it for as long as he did. But one day I asked Inés to get 1½ pounds of ground meat and the rest in cuts of loin and steak. I checked the weight and it turned out the butcher had sent only 1¼ pounds of ground meat. The following week I weighed the meat from four different orders and each order was a quarter-pound short.

When I was sure, I went to that man's shop and exploded, "Look, Albino, I know you've been giving me short weight on that lousy meat you sell."

"Short weight? Me? Never!" he protested.

"Yes you do! Look at this ground meat—a quarter-pound less than I asked and paid for! I'm not asking for any extras, just what I've paid for. Either you drop that racket, or I'm going to complain to the authorities and you'll go to jail."

I would have complained too, and not just for my children's sake. People say that one shields oneself by complaining "for the sake of the children." Well, I'm honest; I say right out to anybody's face that meat is essential for both children and adults, and it's barefaced robbery to sell people short on such a basic food.

After I faced him with the facts, Albino always sent me the correct amount of meat. But then he went to the cane fields. He left a substitute who didn't know his system and we were worse off than ever. One week nobody got their ration of meat or fish. Can you imagine what it's like to be a whole week without a taste of meat? It's deadly! The man handed out a slip of paper to every client who had not received his meat ration and in some of those papers he wrote that the meat had been delivered. What a lie! Obviously the man must have been stealing. Finally about twenty or thirty people who hadn't gotten their week's ration took him to trial. The trial is still pending but they did give us that week's supply of meat. For us at home that meant an extra 8½ pounds, so we could eat meat every single day that week.

Before the Revolution, people had a much more varied diet. They could eat salt codfish, canned sardines, pork, and chicken as well as beef. Before 1959 poultry was the cheapest kind of meat. Today one little chicken costs 65 *centavos* a pound; that's over 1 *peso* for each chicken.

Most people in Buena Ventura never see chicken. Last year I got chicken only twice with my ration book, but that's because it's usually earmarked for sick people and those over sixty-five. Children under two are entitled to one chicken a week, which would make four a month, but when Eufrasio turned two, he'd had chicken only twice on the ration book. Some children never taste chicken again after they get to be two years old. Eufrasio wouldn't either if I didn't have a small flock of my own chickens in my backyard. There are people who would like to do the same thing but don't have the opportunity—or my initiative and industry. I had to tie up 200 *pesos* that I needed for other things, and now I have to buy corn for the chickens for 1.50 *pesos* and chicken feed for 2 *pesos*. If you stop to figure it out, by the time they get to my table those chickens cost me over 20 *pesos* apiece, but at least we get to eat chicken oftener than we would otherwise.

Sometimes I'll tell Esperanza to kill a chicken and make soup. So at midday we eat the broth and have the boiled chicken with bread for dinner. On special days, like my saint's day or whenever we have company, I may kill about six chickens if I don't have any other resource. But my chickens are like money in the bank to me, and if I killed six chickens every two months I'd soon have none left. I can't risk that. Whenever I can, I get a small pig, a goat, or a turkey.

As I understand it, fish consumption has gone up tremendously. Very few people ate fish before. They could afford to all right, they just didn't like it. Nowadays it's unrationed and they eat it as a substitute for meat. Fish comes frozen but it's lousy quality because it has so many bones. People speculate with fish, too. I've seen people here exchange it for condensed milk. I usually spend about 2 *pesos* a week for 3 pounds of fish. It comes once a week, on Wednesdays, and we eat it the same day. Where would we keep it? Esperanza cleans it and fries part for dinner. The rest she makes into fritters or serves with fried eggs. Most people can't spare their oil to fry, so they boil the fish and add a little bit of *sofrito*.[29]

In my home there's no shortage of eggs. We're entitled to three eggs a week per person, but I only buy half the allotted ration because we're not very fond of them. When we get dry wine I sweeten it and beat in one egg yolk for each child to take away the egg taste. They drink it first thing in the morning on an empty stomach. Otherwise we always have some left over at the end of the month.

It seems to me that the quality of eggs has deteriorated since the Revolution. The eggs we get today have no food value, all they do is give the kids indigestion. I think it's because the chicken feed isn't as good now. Last week we bought a batch and we threw practically every one away because they were spoiled. Yet they're 96 *centavos* a dozen, which means you pay 8 *centavos* for one egg. Before the Revolution you could get thirty-three eggs for 1 *peso*.

Some people in the *reparto* speculate with eggs, selling them for 30 or 40 *centavos* each, instead of the official price of 8 *centavos*. I don't do it, because you get involved in something like that and first thing you know a cop grabs you. Why take such risks?

It's a shame, the food shortage, and that's the truth. Still, people joke about it. They have funny names for different kinds of food. Bread we call "I hate you but never will I forget you." Why? Do you know what it is

29. A combination of salt ham, fatback bacon, green peppers, small sweet peppers, and tomato sauce used to season many foods.

to have to eat bread with nothing but saliva? If you have a bit of butter, you butter it and sprinkle it with salt because there's no garlic.

After you finish your bread, you can wash it down with "rooster soup." Know what that is? Sugar water—just plain water with sugar in it. What a life! Fried eggs are "the persistent Vietnamese guerrillas." "Summer romance" is chicken; "black tears" means black beans. Jerked meat is "If I've ever seen you, I don't remember." When we get pork, which is about once a year, we call it "dreams of youth."

That's Cubans for you! No matter how sad or hard up they are, they find a funny side to everything.

Cigarettes are rationed too. Each adult gets one pack a week, at 20 centavos a pack. There are five adults at home, so every Thursday I get five packs of Competidoras for 1 peso. They don't last. Esperanza goes nearly out of her head with the desire to smoke, but she manages pretty well by smoking Populares and other stronger brands. That way she makes them last until the following Thursday.

You can buy cigarettes on the black market because many people who don't smoke buy their allotted ration anyway and then sell it.[30] They charge 1 peso or 1.50 a pack. Marta used to say to me, "What, 1 peso for a pack of cigarettes? Not me!" The most she ever paid was 50 centavos. I'm entitled to a cigar ration but I've never been a steady cigar smoker. I like to light one after dinner but it isn't a vice with me.

We get two soft drinks per person a week. Whenever it comes in we get a full box, twenty-four bottles, for 1.20 pesos. There isn't much black-market speculation with soft drinks. If they're being sold legally in the stores you buy them; if not, you do without. We always buy it, no matter what it is. Before the Revolution there were all sorts of different flavors—Jupiña, Oranche, Canada Dry, Materva, Salutaris, Pepsi-Cola, Coca-Cola, Spur-Cola, Royal Crown Cola ... a whole variety of soft drinks. Today all we can get is an orange-flavored drink and cola.

Some places in the street sell natural fruit drinks. For instance, mango or mamey juice or coconut water. But who's going to leave the reparto with seven kids trailing after him and go all the way to Havana just to buy a drink that isn't even cool? There are so many bars with frigidaires using up electricity, but do you think that any of those fellows earning a salary there ever think of putting the drinks inside to cool? Oh no! They think that because people can't get soft drinks anywhere else, they'll take them warm. That's not right! Let's put them in the refrigerator and serve decent drinks.

30. For a frank discussion by Fidel Castro of the "mini-commercialism" created by the rationing of cigarettes, see Granma Weekly Review, May 16, 1971, p. 6.

Some people in those bars give you water straight from the faucet when you ask for a drink. Sometimes they even tell you they don't have any. That's how mean we are to one another. And who are we hurting? Ourselves. It wouldn't do the government any harm if those people served cold drinks. But instead of solving a problem, there are men who put twenty difficulties in your way and only succeed in making people feel bitter.

When people say they lived better before the Revolution they're telling the truth, because things were cheaper then. The clothes my *papá* could buy then for 30 *pesos* I couldn't buy now for 300, even if I could find the goods in the shops, which I can't. We're all short of clothing. After the Revolution they said all would be as before, but it wasn't, and every day the situation gets worse. My two youngest boys get clothes on the rations, but Manolo and Omarito aren't entitled to any more this year, so they don't have one decent pair of pants between them. I buy trousers from my rations and have them altered for the boys. They're good trousers but the boys have torn them badly; I'm always punishing them for not taking proper care.

As for me, my work department gives me two complete changes of clothes a year, two pairs of pants and two shirts. This year, when clothes and boots were supposed to be distributed, we only got boots. We're still waiting for the clothes. All I have left are two pairs of work pants which are already singing "The Peanut Vendor." I do have work shirts but I can't buy any more because I used up my clothes ration buying pants for the boys. I have two white shirts to wear when I go out, but only one has long sleeves. I have plenty of underclothes except for undershirts, which I hardly ever use anyway.

Esperanza is short of clothes because she also uses hers for the girls. She's barely got one decent dress for herself, but she hardly ever goes out. Some of the people at home, my wife's brothers for instance, have been given clothes elsewhere. The work centers they belong to distribute one set of clothes, I believe, every six months.

We do get a ration of corduroy. That came in just recently and Esperanza went to buy it. I've never gone to get that sort of thing because I don't like to stand in line. Esperanza gets along well with people, so she waits in line. She's polite and well-bred. She never went to school or anything—she's learned by experience, stumbling and making mistakes. But I'm apt to get into some kind of trouble in line. Suppose I've been waiting since early morning in front of a store that opens at 12:30 and then some fellow tries to force his way ahead of me. Of course I can't let him get away with it. I don't yield my place, so then he tries to force me out, and before I know it I wind up at a police station.

Among common citizens the food shortage is the main grievance— that, and waiting in line. Nobody bothers about political problems or complains that we lack freedom because there are no elections. Nobody talks about personal liberty, though they should. The Revolution has its flaws in those areas too.

People make complaints about the scarcity of things, but if you can't right a wrong why go around talking about it? Of course people should take a stand on one side or the other, but if I complain I only make things more difficult for myself. I'm not going to change anything by talking. After all, it's the masses who decide, right? Whenever I hear someone bitching about the way things are, I tell him, "Rebel, *compai*, pull up your pants and go to the mountains to fight if you feel that way. See how soon you get covered with lead from head to foot. If you don't fancy that, then shut up and wait for better times."

That's my way of getting rid of loudmouths, see? If I can make him fight, they'll kill him so he won't shoot off his mouth anymore. On the other hand, that's also my way of advising him not to say things that might get him in trouble. I open his eyes in one way and pull the wool over them in another, hoping that way he gets rid of his horns.

There are other people here who tear off the upholstery from bus seats and think they're going to overthrow the government that way! How can anyone be such a fool? The government can have 50,000 bus seats reupholstered and never be the worse for it! But to do such damage is the work of a *cabrón*. If I ever saw any son-of-a-bitch do such a thing I'd take him straight to the police station. Besides, such tricks can backfire. Any day the offender might happen to get on that same bus again and a seat spring might tear his pants. Life has such turns, you know.

I wouldn't call these *cabrónes* counterrevolutionaries. I'd call them greedy, that's all. To me a *gusano* is a man who gets together and leads a band of counterrevolutionaries whose object is to overthrow the government, and of this kind of *gusano* there are none.

Frankly, there's no lack of money in my house, but there *is* a lack of material comforts. If you have money, you can live better buying things on the black market. Just walking down the street on your usual errands you always run into friends and acquaintances wanting to sell something without papers. For instance, people who plan to leave the country will sell their things before they apply for permission to leave. But suppose I had 1,800 or 2,000 *pesos* in my savings account and I had a chance to buy something like a set of bedroom furniture. The state still controls savings accounts today, and in order to draw out more than 250 *pesos* I must first explain why I want the extra money. I would have to say how much the bedroom set cost. That way the state controls prices as well, see?

Anyone selling something privately has to have a permit from their block Committee. Suppose you wanted to buy a bedroom set. Nowadays a bedroom set costs 1,200 or 1,300 *pesos* retail, but you may buy it secondhand cheaply from someone, say a man who's broken up with his wife. You would then make out a contract with the seller stating the price, and you would both go to the Committee in his area to get the contract approved and get a permit. The Committee calculates the "reformed state value" of the set according to their price list, and if your price is fair the sale is made. Actually, I think the CDRs have no idea about the value of things, but they allow you to sell anything as long as they think you aren't charging too much for it.

Then, when you buy the furniture, transporting the object is a problem. You have to get a certificate from the CDR stating that it is to be moved from one place to another, and a chauffeur is authorized to do the job. When the refrigerator or whatever arrives, you give the Committee the paper and that's all. But after you get it you have other problems, like the neighbors flocking in asking to keep their food in it.

Some things, like bedroom sets and refrigerators, are so hard to come by that people will get around the Committee's price controls and pay the earth for them. Suppose I had 10,000 *pesos* and was looking around for someone to sell me a refrigerator. I wouldn't worry about the price. I'd get a contract approved by the Committee but I'd settle the actual price secretly with the seller. And who's to say the price in the contract is the one paid? Of course in order to pay I'd have to have the money in my hand, not in a savings account where I couldn't get at it. So I keep a few *kilos* put away at home, within easy reach. That's why I don't keep 1 *kilo* in the bank.

In my own home our most urgent need is for more beds. When Esperanza first moved into the house there were three beds. None of them had springs or mattresses, only cardboard made of sugar-cane bagasse and a few thin quilts to lie on. At that time there weren't so many—only Esperanza, her daughter Marilola, her sister Inés, and her brother— four people altogether. Now there are nine of us. One of the beds is a wreck. The quilts are worn out so we cover the cardboard with jute sacks.

Esperanza sleeps in one of the two beds with Marilola, Delmira, and the baby girl. I can't sleep on the same bed as the little girls, so I say, "All right, I'm the man of the house, I work and need my rest. It's against nature but I'll be the one to sleep on the floor." I have no mattress either, only a bedspread to lie on and a sheet to cover me.

The boys—all four of them—share the other dilapidated bed. Two big boys and two little ones in a three-quarter-size bed! They have to lie across the width of the bed and can't stretch out so they don't get any rest.

About two years ago I went to the Ministry of Social Welfare with some blanks I'd filled in, stating what I needed. I wanted a single bed, a double bed, two couches, a bedside table, and a cupboard. We need a cupboard because the closet where we keep our clothes is very damp and the clothes get mildewed. The comrade I saw at the Ministry told me that my problem didn't come under her jurisdiction, that she only dealt with cases of natural disasters, fires and such. She told me to go to Victoria, the social worker who was assigned to the *reparto*. I went to see her but she didn't solve my problems either. In fact, that social worker did me a lot of harm.

It turned out that Victoria was involved in some shady deals with Minerva Ruz, who is president of one of the block Committees in the *reparto*. Minerva had a lot of influence with the social workers and played little political games with them. When I first went to live with Esperanza I had just come from Matanzas, and at that time things were really hurting in that province. Minerva made the social worker believe I was a counterrevolutionary who had been an *esbirro* in Matanzas. An *esbirro* was anybody who'd been in Batista's army or had committed abuses or crimes against the people. Malicious gossip—that's Minerva's specialty. Comrade Victoria believed Minerva's story, and without knowing anything about me and without bothering to investigate, she went ahead and slandered me politically.

None of my papers ever reached the Ministry. When I had no news of my request, I went and talked to her. She assured me she had sent the blanks to Social Welfare, but I know that's not true because we never received an answer from them. Later on, I noticed that if you wanted Victoria's help, you had to be in her good graces.

Once Social Welfare placed a supply of sewing machines and cribs with Victoria, who was to distribute them where they were most needed—to the mothers with the most children. But Comrade Victoria didn't do that. I think she gave them to the people who traded their supplies with her and would send in requests for anything they wanted. That way some people's needs were met. But whose needs? Those of her friends!

Once I came right out and told Victoria what I thought of her—not just because of my own case, either. I told her that if I and other neighbors who hadn't gotten her help should get together and complain to her superiors, she wouldn't have a very good time of it. I guess when I said that she decided, "The only thing to do with this fellow is to sink him completely."

I was out of a job at the time. What I call a job is having steady work which you go to every day. I was working only three or four days out of every fifteen, and what with Martita's death, taking the boys here and there—all those expenses—I was very short of money. Every worker is eligible for emergency aid to deal with urgent needs at short notice, and Victoria distributed the money from this fund to the people in the *reparto*, giving emergency aid to many. I myself could have qualified for it but I told her, "I don't need that, I have two strong arms to work with."

When I saw I would get no help from Victoria, I went to Tomasa, who is president of my block Committee. She wrote a letter expounding my needs and I took it to the *Poder Local*,[31] where Serafín, the comrade who works at the bank in Old Havana, stamped and countersigned it for me. The following Monday I went to a place on Porvenir Street, but they told me I was in the wrong building and sent me to a warehouse on Via Blanca where the furniture is stored. I went there and waited until almost 1:00 P.M., when a comrade told me, "Man, don't waste any more time waiting. They haven't brought any stuff here for the past three months."

I couldn't buy a bed because there were none to be had and that was that. I can't buy a frigidaire for the same reason, and God knows we need one. We have to buy all sorts of perishable foodstuffs like meat, milk, butter once a week, and week after week they've spoiled because we must buy more than we can eat right away.

Three of my boys—Manolito, Alfredito, and Eufrasio—have bronchial asthma. It's a hereditary illness, and now Angelita has it too. The doctors prescribe suppositories for that illness and they always tell me, "Keep them in a cool place." A suppository has to be kept cold, otherwise it melts and then it's impossible to insert.

Well, I ask you, we don't have a frigidaire, and you can't buy ice unless you get up at 2:00 A.M., so where can I keep them? I can't even keep them in a neighbor's house because none of them has a refrigerator. If I could keep a supply at home I could treat the asthma myself, but as it is we have to take the kids to the hospital whenever they get an attack.

I'd like a TV set, a record player, and an electric heater, too, but the only electric appliances we have are the radio and the iron. The radio is in terrible shape. It looks like a monster because I fixed it myself and it works by whim. As for the iron, about six years ago I found it in a trash can. I mended it with wire pins and got a new cord for it and it still

31. Introduced in 1966–67, *Poder Local* (Local Power) was the national agency for coordinating local government functions. It was designed to decentralize administrative decision-making so that localized problems could be solved at the local level. Its administrative base was the sectional level in urban areas and the municipality in rural areas. The base-level offices were run by committees of delegates from local units of government ministries, the Party, and the CDRs. Two CDR delegates were elected (apparently in public assemblies at the zone level) from each zone in the sectional to serve as intermediaries between municipal administration and the people. *Poder Local* had jurisdiction over seven administrative "fronts": commercial services, communal services, construction, economy, supplies, transportation, and organization. There was considerable overlap between the areas of responsibility and the "fronts" assigned to the CDRs, causing some rivalry between the agencies. (This description is based on Oscar Lewis's 1969 interviews with a *Poder Local* official and on Booth, "Neighbourhood Committees and Popular Courts," pp. 56–57.) In 1974 the Cuban government was in the process of implementing a new administrative system, *Poder Popular* (People's Power), which will supersede the authority of *Poder Local*. Castro said the primary objective of the system is to control at the grass-roots level all production and service units that serve the community. (*Granma Weekly Review*, Aug. 4, 1974, p. 4.)

works. When something gets out of order it takes a long time to have it fixed through the *consolidado*,[32] so I do whatever repairs I can myself.

One thing I would not buy now, even if I could afford to, is an automobile. It's too difficult to get spare parts and to buy gasoline, but more than anything else, even with all the cars now in use here, there isn't one in good condition. They spend more time at a mechanic's shop than rolling down the streets.

For every 100 *pesos* I had before the Revolution, I have 300 today. The purchasing power of the nation has increased by 100 percent. Most families in the *reparto* have at least one wage coming in regularly, but there is less abundance because of the blockade.

Of course wages do vary, depending on the kind of work one does and on one's place in the scale.[33] A single man may earn 200 *pesos* and have no relatives to support, while a married man with five children may earn only 85 *pesos*. How do those men manage? I myself earn 200 *pesos* but I have seven children and I honestly don't know how to manage.

There are times when I've spent 15 or 20 *pesos* at the grocery store and come out with nothing to eat—only detergent, bath soap, laundry soap, toothpaste, and twenty other trifles. There are many like me, who walk out of the grocery store loaded with stuff, yet that night they have no dinner. To make ends meet, once in a while I may have to sell a can of milk. If I sell five cans I get over 7 *pesos,* and with that I can buy my quota of rice and lard. Of course my children get less milk, but by selling a single product I manage to buy two. I object to a man having to sell his children's nourishment to fatten someone else's belly.

Actually, it's Esperanza who manages the money in our house. Every month I give her more than 100 *pesos*. I tell her, "Save a few *kilos* in case of any emergency so we'll have money to go to the doctor," and so on.

She does all right, I must say. Naturally she can't buy everything we need since I don't earn enough, but she'll buy a lot of stuff all at once and for the next fifteen days she doesn't buy anything at all. That way she saves enough for us to fall back on. It's easy to save money in Cuba today. There's really nothing to spend it on.

Today people are hurt and disillusioned with Fidel and communism. They've struggled and made sacrifices to attain the revolutionary ideals, but where is it getting them? There's still lots of poverty and lots of work too. Each day we have to work harder; we're yoked and driven, yoked

32. A general term of reference for any consolidated enterprise. Here it is an abbreviated way of referring to the state-operated repair-service centers.

33. In 1969–70 Cuba had several wage scales. Workers were classified by their occupational sector (i.e., agricultural, nonagricultural, administrative, or technical and executive) and by the skill level required by their jobs. Wages ranged from a low of about 65 *pesos* a month (grade 1, scale 1) to approximately 844 *pesos* a month (grade 8, scale 4). (Hernández and Mesa-Lago, "Labor Organization and Wages," pp. 227–29.)

and driven, all the time. For example, on Sunday, night combat training begins. A little combat training never killed anybody, but the great majority don't like the idea of giving up their only day of rest.

The government has closed down the bars and that really kills the young people.[34] They need a chance to relax sometimes. We work until noon on Saturday, so why not open up a few bars where people can go in the afternoon to hear records and take a few drinks? Many of the cinemas were closed down when they took the equipment to show films in the schools. Those theaters have never opened again so now there are fewer film shows. I don't understand why they can't buy more movie equipment to make more amusements available. After all, we trade with socialist countries, and one of them, East Germany, is one of the greatest manufacturers of electronic equipment in the world. They produce movie projectors, radios, and all that kind of thing. So why can't we buy it from them?

With all these deprivations, naturally people are becoming disheartened. They're tired of working so hard and never having a moment's rest. Our leaders should understand . . . machines are made of steel and if you don't look after them they explode. Men are but flesh and blood. If they don't get plenty of good food and rest, they waste away.

Today in the *reparto* you'll hear lots of sayings and songs complaining about the new system. One of the sayings goes, "Now you've got them in your home, you want to move out, eh?," meaning that before the communists came to power everybody was in their favor, and now that we have them everybody wants to get away. Another, "If they put twenty ships in the harbor, *el comanducho* would be left all by himself." *El comanducho* is Comandante Fidel.

There were rhymes like *"Con chícharo y pan, los diez millones se van"* and *"Si nos dan codito, trabajamos poquito. Si nos dan filete, trabajamos hasta las siete."*[35]

And it's true, you know. Anywhere in the world you need good food if you're going to work hard.

34. Nightclubs and bars were closed late in 1967, during the official period of mourning for Che Guevara. In April, 1968, 3,900 privately owned bars were nationalized as part of the revolutionary offensive announced the previous month. Since the Christmas holidays of 1968, some nightclubs have been open several nights a week, but the bars, which the government regards as hangouts for "loafers," have remained closed. (Booth, "Neighbourhood Committees and Popular Courts," p. 94. Also see *Time,* Apr. 19, 1968, p. 36.)

35. "The ten million have fled, along with peas and bread" and "If you give us little, we work little. If you give us steak, we work late." *Codito* may also be translated as "elbow macaroni."

Chapter Seven

New Homes, Old Ways

BUENA VENTURA WAS SET UP after the Revolution when they did away with Las Yaguas. There are about 200 of us from Las Yaguas living here in new houses given to us by the government. It's true the house I live in isn't mine exactly—the papers aren't in my name—but it's as good as mine. I live in it, don't I? And we share everything in it, don't we?

After the Revolution whole new towns were built for people like us, people who'd never even dreamed of living under a roof of their own or having a patch of land to plant. In Las Yaguas we lived in houses that had dirt floors, no bathrooms or toilets, where the children slept in the same room as their parents, and men and women were doing it practically on top of their children. That's a dirty and disgusting thing and sets a bad example for the children. It was because of those crowded sleeping arrangements that you'd see ten- or twelve-year-old girls who already had lovers. They did as they saw their parents do. With new housing conditions their lives have changed completely. They have things they never had before—like privacy.

Yet even after that slum had been destroyed there was still no peace in the new *barrio.* Today we still have some families who have a history of trouble with the police and who give us no peace. There's Sulema's family, Juan Tomás's, Lina's, and Jacinta's, to name a few.

Sulema's daughters are all loose women. They can't take life seriously. They like a libertine way of life—drugs, drink, hotel rooms. Most of the addicts come into the neighborhood by way of that family. They have a whole pile of friends who are thieves and marijuana smokers. Those girls bear children to this man and that, and before they know it they've had forty babies who are nothing but a burden on the government. What kind of education do they give their kids? No sooner are they up and their cunts washed than they're off, sitting in the park until 2:00 or 3:00 in the morning. How can a woman like that run a house? What kind of example can she give her children?

Juan Tomás is another one. His house is a sink of iniquity. Gamblers, thieves, and *santeros* gather there. Juan Tomás is himself a *santero*. The minute you go in you see a St. Barbara painted on one wall and a different saint on another wall. There are more saints than you'd find in the Vatican! I don't understand. Those people have 100, 200 *pesos*, they have more than the rest of us can lay hands on. Where do they get it? None of them works.

Sita's house is as bad as Juan Tomás's. It's a gambling den. She sells marijuana, liquor, this and that, all of it illegal. Her children bring vegetables from the country and she sells them out in the street. She's suspicious of everyone, naturally, since she's afraid of being investigated. Celina is Sita's daughter. Her house is a hangout for thieves and junkies.

Jacinta is another one whose house is a den of thieves and gamblers. She claims she can't work because she has seven fibrous tumors in her womb. I think that must be a lie. A woman with seven tumors would either be a bedridden invalid or be dead by now. Why, she'd have such a hemorrhage every time she menstruated that they'd have to stick a stopper inside!

It's only to those people that the police go today. How come they don't go to *my* house? Or to the house of any other law-abiding neighbor? Because as long as you obey the law, the police will leave you alone. They go to Juan Tomás's and Sita's and to the house across the way because all you find in those places is rottenness. I'd kick all those people out if I could. Then the place would be as good as a bag of gold. That's been my opinion for a long time. Even the comrades at the regional office of the CDR think so.

The CDRs are supposed to keep the peace in the barrios, but let me tell you, they have a long way to go. There are some places where you would have to set up a machine gun on every corner to do any good— then the law of the strongest would rule, just like the Wild West. Buena Ventura isn't really so bad—if there are problems it's because of some rottenness at the core, I mean the presidents of the block Committee, people like Minerva Ruz.

In Minerva's block there are a number of problems which she does nothing to resolve, because if she did, she'd have to take steps against her friends and relatives, people under her jurisdiction who do nothing but play bingo, dominoes, and baccarat day and night. Minerva will tell you she struggles for law and justice. Why so she does, but for her relatives.

Now let's tell the hard facts about Minerva. What she does isn't any struggle for justice. It's a struggle to defend the nephews who give her 3 or 4 *pesos* now and then and the friends she can count on for a free meal and a couple of *pesetas* when she's broke. Her nephews are a bunch of hooligans, marijuana smokers and thieves, every one of them. There's her sister Salomé's son, Pedro the Bad. He's a thief and has been jailed several times as a dope pusher. He's in jail right now. There was one family who were intimate friends of Minerva. They were called "The Charities" and Minerva put up a great fight on their behalf, defending the no-good sons. I didn't know them all, just the ones who were notorious for their delinquency. Those are the kinds of people Minerva fights for. Her protégés are all old cronies, and fit company for her, too.

Minerva is a spiritist, a religious fanatic. If she has a headache, she's sure someone must have thrown a powder in her way. If her feet swell, it must be due to sorcery. She has a lot of necklaces—one with beads of many colors, others for St. Barbara, the *Virgen de la Caridad*, the *Virgen de Regla,* and a white one which she says is for Obatalá.[36] Then there's the necklace of flags, for wartime. That one is for the male *santeros.* Every twenty days she gives away 20 *pesos* in coins for the dead, yet she doesn't have the money to eat three meals a day. What's that if not fanaticism?

Minerva's *mamá*, Idalia, was once a slave and everyone believed she had spiritual powers, so they believe Minerva has spiritual powers too, and they're scared of her. It's true she holds seances, casts "spells," and throws powders around while she calls people all sorts of obscene names. But if she has occult powers why doesn't she use them to reform the twenty or so bums and delinquents in her own family so they'll go straight and stop making their poor mothers suffer so?

Minerva lives alone and doesn't have enough to eat. She has to keep strictly within what she's allowed in her ration book, so why doesn't she use her powers to get herself more food? She criticizes the government for the food shortages. Well, if she has this power and sees Fidel up there, ruling, why can't she use her powers to get him out? Where is her power if she can't do that? That's the way I analyze Minerva's claims, and that's why I doubt them. But lots of people believe that old-fashioned nonsense. I say life is real, not fantasy. At least I've always lived realistically. If I need to go out and work to earn my 4 *pesos,* I'm not going to stay home and let comrades do my job for me just because a spirit told me I shouldn't work that day.

When someone belongs to the Party and is head of a Committee, shouldn't they work to unite the neighborhood and make it prosper? But how can it prosper when Minerva belongs to such a backward religion? That cult is against science, against modern life in all its aspects. How does being a communist fit in with believing such stuff? It's too great a contradiction. Yet Minerva thinks she's such an intellectual and she claims to be so revolutionary, so fervent a communist.

It's true she's been a Party member for years and was active in the early days of the Revolution. She's the widow of Montano, who used to lend me books about socialism. Montano came from a big family. Many

36. See Benedí, n. 49. Each *santo* is associated with certain colors and/or emblems. Religious practitioners often demonstrate their devotion to a *santo* by wearing (in jewelry or clothing) the colors or symbols of their particular saint.

of his women relatives worked at La Corona cigar factory. Minerva worked there too as a tobacco stripper, but that was many years ago. When he and Minerva lived together they acted like strangers to each other because Minerva neglected him. She's the kind of woman who sits in the corner gossiping till 2:00 or 3:00 in the morning. A man whose wife doesn't look after him might as well have no wife at all. Then Minerva was unfaithful and they separated. Six months later Montano died. That was before the Revolution triumphed.

When Fidel came to power, Minerva was one of those who thought they'd get the best of everything, and a good position without working for it. They said to themselves, "Oh, when I go back home I'll be a captain or at least a lieutenant and drive two "ducks' tails,"[37] and I'll have 1 million *pesos* in the bank. . . ." Well, that isn't what happened. The state gives her a pension of 60 *pesos* a month, so she's poor. Now Minerva is a revolutionary from the lips out—all she's willing to fight for today is her own belly.

Before the Revolution, when Las Yaguas was to be eliminated, there was a fight to save it. The land in Las Yaguas didn't belong to anyone since it had been abandoned by the original Spanish owners. That's why the poor began to build their shacks on it. But Luyanó was an industrial zone and the value of the land went up. Then there were people who wanted to build on the land and do away with Las Yaguas. To get the squatters off the land they had the *reparto* declared unsanitary and no doctors were allowed in. That's when Manolo Castro[38] and Chibás[39] began to defend Las Yaguas. Chibás wanted the government to build little bungalows for the people who lived there. He went to the *reparto* many times alone, without guards, or with two or three of his friends. But the people in Las Yaguas were ignorant and didn't know how to appreciate what those men did for them.

Minerva says she was a real firebrand in those days and was active in the defense of the *reparto*. That's Minerva's way, always bragging. But the ones who really worked hard to save the *reparto* were Manolo Castro and Eduardo Chibás, who were members of an FEU committee.

---

37. Slang term for a Cadillac.
38. Manolo Castro fought against President Machado as a student member of the *Legión Revolucionaria*, then became a police lieutenant under Grau in 1933. In 1945, during Grau's second presidency, Castro was named president of the University Student Federation (FEU) and, in 1947, national director of sports. He was implicated in a number of crimes and was himself murdered in 1948. Fidel Castro (no relation) was one of many suspects rounded up and let go for lack of evidence. (See also Benedí, n. 60.)
39. Eduardo Chibás, revolutionary son of a wealthy family and treasurer of the *Directorio Estudiantil* that opposed Machado, supported Grau until 1947, when he broke away from the *Auténtico* Party and formed the more radical *Ortodoxos*. Chibás was widely regarded as a politician sincerely interested in the Cuban people. He died on August 5, 1951, after shooting himself at the close of a radio broadcast.

Be that as it may, Minerva was chosen to lead the CDR of her block in the new *reparto*, Buena Ventura. Now she's boss all right, boss of the underworld. The only people she controls are the low-lifers, no one else.

You can divide the people in Buena Ventura into three classes—first, second, and third. Nearly all the people in Minerva's block are third-class—only five or six of them have no police record. I would classify Minerva herself as second-rate, because if someone shields marijuana users, it must be because she smokes it herself.

Minerva's block has an alley where she and three other families live. Orlando lives next door to Minerva. He's second-rate—cat-piss, a brazen good-for-nothing, a black who lives with a tramp named Neftalí. His first wife died of lung sickness and now Neftalí has it too—incurable. She's dark and believes in witchcraft and always wears beads and other charms.

Once Orlando was looking for a job and Minerva gave him a letter of recommendation to his work center. After that she believed she had something over him. She thought she had a right to make him live out the rest of his life groveling at her feet. Then she found powders, pounded peppercorn and such, scattered in front of her door, and because of that she lost the courage to call Orlando to order. She claims that Neftalí works sorcery on her.

Two doors down from Orlando lives Abelardo. He's been Minerva's crony all his life, ever since he had the little restaurant in Las Yaguas where they worked together. All the delinquent types, the marijuana smokers, flocked there for their meals, that's the kind of customer he had. Moreover, Abelardo is a *maricón*, the kind that gives and takes. Some queers are only on the receiving end and pay to have it done to them, but Abelardo pays to have it done to him and pays to do it to other men. He's second-rate.

Next to Abelardo lives an old man called Miguel. We all call him "Lovely Water" because he's effeminate. He's always complaining that he's been robbed, but the thieves are the boys he takes in there to screw. That bird is in the lowest class.

If you keep going down Minerva's street you'll come to another alley. In the first house lives Crazy Tita and her family. Those people bear the surname Sarmiento, which used to be famous in Luyanó. The whole family is rotten—sexually rotten—relatives lay relatives. Rodolfo screwed Tita and she bore him that little idiot boy, Miguelito. Tita is now married to Cándido, a young mulatto who's as crazy as she. They call him Sherlock Holmes because he always has a pipe in his mouth, so they call her Dr. Watson. I place those people on the lowest part of the scale. Tita's daughter Sita lives next door to them. Her family are second-class. Bums, all of them.

I'd place Lisa, Sita's neighbor, in the second class too. She's fat and looks Spanish. Once I put that woman in a terribly embarrassing situation. At that time she was living with a colored man, Antonio, who worked on the docks. One day she sent for me to fetch her something from the drugstore. When I went in, I saw blood all over the floor and a little bundle lying there. I thought she needed a doctor, see, and I ran out and called the cops to take her to the emergency clinic. Well, it turns out she was having an abortion and my calling the cops put her in a real fix. Poor woman! Well, at least it did no harm, she came out all right. That woman has suffered a great deal on account of her children—one of her boys is a born queer.

There's a bunch of old men living in Minerva's block. There's Nilo, Neno, and Benito, who was the cook for a fritter stand in Las Yaguas. Old Benito has his little pile of *kilos* stashed away. Then there's Nicolás,[40] and next door to him a colored man, Baldomero, who's a *palero*. Fajardo is another. He has his faults but he can be classified in the first rank. He's never been a bum or a delinquent. Recently he's been having trouble expressing himself because his tongue is partially paralyzed as the result of a stroke.

All these old guys used to play dominoes until 10:00 at night, and people started saying how come if the old fellows could see well enough to recognize the numbers on the dominoes they couldn't stand guard. Of course they can't stand guard! Most of them can hardly see at all. They don't go to the doctor but any day they'll be singing "The Peanut Vendor." Well, Minerva had it in for them and she made them give up their domino games. I think she even brought the police.

Nicolás . . . now there's a man who's had his willpower undermined by Minerva. I think she has a hold on him because she knows something of his sorcery activities or else he fears she could expose something about him to the other people in the *reparto*. Whatever it is, Minerva pressures him and he gives in. She can do anything she likes with him. I believe she blackmails him.

There's not a grain of decency in Nicolás and that's the truth. A man's morality is the most honorable part of him and that fellow has none. He and his wife used to steal things and sell them in the neighborhood. Not only that—they're always asking the neighbors for a bit of alcohol or kerosene for the lamps, a cup of sugar, or a can of milk. Then, when they get stuff from the grocery store, they don't pay them back.

Nicolás's wife, Flora, is no good either. She's cat-piss, a shameless bitch. A little dark fellow made an exchange of houses and moved in across the way from Nicolás and took Flora in to live with him. It was up to Nicolás to act like a man whose self-respect was wounded, but he didn't

---

40. Nicolás Salazar, whose story appears in Part III of this volume.

do a thing. In fact, he's such a dirty, low-down character that when the woman decided to return, he took her back.

That wasn't the only other man Flora lived with. She sleeps with other men either for pay or for pleasure, and why? Because a woman with a husband who won't give her money to get a dress on her back has to get money somehow. And if she's none too bright, what way would she take? The easiest way of course. And what's the easiest way? To sleep with a man who's willing to pay 10 *pesos* for it.

Nicolás is a guy who has always worked for his living. He likes to work, but when he falls in love with a woman he forgets about his job and everything else. He'll quit work just to keep a watch over his wife's ass. That's his weakness. He and Flora are both third-rate.

If you look at that block, you'll find the only honest, first-class people are Raquel and her husband, Sabino. They live in the last house in the alley. Then there's Goyito. I don't know his surname. He works in food supply for markets, supermarkets, and so on. He's first-rank.

Minerva is looking for trouble. Any time now, the Committee is going to be taken away from her. She lives in fear of any investigation of the workings of the barrio. It wouldn't be to her advantage; if you have a bad record you have no right to new promotions. That's what she's so scared of, and why she doesn't want any investigation. Yet just recently, she accused another Committee of inaction. She got it into her head that the members had no history of being revolutionary or militant communists like herself. Now, even supposing you're an old Party member, if your own Committee does nothing, you can hardly accuse another Committee of inaction, can you? Because who is dirty? Why your Committee of course!

Not all the block Committee leaders are like Minerva. Take our friend Tomasa, president of the Committee of our block. Anybody in her jurisdiction who commits a crime or gets into trouble is dealt with by Tomasa herself. She has turned in a lot of people on the block and makes a lot of enemies for herself that way. It's thanks to her that the crooked ones don't get away with it. Today there are thirteen or fourteen families there, good citizens, clean, without a past, who are first-rate people.

Minerva and Tomasa do not see eye to eye. Minerva got it into her head that Tomasa and I shouldn't be friends. Tomasa was married to Aurelio Del Río, who belonged to the militia and worked for the police department. Minerva got together with him to make trouble for me. I knew all about it beforehand, because José Manuel, Minerva's brother, warned me that she and Aurelio were plotting against me. Minerva's like that; she doesn't fit in anywhere. That's why she and her doings are always on everybody's tongue.

I was working in Batabanó at the time and I used to pick up plantains and tubers to take home every day to give to Esperanza and various neighbors. Well, Aurelio came one day to accuse me of selling contraband pork. The man was mistaken, even if he did belong to the militia, so I said, "Now don't go making any mistakes. I know all about your past but you know nothing about mine. I have never sold or smoked marijuana as you have, so don't go accusing me. Why haven't you had the balls to stop me and ask me what I'm carrying?"

"Now, now, Fredito, don't get upset," he pleaded. "I only called you because I'd been told those things about you."

"Well, let me tell you that if any *maricón* on the Committee tries to make trouble for me, I'll kill him like a dog. It isn't *my* trouble I care about, it's the harm it would do my children, because I'm both father and mother to them. So don't go thinking I'll put up with that kind of queer's tricks!"

"I've given you enough rope," he says, addressing me very improperly as *tú*. All right, he had a position of authority but he had no call to speak to me in such a familiar way. I came right out and told him, "*Tú* is the way you address a dog. I have a name and surname and you know what they are."

"You're mistaken," says he.

"Oh no," says I, "you're the one who's mistaken, and let me warn you, I'm a hard bone to gnaw."

"Not for me, I always keep a thirty-eight handy," he says.

"Look, I don't fool around. As you well know, I always have a forty-five. All you need are balls enough to press the trigger—and you've got no balls, kid. You're exactly the same as your whoring wife!" I told him off because people were swelled up with their own importance and you had to talk to them like that.

Soon afterward the police car came to take me to the station. There I saw a man who was a psychologist or something of the kind. He asked me a lot of questions, then he said, "But *chico*, why do they bring you here? It says here that you sell pork, but nobody has ever caught you red-handed. It says you sell plantains, but your neighbors say that you give some away and keep the rest for your children."

"That's not all," I answered. "The man who made that accusation has himself eaten my plantains. The only thing I regret is that they didn't bust in his guts!"

The man who interviewed me was a lieutenant, and he called Aurelio Del Río at once. He gave him a tremendous talking-to right there in front of me, accusing him of plotting against decent men instead of trying to get the thieves and marijuana peddlers who swarmed all over the place.

Aurelio and I returned together to the *reparto* and Minerva and Tomasa both saw us. He had a terrific quarrel with Tomasa, packed up his things, and left the neighborhood before daybreak. He was ashamed or embarrassed I suppose. Anyway, he abandoned Tomasa. Minerva told her that I was the one who had broken up her home. It was quite a while before Tomasa understood it was a bunch of lies. She and Minerva were friends and then, from night to morning, Minerva quarreled with her. Now Minerva slanders Tomasita wherever she goes.

Afterward Tomasa came right to my door to beg my pardon. "I'm glad you're finally convinced," I told her. And now the only house in the block where Comrade Tomasa visits and has dinner with the family is my house. Many's the time she's told me, "I don't know how I could ever have been so mistaken about you. I must have been blind."

As for Minerva, as I see it, one who has as much learning as she does should encourage fraternal feelings among people and spread a little of her knowledge, teaching those who have less education. But Minerva does the exact opposite. She's a malicious gossip and a sneak. If somebody has something against you, they should tell you so to your face, not go around dropping hints behind your back as Minerva does. When she sees two families on bad terms with each other, does she try to make peace between them? Hell no! She fans the flames and inevitably sides with the one who's in the wrong.

And she considers herself an intellectual! I don't understand how that woman's mind works. She'll begin to hate people for no reason at all, without their ever having harmed her. Take the case of Socorro Ibáñez. Two or three years ago she and Socorro were inseparable friends, as close as fingernail and flesh. If they had only one plate of food between them, they'd share it. And then, overnight, the friendship broke up— Minerva stole Socorro's husband, Barbudo. The affair with Barbudo lasted about as long as a noisy dance at a school door. One fine day he simply walked out on her—he wrote a bill of sale to both those women.

Now Minerva hates Barbudo's guts. God knows why. I don't understand the woman. She's always looking for a quarrel. Either it's jealousy or something I can't fathom.

Tomasa confides her troubles to Esperanza, and at the moment she feels very hurt because of the way Silenia has treated her. She and Silenia used to be great friends. Whenever one of Silenia's children was sick, Tomasa would prepare a remedy and stroke[41] them to make them well. She really loved those kids. One of Silenia's little ones died and Tomasa wept for him as if he had been her own.

Then Silenia's husband, Baldovino López, who is twenty-nine or thirty years old, began to make trouble for Tomasita. He and some other fellows took to gathering at his house to play dominoes until 2:30 or 3:00 in the morning, night after night, keeping everyone from their sleep. Now I've played dominoes myself, and nobody can put anything over on

41. A gentle stroking or passing of the hands over the painful area, a technique widely used by folk healers.

me. You may stick to dominoes until 2:00 or 3:00 A.M. for one day or maybe two just because you enjoy the game, but there has to be some kind of incentive to keep you interested night after night. Baldovino's place had the atmosphere of a gambling den. He was the only person on the block who played at the game and he did it just to mock the Committee and to challenge Tomasita.

I told her, "How can you put up with those people? As president of the Committee you have the authority to stop it, because the day the patrol car comes around and catches them playing dominoes, you're the one who's going to be in trouble."

Well, she didn't mention the matter to them. Instead she sent Ramón, a friend of her husband's, to speak to them. After that they stopped playing dominoes, but things didn't get better. The bastards still kept on meeting and kicking up a racket until 1:00 A.M. every night.

One night I protested to Baldovino myself. At around 1:30 A.M. I went out in my undershorts and called Baldovino over and told him he'd have to pipe down because, first, I had a sick kid at home and, second, some people had to get up at 4:00 A.M. to go to work and couldn't sleep with all that noise. "Tomasita has already called your attention to this," I said. "She could ask her husband to speak to you, but she's afraid of what he might say and do, because he's kind of rough."

Actually, Tomasita's present husband, Rubén Del Valle, is gentle as a lamb. He's always soothing his wife: "Tomasita, don't get upset . . . Tomasita this . . . Tomasita that. . . ."He's black but he keeps her damn well and loves her better than he loves himself.

Two days went by without any noisy gatherings at Baldovino's place. Then they set up a game of dominoes and played until 2:00 A.M. I don't complain anymore because I know that people nearly always pay for the wrong they do. But Baldovino and Silenia, who has turned very bitchy toward Tomasita, are a bitter pill for Tomasita to have to swallow.

When Tomasita's daughter Cuca killed herself, the proper thing for Silenia to do would have been to pay a visit and offer her condolences, right? Especially since she owes such a debt of gratitude to Tomasita. Silenia should have gone to her house and told her, "How sorry I am for your trouble." But no, she and her husband couldn't or wouldn't go to the wake, but that very night they were laughing their heads off and kept the radio turned on until after 2:00 A.M. Is that the way to show consideration for a friend's feelings?

When that stuck-up Justina moved into the block, she became very friendly with Silenia. And now Justina too makes nothing but trouble for Tomasita. Justina's brother works at the DTI[42] and she uses that as a

---

42. *Departamento Técnico de Investigaciones* (Department of Technical Investigations), the subdivision of the Department of Public Order responsible for criminal investigations.

means of pressuring the Committee. She criticizes other people, but I've learned from bitter experience that her kind always turn out to be vicious and degenerate. Justina pretends to be virtuous but she's a drug addict. For her there's nothing more delicious than a smoke of marijuana. The people who visit her house are a bunch of hoodlums—the one who isn't a thief is a junkie or a queer. Justina's neighbor Arsenio is a *maricón,* and the things that go on in both their houses are a scandal.

I said to Tomasita, "Look, in those two houses there are strange goings-on. You shouldn't permit drunkenness except at authorized fiestas. Much less can you allow marijuana. I want you to know that in Justina's house they're not only smoking marijuana, they're also selling it: I'm going to tell her to be a bit more careful and put an end to that scandal. That way she won't think I'm a poor dope who doesn't realize what she's up to." And I did, too.

Let all those people who visit her keep coming. I know her past. It's shameful. That woman boasted she was an actress and had worked on TV, but I never believed that story. It seems awfully unlikely. She has an attractive face but her figure isn't worth 2 *centavos.* She's a real tramp, just like the woman who lived in that house before her.

That little room has quite a history. The previous occupant of Justina's house was Debra, a little bitch in the life. After her husband abandoned her, she told everybody she had a job, but actually she was well on the way to being an out-and-out prostitute, charging 4 *pesos* a throw. That was just before she exchanged houses with Justina.

Debra's backyard adjoined my garden patch, and I had given her a bit of the land I'd planted on condition that she allow my kids to play there, because they don't have a big yard to play in. At the end of each block there's a plot of land that doesn't belong to any of the houses. Many of those plots are rats' nests because the neighbors dump their garbage there instead of in cans where the garbage truck could pick it up. That's a habit they brought from Las Yaguas. Well, when the *reparto* was newly built there were two social workers in the area, both girls. I spoke to one of them about the plot next to our block and asked for a permit to clean up the place. They gave me one, so I cleaned it up and planted sweet potatoes there. The neighbors began to talk. "What does he think he's doing?" one said. "Nobody can claim that land."

"Let him work," said another. "After he's cleaned it up, I'll take it. It's mine." There were all sorts of comments of that sort.

I didn't care. I paid no attention to the talk. My potatoes grew and I gathered heaps of them. Most of them I gave away because there were more than we could eat; they would have rotted if I'd kept them.

Debra fenced in the piece I gave her, but when she exchanged houses with Justina, do you know what that brazen liar did? She gave Justina to understand that the planted land would be for her use.

One morning after Justina moved in, I was awakened by a strange noise a little after 5:00. I got up and saw a guy inside the fenced plot so I got my little gun, thinking, "If that man is a thief he'll lose his taste for stealing." But no, it was Arturo, Justina's husband, who was just looking over the place.

We got to talking and he told me that Debra said the land was his. I explained to him I had a paper saying that piece of land had been given to me to plant, so it was mine. The man accepted my explanation and there was no problem; in fact we became friends. His wife was another matter altogether.

One day she asked to borrow my spade to work in the yard and I loaned it to her. I didn't care if she used my spade, but I did get annoyed because she dumped all the grass cuttings and garbage from her yard into mine. I always keep my yard clean without any grass growing in it. I have a line of plantain trees right next to the fence and she killed the sprouts.

When I went out and saw what she'd done I was furious. I yelled, "Damn it, I wish I knew what whoring bitch threw that stuff in here so I could shit on her whoring mother's heart!" I spoke like that, without naming names, so that whoever had done it would come out and protest.

Justina came out and said, "It wasn't me who did it."

"Is that so?" I broke in. "Well, let me tell you, you're the lying daughter of a great whore and you'd better get busy carting away all the trash you dumped in my yard; if it isn't cleaned up I'm going to bring the patrol car here. Decide what you want to do about it." I went away and around 5:30 P.M. returned to get ready for work and found the yard clean.

For a while Esperanza was friendly with her, until Justina took advantage. Justina let days and days go by without going to get her daughter's milk ration. When she ran out of milk she'd go to Esperanza to borrow a can, and like a fool my wife would let her have it. I kept count, and when she'd "borrowed" six cans of milk I said to Esperanza, "Look, chica, have you been eating shit or what? When she gets around to collecting her ration she's not going to be able to spare what she owes you. And then do you know what she'll do? She'll find some pretext to quarrel and break off the friendship, then you'll never get your cans of milk back."

It happened just as if I'd been looking at it. Not long after, Justina found a pretext to quarrel and break off the friendship. As I say, I won't allow anyone to take liberties with me. Like everybody else, I live planning and budgeting my purchases according to what I'm allowed in my ration book. So I spoke up to Arturo: "Excuse my frankness," said I, "but it seems to me you have a bit of a nerve and so has your wife. You should understand that everybody has to plan strictly how to use their rations."

"No, no, no, don't worry. I'll return the milk we owe you." He went right away and bought the six cans of milk and gave them to us.

Arturo doesn't live with Justina, he just visits her and spends the night now and then. Once Justina asked me whether I knew a spiritist or a *palero*, somebody trustworthy, because she wanted to have a "job" worked on Arturo. Well, I saw her intention as clearly as if it had been my own. The "job" she wanted was to make her husband stay with her every day. Fortunately I couldn't help her. What spiritists do I know? She knows more about those things than I do.

That woman's a real tramp. Once she tried to set her cap for me. It was the first day of the year and she was standing in the doorway drinking a glass of sweet wine with my brother-in-law Macho. "Come on over and have a glass of sweet wine with us," she calls to me.

"All right," I said. They gave me a glass of wine, which I drank, and then we went into the house. She shut the front door so nobody else could come in.

Now Macho was in love with Justina and he'd already given her money, which she had accepted. Justina knew that a man isn't going to give his money away for nothing, so from a moral point of view she was obliged to go to bed with him. But she wanted to shake him off because she was expecting Arturo to spend the night there. So Macho was a problem for her, get it? That's why she invited me over. I was the only means she had to prevent Macho from getting on top of her that night.

Now I've never been interested in Justina as a woman. I never make passes at any woman who visits my home. I'm the keeper of the whole family's morality, because if the main beam is twisted, what can you expect of the kids, for whom I must set an example? One has to be very careful and think before one acts. But at about 1:00 o'clock Justina accuses me of wanting to screw her. She starts making a fuss, pretending to be offended and saying, "Oh you, you want to screw me."

I hadn't started anything. She was simply trying to wriggle out of her bargain with Macho.

"Look, *chica*," says I, "why should a man want to screw a tramp like you? Besides, Macho here is the one who's entitled to sleep with you tonight because you accepted his money." I came right out and said it to her face. That's how the argument began. She claimed I tried to force her, but if she resented that, wouldn't she, as my wife's friend, have gone straight to Esperanza with the story? But no, the whole thing was a drama she cooked up herself. Finally Tomasita intervened, but the matter went no further. I would have liked to see it brought up before the highest possible authorities, right to the police station.

Next day her husband, Arturo, went to see her. He didn't ask to see me but I thought, "Better wait, because if she says I tried to screw her, he'll have to call me to account, if he's a man." But no, nothing of the kind! The matter was dropped. Later I analyzed the situation—psychology is the most perfect thing that exists in the world—and now I know her story. I came to the conclusion that Justina was jealous of my wife. You see, Justina thinks she's a very goddess of beauty, and it upsets her that she doesn't have a man to give her warmth or to support her. Instead she has to beg from her family. What's more, Justina is a racist. That's strange for a woman who's slept with twenty different blacks.

I read her thoughts this way: she sees Esperanza living well and she thinks, "This black woman has a white man by her side, he works for her and she has everything she needs, while I, who am whiter and prettier, do not." So she tries to break up Esperanza's home.

How cynical can a woman get? So you see, it isn't on account of some little argument or other that I criticize that woman. No, no, it's her falseness I object to. I disapprove of her meanness and perversity. But I have no interest in her as a woman—there's nothing to that story. After that incident I never again had anything to do with Justina. I don't even look at her.

The most peaceful block in the *reparto* is the República block. There are six families there who are first-rate. First, there's Manolo and his neighbor Ramiro, who keeps himself busy making little tin pitchers out of condensed-milk cans. Next to him is La Mulata. She used to pick up vegetables that fell from the trucks at the marketplace and sell them in the *reparto*. Her neighbor, Dámaso, also used to work in the marketplace as a helper. He's never had a steady job. The longest he ever worked in one place was a bit over five months, and then he just walked out. He lives by getting a *peseta* here, a *real* somewhere else, whatever he can pick up. Next to him is Edelberto's family. Edelberto lives with a little mulatto woman who has borne him several children and who has also borne several others who are not his. They have cultivated the little plot of land at the corner. Then there's Salomé and her mother. None of those families have police records. Edelberto's other neighbors are Asela and Ovidia. Asela has been a dope pusher and a tramp so she belongs in the second rank.

In the block at the back of the *reparto* live Alejandra Díaz, her sister's family, two *guajiros*, and Rufina and her husband. All those people are first-class except Rufina and her children. They have a very dirty past. Rufina is an adulteress, a whore, and a lesbian. She was unfaithful to her first husband, and her buttocks are all scarred because he cut them up. But she's still attractive. She seems to be in love with her present husband but she's as much a lesbian as ever. She likes to feed on both sides of the fence.

You'll find others like her in the *reparto*. Take my friend Alejandra Díaz. I knew Alejandra before I was married to Esperanza. She's a mulatto and has led a pretty loose life. She's married to a guy named Caoba. He has a job in market supply and earns around 200 *pesos* a month. We Cubans have a saying, "Some are born to wear horns as sure as lightning flashes from the skies." Caoba has always been the head of the house, but it seems he has some sort of trouble with his member and Alejandra has never been faithful to him. She's an ardent woman and has several other men who visit her. She really squanders money buying liquor for them. She goes for young men. Whenever she falls for one, she gives him anything to go to bed with her—she'll even pay him.

Caoba makes a show of leaving Alejandra and has disappeared for a few days, but he's one of those people who never gets rid of their habits, not even when something earthshaking happens.

Alejandra once thought Esperanza was the one who had given her away to Caoba and she started avoiding both of us. She began to talk her head off about Esperanza, saying twenty trashy things about her, such as, "That Esperanza has gotten stuck-up since she's living with Fredo and is well off, but she used to be a nobody. She won't talk to people now, that's how proud and vain she is." Women's gossip, foolish trifles.

Then Alejandra lost her purse with 50 *pesos* in it. Esperanza found it, and like a fool she returned it to Alejandra. When I heard about it I said to Esperanza, "You're a dope. You should have waited till I got here. I would have spent that money on beer and burned the wallet. I wouldn't have returned it!" And I wouldn't. Alejandra would never have gotten it back.

Anyway, Alejandra also likes women now and again. There are a whole bunch of *tortilleras*[43] in the *reparto* and they're the ones you would least suspect. But I can name all of them for you. There's Jacinta, who is a hardened lesbian, Rufina, and my friend Alejandra, who falls to that level just once in a while, and then there's that fat one who lives on the corner, and Rodríguez's wife, whom they call Gata. That one is both lesbian and whore. Officially Rodríguez is her husband, but that's just to keep up appearances. Gata has a white man, and he's the one who scratches where she itches and to whom she gives her all. She and the others make dates with each other and gather in different houses to commit immoral acts. I mean, sex between a man and a woman is natural but not among several women. I can't imagine what pleasure they get from it.

In that same block at the back of the *reparto* lives La Fuente, Mirabal, and a fellow they call "the Bear," who dabbles in sorcery. He keeps pretty quiet about it but I know he's one of them. They're all second-rate people. Arsenio Martínez, another queer, also is second-rate. Some other queers who come here live outside the *reparto*. Eventually the lung

43. Slang term for lesbians.

sickness will kill all those people. The ones who don't die of phthisis die insane from taking drugs.

Men and women of the life like to take all sorts of narcotics; they smoke marijuana and even smear salves over their organs to make their sensations keener. A man I knew once bought a salve with cocaine in it. Before having intercourse with his wife he'd rub some of that stuff on his penis, then he'd kiss her and tell her a lot of sweet talk to give the salve time to take effect. It was meant to prevent the man from coming and to make the woman feel as if she had a great thick column inside. Fellows who used that were supermen in bed. Some men adapted their wives to it, and in the lower parts of town there were women who claimed that their husbands gave it to them as often as five times a day! Can you imagine an organism functioning like that five times? It's possible, yes, but difficult, very difficult.

Other fellows would use camphor salve, or toothpaste because it has menthol. They thought those things would make the women sexier. I've never tried any salves. Not me! They'd recommend it to me and I'd say, "Hell no, not even if I was crazy!" Maybe those things were beneficial, but if you used them for a long time, one fine day *bang!* the horse would fall and God himself couldn't get it up again.

One thing that has always been famous in Cuba are the eggs of the carey, which is a very large turtle. The male is so potent he stays on top of the female during the forty-one days it takes her to lay all her eggs in the sand. Well, people here gather the carey eggs and sell them for a fortune. You dry them and put the powder in your coffee or in a glass of milk and drink it. I've heard of men who've been hospitalized on account of that.

Recently a soldier, a sergeant I gather, from his uniform, moved into Alejandra's block. I know nothing about his past. I'd have to analyze that very well indeed before I'd attempt to classify him. He'll probably turn out clean though. The soldiers of the Revolutionary Army are very superior. I have nothing but praise for compulsory military service and the militarization of the schools. In one year a young boy of sixteen who joins the military service has a lot of thoughts driven from his head. He goes to military school and comes out a man, not a weakling or a thief or marijuana smoker.

The Cuban Army today is superior to Batista's army in its capacity for work, in military skills, and in discipline. Before the Revolution soldiers never treated citizens with respect or did an act of kindness for anybody. They considered themselves kings of the world. Wherever they went they were served first. Today a soldier can't shove in ahead of you but must take his place in a waiting line like everybody else. Even the meanest recruit will treat you with respect. The soldiers don't mistreat and exploit people as Batista's army used to. On the contrary, the new army is generous in its dealings with the population. It lends a hand wherever it's needed to help the country get ahead. In times of natural disaster—hurricanes, for example—they rendered great service to the nation. I was glad to have a revolutionary soldier in the *reparto*. He got along with his neighbors, Alejandra, Rufina, and the others.

Also on the soldier's block were the two poorest in the *reparto*, Ovidia Blanco and her sister Ana. Ana lives in the most wretched conditions you can imagine; the inside of her house is falling to pieces. The house is built on a corner lot that I like. Once I offered her my house, freshly painted, plus 300 *pesos,* in exchange for hers. The exchange would have been perfectly legal; exchanging houses is allowed because it doesn't affect the institutions of the Republic in any way. When she refused, I thought, "Maybe it's just as well. Why should I want to go moving elsewhere when I have a plot of land planted and room to raise my chickens right here?"

Ana has a brother, Juanito, who is a hopeless drunk. Once, around Christmas, I suddenly found myself in trouble with the law because of him. It all started because Esperanza persuaded me to lend 20 *pesos* to Ovidia.

"Listen, Alfredo," Esperanza said to me, "Ovidia's rations are ready at the grocery store and she owes me 5 pounds of rice but I'm embarrassed to ask for it."

"What!" I exclaimed. "How can you lend 5 pounds of rice to that woman? Suppose she doesn't have enough money to get her rations from the grocery store and can't pay you back. What are *you* going to eat then, eh?"

"That's what I'm trying to tell you," says Esperanza. "She wondered if you could lend her 20 *pesos* so she could collect her groceries."

Well, we had already bought the children's toys and had them hidden in Tomasita's house where the kids couldn't find them, so I answered, "Well, there's nothing we can buy at the grocery store until a new consignment arrives, so give her the 20 *pesos.* One thing, though, tell her that as soon as her check comes, I want my money back."

So with our 20 *pesos* Ovidia got all her rations out of the grocery store and paid us back the 5 pounds of rice. On December 23 she got her money order. She said to me, "When you have the time, come by my house so I can pay back the 20 *pesos.*" I went, but no sooner had I stepped inside her house than Ovidia locks the door behind me. A few seconds later, *tun, tun, tun!* someone bangs on it. I open it and there are this man and a policeman saying something about a stolen sow.

"Stolen sow?" says I. "What are you talking about, comrade? Nobody here has stolen anything."

"Maybe not, *compadre.* All I know is that the stolen sow is here!"

They told me that Ovidia's brother Juanito had stolen a sow from a pigpen while drunk, and after practically tearing the place apart he'd dropped his I.D. card there. Then the policeman said, "The sow is out in the backyard."

"All right, open the door and look," I said. "But don't stand there talking to *me* about it. I have nothing to do with it." They went into the backyard and there was Juanito with a whole array of bottles of alcohol by him, busily scraping away at the hide of a dead sow. He looked crazy.

"Oh my God," I thought, "everybody's going to get arrested now!"

"Everybody in this house is under arrest," says the policeman, and he herds us all to the station.

It turned out that Juanito had had a quarrel with his brother-in-law El Gordo about whether or not they should kill a sow for Christmas. The sow belong to El Gordo and he was not for roasting it. So, would you believe it, Juanito sneaked into the pigpen and grabbed a sow, only instead of taking his brother-in-law's, he took someone else's. Fortunately Juanito admitted he was guilty, but the lieutenant wanted to screw me up by insisting that I had taken part in it.

I had to stay overnight at the police station, but then they let me go. The day of the trial, I was in the courtroom waiting when the prosecutor called, "Alfredo Barrera!"

"Present!" I answered, and they led me into the courtroom. My God, I was sick to my stomach. They'd charged me with robbery and I didn't know whether I'd be found guilty. If you're jailed for fighting or something, that's not so bad. But robbery! I'd heard about the sentences dealt to people charged with theft and I'd passed by the prison farms, so I knew what I was in for if they found me guilty. My balls climbed right up into my mouth because I'd never been involved in anything like that. I said to myself, "Oh my God—jailed and in such circumstances!"

But they let me go free and Juanito too, though he was under some kind of legal condition—parole I think they call it. So I got off all right, but every time I think about that darn trial I feel sick.

The truth is, there's much, much more justice now than there used to be. Suppose, in the old days, I stole a chicken and the cops got me. The judge would fine me 31 *pesos* and turn me loose in the streets. But if you were arrested you lost your job, so after I was free I would have no choice but to steal again. Then I'd be arrested again and get twenty days, or I'd get a little lawyer to defend my case and I'd be free in the streets once more.

Today there's morality. If a man is found guilty of a minor offense, he's sentenced to work on a prison farm, or he can attend classes at a military school. No matter how you look at it, this is better than before. This way, a man who has gone a bit wrong or has a weak mind can study and reform. He changes completely. While he's in jail, the state gives his family a pension to live on so he doesn't have to worry about them and his mind is free to study. When he gets out, his job is waiting for him at his same work center. If it's been filled, he's sent to work somewhere else. Once free, that man can set a good example to other unbalanced fellows who want to take what doesn't belong to them and whose stealing only harms the rest of the population. I see the whole thing very clearly and I think the People's Courts[44] are good.

There are some people for whom the Revolution provides a mask of decency. A neighbor of mine in Buena Ventura is a habitual petty thief. That guy is apt to steal a pair of undershorts worth only a few *centavos*. I call him a lowdown pilferer. If a man must steal, let him do it on a grand scale, let him rob a bank of 15,000 or 20,000 *pesos*.

Anyway, this guy chooses to live as a public charge and the government lets him. He puts his spoon away in El Príncipe prison oftener than he does at home. He has a wife and children, but he doesn't have to spend a *centavo* on them. His wife, obeying his wishes, sold their house. Homeless, the government supplies her with relief to the tune of 130 *pesos* a month. It has provided scholarships for her children, and those scholarships include not only schooling but the food they eat and everything else. Yet in spite of all those benefits, that man refuses to mend his ways. If he had any feelings, any morality, he'd see how much he owed the Revolution, but no, he uses it only as a mask of decency.

He's out of jail now, and the other day I said to him, "Take off your mask, man. They have disguised you as a decent man, and now you must choose one path, be it straight or crooked. A dog has four paws but that doesn't mean it can walk four different ways at once. The same holds for you. You have to make a decision, one way or the other."

There are a number of people like him here who will never change. Do you know why? Because they don't understand the Revolution.

In Buena Ventura we still have many problems because we don't have all the necessary services nearby. If you want to phone, you must go to the local MINCON,[45] which is a block and a half away, but that's no problem. We don't have a dairy, a cafeteria, or a pizzeria. Not that we eat pizza anymore, because the ones they make now are very bad.

The post office is a long way off—you have to change buses to get there. We get our mail delivered each day, but if you want to buy stamps you have to go all the way to the post office.

44. The *Tribunales Populares* were neighborhood courts, first established in Havana on an experimental basis in 1966 to hear minor civil and criminal cases involving "antisocial behavior" (e.g., petty theft, drunkenness, disorderly conduct, juvenile delinquency, health and sanitation code violations). The cases were heard by a panel of three lay judges who, in theory, are popularly elected at the community level, after nomination by the CDR or the Party. In 1974 the People's Courts were incorporated into Cuba's new judicial system. (*Granma Weekly Review*, Feb. 19, 1974, p. 3.)

45. *Ministerio de Construcción* (Ministry of Construction).

The barbershop is also far, and you have to get there very early to get a turn because there's always a crowd. Haircuts are 80 *centavos* apiece. The four boys and I are the only ones at home who go to the barbershop. My wife doesn't go to a hairdresser—she runs a comb through her hair and that's it.

There are no dry cleaners in the *reparto*. When I send my pants to be cleaned, it takes days to get them back. I don't remember how much they charge because Esperanza is the one who tends to such things. And there are no carpenter shops or watch-repair shops, either. In my opinion it would be very useful if we could have a mobile service squad with a carpenter, an electrician, a mason, a plumber—each with two or three assistants—to tend to repairs. They would provide maintenance for the *repartos*, especially remote ones. Once they were through in one place, they would move on somewhere else. That would be perfect.

The polyclinic near us gives good service. We're always rushing over at all hours of the night when one of the children gets an attack of bronchial asthma. If you go during the day though, you have to get up at dawn to get a turn. And if you take your prescription to the social worker, she'll stamp it so you can buy the medicine at a 50 percent discount.

The drugstore where I buy medicines gives good service too. If they don't have the medicine you ask for, they phone around until they find it. That's what I call good service. The drugstore is a long way from home, but transportation is very good because the bus passes right by the *reparto*. They don't run at night though, and there's no taxi stand, so in emergencies there's no transportation to the hospital.[46]

The people here should look back and compare how they live today with how they suffered in the past. There's no comparison between the old system and the new one, and there have never been so many opportunities. Everything has changed, and these people are frightened by it. They refused to join the collectivity because it's strange, different. It hurts them and makes them sick because it requires that they start a new life and adapt to this new society, and they can't. Their minds are too corrupted and there's no room in their heads for anything except trade and vice. So they're still living in the midst of the same old rottenness. Well, the people from Las Yaguas have always avoided the tree that gives them shade in order to huddle under the barren one.

46. There is free ambulance service.

Chapter Eight

My Family Today

ALL MY FAMILY DID WELL under the Revolution. None of us has any reason to complain. When they tore down Las Yaguas, *mamá* and my sisters Angelita, Manuela, and Berta were each given new homes in the *reparto* Algeria. None of them had owned a house before. *Mamá* now lives there in peace with her husband, who has a steady job. What more could she ask for? If she's not satisfied it's beyond me.

SEÑORA LORDI:

I'm very happy about our present government and that's the truth. For one thing, it took me out of the mud-hole I was living in and gave me this house. The roof of my old shack was made of palm leaves, and no matter how much you worked to make it waterproof, the thatch would crack open in the sun and then leak when it rained. My present house only has two leaks. That's really too bad because it's such a good house. We can't get the materials to fix it, though. We can't even get paint to make it look nice. After the hurricane, my husband went to *Poder Local* to ask for a small bucketful of cement to cover up a crack, but they said they couldn't give us any. I hate to see the house the way it is, knowing what a good one it would be with just a little cement and paint.

Even so, I love the house. We have running water and a toilet and my furniture looks so nice. When it rains, I cover the furniture with plastic to protect it. And when my grandchildren come I don't allow them to touch anything.

I really take care of my things. My daughters didn't take after me that way. Each of them got furniture every bit as nice as mine when they were married, but they just won't bother to keep their things in good shape.

It would cost me 500 *pesos* to replace this furniture, and besides, you can't get new furniture anymore. People say these things were a gift from Fidel, but I tell them, "Look, this is no gift, we have to pay for it."

BARRERA:

When Angelita moved into her house in Algeria, it shone like an ounce of gold. Nobody had lived in it before. Her husband, Felipe, was in charge of the paint at the *reparto* so they were able to choose their favorite colors. At first she hung a few ornaments on the wall and so on—new brooms sweep clean, you know—but it's a mess now. My house is the way it is because I can't help it. I'd get new things if I could but I can't. Besides, I've got seven children who don't take good care of things. Angelita has seven too, but she and her kids are pigs, that's what they are!

When I go there and see the mess, I explode and tell her off. I say that there's no excuse for living the way they do. "Oh, that's all the government's fault," she says.

"It's not the government's fault," I answer. "It's yours. If you'd taken care of the things they gave you, you'd be living decently. This house is a mess because you're a slob. If only your husband were a real man, with character and principles, he wouldn't have allowed you to sink so low."

Actually it isn't Felipe's fault—he even has some paint put away to paint the house again—it's Angelita who's to blame. Her children pissed in the bed and started breaking this and soiling that. Angelita, too, tore up this, that, and the other during the quarrels with her husband. Every time she gets angry she breaks something. That's how she's destroyed everything in the house.

Of all my brothers and sisters, I've always got along best with Angelita, but she's bad-tempered and harsh with her husband. She's more like a man than a woman. Felipe is Angelita's second husband. He's a mulatto and is the father of five of her children. She has no reason to complain because he has always lived for his wife and for his home.

Angelita believes in witchcraft, and some spiritist put the idea in her head that Felipe's first wife was casting spells on her, trying to break up their marriage. That's why she quarrels with Felipe. She won't do anything for him. She's used to him coming home from work and cooking dinner for the kids. Many times Felipe even had to go eat at *mamá's* house because Angelita wouldn't cook for him. She won't even save food for him when she does cook.

That kind of thing is hard on Felipe, so naturally they have problems. Whenever they quarrel, as if it weren't enough to smash up the house, Angelita takes it out on the children too. When she scolds them she doesn't explain things gently, she cusses them out. The language she uses! "Hey, you son-of-a-great-whore, what in balls is the matter with you, you damn bastard!" That's the way she talks to those kids. One day Angelita got so mad at Felipe she tore up the doctor's letter to add the new baby to their ration book. That's not right. If a married couple quarrels, they shouldn't take it out on the children.

My sister Manuela's a much better mother than Angelita. Her trouble is that she's never found a man who could make a woman of her—who'd say, "Look, you must do this for such-and-such reasons." She's had only dirty, sloppy men who haven't had a strong fist to control her. That's the reason why she has failed all along the line.

Manuela was married to Roberto, a boy who wasn't from Las Yaguas, though they set up housekeeping there and did fairly well. They were poor but never lacked food or clothes. He was a crazy fellow, rattle-brained and loose-tongued. He drank a lot and never had a steady job. Manuela's wasteful ways annoyed her husband but he was to blame, because he was weak and foolish and had set her the bad example. In the old days you could buy a new shirt for 79 *centavos,* so when one got dirty it was easy to throw it away and buy a new one. No single fellow living away from home ever bothered to have his shirts washed because the laundry charged 20-odd *kilos* for washing, starching, and ironing a shirt. What was the point when for 50 *kilos* more you could buy a new one? Well, it seems Manuela took up that habit and they quarreled about it. She was the kind who, when she bought a new dress, would lose interest in the ones she already had, so she'd wear the new one every day for a month until it was only fit to be thrown away.

After the triumph of the Revolution, when everybody made a great rush to get a new house outside Las Yaguas, there was no established law enforcement, so there were many large-scale burglaries. The empty houses and apartments were sealed and people began breaking the seals and moving in.[47] I broke one myself to get an apartment but I gave up the idea. I thought, "Suppose the owner shows up? Before I know it I'll be in trouble, and who knows what can happen with the law these days?" About six months later Fidel made a speech and said there was a law to punish those who broke house seals. That held people back, but even so a few managed to take over a place illegally.

On Arroyo Street there was an empty apartment that wasn't sealed. I said to my brother-in-law Roberto, "Say, would you like to live in that apartment?"

"Yes," he said at once. "Do you have it?"

"Yes, I do. But I'll give it to you on condition that you never set foot in Las Yaguas again."

Well, we went there and broke down the door. The following night he, my sister Manuelita, and her daughter Bárbara moved in. The house had good furniture and a gas stove, a crib, and everything they needed. Having all those comforts influenced Manuelita's lazy spirit; she changed in many ways. You could see the emotion reflected in her face.

47. The Urban Reform Office sealed the entrances of vacated houses and apartments to indicate they were being held in reserve for future allocation.

When she had things of her own she kept them clean and wanted the place looking nice. Roberto changed too. He stopped drinking and lived decently and in peace. He got a good job in Transportation and would go to the country and bring back cheese and twenty other things for his wife and children.

They lived quietly in that apartment for two or three years. Then came the relocation of the people of Las Yaguas to new housing in different *repartos*—Algeria, Buena Ventura, Bolívar, and so on. Manuela had left her old room in Las Yaguas locked up, so in due course, María, who was the one in charge of the housing census, called my sister for an interview and offered her a new place. Just think, the Committees had already been formed and they recognized Manuela's right and all!

I was living in Matanzas at the time. I made a special trip to Arroyo Street to talk to my sister about the house.

"Look, Manuela," I said, "Roberto is content; he's working and taking care of you, so don't make the mistake of leaving this place even if they offer you a new house. If you move out of here, he'll find himself in the same surroundings as in the past and he'll go bad again. Tell him to get the Committee to arrange the papers so you can stay in this apartment and start paying rent on it."

Manuela did exactly what I'd advised against. After they moved to Algeria, Roberto was drunk every day, fighting and using bad words, as I predicted. The man fell into all the old bad habits.

As I understand it, Roberto had a quarrel with Bichi, a *compadre* of his, and also had problems with a boy by the name of Fermín. So Bichi and Fermín got together and the two of them shot Roberto dead. On the day of the funeral, Manuelita came to me and said, "Brother...."

"Stop!" I said. "Don't talk to me about this because I told you what would happen. I opened your eyes but you wanted to go back. If you had only stayed in your apartment. How lovely it was! Everything neat, clean, decent. But no, you had to leave all that and come to this rottenness. Now you have no husband, you have to work and support your children. Now you can go shit on the hour you were born."

"No, it was because Roberto wanted it."

"So what if he did? You were his wife; it was up to you to change his mind and tell him, 'All right, you can go but I'll stay here. If that means we separate, then we separate.' He would never have separated from you. You didn't know how to be a real woman. You should have stood your ground but you didn't." I told her all those things the day he was buried.

Then she said to me, "Well, what now?"

"Now you're on your own. As your brother, I may give you 20 *pesos* now and then when I can afford to, but don't expect me to do it every month, because I have my obligations too. I can't take from my family to give you money."

I don't know how she arranged it, but she started getting financial help from Social Welfare. Bah! So now we get back to the same old shit. That very Bichi who had been Roberto's sacramental *compadre,* who'd taken one of Roberto's children to church and poured holy water on his head, who had later had a hand in his killing, then goes and courts the wife and sleeps with her. That man was a provocateur, an instigator of fights. He's a *ñáñigo, palero,* and a whole series of things, but he only earns 85 *pesos* a month and there's no getting him out of that rut. Well, it so happens that man is today my sister Manuela's husband. She went to live with him and bore him a child. Now wouldn't you think God or some saint would punish something like that? I ask you! That's why I have no use for religion.

Manuela has children by Roberto and by Bichi, and a thirteen-year-old daughter, Bárbara, by another man. My sister thinks Bárbara is her slave. There's a tough problem concerning the girl and Bichi and also my sister Angelita. It's an interesting story and at the same time dirty and repugnant.

Manuelita and Bichi are members of *El Lazo Africano,* an African religious sect. Bichi is president of that society, the *padrino,* they call him. The rest are godsons. They all have those iron pots full of images and stones. Bichi and Manuela go to spiritual masses and also hold them in their houses. One day Bichi said to Manuelita, "I want Bárbara to go with me to a mass."

Bárbara is a pretty, white-skinned child, and Bichi is one of those dirty blacks. I knew his intentions toward the little one. The result was he took her to a hotel and she realized that it was no spiritual mass the man was taking her to. She got away and went straight to the police station, where she accused him of wanting to violate her and having tricked her. He didn't get a chance to do anything to the kid. Lucky for him, because then it would have been a whole different thing.

Well, in spite of all that, Manuela, the girl's own mother, now believes that that man is a saint. At first she also made charges against Bichi and he was forced to move out of her house, but then Manuela was left all alone with Bárbara and the little children. After Bichi was brought to trial before the People's Court and the process of law had been going on for a month, Manuela changed her story. She says that Bárbara is lying, that Angelita put the idea into Bárbara's head to make her accuse Bichi, that they invented the whole thing because Angelita doesn't want Manuela to live with Bichi.

Think of it! Can you imagine anything dirtier? What a rotten mind! How can she defend him now after she'd already accused him herself? She talks backwards and forwards. The judge believes the first story. So what does Manuela think she's doing anyway? I don't know where it's going to end up.

Manuela, the child's mother, is now trying to get Bárbara to take off with the first man who pays any attention to her. If Bárbara does, it won't be because she loves the man but because her mother forced her into it. That's how far-reaching the consequences of this might be. To push the kid into something that would be all wrong for her! There's a lot of counterpoint here.

Bichi was still president of the society, and a short time after all this blew up, a man called Bernabé, who is Bichi's *padrino de palo*,[48] showed up at my house and asked me not to do anything about Bichi. He told me, "The point is that all the godsons who belong to the society are going to meet and expel Bichi and take away the powers we have given him."

I told him I could hardly be less interested in the problem. What interested me was my own children, not anybody else's. I said I appreciated his advice but there was no need for him to have come at all.

My sister Berta is married to a fellow named Alberto. They too live in a new house in Algeria. They married young and have been through good times and bad. They've had their quarrels and separated but they're back together now and living at peace with each other.

Berta is good-tempered, although she cusses out Alberto sometimes and talks dirty. He's very different, a nice, cleancut fellow. She's clean around the house and takes good care of their three children. Whenever one of them gets sick, she rushes him to the doctor without waiting for anybody else, which is the correct thing for a mother to do.

Alberto has his job and has settled down. He's integrated in the Revolution and is a chauffeur for the Party. They're poor and often have to go to great trouble to get the things they need, but he supports Berta as well as a poor man can and gives her whatever he has.

Anita and Julio are living in Bella Vista. I don't see them much because I've never gotten along with my brother-in-law. He's selfish and stuck-up. Once before the Revolution, when I was out of work in October, Julio got me a job wielding a pick and shovel. I'd been working under contract as a plasterer but the month of October was always bad. I was hoping for better times in December, when everybody fixed up their houses for the Christmas season. One could work night and day then and lay aside a bit of money for Christmas and the Day of the Three Kings. So to fill my time until December, I worked with Julio.

When you're poor you can't be too proud to share things with others. As the saying has it, "Each hand washes the other and both wash the face." During those three weeks I always shared my lunch with Julio. One day the lunch *mamá* had cooked for me was spoiled and I was left with nothing to eat. Julio had a lunch pail with black beans, rice, and chicken. He shared his beans with the rest of the fellows and didn't give me even a spoonful.

48. Godfather at Bichi's initiation into the *Palo Monte* sect.

Julio was the kind of man who acted as a stooge for the bosses and who browbeat the workers to make them produce. At the end of the third week he told me they couldn't keep me on there. On Friday, when I got paid, I gave him 5 *pesos* as a gift with the words, "Take it to buy yourself some beer." That was like stabbing him, because he had kicked me out of the job to make room for a couple of his friends. After that I had nothing more to do with him.

Today Julio is integrated in the Revolution and works for the Ministry of Education. He and Anita have four children. In spite of their squabbles they're still together. The last time I saw Julio was on Mothers' Day, at my mother's house.

ANITA VALVERDE:

Julio keeps after me to get my papers in order so we can get married, but somehow I haven't gotten around to it. He nags and nags about it. "Suppose anything happens to us before we get married? The kids will have no rights and no protection," he says.

"All right, all right! I'll do it. But I don't understand why you're so bent on getting married after we've been living together all these years."

"It's for the children's sake," he tells me.

The truth is, I don't like the idea of getting married. Not that I have any complaints about Julito—he's sober, a good family man, and better than bread. He's very loving to me and his children and to Alfredo, my eldest, who isn't even his own child.

When we came to Bella Vista, I and my daughters Lela and Sonia enrolled in the Women's Federation and the Committee. We stand guard sometimes, one or another of us. I went to work at the *Cordón de la Habana* for five months. Lela looked after the kids, but Julio didn't like it. He said I should stay home and look after them, so I quit. Anyway, Lela got a job at the cookie factory and couldn't help me out anymore.

Julio, too, stands guard at his work center and goes out to the country three times a week to do volunteer work. He works eight hours at it, unless it rains; then he comes home early. He was working at Nueva Paz during the whole of the *Quincena de Girón*.[49] During that time he came home for a visit only once and then only because Lelita broke her arm. But seeing it was nothing serious, he went back right away, at 4:00 A.M. that morning.

He's going away again this year. It's no hardship for me: his salary gets paid just the same. All I have to do is go to his work center and collect it. We do all right and are quite happy even with him away.

49. A two-week worker-emulation period commemorating Playa Girón. (See Benedí, n. 83.)

Sure, I miss him and so do the kids, but he's helping the Revolution. As he says, we must all help to win the battle of the sugar-cane harvest.

I feel happy and proud that my husband does volunteer work. When one of the other women says, "My husband is out working in the cane," it gives me a good feeling to say, "So is mine."

Julio is the union coordinator. He was also a militiaman but quit because of his stomach trouble. All three of my children who are still at home go out to do volunteer work. My son Julito, who is fourteen going on fifteen, studies at the Veterinary School. He doesn't have a scholarship but he works at the Hotel Vedado. He gets paid 74 *pesos* and has his lunch there. Just recently he went to Camaguey to do volunteer work. Sonia is in secondary school—she'll be sixteen in July.

My son Alfredito lived with us until just recently. He got married in October and moved to a house near the tractor factory where he works. He's the union coordinator there and is responsible for collecting the money for the mutual fund. That money is used to help the families of workers in case of emergency. He also volunteered as a *permanente*[50] to cut sugar cane. The poor boy is working very hard right now—twelve hours a day, from 6:00 P.M. to 6:00 A.M. He's supposed to work from 3:30 P.M. to 11:30 P.M., but he's the one who gets called whenever anything comes up.

He's a Vanguard Worker and a member of the Young Communists. He's only twenty-two and he's already been nominated for Party membership. But he says he wants to wait a bit before he takes on that extra load.

BARRERA:
Celia lives near Anita in Bella Vista. Celia is married to Baltasar, the brother of Felipe, who is married to my sister Angelita. Things are going all right with Celia at the moment. They have six children and Baltasar did everything he could to get the new house. As long as she lives Celia should be grateful to the Revolution for having provided her with a good house, a frigidaire, a TV set, and all sorts of comforts. Not only that, all her kids are in school now. She and her husband both have jobs at the Ministry of Public Health, and Baltasar belongs to the militia, too.

My sister Adela is over thirty and is married to a black, Reinaldo Fernández. They live on Heredia Street and have two daughters, Edita and Fina, one married and the other getting ready to be married. She's studying to be a nurse. They turned out to have good heads on their shoulders and are quiet, well-behaved girls.

Both my sister and her husband are integrated in the Revolution. It

50. Long-term volunteer for productive labor.

seemed that Reinaldo was ready for the Revolution from the very first. He joined it at once and was in the fighting. He has injuries in one hand and one leg, but even so, he works. My sister worked as a cook in the home of Alcover, the government official who had helped me.

Reinaldo is from Oriente. He happened to be one of the few good, clean *orientales*, which was lucky for Adela. But he himself has told me, and I know from my own dealings with them, that people from Oriente are no good. Eighty per cent of them have treason in their blood. They're slippery customers, creeping and crawling to you, dragging themselves along the ground like the *majá* snake. Then, when they're sure of you, they tear you down and use you for their own benefit. They're hypocrites, every one of them, black or white. Money, that's all they care about.

I've seen what happened to friends of mine who received *orientales* in their homes. At first everything went beautifully, but as soon as those *orientales* got jobs they became enemies of the people who had helped them, even trying to rob them of their money and belongings. Two or three of my friends have had their marriages wrecked by *orientales*. If there's a woman in the house, they try to make love to her. And if it's a woman from Oriente, she destroys the man's house, damn her! That's the reason why I don't get along with them.

Every *oriental* who comes to Havana claims that back home he has a farm, cattle, a number of coffee trees. I've been in Oriente seven or eight times and seen what it's like—poverty and nakedness everywhere. Listen, the people in Las Yaguas were well off compared to the *orientales*.

And in spite of all their defects, they do nothing but criticize the people of Havana! They criticize us because we bathe practically every day. True it's cool there, but they don't bathe even in the heat of summer. They claim that "the bark protects the tree."

The last time I was in Oriente I was employed by the Ministry of Labor to do some plastering. We found that the Revolution hasn't made many changes there. Of course you can't build a town and transform a place overnight, like the remedy of Mary Magdalene. It's the policy of the state to eliminate all large slums, so eventually they'll be torn down and new houses built, but so far they've done nothing to eliminate the slums.[51]

I can't imagine why all my sisters have been drawn to the black race. Ever since they became señoritas I had hoped they'd find themselves

51. In 1969, in Santiago de Cuba, we visited a family living in a small prefabricated house that was part of a new development covering several city blocks. The woman we visited had previously lived in a slum, and she and the other residents had been promised new homes by Fidel Castro. "He kept his word," she said. Nearby was the José Martí development, a group of apartment buildings constructed from precast concrete which, we were told, was made in a factory presented to Cuba by the U.S.S.R. RML.

honest, hard-working husbands and never marry colored men. Not to belittle the husbands they have, but I hoped they'd be white. I didn't want all that blackness in my family. That's why I bear a grudge against my sisters.

There's a certain unreasonableness on my part in this because I too married blacks. Maybe it's a curse that Fate or God has put upon me. Still, for a white man it doesn't look too bad—but a white woman? Of course nowadays, wherever you look you see a white woman with a black man, but I'm against them marrying, even if he's an intellectual or a scholar or a doctor and a good guy to boot. After all, a person's social position may change but his personality doesn't.

How is it possible that I, who twice preferred dark-skinned women as wives, should turn out to be a bit of a racist after all? Oh yes, I admit that I have some racial prejudice. Perhaps that's because I've moved among a very low class of people. I like the decent middle-class blacks but not the lowness of the working class. In Las Yaguas there were some who were rotten through and through, not worth one copper *kilo*, so low-down they didn't deserve to be alive. You'd have to search a long time before you'd find a white person who behaves as badly as some of those blacks, or who has such low sentiments. For instance, only the worst white rabble would go out in the street with open shirts displaying tattoos all over their bodies, but among blacks it's common.

What I dislike most about blacks are their foolish superstitions. There isn't one of them who isn't a *santero* or a member of the *lucumí* cult or something of the kind. There's nothing a member of such cults likes better than talking about them. I can't stand such tomfoolery.

It's only Cuban blacks I object to. Black people in the United States are all right—at least they're not superstitious. If there's racial prejudice in the United States, then it must be the blacks' own fault. It's a long time since I read the history of the United States, but when you consider the problem of the South, it was the blacks' own cowardice that led them to failure. I figure they're guilty of the evils they suffer because they were cowards.

I understand that there's a stable wage scale in the United States, a standard according to the kind of work each does, and I'll bet the blacks try to get those jobs at lower wages. That's why the workers dislike them. That very thing happened here in Cuba before the Revolution. By means of flattery and chicanery the blacks got in at the bottom, so I say it's all their fault. They were the ones who agreed to work for lower wages, weren't they?

Frankly, I'm against that sort of thing. That doesn't happen in Cuba anymore. Now blacks are on an equal footing with whites. But I think blacks have been given too much power here. In the work centers and every aspect of life they've been given such authority they think they're gods.

Before the Revolution there were many blacks in Batista's army. Batista himself was a mulatto but I don't think that had anything to do with it. No, the army was a comfortable life. The soldiers knew nothing of hard labor or sacrifice; they lacked a well-organized political conscience. It was an army of 30,000 to 40,000 men, earning a salary and eating good meals without rendering any service to the nation. Blacks joined because they were sure of three meals a day and a salary, and they walked around carrying pistols so they were respected. Some are even in the higher ranks—lieutenants, sergeants, all ranks from corporal on up. It's not that white men have less merit or ability, but it seems the colored class has more of a liking for army life.

You know, lots of people say of me and my brothers, "*Caramba,* how is it that you boys grew up in that slum amidst such corruption and vice and aren't a bit affected by it?"

The answer to that is, the tree that is born crooked stays crooked, but the one that is naturally sound will grow straight, even in a mud-hole or a garbage dump. And that's the way it was for my brothers and me. None of us has any reason to complain now. We've all benefited from the Revolution in some way, and all of us are integrated.

My brother José is living in Algeria *reparto* with *mamá*. He's about twenty-one and still single. He joined the Centennial Youth Column[52] and now he's completely changed. He's working steadily and has even become a driver of heavy equipment. I don't know how much he's earning but I understand that the young fellows who join the Column earn something while learning the job and get a raise as soon as they become expert at it.

Even though José is now working and is integrated, *mamá*'s husband wants to get my brother out of the house and they've quarreled about it. The man has no right to do that because, one, the house belongs to the old lady and because, two, he knew she had children when he took up with her, and, as we vulgarly say, when you take over the cow, you have to take over the calves too.

My brother Andrés is thirty-five years old. When the Revolution began he was twenty-five, a man who had no idea of morality, of what life was like, of what it meant to struggle for a living ... in short, of anything. But after the Revolution Andrés gave up all his old ways. It improved him in 99 percent of the aspects of his life. He joined the

52. The Centennial Youth Column, organized in 1968 to celebrate 100 years of the Cuban Revolution (dating from the beginning of the War of Independence in 1868), was composed of young people between the ages of seventeen and twenty-seven, recruited to work in agricultural production. The *columnistas* received room and board, clothing, and a monthly allowance, and in addition were considered to have fulfilled their military obligation. In 1973 the Youth Column was merged with other paramilitary labor groups to form the Army of Working Youth, under the Ministry of the Revolutionary Armed Forces (MINFAR).

militia and it made a man of him. He even volunteered to cut cane. I was flabbergasted when someone told me, "Your brother is going to cut sugar cane."

"No, no, that's not true!" I exclaimed. "Even drunk I wouldn't believe that story. You must be joking."

"Well, he is. Take a look at this paper." He showed me the leaflet telling about the farewell to the cane-cutters, and, sure enough, it said Andrés was going and his old lady would get half the money he was paid there.

"Unbelievable!" I said. "How come that lazy bum volunteered to cut cane? I bet he'll be back at the end of three days." Three days? How wrong I was! He got a taste for it. He's already worked at seven or eight of the people's sugar-cane harvests. Now he has a regular job at the Ministry of Labor and is about to be made a Party member.

I don't know where Andrés learned about communism. It wasn't from Benedí or Montano because he never knew those people, but when Andrés was about twenty, he was living at my aunt's house at Córdoba and helping her with her lunch pails. Every night when we played dominoes with the Spaniards and Catalans who lived on Pasaje de Córdoba, Andrés listened to them talk about socialism and may have been influenced by them. Now he's devoted to the Party.

My brother's loyalty to the Party even brought on a break with his wife. They separated because she asked him how long he meant to keep on neglecting her, and did the Revolution mean more to him than she did. "If this is the kind of life I'm going to lead married to you," said she, "I'd better leave before I'm unfaithful to you." So, despising wealth and comfort, she left her husband to take up with a fellow who has nothing and who is practically illiterate to boot. But at least she was honest, and in spite of everything, I think she deserves a monument for it.

On Mother's Day I saw Andrés at *mamá's* house. We hadn't met for three years and we had a long talk. *Vaya!* It was an emotional meeting that brought tears to my eyes. Andrés did most of the talking. There he sat, telling me about his doings in detail and giving me advice.

"Hey, wait a minute!" I said. "How come you're giving me advice now when I used to be the one who always advised *you?*"

"Well, brother," he says, "this just goes to show you how things change. As you know, I'm now on the Party's list of candidates because I've worked in the harvest for nine years running. Besides that, I've accumulated merits by my revolutionary activities in various fields. Now that I've earned this great honor, I'll struggle and consecrate myself to the Party more than ever."

That's the way he expressed himself, and I was especially happy because he was my brother and we've always been close to each other. I was overjoyed at his success. For a head like his, crazy from the start, to become a member of the Party! It meant that if he still had a taste for drink, he'd have to eliminate it, see? He'd have to be more measured in his tastes, and settle down, especially in regard to women. Besides, I know that as a Party member he could be of help to me if I ever had a problem or needed something. I was really impressed and pleased but I think my emotions came more from the fact of meeting him again after such a long time.

I myself wanted to go to a school of self-improvement, but after I had enrolled and bought notebooks and everything, I backed out. I was embarrassed, that's why. I really wanted to learn how to write music. I compose music sometimes, see? I don't play any instrument, but now and then music comes to my mind and brings me peace for a little while. Well, I wanted my music to be copied so other people could hear it and so I could be recognized as part of the culture.

SEÑORA LORDI:

Of all my children, Andrés and José are the most integrated in the Revolution. Andrés is the manager of a grocery store now. Every time he comes to see me he gives me 5 or 10 *pesos*. He's on the point of becoming a Party member. He only has one child, Andresito, who's about the age of my youngest daughter, Susanita.

José is twenty years old. He's in the Centennial Youth Column. He likes it and they treat him very well. He works on two different shifts. This week he's on from 5:00 in the morning to 4:00 in the afternoon; next week he's on the 2:00 P.M. to 12:00 midnight shift. José told me that as soon as this sugar harvest is finished they're going to take the Column to Camaguey to make repairs on sugar mills. And I answered, "All right, goodbye."

I've been lucky with my sons and husbands. They've all been homebodies. Look at Fredo. He comes straight home from work. And José, my youngest, who's still living with me, comes straight home from work, takes a bath, eats, and goes right to bed. And look at the husband I have now. Norberto comes home from work at 4:00 P.M., eats, goes to bed, and sleeps till next morning at 5:00, when he gets up to go to work. My only troubles have been trying to scare up a couple of *pesetas* for food when Norberto was out of work. Aside from that, I've had no problems and am very happy.

All of my husbands have been believers except the first one, Rafael. That one was a terrible unbeliever—he didn't even believe in the mother who bore him—and was always cursing and speaking against religion. But he couldn't interfere with my beliefs. God forbid! Sometimes he'd even say, "I shit on God!" And I'd say to him, "Stop shitting on God because He's up there ruling all of us down here in the world. If you keep on swearing like that you'll bump into something with your cart and break a leg."

"Ah, God doesn't exist!" he said. Well, he got his, exactly as I had foretold, and broke his leg. I don't even feel like talking about that devil or hearing his name.

My husband Alfredo believed deeply. His favorite saint was St. Lazarus. Vicente had great faith and so does Norberto. Norberto's favorite is St. Barbara. He's crazy about her. That's his thing. Whatever he wants, he asks St. Barbara for. He's done that since he was a child. His parents were oldtimers, not modern.

I believe in all the saints, but my favorite is Yemayá, the *Virgen de Regla.* I have her image right here. She was my guardian, that's the reason I like her so much. Other people have other favorites; many prefer the patron saint of Cuba, the *Virgen de la Caridad del Cobre.* If you ask a boon from a particular saint and get it, naturally you become more inclined to that saint than to others. It becomes the saint of your devotion because it protects you and gives you what you want. I like Yemayá best because whenever I've been in trouble, had someone sick or something, I've asked for her help and gotten it. I once made a vow to Yemayá that if she got me out of the muddy place where I was living and into a weathertight house where I could live in peace, I'd adore her all my life and light candles before her shrine.

On September 7 every year, everybody in Regla has fiestas in honor of Yemayá. And on the 8th of each month I go to the church at Regla, and then I spend a long time walking beside the sea. It's so beautiful. I've always loved the sea. Old people say Yemayá is the owner of the sea. I wish I could read her history—I'm dying to know more about her.

It's been more than a month since I last went to church because the one we go to is sometimes open and sometimes not. They always open it on July 16, because that's the day of Our Lady of Carmel. I go to the special church celebrations whenever I can. Those are my only fiestas. I don't make any offerings except flowers to the saints.

About four months ago I decided to bring down a *santo* because my vows had been granted. I haven't made any new vows lately because I haven't had any problems. I'm content for the present because my family is doing all right.

I went over to my godmother's house and they made the rite for me. In it they use holy water for the baptism and the initiation of the *santo* and to wash the ceremonial objects. The godmother blesses the water with *Pater Noster, Ave María,* and so on, just like the priests in church. Then she lights a candle to the *santo.* They cut some people's hair but didn't cut mine. It all depends. Suppose one of my children— dear Lord protect them from harm!—should get sick and I should vow to some saint that his hair will never be cut until he reaches a certain age. When he gets to be that age, I have it cut. Some people vow to have their hair cut when they get their *santo.* It's the same principle.

The necklaces are bought by the initiate and put around his neck during the ceremony. I've had mine about twenty years. The red-and-white one belongs to St. Barbara, or Changó; the blue necklace belongs to the *Virgen de Regla,* and the blue-and-white one is hers too. The yellow necklace is for the *Virgen de la Caridad del Cobre,* and I have one for the *Virgin de la Merced* too. You'd walk a long way trying to find a place where they sell these necklaces now. All those stores have closed down. You couldn't get them even if you were willing to pay 100,000 *pesos!* As for the white cloth needed in the ceremony, I simply bought white yard goods instead of colored when my ration of cloth was due.

Lots of people attended my *fiesta de santo.* Many were friends of mine. It was just as if you were celebrating a child's baptism and invited everybody in the neighborhood. The ceremony wasn't very expensive, only 50 or 60 *pesos.* I bought a few flowers, candy, and soft drinks, the kinds of things you serve at a party. If you want to have a big *fiesta de santo* you usually have a cake made, or you can kill a couple of chickens and invite the other participants to dinner.

I'm only entitled to eight soft drinks every time my turn comes, so I saved them up for my fiesta. Of course I had to return the empties before I could buy new ones, so I poured the drinks into old wine bottles and took the empties along to get the new ones. I saved them up until I had about forty. Sweets can't be hoarded so I bought all I needed the same day. My daughters Anita and Susanita helped. We had to stand in line at several candy stores to get enough.

Some of my girls aren't believers and some are. Celia is, and her favorite saint is *La Caridad del Cobre.* Berta is not what I call a believer. She believes only when she's in some sort of trouble. I don't know what Susanita believes, that's up to her. As for me, I believe in my little Virgin and will until I die. What my sons believe, I do not know. They're all grown by now and each has his own opinion.

None of my daughters got angry about my getting a *santo.* My daughters can't boss me around—they're married women and their husbands rule them, but they don't rule me.

I know many white people who are believers and have their *santos.* Most of us are believers because we were born in the midst of believers. Perhaps Fidel doesn't like to have us believe in religion, but he has never interfered with us. Maybe I'm outside the law, but what harm does it do if I believe in my saints and put flowers before them? One must keep the law, but what does law have to do with religion?

I heard that a dove perched on Fidel's shoulder, but when I repeated the story somebody told me, "Don't say that; Fidel doesn't want people to believe it."[53]

53. During Castro's nationally televised triumphal address at Camp Columbia on

"That's a lie!" I protested. "Fidel couldn't have said that, because if a dove perched on his shoulder it was sent by the Most Holy. It was a messenger of God Himself!" Maybe, for some reason, Fidel can't admit he believes, but deep inside I'm sure he does. God wouldn't send a dove to him unless he were a believer.

Every human being has faith in something. You can have faith even in a plant, as I have faith in the guava plant growing out there. Why? Because it's a good cure for diarrhea and all sorts of stomach troubles. People have faith in that plant because it cures. These remedies were given to us by God. Whatever is found in nature is God's gift to us.

I hope God will grant me health for at least two or three more years—so I can see my youngest daughter married. After that, all I want is to live in peace—and to get some paint and cement, a new mattress, and a refrigerator. Then, when I close my eyes and die, I can leave Susanita a nice home of her own. I hope she takes good care of it.

Those are my only dreams and hopes just now. In any case, His will be done.

BARRERA:

Mamá used to hold seances but I never attended any of them. My first wife, Martita, was a spiritist and held seances too. So did Esperanza, because they told her she had powers she must develop. And now, just recently, *mamá* was presented to a *santo*.

The *santero* of the *lucumí* cult told *mamá* she should make the fiesta for the *santo* because she's always been subject to attacks that made her lose all notion of things. Whenever *mamá* got a bit sick she'd say she had one of those spells. Those religious myths, bah! I think she must have some kind of heart condition—I certainly don't believe there's anything spiritual about it. But the *santero* told her to do it, so she did. It cost her a good stiff price but I helped by giving her 50 *pesos*.

A few days after *mamá* was made a *santera*, I went to see her. She seemed awfully thin to me, but perhaps I wasn't used to seeing her hair tied up in a kerchief or all kinds of beads hanging on her.

"When are you coming back to see me?" she asked.

"Oh, next week," I promised. Actually I didn't go back until about five months later. When I saw her again she still didn't look well. She paid her 1,000 *pesos* to become a *santera*, but frankly, I haven't noticed that she's any the better for it. She lives as she always has and her health isn't at all improved. She still gets the same dizzy spells; she hasn't solved a single problem. If she had spent that much money on other things, she

---

January 8, 1959, someone in the audience released two white doves, one of which alighted on Castro's shoulder as he spoke. This was interpreted by many Cubans as an omen from God. (Ruby Hart Phillips describes this incident in *Cuba: Island of Paradox* (New York: McDowell, Obolensky, 1959), p. 406.)

could have solved twenty problems with it. Well, everyone has his own religion and *mamá* fell for that one. She really believes in all that stuff. From the moment you set foot in her house you see pictures of saints all over the place and a table with a lot of glasses of water and flowers. It's fantastic! But it makes her happy. I don't buy it, but who knows, maybe one of these days you may see me walking around dressed in white too, a saint no less! Life is like that.

Chapter Nine

Life Goes On

A COUPLE OF YEARS AGO, my brother-in-law Felipe got me a job in Maintenance at the National Hospital. I was working with two comrades, Homero and Martín. At first they were quite friendly with me. We went to the dining room together and shared a dressing room. Then, all of a sudden, things started to look bad and I began to have problems with them.

They were always trying to pick a fight with me, making pointed remarks about people who held two jobs and asking how come I got out of work at 3:00 in the afternoon when they had to stay until 5:00. What they didn't know is that I'd been authorized to have two jobs and to leave the hospital early so I'd have time to go home, bathe, change, and eat before going to my second job. They also didn't take into account that I worked straight through from early in the morning until 3:00 P.M. without taking an hour off for lunch or fifteen minutes for a snack in the afternoon like they did.

That was only the beginning. After a while they began to gripe because I earned a lot more than they did. That was what really caused it all. How come, they asked me, I got 157 *pesos* a month when I was new, while they, after working there for nine years, only earned 116? Of course they didn't consider that different jobs draw different wages. They worked under the title of "floor scrubber" while I was an experienced plasterer.

Matters got worse when I started to lose things from my pockets in the clothes I left hanging in the locker room. One day I lost a jar of brilliantine and I said to them both, "Gentlemen, that jar of brilliantine must be found. Only three people have the keys to this room, you two and Felipe, so one of you must have taken it and I want it back."

Now if one day you lose your brilliantine, and the next day Martín, who hasn't used any for over a month, turns up with his hair all slicked down and shiny, who would you suspect, eh?

I didn't mention the brilliantine again, but then I lost 10 *pesos* from my wallet. *Concho!* I had over 120 *pesos* in my wallet that day and it was hardly likely that a thief would steal only 10. But a low-down pilferer would, to make it look as though I'd lost it. So things kept getting lost and nobody ever knew anything.

Once I had to go up to the roof, and there I surprised Homero opening the door to the supply room. "Hey," I called out, "where are you going?"

"To get some paper, so I can go to the toilet."

I let it go at that and nothing happened that day. The next day they sent me to do a job at the Medical Sciences building. I went, finished my job, returned to punch my card, and went home. Bah! There was trouble, because they said a sack of plaster was missing. I was the one who always got the plaster. They'd give me a piece of paper that I had to turn in whenever I collected the plaster, but I was away that day, so if some plaster got lost it was none of my doing.

Those two guys did their best to make my life unbearable. I thought of taking the case to the union local and from there to the Labor Council.[54] Those were the official channels through which I could have made a formal complaint against them. I had nothing to worry about because I didn't have any bits of shit to hide. But they did. I knew that if I made an official case of it those two would spend some little time in the shade, whether in jail or on a prison farm. But I did nothing.

For one thing, it was now a matter of my manliness, in the sense that I had to get the better of them on my own. Also, I felt I absolutely could not make a row. It wouldn't have been fair to Felipe. So out of manliness, because I didn't want to harm anybody else, I was silent. But *concho!* I only harmed myself.

One day I had an argument with Homero and was on the point of hitting him. I came right out and said to him, "I'm going to leave this place, because if I stay I'll break your head sooner or later, and I don't want to blot my brother-in-law's record because he was the one who got me the job here."

I went to Jorge Pardo, who was in charge of all the departments, and said to him, "Jorge, I want you to change me to another department,

<hr />

54. The *Consejos de Trabajo* were established at the enterprise level and were composed of five members elected by the workers. Members were required to have a socialist attitude toward work, be disciplined, and have a good work record with no instance of absenteeism. The Councils handled violations of labor discipline: tardiness, absenteeism, disobedience, negligence, lack of respect for superiors, physical offenses, damage to equipment, fraud, and robbery. Decisions of the Councils could be appealed to the Regional Appeal Commissions and, at the highest level, the National Revision Commission. The manager of an enterprise could, under the law, impose disciplinary sanctions without hearings by the local Council. And the Ministry of Labor could dismiss members of local Labor Councils, recall cases being heard, deny appeals procedures, or annul a Council decision. (Hernández and Mesa-Lago, "Labor Organization and Wages," pp. 221–22.)

maybe Cleaning, anything, so long as I don't have to work with either Homero or Martín."

Well, Jorge sent me out of Havana to work; five times I was sent out to the country, and then, when they were about to send me for the sixth time, I said to Jorge, "Stop, will you! Let somebody else go to the country this time because I'm not going. Those jobs are supposed to be assigned to men with no children. Homero has no children; Martín has no children; yet *they* never get sent out. But I do, just because I have no relatives among the bosses, because I have no strings to pull."

I almost signed up to go and cut cane, to get away from my job. The captain of the maintenance brigade was desperate because all the other organizations had at least one "millionaire brigade," and there were we, with fifty volunteers, yet we had never cut our million *arrobas* and won the flag of the million.[55]

I was about to sign up but then I learned that Homero was also going. I thought, "If I go I won't be able to resist cutting that *cabrón*'s throat with one stroke of my machete." Besides, the guys going were a greedy bunch of deadbeats. I mean, they'd go spend fifteen days in the country and come back without having done a lick of work. After ten or twelve days in the fields, they'd pretend to be sick. Those deadbeats spoil things for a guy who really wants to work. The way I look at it, there's no excuse for a strong, healthy man who promises to carry out a task and doesn't. He has no shame if he makes the government spend money on his fare and equipment, and then he quits after only fifteen days.

When you volunteer to cut cane, the state gives you a roof over your head, three meals a day, and tobacco. Volunteers usually eat better than they would at any work center in Havana because they get sweets, too. It's only with twenty difficulties that you can get candy or any kind of sweets in Havana. Out in the country you don't have to wait in line or anything. The state also gives you one pair of boots and two changes of clothing, which are renewed each year. They spend a lot of money on those fakers.

Some of the volunteers are so brazen, they take their new boots and sell them for 30 *pesos*. It's forbidden to sell them but they do. They keep on using their old boots, and if anybody asks them they say, "These are the ones they gave me this year." Other volunteers take their new pants and sell them for 25 *pesos*. The government's been too soft with that kind of thing. What they should do is tell those fellows, "You were given these clothes for working in the cane. If you sell any of them, you'll get no more. You'll have to work with what you have."

One time Fidel went over to Pinar del Río and got mad as hell at what

---

55. One *arroba* is equal to 25 pounds. Thus to become a "millionaire brigade" it was necessary for the volunteers to cut 25 million pounds of sugar cane during the harvest period (January-May). Brigade size varied upward from twenty members.

he saw. He told the guys there, "All right, all these bastards on the truck here can go to hell." He really cleaned up that place.

I saw lots of those deadbeats in 1960 when I cut cane for three months in Oriente. But I was assigned to a squad where the least efficient man cut 300 *arrobas* of cane a day and I had to work hard not to look bad in the eyes of the other comrades.

That was the first time I had cut cane or even been in a cane field. In the beginning my hands were covered with blisters, my whole body ached, my legs felt shaky, I kept slipping and falling, but little by little I got used to it. It's odd I should have found the work so killing. I'd done hard physical labor all my life but never anything like that. I did it though, and now I have that experience. It never hurts to learn something new.

When a call was made for volunteers many people from Havana went. According to the law, volunteers cutting cane must be paid whatever they earned at their regular job. The majority of them were earning upwards of 200 *pesos*. The *guajiros,* having worked in the cane fields all their lives, were much quicker and better at it, but they earned only 3.18 *pesos* a day, or about 90 *pesos* a month. When they asked the city guys, "How much do you earn?" one would answer, "Two hundred *pesos."* The next guy would say, "Four hundred, and I'm not about to kill myself cutting cane, either. That's a job for peasants."

What could the *guajiros* think? They decided that if there were men earning 300 *pesos* for doing nothing, why should they put themselves out cutting so much cane for only 3.18 *pesos* a day?

That system is still in force, and out in the country people feel it like a kick above the liver. To my way of thinking it's a great mistake, because it kills the farm workers' faith in the Revolution. It seems to me that the volunteers should have been paid according to the yield of their machete. At that rate most of them wouldn't have earned enough to pay for their *café con leche* but the *guajiros* would have felt much better.

I didn't go again to cut cane, but to punish me for complaining they sent me to work in Oriente Province for forty-five days. The change of drinking water in Oriente affected my stomach and kidneys and when I got back home to Havana I was sick. I went to the doctor to get a medical certificate. It wasn't that I didn't want to work—I've never liked to get money I haven't earned—it was that I couldn't. But the doctor said, "No, I will not give you a medical certificate."

Says I, "Look, doctor, don't play around with me. If I don't get a certificate I'll lose my job."

He wasn't one of the new crop of doctors promoted by the Revolution. He was an old fellow who put all the obstacles he could in people's way, not only for me but for several of the other fellows who worked there.

I was sick for twenty-eight days with diarrhea and stomachache, and I kept going back for a medical certificate, but the doctor refused to accept the days I'd spent at home before seeing him because he thought I'd been out too long. Finally that doctor was transferred, but the new doctor gave me a certificate that was good only for the days he'd been substituting for the other doctor.

At my work center they knew I was sick, but without a medical certificate Jorge refused to credit me with the days I'd been absent. I stayed on until one day I thought, "Oh, what the hell. I'm not going to work here anymore." I left without even going to get my vacation money. I was fed up with those pigs, those sons of a whoring mother and their carping and criticizing.

When you want to change jobs you must have some reason. The state makes its demands and the needy one invents his tricks. So I had a talk with Jorge and he gave me a document from my work committee saying that what I earned at my job wasn't enough to meet my expenses. I went to the regional committee, who stamped the document, then I presented it at the offices of the chief of Personnel and talked with someone there, and he approved the transfer. Officially I still have that job at the hospital, because they haven't given me my release yet, but I signed a contract for a job as a garbage collector. I've been working on a garbage truck for the last two years. It's killing work and now I want to get out of it.

The street-cleaning department is divided into separate groups, the men with carts who sweep the streets, those in trucks who collect leaves and brush, and those who collect the trash from the boxes where the carts dump the street sweepings. These people earn 90 *pesos* a month. Garbage collection is a special division that serves residences and we get 200 a month. But that work is cursed!

The truth is, nobody likes the job of garbage collector. Usually, all those who work at it are just avoiding other obligations like guard duty, because garbage collectors are not required to do it. I'm one of those, because I hate guard duty and that whole series of obligations this system makes us take on.

Our route is in a seventeen-block district. The work has been doubled, because where there used to be six trucks there are now three, each with six men running behind it. There's a big risk of infection in that job and the sooner we get it done the better. We figure it should take four or five hours to complete the two routes, but the amount of garbage varies from day to day and so does our schedule.

Sometimes we don't finish until 8:00 P.M. If the truck breaks down we have to call a mechanic and wait until it's repaired, and that really holds us up. One day you may feel like working fast and getting it done within four hours, but unless everyone feels the same, it doesn't do much good because you find yourself working in a vacuum. When one man is absent, the work has to be done by the rest of the team. The government used to give us substitutes but not anymore. There's a lot of absenteeism. It always happens that the day there's more garbage three or four are absent, so it's hard work and we can't keep to a regular schedule.

A four-hour shift doesn't sound bad—until you stop to think that it's four hours spent slinging filth. It's no picnic having to plunge your hands into all kinds of shit that people throw away. Not that garbage collecting has to be all that unpleasant. It depends on the circumstances. In the United States garbage collectors wear a white uniform and have all the equipment they need. Every building has an incinerator so that the only thing your hands touch is clean ashes instead of filthy garbage. And they earn almost 500 American dollars a month! That's a very different proposition.

Garbage collecting isn't mechanized here. It's all done by hand. The regulation cans are enormous iron ones made in Russia—it's lifting those heavy weights all day that makes the work especially hard. It was suggested that we get rid of them, but if we did, what would we replace them with? Before the Revolution, if your garbage can rusted and the bottom fell out you could go buy a new one at the hardware store, but things have changed. If they take away the iron receptacles, the garbage would be dumped out on the street. So we haul those Russian cans and it wears a man out.

People make the job a real headache. Some leave the trash can right in front of their door instead of near the curb. On a day when there isn't much garbage, we walk over and pick it up, but when there's a lot of work we take only the cans we can get at quickly. For three days we may go all the way to someone's door to pick up their garbage only to have him get mad because we can't stop for it on the fourth day. Then they tell everybody, "Look at that whore's son of a garbage collector! He rushed by and didn't pick up my garbage."

People will curse your mother and you have to put up with it. They'll even accuse you of stealing. One neighbor will take the garbage can belonging to another and paint it a different color so it won't be recognized; then *we* are blamed for stealing!

It's killing work all right. Do you know what it's like when it starts raining and we have to keep on working just the same? The city of Havana must be kept clean, come rain, come hurricane.

The comrades who work with me on the same truck are Piche, Angel, Rosales, Jesús, Camilo, and Fernández, the driver. There's comradeship among us because we all want the same things: to finish the job on hand and to earn money to support our families. I'm most friendly with Piche and Angel. If we buy soft drinks, one of us always pays for all three. The others usually go "American style," each paying for his own.

There is one, Rosales, whom we call "the Lip," who's been treated to a drink by everyone on the truck, but he's never treated any of us to so much as a glass of water. You can't get a cup of coffee worth 3 *kilos* out of that man, yet he's always boasting that he has 300 or 400 *pesos* stashed away. Well, he's the kind who'd go without food so he wouldn't have to shit.

"The Lip" has been working at the same kind of job, street-cleaning and so on, for twenty-five years, and he avoids the rest of us. When we first arrive at work we pass the time of day for a while before we begin. Someone might tell you about a problem he had with his neighbor, or something that happened at the work center. I do my share of the talking, too. We kid around a lot, but "the Lip" holds himself aloof. I figure it's because he's henpecked by his wife. She dominates him and forces him to be home by midnight.

One guy, whom we call Batabanó because that's where he's from, is always kidding around. A lot of the jokes are about the *santeros* in the group. All of us are Catholic but some are *santeros* too. They wear necklaces and knotted chains to ward off evil. My best friend, Angel, is one of them—that's why I've never been to his house. I won't have anything to do with those "saints."

There's one guy, Camilo, who brags about being a *palero*, a saint-maker, and we kid him a lot, asking him if today he's going to make Fernández's leg swell. Fernández is always complaining of swollen legs—that way he gets off work—and, well, Camilo wouldn't actually harm any of his comrades but sometimes we start kidding and what we say comes true. Just coincidence, see?

"The Lip" is the only white man in the group other than me. Jesús, Fernández, Camilo, and Piche are all mulattoes. I never visit any of the fellows at home, but I went to Jesús's house once. I'd been complaining of the trouble we had at home getting kerosene for cooking and he promised to sell me some.

"Give me 5 *pesos* now and go by my house tomorrow to get it," he told me. He wrote down his address and next day I went there. He gave me the kerosene, telling me a story about how difficult it had been for him to get it for me. Only a few days earlier he'd been telling us that he had quite a bit of kerosene stored at home, so I knew it was no trouble for him to sell me some. Even so, he didn't return any change from the 5 *pesos* I'd given him. Of course he deserved something for having offered to sell me some at all, but he really exploited me because at 9 *centavos* each, those ten little bottles of the stuff weren't worth even 1 *peso*. I had to take it. What else could I do? But the thing is, we worked together so he shouldn't have overcharged me that much.

Life has some funny turns and I caught Jesús in his own trap. He'd bought a Japanese electric iron which broke down. When he took it to the *consolidado* to be repaired he found he'd have to wait months before they got around to it, and the iron was urgently needed at home, so he brought it to me.

"Fix it and then tell me how much it costs," he said.

I did as he asked and charged him 10 *pesos.*

"What!" says he. "Oh no, that's much too expensive."

"Sure it is, but so was the kerosene you sold me. I paid it because, after all, you'd done me a favor and solved a problem for me. Well, this time I solved your problem. Turn about is fair play, so hand over the money."

None of the group working on the truck with me is a Party member. We make jokes about Fidel's speeches. When he talked about 1980, 1990, and so on, we kidded about it and said, "Sure, it's a 100-year fight and so far we've had ten years of blight." In fact, some of the men are a bit *gusano*-ish, because they don't share all those communist ideals. Heck, I don't share them myself! We belong to the Committee to keep people from talking and because we need identification papers. You see, in my line of work you find lots of good stuff people throw away, and when you're carrying a bundle late at night you're apt to be stopped by the police. If you don't have a card from your Committee, you're picked up and taken to the station. Garbage collectors have the reputation for being a pack of thieves.

A few days ago I found a kerosene lamp in perfect working condition, complete with socket, plate, and wick. It was an old-fashioned lamp of a kind I'd been searching for for ages to use in case of a hurricane. I prefer kerosene to petroleum because petroleum smoke stains the ceiling. I was overjoyed to find the right kind of lamp. I keep it in the bedroom. We garbage men take a lot of the useful stuff we find but also leave a lot, because we think it might have belonged to someone who died of a contagious disease.

Although we belong to the Committee, all the fellows at work avoid voluntary labor. Of course one must do the officially designated duties, but those other things are not compulsory. I, for one, do everything I can to avoid standing guard for the militia. Today that's the only duty I perform for the Revolution. Why? Well, after all, when all's said and done, why should I do more?

We go to meetings at the work center, for a session of self-criticism or to talk about the Revolution or about the things that are needed. There's a lot of talk about the government and most of it is unfavorable. For instance, the men complain about having no substitutes. Also, that everybody used to get two changes of work clothes each year, but nowadays you can't get so much as a pair of pants. And when you go to the union local to get something, they put twenty obstacles in your way. What a system!

During one of the sessions they were proposing people—those who worked most and behaved best—for Party membership. One of the comrades, Marcelino, brags all the time about being a great revolutionary, and someone proposed him. The assembly agreed to hear his case, and one of the presiding Party members asked him, "Do you believe in God?"

Marcelino thought for about fifteen minutes before finally answering, "Well, yes and no." What a silly answer! I mean, either you believe or you don't.

Then the comrade said, "No, Comrade Marcelino, you can't belong to the Party because you obviously believe in some religious sect, and we in the Party do not permit any kind of religion."

Then they asked my opinion of the comrade. I answered, "I've only known him the short time we've been working together. It seems to me he has good aptitudes, but in my opinion there are two things that should bar him from being a Party member. One, he's a drunkard, and two, he trades with country people and there's no room for profiteers in the Party."

My saying that got him into trouble, but it's true. He picks up old clothes people throw away, launders them, and goes out to the country and exchanges them with *guajiros* for flour and beans.

Last week I was working on the late shift, from 7:00 P.M. to 11:00 P.M. On Monday night we finished the rounds and I got home at 11:30. I'm on a good bus route—it comes quite frequently. I like to get home early, not because I'm henpecked but because the water is cut off after midnight and not turned on again until 6:00 A.M. and I like to take a bath before I go to bed. Do you know what it's like to go to bed with the stink of garbage on you?

Esperanza always waits up to open the door for me at night. She's got plenty to keep her busy till that time—if she isn't ironing, she's cleaning up the house.

When I got in, I bathed while Esperanza prepared bread and *café con leche*. If I don't eat what she sets before me she protests, "I'll never prepare anything more for you to eat. What's the point? You just leave it."

The kids are all asleep when I get home but Eufrasio, the three-year-old, seems to sense when I come in and *bang!* he wakes up. That kid is like a magnet. Maybe he's dreaming about me, but whatever it is he wakes, knowing I always have a bit of candy for him. I buy candy for the kids as often as I can. I stand in line while the truck drives off to unload the garbage. Some comrades who don't eat candy also stand in line for me and let me have their ration.

Well, Eufrasio woke up and Esperanza brought him in and chatted with me while I ate. Then Esperanza got kind of romantic. About 1:30 A.M. the kid fell asleep and we had a chance. We got on my mattress on the floor and stayed there awhile. Afterward Esperanza got up and washed, then I washed. We always keep a pail of water handy. Esperanza fell asleep after 2:00 A.M. but I couldn't get to sleep all night long. I lay there, half awake, thinking about the things that had happened to me that day. I thought about Hermelinda, my girl friend. She was sick and had left two or three messages for me, but I hadn't been to see her. I felt I'd let her down.

The next day I woke up at 4:00 A.M., at cockcrow, with the sound of footsteps on the sidewalk; from 4:00 on people tramp by steadily. Some work out in the country and the truck that picks them up passes by pretty early.

I got up, looked over the yard, and planned what I would do about the henhouse. After that I went back in and lay down again. I turned on the radio and listened to the news on *Radio Reloj*. Then the kids woke up and got ready for school. For breakfast they had some hot dogs I'd brought home the night before. They love them in the morning and had them in addition to their usual breakfast of bread and milk and an egg beaten up in a glass of sweet wine. We always eat something salty for breakfast.

After the kids had left, Tomasita came over. Every morning she shows up to drink coffee and ask for cigarettes. "Esperanza, could you let me have a cigarette?" That's her habitual greeting. Then she regales us with bits of gossip she's picked up around the neighborhood. Every time she quarrels with her husband we hear about it in detail, or else she jabbers on about her little aches and pains! God, how I hate to have somebody always jawing about the same old things! I say, if you feel poorly all the time, go to a hospital where they'll take care of you! What good does it do you to bore other people with your complaints?

Actually it's Esperanza she talks to, but if I'm sitting there I have to listen. On Tuesday morning when Tomasita walked in, I got up and went out to my garden to look over my plants. I have to build a new fence soon because the one I have is run-down. Later on I went over to MINCON and talked to a comrade there, Mercurio, about my kid's bicycles. The tires on the small bicycle were flat and broken. They had American valves which I couldn't replace so I wanted to change the tires for larger ones.

Mercurio told me to bring the tires in and he'd change them for free. I brought them to him and gave him five cigars as payment. A neighbor had given them to me but I hardly ever smoke them so I thought I might as well give them to Mercurio.

At first I was "between two waters," as we say, about getting bicycles for my kids. They were really anxious to have them but I was scared they'd fall and break an arm or a leg. Finally, at Esperanza's urging, I agreed. The Day of the Three Kings was coming and there were long lines of people waiting to buy them. I couldn't stand in line days on end so I thought, "If I can get a couple of secondhand bikes in good condition, I'll buy them."

One of my wife's friends, Clara, had a couple of bikes her grandchildren had outgrown and she wanted to sell them. Clara had paid 130 *pesos* for both bikes. She had one grandson living with her, so she bought one bicycle for 70 *pesos* in his name. She couldn't spend sleepless nights waiting in line any more than I could, and she paid a fellow 10 *pesos* to stand in line for her. Since she was entitled to only one bike, Clara paid someone for the right to use his ration book to buy the other bike, which cost her 60 *pesos*.

Clara sold the two of them to me for 160 *pesos*. I thought that was pretty reasonable, since they were still almost new and I didn't have to wait in line. Those are small transactions which are not reported to the Committee of the *reparto*. The state is on the lookout for the buying and selling of furniture, frigidaires, radios, TV, but they don't bother about bicycles.

My neighbor, Baldovino, couldn't afford to buy his kids bicycles. Each year when the Day of the Three Kings approaches, his wife, Silenia, says, "I'm going to visit all our aunts and uncles to see if I can't make a collection to buy Benito his bicycle." Benito is her oldest boy. Well, Silenia's been saying the same thing for the past three years and still no bicycle, so you can imagine what a blow it was to her motherly pride when she saw my two kids with theirs. It's kind of hard on her, I realize that, but she kept needling me about it, accusing me of starving the kids so I could pay for those bikes. I finally got fed up and told her that neither I nor my kids ever went hungry to pay for any luxury article.

Well, at noon on Tuesday the kids got home from school and their *mamá* served them some rice, ground meat cooked with spices, and plantains. After lunch they drank milk and ate same mangoes a cousin of theirs had brought. I hardly ate any lunch. I had to hurry and climb up on the neighbor's roof to get my kids' ball, because two or three boys had seen it there the day before and the neighbor had given them permission to climb up and get it. By the time I got back down, the food was cold and what little appetite I'd had had disappeared.

At 3:00 in the afternoon I lay down to rest a bit before going to work. Then I bathed while Esperanza prepared supper and set the table—we put a tablecloth on the table but we don't use napkins or any of those niceties—then, with my permission, she served the kids. The children usually eat supper before Esperanza and me. That way we can be sure that if there isn't enough to go around, at least they won't go hungry. But they have a habit of eating twenty trifles between meals and then leaving most of their supper, so I'm always urging them to clean their plates. They have no excuse for leaving any food because Esperanza is a good cook and has a real knack for seasoning.

When they had eaten Esperanza served me, but do you know what those little rascals did? As soon as I started eating they swarmed all over me. I've gotten into the habit of giving them little bits of my food and they'll say, "*Ay, papi*, it's my turn, you haven't given me any yet." Then one of the others will start to cry, so I have to give him some too. It's getting to be one heck of a bother.

After supper I drank my coffee, rinsed my mouth, picked up my gloves and sneakers, and at 5:55 left to catch the bus to work. Usually the bus is very punctual, getting to the bus stop at 6:05, but I don't know what happened that day. There was no bus at 6:05, then two came together at 6:30. By then it was too late for me to get to work and sign in at 7:00. By the time I'd have got there my comrades would have done two full streets. They don't care whether I get there early or late but I take great pride in never being late for work. So I turned around and went home. When I got there Esperanza said, "What's wrong?"

"Nothing, I just missed my bus," I explained.

They'll deduct a day's pay from my wages because I missed work on Tuesday. The government has acted very badly about absenteeism. We used to get full wages whether we missed a day or not. Then, for a while we were docked 5, 10, or 15 percent of our wages for absenteeism. There was a lot of griping and I guess they thought things over and decided those economic sanctions were too tough, so they eliminated them. Now they dock us just for the days we miss. But absenteeism is as bad as ever.[56]

I should have phoned in to say I wasn't going to work, but the supervisor, Mango Gómez, hasn't the moral right to bawl anyone out. His title is "district chief" but he doesn't belong to the Party. He's black and just a brazen, greedy son-of-a-bitch. That man thinks he's a superman; the power has gone to his head. According to the rules, he's supposed to stay at the work center until the last garbage truck returns. But hell! At 10:00 A.M., before even the first truck is back, he goes home to sleep. On his way out he says to the night watchman, "If there's any trouble, call me." One of these days there's going to be a big fat accident and then he'll really be in for it!

"Now that I've got the evening off I'll go see Felipe."

"Ask your sister if she can spare a few onions while you're there," Esperanza said.

I got on the bicycle and went to the *reparto* Algeria. I chatted with my brother-in-law and he told me there had been a fire in the hospital building where I used to work. Then he said that a number of comrades had been transferred to other departments because of illness and that

---

56. After a long campaign against absenteeism and vagrancy, the government passed an anti-loafing law on March 15, 1971. Under this law, all men between the ages of seventeen and sixty, and all women seventeen to fifty-five who are physically and mentally able, must work. Those who do not are considered to live "parasitically" and to be guilty of "antisocial behavior." Persons absent from work fifteen days or more without due cause, and persons who have been reported by their work centers to their Labor Council two or more times, are subject to sanctions under the law. This can take the form of internment in a rehabilitation institution (work camp), or a period of home arrest coupled with supervised work at their work center. Sentences can be suspended if the individual shows improvement. (For text and discussion of the law see *Granma Weekly Review*, Mar. 28, 1971, p. 2. Also see Lowry Nelson, *Cuba: The Measure of a Revolution* (Minneapolis: University of Minnesota Press, 1972), pp. 121–26.)

they were short of personnel. He scolded me for having walked out on them, so I said, "I'll go there next week to see whether they'll take me back."

Esperanza and I live together but we aren't happy. I knew from the very first that I wouldn't be happy, yet I chose her with my eyes open. I don't want to belittle Esperanza. She's a good woman and quite well-behaved and polite. Not that she ever went to school or anything—what she's learned, she's learned from her own mistakes and hard knocks. Anyway, she knows how to get along with people. But it seems to me that she must have some mental difficulty—she's so very reserved. She often does things behind my back and that makes me angry, though she's affectionate enough—really I'm the one who's harsh—and she does respect me. Lack of respect would upset me even more than lack of love or understanding.

Esperanza and I share our lives to a certain extent but not with the understanding and actions I'd like. I've sacrificed my own feelings and that's no lie, for I've never been understood. That's what I've always longed for. Even if my women haven't loved me, if there could at least have been mutual understanding between us! I think two people who understand each other for twenty years are happier than a couple who love each other for five. That's the truth as I see it and that's why I say it's better to have understanding than passion.

A man's heart is practically like a guitar—only the one who knows how to play it can understand it. The strings are very sensitive and I, too, am sensitive and a bit melancholy. There are certain times of the year when I'm overcome with sadness. This melancholy of mine is my perdition. It's going to destroy me one of these days.

Esperanza is twenty-eight and she makes demands on me because she's young. She's a hot woman, but even so she can't behave correctly in bed. I know there are people who consider that a black woman's organism is hotter than a white woman's. But I know from experience that a white woman may be as ardent in love as a black or a *mulata*. You can't judge a woman's passion or coldness by the color of her skin.

I've never mentioned Esperanza's color to her. On the contrary, she's the one, poor thing, who often says to me, "When all's said and done, I know I'm black and sooner or later we're going to break up because of that." Maybe it's her woman's vanity that makes her think so, to explain to herself a certain lack of love and sexual attraction that she notices in me.

The conditions at home make it difficult, often impossible, to fulfill my physical needs. How can a man go to bed with his wife while children swarm all over the place? But I've never taken Esperanza to a *posada* or a hotel. No. How could I do such a thing to a woman with whom I've established a home? No matter how much a man needs a woman he can't take his wife to such a place. That would be an awfully low-down thing to do.

We manage to have intercourse at home in the daytime when the children are away at school, although we have visitors practically every day. We have to take care to lock the doors. A man gets tired of it and that's the truth. All those things kill love. Under such conditions, who could help being disillusioned and feeling that he isn't attracted to his wife? Then, when we have sex, afterward I start thinking that it's only a kind of duty the wife must perform for her husband, or a way of playing up to him.

To tell the truth, my girl friend, Hermelinda, helps me a lot. She's thirty-two years old, white, and much prettier than Esperanza. She has a better figure and better manners too. She behaves so well, she's so charming . . . she has all those virtues and yet in the sex act she's easy. Before you've done much to her she's already practically through.

Hermelinda works for MINCIN.[57] I only see her now and then because she usually has to work when I have my day off. Sometimes, though, she manages to exchange shifts with another woman, and then I rent a car and take a room in a *posada* for half a day.

I feel it's shameful to take her to such places but what else can I do? She lives with her mother and sisters in Poey. They know nothing of her affair with me, so there's no way I could be with her there. I could take her to a hotel instead of a *posada,* but at a hotel you have to request a room for a specific number of days or weeks. Besides, some *posadas* provide more comforts than many hotels do. The one we go to, for example, has some rooms with air-conditioning, telephone, and radio. Of course you pay extra for that. A room with air-conditioning costs 2.50 *pesos* for two hours. If you'll settle for a room with just the bed and a mirror it will cost you 1.60 *pesos.*

Like everything else, you may have to wait in line for a room, but if you go at 2:00 P.M. you don't have much trouble. They ask to see your *carnet*[58] and I always show mine, but Hermelinda registers under an assumed name. There really is no reason to deny her real name, but we do in case something unusual should happen that might get her in trouble.

Esperanza has no suspicion of the affair, but one night I went out without telling her where I was going and she got jealous. When I got home late she started to quarrel. She has her fits of jealousy but I never pay any attention to them. I simply say to her, "All right, if you think I'm doing anything like that, go ahead and think it. That's your problem." I lie down on my mattress on the floor and listen to her go on and on.

57. *Ministerio de Comercio Interior* (Ministry of Domestic Trade).
58. Worker's identification card.

There's a lot to be taken into account when you have an affair. I feel I should be very careful and discreet and not upset Esperanza for no reason at all. You see, Hermelinda has made many propositions to me, but I'm too grateful to my wife to leave her. It's not the children that stop me. They're no problem, because if I ever fell so much in love with another woman that I wanted to leave Esperanza, it would not in the least affect my children. I'd never in the world deprive them of the money I earn in order to keep someone else. No, it's not the children, it's gratitude to Esperanza. She has stuck with me through thick and thin and I'm grateful to her. That's about all that binds us together now.

No, I don't love Esperanza. What irony! The word "love" means a great deal to those who are not loved, and nothing to those who are. Love is a brief illusion. Today you fall in love, tomorrow you have children, and you may have an affectionate wife, but there is always some one thing that keeps you from saying, "I'm happy." I believe that happiness doesn't exist except for just an hour or a day. After that there's nothing but destruction and pain.

God knows if someday I'll be happy. Life has never been good to me. For every day of peace and joy I've had ten or twelve of sorrow and pain. A heart that has suffered too much and taken many blows from life can never be a happy one. I live with the memory of my sad and painful past, and whoever lives on memories lives in torture. Maybe some wounds heal with the passing years, but I think my wounds can only be cured by death.

Sometimes I think, "Why should one make so many sacrifices to live? If you die you go to your eternal rest and never again have to worry about anything." But when I look at my children and think of their love for me, my courage to keep on struggling is renewed. Many times I think, "*Coño*, if only Marta were alive to see what she longed for." It was her dream, as well as mine, to see the children going forward as we walked behind.

The one happiness I've prayed for from above, if something exists there, is that I see my youngest grow to be twelve or thirteen and able to fend for herself. My ambition for the children is that they have the opportunity to attain their goals and choose careers according to their ability. My eldest son, Manolito, is now ten going on eleven and is doing quite well in school. He's got a good head, that boy—he's alert and quick-witted. Only in the fifth grade and already he's interested in book-learning and medicine. Twice he's been promoted to a higher grade in the middle of the school year, and so has Omarito.

Omarito is nine and he's in fourth grade. Manolo is more clever and mentally wide-awake than his brother. Not that Omarito is less intelligent or stupid in school, but in everyday things he's quiter and more reserved. Manolito even moves more quickly than Omarito.

The girls, Marilola, who is eight, and Delmira, six, are also in school, but Marilola is backward. She should at least be in the third grade, not in the second as she is. The others are still too young to be in school.

Not one of our children is as dark-skinned as Esperanza. All my children, Manolito, Omarito, Alfredo, Eufrasio, and Angela, are lighter than I. Esperanza's two girls, Marilola and Delmira, are darker and have features which degenerate toward their mother's side of the family. As far as hair goes, only Eufrasio's degenerates toward Esperanza's. The rest of them have good hair like mine.

For Omarito and Manolito, their *papá* is everything. They're indifferent to their mother and are interested only in their father, just as I was. As for me, I want and pray only to be granted the joy of seeing all my children grown. That's the one thing that could bring me satisfaction and happiness.

I have nothing but praise for what the Revolution has done in the field of education, and I say so with no political passion whatsoever. Before the Revolution there were maybe 10,000 or at the very most 20,000 in school. Children were generally neglected. I'd say about 99 percent of them were completely without care or supervision. All that has changed. Nowadays children are looked after, and the teachers like the kids, too. At any rate, we have no complaints of any kind against our kids' teachers. There are more than 300,000 students studying on scholarships that provide them with tuition, three meals a day, clothing, and a place in a dormitory.[59] Now you have to sharpen your pencil to figure out how much it costs the state to take care of all those youngsters.

Medical services, too, have improved by about 50 percent since the Revolution. The government has built a world of hospitals and they're building still more. They're handsome buildings, too, and very practical. All the polyclinics and hospitals are integrated.

Everything has its pluses and minuses, and I agree with the Revolution in some of its aspects but by no means in all. I used to read many books that make the whole revolutionary process sound very pretty. Yes, but I'm a realist, a man who has his feet on the ground, and I idealize nothing, absolutely nothing. I myself have lived through good and bad. I've seen that some people are born to ease and plenty, and for them life is a wonderful gift because they've been spared pain and hardship. They've never had to break their heads trying to solve insoluble prob-

59. K. S. Karol states that in October, 1968, there were 244,718 scholarship students and 160,818 semi-boarding students. (*Guerrillas in Power*, p. 596.) The highest government figure we have seen on the number of full scholarship students in that same period is 185,932. (*Atlas Nacional de Cuba* (Havana, 1970), p. 114.) This compares to 1974 figures of 332,900 boarding-school students and 318,400 semi-boarding-school students. (Fidel Castro, quoted in *Granma Weekly Review*, Dec. 15, 1974, p. 2.)

lems, their cheeks have never grown hot with the shame of poverty, their flesh has never been crushed in the grip of pain. To them life is a garden of roses. But I've seen others who have lived in bitterness and suffering, and to whom life is nothing but a ball of shit.

I used to feel that way myself. I'd say to myself, "Life is only a ball of shit and you must put up with it and live as best you can." The way I saw it, all we suffered, all the tears we wept, and all the foolish troubles we bore were in vain. Sooner or later it was all over. No man is a seed that springs into life after he's buried. Often, very often, I'd say to myself, "What's the use of living when your life is nothing but suffering? Better not to have been born at all, better to die."

I had good reason to think that—things my own mother did to me, things that have happened to me. But I kept on struggling for a less strained, more restful, peaceful kind of life. I must live for the future because that's where my children's welfare lies. I don't matter. I'm a withering tree that rots and decays with the passage of the years, but I want a future for my children. After that, let death come and put an end to me.

I've analyzed not only my own life but the lives of others. I've known people from the low, middle, and upper classes of society. I've seen as much meanness and hypocrisy among the lower as among the upper classes. In the upper class, a man who has thousands of *pesos* strives for millions. In the lower class, those who have nothing want everything. Before the Revolution each looked out for himself. People were willing to sacrifice themselves for the sake of their own comfort or their own aggrandizement, and more often than not they ended up destroying themselves.

In those days I lived with a veil before my eyes. I didn't have any exact idea of the different paths one can take in life; now I do, because the Revolution made me face a new panorama. Now I analyze the condition of the country as a whole, my own needs and the needs of others, and my eyes have been opened. I've come to think that it's better to work for the collectivity. Today people struggle and make sacrifices with a collective end in view. In a collectivity like Buena Ventura, where there are 200 families, we're all united, and it seems to me we live more serenely, more at peace with each other, with better mutual understanding, than before.

I have great hopes that my children can expect more than the children of Las Yaguas did. Our future in Cuba will be quite different from our past. Our society will be fair and equal, though we still have a long way to go. Then we in the fatherland will set an example to countries in Europe and Latin America whose people live in worse poverty than we had here in Cuba. Already in Cuba money no longer rules. No, that's dead and past here, and in a way I think that's good. Men cannot have the same ambition to have such great sums of money—today things are very different. Oh, I still have my unmet needs, but let's leave those out of it because now we're working for the future. Of course, sometimes I have my doubts. Who knows what the future really holds? But maybe this new political structure will indeed completely change our country's destiny.

PART III

Nicolás Salazar Fernández

Chapter One

Papá's Burden

I WAS BORN IN LAS YAGUAS on September 19, 1938. It was an immense barrio, crowded with a lot of shacks of *yaguas,* tin, and tarpaper. One section was called Havana and another Matanzas. Matanzas was on low ground, down by the river, and was muddier than Havana. It didn't have any public water taps; you had to cross the river to Havana for a pail of water. People in Matanzas were worse off, more screwed up—"the ones who came last," they were called. They came from slums like Cueva del Humo and Isla de Pinos, or from the country. They had no houses and no place to stay, so they got materials and built right in the middle of the mud-hole, at the foot of Loma del Burro.

There were few legitimate businesses in Matanzas, but liquor was sold everyplace—in grocery stores, from stands—and you could find forbidden gambling games. At around 7:00 at night, people would flock in to drink and gamble. Some houses had four gambling tables inside and three outside, with four or five people at each table. Gambling was sure profitable and the owners of gambling joints were well off. Gabino, the barber, ran domino tables, and the Alonso family had a cockpit in their house and also tables where they played for money. Those people lived in cement houses with cement floors, and they had chairs. Some even lived outside the barrio. Their clothes and shoes were better than anybody else's and money always jingled in their pockets.

The Havana section was easier to get around in. It had more problems, though, with so many people crowded together, rubbing shoulders and always getting in each other's way. Many people came there just to shop. In the center, on Havana Street, there were a lot of stores—Joaquín's grocery, the bar, which was open until 10:00 at night, Naran-

Nicolás Salazar's life story is based upon 1,034 pages of material gathered in twenty interviews, one of which was conducted by Oscar Lewis and the remainder by the Cuban assistant Rafael Salinas Madrigal. Flora Mir Monte was interviewed six times by Elsa Barreras López and once by Oscar Lewis, for a total of 326 pages. Salazar's mother was interviewed once by Oscar Lewis.

jo's grocery, Benito's fritter stand, Santana's stand where he sold *café con leche* and crackers. There were also the charcoal store, the Chinese grocery, the Cuban grocery, and Montojo's grocery. Besides food, the grocery stores sold lamps, shoes, and so on. If you wanted to pawn or sell a piece of jewelry, they were the ones to go to. Where we lived, in upper Guillén, near the Manuel Pruna exit of the Havana section, the only store was Chelo's little stand, where he sold candy, soft drinks, and coffee.

The best store in the barrio was Joaquín's. He was a man with a conscience and was loved and respected by all. You could tell him, "Look, Joaquín. I'm broke. My kids are sick and hungry."

"All right," he'd answer. "If you have a piece of jewelry or anything else you can leave to guarantee a loan—a pair of shoes or pants—I can let you have 20 or 30 *pesos* or whatever you need."

I could get a pair of shoes from him just by saying, "Look, Joaquín, my shoes are so worn that my feet drag in the dirt. I need to buy a pair on credit. I'll pay you later."

"Take the shoes," he'd tell me. "They're worth 1.50."

Joaquín would even give *papá* credit when he went there without a *kilo* on him. Joaquín would let him have 4 pounds of rice or lard and write it all down, and as soon as *papá* had money, he paid him.

The storekeepers of the barrio lived well. Many of them, like Montojo, had stores in their homes. Others had separate houses, like Toledo, the owner of the little bar, and Santana. Those people had frigidaires and everything. A guy who owned two businesses, a grocery and a restaurant, near the entrance to Las Yaguas, even had a tile floor. He kept his restaurant in very good condition, with tables and all.

The house *papá* bought in Guillén was nothing but a tarpaper-and-lath shack with a tin roof and a dirt floor. He reinforced it with wood and divided it into two parts. I slept in one little room on a folding cot, with my older brother Juan. *Mamá,* my old man, my little brother Ernesto, and the baby, Alvilino, slept in a large bed in the other room. Later *papá* built a wooden platform in the kitchen for all of us boys to sleep on.

Other people had electricity but we didn't. An electric meter cost 3 *pesos* a month, even if all you had was a light bulb and no radio or anything. At that price we didn't want it.

A woman called Lilia, whose husband worked in the telephone company, lived nearby. Another neighbor was the seamstress Basilia, who owned a sewing machine. Next door to *papá*'s side of the house lived Miguelito and his family. I don't know if his wife was a prostitute, but he'd turned their place into a whorehouse. He kept a bed in the parlor and set up chairs and stools outside. People sat around waiting to get in.

Behind our house, right across from the window of our room, was old Fish Head's shack. He also kept a whorehouse and was robbed several times by the women who came there with men. Farther up in Guillén, near the exit, a man named Pablo had built several houses and divided them into tiny rooms. That was a whorehouse, too.

Many prostitutes came down to the barrio or they lived there. You could see them sitting in front of the houses after 5:00 in the evening, waiting for customers. Sometimes a man would show up with a bottle of rum, and after a few drinks he'd rent a room from Fish Head or Miguelito or Pablo for 80 *kilos*. The women charged 1 *peso* for their trouble, but by 1956 some young, good-looking ones charged 2 and even 3 *pesos*. A fat woman of forty charged less.

I also knew a lot of pimps. The pimps posed as the girl's husband and were always fighting. One of the Alonso boys had a little *mulata* hustling for him. He was real mean to her and beat her when she didn't bring him money. The pimps never worked and spent their time playing dominoes and baccarat. They also sold marijuana. People in the barrio smoked it as if it were tobacco, and outsiders came in to buy it. Sometimes four or five fellows got together and smoked it right in front of our door. "No, gentlemen, you can't smoke that stuff here," I'd tell them. "If the police should happen to come by and find you, they'd arrest me too."

I'd been told that marijuana carried you right out of yourself, that it made you feel up in the clouds as if you were somebody real big. But *papá* always said, "Don't smoke that stuff. It will either give you the lung sickness or make you insane." One day, a fellow I knew in the barrio was smoking it and he said, "Here, have a drag and see if you like it."

I said, "No, not me!" But I took two or three puffs anyway. "*Chico*," I said, "I've heard this stuff makes you feel different but I don't feel a thing," and I gave it back to him. Perhaps it was poor-quality marijuana. They often mixed it with common grass and sold it as pure. That was the first and last time I tried marijuana.

The pushers didn't exactly lead peaceful lives, not that the neighbors interfered with them, but now and then the *delegados*, the police in civilian clothes, raided the barrio looking for them. They'd drive up and run along the streets of Matanzas, where the domino tables were, shooting their guns and attacking anybody around. A fellow might be standing peacefully on the street corner and he'd be challenged: "What are you doing here? Do you live in the barrio?"

"Sure. I live up that way."

"Where do you work?"

"Well, I . . ." and *pam!* they'd punch him in the face or kick his shins and run on. Maybe they'd arrest him just for the hell of it. Whenever I heard shots, I got scared and ran.

The pimps and pushers often fought among themselves. Once a man with a razor ran into the wake for Lino Ortíz Paseiro's little brother. A wounded man, bleeding and with no shirt on, chased him right through the parlor, out the back door, and straight up the hill behind. The guests got out of the house and the relatives of the dead child tried to catch the one with the razor. Then the guy with all the razor cuts walked away. People offered to take him to the hospital, but he said, "No, no. I'll go alone." With about fifty razor cuts on his body! Later on they caught the guy who did it.

When I was about twenty, a fire once brought the cops down. I was on my way home at about 6:00 A.M. when I heard people yelling, "Fire! Fire! Fire!" I went and called *papá*, "Listen, there's a fire down there."

He said, "We know about the fire but it can't reach us; it's way down where those thirty-seven little shacks are."

Instead of going to bed, I went to see the fire. By that time it was pretty well under control. A fire truck had arrived, also a police captain, a lieutenant fireman, and so on. But the wooden shacks had turned to ashes. The police were asking everybody how the fire had started, but nobody was giving any explanations. I took off fast. I thought, "Better go while the going's good, before they get me involved in this." Later they gave 30 *pesos* each to the people who lost their homes. That was enough to buy or rent another shack from the barrio mayor or the supervisor. But some had to stay with relatives until a house became vacant.

There were many quarrels among the women in the barrio about whose turn it was at the water tap, and about everything else. The young girls made fun of the old people who passed by, and threw things at them. They'd yell and scream and curse and tear each other's clothes while people crowded around to laugh and see the show.

Many fights would develop whenever there were religious fiestas, like when someone became a *santero* or when *El Palo* members were going to "mark" someone. I don't know much about the *Palo* sect, but when a person is going to join, they mark his back with several stripes. And to find out something about him, if he's a queer or a bad son or a bad father, someone calls out, "Does anyone here know so-and-so?" Then someone jumps up and says, "Yes, I know him from way back, he's a such-and-such, he did this, he did that. . . ." Because they say you can't belong to this religion if you're effeminate, or not a good father or a good friend. So the quarrels and fights began, because sometimes the one who wanted to join came with four or five friends, armed with knives and razors. Then the barrio supervisor, Pérez, would show up and mix in the tangle, hitting out with his sword, breaking it up and throwing them all out.

Once in a while a fiesta went peacefully. They'd beat on drums and dance till long after midnight. A lot of people hung around, even non-believers, because they served food, beer, and soft drinks. A few stayed out of curiosity. I just kept away.

When a believer made a *fiesta de santo*, they'd also beat drums, and women danced in the street. The one who was making the *santo* had to pay for everything—the animals, the cocks, the meal ... and there had to be food for all who came. It was really hard for such poor people to scrape up so much cash. But if a *santero* told them to bring down a *santo* for the sake of their health or well-being, they'd sacrifice themselves and scrimp to do it.

The fact is, *santería* and spiritism were the strongest religions in Las Yaguas. The tools and iron kettles from their rites could be bought anywhere. There was a colored woman, the *mamá* of a family we called "the family of the saints," who was a *santera*. She made a *fiesta de santo* and after that she dressed all in white. There was a tamale vendor who had also brought down a *santo* and wore white. Whether they were real *santeros* or fakes I don't know, but they all lived by exploiting others. I knew them by sight, but I had nothing to do with them.

We lived next to a certain footpath which *papá* told us not to go on. "It's the pathway of sorcery," he said. We were always finding dark *kilos* scattered about there, or a bunch of bananas tied with a red ribbon. "Don't eat those bananas, piss on them," *papá* would say, because the urine would kill whatever power they had. So we'd urinate and *papá* would cover his left hand with paper and pick them up and throw them away. He said his left hand wouldn't receive any of the evil but his right hand would. We never ate anything they left but after we urinated on the money we took it to buy candy.

I never mixed into *santería* or any of those things, and really, neither did *papá*. He didn't take us to *santeros* or spiritists when we got sick so they could pass their hand over us, or make the sign of the cross with a twig of sweet basil, or anything like that. It wasn't until I was older that I found out they put powders in the doorway of a house and do cleansings with chickens and doves and then throw them where the other person will step on them.

My *papá*, Juan Tomás Salazar, was a peon, an unskilled laborer with no trade. He was a car washer and chauffeur at the Portocarrero garage. Then, under Grau's administration, he did different jobs for Public Works and in private construction. *Papá* went to school but only through the second grade. He can barely read and all he can write is his own name. Like *papá*, *mamá* grew up in the country, in Matanzas, but she can't read or write at all. She just stayed home and looked after us four kids. She'd put us into wooden boxes to keep us from running out to the street.

The only one in *mamá*'s family who's had a bit of schooling is her sister Emelina, who lives in Cantel as a tenant worker in an agave rope factory.

After the Revolution, the factory was taken over and re-named for a martyr. The tenants used to pay 9 *pesos* a month to live there; now they own the place.

I never met *mamá*'s parents—I don't even know her mother's name—but once *mamá* took me to visit Aunt Emelina and I asked about their father. I knew he'd died at the age of sixty-eight, blind and begging for charity in the streets. My aunt showed me his photo hanging on the wall. "That's Mateo Fernández, your grandfather," she said. He was the image of a hard-working peon, short and rugged, with the round shoulders of a man who'd labored long in a stooping position. He wore rough work clothes and a country man's straw hat. He must have worked in the sugar cane, hoeing and planting and cutting.

Mamá told me that my grandfather had also worked in the rope factory, cutting the agave and laying it out to dry. Grandpa could always get jobs there for himself and his daughters because so many of their friends worked there. *Mamá* worked in the factory as a young girl and earned 1 *peso* or 1.25 a day.

Papá's father also died before I was born but *papá* told me all about him. He was a *guajiro* and worked for *colonos*[1] at low wages all his life. But he liked country life and enjoyed work—in fact, he couldn't sit still a minute. He'd throw his tools into a sack and go from farm to farm looking for work. He took *papá* with him and they'd follow the sugar harvest from province to province, planting, plowing, hoeing, and cutting cane. They worked for four to seven months, depending on the length of the season. When *papá*'s brothers were older, they too had to go off to earn money for food, clothes, and medicine. They must have been awfully poor if they had to leave Grandma Eulalia alone for such long periods.

During the "dead season," when there was no work in the cane fields, Grandpa worked building boats in a shop at the docks of Matanzas, or he'd make furniture at home. He could read and write and he even learned about decimals and metric measurements from his carpentering.

Papá was very young and didn't have a regular job when his father died of a heart attack, so he went to Havana, where his sister Dora lived in a *solar*. My Aunt Dora was the janitor there and she also took in laundry. Through her, *papá* was able to rent an apartment for his mother in *reparto* Aranguren, and he got a job in the city to help support her.

Grandma Eulalia had only worked as a washerwoman for soldiers and laborers, but she taught *papá* to print his name when he was little and

---

1. Sugar-cane farmers; refers to all cane growers whether they owned or rented their farms (*colonias*).

kept him practicing till he got the hang of it. She was very devout. She made her children cross themselves and pray before meals and before going to bed. She had an altar at home for the *Virgen de la Caridad del Cobre,* the special saint of her devotion. She never talked to us about religion but she practiced it right in her house by setting glasses of water and sunflowers on the altar.

When I was eight or nine, *papá* visited Grandma almost every two weeks because she was a sick woman. Her legs were swollen from varicose veins. She walked very little and hardly talked, but she'd want to know what we kids were up to and if we were sick or well. When *papá* said, "All right, kids, let's go call on the old lady," we'd happily rush to get dressed. Grandma always sat in an old-fashioned cane rocking chair, and whenever we came she looked happy to see us. *Papá* would ask her, "Well, old lady, how are you?" Then he'd tell us, "Kiss your grandmother."

"Yes, come up close, children," she'd say, and lift us to her lap and play with us. She usually had candy and cookies and she gave us pennies that she kept tied in a handkerchief. "Here," she'd say, "so you can buy candy after you leave." After a while we'd run out and play, or we'd visit Uncle Emerio, who lived down the hall. He'd play with us and give us money too.

Papá would sometimes go across the street to San Antonio's pastry shop, where they'd give him a big bag of broken left-over sponge cake and he'd bring it back for us. Like all kids we loved getting sweets and being away from home, especially because Grandma's apartment had cement walls and a floor and her neighborhood was so different from Las Yaguas. But it wasn't just the cake or the place. We were truly fond of Grandma, and it was so nice to be with her that we could hardly tear ourselves away. We'd kiss her goodbye, then she'd give *papá* all kinds of instructions: "Take good care of the kids; don't let them get wet; be sure you get home early." When *mamá* left us, Grandma gave him even more advice, though she died not long after that.

Mamá and *papá* had a lot of quarrels and I never knew why. But *papá* told me what provoked their break. One day he was calmly reading the newspaper when *mamá,* without any reason at all, walked up to him, slapped his face, snatched the newspaper out of his hand, and threw it away. That did it. *Mamá* says that when she and *papá* got into an argument, he'd hit her. He did, but always because of something *mamá* did, never for the hell of it. *Mamá* had a habit of setting the kettle of food on the floor and *papá* didn't like that. It also bothered him when she put her hand into the food or left dirty clothes scattered around.

The truth is *mamá* had been carrying on an affair with Antonio, a stonemason in the barrio, and she finally took off with him. When *papá* was out, Antonio would come and say to *mamá,* "Don't be a fool, Ana, come live with me. That man's too rough with you. I have a room of my own and can support you with my trade. With me you won't have such a hard time." He kept it up until he convinced her to leave us.

Papá had words with Antonio more than once after that and Antonio told him, "You mistreat that woman. It isn't right when she's borne you so many children and has such a hard time." But *papá* didn't want to give up *mamá* after sixteen years. For all their fights, it never entered his head to leave her. He even went to a *santero,* who told him to put a little bird in a cage and do a job on it to get *mamá* back. *Papá* did everything and paid good money but it did no good. He saw he'd been deceived and lost the hope he had.

We'd sneak over to see *mamá* when *papá* left us alone at home. "Try to visit me when Antonio is out," *mamá* told us. "If there's a bite of food in the house, I'll give it to you." If Antonio saw us he'd get mad and scold her and try to pick a quarrel with me. He claimed I went to try to get her to break with him. But she never asked Antonio to bring her to see us, or bought us clothes or gave us food.

One time—it may have been after Ramona, my stepmother, moved in—*papá* sent the four of us to live with *mamá*. It was raining and we got there sopping wet, but *mamá* turned us all away, except Alvilino. She didn't want to do it. With the tears running down her cheeks, she told us, "I don't give the orders in this house and Antonio doesn't want you here." *Papá* and Antonio quarreled about that and *papá* said, "She's the boys' mother. It's up to her, not me, to look after them."

"Well, I can't have them in my house, it's too small and there isn't room for them," Antonio objected. But the argument never got beyond that and *papá* took us home. Alvilino stayed because *mamá* wanted him, but he broke out in a rash and refused to eat, and *papá* went and got him, too.

I was young and innocent then and really didn't understand things, but I thought it was wrong for my parents to separate over a quarrel— and after living together so long! I also felt very bad about having a stepmother and stepfather, but especially about *mamá* not wanting us. When a woman leaves her husband for another man, the first thing she should say to him is, "I have children. If there's no room for them in your house, there's no room for me."

The same thing happened to *mamá*'s daughters by her first husband, David. She had left him because he wouldn't give her anything and she worked until she took up with *papá*. When *papá* decided to go to Havana, *mamá* wanted to bring along the girls, who were nine and ten. David refused, *mamá* cried, and *papá* and David had a big argument. *Papá* insisted the mother had the right to the daughters. In the end, *mamá* left them behind in Matanzas and didn't bother with them for years.

Mamá's trouble is that she doesn't have a will of her own and has never been able to run her own life. She drifts wherever the current carries her. Ever since she took off with Antonio, he's had her under his thumb. When they first got together, Antonio worked and took care of her. Later he quit his trade and began living off her while he mended shoes and did odd jobs at home. I don't mean that *mamá* ever had to go out with men to get money. Not that I know of, anyway. She always managed because she had many friends in Luyanó and one day she'd wash somewhere, another day she'd starch or iron somewhere else. So he depended on her.

No matter what *mamá* is, she's still my mother. We have a saying: "Though she be like vinegar, a mother is always a mother." She's the one who bears the child and stays with him when her husband goes to work or to have some fun. My *mamá* hasn't shown a mother's love for me, but I love her anyway and so do my brothers. Before she left *papá* she made plenty of sacrifices for us. A woman who's borne a child and gone to a thousand troubles for him and stayed with him until he's seven or eight years old has done enough. There's nothing worse than having to wipe a baby's bottom, feed him when he doesn't want to eat, and rush with him to the doctor when he's sick.

A stepmother is not the same. Mine never bothered about me. When I had a feverish cold, she'd come into my room and ask, "What's wrong with you? Are you sick?" That's all. I had to tell her, "I'm sick, Ramona, could you make me a cup of coffee?" or "Could you prepare some herb tea for me?" I even had to ask her to tell *papá* I was sick so he'd come in and see me, otherwise she wouldn't mention it.

I'm fonder of *papá* than *mamá* and feel closer to him. For many years he ran with us to the doctor and never abandoned or neglected us. He was a good father—he struggled to raise us, cooked our meals, washed our clothes, gave us good advice, and played with us. He got us clothes, even if it was only one pair of shorts and one pair of shoes. I remember how he took us to La Cueva del Humo, to the house of an old guy called Sergio who sold secondhand clothes, and got three or four pairs of boys' pants and a pair of shoes for 40 or 50 *centavos*. He pushed in wherever he could get food for us and we never had to go hungry. But sometimes we had to wait to eat supper until 10:00 at night, when he got home from work.

On Christmas *papá* couldn't even afford to buy food for Christmas Eve supper. Some people came around giving out boxes of food or tickets to go to the police station or store to get food. The police supervisor went from house to house giving tickets according to how many were in the family. *Papá* would get two tickets. Every family in Las Yaguas got a box or two packed with pork, rice, black beans, nougat, sweets, grapes, and 1 *peso* to buy condiments. It was no feast—we had no wine or beer, but at least we had something to eat.

There weren't many Days of the Three Kings we celebrated either. To us it was just another day. I knew what the Kings were and I also knew that my *papá* couldn't buy presents for us. If we got a toy it was something old that someone gave him. At Aunt Dora's house we'd get a ball or some little trifle she saved for us. The only toys I ever had were balls, bats, and little trucks. On the Day of the Three Kings my brothers and I would play with other kids' toys.

We were scared of *papá* because if a neighbor complained that we'd been throwing stones or broken something or if we played in the dirt and messed up our clothes, he'd hit us hard with a belt—barbarously hard. If we got into any kind of mischief, broke a glass, wrinkled the bedclothes after the bed was made, or peed inside the house, he'd say, "I've told you not to do that, go out into the yard!" and he'd whale the daylights out of us. He was kind of brutal.

Papá's a changed personality now—just the opposite—he even plays with his little daughters. I've never understood why, but that man was never as bad-tempered with Ramona as he was with my *mamá*. *Mamá* says, "It's a fact, Juan Tomás has sure changed. He does whatever that woman tells him to. He was really different with me." *Mamá* always had to do as he said, but now *papá* mostly does what Ramona wants. He may say no once or twice but then he gives in. Not that Ramona throws tantrums or browbeats him. No, she just goes ahead and does as she pleases.

Mamá never punished us when we were little. She'd threaten us and say, "Calm down, kids. If you don't stop right this minute, I'll tell Juan Tomás when he comes home." But she never did. I was lively and mischievous and often played tricks, like hiding from *papá* when he wanted me. I was always out in the street playing with Ernesto and two kids, Rubén and Victor, called "the twins." Their parents were very strict and really brought those boys up right.

We played tricks on El Chino, who had a restaurant on our street. We'd grab the corners of a tablecloth and pull, then run when El Chino came at us, mad as hell. Or when we rented a bike, we'd upset people's baskets full of stuff and pedal off as fast as we could. We'd also go into the Cafeteria América, three or four of us, and order candy. Then we'd argue about who'd pay until the storekeeper was confused and we'd run away. He'd rush out, "Stop them! Grab them!" But we scattered and ran in different directions until we shook him off. Actually, the owner let us have the candy for the fun of seeing us run away. We played the same trick at the bread and pastry shop.

We could even get into the movie theaters without paying. When I wanted to see a picture I'd say to the other kids, "Well, gentlemen, let's go to the movies!"

"Yeah? What'll we do for money?"

"Never mind about that. Just watch me. When I go in, everybody follow me."

The doorman would be standing next to that thing where they throw the used tickets and we'd hang around watching him, pretending to look at the posters. The minute he turned his head away, one of us would say, "Let's go." But the usher usually saw us and followed us in. He'd search for us with his flashlight and we'd hide under the seats or in the men's room. Most of the time they caught us and put us out, but it was so much fun we kept right on doing it.

We never got into mischief with girls or anything like that. Only boys played out in the street and all we thought about were movies, candy, and bathing along the Malecón.

Through a politician named Valdéz, *papá* applied for scholarships for Ernesto and me to study at the Colonia Hershey. It was a boarding school for children whose parents had political pull. In return, *papá* had to hand over his identification card to the politician, to assure him *papá*'s vote if any elections were held. Through bigger politicians than himself, Valdéz got the scholarship for us.

Papá sent Ernesto and me to study because we were the cleverest and most wide-awake of the lot, and he hoped that sometime we'd be of use to him. With us in boarding school his burden was lightened. I was very happy to go because I expected it to be nice. It turned out we *were* much better off there because every single day we had breakfast, lunch, and dinner, even a mid-afternoon snack. At home we ate only once a day.

The boys' and girls' barracks at the Colonia Hershey were divided by a street, with boys on the left and girls on the right. The wooden barracks were very well made and had tile roofs. We had canvas cots to nap in at siesta time and everyone had his own iron bed with a blanket, a sheet, a pillow, and a cotton quilt to cover the springs. Between every two beds was a cabinet with one shelf for each boy.

We rose at 7:00 in the morning, made the beds, and were taken down to breakfast. Then they marched us to the classrooms in formation, by company, with a teacher leading each company. The teachers always had rulers in their hands. Our teacher waited for us at the door of the classroom and gave us a notebook and pencil before class started.

The first things they taught were the alphabet, arithmetic, Spanish, and history—how Columbus came to Cuba and so on. We really didn't get much of an education. Classes were over for the day around 10:30 A.M. We went to lunch, then sat around in a park for half an hour; it was forbidden to leave the paved square. We were taken to the barracks for a nap and had to lie on our backs, face up, the whole time. If we drew up our legs or lay on our sides or stomach, the teacher in charge would strike us with a ruler or a long cane. We slept until 2:00 P.M., when we had a snack of cold milk, sweets, or a soft drink. Around 3:00 they'd take us out, sometimes to play ball, to ride on the merry-go-round, or to play on the seesaw and the slide, or just to run around.

Next we were taken to the workshops, where we had a choice of carpentry or ceramics. I chose carpentry and learned to make toys, doll houses, and knickknacks. In the girls' workshops they learned to cut and sew, embroider, and do other kinds of manual work.

Five of us sat at each table for dinner and were served a dish of rice and a bowl of soup. The teacher pointed out the kid whose turn it was to serve, and he would rise and serve the rest. We each had a fork, knife, and spoon and were taught to use them. We weren't allowed to eat with our hands, or put our mouths to our plates, and we had to be careful not to spill things. The table was cleared by the boy who served and he was expected to leave it clean and neat.

Discipline at the *colonia* was very strict, and any boy who acted up or got impertinent was hit with a ruler. They'd also make us kneel on scattered grains of corn with our arms held straight out at right angles. I was struck only once in school, when I raised my knees at nap time. The teacher was on me like a flash and hit me on the thigh with a ruler, saying, "Get those legs down!"

Sunday was visiting day, but in the six months we were there, *papá* only came to see us three times and he never once brought us a gift. We had everything we needed, but other fathers brought their sons gifts, and even if it isn't something big, a fellow likes to get a gift when he's away from his family. On Sundays, when we heard the boys called, one by one, through the loudspeaker, it made us sad that everyone else had visitors. I'd say to my brother, "I guess *papá* isn't coming to see us this Sunday. Just look at what time it is and our old man hasn't come yet." You can imagine how sad and disappointed we were.

I remember the first time he visited us. We were out in the yard when someone told us, "Your father is here to see you." And there was *papá*, hat in hand. We sat beside him and he asked how we were, how they treated us at school, and whether we liked it there. Then he said, "Don't go running away now. If you do, I can't bring you back here. Behave yourselves."

I liked living at the school and I think it did a lot for me because I learned the rules of good deportment, correct grammar, respect for my elders, not to say bad words, to brush my teeth instead of just rinsing out my mouth, to comb my hair in the morning, to put on my shoes and clothes by myself. We had to leave school when the government changed hands because the politician Valdéz was out and we lost our right to the scholarships. That ended our chance to study. At least we completed the second grade.

The situation at home was very bad when Ernesto and I were at school. *Papá* was working twelve or fourteen hours a day and earning only about 2 *pesos* a day. Often as not, when he went to pick up his wages they refused to pay him. But at least he did have a job. In 1948 he lost his job and from then on he began to beg alms. He was about forty-seven years old and he kept on begging until 1959.

Now and then *papá* did odd jobs, like carrying things in his handcart from the marketplace to Joaquín the grocer, and Joaquín would give him 2 or 3 *pesos* or some rice or beans. But it wasn't steady work and he had to go on begging. What else could he do with no job and four children to support? It wasn't that he wanted to beg, but there was no other way out. Right now if I should find myself unemployed, unable to get another job, and with two or three kids to support, I'd go to anybody to beg a bit of food for them.

So that people would take pity and give them something to eat, he'd take Alvilino and Juan from house to house, knock on the door, and say, "I came to see if you could help me with a bit of food or something." Then they'd drop the food in an empty can he carried, give him a shirt or a pair of pants or 20 or 30 *centavos*. He kept on until he had 2 or 3 *pesos*. If it got late, he'd sit down on the curb at a park or anyplace, heat two or three cans of Spanish sausage he carried in a sack, and feed my brothers with a spoon he brought along.

When I was about ten, I'd go out with him too, but I was ashamed and always stayed outside the fence when he went into a house. He'd tell me, "Go in," but I hung back. I simply wasn't made for begging, and when I refused to beg he'd spank me.

Sometimes when *papá* took us into a café to get a drink of water, the man there would take in the picture we made in our old, secondhand shoes, patched, ragged shorts, and mended shirts and give one of us a *peseta* and the other a half-*peso*. We never went barefoot, because when our shoes wore out, *papá* would have a talk with Joaquín. Besides, *papá* was often given old shoes at the houses where he begged and he mended them with some shoemaker's tools he had.

When we kids were a bit older, *papá* sent us out to beg alone. *Papá* would tell me, "Go up to that house with your older brother and knock on the door."

"No, no, I can't!" And he'd slap me a couple of times and threaten, "Just wait till we get home, then I'll hit you really hard!" My brother Juan would go alone and *papá* would say, "Try to be like Juanito. He isn't ashamed to beg. See, today he got over 1 *peso*. You and Ernesto are two little shit-eaters. Just see how people give things to Juanito." When we returned home, I got spanked again.

Little Alvilino also found it easy and would hang around and act cute until people were sorry for him and gave him a *peseta*. But Ernesto and I were too embarrassed and we refused. I had this fear, shame . . . this terror of everything. I'd think, "*Coño*, suppose they kick me out?" Being a little kid, I never really stopped to think whether begging was a good or bad thing. I only said, "No, *papá*, I won't beg."

Papá would threaten us, "If you kids don't beg, you'll get no dinner."

"I don't want any," I'd say. He fed us all right, but Juan was given better food. Ernesto and I never asked people for money, but sometimes they'd be sorry for us and give us a *peseta,* a half-*peso,* or even a whole *peso. Papá* would snatch it away and I'd protest, "It's mine, they gave it to me."

"You've no right to have money of your own. They gave it to you because you're with me. I'm the beggar. You did nothing to deserve it. Juanito can keep his money because he helps me."

One day we were out begging and I got 30 or 40 *kilos. Papá* took us to a cheap Chinese restaurant at Teresa Blanco and Luyanó and told me, "We can all eat with that money."

"I'm not hungry and I'm not going to pay for anybody's dinner," I answered. "I want that money for the movies. It's *my* money!"

Papá took off his belt and said, "Either you go in and eat or I'll kill you right here." He took my money and struck me several times across the back with his belt. Then a policeman came and said, "Hey you, don't hit that kid so hard!"

"That's none of your business, he's my son. What's it to you if I whip him? If I killed him it would still be none of your business!" *Papá* made me go into the restaurant, but I just sat there without eating, though my back was covered with welts. I really cried that day. It was only right that he whaled me because I disobeyed him but I wasn't bad enough for him to hit me that hard.

The next morning I slipped out of the house and went to *mamá*'s. I told her what my old man had done to me and showed her my back. She put rubbing alcohol on it, lamenting, "What a savage Juan Tomás is. To beat you up like that just because you didn't want to eat!" Then my stepfather Antonio caught sight of *papá* coming down the street to get me, and he and *mamá* went out to talk to him. Antonio said, "*Chico,* that's no way to spank a child."

"That's none of your business," *papá* answered angrily. "I'm the one raising those kids and I'm responsible for them. If he doesn't eat, it's my son, not yours, who will starve to death."

Antonio said, "All right, do as you please. I won't interfere." But he told me, "He won't spank you now that I've talked to him."

Then *mamá* said, "You're too rough with the kids, Juan Tomás. Don't hit them so hard. If Antonio had a bigger house, the kids would be with me." *Mamá* and Antonio were both polite to *papá* because they knew he took us along wherever he went and took care of us. I mean, *mamá* couldn't make any demands on him because he was being father and mother to us.

Papá said to me, "I'm not going to spank you now. Why should I? I already did." When we got home he put rubbing alcohol on my bruises too and said, "You don't have to go telling Antonio or anybody else what

I do to you. I'm your father and I'm the one who's raising you. What I do to you is none of Antonio's business."

One day when I was about eleven, *papá* said to me and Ernesto, "You boys are pretty big now so it's up to you to do something to help out. I'm out of a job and you boys do nothing but bother me and sneak out of the house to raise hell. Next thing I know, I'll get in trouble with the neighbors. I'm going to prepare two shoeshine boxes so you can go out and earn some money. When you come home, you must give me what you've earned so I can buy you shoes, clothes, and whatever else you need."

But before I gave our old man the money, I always hid 1 *peso* for candy and movies on Sunday, because the most he ever left us was 1 *real* or, at the very most, 1 *peseta*. He'd often have to spank me before I'd hand over the money I earned. My brother Ernesto was different. If he only made 1 *peso*, he'd hand over his whole day's earnings before *papá* even asked for it. Ernesto won *papá* over that way, and that's why *papá* was fonder of him than of me. If *papá* was given only one pair of boys' pants, it was always for Ernesto. If he was given two pairs, Ernesto would get the best one. That's something I had to accept. But I didn't understand it.

My stepmother preferred Ernesto too, because he never interfered with her. I was always butting in and finding fault with everything she did. She resented my good advice. I'd tell her, "You should stay home, not go out with *papá*. You should send your kids to school. . . ." She'd wash out Ernesto's socks or shorts and never do it for me. Even *mamá* made a bigger fuss over Ernesto when she stayed with us, and worried when he was late from work. "*Mamá*, stop worrying. Ernesto is safe," I'd tell her.

"But it's so late and he isn't home yet. Just look at the time!"

"He's at work and he's better off than I am."

"But he's so young and something might happen to him out in the street, poor kid." Not that she wasn't nice to me. As long as she lived in my house, she'd wash my clothes and look after me, but she really felt more for Ernesto. I guess I was jealous of him.

As for Juan, I never minded when he was treated well or held up to me as an example. I felt sorry for him and tried to help him, because he was mentally retarded, abnormal from birth. When Juanito was little, he lived for a time with his godparents, then with Aunt Dora. She noticed that he was slow and quiet and didn't like to hang around with people. He was a loner. When we went out begging, he'd hang back and walk alone. Sometimes he stayed away from home for days and *papá* would tell us, "Go look for Juanito. How come he didn't come back with you?" We'd find him sitting on the curb somewhere, picking up cigarette butts and bits of paper. Juan liked to smoke but he wouldn't spend a *peseta* on cigarettes or a piece of candy or a movie. That's why *papá* let him hold on to his money and also because whenever *papá* needed money, Juan gave it to him. *Papá* says Juanito has always treated him best, that Juanito and Ernesto have given him the most money and are his best sons. He says I've been the least good to him.

Ernesto and I got along well. We never quarreled about money because when we left the house we'd agree, "Let's go to such-and-such a place in Havana today and shine shoes until we've earned such-and-such an amount. Then we'll come back home." The only thing that bothered Ernesto was to have me take his things or borrow his clothes, though we never had serious quarrels, we just argued. But no matter what he said, when I didn't have a clean pair of pants I'd take one of his.

The life of a shoeshine boy was hard in every way. There were a lot of other shoeshine boys to compete with and the cops wouldn't allow us to go into tourist bars, the only places we could hope to make some money. The waiters would throw us out. But it was the cops I was really scared of. They carried whips and they'd hit us with them. Many's the time we got whipped out of the bars and restaurants near the docks, where we hung around waiting for the American sailors, our best-paying customers. Some would give us 25-*centavo* pieces, others gave 40 *centavos;* that's why we all wanted to go there, even if it meant getting hit. We'd also go around to Galiano, by the América cinema, the cafeteria, and the bakery. Then we'd turn the corner into San Lázaro and down Obispo Street to the post office, where we shined the high boots of the telegraph company messengers. We charged them 25 *centavos* for a shine and they paid us at the end of the week.

Some things we did out in the street were fun. Shoeshine boys went around in groups of three or four. I and my group, Arturo Sedano, Celiano Medina, and Ernesto, would sometimes go bathing along the Malecón and in the swimming pools that admitted us. Mostly, though, my memories of that time are unpleasant. Just getting something to eat was a problem. I never took along food, so I'd have to wait until I earned enough to go to some cheap Chinese restaurant. I and the other guys would sit down, but the owner wouldn't serve us because he thought we wouldn't pay. Lots of boys did that, see; they'd eat, then run out. My group never played such tricks but the owner avoided us just the same.

There were nights we had to sleep away from home, hungry, because we hadn't earned a *centavo*. Our old man would scold or spank us because he thought we spent the money on candy and trifles. So we'd pick out a store or building with an open hall, spread cardboard on the floor, and sleep there with our clothes and shoes on. Some nights the police chased us away and we'd have to find another store to sleep in. Then the cop from that block would show up, kick us out, and we'd look for another place. When we saw one of those shiny blue-and-white cars coming our way, we'd run.

One night a patrol car drove by and a policeman made us get in. They drove us to the old Fifth Precinct station on La Zanja. There another cop said to us, "You've been charged with sleeping in doorways, hanging from the back of moving buses, throwing stones, and doing mischief in several stores. You'll have to wait till the captain gets here and decides what to do with you." And we hadn't done anything except lie down in a hallway to sleep!

At 5:00 in the morning the captain showed up. "Ah, so you're the little gang that hangs around Galiano and Prado bothering people, no? Well, you know you're going to be sent to Torrens, don't you?"

Torrens was a reformatory for minors. It was divided into Old Torrens and New Torrens. The cops told us anybody who made trouble would be sent to Old Torrens. That's where the worst delinquents were sent and they were beaten, locked up in a cell, and all that. Most of them were over seventeen and eighteen years old and we were only twelve and thirteen and would never be able to defend ourselves against them.

We were sent to New Torrens for a few months. We were terribly mistreated there because those delinquents were the kind who turn on you in a gang, with their fists, or with a knife or any handy weapon. The gangs were always on the watch to lift anything somebody else left around. We were told, "You can't keep anything here—if you have something, be careful or it will get stolen." They'd snatch away from the weaker boys whatever their folks brought—candy, money, or anything. Some of the tough boys had knives, others made sharp instruments. Those guys would stick a knife into you or cut you with a razor without a second thought. Sometimes they even killed.

Those things made it very hard to live among them and we hated to be locked up in there. Arturo and Celiano, who went in when we did, joined Ernesto and me and we formed our own gang to defend ourselves in case a fight started. We tried to stick together as much as possible. We were scared to death in that place.

The reformatory kept us very busy from 7:00 in the morning on. Until 10:00 we had classes, but we didn't learn a thing because we were so terrified and anxious to get out. At 10:00 they'd take us to the patio and distribute hoes and three-pronged rakes for us to work on the grounds. They worked us very hard compared to the Colonia Hershey. Anybody who didn't work had to stay inside the pavilion and was forbidden to have visitors. My brother and I never refused to work. I always followed orders.

Those in charge didn't treat us at all well. We were expected to keep discipline at the *colonia,* but it was completely different from Torrens. Here the rules were very strict and discipline was the main thing. We couldn't talk while in formation and we had to march in and out of the pavilion. The beds had to be made up neatly and be exactly in line with each other. Clothes had to be neatly put away in the cabinet. No talk was allowed at mealtimes. If you talked, you got hit with a ruler and had to stand up till the end of the meal. The food was good only on Saturdays and Sundays. The rest of the week they'd give us rice, soup without salt, and vegetables. Sometimes we'd have only the boiled vegetables. The servings were so small, just one little round aluminum plateful, and an even smaller bowl of soup.

Smoking was absolutely forbidden. If they caught a boy with a cigarette, they'd hit him with a ruler and punish him by locking him in a cell where he had to stand up most of the day. At mealtimes they'd push his food in under the bars and some of the boys would get mad and throw it down without eating. I was never sent to that kind of cell, but when I passed by I could see other boys inside. They had no shirts or shoes and there was an iron bed stuck fast in the concrete floor, with only the bare springs to lie on.

My friends and I tried to behave well, but it was difficult to avoid getting beaten and punished in such a place. I'll never forget the day the four of us were caught talking in formation. We were all taken to the end of the pavilion and locked together in a cell for almost the whole day. What a horrible place, with nowhere to sit or lie down, not even a single bench, nothing. It measured 4 by 4 meters, had iron bars on every side, and the door was padlocked. That day I thought a lot about home and the freedom of the street. How different it was at home with *papá*, and me wandering at will around the barrio!

On visiting days the boys would gather in the street lobby of an enormous theater. That's where the parents visited their sons. Most of the time nobody came to see my gang. My old man seldom came, and in all the time we were there *mamá* never showed up once. For one thing, she didn't know how to go anywhere by bus, and Antonio wouldn't let her go out alone. Besides, *papá* didn't bother to tell her we were in Torrens so *mamá* found out from a neighbor.

You see, *papá* didn't want us to grow close to her any more than Antonio did. *Papá* went out of his way to keep us apart from *mamá* and he'd often say, "Your *mamá* is a shameless woman who abandoned you to go live with another man, then kicked you out of her house when you went there. You'd be pretty shameless yourselves if you wanted to see her. Forget about her, pretend you don't have a mother. I'm both mother and father to you boys. I, your *papá*, am rearing you." *Papá* always harped on that.

But we weren't shameless. We just wanted to keep in touch with our old lady. It wasn't her fault she couldn't take a bus without getting lost, because she's illiterate and none too smart. But I've heard that she'd cry for us and *papá* wouldn't tell her anything. During those six months, Ernesto and I were awfully homesick and heartbroken because we had no visitors.

At the end of our term, in 1951, Dr. Irma Celeya, the lady director of Torrens, realizing we had committed no fault and broken no law, had us transferred to the Casa de Beneficencia. Of all the institutions I've been in, the Beneficencia was the best. There we had classes at night, the food was the best we ever had, and so were the beds. They gave us everything—a blue uniform, one pair of white pants with a blue stripe down the sides, two pullover jackets, two white shirts, and a khaki army shirt. No one hit us, and when they scolded, they did it gently.

In the afternoon we were taken outside on the grounds to play. I learned to play soccer and basketball. At 5:00 or 6:00 P.M. we were taken to the social center to watch movie cartoons or play games. They had sets of checkers, dominoes, parcheesi, and Chinese checkers. Sometimes I'd play checkers or watch others play games and so pass the time.

Boys who behaved themselves in class and in the dining room were given weekend passes and could stay home from Saturday until early Monday morning. Out on a pass, Ernesto and I paid a call on *mamá*, and sometimes our old man would take us to Aunt Dora's or Aunt Teresa and Uncle Fabio's. Afterward we'd go to the movies.

On Sundays when we didn't have passes, we'd be taken to the church at the entrance to Beneficencia for Confession and prayer. We didn't have regular classes until the second year, and the whole first year were taught nothing but religion. I had a hard time learning the catechism because you have to get it all by heart, and when I made a mistake, *pam!* they'd hit me with the ruler and say, "Read it again and keep at it until you know it word for word." My brother and I learned the catechism, the *Pater Noster,* and the *Ave María* thoroughly.

We made our First Communion dressed in white pants and a white pullover. I was very scared because I didn't know what making one's First Communion was. I thought the wafer was something they stuck in your mouth that made it swell up. When the priest tried to lay it on my tongue, I turned my head aside and burst into tears. "But my son," the priest said, "this won't hurt you. It's soft and smooth. Open your mouth." I swallowed the wafer, still sobbing. A nun noticed how nervous I was when we left the church and told me, "Calm down, that didn't hurt you. It only means that before you were not a son of God and now you are."

In honor of our First Communion we were excused from military drill. They said, "Go play in the park if you like."

I went to church often after that because I liked to feast my eyes on the colors of the walls and altars. It was pleasant to see the priest lift the chalice high, then cross himself and ring his hand bell.

On Thursday nights at Beneficencia a movie was shown. Chairs were lined up on either side of the room with a passage in the middle. On one side sat the boys and on the other the girls. I was about fourteen and already felt a man's vigor and desired the female sex. So when the lights were out, I'd sneak over to talk to Nereida Quesada, my first sweetheart. We never even got a chance to kiss, and just talking was a risky undertaking. If we'd been caught, we'd have gotten a good scolding.

Everything there was so strictly supervised, even masturbation was a problem. The toilets had no doors and there was always a corporal at the entrance. Two boys were not allowed to go into a bathroom together. When one went in, the other had to get out immediately. The showers were divided by panels but they had no doors either. So I could only masturbate on Saturdays when I went out on a pass. I'd go into a toilet, or get into the self-service elevator of a building and stop at any floor. Then I'd masturbate into a piece of paper I carried.

I left Beneficencia during my second year and was on the streets of Las Yaguas shining shoes again. Then *papá* sold our house and we moved out of Las Yaguas to a small plot of land my uncle gave him. It was there that my youngest brother, Alvilino, was killed. It happened because my stepmother refused to stay home with the younger children, even though *papá* asked her to. She said, "I'm going with you. I won't stay alone in this dark place." I was on my way with Ernesto to Obispo, to shine shoes. Juan was there too. I was about fourteen, Ernesto must have been about thirteen, and Alvilino was six. We all set off, using a kerosene lamp because we lived very far from downtown, near *reparto* Solita, in a grove of mango and avocado trees. It was still dark and really scary. *Papá* was carrying Carlita, leading Alvilino with his free hand, and Genaro was clinging to his pants legs. My stepmother held the hands of the other boy and girl.

We were standing by the side of the road, waiting to cross over, when the bus for La Purísima Concepción Hospital stopped. Alvilino slipped away from *papá* and started to run across the street. It was on a hill and the street had only a very thin coating of asphalt over the granite. Alvilino's shoes had been patched by *papá* with pieces from another old pair, and there was no rubber on the heels. He slipped and fell in a sitting position. Just then a bus came from behind the parked one, knocked him flat, and drove its front and back wheels over his head. He was torn to pieces. It was a horrible sight.

Papá threw himself on the traffic policeman, snatched his revolver, and tried to shoot the driver with it. My stepmother stood there nervously and the kids yelled. But the accident wasn't the fault of the driver. It was the kid's own carelessness that caused it. When the Red Cross came they spread a sheet over the body, which was lying in a pool of clotted blood.

At the Díaz-Sierra Funeral Home, where they took the body and held the wake, the bus driver went up to *papá* and wept as he talked with him. *Papá* adored that child and the man knew it. "Leave it to me," he said to *papá*, "I'll take care of all the expenses." He knew *papá* was a poor man, unemployed, with nine people to support. The driver's relatives were upset too. They offered *papá* money but he refused it. So they bought a wreath for the funeral and paid for the funeral car. They begged *papá* not to press charges because the driver was the father of a family and was very sorry for what had happened.

For a long time after Alvilino's death *papá* was not himself. It affected him deeply. My relatives felt bad when they came to visit, to find *papá* taking things so hard, refusing to eat... in torment. He blamed my stepmother. "You see, Ramona," he said, "if you'd stayed home as I wanted, this wouldn't have happened." I also blamed my stepmother: "It's your fault I lost my brother. If you had only minded *papá* and stayed home. But no, you always have to be chasing after him!" Ramona admitted it, too. "Yes, it was me, it was me. I know it's my fault."

Ramona became awfully nervous and claimed she saw the ghosts of Alvilino and others. The darkness of the place terrified her, and she insisted on moving away. To please her, *papá* moved back to Las Yaguas.

Chapter Two

Struggling Along

WHEN WE MOVED BACK to Las Yaguas I was sixteen, already a young man, but I had no knowledge of life, no experience. I lacked discipline at home. *Papá* let me go my own way and I went astray. I was shy, easily embarrassed. I felt so ignorant that I kept to myself. I couldn't talk with people as easily as I do now. I'd sit all alone and think of the sad picture my father and the rest of us made.

I found it very hard to get a steady job. My brother Ernesto was different. He got a job as a waiter at the Concordia café on the Calzada de Luyanó. Nestor, the owner, would see him go by with his shoeshine box and got to like him, because Ernesto ran errands for him and helped around the place. One day they offered my brother a job and he accepted. They paid him 40 *pesos* a month, and sometimes he slept there.

Instead of looking for work, I'd go to the market at 5:30 or 6:00 in the morning, when the trucks were unloading. I'd take along an empty sack and fill it with food that fell to the ground—three or four bananas, plantains, tubers. Then I'd get a bone in the meat market or they'd give me a fish head, and none of this cost me a thing. I didn't have 1 *kilo* to spend, not even for the bus, and I'd walk all the way home. I'd give the food to my stepmother and she'd make me soup, which was my lunch and dinner.

Sometimes I couldn't find anything to eat. I'd go hungry all day long. But when Ramona and *papá* came home from begging he'd tell her not to feed me.

"He's a big boy now, yet he won't work," *papá* would say. "I wonder when he'll quit stalling and find a job."

"But *papá*, couldn't I have just a little bit of food?"

My stepmother would butt in, "No, don't give him anything. He doesn't want to work. He's grown up now. Let him get a job."

Once in a while *papá* said, "But these are my children."

"Your children! You're always talking about your children. And what have they ever done for you? Look at this son of yours—big as he is, he doesn't work for a living. What do you mean to do, support him all his life?" *Papá* didn't answer and he didn't give me any food either.

So I'd shut myself up in my room and cry. Lalo, who lived across the way, would tell me, "Don't cry. That screws up your nerves something terrible. Come on over. If I can find a bite of food, I'll give it to you."

Lalo was our nearest neighbor. He lived in a house with a kitchen, parlor, and one bedroom, all with dirt floors. He was a bottle-seller and his wife, Daria, took in laundry to help him out. Lalo was hard up because he had so many kids. They had credit at Joaquín's store, and when business picked up they'd pay him. Business was very bad then, and Lalo had sunk as low as the floor. So he told me, "I can't offer you a job or give you as much as a bite of food either." But we struck a bargain. Sometimes I'd run errands for him, other times I'd look after his little kids, and he taught me the bottle trade. I'd go out with his handcart and help him buy and sell bottles. For that, Lalo paid me 2 *pesetas,* 3, whatever he could afford. I'd use it for the merry-go-round, or to go to the cinema. I was still very fond of movies.

One day Lalo said, "Look, kid, things are bad. As you know, the bottle business has its ups and downs. I can't keep on feeding you, much less give you money, when there are days I don't earn enough to feed my own family." By then I was seventeen, so I began to search for other ways to support myself. Some of my friends in the barrio were car washers. They'd call me and say, "Here's a car to wash. Do it and I'll give you 80 *kilos.*" Humberto, a friend of *papá*'s, had a small coffee shop where he sold *café con leche* at 7 *kilos* a cup, and bread and butter at 5 *kilos*. Now and then he'd call me to help him, and he'd pay me 1 *peso,* 8 *reales,* or whatever he wanted.

Things were really tough in the 1950s. As we say, "The street was very hard." There got to be quite a group of us who substituted for patients waiting in line at the Hijas de Galicia Clinic. They'd give us their number cards, pay us a *peso,* and we'd hold their places in line while they went home for a good night's sleep. In the morning they'd pick up the cards. There were often quarrels about whose turn it was, and the directors of the clinic asked to have two policemen assigned to keep order. One day they checked everybody's cards. We all said we were there visiting sick relatives, because if we'd said we were being paid to wait in line, we'd have been clapped in jail.

One time I was in the clinic cafeteria with a bunch of guys, just having *café con leche* and talking, when the two policemen, Córdoba and "the Axe," walked in and shouted, "All right, stay where you are everybody! Don't any of you dare make a move!" I stayed where I was. They began searching me and questioning the guys sitting at the counter.

"Where do you work?"

"Well, I. . . ." *Pra!* a blow. I slipped out, plenty scared. Outside the people were yelling, "Beat it, the *delegados!* Go that way! Go this way!"

Another time, around 11:00 P.M., I was sitting alone in the Concordia café, waiting for Ernesto. Then I saw Córdoba's Dodge drive up and stop at the café. The police got out and started hitting everyone with rubber clubs, the kind we call "ox's prick." Everybody ran, scattering this way and that. I saw Córdoba coming at me and I stood up and put my hands behind my back. "What are you doing here at this time of night?" he asked.

"Waiting for my brother to get through working so I can see him home."

"Don't you know it's against the law to be sitting in a commercial establishment after hours?" said he, swinging the rubber club. I started running before he finished talking and headed for the barrio.

I was tired of being pushed around and having no steady job. I had no decent clothes, my stomach was always empty, and I had dark circles under my eyes. I asked a tailor, a friend of mine who lived near us, "*Chico,* what can I do? I want a job but I can't get one. I just haven't had my brother's good luck."

He said, "Go to Abelardo's restaurant here in the barrio and tell him I sent you. Even if he can't pay you, at least you'll get your meals there and you won't go to bed hungry the way you've been doing. Just look at you!"

Abelardo told me, "I can't pay much but I can give you your meals and 10 or 12 *pesos* a month, maybe as much as 15 when I have a lot of customers. But that's all I can do for you." I accepted because at least my meals were a sure thing.

I worked at Abelardo's, on and off, until he had to close down for lack of customers. There I learned how to serve customers at the counter, to dish out food, and so on. I also emptied out the dirty dishwater and got fresh water from the public faucets, because the restaurant had no running water. I made seven trips a day to fill the tanks of the restaurant and of Abelardo's house. I was only nineteen then, in the full flush of my youth and strong as a mule.

One day I was on my way to Abelardo's when my *mamá* came crying and complaining that Antonio was too demanding and forever picking on her. He'd forbidden her to visit some neighbors and accused her of having an affair with the man of the house. But the real reason Antonio objected was that the neighbors told *mamá,* "Don't be a fool, why should you break your back working? A woman like you with grown sons!" They pointed out how Antonio mistreated her, carping and criticizing, and taking the few *kilos* she earned. He'd fight with her if she bought herself candy or a soft drink. Those people were opening *mamá*'s eyes.

"Well," I told her, "if you're fed up with Antonio, bring your clothes over here. You're welcome to stay with us." So she moved into the room with us boys.

A few days later Antonio began to hang around the house. "They've gone and put a bug in Ana's ear after she's lived all these years with me and I've been so good to her," he'd say out loud.

"Look, *mamá*, just let him talk. He'll get tired," I said. I urged her to go with me to Matanzas so I could meet my half-sisters, Meira and Eugenia, and we left. My sisters were glad *mamá* was separated from Antonio because neither they nor anyone else liked him. They advised her, "Look, *mamá*, an old lady like you shouldn't have to go out and work."

When we got back to Las Yaguas, *mamá* stayed on with me and I brought her food from Abelardo's. Since I wasn't earning much, she got a job as a laundress and ate lunch at her employer's house. She'd go out in the morning and be back at 1:00 or 2:00 in the afternoon. On wash days they paid her 2 *pesos*, and when she ironed it was 3 *pesos*.

"This little job will help you make ends meet," I told her. "Buy yourself clothes or anything you need." But when she got paid she tried to give me the money. "That's yours, *mamá*, keep it," I said.

"No, no," she protested. "When I was with Antonio he was the one who managed the money."

"So what? Antonio isn't here. That's your money and you can do as you like with it. You can buy yourself as much soda pop as you want now." A month later she went back to him.

At the age of nineteen I still hadn't known a woman sexually. At Abelardo's restaurant I met a guy called Roger who was a waiter there. He said, "I'm going to take you to a place where there are good-looking dames to be had for 1 *peso*." He bought a couple of condoms and handed me one, saying, "When you begin, put this on." But I didn't know how to put it on. The truth is, it was the first I'd ever seen.

In Guarina the women would stand at the doorways in the alley. There were no rooms. When they got a man, the couple would go into a small park, the woman would lift her skirt, and they'd have relations quickly, standing up. When we got there Roger said, "Pick out the one you like."

A stout *mulata* came and asked if I was looking for a woman. "Yes," I said.

"First time I ever saw you around here," she said.

"Yes, I've never done this in my life."

"Well, well!" says she. "Come, I'll teach you how to do it."

She led me into the park, but when she got in position I told her, "Wait, there's something I want to put on first." I fumbled around with the condom and she said, "You don't know how; I'll put it on for you." So she got my member to stand up and slipped the cap on it. Then she turned around with her back to me, grasped my member, and introduced it into her parts, just like that.

I just stood there and the woman said, "Move, kid, move. Praise be! Your friend is almost through and you haven't even begun. Goodness, you're turning out to be expensive for me."

In the midst of all this a police patrol drove by. One of the cops said, "We're coming to pick up the cock."

"Come back later," the woman called.

They turned off the headlights and left, but after that interruption I couldn't manage to get going. I was so upset I lost my erection and that damned cap fell off. What the hell. I picked it up, wrapped it in a piece of paper, and stuck it in my pocket. As we left, Roger asked me, "Did you manage to do it, kid?"

"No, I couldn't do a thing. She started quarreling with me and got me all confused. But at least I still have the cap to use next time."

"Hell no, kid! Throw it away. Once you've used one of those it's no good anymore."

Another time, I went alone to Atarés at about 10:00 at night. I walked around and found a tall, slender *mulata* who called, "Hey, young fellow, come here!" You're looking for a woman to lie with, aren't you? How much can you pay me?"

"All I have is 80 *kilos*."

"No matter," said she. "With you I'll have the cross made today. Just don't tell anybody you paid me only 80 *kilos*, because if you do I'll have to charge everybody else the same."

She took me to a room, undressed, and said, "Take off your clothes too."

I stripped down to my undershorts, then I lay down beside her on the bed. She herself got it hooked up in her and started to move, giving me instructions all the time. "See, you move this way and that. Kiss me here . . . now here. Touch my breasts." I was so jittery I couldn't even touch her breasts. I had an erection but much good it did me! All of a sudden I came.

"*Muchacho*, so quickly!" she exclaimed. Afterward she said, "Whenever you feel like it, come here and ask for Amelia—that's me. Everybody here knows me."

By the time I was twenty I'd gained a lot of experience and knew more about life. When I went out with a woman, I was clever enough to play the trick of holding back instead of coming right away. I learned that from the other fellows. "Don't be a fool," they said. "You have to pay 1 or 2 *pesos* for it, so get your money's worth. Don't let yourself come the minute you get into a woman. Get all the enjoyment you can."

To keep from coming too soon I'd think about my job or anything in the world except the woman I was with. I'd flop down on the bed and I'd let her push and pull and move but I wouldn't come. The woman would say, "What's wrong with you? A young fellow like you, why don't you come?"

"Yeah, that's right," I'd say, but I'd hold back. I'd take it out and stick it in again, and when I thought I'd been there long enough, then and only then I'd let go, and *bang,* I'd come.

While I was working at Abelardo's restaurant, I met Vera, a woman of the world who sometimes went there to eat. She was nineteen or twenty, not pretty but not homely either. She was slim, not very tall, with chestnut hair and big brown eyes. Her right arm was smaller than her left and sort of dried out, a defect she'd had from birth. But that didn't keep her from working. She could wash, iron, and cook.

It was Abelardo who pointed out that Vera liked me. "It looks as if that girl wants to be friends with you or something, the way she smiles at you and wants you to wait on her," he said. At first I paid no attention to her, then we talked and got to be friendly. One day we ran into each other on the street. She told me about the two children she had by a man who beat her and mistreated her. She had no home, not even a place to sleep, and had to spend most nights at a whorehouse.

I had a room of my own in Las Yaguas by then, and I suggested she go live with me. It was no secret to me that she was a prostitute, but I thought she would settle down and live a normal life. She spent that very night in my room. Next morning I introduced her to my old man. We lived together over two years.

I don't think Vera particularly liked me or wanted a man but she needed a place where she could cook, eat, and take a bath, and I didn't have much experience and wanted a woman. I knew she wasn't perfect but that only made me sorry for her. I thought I could change her, and after a time I got fond of her.

From Vera I learned what a woman is really like and how to treat her. I mean I got to know deeply the ways of a married woman. She taught me to wash after having sex. She also got me to take off all my clothes, saying, "We're husband and wife, why should you be embarrassed?" She knew a lot about sex. She'd say, "Lie down on top of me and move like this and like that." Sometimes we'd lie on our sides and do it like that. She taught me to tickle her and kiss her ears and neck. But she didn't like to be sucked. When I sucked on her neck she'd get out of bed, mad, and go out in the street. She wouldn't let me suck her tits either, because she claimed that makes them loose and flabby. Later on, I did those things with other women.

Every day Vera would cook and clean the house. By 5:00 in the after-noon she was bathed, dressed, and ready to walk the streets. Before she left, she sometimes gave me money for carfare, cigarettes, or whatever. Other times, if I needed a *peso* or so, she'd refuse, so I'd sneak it from her purse. She'd pout and get mad and insult me. "Why did you go and do that? You should have asked me. You have your money and I have mine. I never ask for 1 *centavo* of your money for anything."

"Well, I needed it so I took it," I'd answer. "If you like, I can pay you back later."

But whore that she was, she never asked me for a *peso* and she bought food for both of us. She'd stop by the clinic, invite me down to the cafeteria, and pay for my *café con leche* or my breakfast. I really didn't need much money then. If I worked a night at the clinic, I'd have enough money to eat and 2 or 3 *pesos* in my pocket.

Even so, I wanted her to stay home and quit walking the streets. The very morning after she moved in, I told her, "I expect my women to look after me, take care of the house, wash my clothes, and cook. I don't care about your having been a woman of the streets, but *chica*, you can quit now, can't you?"

"No," she said, "I can't. I'm used to drinking beer and listening to jukebox music and dancing. I can't live without those things anymore."

"I won't ask you to quit all of a sudden, then. You'll lose your taste for that kind of life little by little, so all I ask now is that you be home by midnight." I warned her that she'd have to sleep outside if she was late. "I'd rather have no woman than one who spends all her time in the street." But she'd come back late, bringing me a *maltina* or a sandwich or some little gift, and sweet-talk me into letting her in. Next day she'd beg me to let her go out, promising to come home early, and I'd always give in.

After a while I noticed that when I wanted sex, Vera would satisfy me just to get it over and get rid of me. "Not that way," I'd tell her. "You aren't doing this like a woman who's enjoying herself."

"Hurry up, come!" she'd say.

That would get me angry. I'd say, "You wait till I'm good and ready. I'm not one of your clients." After that, three or four days would go by without our having sex. Then she'd tell me, "All right, I won't get drunk tomorrow and I'll do my best to come home early." She'd get back before midnight, sober and happy, and do her duty by me.

Sometimes she stayed out two or three days at a time and there I'd be, worrying my head off. Once she and some other streetwalkers got caught in a police raid. For a month I didn't know where she was, except that people said she must be in jail. When she came back she looked thinner and her hair was cut short. She complained, "There I was, in jail, and you didn't even come to see me or try to find out where I was. You say you love me—some love!"

Well of course I didn't try to find out! I knew that if I went to the police station investigating, they'd clap me into jail as her pimp.

That day I gave it to her straight. "Here you are making me act like a pimp," I told her. "If you must be a whore, at least don't peddle your wares in the barrio. Go hustle if you must, but if I catch you at it here in Las Yaguas you and I are going to quarrel." Hell, I had nothing to do with pimps and was embarrassed to look like one.

"I've never said you were a pimp. You're my husband. I help you out because I want to," she said.

"Some help! If you really wanted to be nice to me, you'd quit hustling."

"No, no, not that. I get bored staying home." I guess that was true, because she walked the streets when she was married to her former husband too. She just wanted her life to be one long fiesta—with plenty of money—a real woman of the gay world.

Many times *papá* said to me, "That woman is not good for you. She's a common whore."

"I'm trying to reform her," I'd answer.

"Well, that's your business," he'd say. The neighbors, too, all told me to leave her. "Here you are, playing the part of a pimp, and that's not right because you aren't one. You're just looking for trouble. If they catch you, you could go to jail."

I guess I was too soft with Vera. She was running around like a crazy cunt, coming home when she felt like it, and I let her get away with it. I should have told her from the start, "It's the streets or me." But she knew I wouldn't beat her or force her to do anything, so she took advantage of me, played me for a fool, and did as she damn well pleased.

One morning I woke up and she still wasn't home. I made a heap of her clothes in the yard, poured a bottle of alcohol over them, and set them on fire. About 3:00 that afternoon she showed up. "Are you mad at me?" she asked.

"No, I'm only asking you one thing, get out and stay out!"

"All right, I'll just go in to get my clothes."

"See that heap of ashes? Those are your clothes."

She burst into tears. "How could you do that to me?" That very same day she moved out.

I wanted to be a waiter like my brother Ernesto, so I went to see Luciano Ramos, the owner of a little coffee shop. I told him I needed a start at a café and offered to do any work for whatever he could pay. He accepted and started right in teaching me. "Look," he'd say, "this is the way to serve *café con leche.*" He showed me how to make coffee with two different coffee-makers, the *Royal* and the *Nacional.* He also taught me to make sandwiches and how to wait on a customer. On Saturday or Sunday he'd ask, "Do you have any money?"

"No."

"Take this *peso* so you can go to the movies" or "Take these 2 *pesos.*" I didn't earn fixed wages because I was still learning. Sometimes he gave me a shirt or a pair of pants. They were always too large because he was so fat. I'd save up money, *kilo* by *kilo*, until I had enough to have the clothes altered by the tailor who lived near me. "I know you have no money so I'll only charge 1 *peso*, although an alteration is worth more," he'd say. Then he'd cut the clothes down. I was always neatly and decently dressed.

After I'd worked three months for Luciano, I told my brother I'd like to work where he did and learn more about serving in a cafeteria and bar. I wanted to know about mixing drinks and so on. Ernesto spoke to Nestor, the owner of the Concordia café. He didn't object to my working there. But if he'd known Ernesto and I were from Las Yaguas, with the reputation the place had, he wouldn't have kept us on. Just hearing we were from there was enough to make a man's hair stand on end. There was a lot of talk about people from Las Yaguas stealing on the job. No matter how honest you were, they all thought you'd dip your fist into the cashbox or take things. Any guy from Las Yaguas was bad, a delinquent, because that was where the worst scum of Havana found its way.

If I admitted where I was from, people would say, "From Las Yaguas, ugh! How come you, who are so young, live in that barrio of indigents?" And they wouldn't want to have anything to do with me. Things like that made me ashamed. So we lied to Nestor and told him we were from the country.

In spite of all handicaps, I started making some headway. Nestor gave me the job of dishwasher and paid me 25 *pesos* plus my meals. I also learned about waiting on tables. I had to remember what dishes were being served each day and what they cost. I learned to add up accounts without using pencil and paper. I got to be very quick at it and rarely made a mistake. I stayed there until I got a job at a cafeteria on Ensenada, but it didn't last long because the owner went bankrupt.

Early one morning Carlos Marrero, a *guajiro* who lived in the barrio, said, "Come along with me, I'll teach you to buy and sell flowers. Afterward you can go out with me and carry a flower basket." We set out by bus for the gardens at Cuatro Caminos, where they grew gladiolas and all kinds of roses, and we brought back big bunches wrapped in paper. We'd arrange them in baskets and at 8:00 or 9:00 o'clock we were ready to go out and sell them. By 1:00 or 2:00 in the afternoon we were finished. For that half-day's work Marrero gave me 2 or 3 *pesos* and paid for my lunch, cigarettes, and coffee. He also paid for the flowers, the baskets, and other expenses.

When the flower business dropped off, Marrero told me, "Look, I'm going to rent a handcart so we can start another business. We'll get up at 3:00 o'clock in the morning and go buy papayas. The cafés buy a lot of them for fruit shakes. We'll get the cheap ones that are a bit overripe and the green ones with a little defect. We can buy those for 1½ or 2 *kilos* and sell them for 3 to 9 *kilos*."

We'd go to the marketplace and Marrero would buy 100 or 200 papayas, enough to fill the cart. By the time we got to Luyanó we'd have sold most of them. When there was no *papaya* in the market we'd buy avocados or oranges, about 100 at a time, and sell them at two for a *medio*. When the fruit business got bad we'd go back to flowers. That was just about the time of the Revolution, at the end of 1958.

Chapter Three

Beginning to Understand

I HAD NO IDEA WHAT was going on in Cuba. I wasn't in favor of Batista but neither was I involved in the Revolution. My aims were to go to the movies, to have money in my pocket, to dress well. I didn't give a thought to anything else. I was just drifting along, not able to understand reality as I do now. I could see how Batista, or those who served him, mistreated people. I witnessed the attitude of soldiers who went to the barrio in search of women. I saw those things all right, but I didn't have the developed conscience to understand them.

The only thing I was sure of was that I didn't trust Batista. I got nothing from Batista and neither did my family. None of us had a post or government job or was an officer in the armed forces. We weren't in the police or in politics. My brothers and I didn't even know what a voting card was. We never voted. *Papá*, who knew more about politics than we did, had nothing to do with Batista. But I can't say I had any faith in the triumph of the men in the Sierra, nor could I have imagined all they were going to do. I'd never seen that genial lawyer called Fidel Castro and knew nothing about his ideas or the benefits he would bring to the poor.

In the face of the Revolution I was unbelieving, ignorant, childish. All I knew was that a group of men were fighting in the Sierra Maestra under Fidel Castro and that many had fallen when the *Granma* landed.[2] But I was sunk in a fog of confusion and believed all the fool things people in Las Yaguas said—that Fidel could never win stuck up in the mountains, especially since Batista had so many troops, tanks, and cannons. Anyway, that's what people over forty said. I was so confused that when my

---

2. *Granma* is the name of the launch that brought Fidel Castro and eighty-one other members of the Twenty-sixth of July Movement to Cuba from exile in Mexico. The *Granma* landed on Las Coloradas Beach in southwestern Oriente Province on December 2, 1956. The twelve survivors of the landing escaped to the Sierra Maestra and formed the nucleus of the Rebel Army.

brother Ernesto joined a revolutionary combat battalion I told him, "You're crazy! How can you do such a fool thing?"

A young fellow I knew, who lived in Las Yaguas, was also against Batista. He said he had a gun and would join Fidel's forces in the Sierra Maestra or the Escambray. Other comrades who grew up in the barrio, like Raúl and Andrés, who's now in Pinar del Río completing a course to become a lieutenant, met with some guys in the basement of the Catholic church. There, in a place for social activities and recreation run by *Acción Católica*,[3] they'd talk about recruiting young people and plan secret activities and sabotage.

Comrade Osvaldo Morante took part in all such actions in the barrio of Luyanó. He laid everything on the line, including his life, and sacrificed it all for the cause. We named our CDR after him. Comrade Junípero and his twin brother also made a great contribution, doing sabotage and other activities in the underground movement. They set garbage cans on fire, raised flags, and set off petards in the barrio, around the Calzada de Luyanó, in factories, and in places like Toyo's Corner, where large numbers of people congregated. That little old barrio of Las Yaguas did its bit for the Revolution against the yoke of the oppressor.

The revolutionary comrades were my friends but I never thought of joining them. I didn't participate in any of their activities or in a single act of sabotage. They let me in on their secrets because they knew I wouldn't repeat anything. "These matters can't be talked about," they warned. I wouldn't have let a word cross my lips—not for money or anything—because all of us would have been harshly punished. I took risks for the sake of my friends without understanding the Revolution's militant position.

One night at the end of December, Carlos Marrero and I set out to buy flowers. I said, "Carlos, this is December 31 and Fidel is expected to reach Havana tomorrow. We shouldn't be going out tonight." His wife, too, begged him, "Don't go out tonight, Carlos." But he insisted, "Yes, yes, we have to go buy flowers. If not, I'll have to spend this money for food tomorrow and then I won't have any to buy flowers with. By the day after tomorrow we'll have neither food, money, nor flowers. So how are we going to eat?"

As we walked with our basket, we saw soldiers wearing the Twenty-sixth of July armbands. The streets were full of students, Rebels, and people who'd been working in sabotage and the underground. When we

3. Catholic Action was a Roman Catholic youth movement founded in the 1930s. While it did cooperate temporarily with Castro, *Acción Católica* was more moderate in its opposition to the old system, and many of its leaders left Cuba after 1959.

reached the clinic of the Centro Gallego near Concha, somebody said, "Halt! Who goes there?"

"We're just going to the marketplace to buy flowers."

"All right. Pass." On top of the wall was a bunch of men and young fellows in civilian clothes armed with revolvers and rifles. Havana wasn't the safest place in the world just then. The police were all over, arresting people, but when we got to Cristina I was sure startled when somebody called, "Halt!" and pointed a gun at me. A man with a helmet and armbands told us, "Step aside. Get behind that column." I saw a crowd of young fellows, guns in hand, who shouted, "Long live Fidel!"

"*Caramba*," I thought, "the Revolution has won!" A truck was driving down the road and some of the men yelled, "Stop that car." Then they shouted, "Turn off your headlights!" A captain of the dictatorship and several national policemen were running away in that truck. Fidel's men ordered, "Everybody out." They disarmed the captain and the policemen and put them in a station wagon. Two Rebel troopers armed with rifles got in and they drove off.

The other Rebels told us, "You may go on now." At the marketplace we found all the entrances roped off and guarded by armed men. I said to Carlos, "Let's go in and have a cup of coffee or something." But the guards said, "No, you can't go in."

"What do you mean, we can't go in?" They didn't say a word—just showed us their revolvers and rifles. So we took off for the flower stalls and sat down there. A Public Works truck full of Rebel soldiers stalled right in front of us and we had to push it. When I saw all those guys wearing the black-and-red helmets of the Twenty-sixth of July, I guessed Fidel had arrived in Havana.

I began to understand Fidel's ideas after the Triumph when I joined one of the sanitary brigades that were being organized by the Public Health Ministry. They sent me to a remote place in the hills of Pinar del Río to participate in the planting of pines proclaimed by Fidel. It was part of Fidel's plan to plant 100,000, 1 million, or 10 million pines. I forget which.

I worked as a kitchen helper there. The food was good, and those of us in the kitchen ate whatever and whenever we pleased. For the others the food was strictly rationed—one ladleful of rice, one tablespoon of beans, one slice of bread, three little pieces of meat—and no seconds.

Things were bad there. A lot of people came from Las Yaguas and elsewhere to work a couple of weeks, long enough to get their pay and gamble it away. Some stayed in camp and gambled while the brigades planted pines and cleared away underbrush. Those in charge let them gamble because they were a bunch of tough, razor-toting blacks. Only the guards, who were from troops quartered right there, dared to interfere. A lieutenant had them encircle the camp after dark and then he turned the lights on. Two men were surprised playing dominoes, cards, baccarat—some even smoked marijuana! Money was often stolen. When a thief was caught, he was taken to troop headquarters and turned over to the police. There were a lot of fights, too.

I had a fight with a great big black who wanted to box with me. He started throwing punches as though he was kidding, but he hit hard. "Quit, *chico*," I protested. "I don't like these little games." He insisted, until I lost my temper. Then he pulled out a knife and lunged at me. I struck the underside of his arm. That deflected the knife but I got a cut on my forehead anyhow. He pushed me and I fell. As I scrambled up, he ran.

I ran after him yelling, "Stop, bastard, stop!" But the other comrades saw I was bleeding, so they got me and took me to the office. On the way they warned, "Don't say that you got hurt in a fight. The soldiers don't want any fighting here. If they found out what really happened they'd have you both locked up. Tell them you stumbled and hit your head." It's better to keep your mouth shut in a situation like that. If the people in charge couldn't control things, what could I do? I told the guy at the office that I fell and hit my head. So they treated the cut and let me go. Later the guy apologized for cutting me and we shook hands.

Every fifteen days, around payday, we were allowed to go to Havana, though I sometimes let a month go by so I could pile up money, but with the gambling. . . . Hell, they figured out all sorts of ways to snatch your hard-earned money! Seeing how bad things were, I quit after seven months and went back to Havana.

I'd heard that anyone who worked at the camp was eligible for work with Public Health in Havana. I had to see Dr. Diego Cepero several times before I got a job digging ditches. I earned 92 *pesos* a month and bought shoes and clothes—two changes of khakis, two pairs of shoes. My old man didn't ask me for money, but I knew he needed it so I gave him 10 or 12 *pesos* out of each paycheck. On payday I'd go to the waterfront and drink beer with the fellows who worked with me, and I'd spend 25 or 30 *pesos*. Then we'd go to a barrio of whores in Pila or Pajarito.

When they organized the militia in 1960 or '61, LaVilla, a friend of mine, asked me to join. "Well, I'm willing," said I, "but I don't know what it's all about."

"That doesn't matter," he told me. "I'm in charge of the unit. I'll teach you how to shoot a rifle and how to hold it when you stand guard at the door and all that." So I began to stand guard in El Vedado, the area covered by the Public Health militia, and at the Plaza Cívica when Fidel spoke. From then on I was an active militiaman.

LaVilla and my other comrades in the militia explained the Revolution to me. I began to understand Fidel's ideas better. I put forth my maximum effort and always tried to be the last to quit work. I told

La Villa I was anxious to join the Army of the West[4] to have a better chance to get ahead. "Don't worry," he told me. "I'll do all I can to help you join up." He explained that the Army taught more than firearms and military matters. It also gave cultural courses for self-improvement.

I didn't really know the reason for many of the things I was doing. Mostly I followed LaVilla's advice. "You see, comrade," he said, "I have clear ideas about political matters. I'm the one who's responsible for you. I know you're kind of dumb about these things, but that doesn't matter. We're comrades, so I'll teach you."

There was no volunteer work then. There was still sectarianism and favoritism toward friends. A lot of guys were negative and weren't for the Revolution, and they talked all kinds of nonsense. They'd tell me I was a dope for standing guard because I wasn't going to get any extra pay. I answered as LaVilla had advised me, "I do it because I'm aware of the times I live in. I stand guard of my own free will, to protect my work center, not because I wish to be paid."

Papá kept on begging until 1959, when Public Works started to take a labor census. I'd been telling him, "It's not right. It's shameful. *Papá,* you must find a way to quit begging. Everybody here in Las Yaguas knows what you do. It's too embarrassing. Tomorrow we're going over to Public Works."

"Not me. What for?" he answered. "I've already been to those shacks they set up for the labor census and they haven't called me yet."

"But tomorrow I'm going with you to see the head of Personnel or whoever one has to see. You used to work there and you have a right to a job there again. This new government recognizes your right to that job."

"Stop butting in," snapped my stepmother. "Juan Tomás is better off begging."

"It may be better for you but not for him. He's only fifty-six and tall and strong with no physical impediments."

He finally agreed to look for a job, so one morning at 7:00 I took *papá* to Public Works. Ramona began to rage and scream. She slammed the door and said she was going back home to Cárdenas. "I'm going to leave you because you let your son tell you what to do. You pay no attention to anybody but your sons."

At Public Works we saw a comrade called Ricardo who was head of a work squad. He sent us to the office, and they looked up *papá*'s record to see how long he had worked there. After a time, they called him to work on the buildings going up in front of the National Hospital.

---

4. *Ejército de Occidente,* one of the Revolutionary Armed Forces' three field armies.

I said to my stepmother, "See? If *papá* had paid attention to you, he wouldn't have a job now."

When the government created the plan to eliminate Las Yaguas, I found out that *papá* had signed a contract in 1957 to buy a small lot in Aranguren. I had no idea, nor did anyone else, that he'd bought that land and was paying 9 *pesos* a month for it. He'd tell my stepmother, "I'm going up to Havana today, I'll be back early," and he'd go to the office to pay the installment. Just from his alms, he put away 1 *peso* or 8 *reales* every day until he had the payment. He saved another 200 *pesos* from 54 Ernesto had given him plus 10 or 15 *pesos* a month from Juan, who also had a steady job. The extra money was for wood to build a house. He kept the money at home but none of us knew about it.

Then the government people came and offered him a house in Buena Ventura. "Give your land to the Revolution and we will build you a big house," they told him.

"No, I don't like the idea of giving up my land. I'll build there. I don't want a big house." He was a bit reluctant because he'd already paid 1,200 *pesos*, only 400 short of the total price. But mostly, he didn't want to live with people from Las Yaguas. People there poked fun at *papá* because he'd been a beggar. They called my stepmother ugly nicknames and played nasty jokes on her—sorcery, she said. One day some boys of fifteen or sixteen caught a pigeon and passed it in front of her. "Now you're going to die," they said. Well, that simply terrified her. Poor *papá!* He had to face all those problems and quarrels and was fed up with Las Yaguas.

If he had to live with them, he told a social worker, he didn't want a house. Finally, the government said he could keep the land, that he'd already paid enough.

They tore down Las Yaguas in 1963. My brothers and I helped *papá* pick up several truckloads of wood and tin from the demolished houses. He fenced his land with it and built the house. It has a living room, one bedroom, a kitchen, and a latrine. He has electricity and a clock, and running water that he has to pay for every month. Still, the place is nothing but a shack, with a dirt floor and a leaky tin-and-tarpaper roof. The social worker went there many times to convince him to move. He refused.

When he saw the government houses he told me, "I was wrong. I'd have been much better off if I'd given up that land and gotten one of these in exchange." Sure, he would have had to pay rent. But the government houses are a better bargain. They have bathrooms with inside showers, kitchens, dining rooms, parlors, modern furniture, beds, and everything. *Papá* has two girls, my half-sisters Carla and Patricia, who are seventeen and eighteen, and Genaro. The boy is now nineteen; he's done his compulsory military duty and has a job. Papá would have had a bedroom for the two girls, one for the boy, and one for him and Ramona. And there he is, living in that shack in Aranguren, at the end of the bus line.

Papá is a night watchman now, with the Ministry of the Interior's Front for Vigilance and Protection. He's in a study program in CUJAE[5] so that he can advance. His unit has to take self-improvement courses. *Papá* was enrolled as a member of the CDR by some people who came to his house, so I can say he's integrated in the Revolution.

Gilda was a woman of twenty-nine who lived behind Lalo the bottle-seller's house. She had dark skin and straight hair. Every afternoon when I passed her house she'd ask, "How are you?"

"Hell," I thought, "that woman seems interested in me."

One night she called, "Come here."

"What?" says I.

"Now don't get mad at me—could you spare me a cigarette?" So I gave her one. Then she said, "How handsome you look tonight, all dressed up. Where are you going—the movies?"

"The movies, yes."

"Well, come by here tomorrow, I have to talk with you."

Next day I was dressed up by 6:00 in the evening and at 7:00 I went to her house. "What was it you wanted to talk to me about?"

She said, straight out, "I like you. Would you like to get together with me?"

"I can't do that. You have a husband and I know him, a guy named Felito."

"Yes, but he isn't living with me anymore."

They had six children but he got mad and left her and refused to support them. Gilda took him to court but didn't get anything. Finding herself abandoned and with no means to support the kids, she started begging. Sometimes she'd send the kids out to beg too. She'd had so much trouble in her life and was deaf from a blow on the ear a man gave her when she was a kid.

Two days later I went to see Felito. He was out so I talked with his *mamá* and brother. "What do you want to see Felito about?" his brother asked.

"I'm thinking of getting together with Gilda, and I'm not sure they broke up for good."

"Oh, he left her long ago, those two will never get together again."

So I went to Gilda and told her, "I talked with Felito's mother and brother and they told me he'd never come back to you. I'll think it over

5. *Ciudad Universitaria José Antonio Echeverría* (José Antonio Echeverría University City).

and figure out if you're the right woman for me to live with. I've already failed once and had to separate from my first woman."

"Swell, think it over," she said. "But let me tell you one thing: I'm better than Vera and I'll really look after you."

After seven days I'd analyzed her and we decided to get together. I packed up my clothes and moved into her house. That was sometime in 1961. From then until I left her, I supported her and her four younger children. The two eldest lived with their grandmother. I told her she didn't have to beg anymore; in fact she had no reason to leave the house. She was willing to stay home, very different from Vera, who I was never able to control and who didn't give a damn. Gilda was good to me, kept my clothes clean, and had my lunch ready when I came home from work. We'd leave the kids with her mother in the evening and go to the movies or sit awhile at Maceo Park.

After six weeks together Gilda and I hadn't had an argument, much less a fight. She was happy and often said she liked me. But one day I got home from work and saw her kids taking food out of the pot with their hands. "I don't like having the kids paw over the food we're going to eat," I told her.

"Go to your mother's cunt!" she yelled. "What my children do is none of your business!

"None of my business! And who pays for that food? Me!"

She cursed my mother again and I hauled off and hit her pretty hard. Then I threw out the food, pot and all, packed up my clothes, and left, mad as hell.

Gilda went several times to *papá*'s house. "Juan Tomás, I came to ask you to talk with Nicolás. I want him to come back to me."

"I can't interfere," *papá* answered. "If he doesn't want to live with you, I can't make him."

From then until 1966 I never went to bed with her. In 1966, after I was married to Flora, Gilda came to my house one day to ask me for food for the kids. I gave her 4 pounds of rice, two packs of cigarettes, and 2.80 *pesos*. Flora had gone out so I took advantage of the opportunity.

In 1962, after separating from Gilda, I quit my job in Public Health. I was tired of always doing the same kind of thing, so I started to work on my own in the barrio, running errands and selling fruit in the street. I kept this up until Nelia, the barrio social worker, talked to me about getting a job in the construction of the new housing they were building for us. She said, "There's a need for as many men as we can get to work building the *repartos*." I went to a work center right in the barrio and they gave me a slip of paper so I could start working.

I got a steady construction job, but we'd also go out in brigades to lend a hand in the new *repartos* where the work was going too slowly. I worked on the same one El Che had worked on, as well as the ones in Marianao and Bolívar. In February, 1963, Nelia sent several of the men in Buena Ventura to work at the CUJAE. We were digging deep down for the building foundations and it was very damp and foggy in that mud. After eight months I went to the union and told them I felt sick and couldn't work there anymore.

"You can't get a transfer unless you bring a medical certificate because this is your work center," they told me. So I simply went home and never went back.

By then I'd moved to Buena Ventura. There I ran into Santiago, a young guy everybody calls Guito. He was a bottle-seller with a handcart. "Look here, Nicolás," said he, "you're out of a job, so I'm going to teach you my work." I needed practice in the business so I agreed. We'd go out at 8:00 every morning. First we'd buy jugs from José Dávalos for 15 *kilos* to exchange for bottles. A woman would come up and ask, "How much is that jug worth?" We'd answer, "Four quart bottles or six smaller bottles." We'd sell the quart bottles at a collection center for 18 *centavos* apiece. There were days I made 5 or 6 *pesos* on them. We'd split the profits exactly in half.

Wine and beer bottles we'd buy for 2 *kilos* apiece and sell them at a depot in Luyanó, where they paid 12 *kilos* for them. Around Christmas, when people bought bottles to use for the holidays, they'd pay as much as 18 *kilos*. In January the price would go down to as low as 10.

Some people used oil jars in their business. They would buy clean, empty jars for 12 *kilos* apiece and fill them with grease for car brakes. Santiago and I once made a sale like that for 20 *pesos*. Bottling perfume, nail polish, and hair oil was another large-scale business. They'd take animal fat, mix it with a few drops of perfume, and sell it for 50 *centavos* a bottle. We'd buy the little perfume bottles dirty and unwashed and sell them to a guy named El Machetero. He drove up with a friend in a hired car and picked them up. He'd pay 6 *centavos*, a *medio*, 4 *kilos*, depending. There were times we had as much as 75 *pesos* in perfume bottles stored at home. We really made a tidy profit on them.

We bought tin pitchers, too. We didn't want to pay much for them so we'd pick up empty tin cans of *Pelargén* powdered milk and condensed milk practically anywhere. We gave the cans to Dávalos for nothing, and he lowered his price for making them into pitchers. He only charged 1 *medio* for putting on handles. We sold them for 10 or 15 *centavos* apiece but hardly ever made money on them. Mostly we exchanged them—one pitcher for 10 or 15 *centavos*' worth of bottles or broomsticks. We had a number of broom-makers as clients who paid 10 *centavos* a broomstick. When we had ten or twelve broomsticks, we'd load up our handcart and take them over.

The times we were most hard up for money, we'd go out into the street with a supply of homemade lollipops. We made those by pouring hot syrup into cone-shaped paper molds. When they cool, you put the sticks in and carry them on a board with lots of little holes in it. Kids love them. When they asked, "How much?" we'd say, "We exchange them for bottles." Then they'd run home, get empty wine or beer bottles, and exchange one lollipop for one bottle. I didn't sell lollipops for money except toward the end of the day if I had a lot left.

After a time Guito told me, "Now you know the work well enough to be on your own. You'd better get a handcart and go into business for yourself. You'll earn more that way." So I borrowed *papá*'s handcart. Guito and I would start out together, then go our separate ways—to Jacomino, Layanó, Dolores, El Cerro, and Santos Suárez, a different barrio every day. You have to give people time to accumulate empties in the yard.

I'd push my cart along, singing out, "Bottles!" When I got tired I'd stop for a drink or a cup of coffee. I'd buy cigarettes and a drink of *guarapo*[6]—there were still juice stands at the time. Some days I ran into a client who said, "Hey, I have a heap of bottles at home. Let's go there and I'll sell them to you." I'd fill my cart, sell my load at the bottling plant, and get home by 1:00 or 2:00 in the afternoon. On a good day I'd make 7 or 8 *pesos*. I had bad days too, when I walked all over a barrio and made only 1.50 or 1.60. After work Guito and I went to my house to put away our carts. We never left them anywhere for fear someone would steal them or take a wheel.

At the end of 1963 I had to quit the bottle business because the prices had gone down so low. They paid 3 *centavos* for a 1-liter milk bottle. Sometimes I had to sell two carts of bottles to make 4 or 5 *pesos*. Even the days I earned that much became few and far between.

Then the government decided to close the bottling plants. The comrades of the *Poder Local*[7] told the plant owner they needed his building. "Don't bring me any more bottles," he told me. "I have to turn the plant over to the government and can't buy any more." I heard the same from the bottlers at Luyanó. "We're only buying from our regular sellers and no more." They were afraid the ax would fall when they least expected it. So I pushed the handcart back to *papá*'s house.

Neither Guito nor I felt too good about the revolutionary government's expropriation order; in fact we were both bitter. Guito, who'd been in the business for years, said, "*Chico*, we're really screwed. We'll have to find some other kind of work because now that Fidel doesn't want bottle buyers in the street, the business is all fucked up. Now they're going to make us work in construction for 50 *centavos* an hour, which means all we'll earn is only a bit over 3 *pesos* a day."

6. Sugar-cane juice diluted with water.
7. See Barrera, n. 31.

"Damn it," I'd say, "we're really out of luck. We're going to have to dig up concrete with a pick or a spade, now that street vending is banned."

When you come right down to it, Guito and I were among those least hurt by expropriation. The big businessmen who bought broomsticks and mattresses, or who bottled stuff and manufactured nail-polish brushes, made a lot of money—they owned automobiles and dressed elegantly—and had more to lose. All of us had to look for jobs on our own, or list our names with the plant owners. The lists were turned over to the government and the men were relocated. Guito got a job as a street cleaner in JUCEI.[8]

Early in 1964 I ran into a fellow who worked in the Ministry of Industry. He offered me a job and told me what I had to do to get it. I filled out an application blank and went to the office for an interview with the head of Personnel. They hired me as an assistant on a concrete mixer. I had to pour cement, sand, and crushed stone into the mixer. They paid at the rate of 1.50 *pesos* an hour and I could work twelve, fourteen, or sixteen hours if I chose.

By the time I got the job, I was already living with Eva Rita. She was from Las Yaguas but I ran into her at Lilia Betancourt's. Rita was in her early thirties. She was dark, slender, not very tall, neither ugly nor pretty. I'd call her nice-looking. I asked who she lived with and she said alone, with her *mamá*. I started seeing her regularly. She was a whore, but only for a few men friends she'd met at dances and elsewhere. Some of the neighbors said to me, "But Nicolás, what can you be thinking of, courting Rita? She's a sick woman. She's lived hard. You can do better than that."

We kept on seeing each other and agreed to get together. One afternoon she brought her clothes to my house. We cooked and ate together. When we went to bed she started to lie down with her clothes on. "You came here to stay, right?" I told her. "Well, that means you're my wife now, so take off your clothes." She did as I said, then crept into bed and lay there quietly. She was pretty well preserved for a woman her age. Her breasts and body weren't bad at all. I stroked and kissed her and took off her panties. She was still shy and didn't seem to feel any sexual desire. I had to do everything.

"What's wrong, are you nervous?" I asked.

"Oh no. I'm just embarrassed to be doing this with you."

"Don't be. I'll be nice to you, my child."

She became more trusting and started to warm up. We had intercourse bare, with no protection. Afterward I said, "I like a woman who washes after she's through relieving herself in any way, and before going

8. See Benedí, n. 26.

to bed and when she gets up." I explained that I expect a woman to keep the house neat and clean, too.

Rita was shy at first because she didn't feel well. But even when she felt better I had to tell her, "Kiss me . . . now hug me . . . say something to me. . . ." Otherwise she'd just lie there like a sack of potatoes. She never asked for sex. I had to say, "Come on, I want to go to bed with you." Experienced as she was, she didn't enjoy it. She was clumsy in the kitchen, too, and as slow as a stiff. She'd never had a home or husband before and didn't know how to cook, clean, or wash clothes. Mostly she wanted to lie down. I'd ask, "What's wrong?" and she'd say, "Nothing, I feel bad." Then I'd have to do the housework.

She had the nerve sickness, it turned out, the kind when a person has convulsions and can't speak. She'd tremble, especially in her arms and legs. The sickness gave her inferiority complexes that made her hold back in sex. She was afraid of everything—she wouldn't take a bus for fear she'd fall down or get killed. So I took her to Mental Health. She was put under treatment and improved. I didn't have to nag or force her to do the housework anymore. She became calm and noble-hearted. She never asked anything for herself, much less demanded it. She'd kiss and caress me, and got to the point of saying, "Hug me, Nico. Take me." She was very good at sex because of all the practice she'd had in the streets. Besides, she really worked at it.

Then she got some ovarian disorder and I got a turn to see a gynecologist at the polyclinic. We were on our way there when she began to cry and whine, "No, I won't go." I had to sit with her and calm her before she went on the bus. The doctor said she should have certain blood tests and vaginal tests but Rita wouldn't go through with them. She even tore up the doctor's prescriptions.

The problem was she'd developed a fear of doctors. She wouldn't have any kind of treatment and began to backslide. We quarreled constantly. "Look, *chica,*" I'd say, "you're better now, but you have to keep on going for checkups. And every Monday you must go to the Mental Health clinic. Now you've started drinking again and doing everything backward. I can't stay with you if you don't try to help yourself. Why should I keep on pouring water into a basket?"

"Oh, I'll go, I'll go," she'd promise. She simply wanted me to take her everywhere. She made me lose time from work, too. I'd rub her down with alcohol, give her pills, and just generally take care of her until she calmed down. Then I'd go back to work. Rita was nothing but a stumbling block in my life. It was her fault that I quit my job.

When the factory we were working on was completed, we were transferred to Buena Ventura to construct a warehouse. Then I was told they were sending us to a farm a long way from Havana. I told the comrade,

"*Chico*, I can't go. I have a sick wife and I can't be so far from home." I didn't go back to work again—not that it was right to walk out after so long. It was a hard choice, but in the end I didn't mind quitting and starting the struggle all over again.

I went back to doing odd jobs and running errands for the neighbors. Like I'd get Inés Ceballos's fifteen cans of milk from the grocery store when her ration came around and she'd pay me a *peso*. That's the way I struggled along until October, 1965. Then someone said to me, "Say, would you like a steady job? Go to Monte Limbo. They're hiring people and paying well." Monte Limbo was where all the commercial buildings were being repaired. I asked Carlos Cueva, who'd been my neighbor, to come along. He'd been working on the terminals being built for the motorized police, but in 1965 they assigned him to the country and he refused to go. His grandmother supported him for a year and his *mamá* gave him a little something too. We were willing to work at anything, anywhere we could find it.

At Monte Limbo there were several engineers in charge of construction. They hired their own personnel and Carlos and I signed contracts for a month. We did repairs on a house and worked twelve or thirteen hours a day at 63 *centavos* an hour. When that was finished, Carlos and I decided to go to the municipal office to see if we could get work. None of the people we wanted to see were in the office that day, so we went to the provincial office of the CTC. As we were leaving there a comrade said, "Call the comrade in charge of the construction union, maybe they can get you a job." At the union office a comrade sent us to apply for work in the Carpentry Enterprise. When we got there I said, "This comrade, Carlos Cueva, was assigned to the country and he didn't want to go. He's been out of a job for a whole year. I think one year is punishment enough, comrade. He needs a job and so do I. His grandmother has had to take in laundry to support him all this time. And I have a home and wife. We came to see if you would give us a chance."

They assigned us to a warehouse in Santos Suárez. The pay was 42 *centavos* an hour, about 48 *pesos* every fifteen days. "We'll have to work with pick and shovel," I said to Carlos, "but let's go anyway." We took it because we were out of work.

The first two weeks on the job neither of us had money, and we had to walk to work. We were always early and would sit down until the place opened at 7:00. Then a truck would arrive to take us to the factory, where Carlos, the driver, and I would load 400 cans of paint and then unload them at the warehouse. Or we'd have to check the number of gasoline containers, rubber tires, cameras, and boxes of nails in the warehouse. I really liked working there. Then the Carpentry Enterprise transferred me to the former Ministry of Justice building, which was being repaired and turned into the presidential mansion. From there we were sent to Santa Catalina.

I began work with the Carpentry unit as an *operario;*[9] they do the hardest work for the lowest wages. We had to carry wood and equipment, and putty and sandpaper windows, floors, and walls. We breathed in the dust and got it in our ears. We had to scrub and shellac the floors when the painters finished. And let me tell you, those painters sloshed paint around like soap and water. My aim was to be promoted to carpenter's assistant to earn a bit more, because 42 *centavos* an hour was too little.

When the project at Santa Catalina was about finished, a comrade said to me, "Don't be a dope. Volunteer for the cane harvest; you'll be better off there."

"I've never gone to the cane fields," I said, "but maybe you're right." Then in December, 1965, a comrade came around to make a census of cane volunteers. I filled out an application. I had to put down my name, address, wages, the size of my pants, shirt, and shoes, and the amount of money to be withdrawn for my family. The other volunteers told me, "Working in the cane will kill you. You aren't used to it and anybody can see you aren't strong. You probably have tuberculosis."

I didn't argue. I wasn't sick at all, but I was terribly skinny. Hell, I'd signed up mainly to get free meals, and free clothes and transportation, too.

I went home and told Rita, "I filled in the blanks and I'm going out to work in the cane harvest."

"But that means I'll be all alone," she whined.

"No it doesn't. If you want company you can go over to your *mamá's* house. Here's a slip of paper. Take it to the unit and they'll pay you an allowance of 30 *pesos*. I signed up for you."

I didn't feel bad about leaving her. It was like laying down a burden. I only worried she'd do some fool thing like take poison or go out and leave the door open.

I reported to the unit on January 19, 1966, with my clothes and tooth-brush packed in a box. They took us to the Plaza Cívica by station wagon and checked us into the Leylands.[10] There were thirty-two men in my bus but I only knew one guy, an assistant carpenter from my unit.

The Leylands started off. Everybody was happy and they played rumbas. We had one hell of a good time. During the trip I was thoughtful. "I wonder how the work is. Where are we going? How far?" I worried. "If I can't do the work, if I'm not strong enough, I'll have no choice but to go back. Well, I'll do my best anyway. I'll bend my knee to the ground rather than turn back."

The trip took only twelve hours. We went to Camaguey instead of to Oriente as I had expected. The buses stopped at the sugar mill and they

9. Unskilled worker.
10. See Benedí, n. 106.

transferred us to trucks. We got to La Caridad camp about 9:00 P.M. It was dark but you could see the place was a mess. We were put in little palm-leaf huts that were really sheds for fertilizer and empty sacks. The camps were not well organized then. Nowadays when a group arrives, the beds and quilts are all ready. We had nothing to sleep on, not even hammocks.

The comrade in charge of our brigade was Rolando Torres, an aspirant to Party membership. "This cannot be," he told us. "You can't sleep on the bare ground. I'll get some hammocks or something." He took along some comrades and returned with hammocks, lanterns, and hammers. There weren't enough hammocks so the guys who grabbed from the heap first got them. That left four or five men to sleep on piles of straw and newspaper.

Next morning, as soon as the comrades woke up, they pitched into Rolando. They took everything out on him and complained angrily, "We came here to cut cane, not to sleep on the floor and live like pigs in a sty."

"How are we to cut cane?" we asked. "There's nothing here except potatoes, sweet potatoes, and other vegetables."

"*Chico,* it's not my fault," he answered. "It's the farm's fault. I'm going to see the man responsible to the Party here, to get things straightened out." Then a truck drove up and left sacks of rice and other food. Rolando assigned some comrades to cook our first lunch. What a queue formed! There weren't enough plates and spoons to go around and the lunch was lousy, badly cooked, and so was dinner. Many of the men left their plates full and went to eat at the nearest town. Later we sat around alone. Some played checkers, others chatted, and others griped, "I'm going back to Havana . . . I'm going to pack up my things and go. I didn't come here to be stuck into a kennel like a dog, I came to cut cane. . . ."

Comrade Rolando ran all over to solve our problems and get us placed. He even made trips to the Party's district office. It was two days before they paid any attention. A group of comrades drove up in a jeep and got out. One from the UJC had a gun in his belt. He said, "Look, comrades, you'll have to stay here until you get assigned to cut cane somewhere."

Later that day the Party representative and the man in charge of the farm showed up. The Party man told us we'd stay there three days, resting until the cutting started. We'd get paid for those days. He had the hammocks gathered up and sent us cots. He also sent a real cook. I let myself be led by what the Party comrade said. I thought, "Here I must do as the majority does. If everybody takes off for Havana, I'll go too. But I'll wait till the last possible moment. After I took the step of volunteering, I don't want to draw back unless I have to. I'll wait until Rolando, who's in charge, tells me what to do."

The next day Rolando told us a truck was going to take us to La Rivera, a kind of *batey* or compound in the country, with several houses.

Rolando drove there in a truck loaded with supplies. He distributed a pair of pants, a shirt, and a pair of boots to each of us, and said, "Gentlemen, we start working tomorrow morning, so check your things. We'll get up at 5:00, eat breakfast, and then go out and cut cane." He gave us gloves, machetes, and files. We sharpened our machetes on a big stone he'd brought, and honed down the cutting edge with a file.

At 7:00 A.M. we walked 1 kilometer to the cane fields. This was the first time I'd ever been in a cane field but many of the men were old hands. Rolando himself was from Oriente. He'd been a volunteer several times. He divided the men into groups of three and four. "I'm going to put you in with a couple of experienced fellows," he told me. "That way they can teach you the work." He took the machete from my hand and said, "Watch. Grab the top of the cane like this, then cut."

My two comrades were older guys, Domingo Ferreiro and Emilio Pujadas. They went ahead steadily cutting cane. The standard then was to cut an average of 80 *arrobas* per man a day. I was soon left behind. All of a sudden, *pran!* I cut a finger with my machete. Comrade Rolando hurried over. "What happened?"

"Nothing. I cut my finger." He put me in a truck at once and took me to the office, where they tended to my finger. Comrade Rolando told me, "Look, nobody wants you to kill yourself or to slice off your hand. We don't expect you to meet our quota yet. Just do what you can. Only cut it well. Pay attention and work steadily without hurrying. You'll soon be able to cut as much cane as the others."

During the first few days I cut about 40 *arrobas,* and badly at that. Rolando cut cane along with the rest of us. "You shouldn't leave that much stem standing," he explained. "Neither should you leave the shoots." I learned and improved until I was cutting 80 or 90 *arrobas* a day. By then I was full of enthusiasm.

Every night after work we'd bathe in our "bathroom." It was in the backyard behind a wall of *guano* leaves. There were no bathtubs so we'd take condensed-milk tins and fill them with water, heat the water over a bonfire, and pour it on ourselves. There were only thirty-two of us and they sent plenty of food. A small room was set aside to store the food. A comrade was assigned to guard it, and at night he slept right in the storeroom. Even after we got to know the families nearby, we didn't remove the guard.

Later on, Rolando was sharpening a machete and got some filings in his eye. He had to go to Havana for treatment and brought back a padlock, so the comrade who served as sentinel was able to go cut cane. Only the cook and an old man who helped him stayed in the barracks during the day. With a real cook the meals were good. They'd nicknamed me "Skinny" when I arrived, but by the end of my stint I weighed 157 pounds.

I'd been in the cane fields awhile and hadn't heard from Rita, so I started to worry. Ferreiro and Pujadas said, "*Chico,* the first time out one keeps thinking of home. What you should do is get it off your mind, forget it. Write to your brother and don't worry so much. You think of going home and next thing you know, you'll quit. Then you won't be able to work in Havana, either."

Comrades who quit in the middle of the harvest were out of a job till the harvest ended. So I thought, "I really can't leave now." I wrote to my brother Ernesto and asked how Rita was. I also asked him to go to my house and take a look in case anybody had broken in.

One day I mentioned to Comrade Rafael, "*Chico,* I don't know what's wrong. My wife hasn't answered my letters. I wrote in February and since then I've sent about five more."

Rafael was from the union local. He was going to Havana, so I wrote out my address for him and said, "Look, go over to my house and see what's happening. Maybe my wife's gone off her head or God knows what."

When he got back, he told me he'd found no one in my house. But the neighbors told him Rita spent her time out in the street, drinking and spending my money like mad. As soon as I'd left for the cane fields, she started to exchange her coffee ration for other stuff and to sell some of the rations. She went to a bar to drink beer and play the jukebox. In fact she was arrested there. She'd been drinking at the bar one night and started to play the jukebox and dance around, making noise. A plainclothesman walked in and asked, "Where do you live?"

"None of your business," she said, so he arrested her. At the station they saw she was high and said to her, "Look, Rita, don't go out anymore. If your husband is helping with the sugar harvest, you shouldn't be going out. Go home and stay there." She was lucky they were so kind to her. If they'd taken it into their heads to send her to jail, I wouldn't have known where she was until they called me up for her trial.

I told Comrade Rafael, "*Chico,* when you go to see the paymaster, please ask him to cancel the allowance I've been sending her."

After forty-five days I got a pass and went home. I talked to my neighbors, Abelardo, Miguel, little old Gisela, and Minerva Ruz. "*Chico,* she's really living it up," they told me. "She goes out with any fellow who asks her and hardly sets foot in the house. But don't be a fool. What's a young fellow like you doing with that woman, anyway?"

"I'm sorry for her," I answered.

They said, "Being sorry isn't going to solve any problems. She's used to the streets because her mother let her do as she pleased ever since she was a young girl. She's a lost cause. She could be doing very well with you and look at the way she acts up."

"She won't pay any attention," I replied. "She refuses to go back to the hospital for treatment. It's not my fault she acts the way she does." Not that the neighbors blamed me. They always had a mighty poor opinion of her.

I can't say for sure that Rita went into prostitution. But she wanted money for drink so she must have decided to get it from anybody willing to fork it out. It was only logical and I'm not passing judgment on her. But I hadn't expected her to do any such thing. My only purpose in cutting off her money was to drive her to her mother's.

I went to her mother and said, "Look, when it's Rita's turn to get rationed goods, send me a telegram saying the things have arrived. If she's short of money, tell me and I'll send her 10 *pesos*. But that's the most she'll ever get from me." Even if she went around with other men I couldn't abandon her. I'd promised her mother and brother to stay with her. It was my duty to support her, no matter what.

I returned to camp. After about a month, they moved us to a larger, more comfortable camp. All the volunteers from Carpentry ate there in a collective kitchen—so did the union officers and several brigades from Waterproofing and Painting. The field chief came around on horseback with Party comrades to give us our directives. They told us that a number of comrades from Waterproofing and Carpentry had very low averages, below the mandatory 80 *arrobas* a day. Comrade Rolando and the comrades from the union local told them, "Some of the comrades are new to the work and we cannot demand more from them." The comrades from the Party argued back.

Right after that several comrades quit and returned to Havana. They refused to cut more than 60 or 70 *arrobas*. They'd simply stop working and loaf around. Whole work groups of three or four did that, so in the end they had no choice but to leave. There was even a comrade who, without consulting anybody, got himself a horse and bought chickens and bananas from the country people, then loaded them on his horse and sold them in Havana. When he was found out, they spoke to him and he had to go home too.

The harvest was over in June. My work group averaged at least 350 to 400 *arrobas* of cane a day. That was almost a cartful. Comrade Rolando told us, "You're doing all right. If you cut that much a day among the three of you, that means each of you must be cutting over 100." The truth is, I was lucky to be assigned to the same group as my comrades. I cut 70 to 80 *arrobas* a day and they cut the rest. It was collective work, all averaged together, and that saved me.

By the time I got back to Havana in June, I was determined to make Rita behave herself. "All right," I told her, "either you live with me or you live out in the streets. So try and straighten yourself out or back to your mother you go." She settled down a bit and did the housework. But pretty soon she was getting drunk and making scenes. On top of that, she turned jealous. She fussed when I went out or talked to Sara across the street. If a woman borrowed a cup of sugar or wine, she suspected something. I'd say, "But Rita, after all the things you've done to me, how can you make a fuss about my talking to another woman?"

By August I'd had enough of her. Besides her bad temper, she never felt any sexual desire. "Look, *chica*," I said, "I'm through." I packed her belongings in a shopping basket early one Sunday morning and walked her over to her mother's. "Here's your daughter. I'm leaving her with you. She refuses to take treatment, she won't do her work in the house, she won't even keep herself clean. She's a pig."

Then I went to OFICODA and let them know she was off my ration book.[11] I took the official notification to her mother. "Here," I told her, "take this so you can include her in your ration book." A few days later Rita began to hang around my house and insult me. Some people in the *reparto* egged her on. "Don't be a dope," Lola Silvina told her. "That house belongs to you. Don't let him take another woman there." Rita did everything to upset me then. She was looking for a chance to get me arrested so she could claim the house. I locked up the place and went to *papá*'s.

I wanted to make more money so I got myself transferred from the warehouse in Santos Suárez to a job where there was more profit in it for me. I worked from 9:00 A.M. to 6:00 P.M. but they counted it as ten hours.[12] That way I earned 56 or 58 *pesos* every fifteen days, 50 after deductions. The people in charge came by a lot and always saw me hard at work. After the project was finished, the outstanding workers were promoted. They made me a carpenter's assistant and my salary was raised to 56 *centavos* an hour. The work is easier for an assistant carpenter than for a laborer, but there's more responsibility.

Time passed. Rita no longer haunted the neighborhood, so I moved back into my house. But I hadn't heard the last of her. Her mother came to me when I was already living with Flora, and asked me to help get Rita to the hospital. So Flora and I took Rita to the police station and the police took her to Mazorra.[13] She's back with her mother again but she quarrels all the time and refuses to go outside. She's full of complexes.

11. See Barrera, n. 19.

12. According to Hernández and Mesa-Lago, "Wage rates for those performing their jobs under harmful conditions are increased by 20 percent, and for those laboring under extremely arduous or dangerous conditions, by 35 percent." ("Labor Organization and Wages," in *Revolutionary Change in Cuba*, p. 229.) There was a risk of injury in Salazar's new job, but the exact nature of the work has been deleted from his work history as a means of protecting his identity.

13. A mental institution in Mazorra, a small suburb of Havana.

Chapter Four

Flora Mir Monte

I MET FLORA MIR MONTE at *papá*'s house. Flora's the woman I live with now. She and her family were all born and raised in Guines. Her parents and her brothers had a laundry, but the family was very poor. There weren't any luxuries in their house. They couldn't even afford separate beds for Flora and her brother Cirilo. Their parents spoiled them, too, because they're the smallest. They allowed Flora, a young unmarried girl, a señorita, to go out alone and return late at night. Worse yet, they let her go alone to Havana. Then they saw that Flora's belly was growing. "Who's the father?" they asked.

"He's my sweetheart, a boy I meet secretly. He's going to marry me," Flora said. The truth is she and Cirilo were having sexual relations, but she was ashamed to confess.

What kind of parents would suspect a son and daughter unless they're dirty-minded to begin with? Omar, the eldest brother, figured things out. He noticed Cirilo brought Flora candy and cloth for dresses. Then Cirilo took her to Havana. He'd never done that before. One night Omar caught them having intercourse standing up. He called the whole family together and told them. What a scene! Omar went at Cirilo and Flora and practically killed them. The parents scolded and called them twenty names. They were terribly embarrassed. Even the neighbors knew all about it, and the parents didn't know how to face them. Cirilo was so crazy about Flora he insisted on going on with the affair, so their parents kicked them out. "If you're going to live together, you can't do it here. You'll have to go somewhere else," they said.

Flora gave birth to a boy but not in her parents' house. Oh no! She went from one relative to another, but nobody in Guines wanted the responsibility of keeping her. They were so ashamed of the bad reflection Flora cast upon the family. She and Cirilo went from place to place and she got pregnant again. So they went to their Aunt Ramona, who is my stepmother, and told her and my *papá* that some man had gotten Flora pregnant. *Papá*'s an ignorant man; he swallowed the story and took them in. Ramona and he were sorry for them. But that very night Flora and Cirilo calmly got into the same bed. "I can see you lied to me," *papá* said. "It was you and nobody else who gave Flora that belly. Now I know why you have no place to go and why you had to quit your job at Guines. But I'll help you and let you and Flora have a room here with us." *Papá* kept on helping them—even when Cirilo got very sick with that illness they call poliomyelitis—because the fellow was mentally retarded. He simply wasn't all there.

One day I had a talk with him. "Look, Cirilo," I said, "there's more than enough work here. You have experience as a presser so there's no need for you to go wanting. You have a child to support. It's your duty to face up to things. Go to any laundry and tell them you're an experienced worker. Don't tell them about your personal problems. That's none of their business." He followed my advice and started to work right away.

FLORA MIR:

From the time I was small, Cirilo was the one who liked me best and was most affectionate with me. I was fond of him because he always got mad when they tried to spank me. "Don't spank her, she hasn't done anything," he'd say. I was his favorite sister. He always shielded me. When *mamá* wasn't home, he'd promise to take me to Havana and buy me all sorts of things. He and *mamá* were the most loving with me. The best they had was for me. *Mamá* loved all her children equally but she indulged me more. She hovered over me and didn't want me to do a lick of work around the house because I'd been a sickly child.

I had measles and whooping cough and then, when I was eight or so, I started getting intestinal parasites. I had the worms so bad, sometimes I'd spit them out. So *mamá* gave me bitter herb tea and hung three cloves of garlic on a string around my neck to keep the worms from coming up through my mouth. They took me to the doctor, too. I kept having injections, pills, and analyses for three years until I was cured.

I was ailing and skinny and my parents were sorry for me. They indulged me more than the others. "*Papá*, give me 10 *pesos* for a pair of shoes," I'd beg. Then I'd burst into tears.

Mamá would cry, kiss me, and say, "Quick, old boy, give Florita some money so she can go out and enjoy herself when she gets well."

I wet the bed until I was nine because I had a weak bladder—that's an illness too. *Papá* cured me by heating bricks or a piece of iron for me to pee on. The piss would turn to steam and little by little those heat treatments worked. The heat got into my bladder and cured it.

Once I dreamed I slipped and fell into a river. Next morning when I woke up I found I'd peed all over myself. That's the only dream I remember from my childhood. I hardly ever dreamed. What would I dream about when there were never any thoughts in my head?

Mamá and *papá* spanked me for wetting the bed. Sometimes I tried to blame it on my little brother Esteban. The fear of wetting the bed hung over me. But that wasn't my only fear. I've always been a scaredy-cat. I was afraid of the dark, too. Even now I don't like to sleep without a light because I feel that a man is hiding in the shadows.

I was afraid of policemen, too. Whenever I saw a policeman, I'd run away screaming. It was *papá* who made me scared of the police. When I didn't want to go to school he threatened, "I'm going to fetch a policeman and he'll take you to jail."

I was also afraid of the station wagons that drove around, advertising different things through microphones. I'm still afraid of lots of things. Mice, frogs, black widow spiders, snakes, scorpions, and lizards all scare me to death.

I loved both my parents but I loved *mamá* just a tiny bit more because she protected me and kept her mouth shut lots of times when I got into mischief. When *papá* wanted to spank me, she'd say, "Oh, let her be. Can't you see how skinny she is?"

Papá was very affectionate even if he did spank us. He'd kiss me and say, "My child, be quiet so I won't have to spank you. It hurts me to spank you because you're sick." He showed the most affection for me and Esteban. When we got sick or needed anything, he never told us he had no money. He always said yes and gave it to us right away. I love him because he's been a good father.

Papá is a big man, about as big as Nicolás. He used to be stout, red-cheeked, and very strong. Now his hair is gray and he has none of his own teeth left. He started getting them pulled while still a young man. He's had meningitis and can't speak clearly. He also has bronchial asthma, kidney trouble, and heart trouble. He goes to a doctor and gets injections.

My father has faced all sorts of problems and achieved all the goals he ever set himself. His family never had any bad trouble, because when the situation gets critical he manages somehow. When *mamá* was pregnant with me, and before, too, *papá* worked on street construction. He worked hard, but all they paid him was from 40 or 50 *centavos* to 1 *peso* a day.

Mamá told us she had two abortions and a miscarriage because *papá* was having a bad time. She had only two dresses then. She'd wear one all day, wash it at night, and wear the other dress the next day. We didn't have any nice clothes when we were little. *Mamá* boiled sugar sacks and made our clothes out of them. A lady whose laundry *mamá* did gave us the clothes her own children outgrew. But as bad as things were, none of us ever went to bed on an empty stomach. *Papá* would buy food after work and *mamá* would start to cook at night.

From the time I was born until I was eleven, *papá* worked at a hardware store. He earned 50 *pesos* every two weeks. My brother Omarito started to work as an assistant at the hardware store when he was nineteen years old. He earned 20 *pesos* every two weeks. On pay-days he'd give me 1 or 2 *pesos*. He was nasty to me, but he wasn't stingy.

Papá always managed to get us toys. When boxes of toys arrived at the hardware store, some were always damaged and they'd give them to *papá*—little cars and other toys for the boys, and dolls, tea sets, and so on for the girls. My prettiest doll was big and blond, with blue eyes. I also had a doll carriage and a crib. The truth is our old man has always been a good, kind father to us kids. Anything he had, he shared equally among us; he gave us presents on the Day of the Three Kings and on our birthdays.

Papá has a happy, playful temperament. He's never bitter and never gets angry. It made him sad when he had to spank us, but he'd get over it and play and laugh with us. Esteban and I would run our fingers through his hair and kiss him; we'd press his face between our hands and swarm all over him.

My old man quit the hardware store and was unemployed during most of 1958. He quit because he couldn't bear the owner any longer. My brothers said, "Quit, *papá*. We can give you money for food and things." We owned the house we lived in so we didn't have to worry about rent.

After that, sometimes we had our food set aside in the grocery store but couldn't go get it until Cosme and Omarito and Cirilo got paid. Cosme earned the most—they paid him 80 *pesos* a month at the bar—so he helped *papá* most. *Papá*'s friends helped too, because he had never refused to help a friend in need. That made *mamá* mad. "What a man!" she'd say. "He's too good. He always says yes to everybody—he can never say no."

I started going to school when I was five. It was a big school with four classrooms and lots of desks. *Mamá* brought me there the first day. I wore a pink-and-white flowered dress, a hair ribbon, and shoes and socks. The first few days I cried because I missed *mamá* so terribly.

I went to school with my brother Cosme. We took along sandwiches of guava paste, omelet, or beef. Sometimes *mamá* gave me a roll with salami baked in it, or cookies filled with cream cheese, like the ones they sold at school. When it was snack time Cosme would give me his. Sometimes *mamá* gave me money for a snack at school, sometimes *papá*, so I'd have money every day.

I stayed in that school about two years. I had to repeat the first grade twice. Then I passed to second grade and to third, which I also had to repeat. I never did like school. I started getting terrible headaches when I was about eleven. I'd throw up and they'd send me home. I missed a lot of school that way.

None of my brothers and sisters completed elementary school. Cirilo never went to school. He can't read or write but he can add and subtract. None of us liked school and that's the truth.

My parents didn't have much book-learning either. *Mamá* knows more than *papá*, enough to pick up a newspaper and read it. She went about as far as the fifth grade. *Papá* only got to second grade, but he's a whiz at figures. He had to quit school because of the meningitis. But he was always interested in my school work. After school I'd run to him and show him my notebooks. He'd kiss me and say, "Good, my child. I'm glad you're learning." He was interested in how I behaved, too. If they told him I had cut school or misbehaved, he'd spank me and send me to bed without supper.

At home we've always been Catholics. *Mamá* had one of those large pictures of Christ on the wall and she went to church a lot. I used to go to church every Sunday with my friends. I went because I liked to and because I wanted to take Communion. I made my First Communion at the age of nine. My parents couldn't afford a special dress so I wore my best dress, a sleeveless pink flower print with a ruffle, and strapped shoes and white socks. My friends all wore long white dresses, veils, white shoes and gloves. I felt terribly sad and said to the priest, "Look, *padre*, I'm not going to make my First Communion after all, because I'm ashamed to go in these clothes." But I did it and the day went well.

I was twelve when Fidel came to power, and that's when my family bought the laundry. It cost *papá* and my brothers about 800 *pesos*. They saved up for a long time, each putting whatever he could in the kitty—20, 40, 60 *pesos*.

The laundry belonged to my brothers. *Papá* just helped. He earned only 40 *pesos* every fifteen days. My brothers bought the washing machines and irons and paid for the license to buy supplies wholesale. The building was made of concrete and had a shop in front. The whole family worked at it—even I helped by sorting the clothes. *Mamá* waited on customers.

The truth is the laundry made money—about 360 *pesos* a month. From 1959 to 1965 we were well off. We bought a parlor set that we badly needed because ours was worn out. It was a good buy for 250 *pesos*, secondhand but in good condition. It had a glass display case, a table, a mirror, two rocking chairs, two large armchairs, and the sofa. *Papá* bought a new spring mattress for the bed for 60 *pesos*, sheets for all the beds, and towels. If we needed clothes or shoes, *mamá* would go to the store and buy them, just like that.

My old man always had 50 or 60 *pesos* set aside for emergencies. He saved 20 or 30 *pesos* a month when he worked for others. When somebody was sick, he had money to pay the doctor. A private doctor charges 5 *pesos* for a consultation. *Papá* could even afford to have the doctor come to the house.

My parents got legally married after the Revolution. The government sent people from house to house asking couples who lived together if they wanted to get married, and my parents decided to.

Papá has been a very good husband. In all *mamá*'s sixty-six years of life, she's never had to take an outside job. After my sister Marta was married, I was the only girl at home. I was eleven then, so any time *mamá* got sick, *papá* cooked for her, cleaned, and took the clothes to be washed. He didn't want my *mamá* to get upset or work too hard.

Papá was as affectionate to *mamá* as Nicolás is to me. Even more I'd say, because he never did anything to upset *mamá*. Sure, they had their arguments, like all married couples, but they only disagreed about us kids.

Papá never missed giving *mamá* a gift on Mother's Day and her birthday—like panties, or cloth for making dresses. He gave her the lovely bronze statuette of St. Barbara that's in the parlor. It cost him 20 *pesos*. Another time he bought a dish with the picture of *La Caridad del Cobre* because *mamá* is a devotee of that Virgin.

Mamá looks very old and faded now. She was plump but now she's thin. Her illness is wearing her down. There's something wrong with her liver and bile duct, and she vomits very often.

Mamá has a lot of dignity. She was never the kind to run in and out of neighbor's houses to gossip or wag her tongue. She and *papá* never had problems, such as *mamá*'s putting the horns on him. She's not a rattlebrain like some of her sisters. *Mamá* and Aunt Fermina are the only virtuous ones. The rest have taken on several husbands. All their children have different fathers.

If a woman is living with a man she doesn't like, it's only fair that she get herself another husband. But my aunts themselves were often at fault. Not that they were prostitutes—they never were—but why should a woman with a good husband need to run around?

From the time I was eleven I was dying to grow up so I could use makeup and wear tight skirts. I loved to play house, and I borrowed my sister's high-heeled shoes and painted my mug. If I saw a young girl whose breasts already showed, I'd say, "Oh, I wish my breasts stuck out like that so I could wear a bra!"

I'd put on a wide skirt, draw a belt tight around my waist, and fix up my hair. Then I'd sashay in front of the mirror, sticking out my bottom and wiggling my hips. I darkened my eyebrows and painted on eyelashes. I loved to wear rings and a wristwatch.

At thirteen I was fed up with school, so I quit and *papá* spanked me for the last time. I went to my grandfather's house and stayed there about fifteen days. Grandpa was against me too, but he treated me well. He always said at mealtimes, "Heap Florita's plate. Heap it up good so she'll fill out."

Mamá kept sending me messages by my brother Omar: "Tell Florita to come back home. I miss her terribly."

When I became a señorita at the age of fourteen, I had no idea what was happening. I saw bloodstains on my panties and said, "*Mima,* look, I must have hurt myself!"

"No you didn't, child. You got your period." Then she told me that a woman gets her period every month and that it's a terrible thing. When you have it, you can't walk barefoot or do anything rash. *Mamá* warned me to be very careful of men because once a woman loses her virtue she's dishonored forever.

My cousin Idelisa talked to me all the time about what men do in bed, how they did it naked, how to kiss and press a man, what to do with your tongue, and I don't know what all. I'd try to imagine what it felt like. I'd put my finger down between my legs on that little knob that sticks out and do . . . *that* to myself.

"How I wish I were old enough to have a sweetheart," I'd tell my cousin.

"Child, don't start thinking about that now," she'd advise. "That's still a long way off."

As a señorita I often thought, "*Coño,* I'm really hungry for a man." I daydreamed about my future and longed to find a young man who'd love me. Then we'd get married and have babies. I loved babies, and still do.

I began to know some of the boys in the barrio. The first man I was attracted to was Orlando, the clerk at the grocery store. I was fourteen and he was twenty-five, dark and handsome. I've always gone for dark men. Every time I went to the store for my mother, he'd take my hand and say, "Ummm, how warm and delicious your hand feels!" If he was drinking soda pop, he'd give me half.

Orlando and I were sweethearts for six months. We'd meet in back streets, in the movies, or in the park, so my parents wouldn't find out. Then I found out that he had another sweetheart and I told him we were through. I haven't seen him since.

One day my brother Cirilo took me to Havana. He was twenty-five and had never had a sweetheart; he was so shy he didn't dare talk with girls. I was fourteen years old and that's when I made my first slip. Look, I'll say it straight. I'm ashamed to admit it, but it was my own brother Cirilo who dishonored me. I was Cirilo's first wife and he was my first husband.

We got to Havana around 9:00 in the morning. First we went to a bar and he kept giving me drinks until I got dizzy and a bit high. He took me to the hotel at Cerro and Arango around 11:00 in the morning. My head was going round and round. From then I remember nothing—I was too drunk—except that I felt it when he got inside me. I remember that he kissed and squeezed me and kept saying he liked me a lot. I thought, "No, this can't be, he's my brother." It was the first time I'd had sex with a man.

"Don't tell *mamá* about this," he warned. "If you do she'll kick me out of the house. You can't tell this to anybody."

When my head cleared and I realized what I'd done, I thought, "Now it's all over with me. I'll kill myself, I'll set myself on fire. If *mamá* ever knows this, she'll kick me out. . . ."

We left the hotel at 8:00 that night and hurried over to the shops before they closed. Cirilo bought me shoes, a blouse and skirt, panties, brassieres, a petticoat, face powder, and nylon stockings. I was loaded down with parcels. I wasn't quite so drunk anymore but I felt kind of sick.

When we got home at around 11:00, our parents were in the kitchen and my youngest brother was sitting in the parlor. They didn't realize what had happened until days later when they saw my new clothes. "What in the world were you thinking of, *muchacha?*" they said. "You must be insane!"

Mamá told us to get out of her house. "I'm sorry," she said. "You're my children but I can't have you here. How could I hold up my head in front of the neighbors if they found out you two were carrying on like that?"

Cirilo and I went to live with Aunt Ramona in Havana. Cirilo stayed there about two years, although I broke with him after only one year. He was always quarreling, terribly jealous, and always objecting to my clothes. He said my skirts were too short and too tight. He wouldn't let me go out, not even to the grocery store. During that year I left him several times and went back home to live. He visited me often at home but I told him I was through.

The truth is, I didn't feel at all attracted to Cirilo. He could excite me but not get me really hot, you know, so hot you feel kind of scared. He was passionate but not like some men. His kisses didn't have the flavor other men's do. Besides, he was my brother so I couldn't feel as proud of having him for a husband as I would have with another man. I loved him as a brother but the only reason I had him as a husband was that he got me drunk and dishonored me.

I was back at home when I had my fifteenth birthday. It was a happy one. We had a party at Marta's house and it was a family affair. Omarito, Esteban, Cosme, and my parents were there, and so was my brother Cirilo.

I wore a new beige dress that cost 45 *pesos* in Havana. The under-skirt alone cost *mamá* 10 *pesos*. *Mamá* and *papá* gave me the dress. Cirilo gave me beige shoes and stockings. Shoes were unrationed then and mine cost 7 *pesos*.

My hair was trimmed, set, and combed into a pageboy hairdo at the beauty parlor in Guines. It cost 1.80 *pesos* and was also a gift from *mamá*. My sister shaped my eyebrows with a razor and I did my nails.

As soon as I was dressed, I went to Havana to have my photograph taken. We went in a rented car. The chauffeur waited until we were through. *Papá* paid him 15 *pesos* and gave him supper and beer. The photos were later ruined at Aunt Ramona's house. The roof leaked and the pictures got wet.

The cake at my fiesta was another gift from Cirilo. *Papá* contributed a whole roast suckling pig, rice, black beans, tomato salad, beer, soft drinks for the girls, and ice to keep the drinks cold. We danced until 2:00 in the morning. I danced with Cosme, my brother-in-law, *papá*, and Cirilo.

In Guines I went out almost every night with my two girl cousins, and also on Sundays because then the parks were full of people strolling. One night we were sitting in the park and I met a fellow called Segundo Varela. We sat in a quiet place where few people went. There were no kisses that night, only talk. Segundo tried to kiss me but I said no. "What's wrong with it?" he protested. "I like you."

"No, no. How can I kiss you when we've just met? I don't even know who you are or where you came from."

I saw him again two weeks later. I was in the store when he came up behind and touched my shoulder. He asked, "What are you doing here?"

"Buying a pair of shoes." I was alone. I'd promised *mamá* to return home right away, but instead I went to the movies with Segundo. We kissed and kissed until we got hot. Then he said, "Look, *chica*, let's go somewhere and have a beer." We got on a bus near the Guines funeral parlor and arrived in Havana at 8:00 in the evening. Segundo took me to a hotel, and the room we got had a bed, dressing table, two bedside tables, and a private bath with bidet and washbasin. There were even slippers under the bed.

"Take off your clothes, darling," Segundo said.

"I can't. I'm ashamed."

In the end he undressed me. When he started taking off my panties

I grabbed them and we struggled a bit. My heart beat as if it were going to pop right out. *Ay,* how embarrassing that is!

As soon as I was naked he grabbed me and we began to hug and kiss. His skin felt hot against mine, with the warmth men's skin has when they're excited. His mouth was sweet. He caressed my neck and tightened one arm around my waist while he kissed my lips, my breasts, my back. He kissed as I'd never been kissed before. I pressed him to me, and I bit him around his waist and hips. When I felt him inside me I went wild with desire and pleasure. He was so excited and he's so big!

We had intercourse first lying face to face, then with me lying on my back and he on top. He kept saying, "My life, my love." And he said intimate things about me too—that he liked my cunt, that I had pretty buttocks, that he found me attractive. I've always been a good-looking woman and at that time I was plump. I weighed 130 pounds. I was luscious and he knew it.

I told him that I liked him a lot, too, but that his... you know... was too big and thick. We'd tell each other, "Baby, give me your tongue... give me this... give me that...." I said to him, "Give me your milk." The third time we did it, with him flat on his back and me on top, I said, "Go easy on the sandpaper."

The only position I refused to take was face down. I hate it that way, it's a lousy position. Just once I tried that with Nicolás, but he went in through the front if you know what I mean. Even then I got a hell of a pain down there.

It must have been about 11:00 that night when Segundo took me back to Guines.

I went home alone and *mamá* asked me, "Where were you?"

"Me? Over visiting Grandpa. Then I went to the park with my cousin, got to talking, and didn't realize how late it was."

After about two months *mamá* remarked, "Say, your period hasn't come." She prepared all sorts of brews for me to drink but nothing brought on my period.

"I can't imagine why it doesn't come, *mima,*" I told her.

"Hm, I don't like the looks of this," was all she said. Well, the long and short of it is, I was pregnant and Segundo refused to marry me.

When my brothers and *papá* caught on to what was wrong with me, they scolded me constantly. They were puzzled, too. "How could this girl have gotten pregnant right here at home? She never goes out except with one of her cousins." They kept telling me how bad I was. They didn't hit me because *mamá* said they might hit me too hard on the hips and that would be dangerous. In that way she protected me.

Mamá took me to a doctor and even put 100 *pesos* in his hand for an abortion. I didn't want one but *mima* insisted. "Your *papá* is angry

enough as it is. You know he doesn't want you to have that baby." In
the end the doctor refused, saying, "This girl is five months pregnant
already. If I do an abortion on her now, I'm the one who goes to jail
for it."

"In that case," *mamá* said to me, "there's no help for it. You'd better
just stay with us till the baby's born." She said I was too young to take
care of a baby and start my struggles so soon. I wanted it because I
adore babies. They're so pretty and have such silky skin. I felt well and
very happy about having a baby. I wanted a girl because you can dress
them in prettier clothes, but I made up my mind to accept whatever I
got. Sometimes I'd be afraid of giving birth but *mamá* said, "*Muchacha,*
don't worry about it. You're carrying your baby low and that means an
easy labor."

My son, Segundito, is almost six years old and my parents have
brought him up since he was a baby.

After the baby was born, Cirilo begged me to go back to Havana and
live with him because he still loved me. He promised he'd change and
not quarrel with me anymore. "Besides, your aunt cries because she
misses you so much," he added.

"All right," I said, "I'll go back." Not because he made me hot
but because he was kind to me and bought me lots of clothes.

When the neighbors found out, they talked twenty kinds of garbage
about us. They said it looked very bad for a brother and sister to live
together like that, that such things shouldn't be, that they couldn't
imagine what pleasure we could feel in bed with each other. But heck,
I was young and naturally I felt sexual desire—you know, the urge to
do that.

A year and a half later I got pregnant with my daughter, Adelaida. I
was happy and hoped I'd have a girl. By then *mamá* received me when I
went there with Cirilo, even if I was pregnant. She'd save the best food
for me, *maltina,* milk, and any other little delicacy she had.

Papá's laundry was closed in 1965. They told us it would be closed
for a few months but it never reopened. It wasn't expropriated
though, because nobody outside the family worked there.[14] The
equipment had to be stored. They never paid any money in compensation but they did give them all jobs. Omarito was put to work in a
laundry. They gave Cirilo a job in Havana because he was living in
Aranguren, and *papá* was employed in a dry cleaner's. Before that he
worked in a bar, but the bar was closed down. Esteban sometimes
helped out too. Now he's working in a restaurant.

14. Although all large businesses had been nationalized before 1965, approximately
55,000 family-owned and -operated businesses, accounting for 25 percent of all goods sold,
were in operation until the "revolutionary offensive" of 1968. (*Time,* Apr. 19, 1968, p. 36.)

Salazar:

After the baby girl was born, the quarrels between Cirilo and Flora started. He beat her, threw away her things. . . . She hit him, too. Their life was one dogfight after another. He'd lock up the food before going to work and leave her hungry, and the baby often went without milk. Even the roof of their room leaked. Then Flora got pregnant again. The whole thing was a mess. *Papá* was afraid the neighbors would start to complain. So he told them they couldn't stay unless they stopped making scenes.

Flora and her brother hardly said a word to each other after that. He slept on the floor and she shared the bed with the baby. A number of men took advantage of the situation. They knew Cirilo was on the night shift. They'd visit Flora and give it to her good and hot. She got her pleasure from them because she couldn't count on her man. Some guys pushed open the door and took her by force.

"No, no, you can't do that," my stepmother protested. They'd threaten to beat her up. They got away with it because *papá* worked nights. He didn't interfere when he was home either. Flora was of age and had her own room. Besides, it was none of his business.

I noticed Flora stole looks at me while she cleaned the house or washed dishes, even when Rita was still with me. One time she dropped a plate because she was so busy watching me. I realized then she liked me. She was a pleasant girl and had all her teeth, so I got interested in her.

I had to cook for myself after I left Rita, so I'd go to *papá*'s and ask Flora, "Hey, could you spare me a cup of coffee?"

One day my kid sister told me Flora liked me a lot and wanted to talk to me. "Well, why doesn't she tell me herself?" I asked.

"She's ashamed to."

So I asked Flora what she wanted. "I can't tell you," she said, and laughed. After that we felt more at ease with each other and began to play. I pulled her to me. "Come here!" I said. She answered, "Oh no, no!" and laughed again. I finally pulled her close, picked her up, and sat her down beside me. "Well look," I said. "Let's make a deal. If you want to be with me, I'll observe you for a while. Then maybe we can get together."

Flora was a simple little country girl, a *guajirita* without malice. Not like the girls from Havana. I was attracted by her shyness and quiet ways. She was good at housework and was a very good cook. She's young and that pleased me too. She wasn't really promiscuous. At heart she's a one-man woman. She slept with all those fellows because she had to get sexual relief somehow. Besides, she was inexperienced. She thought one of them would take her out of there.

Ramona was forever telling her, "Aren't you ashamed to live with your brother? It's a scandal! Why, your own mother doesn't want you in her house! As long as you live with him, you can't set foot there or at your sister's house either." I knew she wanted to break with her brother. None of the guys who lined up to sleep with her would give her a home. So I decided to take her home with me.

Once I'd made up my mind, I told my *papá,* "See to it that there aren't any more quarrels and don't let any other man come to bother Flora. She's made up her mind to go straight and live with me. Look out for her. If anyone comes and makes a fuss, tell him to leave Flora alone." I said the same thing to Cirilo. I didn't live there and I worked nights, so that's all I could do. Then, to win her over I started to save little gifts, like a sandwich or a malt beer they gave me at work. I'd take the stuff over right after I finished my shift, before Cirilo got home. But Flora didn't have much appetite and went for days without eating a real meal. She was so upset by the fix she was in. I told her to be calm. I talked to her about leaving Cirilo and about Adelaida, her daughter. Cirilo had never recognized her as his. "You must think of your daughter," I urged Flora. "I'm perfectly willing to register her as my own."

Papá tried to persuade her too. "You won't be badly off if you get together with my son," he said. "At least he has a house of his own. Besides, you won't be in the shameful situation of living with your own brother." But she was afraid to make a decision. She was terrified of her brother.

One day I simply said to her, "You and I are going to get engaged. From now on nobody else can come here to be with you." That very night I went into the bedroom with her and we had intercourse. There were three other fellows waiting for me to get through. One of them said, "As soon as she's free, you go in, then you."

"Gentlemen," I said, "nobody else is going into that house. That girl is going to be my wife. Now beat it!"

Then *papá* said, "Yes, you must go now. Out, out!"

I went to see Flora one night before I left for work. It was after 8:00 but she hadn't eaten. I asked why not. She told me she'd cried the whole day. "Look, Flora," I said. "You have to put an end to this. I'm due at work by 9:00, but I want you to make up your mind right now whether you're going to be my woman. The only thing is, as long as you live with me you must behave yourself. You think about my conditions and I'll think about yours. Let's try to come to an agreement. If you don't want to live with your brother, there's no law to force you to. I have some money here. I'm going out to hire a car. Pack up your things, but be sure not to take anything of his. We can take the crib apart and carry it with us in the car."

I went out and got a car from a neighbor to move us to Buena Ventura.

FLORA MIR:

My daughter was a year old when I met Nicolás. His father was married to Aunt Ramona, and Nicolás came there to visit. He dressed well in a long-sleeved white shirt, gray pants, and well-shined moccasins. He was always shaved and kept his hair neatly cut and combed. He looked handsome.

I began to fall in love with Nicolás but I didn't let on. I'd say to his sister, "Gosh, your brother's a bad one!"

"Huh, you've got the itch already," she said. "You're nuts about him. Let him know, *muchacha!*" I had my chance to flirt with Nicolás because Cirilo worked at night. But I sure don't tell a man I like him just like that. If I did, right off, he'd think I was a tramp.

Nicolás kept sending me little messages through his sister. Finally I told her to tell him I liked him a lot and thought he was a delicious hunk of man. Once I was washing dishes and dropped the whole lot on the floor. "Glory be!" says Nicolás, "why don't you concentrate on doing the dishes instead of staring at me?"

"I wasn't staring at you!" I protested. But I was. I'd been looking straight into his eyes because I was so attracted to him.

He started to court me in the patio of his *papá*'s house. One day he found me sitting on a bench there, eating cookies. He asked for one and I gave it to him. Then he began to kiss my back and my face. "Kiss me," he said.

"No, I won't!" I replied.

That night he was sitting in a rocking chair. All of a sudden he pulled me down on his knees and said, "Come on, let's go to your room. There are lots of things I want to talk about with you."

Cirilo and I had a little room right beside my aunt's. We had our bed there, Adelaida's crib, a rod to hang our clothes on, a tin tub to bathe the baby in, and all the rest of our things.

Nicolás lifted me up in his arms, carried me into the room, and threw me down on the bed so hard that one of its legs broke.

"You'd better fix that leg in a hurry or we'll be in one awful mess," I told him. He took the hammer and fixed it.

It was already dark, about 8:00 in the evening. The light in the room was out and my daughter Adelaida was asleep. We sat on the bed and Nicolás whispered, "I like you so much. Oh, how I need a woman of my own!"

"I like you very, very much and you're so handsome and attractive," I whispered back. He kissed me and I kissed him. I found his lips delicious. He was really hot by then.

He took off my clothes. Then he took out his cock and put his fingers in me. He bit me and I bit him, we kissed and sucked each other's back. The first time I was lying across the bed with my legs out over the edge and Nicolás on top of me. We began at 9:00 and finished at 10:30.

I was satisfied and I could tell Nicolás was too, because he said, "I'm going to take you home to live with me. You'll see how well I keep you." We got dressed and went to a movie in La India. Halfway through the picture we left and he took me to his house in Buena Ventura. We got there around midnight. "How do you like the house?" he asked.

"It's real pretty," I answered. Nicolás gave me coffee. Nicolás's brother Ernesto and his wife lived there too.

Ernesto said to his wife, "Hilda, prepare some supper for our guest."

"No, no, I'm not hungry," I said. So they brought drinks instead. We stayed there until 2:00 in the morning.

I got home around 3:15. That was plenty early because Cirilo wasn't due home until 6:00. I'd done my hair in an upsweep, so I combed it out, washed off my makeup, and undressed. When Cirilo got home there was no way he could tell I'd been out.

I hadn't had sex with Cirilo for exactly one month. It was no fun to sleep with him anymore. I felt no fever, no love. I felt only disgust when he touched me. I could hardly stand to have him close. We still slept in the same bed but that's all we did, sleep. When Cirilo tried to start something, I turned away. I even wore a blouse and underskirt to bed. Nicolás left marks on my body but the blouse covered them and I wasn't about to let Cirilo take off my blouse.

Cirilo went to work at 7:00 P.M. Nicolás would come by for me at 9:00 or 10:00 and we'd stay out till 4:00 in the morning. Then I'd go to my room and he to his *papá*'s part of the house to sleep. Nicolás's *papá* and my aunt knew all about it and they kept their mouths shut. But the gossiping neighbors drove Cirilo crazy and he started to beat me. I told him, "If you beat me, I won't stay with you." When I refused to have sex with him he'd get mad enough to kill me. I said I didn't like him anymore and he couldn't stand it.

"You bitch! You daughter of a great whore!" he'd yell, threatening me with a stick. He beat me, sometimes with a strap, sometimes with a stick. He'd hit me just anywhere: on the back, waist, thighs, even in the face. He'd hit me morning, noon, and night. The neighbors said I was a shit-eater to put up with a man who beat me. One day I grabbed a stick and hit him on the hand so hard that he cried. The other times he hit me all I could manage was to slap his face. I couldn't go on living like that. So I took off with Nicolás and moved to Buena Ventura.

When we got together my parents were overjoyed and decided to let bygones be bygones. They'd gotten over their anger at what had happened with my brother and Segundo. Now they accept me as a daughter and are affectionate with me and my kids. They ask me to dinner and have never stopped giving me money.

Cirilo doesn't come around bothering me anymore, not since he got himself another woman. He and his wife live in a little room in Aranguren, next door to Nicolás's father. Cirilo's wife speaks to me but I don't speak to her. She came here the other day with my sister-in-law, but Cirilo never comes here. He's happy with his new wife. They haven't had any children and they go to dances and all sorts of places.

SALAZAR:

When I took Flora to Buena Ventura, I wanted to have a celebration, so I brought along my sister's father-in-law and the driver's wife. We got to my house at 10:00. I had a bottle of *aguardiente*. Everyone began to drink. Flora was tense, afraid her brother would come and kill her. The rest of us drank and talked till 4:00 in the morning. After everybody left I tried to cheer Flora up. I talked to her about my likes and dislikes. I told her about Buena Ventura. But I was exhausted so we didn't have sex on our first night as husband and wife. Nothing can happen between a man and a woman when there's no tranquillity of spirit between them. Besides, I had plenty of other things to think about.

The next day I made sure to go to Minerva Ruz's. "Look," I told her, "I'm through with Rita. You already know she hasn't been living here for some time. I took a new woman, a woman I can get along with."

"I'm not interested in such things anyway," Minerva answered. But Victoria, the social worker, said, "You can't do that. That house is for a single person. You can't bring a woman there."

"Well," said I, "you can't expect me to live alone all my life. And now I've found the woman who suits me."

Rita had several talks with Victoria after that. She tried to get her to work on me and make me leave Flora. But I stuck to my guns, though Rita's friends, like Celina and little old Gisela, disapproved. Every time I met them they'd say, "What a son-of-a-bitch you are to kick Rita out and bring another woman in her place! Rita is the one who has a right to that house."

"You think so because you don't know how Rita behaved," I'd answer. "I'm the one who knows, and I suffered from what she did. Besides, it's none of your business. I can bring to my home any woman I damn well please because I'm a *macho*."

I'd run into people at the butcher shop who asked, "Hey, what about Rita? Is it true you kicked her out and took on another woman?"

"Well, gentlemen, that's no business of yours," I'd tell them. "That's a personal matter."

I went to see Flora's relatives the day after she moved in. I talked with her parents, brothers, and sisters. They all approved of the match. My family approved from the first. They knew all about Flora's problems and said I'd done the right thing. We both felt calmer after that.

In the afternoon, at about 2:00 o'clock, we went to bed and did it. We were both sincere and really attracted to each other and I know Flora felt pleasure. We had intercourse in a natural way, without doing anything bad. I didn't kiss her ears or suck her tits to fire her up. I didn't use any of the low tricks an experienced man uses. She meant something to me, so I didn't excite her with my finger or turn her over on her stomach and get into her intestines. You don't do those things to a woman you truly love. It would corrupt her. When we finished, she washed herself and we rested. Then I took her out to show her the way to the grocer's and the butcher's.

It was almost dark when *papá* arrived to tell me Cirilo was waiting for me at the corner. Flora ran and hid in the bedroom. I told her I wasn't looking for a fight. "I'm simply going to explain things to him. If he refuses to understand, I'll use other methods." Then I pushed the door open and went out to meet him. *Papá* insisted on going with me.

"Flora doesn't want to live with you anymore," I told Cirilo. "You should be ashamed of yourself, living like that with your sister!"

"All right, I'm going," he said angrily. "Tell Flora I'm no longer responsible for her or for the kids. I never want to see them again!"

Next day he was back. I took him up into the house and said, "Look, those are your children. You shouldn't turn your back on them even if you did wrong in begetting them. You may come here to see them whenever you wish. Just tell me when you're coming. If it bothers you to meet Flora, I'll send her to a neighbor's house. I'm the man of the house. Flora must obey when I give an order."

He repeated what he'd said the day before. "I don't want to see either Flora or the kids again, ever."

I had to take on the responsibility for two of Cirilo's children—Adelaida and Emelina, the child still in Flora's belly. I registered them with my surname. Flora had so many boyfriends, I've no way of telling if Emelina was Cirilo's. You'd have to make a clinical analysis for that. Flora and Cirilo's first child, the boy, was no problem. He was very skinny and had a lot of colds so Flora's *mamá* raised him from then on. He's a big boy now, almost six. When somebody asks, "Who's your *mamá?*" he gives his grandmother's name, Elida.

Cirilo got together with my former wife Vera two months after Flora moved to my house. Vera had quarreled with her husband and was wandering around. She'd visit *papá* and Ramona because she hoped to run into me. One night she stayed over, with every intention of moving in. Ramona had a talk with Cirilo the next day. He lived next door in a one-room shack he'd built. Ramona pointed out he was alone and asked if he'd like to live with Vera. Then she introduced them. I'm sure Cirilo thought, "So that fellow got together with Flora, eh? Very well, I'll get together with Vera." He figured I'd get jealous, see, and maybe leave

Flora and try to get Vera back. Besides, he wanted to make me mad. After Cirilo lived with Vera awhile, he told her, "Look, I'm going to marry you so you'll calm down." She agreed.

I warned Cirilo, "Watch you step. You don't really know that woman."

"I know what I'm doing," he assured me. "She promised she'd settle down with me." Flora talked to Vera about it too. "You aren't really going to settle down after you marry Cirilo and you know it," she said. "You got together with him only to boss him." And it was true. Vera made Cirilo do whatever she wanted.

They got married legally, at the Wedding Palace. But they quarreled all the time. As soon as he went to work, she was in the streets till 11:00 or 12:00 at night. One time she packed up all her things and left for her sister's house. Cirilo went to get her and they made up. They kept breaking up and getting back together until a short time ago.

Vera encouraged Cirilo to go cut cane. She told him, "Don't come here, stay at the shelter; you'll be more comfortable there." Cirilo pretended to take her advice. But he turned back and surprised her with another man. "At last I've caught you!" He said. "So that's why you encouraged me to go cut cane, so you could be free."

Cirilo wanted a divorce but said she'd have to sue him. The law says she gets the house and everything in it if he sues her. But if she sued, he got to keep everything. She went ahead and did it because she didn't have any more sense than morals. Cirilo met her at the office in La Solita and they talked. He asked whether she wanted to repent but she said no, she had no intention of repenting. So they asked for the divorce. Cirilo was asked if he wanted to make any accusations against her. He said no, all he wanted was to get rid of her for good and all.[15]

Cirilo returned from the cane fields last month. He stopped by especially to tell me about his problems with Vera. He and Flora don't speak so it was just as well she'd gone to the grocery store. Cirilo saw his kids but he didn't pay any attention to them.

15. Until 1975, couples seeking a divorce declared their intention before a civil court and the marriage was dissolved within approximately thirty days, provided there was no cohabitation during that period. Men were obligated to pay child support and alimony. Contested divorces were heard by a judge. (*Area Handbook for Cuba* (Washington, D.C.: Government Printing Office, 1971), pp. 110–11.) The new divorce law (effective March, 1975), part of the new Family Code, makes divorce obtainable only by judicial decree and states that when a marriage is "declared null and void, the partner whose bad faith brought this about will not share in the distribution of joint property." Where this condition does not apply, the property may be divided equally between the two partners, with this exception: the partner having custody of the children may be awarded use (not ownership) of "certain domestic items of common property which [the court] feels are needed or convenient for the education and upbringing of minor children...." Husbands and wives have equal rights and obligations in child-support and alimony payments. (The English translation of the full text of the Family Code appears in *Granma Weekly Review*, Mar. 16, 1975, pp. 7–9.)

I was at work one day when Comrade Rolando came by, rounding up volunteers for the sugar cane. "Well, comrade," he said, "we can count on you again this year, right? I brought the blanks for you to fill in."

I said, "I guess so. It's a good thing for me, in fact, because I need to save up some money." Stuck away in the country, there's nothing to spend it on. As soon as I filled in the blanks they gave me a shirt, a pair of pants, and boots. They paid me for the days I'd worked and gave me three days off to get ready. I told Flora, "I'm going because when I return I'll have more money to buy you and the girls the clothes you need. I'll have almost no expenses there, so I can save 100 or 200 *pesos*. Besides, I'll leave you an allowance of 30 *pesos* from my wages."

I remembered how Rita had acted when I was away, but I thought things would be different this time. Flora was pregnant. Her mother said, "Nicolás, if you go to work in the cane, Flora can stay with me." Flora packed her stuff and went. There was no possibility of her going wrong or making a slip. I locked up the house and left on January 7, 1967.

The camp was on a *central*[16] in Camaguey that was part of a state farm. A Party comrade and a cook were waiting for us with the dinner prepared. Afterward we chose our beds and put away our things. The next day things were pretty disorganized. The comrade responsible for assigning us to our *central* didn't show up, so we sat around and did nothing but eat for a day and a half. We usually got the first day off anyway, to rest up from the trip. On the second day that comrade came with machetes and files for sharpening them, and we went out to cut cane after lunch.

Rolando, who was in charge, woke us up every morning at 5:00. We all had toothbrushes and tubes of toothpaste and we'd brush our teeth before going outside. Meanwhile, the cook had been in the kitchen since 3:00 or 4:00 preparing our breakfast of *café con leche* and bread. We ate in the kitchen.

We had pretty far to go so we set out at 6:00 A.M. We got there at 7:00 or so and went right to work. We cut cane until 9:00, then had a fifteen-minute break for a snack. Every day they'd bring a box of sponge cake or something and we'd each take one. Some Haitians would ride in on horseback to sell candy, cigars, cigarettes, and *raspadura,* a cake made with crude sugar. We'd all buy from them. At 11:00 we went to lunch. Rolando was usually off working on some of our problems, so any comrade with a watch could announce lunch. They played fair and called us at 11:00 or five to, never earlier.

We had to be back at work at 1:00, and we cut cane until 5:00. Then

16. A sugar-mill complex, including the adjoining cane fields.

we bathed and ate our dinner. There was no radio or TV there, only dominoes and parcheesi. That was our main amusement. The camp had a truck. Sometimes they'd say, "Any comrade who wants to go to town, get in." I'd go to see a movie every Sunday and sometimes on weekdays. Once in a while a mobile film unit came to the camp and showed movies.

It was the rule that you had to cut an average of at least 120 *arrobas* a day! Of course, somebody who dawdles at his work or stops often to smoke or rest or chat won't be able to cut that much. But working normally, any comrade can cut even 140 or 150 *arrobas* in one day. They'll make allowances for a beginner, but a person who doesn't go beyond 40 or 50 *arrobas* is plain irresponsible. He won't ever improve. He's a drag on others and has no place in the harvest.

The quartet I worked with cut 500 to 550 *arrobas* a day, but a number of comrades fell below the quota and were sent back to Havana after a month. They weren't allowed to work on their regular jobs until the rest of the comrades in their group returned. I think that's perfectly fair. Fidel himself has said, "A comrade who goes out to the fields to stroke the cane and chat with the others would do better to stay home."

In the past, the cane workers had to stop cutting to make bundles of cane and help load them on a cart. The carter owned the cart and oxen and was paid 43 *centavos* for every 100 *arrobas*, so he'd pile on as much as he could. Loading made the men's backs ache and they couldn't work as fast as they do now. Now to load cane, you only have to clear a path alongside the cut cane and throw down the stalks so they lie in a row at right angles to the furrow. Then the crane comes by and lifts the cane into the cart.

Our biggest problem was walking to work. At first we were only about ten city blocks from the cane. But after a month of cutting we had to walk 3 kilometers through the mud. Comrade Rolando brought that up with the farm management and the Party comrades. He suggested they let us ride on a tractor or the truck farmers' vegetable cart. They agreed, but sometimes they wouldn't let us know we couldn't have the cart, and on those mornings we'd wait as late as 7:00 or 7:30. Then Rolando would say, "Well, gentlemen, let's start walking. We're late as it is." We'd go, angry and disgusted.

The food at the camp was good. For lunch we had a meat-and-vegetable stew, or a hearty soup of dried peas, boiled potatoes, or sweet potatoes and eggs, all boiled in bouillon. Those things were easy to get because we were on a farm. But the comrade in charge of supplies had a hard time getting other stuff. The higher-ups whose duty it was to supply all the brigades were very lax. For days we wouldn't have coffee or milk. The supply comrade had to keep after them constantly, running back and forth. Once he had to walk all the way from the supply office to the camp with a sack of food. Thanks to the cook we never went without a meal. He rationed things and always had something in reserve when supplies got delayed.

A lot of comrades got fed up but there was nothing they could do. The Carpentry unit wouldn't allow them to work in Havana with "Quit" on their papers. Some left anyway. They'd say, "This place is shit. I'm going back to Havana." Others left because their wages were 10 or 12 *pesos* short. Havana was supposed to pay us through the *central* office, but somehow they didn't send the money complete. "I'll have to go back to Havana and straighten this out," the short-changed guys said. They just took off.

Other comrades went back to Havana because they got sick. There was no doctor in the camp. A sick person had to go to the *central*'s hospital and wait his turn like everybody else, just like in a polyclinic. It was awfully inconvenient. Of course they did say, "The volunteer cane workers first," and they gave us a lower number for our turn, but that was all. The doctors would prescribe any old thing for us, just like for everybody else. The comrades said, "I'm not going to any of those quacks. If I have to go to the hospital, I'll go to one in Havana."

I quit before the 1967 harvest ended. Not because of any gripes. I liked the place. I liked to go to town. I had fun with my comrades. We became good friends and really got to know each other. But I got a telegram that Flora gave birth to her third child on March 1 or 2. I hadn't been home for almost two months and my brigade wasn't due for a pass. So I told Comrade Rolando, "Look, my wife had a baby. She's at her parents' house. That means there's nobody to look after my house. I'm not asking for any kind of a release. I'm leaving on my own. I'll explain my problem at the office. If they accept my reasons, good. If they don't I'll just hang around doing nothing till the rest of you guys return."

"I can't tell you 'Go,' and I can't tell you 'Stay,'" he answered. "That's your problem. If you go, you do it on your own responsibility. But what good do you think you're going to do anyway? You aren't a midwife."

"No, but I want to see my little daughter and see for myself how she's doing."

Many of the comrades advised me, "Look, *chico*, don't quit now. Send your wife a telegram telling her to stay with her parents until the harvest is over." I didn't pay any attention to them. I had a right to a pass after forty-five days of work, but they did it by brigade and it wasn't my brigade's turn yet. They gave me permission to go for five days. "No," I said. "If I go, I won't come back. Five days aren't enough." I waited until payday and I left. I didn't report to the sugar-cane office or anything.

I went planning to return, but when I got to Havana Flora begged me, "Don't go." So I stayed. Besides, I thought I'd better stay because of Flora's goings-on. She'd lived quietly at her *mamá*'s before the baby was born, but afterward she'd leave the children asleep and go off to a party with Hortensia Abad, Celina's daughter-in-law. Celina had kicked Hortensia out because she took to the bad life when her husband was in jail. She abandoned her kids and used Flora to cover up her dirty business, telling her there's nothing wrong with running around and persuading her to go to places like the Tropicana, Prado, and Coppelia. Flora had never been to those places before, country girl that she was, so Hortensia could easily lead her down the path to a life of evil.

Even Cirilo saw Flora at the Tropicana and ordered her to go home, but she refused, backed up by her friends. Later he told me he didn't know I was in the cane fields but thought she'd gone out without my permission. People stopped and told me Flora acted practically like a whore while I was away. Of course she was a whore once, but she'd been more discreet about it.

Flora's *mamá* was looking after the kids but I didn't feel right about it after she said, "Look, Nicolás, I can't keep Flora any longer. I have my own things to tend to. Besides, when the baby soils herself, I'm always the one who has to change her. It's time for Flora to be back in her own home."

I didn't wait to be told twice. "Pack your things right away, Flora," I told her. "Tomorrow we return to Havana."

I got my job back two days after I returned. I explained about Flora's situation to Hugo Porfirio, the head of Personnel. He said, "All right, come back tomorrow to get your working papers." I didn't have "Quit" or anything on them, so I had no problems. Besides, they didn't suspend everybody who quit the harvest ahead of time. It depended on what the union thought of your reasons. They were also short of carpenter's assistants, what with so many comrades cutting cane. They simply couldn't afford to impose harsh sanctions on me. They took whoever they could get and assigned them to rush jobs. In 1967 I worked wherever they sent me.

I got along all right with Flora the rest of that year. I'd go to the grocery store and help her all I could. She was always home when I was.

Chapter Five

Politics and Personal Problems

FOR ALMOST A YEAR after we came to live in Buena Ventura we had no CDR. It was not until one night in 1964 that the people from the CDR sectional showed up in the *reparto*. Alejandra, the coordinator, and Guido Jerez, the organizer, were there. So were Jorge, in charge of Vigilance, his wife, in charge of the Finance Front, and Emilia, in charge of Education. They didn't have an assembly for all the people of the *reparto;* the meetings were held block by block. They asked if we'd cooperate and said, "Anybody who agrees with the Revolution can be a CDR member, and if we organize a Committee on each block, there will be a great number of Committees. So let's do it that way."

It was after 9:30 when they got to my street, and most of the neighbors were in bed. It wouldn't have been right to bother them. So we got fifteen or sixteen people who were awake, instead of thirty or forty from the thirty houses on the block. They asked if I wished to participate. "Of course, comrade, I'd be delighted," I said. "I'm glad to participate in anything for the Revolution because I want to learn more and improve myself." They saw how willing I was and they wrote down my name.

"Well, comrades, who do you think we should name president of the Committee?" the sectional comrades asked. Everybody called out, "José Dávalos," because he's the oldest. Dávalos could tell us who met the qualifications because he knew everything that went on in the barrio. Comrade Alejandra agreed that Dávalos was the right person for the job.

Dávalos said, "No, no. Not me! I don't want to take on any responsibilities. I don't want to be Committee president. Anybody who has that job is bound to get into twenty thousand kinds of trouble with the neighbors."

Comrade Alejandra reassured him, "You won't get involved in any problems. When something comes up all you have to do is report it to the sectional and we'll come right away to deal with it." Minerva Ruz and others chimed in, "Calm down, there's nothing to worry about." I kept my mouth shut, except to say it was an improper time to hold a meeting. "Why don't you wait till tomorrow? Then maybe all the residents of the block will come." But the sectional comrades couldn't afford to delay. They had to submit a list of the organized CDRs to the district coordinators. Those were the orders they got from above and they couldn't wait. They had to obey the orientation handed down to them.

Actually, they almost forced Dávalos into the job. "All right," they said, "you're going to be president. Does everybody agree?" And, *pam!* they wrote his name down in the blank beside the word "President." Then they asked his age, address, and so on to fill in the rest of the form. "We'll drop in at your house tomorrow to talk with you about the CDR," they told him.

Minerva Ruz was elected CDR organizer the same way. Dávalos proposed her name. "This comrade is really good for this," he said. "She knows politics and she knows everybody here. She's the best candidate we have."

"No, no, not me!" Minerva protested. But Alejandra told her, "Yes, Minerva, you know more than Dávalos and you know a lot about politics. You're the best candidate for organizer." Minerva had been a Communist Party member way back to the time of Batista. She says they expelled her because she had an argument with a Party official who'd ordered her to do some work. She told him she was fed up with being exploited, and for that they put her out.

Minerva and Dávalos asked me to be in charge of Public Health. "This guy can help Dávalos with any task that has to be done," Jorge explained. So I accepted. Then they asked us to suggest a martyr to name our Committee after. One of the women proposed the name of Osvaldo Morante, who'd been shot down by Batista's henchmen.

The neighbors sure grumbled when they heard José Dávalos was CDR president. "How can they name somebody who runs an illegal workshop in his house?" Marcelo Quintana said to me. "That guy is not integrated in any way and he doesn't care about the tasks of the Revolution. He doesn't have one single revolutionary quality." Edelberto said the same thing. Dávalos never even listened to Fidel's speeches. The first time he went to the Plaza de la Revolución was after he joined the Committee.

Some of the neighbors said to me, "Look, Nicolás, if they'd elected you and Minerva, we would have been in agreement, but not with Dávalos. Dávalos is a negative person. He doesn't participate in anything and he talks all sorts of garbage. We belong to the CDR because of you and Minerva, not because of him. He shouldn't be president."

"Well, comrades," I'd answer, "there's no point telling me those things. They should be brought up at a meeting with the comrade officers of the sectional or the zone Committee."

But they'd always say, "No, no, I don't want to bring anything up at a meeting. It's all the same to me. If they want to keep Dávalos, let them keep him. Why should I care?"

I thought he was the worst person they could have picked. Why, he was downright opposed to the Revolution. He made no secret of it. "I've always worked on my own and been my own boss," he'd say. "I've earned enough with my workshop to keep myself fed no matter what government was in power." But who else was there? Most of the neighbors were too old for the job. The rest didn't want the responsibility.

When Dávalos was made president he had the idea they'd assign him a salary. That's how much he knew about it! "Listen, Dávalos," I said, "get that thought out of your head. This is strictly on a volunteer basis." He really criticized the Revolution then. He said it was trash, and he wasn't going to be loaded down with responsibilities without getting paid. He didn't go to the sectional for orientation when he was called. "I can't go," he'd say. "I have some jars to make . . . I have to finish this, I have to finish that. . . ." He always gave some excuse, so I had to go instead.

Dávalos didn't even have a fourth- or fifth-grade education and he lacked culture. The cultural level of a directing officer is very important. He's supposed to fill in all sorts of blanks with a lot of facts like, "How many youngsters under fourteen go to the Committee?" "How many over fourteen?" "How many residents does the CDR have in that block?" "How many are integrated with the CDR?" "How many do guard duty?" "How many do productive work?" They also asked the ages of all the residents, the number of unemployed women, the total number of people who are employed. Somebody like Dávalos can't do the work, so I had to do it all.

The cultural level is important for a lot of other things too. Suppose a comrade goes to the Committee to say he's moving or has exchanged houses or he's going to be out of the barrio for a while. The sectional has to be notified in a written statement signed by the president of the block CDR. If something is stolen, the block president must write to notify the comrade in charge of Vigilance at the sectional so he can pass on the information to the DOP.[17]

If your cultural level is low, you get the sort of problems Comrade Tomasa had. She was the president of another block Committee and she couldn't read or write. She didn't even know what was in the forms they sent her. She kept the directives in a desk drawer instead of getting them done. She's shy, too, afraid to talk to the neighbors. When you take a census for the Committee you have to go from house to house talking with people, but she won't do it. She couldn't live up to the responsibility of being president, so she had to quit.

17. *Dirección General de Orden Público* (Department of Public Order), national police system organized in 1961 under the Ministry of the Interior.

The CDR started to function, but none of us knew what a Defense Committee was. They set up a militia to stand guard in the sectional. They put Comrade LaVilla in charge of Vigilance. He told us every CDR member was allowed to participate. I stood guard for the CDR sectional and later did patrol duty in the zone and I checked to see which CDRs had set up a guard and which hadn't.

Sometimes the comrades from the sectional came to orient us but other times they didn't and we'd have to go ask them what to do. We'd sit through their meetings but we didn't understand the orientations they gave us. They'd give us a paper with some directions but we still didn't have a clear idea what to do. We could only carry out the simplest tasks and resolve the most trifling problems. We cleaned up the *reparto*'s community center and cut the grass and weeds in the park. Eventually the sectional saw we were in trouble. Alejandra, then Guido Jerez, lent us a hand. "Well, comrades," he told us, "your Committee is a bit disorganized. The tasks are hardly ever finished and the censuses are left incomplete. Let's see if we can't straighten things out. I'm going to explain to you how to go about running this Committee right." He'd meet with us in Dávalos's house or mine and teach us how to fill in forms.

"Look, you're responsible for the CDR here," he said. "When an orientation is sent, you work on it thus-and-so."

The twenty-eight members we had at that time weren't enough, he told us. He explained all the requirements for CDR membership. The person should agree to belong; he should not have any terribly bad qualities, like being delinquent or effeminate, or exploiting people through *santería*, or selling things above the legal price; and he shouldn't have a negative attitude toward the Revolution. A negative attitude means to criticize the Revolution and the Committee, and to protest at the grocery, the butcher shop, or anywhere. It was our duty to speak up and refute a person who did any of those things. But aside from people like that, every neighbor should be given an opportunity to join.

It wasn't enough just to say you agreed with the CDR; we demanded deeds. You had to cooperate with the Committee all the time, even before becoming a member. We remembered who cooperated in the census and answered questions willingly. We noticed who asked about volunteer work. Then, when we organized volunteer work, we'd say, "Look, let's fill out a form for so-and-so. It's easy to see what a spirit of sacrifice he has and how much he wishes to integrate with our Committee."

We went from house to house evaluating people. For instance, we said to Ramiro Ortíz, "Comrade, we've come in the name of the Revolution to ask whether you're willing to join the CDR."

"No, no, I don't want to belong to the CDR or anything else. I belong to my work, that's all," he answered.

We told him, "Look, this is a directive we were given by the Party.

They said that if somebody doesn't want to join the CDR, they've got to give their reasons."

"I don't have any reasons to give. I just don't like that sort of thing. Write down anything you like." It was plain we wouldn't get him to join and there was no point trying anymore. We didn't take action against him or anyone like him. We simply wrote down their names and addresses. If there's any trouble in the barrio, we know where to look first—among the individuals who aren't integrated.

I don't think it's right to apply pressure to get people to join. "If you don't want to join," I tell them, "you stay out under your own responsibility. But nobody is going to pressure you into it." Then I explain the consequences of not joining. If you don't belong to the block Committee, they won't resolve any of your problems for you. And if anything happens, the people who aren't integrated are the first to be picked up and taken to some faraway place until the crisis is past.

We increased our members from twenty-eight to thirty-seven, and then to sixty-eight after our last membership drive. Before that drive we got a directive to convince anyone who hadn't joined to join up, and to win over his wife, his *mamá,* and everyone else in the family. They told us anybody who wasn't in favor of the Revolution was against it. Nobody could straddle the fence or hide behind it or stay outside. The sectional coordinator went with us so some people joined before we talked to them. Like Lucrecia Romero. She lives with Manolo and his stepfather Hipólito, in the house behind Minerva's. We simply told Manolo about the new directive. Then he, Lucrecia, and Hipólito became convinced and said, "Yes, we agree to join."

We got really well organized by 1965. The first task we carried out that year for our CDR comrades was to talk with the man in charge of the Supplies unit in MINCON. We told him our Committee wanted to find jobs for several comrades. The comrade answered, "Willingly. We have no objection. Make a list and send it to our office. We'll find jobs for them all. They won't be particularly good jobs, mind you, but they can work near the barrio, where they're constructing a building for Supplies. We'll give them jobs according to their physical fitness." We sent over Ortíz, Abel Casildo Benítez, José Dávalos, and several others. They told us that no one over sixty-five could work, so they rejected José and another comrade. Then, Fidel himself sent down a new directive that anybody who wanted to work was entitled to, and those two were also given jobs.

We attended a course on vaccination against polio. Then we vaccinated the children in the area. We also vaccinated dogs, gathered up stray animals, and collected empty containers and bottles. We made an education census of school-age children, too. Later, we went around and talked with parents who kept their kids home from school.

We were even doing volunteer work outside the barrio, like helping on farms on Sunday. On Saturday we'd go around to the member's house. "Look, comrade," we'd tell him, "tomorrow we're going to do volunteer work. I came to ask if you can go with us so our CDR can send its quota. We're supposed to send at least four or five members. There'll be buses at the sectional office to take us there and back. It's only half a day's work." The comrade might answer, "Well, I'm a bit tired but I'll try so as not to make our CDR look bad." If you approached people politely, they might go even if they were tired.

On Sundays, Guido Jerez would come to wake up Minerva, then she'd rouse the rest of the volunteers. We'd go to the sectional and set off at 8:00 for the farm in Nueva Paz or Managua, getting there about 9:00. We'd do light work, weed, pull up *malanga* and such. We'd leave the farm by 12:00 and be back home by 1:00.

We went to do volunteer work four Sundays in a row. The problem was, the same people always volunteered—me, Minerva Ruz, her sister Idalia, Luisa Naranjo, Ramón Betancourt, Sabino Cruz.... There was nothing we could do if others refused. Volunteer work is supposed to be of your own spontaneous free will. You can't go yelling at somebody, "Either you do volunteer work or we'll kick you out ... we'll take your house away...." If somebody won't go, he won't. All you can do is try to convince him politically. Minerva Ruz talked big about taking away CDR cards and doing other things to people who wouldn't cooperate, but that was just talk. You can't take away anybody's CDR card.[18] How can there be sanctions for not doing volunteer work when it's just that—voluntary? I myself have stayed home when I wasn't able to go and nothing happened to me. The only thing that makes me volunteer is my own wish and need to do it.

Besides, some people didn't volunteer because things were so disorganized. The work directive should have come way ahead of time, not the day before. They sent us too far from Havana. The trucks often came late and didn't get us there until 11:00. That gave us just enough time to stir up the ground with our hoes.

Dávalos told me about one time when he went to weed *malanga* plantings. The few trucks they sent were packed tight with people. The comrades from our *reparto* said, "We won't go unless they send a separate truck for us." Several of them got together and went to the Party offices. They got their truck. But the time they worked didn't amount to anything.

18. According to David Booth, "expulsion of a member could be produced in practice only by either repeated public denunciations by the person in question of the policies or leadership of the revolutionary government, or his or her own conviction by a court in a relatively serious criminal case." ("Neighbourhood Committees and Popular Courts," p. 84.)

In 1965 we had comrades assigned to only a few of the CDR fronts.[19] We didn't have anybody for Volunteer Work, Education, or Finance,[20] so we organized a meeting to discuss our needs and hold elections. We met at 8:00 P.M. under the streetlight in the alley. Most of the neighbors were there. The fronts were restructured; they transferred me to Finance and re-elected Minerva organizer. Sabino Cruz was elected for Volunteer Work and Ovidia Blanco for Education. Dávalos wasn't there—he was off working on the Isle of Pines for JUCEI—but he was re-elected president the same way we all were. They asked us, "Does anybody here have any criticism to make against Dávalos? Against Minerva?" Not a hand was raised; nobody said a word. It was the same with all the fronts.

Nobody had had any trouble with Dávalos during his term. Some people went around saying they didn't like him but the majority wanted him to stay. I suspect that was because they knew Dávalos wouldn't interfere with the gambling and a lot of other things that go on in the barrio. The professional gamblers were afraid they might get somebody heavier-handed. They thought, "If Dávalos is replaced, there might be an investigation or God knows what."

Gambling is a real weakness with those guys. I hear them playing for money at Sulema's, even though they lock the door. They go to Bolívar and elsewhere to gamble, too. Not that they live as well as they did in Las Yaguas, where each house had six or seven tables and they collected a percentage of every game. Mostly, only neighbors play now; outsiders come just once in a while. Even I get together with four or five neighbors at Fernando Guerra's house to play dominoes for fun, not for money.

Dávalos has covered up several times when the Technical Department came around.[21] Dávalos acted very differently then. Like the time in 1966 when they came asking about Comrade Tavares, who'd been caught with marijuana in his house and jailed on a two-year sentence. He wasn't in our CDR but his wife was. While Tavares was in jail, they came around asking why that man had been allowed to keep marijuana at home. Dávalos told them he didn't know anything about it. Then they asked Dávalos why Tavares did it, out of need or because he was corrupt or greedy for money. Dávalos explained that Tavares didn't have a steady job and had several children to support. In other words, it was need that had driven him to such extremes.

Another time they investigated Isidro Fajardo, a bus driver who had stolen fares. He was arrested and jailed. But when the investigation came from above, Dávalos said to them, "Look, that fellow is integrated in the

19. See Benedí, n. 82. There were fourteen fronts in 1969–70.
20. The Finance Front was organized in 1964 when the CDR instituted membership dues.
21. Department of Technical Investigations. (See Barrera, n. 42.)

Revolution. He always talks well about the Revolution. I know he's not a thief by nature. Perhaps he did it to help his *papá,* who had nothing to eat." So they found the young fellow not guilty.

"You'd better be careful what you say," I told Dávalos. "Suppose they make a real investigation? They'll find out that not only did Isidro steal the money, but he isn't living here. He only stays with his father now and then and doesn't help the old man at all." I heard that from old Fajardo himself. "I have to go around begging the neighbors for a bit of food because I can't afford to buy any," he said. I'll tell you something else. Isidro stole money from the Committee itself. And what's more, he spent it on taking his sweetheart out to the Tropicana, not to resolve any problems of his *papá* or his home.

That's what Dávalos should have told the investigator from the Technical Department—the truth. And he shouldn't have said that Isidro gave talks in the CDR because he didn't, not once. He never spoke well of the Revolution either. But I couldn't tell Dávalos what to do because I was in a lower-ranking front. I would have told the Department the truth myself, but they wouldn't listen to me. They only question the president in a police investigation. They went to his house, not mine. And they tell him to close the door before they say anything. If I tried to give an opinion, they'd say, "Excuse us, comrade, but we didn't come to talk with you."

Many of my neighbors prefer me to Minerva as an official in the barrio because I always speak in a pleasanter voice. Minerva is a good Committee officer and does her work well, but she has bad defects. She argues and raises her voice, she says dirty words. So as a Committee official she has no prestige in the barrio. People have lost respect for her because of her temper. She's so rude many of them won't have anything to do with her.

If you're going to somebody's house on behalf of the Committee, the proper thing is to say, "If you're free, I'll drop in for a moment to ask some questions and fill in some forms." Then I explain what it's all about. Minerva gives no explanations. She goes right up to people and tells them, "We have to fill out these forms for the Committee. Either you answer my questions or you'll be kicked out of the CDR." Or, "I'm Minerva, the organizer. Everybody has to do what I say."

That's no way to treat a comrade member of the CDR. I can tell from things people say that they're dead set against her. But at the meetings they don't say a word. I guess they don't want to get in trouble or make enemies. I haven't brought it up either. Why should I? But Minerva knows where I stand and she can't harm me.

Actually, a lot of the others are plain scared of her. She's tough. She'll talk back to any man and back it up with her fists. A while ago she had a fight with a *comadre* of hers. It began with words but they were soon pulling each other's hair. Minerva's sister had to step in and say, "That's enough, comrade."

I'm more understanding. When they bring me a problem, I say, "Very well. It isn't in my power to do anything about it, but I'll talk it over with the sectional coordinator." I try to help people when they're sick or in trouble. Like little old Benito, who was at home with an ulcerated leg and didn't eat. "Let's get an ambulance," I told Dávalos. I helped wash Benito and lift him into the ambulance. I've skipped meals and baths to go the sectional meetings or to stand guard. When I made a census of broken plumbing and door locks, my wife waited dinner for me. The comrades know that. That's why I have prestige among them. They trust me more than anyone.

I feel competent to be an official of the CDR as long as the neighbors want me there. Very few people want me out of office. A lot of them might even prefer me as president of the CDR. In fact, once when I was at her house, Comrade Lina suggested that I move the CDR to my place and be president.

I told her, "No, comrade. That's not the way to do it. We must have a meeting with all the residents of the block to see if they want me. But I don't want to be president because people will say I wanted to overthrow Dávalos so I'd have an excuse to throw my weight around."

Some people may think it's a great privilege to have a CDR in your house, but it's really a burden. I didn't want to be responsible for the failures of such a disorganized Committee.

I accept the responsibility delegated to me by the zone Committee; I have no objection to doing it or even to being president. But this is a low barrio and people get politics mixed up with their personal problems. The first thing my neighbors are going to say is that they don't want me as president because my wife put the horns on me, that she's this or that, or that I don't go to work sometimes. Then they'll refuse to stand guard. They won't want me to give talks about the Revolution. I know because it's already happened.

I tell them, "You're mistaken. Personal problems have nothing to do with politics. The CDR is a political organization. Besides, no matter what happened to me, I feel as much a man as ever. Sweeping my house, washing dishes, rinsing out a rag don't make me less of a man as long as I do it for myself. If I did it for three or four other men, for free, that might be different." That shuts them up.

In some ways being a revolutionary has made problems between me and my neighbors. Take Celina Quevado, who lives near me. Her husband, Clemente, works as a garbage collector for JUCEI. There are six members of that family living together, counting Celina's four children.

One day Celina comes up to me and says, "Two of my kids have no shoes. Let's see what you people in the Committee can do about it."

"Look, Celina," I answered, "we're a Defense Committee. We don't have supplies of food or clothing to give out. The Committee is set up to deal with political questions, not to find food or shoes for anybody. We all have a ration book and have to be ruled by it. But I'll talk to Comrade Lina, the sectional coordinator, and tell her your problems. Perhaps she can get you a couple of pairs of used shoes from her neighbors."

Celina let her stepfather move into her house, but he'd hardly been there three months when she quarreled with him and wanted me to get him out. I said, "You took him into your house without first consulting the Committee. You're the one who put his name down in your ration book without a by-your-leave. So it's up to you to get rid of him. Go to the police station and tell them about it. You didn't count on us, so now we can't interfere."

Another one who gives the Committee trouble is Blanca Tavares. She has a retarded daughter. "How come you people in the Committee don't find a place for my daughter?" she asked. "I've been sent so many places by so many doctors and psychiatrists but I still can't get my little girl admitted anywhere."

"You shouldn't bring that problem to me but to the coordinator of the sectional," I told her. "I'd place her somewhere today if it were up to me. But who am I? Simply the finance officer of the CDR, who can't do a thing about that kind of problem."

The CDR stopped functioning in the barrio in 1968. People began to lose their will to work. When we did anything at all, it was something easy. We got a directive from the sectional to collect bottles, perfume containers, silver coins, and canceled stamps. Enrique Cueva and I collected four sackfuls of containers from the neighbors. We did it against Minerva's will. She said we couldn't carry out a task without consulting her first. But she was ailing and hardly ever wanted to work for the Committee.

Last year I went to the sectional to talk with Comrade Lina. "Look, Lina," I said, "we need you to go down and hold a meeting with all the neighbors to get the CDR going. It's stalled."

"Comrade," she answered, "this is a problem without a solution. We've gone there several times to hold meetings. But nobody comes. We send down directives and they don't carry out the tasks. If people hang back and don't try to solve problems, don't do the work, what can we do?"

She's decided we're incorrigible and dropped us. Well, I must admit she's right. I remember that at the beginning of 1969 a woman comrade came down to make a census about who was doing guard duty. The comrade in charge of Vigilance had to sign it but nobody could be found to take on the responsibility. Even the president and the organizer refused to sign, according to Lina. After that, she stopped sending down directives or anybody to help us.

Our CDR had many members who were too sunk in evil or too negative to be acceptable. Minerva has given them membership cards even though Lina told her in front of me that anybody who didn't cooperate shouldn't have a card. We had enough people who wouldn't stand guard or do anything, but Minerva took in more because they were her friends. She even gave a card to a *maricón*. "But Minerva," I objected, "how can you give a CDR card to a fellow who was rehabilitated at a UMAP farm?[22] Everybody knows he's a queer."

"Sure he's a queer, but people here don't know it," she said, "so I'm going to have him in the Committee."

"All right, then do it under your own responsibility," I told her.

Minerva also criticized Dávalos for doing things without consulting her. "Now you've gone and done this and that wrong." She says this to him, when he's the president and she's supposed to be under him! She's won out, too. At least he lets her get away with it because it's to his advantage.

"Whatever the organizer, Minerva Ruz, says, goes," he always says.

I was told by the people up above that you can't stop talking with a comrade or take him to a police station just because of some personal argument. But Minerva does just that to Dámaso and me whenever we tell her the work's done badly, or that we have to cooperate with the DOP or be strict about standing guard. I've also told her to demand that people carry out their duties. She gets mad and fusses at me, blah, blah, blah.

I used to get along with Minerva. We were nice and neighborly. I'd go to the sectional orientation meetings when she couldn't. But she always watches what others do. That's her main fault. She gets personal when she should be helping the Revolution and getting young people to contribute to production or join the CDR.

Lately she's been staying away from the CDR and is angry with MIN-CIN because of problems she had after she lost her ration book. They have a rule: if you lose your ration book, you have to wait six months for a new one. That's because some people buy stuff and burn their ration books. They think they'll get a new one with empty blanks. But things are already checked off when they get the new books. She handed me

22. *Unidades Militares para Ayudar la Producción* (Military Units for Aid to Production), paramilitary agricultural work camps with tighter discipline than other labor camps and a political re-education program. Political prisoners, criminals, religious dissidents, and homosexuals were assigned to the camps until about 1967, when the units apparently ceased to be forced labor camps. In 1973 UMAP was merged with other paramilitary agricultural labor groups to form the Army of Working Youth.

her new ration book. "Look," she told me, "I haven't bought an umbrella, I haven't bought yard goods or a lot of other things they have marked down here."

I went to Comrade Lina about it, but she returned the ration book and said there was nothing she could do. That was unfair to Minerva. She hadn't bought a lot of things she was entitled to. But I said to her, "Look, Minerva, that's a law that applies to everybody. I know you didn't burn or throw away your ration book, but it was careless of you to lose it. Let that be a lesson to you to be more careful."

She kept protesting but she got no results. So she's bitter and causes trouble in the CDR. She discourages people from working. Then they don't cooperate. She tries to get me to go against Enrique Cueva, who was her aide. She says he gives out letters of recommendation for jobs without her say-so. Well, so what? She was sick a long time and didn't want to work. Half the time she's away working in the Rice Plan; that means she's home twenty-four hours and away twenty-four hours. So Cueva did those things when she wasn't around. I've gone over her head too. That really gets her mad. "I'm the organizer here and you're only in charge of Finance," she tells me.

"Sure you are, comrade," I'd answer. "But in this religion your duty is everybody else's duty too. If you can't work at a certain task, then it's up to the rest of us to do it. All of us CDR officers should do the work to set a good example for others. I'm a militiaman and can activate myself in any field I think proper. I don't have to ask your permission to do any work I feel like doing. I'm not accountable to you, see?"

Besides, Comrade Lina has told Cueva and me, "You don't have to bother about the organizer. If she doesn't want to work and a comrade needs a letter from the Committee or there's some task to be done, just get the president's signature and go ahead." The president's signature, Enrique Cueva's and mine are all valid.

Minerva says she won't work for the Committee, that she's going to exchange houses and move, and I don't know what. I pay no attention because I know she won't really do those things. She gets mad and talks big but it soon blows over.

In December, 1967, I filled out the papers to go to my third cane harvest. I was bored with the monotony of my job, with having to rush out and catch the bus and all that, and I was tired of doing everything for the CDR. I had to shake off the burden of my home for a few weeks, too. Besides, cutting cane was good for my health. I always gained weight there. I told Flora not to let anybody in the house and I left.

The departure was better organized this time. The Leyland buses had signs so we could tell them apart. They left in single file and stayed in line the whole trip. In our bus there was a comrade with a drum, another comrade with maracas, and another with *claves*.[23] Some comrades brought along liquor and kept drinking, so we were all very happy.

We went straight to Florida in Camaguey and then to the Agramonte sugar mill, where the sugar-cane office was. A comrade from the CTC assigned us to the different camps. Two comrades from the CTC, one from the Ministry of Construction, and another from the Party had been sent there from Havana. Those four were in charge. They told us, "No work today, gentlemen. Tomorrow everybody up at 5:00 A.M. sharp."

That afternoon everyone did as he pleased. Some played ball, others began to sing and play their musical instruments. Some of us sat down on benches built around the trunks of the *guano* palms to enjoy the cool breeze. Since that place had electric lights, after dinner one guy got out a game of checkers and another one some dominoes, and some of the guys played. Another of the guys had a transistor radio and a group of us sat around listening to it.

That night a group from JUCEI arrived to reinforce our brigade. They moved into the other barracks. Right away a few men started arguing over beds. One guy pulled out a knife, but the comrade in charge snatched it away. "No, comrades," he said. "You two will have to go straight back where you came from." He called for a truck and sent them away. "This camp is organized," he told us. "We won't put up with fights or pulling out knives or swinging a machete against a comrade."

On the second day the comrades in charge got us together to read to us from a little book put out by the CTC. It told the rules and regulations for cane-cutting. We must keep the shelter clean and not make noise after 9:00 P.M. Each man should work seriously at cutting cane, not argue with his comrades, not sit down to rest during working hours, and take good care of his machete. They forbade us to get too friendly with the country women. We could visit the peasants in their homes if we behaved properly. We couldn't buy or keep any animals. "If any comrade disagrees with the rules," they told us, "let him raise his hand and we'll send him away at once. We didn't come here to buy animals, or to interfere with the farmers or flirt with their wives. We came here to cut cane."

We didn't have such strict regulations before. Some guys had bought animals from the farmers and kept them in the camp and nobody objected. They even lent us a truck to bring back the animals. But that year the Party forbade it. All the pigs and chickens in the camp were slaughtered, cooked, and shared with the other comrades, and there was food to spare. The head of the camp said if anybody had already agreed to buy an animal, he could ask the farmer to keep it for him. But when

23. A rhythm instrument consisting of two short cylindrical sticks of hard wood which are struck against one another.

we had to move on to cut cane somewhere else, we wouldn't be allowed to carry so much as a caged lizard on the bus. Anybody who broke the rule would be sent back to Havana.

The Party comrades explained that these rules would keep the *campesinos*[24] from spending all their time raising animals for sale or barter to cane-cutters. They'd live off the profits, and then it would be no use to ask a farmer to cut cane or work on the state farms. "Hell no," he'd say, "why should I cut cane or spade around orange trees or sweet potatoes? I'm better off this way."

I don't think the way they treated the *campesinos* at that time was right. The cane-cutters got extra rations of coffee, rice, beans, and clothing, but the peasants who hoed vegetables or cut down underbrush or worked inside the mill got no extra clothes. That's why they'd exchange as much as 12 pounds of black beans for one pair of pants. Why shouldn't a man who hoes and spades vegetables get a change of clothing? There were plenty in the cane fields who did nothing but hoe and spade, yet they got clothes. Things simply weren't as well organized then as they are now. There wasn't a thing the *campesinos* could do; the order was given and they couldn't say a word against it. But they'd trade a couple of chickens on the sly for a pair of new or used pants.

In a camp near ours the cook exchanged a pair of boots for a can full of coffee. Another comrade saw him and reported him to the comrade in charge. They brought the People's Court[25] from the nearest town to the camp to judge him. The Court decreed the comrade cook wouldn't be allowed out on a pass for six months. Not even for a trip to town.

A committee was established in our camp to punish comrades who engaged in such deals. To be a member you had to be integrated in something—either a member of the union, an aspirant to Party membership, a militiaman, or something like that. The rest of us usually didn't participate in the trials or even know they were held until they were over. They'd ask us to gather in the mess hall and tell us, "We met and agreed to dismiss this comrade for lack of discipline. . . ." They'd tell us why they made their decision. Then the head of the camp would ask, "What's your opinion of this? Do you agree with this comrade?"

There was one case where the man was given another chance because the rest of us defended him. That comrade drank a lot. One day he wore the uniform of his militia battalion to town during working hours. He got drunk and started bothering people. We participated in his trial and they asked us if the culprit should be sent back. Several of the comrades said, "No. He does his work, his production is up to standard; besides, he

24. Men and women from the country; often translated as peasants or farmers.
25. See Barrera, n. 44.

never bothers anybody." So they told him, "All right, we'll give you another chance. Your only punishment will be not to leave the camp for thirty more days. You may not go to town, no matter what."

The Discipline Committee held that trial in our presence because it was about a small matter. When a comrade bought animals, or stole, or fought or insulted somebody, the Committee locked themselves in a room. But I think all the trials should have been in our presence.

I only cut cane for about a month in the 1968 harvest. The mills didn't start grinding for fifteen days after we arrived, so we weeded, watered, and spaded around the edges of the plantings. We also cleared the drainage ditches. About twenty-five days after we began to cut cane, the cook said to me, "I'm going to talk with Sixto to ask him to assign you to the kitchen." I worked in the kitchen the rest of that harvest and got back to Havana in May.

At the moment, our CDR is simply not functioning.[26] Nobody stands guard or does productive work. Nobody does a thing. Everyone still has the same post they had from the first. Until not so long ago I was doing all the work. When members were called to a meeting, I went; when Dávalos or Minerva was assigned to take a census, I did it; when the president and organizer were called to the sectional to be assigned tasks, I went. I can't carry the whole burden by myself, so I gave up too. Now I'm like all the rest.

Practically all the CDRs in the *reparto* are like ours. Not one of them functions the way it's supposed to. In fact, our Committee was the least bad of the four in the *reparto*. At least it functioned, more or less, for a while. The next best was Tomasa's. The other two Committees have always been stalled. They had to eliminate Martinito's CDR and merge it with Tomasa's because it carried out no tasks ... nothing.

The CDR has sent down long lists of needs of the people in our Committee—roof and drain repairs, for instance, but nothing is being done about them. The plumbers did a bad job of laying down the plumbing, so pipes must be raised and the walls of lots of homes torn up. That requires a brigade of at least twenty or thirty people, including two plumbers to be in charge. Comrade Lina told me she was trying to organize masons and plumbers to make repairs on Sundays and on their days off, but nothing happened.

A lot of the neighbors say, "Look at them! They come here to tell us things need to be done but they don't do a thing about it and they're the ones in charge. Why should we be such dopes as to do guard duty and

26. CDR organization suffered across the island in 1969–70 due to the mobilization of manpower for the 10-million-ton sugar harvest.

swallow all that garbage? What's the point? When we need something, nobody gets it for us." That's true in a way.

We send a report to the zone coordinator, then she sends it to the sectional, who in turn passes it on to EMMIU or CONACA.[27] That's where things get held up indefinitely, because, with the problem of the sugar-cane harvest, those organizations are short of men.

We haven't had the support of the superior levels. The zone people didn't trouble much to come down to the base. Say a CDR is disorganized to begin with; if you just cast it adrift, it's bound to get completely disorganized. If you know I'm apathetic and timid, you should push me, get me going, guide me. If you don't, I won't go anywhere.

There are too few people with a revolutionary conscience in our neighborhood. You have to keep at them to get any work done. But the zone Committee is like a man with two different businesses: he never goes to see how one is doing unless he wants something from it. That's what the zone Committee does; they only come when they need us, like when the Party says, "Comrades, we need volunteers ... there's an urgent need for blood donors ... we must make cytological tests. ..." Otherwise they don't bother about us.

Everything could be set straight if they'd restructure the CDR. I talked with Lina not long ago, to ask when they were going to do it. "In a few days," she said. Well, that was more than a month ago. Lina hasn't bothered to come down and hold a meeting in all that time. The CDR is supposed to meet once a week or every fifteen days at the very least. We're going to have a meeting with the whole zone organization to discuss which front is the weakest and how to get things done. We'll orient the members to see if we can't put some life into them. I hope problems will be brought out too. Somebody who thinks a certain person should no longer be president should speak up and say so, right at the meeting, without embarrassment or hesitation.

We need a real revolutionary to lead the CDR. I mean, somebody who's interested in the Revolution and cooperates when he's needed, even to the point of taking up arms. Every revolutionary militant is duty bound to make his contribution wherever the Revolution needs him. He can't say, "No, I won't do this." He doesn't gripe and curse when he has to wait in line for something; he should help organize the line, and mediate a quarrel. A revolutionary should stand guard or do productive work. He shouldn't just wait for his comrade to say, "Come on!" He should take the initiative and say, "Here I am. How can I help you?"

27. EMMIU is the agency which, in cooperation with the Housing Control Commission, razed old housing and had responsibility for the repair and maintenance of new housing. CONACA is the state water-works *consolidado*, which is also responsible for plumbing repairs.

To me, somebody who's sworn the oath of *"patria o muerte"*[28]—to learn, experience, contribute, undertake new tasks, and get new knowledge—is making more sacrifices than the rest of us. A "fatherland or death" revolutionary must put the Revolution before his family and himself. If they send him to do farm work for two years, he does it. If he has to go to Oriente or to the Isle of Pines, he goes. He must do any task they ask him to because he's sworn, "I'm ready to live or die for the Revolution." Someone who's done that can't go back on it, in my opinion, or he didn't really feel it in the first place. They explain the significance of that oath before somebody takes it—whether he's in the Party, the Army, civilian life, or a work center.

The oath is a big step and I haven't taken it. I feel free and independent. I freely choose any step I take according to my own ideas and beliefs. But once I'm incorporated into an organization, my individual liberty ends insofar as any action I take as a member of the organization is concerned. The same thing applies to my work, because everything must be done according to the will of the majority. So if I take one step as an individual, I'm nobody. I must march along with the rest of my comrades.

I feel revolutionary but I don't set myself up as a model for others. I'm willing to make sacrifices but I'm not responsible enough in my work. I don't volunteer every Sunday and I'm not completely incorporated in the sugar-cane harvest. That's where the real revolutionaries are—out cutting cane. They're in the Rice Plan, working in the mud. No, I can't call myself a real revolutionary. But I *am* a *cederista*,[29] and I've benefited from it. I made new friends, like Comrade Lina and Comrade LaVilla. I went to places I'd never seen. Above all, I learned about the Revolution and politics.

28. "Fatherland or death," an expression used to characterize an ardent revolutionary.
29. A member of the CDR.

Chapter Six

They Just Don't Understand

I'M THE KIND OF PERSON whose doors are open to everybody. If I have a bit of anything, I share it. I'm not a jealous fool either. Once a woman is my wife, I put all my trust in her. I don't mind if she goes to visit a neighbor. I trust my neighbors—the ones who are living close to my house anyway. They've kept an eye on my house and have sat down with Flora and given her good advice—the men have, at least. But I still had problems with her.

When we were first married, Flora was always busy doing things around the house. I could hardly get her to stay still long enough to eat. But that didn't last long. She soon made friends with other women in the barrio, who had a bad influence on her when I was gone from the house. The people here still have evil in their minds. They've been taken out of the slums but can't get the slums out of themselves.

Look at Celina Quevedo, for instance. She's done a lot of bad things. She was still living in Las Yaguas when they found her guilty of drug possession—marijuana or whatever—but she'd already moved to Buena Ventura when her case came up. She agreed to a rehabilitation plan, so they sent her to the women's jail at Guanajay for only two years. Her mother, old Sita, lives on the first block of the *reparto*. She took care of Celina's younger kids. The older ones did as they pleased. Celina hasn't been in trouble since she got out, but I don't see eye to eye with people who live off drugs and gambling. They go to gambling joints and even gamble at old Sita's house. Minerva gambles there too.

Contraband and selling things are not allowed, yet people like Celina and her family carry on such activities because there's not enough vigilance. It's wrong because it's illegal, but the truth is you simply *have* to buy in the black market right now. You pay a lot more for contraband goods than they're worth, but right or wrong, you've got to do it. I don't claim to be better than anybody else—I've done it too. I've found myself without oil and paid somebody 2 *pesos* for a 24-*centavo* bottle of oil. I've bought milk for 1 *peso* a can, but nobody would make the mistake of approaching me to buy mild cigarettes or any other luxury article. Nobody can come to me with a pair of pants they got for a chicken and offer to sell them to me for 30 or 40 *pesos,* or a pair of socks for 5 *pesos.* I wouldn't buy them if they did. But food . . . that's something else again.

I've seen Celina buy rice and milk over the legal price from people outside the *reparto,* then resell them for even more. Some of her friends bring cloth for reupholstering chairs right to her home and she sells it. She's not integrated in the Revolution. Of course she belongs to the CDR and has stood guard and done volunteer work, but that's because she was rehabilitated.

Not long ago Minerva Ruz had a big blowup with Celina, whom she used to call *comadre.* Celina lives in our section, on 3rd Street, and Minerva showed up there one time and yelled at her. That's the way Minerva tries to dominate people. She yells them down and makes them scared. "Nobody can come give me orders or yell at me in my own home," Celina told her. Well, Minerva and Celina won't even look at each other now.

Celina was one of those people Minerva handed out CDR cards to, though she was not supposed to because Celina holds consultations with saints in her home. That never bothered Minerva. She's a member of *El Palo* herself and holds prayer meetings and sets out a glass of water with a sprig of sweet basil, and people go to her home for those masses. The belief itself is no bar to membership, but you're forbidden to exploit others and harm a neighbor.

I still see a lot of women in the barrio who've been presented to a *santo,* but the *santero* religion isn't as strong as it was. Claudio is the only practicing *santero* in Buena Ventura. He's not from Las Yaguas but took over his brother's house after the brother died. People from places as far away as Pinar del Río go to him and he sells them a bit of powder for 21 or 25 *pesos.* Only about a month ago, a fellow from the country went to Claudio to try to get his wife back.

Claudio belonged to *El Palo* before he came here, but I've heard a rumor that except for being striped,[30] he isn't anything. That means he's not accepted for all things, only for some. But he uses that to deceive and exploit people. He takes them to his house and gives them instructions. He sells them little figures, materials for saints, saucers of food, seashells.

Of course Claudio is very careful. He won't consult with just anybody. It has to be people he knows well. Police agents come around to investigate every now and then, and he's afraid of being punished for having that stuff. Claudio hides the things behind his patio door and always keeps the door closed. He's roofed over that part of the patio, too, to keep his neighbors from looking down and seeing his stuff.

---

30. Ritual marking of an initiate into the Palo Monte sect.

I think the people must have felt religion more in Las Yaguas than they do here. You saw more of it and it was more alive. Of course, in Las Yaguas *santeros* had more freedom and could get whatever they needed—swords, iron kettles, and so on. Here it seems they're scared and keep all their religious things hidden, because the government has been sending people around to take those things for the Cuban folklore museum. Nobody has come here to take anything, but the word has gotten around.

The government is doing that because the *santeros* have been deceiving and exploiting the people, making them believe they can do wonders for them. Then, too, they've joined counterrevolutionary organizations of *santeros* and spiritists which they use as a means of exploitation.

FLORA MIR:

Ever since I moved to Buena Ventura with Nicolás I've seen a lot of my neighbors. We help one another in case of sickness and we lend each other things. In this block our best neighbors are Baldomero and his wife, Cira. Whenever I need water or oil or salt, Baldomero lends it to me.

When I go visiting, it's mostly to Abelardo's house. I've had a cup of coffee now and then at poor old Nilo's house, and at Fajardo's and one or two others. I get along best with Nilo, with Baldomero's wife, Cira, and with Ovidia. I'm friendly enough with Lorenza Morilla but she's apt to make fun of people. The other day as I was coming home from work she said, "Aren't you the proud one? Walking by, stiff as a ramrod, and not saying hello to your friends!"

It's none of her business how I walk. I walk as I damn well please because my body belongs to me. I stopped short and challenged her, "Come up close and repeat that. And don't go thinking I keep my distance because I'm scared of you. You're far too old to be cute at other people's expense." Did I tell her off!

The home I've visited most is Fajardo's. But I don't go there anymore because I'm not on speaking terms with Telma or Matilde since they made catty remarks about my shoes. I was wearing the high-heeled brown shoes Abelardo had given me. One of the heels had broken so I asked Nicolás to remove the heels and I wore them when we went out. We passed in front of Telma and Matilde and they started to giggle. When we got back home, Nicolás called Matilde over and said, "Look, *chica,* when you have a friend you shouldn't go sticking a knife in her back. What kind of friend are you? I heard you making fun of Flora's shoes, saying the points looked like the peak of Monte Turquino."

"Oh no, Nicolás, I didn't say that."

"Oh yes you did! Look, Matilde, I'm over thirty, too old to be taken in so easily. I've lived longer than you and have had more experience, so don't go thinking you can put anything over on me."

"Now look, Flora is too old not to realize . . . she's twenty-four."

"You're mistaken, you know," I put in. "I'm twenty-two, going on twenty-three, and you've no right to call me an old woman. If anybody's old it must be you." Telma joined in and the three of us quarreled till we practically broke each other's horns.

Telma makes fun of everybody, even old Miguel. Imagine making fun of an old man! If she doesn't criticize your clothes, she makes fun of your hairdo or says you're dirty. I've had to tell her off about the way her Lucila pushes my little girl around. She hits her and tries to pick quarrels with her and I know that it's Telma herself who tells Lucila to do it.

Matilde used to go to my house and listen to *Nocturno* on the radio until I started my new job. After our quarrel she asked me to be friends again. Nicolás said to me, "Look, *chica*, a real friend, if she had two pairs of shoes and saw you had no decent ones, would give you one of hers. It would be better if you didn't make friends with anybody. Stick to your own house and keep your door closed. That's the best way. When I'm out, lock the door so nobody can barge in asking to be friends. You don't know what the people of the barrio here are like so don't risk having anybody screw you up anymore."

Matilde butted in sarcastically, "Yes, sister, it's better to have no friends. You stick to your house and I'll stick to mine."

"Right!" Nicolás agreed. "Why go around looking for trouble?"

There are a lot of quarrelsome people here in the *reparto*. I'd say the worst ones are the families of Celina Quevedo, Ondina, and Inés Ceballos. The police have never had to intervene in any of the quarrels around here but they've been called over to the grocery store because of Telma's, Celina's, and Sita's people.

The nicest house on this block is Raquel's. She owns a frigidaire, a television, two spring mattresses, and a sewing machine. Her little girl has a room of her own with a bed and bureau. They also have a nice dining-room set—the tabletop is protected by glass and there's a china cabinet with glass doors. Their bathroom is very pretty. Raquel really keeps the house up well.

The poorest houses around here are Nilo's, Fajardo's, and Salvador's. Mine is poor enough, goodness knows, but theirs are much worse. The only trouble with my house is that I don't have sheets for the beds and I need to buy a mattress for our bed and another for the girl's bed. I also need a large wardrobe.

Neither Nicolás nor I have any godchildren in the *reparto*. I asked my sister to let me be godmother of her baby girl but she'd already asked somebody else. I have no relatives living here in Buena Ventura, only friends. Acquaintances, I should say, because none of them is what I'd call a friend. I know, since I got in trouble trusting them.

I've given only one party at home since I came to the *reparto*. That was on Nicolás's saint's day, his twenty-ninth birthday. We bought a cake and beer, and filled the sink with ice to put the beer in. Nicolás's brother Ernesto came with his wife and child. We invited some neighbors from the *reparto*, too—old Nilo, and Cira, and a little old lady who used to live next door. Nicolás also gave a piece of cake to Dávalos, the president of the CDR.

I don't know much about the religion of my neighbors, but when I'm sick Nicolás sends for Baldomero, who's a *palero*. Besides knowing how to concoct remedies with herbs and eggs, Baldomero has *Palo Monte* things at home. So do Cira, Onelia, and Inés Ceballos. Minerva has her saint too—Eleguá.

Nicolás's favorite saints are St. Lazarus and St. Barbara. I believe mainly in *La Caridad del Cobre* and in God, but also in St. Barbara. I've asked St. Barbara for things and she has granted my wishes. The last vow I made to her was for my daughter Adelaida, who was in the hospital with inflammation of the lungs. I vowed that if the child got well I'd light four candles to St. Barbara every week. I bought them for a *medio* each from a little girl who sold them from door to door, because I couldn't get any others. Adelaida got well and was out of the hospital in a few days.

I've asked St. Barbara for other things, like good health for my husband and children, which she hasn't granted.

They sell saints in some stores—I don't know whether they're rationed. They used to be sold from door to door, but I haven't seen anyone selling them around here lately. I've never bought a saint in my life. I've no idea what they cost but I bet they're pretty expensive now. I have a St. Barbara that Nicolás won at a fair before we moved here. He has great faith in his St. Barbara; he wouldn't want to sell it. He lights candles in front of her whenever he can get any. He also has *La Caridad del Cobre* that somebody gave to him—Abelardo, I think—about a year ago. I guess it would be worth 4 or 5 *pesos* at the stores.

I always set out glasses of water for my dead relatives. I've two for my grandmothers and one for Nicolás's little brother, who would be twenty-two if he were alive. He was run over by a bus when he was seven. Then there's a glass for my little brother who died. One glass is for my sister Marta's son. When I fill the glass, I mention the name of the relative it belongs to. I change the water every other day after washing out the glasses with soap. I also put white flowers in them. Here in Cuba we have the custom of setting bread out for St. Lazarus, but not for the dead. At least *mamá* never did.

SALAZAR:

Carlos Cueva Bernal and his family are the neighbors Flora and I are the friendliest with. *Papá* was friends with them when they lived near us in Las Yaguas. The old lady did our laundry. One of them, Hilario, sold ice cream and *papá* would go there to buy. *Papá* gave them old clothes to sell, too.

A lot of relatives live in Carlos's house aside from him and his wife, María del Pilar Fabregas, and most of them are mentally ill and retarded. His grandmother isn't all there, his Aunt Coralía is retarded, and so is her son Rodolfo, but at least *he* doesn't talk much. I had to find a place for him at my work center. He was too embarrassed to apply himself, he's that shy. I often help to search for him when he gets lost. Sometimes he walks around singing. I try to bring him home, away from the boys who crowd around and poke fun at him. Carlos, too, is a bit backward. His Aunt Delfinita, Marcelo's wife, is the most normal of the lot.

I feel easy in my mind when Flora visits Carlos's house. "As long as you behave yourself and no problems come up," I've told her, "you can go iron there and chat with Delfinita. It's a good thing to have friends. One never knows when one may be desperate and need a helping hand." I trust that family, not like some I could mention, who are always trying to give people complexes or evil ideas. But I go there just to see Carlos. When Flora and I pass through the parlor and say "Good evening" to the others, they look kind of sour, especially his Uncle Marcelo. I guess they don't like anybody to visit.

Marcelo and Carlos argue over finances. I often help smooth things over. "It looks bad for you folks to quarrel," I tell them. "After all, you're all relatives here. . . ." They're both wage-earners and have clothes and pay their electric bill. They get what they're entitled to from their ration book, but they have only enough for their most urgent needs. They're still poorer when it comes to sense. Marcelo thinks he's boss because he's paying for the furniture, but Carlos is the real owner of the house.

The houses were distributed under the slum-clearance plan. You had to accumulate a certain number of hours' work on the housing project as part of the payment. Marcelo was away with a militia unit and all the work fell on Carlos. He also had to choose the house and get the furniture moved. Those tasks are done by the person responsible for the family unit. But Marcelo and the neighbors told Carlos to put down his grandmother as the one in charge, because she's the oldest. Marcelo took over after that.

The real trouble started when Carlos decided to take a wife. Marcelo's so high-handed he didn't want Carlos to go out, let alone get married. Later Marcelo told María del Pilar the family was against their marriage because Carlos is retarded and a wife was bound to rule him. Marcelo told me there's a lot of evil in María del Pilar. She's cleverer than Carlos and bound to get him involved in some kind of trouble. I've even heard that she was in the bad life.

She wound up at the house of Ramón Fajardo, near where I live. That's where she and Carlos met. He was too shy to talk to her, but several of the neighbors encouraged him to try. *"Muchacho,* you're a grown man and free to choose a woman. If you like her, all you have to do is take her home, introduce her to your folks as your wife, and settle down with her." So one day María del Pilar packed up her suitcase and moved into Carlos's house.

The tables turned then and Marcelo couldn't boss Carlos anymore. María del Pilar won't let him. They all fight about everything instead. Then Marcelo steps in and goes to the police station to make charges. Soon after, Carlos goes there to make *his* complaint against Marcelo and Delfinita.

One night María del Pilar was standing guard at the Committee office. It was about 1:00 A.M. and Carlos was outside talking with me. I guess his baby was crying—he sleeps in the room next to Marcelo's and the partition doesn't reach to the ceiling—and all of a sudden Marcelo and Delfinita got dressed and ran to the police. Soon the police patrol came by to ask why nobody was looking after the baby. We explained the situation and told them Marcelo should have just called the baby's mother. They didn't make any formal charges. The policeman simply said that when one person is on guard, the other should stay home with the child.

They've gone before the People's Court twice about the ration book. Marcelo refused to let Carlos have the ration book. Whenever he saw something could be bought, he'd go down and get it for himself.

When I saw the situation, I told Carlos, "You're my comrade. Come on over to my house, and whatever I have, I'll share with you until you resolve this. You and your wife can stay until 10:00 or 11:00, when it's time for us to go to bed. Then you can go to your place and go straight to bed. That way you won't have any problems with the rest of them."

Flora had no objection to the arrangement, so we shared with them for two or three months. They'd bring along spaghetti, beans, or a can of milk for our kids. It would have run into money if they'd eaten in restaurants every day. I helped out because I know Carlos would help me if I got into the same fix.

The problem of the ration books was solved by the People's Court. The judge said, "Let's make the two families independent of each other. Each shall be given a food-ration book and clothes-ration book." Marcelo was left as head of the family nucleus of six—his wife and son, his mother-in-law, his sister-in-law, and her son. Carlos's ration books include him and his wife and child.

Then they had a big fight about Carlos's new kerosene stove. There was a census of whether you cooked with kerosene or alcohol.[31] Coralía has a Korean kerosene stove, so she told them she cooked with kerosene. They didn't put her or any of Marcelo's family down for a stove. María del Pilar told them she cooked with alcohol. The inspector came to check. He saw she was telling the truth and put her on the list for a new stove. When Carlos brought it home, Marcelo said, "What! You only brought one? Why didn't you bring ours, too?" Then he said, "Nobody can use that one because it belongs to the old lady." He sent her over to the grocery store and the grocer told her she wasn't on the list. Marcelo was so mad he took off his shirt to fight Carlos. Carlos didn't want to use the stove after that. "Use it and don't worry about it," I told him. "Let him do as he likes. He has no right to it."

Carlos's comrades tell me that he's a fairly good worker. "His only defect is that when he's absent he never tells anybody why," they say. He was absent two or three days when he had that big quarrel at home. So they sent him out to the cane harvest as a sanction. The man in charge of the warehouse told me, "Look, I have no choice. We're sending cases like that to work in the cane harvest, to see if that will straighten them out."

Carlos hasn't had any trouble at work since, except when María del Pilar shows up to complain about something. She hangs around the warehouse until Carlos is through. The other comrades don't like that. All the laborers and assistant carpenters laugh at them. They tell him, "What's that woman who looks like a starved cat doing here, Carlos? Is she trying to do you out of your hard-earned money?"

In María del Pilar's presence, they say that Carlos has another woman, just so she'll make a fool of herself. She, poor girl, has no guile and she doesn't know how to hold her own when they kid her. She gets mad and yells at them instead. That makes them laugh even harder.

I've told Carlos more than once, "Don't let your wife go to the warehouse anymore. It's shameful, *chico*. She talks in front of all your comrades about your private problems."

With all I've done for him, Carlos complains about me sometimes. He says there have been times Flora and I haven't helped him. Marcelo used to tell me I was blind if I couldn't see Carlos was the kind of person you shouldn't help because he's so ungrateful. "Yes, you're right, Marcelo," I'd reply. "Carlos is kind of ungrateful. He's tight. He doesn't like to share with anybody."

But I think he's like that because he's retarded. It's made him turn inside himself so he can't understand sharing. Nothing is important to him except his own affairs. He's very distrustful and suddenly gets a complex for no reason.

31. The government discouraged the use of alcohol for cooking because of the high incidence of accidents. Owners of alcohol stoves were offered kerosene stoves in exchange.

I'm no longer on the best of terms with many of my neighbors and a lot of that is Flora's fault. Those friends of hers brought me nothing but trouble. They encouraged her to take up with another man—Ignacio Reyes. Matilde Cabrera is a tall, black girl who likes to dance. She put a lot of ideas in Flora's head and showed her how to carry them out. "You'd be better off with Ignacio," she said. "You'll have a lot of clothes. He'll take good care of you."

Ignacio got Lilia Betancourt and Francisca Domínguez to be his go-betweens. They took Ignacio's letters to Flora and read them to her—a neighbor lady showed them to me later—and they told her how wonderful Ignacio was, that he'd give her more clothes, food, and money than I. What can you expect of women like them? They were both prostitutes.

The worst of the lot was that so-called revolutionary, Francisca Domínguez. She belongs to the Women's Federation. But what kind of comrade would get money by exploiting someone else? Ignacio offered her money to resolve his problem through the *santos,* and she accepted it.

Ramón Fajardo was in it with her. He and Francisca are close friends. When Ramón lived alone she'd go there, cook for him, and they'd go to bed like man and wife. And she used him as a tool, because he has a little box with *santos* and iron pots and so on.

Francisca told Ignacio, "Don't worry, you'll come out all right with me, just watch and see how things are going there." They had get-togethers at night, too. Ramón would tell Flora not to be a dope, that she was very badly off with me, that I'd never get ahead. He harped on the fact that I hit her now and then and he took advantage of all sorts of things to work on her. Flora herself told me the advice they gave her. They practically forced her into Ignacio's arms. "We're judge and jury here and this is where the trial is going to be held," Francisca and Lilia said. "We'll stand by you, no matter what. Don't be afraid, nothing's going to happen to you."

And Flora, well, they bought her conscience, that's what. That kid just doesn't know any better. They say she's easy. Sure she is. She has a weak head. Maybe she's retarded or has some kind of nerve sickness. She just isn't normal. Here was Ignacio offering her castles in Spain and she simply swallowed the bait. Minerva advised her to wait till I got back, but Flora went ahead and took the plunge. She was blinded by those people. They're completely evil and care for nothing but their own self-interest. Otherwise why would they advise a married woman to leave her husband without telling him first?

If Flora definitely wanted to leave me, she should have said, "Nicolás, I don't want to live with you anymore, for such-and-such reasons." That's the correct way to do it. To go off as she did is immoral. An experienced woman considers her children and thinks things over seriously before she takes such a step. A simple little quarrel is not sufficient reason to break up a marriage. Even two quarrels . . . a married couple should think things over, analyze why they quarreled. They should figure out which of the two was right. But Flora doesn't have enough sense for that. Anybody can take her in. She's no dope, of course. But she has no self-assurance. A woman her age needs more malice to deal with the arguments and propositions people present to her. Especially when they use religion to exploit the situation.

What else can you expect from people like Lilia Betancourt, a mere kid standing in the doorway of her house, who comes from a place like Las Yaguas? She treated Flora like a tramp. The day she and Francisca took Flora to Ignacio's house he spent 10 *pesos,* 5 for Lilia and Francisca to divide up and 5 for Flora. Flora was afraid to take the money home so she did it for free. He had what he wanted—my wife in his power.

FLORA MIR:

There's a colored man named Ignacio who lives right across the street from Baldomero, next door to José Dávalos. My so-called friends around here played a dirty trick on me. They advised me to leave Nicolás because he bullied me. He quarreled with me when they visited, and they thought he beat me up and never gave me money for clothes. He gave me money, but only on payday, if he had any left over. Lots of times he had so many bills to pay he'd tell me, "Look, old girl, I can't give you any money this time because I'm broke. Next payday I'll give you some so you can go shopping." People had such nasty minds they thought that meant he wasn't keeping me right. But sometimes he went with me and bought me clothes as soon as he got paid.

So my friends kept after me. "Flora, you'll be happier with Ignacio. He'll keep you well. You'll have lots of clothes and shoes, and he won't send you out to work. He wants you to go live with him but that's up to you to decide."

I found out that Ignacio paid my friends to carry those messages to me. He gave money to Lilia Betancourt, Matilde, Cristina, and Pascual's wife, the *santera,* who lives by the park. All four of them took money for tricking me.

Ignacio would wait till it was Nicolás's turn to stand guard, then he'd run over to visit me. I warned him that we'd better meet somewhere else because the neighbors were watching us. But he'd just say, "So what? Let them!" Or else he vowed he'd stay till Nicolás got home and have a talk with him.

"Now don't you go talking things over with Nicolás," I said. "If you do, I'll have to get out of here and I'm not about to do that."

"Don't worry, I'm man enough to face up to your husband and tell him I want you to live with me," Ignacio insisted. I said yes just to keep him from talking with Nicolás. If I'd stopped to think, I would have said no. Well, I'm so trusting and inexperienced that I listened to my friends and moved in with this guy. That was on December 24 and I only stayed with him eleven days. He was married but was separated from his wife. She went gallivanting to parties all over the place and got drunk. She'd moved out long before I went to stay at his house.

As soon as I moved in, he gave me 40 *pesos* to go on a shopping spree. I bought a lavender blouse that's faded now, a pair of low-heeled shoes that are worn out already, and a ball and a teddy bear for each of my daughters and for my little boy at *mamá*'s. In all, I spent 23 *pesos*.

The eleven days with Ignacio were happy in a way, without Nicolás to quarrel with me all the time. It was miserable living with Nicolás then. He kept scolding me and would say mean things, like, "You're crazy!" He'd say I didn't keep the house clean, that I refused to cook, or that I didn't wash the clothes. Well, I'd just like to know how I could wash clothes without soap? I *do* wash, as long as I have soap or can get some in exchange for a can of milk or a bit of coffee.

Nicolás wouldn't leave me, but he wouldn't stop quarreling either. It was nice to have a rest from that. Otherwise, I didn't care much for Ignacio. He was too old. I just went to live with him to get rid of Nicolás's quarreling and because those so-called friends of mine kept telling me how well off I'd be.

Nicolás found out I'd left him when Ignacio told him. It scared me into a fit, I can tell you! I'd slipped over to Ignacio's house when Nicolás went to buy groceries. He was on his way home when he saw Ignacio. "*Ay*, Ignacio," he said, "am I ever drunk!" That was a lie. He was just pretending because he was happy that day and he'd been out having a good time.

When Ignacio told him about me, Nicolás broke down and wept like a baby, begging me not to take my little girl Emelina away from him. He adores her. Well, to make a long story short, murder was practically committed on our street that day. Nicolás was striding down the street swinging a machete when Manolo Morilla caught sight of him and ran after him shouting, "You must be crazy. Stop! Stop!"

Nicolás waited for him to catch up. "I'm just going to stand guard and I thought I'd take this along," he said.

"And since when have you gone to stand guard carrying a machete? You can't fool me. I know you're up to something. Don't go looking for trouble, *muchacho*. Listen, go back home and leave that thing there." Luckily Nicolás did as Manolo advised. But there could have been murder, with Nicolás killing Ignacio or Ignacio killing him.

I took my daughters along with me to Ignacio's house. Then Nicolás asked me to bring the baby over to see him, so I did. "Let her stay with me," he begged. "I'll see that she has good care. I'll pay somebody to look after her." That was a lie because he couldn't afford it. After a while he said, "Here, take her." But the girls ran across to visit him all the time and he'd prepare milk for them. Ignacio asked Nicolás for his ration book to buy my food and the girls' and then he'd give Nicolás his share.

I didn't go back to Nicolás right away. Instead I went home to *mamá* with my little girls. My brother Cosme's wife, Alba, came to get me. She said, "Come with me, your old lady is sick." Ignacio was away so I gave the key to Minerva and said, "Give Ignacio this key and tell him my folks sent for me and I had to go. But don't tell him where they live."

Before we left, I asked my sister-in-law Alba to do me a favor. "Go ask Nicolás to lend me 5 *pesos*. Tell him I'll pay him back as soon as I get home." I'd spent all the money I had and needed more for the fare to Guines.

Nicolás sent me the 5 *pesos* and a message, "Tell Flora not to pay me back and to quit that foolishness and come home because I still like her." Not long after Alba came back, Nicolás himself appeared. "So you're off to Guines," says he. "Wait for me there. I'm going to your *mamá*'s house too."

I said all right. Then he kissed the girls with tears in his eyes. He didn't make a sound but he couldn't keep the tears back. He really loves those kids.

In the bus my sister-in-law said, "Look, Flora, I lied when I told you your old lady was sick. I thought I'd better get you out of there before a tragedy occurred. Once a black man falls in love with a white woman, he refuses to let her go. If she leaves him, he gets violent."

In Guines *mamá* said to me, "You did right to leave Nicolás. I was told he beat you and that's one thing you should never put up with."

"No, he didn't beat me," I told her. "But he'd get mad and quarrel with me all the time."

"That's reason enough. If a couple can't get along with each other, they're better off separated."

That very day Nicolás came to *mamá*'s house after work. He didn't stop to bathe or change. He hugged and kissed me and played with me in bed. When *mamá* called us to dinner, he said, "Not now. We'll eat later." About 7:30 we got up, bathed, and ate. We talked, then we turned on the radio and danced.

It was very nice, but all of a sudden Ignacio showed up. I don't know who gave him *mamá*'s address. I guess he asked around until somebody told him. He knocked on the door, and when *mamá* opened it he said, "Good evening, Señora. Is Flora here?"

"Why no, she isn't."

"Now look, Señora, don't tell me that. I know she's here."

"Señor, I'm telling you she's not here. But in any case, it's none of your business whether she is or not. I don't know why she left Nicolás, who's so good to her. Nicolás got her out of trouble and gave his name to her daughters. He's a good man and very much in love with her, you hear? How can a dirty black like you dare to fall in love with my daughter?"

"Very well, Señora. Will you be so kind as to let me in so I can talk with your husband?"

Then my sister-in-law Alba, who's hot-tempered, jumped up and yelled at him, "I should say not! The old man is sick. He can't come out to talk to any damn fool who asks for him."

Mamá put in, "I'm the one who solves any problem that has to be solved, and the old man has no say in it. Will you do me the favor to get out of here!" *Mamá* had warned us not to show ourselves, so Nicolás and I stayed in the kitchen where Ignacio couldn't see us, but we heard everything. Nicolás said to me, "Want to bet that I'm brave enough to go out with you and tell that man I want you to choose between us?"

"I'm not scared," says I. "Let's go! I'll tell him right to his face that I don't want to go back to him because I'd rather stay with you."

But *mamá* said, "Stay where you are. Why should you go out of your way to look for trouble." *Mamá* calmed Nicolás. "Trust me," she told him. "I can deal with this as well as any man. I'm strong, even if I am a woman."

Then my brother Cosme went to the door and said to Ignacio, "Get out, you dirty *negro*, you shit! Beat it! Get going before I kick you all the way across the street!" That got the old black out but fast! I've never seen him since that night.

SALAZAR:
What Ignacio did was very wrong. Surely he remembered I was the one who told him that his wife was a prostitute behind his back. I did it because the situation reflected on him as an officer of the union local. He left his wife, but he didn't take my helpful attitude into account when he decided to lead Flora astray. Instead, he took advantage of our great friendship. We were comrades, both members of the militia, both integrated in the Revolution. That kind of thing should never happen between revolutionaries.

When I finally showed up, Ignacio said, "*Chico*, I think the *reparto* isn't big enough for both of us."

"Well, *chico*," I answered, "I was born in Las Yaguas and as far as I know, I haven't done anything wrong. So you're the one who must go. If I ever leave, it will be because it suits my convenience, not yours." I stood firm. I stayed in place, didn't quit my job or stop standing guard. Ignacio saw that I went ahead as if nothing had happened.

I had a talk with Flora and she came back to me. Ignacio was left all alone. When we met at the butcher shop, he'd make faces at me and turn away. He realized he'd done wrong and was ashamed. I stayed quietly in my place in the queue. I didn't make an offensive gesture or look angry. I'd gotten back what was mine.

Some of my neighbors were dead set against my taking Flora back. There were two groups, one that thought I should take her back and one that thought I shouldn't.

Minerva took my side. "No matter what some other people may think," she said, "there will always be those of us who will lend you a helping hand." She knows I've been good to my wife, that I'm orienting her to act right and go by the good path. Minerva's older and used to be in the underworld herself and knows what kind of people egged Flora on.

But at first Minerva tried to use the situation against me. We were discussing the reorganization of the CDR when she said, "You haven't accomplished a thing so far, so why bother now? Remember you have a paper up there."

The paper simply said that a certain man had taken up with my wife and was responsible for her and her children. Minerva had signed it and I took it to Personnel. "That paper doesn't harm me in the least," I told Minerva. "You wrote it to report what happened here and I myself took it up to them."

Minerva's always been the same bossy, bad-tempered woman, a real firebrand. I've known her since I was a child in Las Yaguas. She would hit policemen and guards and didn't care if they socked back or hit her with a stick. She herself told me she was arrested for fighting with a policeman, and she boasted that she once belonged to the underworld. That means stealing, delinquency, doing everything bad. She says that to scare people into doing what she wants. She's told me right to my face, but I answer, "So what? What do I care?"

I can't say she was ever a whore. At least I never saw her walking the streets. Her only real husband I've heard of was a guy with the name Barbudo. That Barbudo used to be involved in bad things. Now, with the Revolution, he's reformed. He's a soldier and leads a completely different kind of life. But from what I've heard, he used to be a hustler. He didn't give a damn what he did.

Most of the people here from Las Yaguas are bad. They're always on the lookout for somebody they can play for a fool or exploit or deceive. But I'm not easily deceived. When you live with people from the slums, more than anything else you need malice—a bit of evil—in your makeup.

It's because I live in a barrio made up of people from the slums that I can't go to the country to cut cane or do volunteer work anymore; my wife and children wouldn't be secure. A man is needed in the house at all times. That's why a woman gets herself a husband. There are some who can resolve their problems and take care of the place until their husband comes back, but my wife doesn't have enough experience to do that and she lacks that little bit of guile you need to survive in a low barrio. If I'd been at home, Flora wouldn't have been won away from me.

Not that I blame the Revolution or politics for my personal problems. The same thing has happened to others, but there are women who don't need to be watched constantly and protected from all comers. They have enough sense not to be influenced by counterrevolutionaries who say, "Don't be a dope, have fun now that your husband is away. You're young, enjoy life!" and all that sort of crap. The people I hold responsible are those with a negative attitude toward the Revolution who took advantage of my sense of duty to create problems for me.

FLORA MIR:

Ignacio goes to Norma's house next door sometimes. But when people tell me he's there, I answer, "Look, that's none of my business. As long as I don't have to see him, it makes no difference to me." He knows full well that I'm living with Nicolás. Nicolás says to me, "You be careful when you're alone, even if it's only for a minute. That man wants to get you back and he's going to try to bamboozle you again."

"Never again!" I assure him. "What happened happened because I was inexperienced, but I never make the same mistake twice."

It was thoughtless of me to have sex with Ignacio. When I thought it over I wished I hadn't done such a thing to Nicolás, who's a good man. I was too impulsive, that's all.

Baldomero told me to put an egg in a glass of water, with the names of all the people who induced me to leave Nicolás. It had to be a whole egg, not cracked or broken. I wrote four names on it—Matilde, Lilia, Francisca, and Cristina—and then put the egg in a jar of water. I've kept it behind my bed ever since. That's to keep them behind me so they can never deceive me again. I'll keep it there until I get well.

I'll never, never leave Nicolás again. He's changed so much. He doesn't quarrel with me anymore and he helps me do the housework and is nice to me in every way. Before, he'd see me up to my neck in work and never lift a finger. Now that I have a job, if the house is dirty and I'm asleep, he cleans it himself. He has to help me because I work too. Besides, I often help him. When it's my free day, I get up at 1:00 or 2:00 in the afternoon, straighten up the house, wash dishes, scrub floors, and if there's any cooking to do, I do it. When I was sick, Nicolás washed his own clothes and mine too, as *papá* used to do for *mamá*.

SALAZAR:

Experience taught me I was too kind, too sincere, too open with my neighbors. I don't bother much with them anymore. They gossip about you whether you do this or that and criticize you no matter what. For instance, several of my neighbors have asked me why I don't clean up my bit of land and why I still live with "that woman." I tell them, "I'll clean my land when I feel like it and I live with Flora because I damn well want to." It isn't my fault that the women who've crossed my path have been kind of free. It's never been my choice. Is it my fault if a woman like that says to me, "I like you, let's get engaged?" People just don't understand.

That includes my neighbor Enrique Cueva. He's out of a job and lives alone. He had a lot of young girls up to no good visiting his place so I began to avoid him. I told him, "I've changed. I don't want anybody in my home." He got angry because we'd never quarreled. He said if I treated him that way I wasn't his friend.

"No, *chico*," I said, "I know none of this was your fault. It's simply that I don't want anybody at all in my house when I'm not there, just as a precaution." We offer each other a cigarette, a drink, or coffee when we meet in the street now, and we talk about our revolutionary tasks in the CDR. We're still friendly, but not chummy.

The same goes for Norma, and old Neno and Nilo. Some of these people have known me all my life. They see me take these precautions. So they say, just kidding, "Hey, Nicolás, you act as if you'd won first prize in the lottery."

Or they say, "Nicolás, what's the matter with you? Why are you keeping so much to yourself lately? We had nothing to do with your problem; you can't go around blaming everybody for it."

"No, folks, I'm the same as ever," I answer. "If you need me, I'm there to help you. But from now on I'll be more careful, that's all."

My next-door neighbor said to me, "Look, *chico*, you can't lock yourself in or forbid your wife to go out simply because of that trouble you had. Let your wife go anywhere she pleases."

"You may be perfectly right, *chico*," I told him. "But that's the way I've decided to live. I'm fed up. What happened has been a great lesson to me. I won't make the same mistake twice."

I'm sure I'll end up in a mess if I get to trust people again. So I keep up my guard. That's your only choice in a barrio where vice still exists. Otherwise you end up like Ramón Betancourt and his family.

Ramón was away working in Cayo Galino, on the docks, collecting raw materials. His wife, Pastora, had an affair with Guillermo, a boy of about twenty-five, who is Alfredo Barrera's brother-in-law. Guillermo gave Pastora a big belly. Ramón told her, "I don't want you with that belly. Get out of here! Go live with your boyfriend." But Guillermo had no place to keep her. So she stayed on at Ramón's house for a while, sleeping in the parlor, alone. Then Guillermo, who works out on the Isle of Pines for the Ministry of Education, got them to give him a house, and he took her there to live.

Ramón lives with his son Lorenzo and his daughter Lilia. Lilia studied at night, but dropped out. That girl's gone to the dogs. She has one boyfriend today, another tomorrow. Several people told me they've seen her hugging and kissing men and all that, outside the barrio. Somebody told me he saw her at the Prado bar. She wasn't acting the way a girl should act. She's real foul-mouthed, which points the same way. Besides, you only have to see the guys she's going with.

We're not friendly with the Betancourt family anymore because of all that. Lilia used to come over and help Flora around the house. But I don't want her here. She's dirty. I don't want to get involved in any problems on her account. I mean, here she is passing herself off as a señorita when she's no such thing. She goes around with people who lead a bad life.

I allow Matilde Cabrera to visit even though she worked against me. She comes over from nursing classes in her white smock and talks or sews. She asks Flora for stuff. They even lend each other money. I have no objections. "You're both young girls," I told Flora, "you should be good friends. What happened is over and done with."

Chapter Seven

Getting Ahead

I WAS THE ONE WHO integrated Flora in the Revolution. I got her to join the Federation of Cuban Women and the Committee so she would make sacrifices and learn what life out on the farms is like with all the suffering and discomfort. She's due for a great experience when she goes to do productive work.

It's only right that women should join in the task of production when there's such a need of workers in Cuba. Besides, it's an education for them. The best teacher anybody can have is work. Work is no one's enemy. It calms you down, it makes you understand many things—sharing, comradeship, and so on. It's a healthy way for young men and women to keep themselves busy and interested, instead of thinking about things they shouldn't.

Women's labor is necessary for the Revolution and it's an advantage for the women themselves. Working women get new ideas. They learn a lot of things besides how to keep house, clean, cook, and wash dishes. The Revolution encourages them to study and improve their minds. Women are more alert than before.

I can honestly say that I'm perfectly willing to let my wife go anywhere, in any manner, to do anything, in spite of the fact that she isn't healthy enough for it. If she can't make a contribution in one way, she can make it in another. I don't trust Flora all that much and there's no telling what she'd be up to, but out in the country she'd think more of her home and family. Here with us she might not give us a thought.

It used to be a man wouldn't let his wife work for anything. "No sir," he'd say, "I'm the one who supports my family." But nowadays a woman sometimes works harder than her husband, and there are even cases where she knows more. They wash, cook, sew, and offer their services in sanitation work. Whole battalions of women cut cane, do all sorts of farm work, and stand guard at night at the shelters for the women comrades in the harvest. I'm all for it. But I had to struggle to convince Flora, because some of our neighbors filled her head with stupid, counterrevolutionary ideas. They told her she'd never see her kids again if she sent them to a *círculo*.[32] "That's a lie," I told her. "Don't go believing those things." They also said she shouldn't stand guard because it was dangerous and something bad might happen to her. I told her she'd be all right and stood guard with her myself to show her how.

FLORA MIR:

Nicolás took me to the Federation of Cuban Women and talked with a girl there, a fat, white one with chestnut hair and eyeglasses. He told them I wanted to work but had no place to send the children. The fat girl said, "There's plenty of work right now. There are vacancies at Marianao Beach, the Social Circles,[33] and in a nursing home. Which do you prefer?"

"Send me to the nursing home because it's near where I live."

"All right. There's only one more thing you have to do. Bring me a letter from your Federation delegation. The letter from the Committee isn't as important as one from the Federation." She took down my name and address and gave me a slip of paper. I went to Fela, a little colored girl who lives in Buena Ventura and works for the Federation there. I told her I was joining up. I asked her to please hurry the business because I needed a job and couldn't get one unless I was a Federation member. I've already started to pay my dues—I used to pay 25 *kilos*, now I pay 2.50 *pesos*.

The same day, I presented the paper to the head of Personnel at the nursing home. "Good," he said. "When do you want to start working, tonight or tomorrow night?" I told him I'd rather wait till the next day.

I'd never had a job before because of the children. Not that I didn't want to. I once thought of doing productive work in the country when Nicolás went to cut cane. I wanted to go too, so as not to be home alone. He could cut the cane and I could gather it and we'd leave the children in the *círculo*. But they told me they'd have no vacancies in the *círculos* till August or September. The woman there said, "Come back on August 5 to see if we can do anything for you. Wouldn't you like the children to go to the *jardín?*"[34]

32. The *círculos infantiles*, children's circles or nursery schools, are part of a nationwide child-care center program under the jurisdiction of the Women's Federation since 1961. The *círculos* accept children from age forty-five days up to five years. The service, intended primarily for working mothers, has been free since January, 1967. In 1969 there were 44,245 children enrolled in 364 *círculos*, with thirty additional *círculos* under construction. (Figures quoted by Clementina Serra, former national director of the *círculos infantiles*, in *Granma*, July 4, 1969, p. 3.) The day-care center capacity in 1974 was about 50,000, with a projected 150,000 capacity for 1980. (Fidel Castro, quoted in *Granma Weekly Review*, Dec. 8, 1974, p. 2.)

33. Community recreation centers organized under the jurisdiction of *Poder Local*'s Communal Services Front.

34. A less formal, less structured nursery school than the *círculo*. In the *jardín* the children spent most of the day at free play in a fenced-in park or garden. They had lunch and snacks at school but went home before the evening meal.

"No, I wouldn't." I liked the *círculo* better than the *jardín* because the kids get plump in the *círculo* and keep regular hours and have everything they need. Besides, they sleep at the *círculo* and you take them home only on weekends.

I told her, "I'd have to take them there every morning and fetch them every afternoon and I have enough to do as it is. I'm not eager to kill myself." So I didn't go to the country with Nicolás.

On my job at the nursing home I started out for work at 10:00 P.M. and got there by bus at around 10:15. My routine was pretty much the same every night. I went to the dressing room and changed into my uniform. Then I took a turn around the ward to see if the old folks were quiet and the bathrooms were clean. At 11:00 P.M. the 3:00-to-11:00 shift left. This shift cleaned the ward at around 8:00 in the evening. All I had to do was sweep the floors and clean the bathrooms.

After everybody on my shift arrived, we'd go to the laundry to get the clothes. Each one carried up the bundles for her own ward. Then we'd all go to the kitchen to work and sometimes I'd look around for something to eat.

Usually I drank some milk with sugar, then would go to the sitting room and get a little sleep until 4:00 A.M. Then I'd get the bedpans and chamberpots from the bathroom. At 5:00 I began to take the patients out of bed. Then I'd get myself some coffee while the patients were having theirs. I took away the dirty cups and made up the beds with fresh sheets. I made fifty-odd beds because that's how many patients I had in the ward. I took off the sheets they peed on and put them in a bundle on a wheelchair. When the water was turned on at 6:30, I started to empty the chamber pots and scrub them with a long-handled brush and *Pinaroma*. I mopped the bathroom floor and took the bundle of dirty clothes to the laundry. Afterward I changed into my own clothes and took a bus home.

In my free time before the work started at 4:00 A.M., I usually chatted with Clara, an old woman who worked in the kitchen. Of all the comrades at work, the one I liked most was the male nurse, Gombal, because he was such a pleasant and really good person. He's colored but fairly light-skinned, not black.

The one I disliked was Remberto, the head of Personnel. I'd asked him to transfer me because my ward was too big and I was far from strong. In fact, I was all screwed up. And besides everything else, the veins in my feet were swollen. I explained to Remberto that I couldn't walk much because of my feet. But he wouldn't budge. "Now you listen, Flora," he said. "You have to stay there until we get a new comrade and that's that! Why don't you like that ward? I can't see anything wrong with it."

"It isn't that I don't like it, Señor Remberto. The patients there are real sweet, especially the old people. They're just like little kids. But

I'm all alone at night and I'm scared every minute of the time, with no one to talk to. It's the loneliest place in the home."

"It's got to be separated from the rest of the place because it's the senile ward. But I'll have another comrade stay with you on the night shift."

Nicolás was pleased about me having a job. He earned only 52 *pesos* every fifteen days and that wasn't nearly enough to cover our day-to-day expenses. We did much better when we were both working. I earned 75 *pesos* a month as long as I wasn't absent.

What I earned I spent on the house. But I wasn't able to buy everything at the store for a while, because every time my number came around, it found me broke and I lost my turn. I bought whatever came to the grocery store and I paid for the baby's milk. I also paid the electric light bill and I gave Nicolás 10 *pesos* for smokes, matches, and for his bus fare.

We owed 10 *pesos* to old Nilo so I paid him back. We'd borrowed it for food and to get the baby's milk. I also paid back the 2 *pesos* we owed old Abelardo and 1 *peso* to old Luis—13 *pesos* in all. I paid back 3 *pesos* I'd borrowed from the old porter at the hospital.

After I started working, Nicolás wanted to quit his job as a carpenter's assistant because it was too far away. He went to the manager to explain that he had to stay home, that I'd been put to work on the night shift in a very large ward and didn't get home till 9:00 in the morning. Besides, he took care of the children while I slept. The manager said, "All right, you may come back to work any time you want." So he stopped working to look after the children until there was a place for them at a *círculo*.

Nicolás gets awfully restless when he isn't working. He got absolutely desperate. He was very anxious to get back to work. He told Nilo and Abelardo to wake him up in the morning but they never did. When he saw that, Nicolás said, "People want me to fall back instead of getting ahead. They want us to remain poor and screwed up."

SALAZAR:

We weren't able to get Flora's girls into a *círculo* or *jardín*. I wasn't their father but I had to take their mother's place. After all, somebody had to give them milk and change them. Somebody had to make breakfast, wash clothes, scrub, sweep, and dust. It was my duty to help solve the problem, so I did it.

The trouble is I worked far away and began to be late for work. I explained my situation to the man in charge. "Take all the time you need," he told me. "Of course, I can't put you on the payroll for hours you don't work, but if you get here at 8:00 or 9:00, don't worry about being late. Your comrades know you have a tough problem. They'll understand."

The comrades did help me. My working conditions were good. I had transportation and free lunch. But I was anxious to give Flora a chance, to see her progress and make a personal change. I decided to ask for a leave of absence. I went to the directors of the Carpentry unit. They admitted that this was a personal problem and they could do nothing to solve it. They understood I had to do it—I wasn't asking for time off to go to the movies, or to Coppelia to eat ice cream, but to meet a real need. They didn't have enough assistants in my unit but they excused me from work.

Flora didn't much like the idea of going to work while I stayed home with the kids. "What's the point?" she said. "The 75 *pesos* a month I earn isn't enough for us."

"It's all your fault that I had to quit my job," I told her. "You should get your work done in time so you could get home earlier."

Flora didn't know her work too well and was slow. She often had to stay late to finish all her tasks. She wasted time, too, stopping to chat with other employees or with patients, getting out at 8:30 A.M. instead of at 7:00.

Of course I understood she was a beginner. She was in bad shape, too. She had anemia. That sapped her energy. She also had liver, kidney, and ovarian trouble. She'd get sharp pains and have to sit down. That slowed her up some. I told her, "Flora, let's go to a doctor. He can give you some shots." The doctor gave her injections of liver extract with vitamins. She improved little by little.

I don't know how to put it, but after a while it seemed to me that Flora wasn't interested in things really important to a wife and mother. She started to think of her home and her husband kind of superficially, automatically. She wanted to rule herself and do things as she saw fit. Her mind was busy with the money she was earning, perhaps with the new dress she could buy with it. She gave a lot of thought to dressing and fixing herself up to go to work. I don't mean only that she was forgetting the problems at home. It wasn't anything as clear-cut as that. It was as if she thought every problem was solved now that she had a job.

I'd spoken to her about her negligence before. The way she'd go to Marcelo Quintana's house to iron one piece of clothing and stay on and on to gossip. But it didn't stick and I brought it up again. I gave her constructive criticism in the course of our little argument. I said we were far from seeing the end of all our problems; we had to keep struggling. But she wasn't frank with me. Instead, with the little brains she has, she started to think up mischievous things to annoy me. Me, her own husband, who's always been so open with her.

The things she does are stupid, not evil, like leaving a puddle on the bathroom floor. She doesn't make a move when a kid pees on the floor. She'll pretend not to see and wait for me to wipe up the puddle. She's really hinting it's my job. If she does mop up she tosses the stinking rag anywhere. She doesn't even flush the toilet a lot of the time. She lets the kids' shit stay there and clog up the drains. What would she do if she had six children, eh? She'd be in some fix, I can tell you! I've often told her, "You're the kind that drowns in a bowl of water."

She's played all kinds of tricks in the kitchen, too, like she'll go to work and leave the pitcher and glass for me to wash. She just wants me to sacrifice more time in the kitchen so I can't drop in on the neighbors. She doesn't even want me to stand at the door, much less go out. She's jealous, see? She thinks I'll do to her what she did to me. "I know that as soon as I'm away at work you're going into some woman's house to have an affair with her," she tells me.

"My child, I'm not that kind," I answer. "You're mistaken. When I have a woman of my own, I don't go around chasing other women. Besides, how could I go out and leave these angels alone? I'm not like you. I wouldn't risk their falling down and breaking their skulls or getting killed."

Sometimes I'd visit a neighbor while Flora was asleep. She'd get mad if she woke up and I was gone. She'd say, "I sure as hell don't want you going to somebody else's house. . . ." And so forth and so on.

"My child, you don't even know why I went," I'd say. "I had to borrow soap to wash the kids' clothes until my next soap ration comes due," or whatever.

Flora has a more jealous nature than I do. She takes the crown as far as jealousy goes. I never go to such extremes. She gets jealous if she so much as sees a girl or young woman standing beside me. One Sunday she fussed because I talked to the girls at the counter of the pizzeria where we went to eat.

I began to remind her of a few things she'd done that I wouldn't put up with anymore. "You committed an immorality with a man right across the street," I said. "It's known to everybody in the barrio. I won't allow you to give our address to anybody or allow anybody into this house again."

But Flora did give our address to the male nurse at the home, without asking my permission. She says she gave him the address because he had a pair of pants for me. He wanted to invite us to a party, too. How does she know what kind of person he is or what ideas he has in his head? Most men will make a play for any woman they can get when their wife isn't around.

I'm sick of it, of men and women doing things with no consideration for anybody else. My wife is so stupid, how would I know what that male nurse had in mind? There are men who give, and first thing you know, well, they'll expect to take their share. This business of giving and not taking anything in return never works. I know that from experience.

I was so angry I told her, "I'm not painted on the wall. I'm your husband and you've got to respect me. I have to know ahead of time who might be coming to my house. If that man showed up when I was out, you wouldn't know how to get rid of him."

"He wasn't thinking of anything bad," says Flora, kind of mad too. "Besides, suppose he asks me to do what you're thinking of? I'll say 'Nothing doing.' Don't keep harping on what happened to me once. That's over and done with. It won't happen again."

"Well, maybe . . . ," said I. "It depends on what he offers, kid, and what you hanker for. Money, maybe. Or candy. Maybe he can bribe your conscience with that. You know what a sweet tooth you've got." But Flora doesn't know how to analyze those things. I tried to explain it to her but she can't psychologize it right.

"Another thing," I said, "the housework is your business, not mine. I'm a good man so I help you out, considering that you go to work, but it's your duty."

Flora went right to bed after our argument. She was angry and kept tossing and turning. I paid no attention. I put a piece of cardboard on the parlor floor to sleep on and listened to the radio. Awhile later she said, "Listen, Nicolás, kick me out if it's too much trouble for you to keep me in your house."

"That's no way to talk to me," I answered. "I'm your husband. I said what I did only so you'd wake up and learn to take care of yourself." I let her sleep alone in the bed. She slept well because she took some pills. Next morning she woke up in a good humor. Flora's anger never lasts.

"We don't have to quarrel or anything," I said, "but you must realize I'm the boss. As punishment, you'll have to get the groceries."

Flora's always doing some fool thing. Like the time a neighbor kidded her and she lost her head and insulted him. I've advised her to stay out of loud arguments. "Above all, don't raise your voice," I tell her. "It doesn't do you a bit of good after the problems you've had. People will only think worse of you than they already do." And how many times has Flora let somebody or other use her as a tool? For example, it's ridiculous to exchange a can of milk for a pack of cigarettes, but she's done just that. The baby's the one that suffers.

There's nothing easier than keeping track of things in the ration book. But people say to Flora, "You don't want such-and-such a thing? Lend me your book so I can buy it. I'll pay you back." And the poor little dope hands it over. It never enters her head they might buy other things too, if she doesn't go with them. She let these people have the clothing-ration book for the whole family when I was away cutting cane. They bought about five thousand things with it—men's socks and shorts and a length of dress goods and all sorts of things we ourselves needed.

With the money they pay her she's bought milk or something at the grocery, or a meal at a restaurant. She had no need to do that. She could have asked my brothers or her aunts. Any of them would have lent her 10 or 15 *pesos* until I got back.

I think Flora's begun to heed my advice and repent of her faults. We only argue about her bad habits. She shouldn't throw around dirty words like *coño* and *carajo* when she scolds the girls. I hate that. It would be much better if she just slapped their bottoms. She does that too, and even hits them on the back.

Flora's trouble is that she wants to rule the house but she doesn't know enough for that. I say to her, "If you had the experience you need as a woman and the firmness of character a grown woman should have, I'd let you do as you please. But after all the mistakes you've made and keep making every day of your life, I can't trust you."

Very often she tries to boss me. Suppose I tell her, "A friend of mine is coming to visit." Right off she'll say, "Oh no, you can't have him here. There isn't enough food to go around."

"Then just find the way to make it go around. I want him to have dinner with us and that's that. You must do as I say."

Many times she gives me a good reason for doing something her way. I admit it. Otherwise I tell her, "Well, I must be blind but I can't see this your way and it has to be thus-and-so." I mean, the man's the natural head of the family. If Flora really knew what she was about and if I had any reason to be grateful to her, I'd honor her and give her whatever pleasure she wanted. But I'm tougher than she is. I'm not the kind to render honors to a king without a crown.

We had a quarrel not long ago. I was talking to her about self-improvement. I told her she should think about going to school even if it's only at her work center. I asked her how far she'd gone in school. "I finished the third grade and got promoted to fourth," she said.

"Listen, kid," I said, "if you really completed the third grade, just answer a few questions." I took some books I had and set her several problems in arithmetic. She couldn't work out one of them. "You may once have studied the third grade," said I, "but you don't remember anything. You'll have to take it over."

"But I did finish the third grade. I did, I did! How can you sit there and tell me right to my face I didn't?"

We had words but I didn't hit her. I haven't hit her for the last six months. I'd slap her face when she called me *maricón* in front of others, but I realized blows never taught anybody. Instead, I relied on words.

I explained that if somebody doesn't qualify in school they tell you straight out. Then you must take an examination. I found out when I took self-improvement classes. Flora realizes now she'll have to take third grade over.

Still, I'm often sorry about our fights. I don't like to scold her. "These arguments between husband and wife are ugly," I tell her. "We shouldn't quarrel like that anymore. You must find a way not to provoke me." But her ignorance and stubbornness make me mad. They force me to tell her two or three truths about herself.

I know Flora's satisfied with me as a man in spite of everything. She says she loves me, and a woman who doesn't like a man doesn't show affection. Flora kisses me when she gets home from work and all that. But I'm always the one who says, "Get ready, Flora. Wash yourself and everything because we sleep together tonight."

Flora is young and wants sex every night. She protests only once in a while. She'll say, "No, I've a touch of my liver complaint" or "I'm menstruating." If I let two or three days go by without doing anything, she'll say, "You have another woman for sure because you never want to sleep with me anymore." I say, "No, my child, one can't do that every day. You have to rest up between times to keep your strength up, especially now that we don't have all the nourishing food we used to have. If my brain is weak, it might get weaker. Besides, you're ill; I would be taking advantage of you if I were on top of you all the time." Sex wears you out if you're at it every night. So we'll let a day go by. "After all, tomorrow is Sunday," we'll say. "We might as well leave it till then."

The kids sleep in the same room, so we have intercourse at 2:00 or 3:00 in the morning, when we're sure they're fast asleep. We do it once, usually. Then Flora feels calm. It's easy to see she's satisfied with me. Not in words but in the sex act itself, when we come to a climax. But one time we did it twice. The next time I slept with her she said, "How come you only want it once tonight? The other night you did it twice."

"It can't be that way all the time," I explained. "I was a couple of nights behind schedule then."

When Flora and I first got together the neighbors said, "Forget about having children, Nicolás; you're *machorro*."[35] None of my other women got pregnant by me. Perhaps they were too old or had ovary trouble. Or maybe I *was* sexually weakened from the lack of some vitamin. But Flora was so young, I felt, "What no other woman was able to give me, this one will." The neighbors tried to discourage me, and Flora too. But I proved that the woman has a lot to do with it. It just took a while, because when we got together Flora was pregnant with Emelina, and I didn't have intercourse with her after the sixth month. A woman's belly is too low then. Her parts expand and sex hurts her insides. There's nothing to do

35. A term usually applied (in the feminine form) to a barren woman.

but wait till the baby's born and the forty-five days have passed. I waited even longer to see if she started bleeding again.

Flora would tell me she wanted to do it. "No, wait just a little longer," I'd say. "Now that you're well, I don't want to risk upsetting your system again."

I didn't have relations with any other woman, either. I'd lie down with my head at the foot of the bed and pretend I didn't have a woman. I controlled myself up to the last moment. I didn't even think of sex.

I got two condoms the day we started having sex again. I don't think washing her parts keeps a woman from getting pregnant. Flora claimed that as long as a woman is suckling a baby she can't conceive. "What difference does it make anyway?" she said. "If I don't get pregnant, fine! If I do, I'll just go to a doctor and have an abortion."

"Let's see if the doctor authorizes that," I told her. "Getting an abortion isn't nearly as easy as you think. Suppose the doctor says no? I just hope you know what you're doing." I thought if God sent me a child, I'd just have to accept it. Sure, I make the baby, but God has something to do with it.

Flora had trouble conceiving. She had coldness of the vagina and ovary trouble—maybe from going barefoot or washing her hair while menstruating—and there's no warmth in the womb then. The cold gets concentrated inside and the woman can't have babies. Anyway, that's how Lucrecia Romero explained it. She said when a man and woman make contact the womb opens up and gathers up stuff that causes conception. But it can't collect enough when it's cold.

Besides, Flora's insides were a mess. Her womb and parts were dislocated. After the last baby, her parts became full of air. She felt it inside her, like a ball that rolled and bounced around. Sometimes her period was very short and scanty; other times it lasted five or six days. There were months when she didn't have a period at all.

One day old Miguel said to me, "Nicolás, you two have been together so long and you don't have a child of your own yet. Your wife must have some kind of vaginal problem that doesn't allow her womb to gather up or conceive. If you want to cure her, fill a basin with boiling water and tell her to squat over it so that the steam can get into her."

I kept after her to try it because I was afraid I'd get old without ever having a child. I even prepared the bath for her. "You can't go to bed until you've steamed yourself," I'd say. "It's for your own good."

After a month she said, "I don't feel that ball in my insides anymore." Then she took the treatments of her own free will. She kept up the injections of liver extract and vitamins, too. She ate her lunch and dinner and stopped going barefoot. She started to menstruate regularly, on the first or second day of the month, and it lasted three or four days. Her womb began to strengthen. She kept the heat inside her and became pregnant.

The neighbors were astonished when they noticed Flora's belly growing. "Eh, now Nicolás is producing," they said. "How come he hasn't ever
made a baby before?" They even said the kid wasn't mine. Lucrecia
Romero told Flora right to her face, "Nicolás never made that belly. How
could he start having children now when he's never had any before?"

Flora got right back at her. "If you're that curious about whether
Nicholás can make babies, go tell him to make you one!"

I complained to Lucrecia's eldest son, and he said, "You're perfectly
right. It was a rude and disrespectful thing to say. And it's none of her
business. I'll speak to her about it."

I told Flora, "If anybody else asks whether the kid's mine, don't say yes
or no. Just tell them it's none of their business."

Once Flora got pregnant we didn't have time to go anywhere. Besides,
she had no good shoes for going out. We used to visit *papá* now and then,
but we stopped because of Flora. She went to the polyclinic seven months
after she got pregnant. Dr. Otero examined her and prescribed some vitamins and minerals. She didn't tell Flora to rest or quit her job, but Flora
couldn't bend down or turn the patients in their beds, and she slept a lot
on the job. She asked for a transfer to the day shift. "But how can you expect me to do that?" the head of Personnel asked. "If you get sleepy and
can't finish on time in the night shift, how would you manage in the daytime, when you'd have to bathe the patients, take them into the dining hall
for lunch, and so on?"

He explained it to me and I said, "You're absolutely right, comrade."
Then I told Flora, "Ask to be transferred to a smaller ward where there's
less work. That way you can get through in time and come home earlier." I insisted the only way we could get ahead was if we both worked.
Anyway, she'd soon get three months' maternity leave. She'd made a real
effort at her job and got along well with her comrades, but they wouldn't
assign her to a smaller ward. So she decided to quit.

"All right," I said. "Stay home until the baby is born. As soon as you
feel well again, incorporate yourself in the work force. But this time it
will have to be farm work. You quit your job so they won't employ you in
any other work center."

I told Flora to go the Ministry of Labor and she did. There a comrade
from the Women's Federation told her if she'd gone there first, she
wouldn't have had to quit her job. She had the right to ask to be transferred to another ward and to work on the day shift. If only she'd talked
to that comrade in time!

Flora lost her permanent job, her maternity leave, and her child's
place as a full boarder in the nursery school. The head of Personnel
didn't want to spoil her work record completely, so he put down that she
really couldn't do her work unless all her kids were in boarding schools.
But nothing seemed to bother Flora. She didn't mind having another
baby either. Pregnancy makes her more easygoing. We don't argue

about what happened to her job. But I want to place the kids somewhere so she's free to study and work. Not just for the *centavos* but for her own sake.

FLORA MIR:

The Revolution has been good to me. It's given me a job and many other things I needed, like clothes and shoes. Those are rationed, but rationing is also a good thing. Before they decided to ration things, people fairly killed themselves standing in line to buy. Now, you go with your ration book and buy whatever you're entitled to and that's that. There's no fighting for your place in line, no quarrels about who got there first.

There are many things for children now that I never saw before. The government wants all the children to study, and they don't want children to be mistreated. They want children to have shoes, good clothes, and good toys.

There's work for everybody now, women as well as men. Before, there was work, but only for men. Now, if somebody doesn't work it's because he doesn't want to.

I like everything about the Revolution ... well, almost everything. Here in the *reparto* the Women's Federation hasn't done a thing these past few months. In all the time I've been here, I still don't have my membership card. Nicolás has gone there time and again to ask for it, only to be told they didn't have any just then.

When the Federation met, I brought up the matter of the membership card. The very first day we moved in, a fellow came around to our place, wrote down my name, and asked for a photo of me to attach to the blanks. So why didn't they give me a card? I've never participated in any activity of the CDR or the Federation or anything else, because I didn't have the card.

Twice I've gone with the Committee to do volunteer farm work. Both times the truck was supposed to pick us up at the sectional office at 8:00 in the morning but it never showed up. Four of us set out from home at 5:00 A.M. to be sure to get there on time. We waited till after 8:00 and then had to go back home.

I stood guard at the CDR before I quit my job. Nobody stands guard at the Committee anymore because nobody wants to. When their turn comes around, people beg off, saying they're sick or something. They're just going to let the matter drop. I wish they'd do something about it and have a regular schedule again to put a stop to the robberies in the *reparto*. A while ago somebody stole old Miguel's radio and last July they tried to break into Inés Ceballos's house.

Of the people in the neighborhood, it's hard to say which are the most revolutionary. Nicolás is a revolutionary because he never criticizes the government. Dávalos is the Committee president but he talks a lot of trash about there being no food and so on.

The conditions of life have improved here in Cuba and we're living well now. The Revolution is a good thing.

Salazar:

Before Flora quit working I went to talk to the comrade head of the nursing-home personnel. I told him I wanted to transfer there. He said it was impossible because it had to be done through a superior organization. My work unit couldn't do it. After all, they were suffering too. I mean, my personal problems were also making problems for them. The man at the nursing home raised other objections too, but I know if I'd gone to certain places in certain organizations, they might have agreed to make the change. Especially as I work with my hands and they needed me. They'd probably have taken into account how inconvenient it was for me to go on that way.

I spoke to old Abelardo to see if he could help me solve my employment problems. I was worried because I'd talked with friends in my unit and they advised me to go back to my work center even if the head of Personnel said I could stay away. They told me unless I got it in writing, the Ministry of Labor wouldn't take it into account. Staying home didn't affect my standing, but I was afraid it would bring me money problems later on. Flora's salary was about a third less than mine. My finances were going from bad to worse.

"You should go to the Ministry of Labor," Abelardo suggested. "If anybody can straighten things out for you, they can." So I decided to go to MINCON, and after that I went back to my job as carpenter's assistant. My unit made out my working papers, then they told me, "You're going to Guanajay. Your comrades are already there."

"Very well, comrade," I said. "But I have a problem: my wife is pregnant and going to the doctor. She'll have to take the kids along with her."

"There's nothing I can do about that. You'll have to go anyway. We need the assistants to help the comrade carpenters. If something starts in Havana after you're through at Guanajay, you'll come back with the rest of your group."

Flora didn't want me to go, but I explained to her, "This doesn't depend on me, Flora. The unit I belong to makes those decisions and I can't do a thing about it." She was afraid of being alone in the house at night. "Just lock up the house and you'll have no problems," I told her.

In the camp where I work now, they organize the workers by companies, squadrons, and platoons. My squadron has a foreman and about seven carpenters altogether. They sent us to Guanajay to assist the *Poder*

Local comrades of JUCEI's Carpentry Department. We live in shelters, divided by jobs—carpentry, equipment, plumbing, electricity, and painting. The shelters are about one city block long.

Our day begins at 6:00 A.M. We have breakfast in the dining room, a large room with cement tables and seats, then at about 7:00 we walk the 2 kilometers to work. We're working on three buildings, three stories high, which are going to be used as dormitories for a secondary school in the country. They were due to be completed by December 30, but we've only finished one and part of another. We haven't finished the woodwork or the window frames; things like that take the most time. They'll have to extend the deadline a bit.

We work till about 11:45 and walk back to the dining room. Everybody has his blueplate there. We all file by the kitchen to get served and pick up our mugs and spoons. There's a tank full of water and a big box of bread from which we help ourselves. We get rice, beans, and meat every day for both lunch and dinner. Also plantains from Artemisa. There are about 500 *caballerías*[36] of plantains because of the Artemisa Plan for their cultivation. The food around there is better than what we got elsewhere. It's more abundant and all that, because we MINCON people, the ones in carpentry, electricity, and so on, have a dining room to ourselves instead of sharing one with the students. We get a snack of cake at 9:00 in the morning, and in the afternoon we get two cookies or cake. We also get a cool soft drink.

Right after work in the evening we bathe. Then I take a turn around the camp to the student quarters, or I play dominoes with four or five other carpenters. We lie in bed and talk till 9:00 or 10:00. We discuss the day's problems, arguments, or the accidents we've had.

A comrade told about how one of the workers was on a trestle that slipped because they used one cement-sack full of sand as a counterweight instead of two. The problem was the assistant had never done that kind of work before. Another comrade in a certain factory in Havana was painting iron beams and got killed by a 13,000-volt electric current when he touched his wet brush to one of the beams.

We also talk a lot about how cold it is and about the job's difficulties. Sometimes the comrades say, "It's true we're far from home and have to stay here the whole week. But we're earning more because we work ten hours a day, and here we get breakfast, lunch, dinner, and a snack." I'm earning 5 *pesos* a day compared to 4 in Havana. I don't have to pay bus fare or get up as early. They give us bedclothes free, and may even give us free clothes, especially boots, because we have to walk on wet earth, which makes shoes wear out quickly. There's also a health officer to take care of any comrade who's sick or needs a shot.

36. One *caballería* equals about 33⅓ acres.

We work till noon on Saturday. After lunch they take us to Havana in a special truck. It brings us back on Monday. So we do see our families and lend them a hand. I do almost all the hard jobs for Flora, like lugging heavy stuff from the grocery. The only problem is she has to manage things by herself. Well, she just has to do the best she can.

The Revolution has a lot of construction projects under way out in the country. Our next job is on some new buildings in the *reparto* Las Cañas and some semi-finished housing projects MINCON is putting up. I'll go there, or to Grande Valle, or to Artemisa. I'll go anywhere I'm sent. I want to work my way up to 83 *centavos* an hour, the top of my wage scale. That's why I try to learn all I can when a new project comes along. Once I told the supervisor, "Say, comrade, I'd like to be assigned to work with the fellow who makes shelves and cabinets so I can learn how to cut and measure and do the finishing."

Things are going to get more modern from now on. Fidel says that in every construction crew at least one worker must be an operator of equipment. MINCON has to use cranes, bulldozers, and tractors because houses must be built more quickly. Everything is going to be mechanized soon. So the revolutionary government is training a lot of crews and starting courses for tractor operators. If I go to the Ministry of Labor, I can ask for my release from my work center. Then I could ask to take a course for tractor operator in the Rice Plan, or one for operator of heavy equipment or crane operator for MINCON itself. Maybe I'll manage a crew someday, or God knows what. I'm determined in my ambition, now that I have a steady job. I can say, "I have this job and nobody's ever going to kick me out or make me change it."

I wouldn't want to be a millionaire or get rich; money doesn't interest me. What I care about is my wife's health and self-improvement, leading a peaceful life, knowing my children have no problems, and being secure myself.

Chapter Eight

Our Socialist Society

FOR ME THE REVOLUTION is redemption. It pulled us out of the mud and saved us from terrible poverty. If the Americans landed here or something, I'd join a combat battalion and fight. I'm not just talking. I'd really fight to the death rather than let them beat me up or make me work like a mule, or live the way I used to, deprived of the necessities.

Even if I didn't like the Revolution I'd have to accept it, because as one of humble rank I've benefited from it. I lived in a shack with a leaky roof; now I live in a cement house full of furniture. So do my brothers, and I think *papá* will have a house like that soon, with the necessary comforts. I used to have to scrounge for a living. I couldn't go to school because that cost money. Nobody got ahead under the old regime except *comandantes*, colonels, and such. Now the government tries to improve the lot of all the Cuban people. They give every worker a home of his own; they try to raise the workers' cultural level and increase their technological knowledge.

Sure there's still poverty under Fidel, but poor, ignorant people aren't treated like animals. We have rights. Nobody can exploit you now because it's forbidden to live off anybody else. Nowadays it's the workers who have the power. Before the Revolution, if you lived in a room and fell behind in the rent, they'd kick you into the street. No poor person is out in the street today. We have the right to stand wherever a rich man stands, and we can make our complaints. Policemen don't come along and beat you up. All they say now is, "You're under arrest, comrade, for such-and-such a reason. Come along with me."

In the old days, if a worker accidentally upset a load of sand or cement, he'd get fired. Now the comrade in charge comes over and explains how to handle a wheelbarrow so it won't spill. Even I, who have been absent so much, haven't been kicked out. You have the right to discuss and argue your case before a commission or a council. In the past they wouldn't let you talk. You started to explain, "I couldn't come because . . ." and they'd say, "You're fired! Sign these papers and get out!"

Before the Revolution, we in Las Yaguas suffered from a lack of medical services. When somebody got sick there was no polyclinic. They'd go to the emergency clinic in Luyanó and wait their turn to see a doctor. You could see those people didn't like to attend us from Las Yaguas. It was worse for colored people. "Those blacks," they'd say; "always fighting!"

If you had a stomachache, they'd give you a pill or an enema. If you needed a drug that cost less than a *peso,* they'd give it to you free, but it was only cough syrup and such stuff. "Sugar water, that's what they give you!" people said. Penicillin, vitamins, anything like that, you had to buy somewhere else and pay full price. Nobody made a special price for poor people. If you needed expensive medicine you either pawned things, borrowed from a loan shark, or did without. A lot of people died because of that and for lack of food. Especially old people with no relatives. Now anybody not working and short of money can get medicines free at any drugstore. It doesn't matter what they cost.

Papá had eleven children with *mamá* and he told me how some of them got gastroenteritis or diarrhea and died. *Papá* took us to the Children's Hospital but he couldn't afford to put us in there. Besides, you needed influence for that. If you didn't have a letter from a doctor or a politician and you weren't a member of a health plan, you couldn't get a bed in a hospital, not even for a child.

If a private doctor ever made a house call in Las Yaguas, I never heard about it. Perhaps they didn't come because the place was so hellish, with the paths muddy and full of holes and twists and turns. Even people well off economically who wanted a private doctor or a dentist would go to his office.

There were no nurses in the *reparto* either. The emergency clinic had only a midwife. A lot of women took stuff to abort right at home, but in the end they had to see a doctor and be cleaned out.

There was a doctor with a jeep on call at the clinic and he would drive over. They never refused to attend anybody, but there was only one doctor for all of Luyanó so you always had to wait. He'd decide if the patient should go to the Calixto García Hospital. Sometimes you had to wait a day or two until there was an empty bed and the ambulance came. You'd have to be awfully sick for the hospital to keep you.

The situation is very different now. If a person's sick enough, you just have to get him to the nearest hospital and they'll find a bed for him. When the baby fell off her chair and broke her head, we took her to the hospital. They made out the hospitalization order in the office. She didn't have to wait at all. I've never had to bring so much as a recommendation from an organization to get anyone in my family hospitalized. The only problem is that beds are as scarce as hen's teeth.

Once I went to the National Hospital with a very bad cold. "You'll have to wait because there aren't any empty beds," the doctor told me. "All right, I'll wait here until there is one," I said. He had them look through every ward for an empty bed. They found one on the fourth floor in a cubicle for people with skin diseases and sent me there. The nurse on duty gave me an injection of tranquilizer and covered me up well. Next morning a doctor saw me. He made a complete examination and ordered an X-ray. I also had blood tests on an empty stomach. Then they transferred me to another ward and brought me a pair of clean pajamas. They took real good care of me for the eight or nine days I was there.

None of us has ever needed a blood transfusion, but I know that *now* anybody who needs a blood transfusion gets it. They send for a relative and ask him to donate blood. If he can't the patient gets a transfusion anyhow from the hospital blood bank. They don't have to pay for it, either.

The polyclinic also takes direct responsibility for vaccinations. They've got a team of nurses that goes around vaccinating children. They vaccinate women and old people, too. Nobody got vaccinated like that in Las Yaguas. You'd get a vaccine only if you got stuck with a rusty nail or something.

The ambulance still comes for those too sick or too old to walk. They forbid the state doctors to make house calls. But you can call a private doctor. Actually, I've never seen a doctor make a house call in the *reparto*. But state nurses often come to check up on patients after they leave the hospital.

It would be more convenient if the doctors made house calls sometimes, but the polyclinic is usually convenient enough. Not that the problem of medical services is completely solved here. The polyclinic where my family is registered should be open around the clock with a team of doctors, but they close the place after 6:00 P.M. and on Sundays. If Flora vomits or a kid gets hurt, we have to go to MINCON and get into a truck,[37] then go to another polyclinic. There, urgent cases are sent to the National Hospital in an ambulance. Our polyclinic stays open until 8:00 or 9:00 at night only during special drives, like the days of the *Jornada Guerrillera*.[38] The problem is that there aren't enough doctors in Cuba.[39] They're swamped with patients at the polyclinic. It serves an area of about 30,000 inhabitants. There's not even a doctor for emergencies

37. The Ministry of Construction had a supply depot in the neighborhood. For most Buena Ventura residents MINCON provided the nearest telephone and means of transportation for emergencies.

38. A worker-emulation period, *Jornada Guerrillera* commemorates the beginning of the War of Independence (October, 1868). (See Benedí, n. 83.)

39. Despite the fact that many doctors (about 1,500–2,000) left Cuba after the Revolution, the country had 1,200 more doctors in 1969 than in 1959. However, the ratio of physicians per person had not improved; the national average was still one physician for every 1,000 inhabitants. The ratio was lower in Havana, where 50 percent of all doctors practiced in 1969. (Leyva, "Health and Revolution in Cuba," pp. 481–82.)

there. They have to leave their patients when an emergency shows up, but with all the cases and shortages, they've never failed us. The polyclinic has begun to transfer patients to clinics closer to home, so they're getting cleared out a bit.

I've noticed that about twice as many people see doctors these days. They go when they have dizzy spells, lesions, falls, vomiting, and little colds. My family still uses home remedies for those things.

The rich used to eat well before the Revolution. But now I've heard them say with their own mouths, "What's the point of having money? We have to buy what's in our ration book, same as you. We may live better than you but we eat the same things, unless we're willing to pay black-market prices."

I haven't had any trouble getting groceries lately. I go to the store and wait my turn on the first of the month. That's when the rice and beans and things arrive. The place is crowded when the meat comes in too. Our grocery serves about 300 families.[40] People get into arguments when there's a long wait. Some leave their place and when they come back they don't remember where they've been standing. They get to talking and forget who was in front of them. The others tell them they have to go to the end of the line. I say, "It's all right. What difference does one person more or less ahead of you make." I've let them take their place in front of me. I go in the afternoon or the evening when there aren't as many customers.

There have to be waiting lines because there's a shortage of goods. We need to honor our commercial treaties; we need agricultural machinery, buses, trucks, so we must plant and cultivate things for exchange. That's why we have to live by certain regulations. I don't like shortages any more than the next person, but I must agree with this policy because I belong to the poor masses, the proletariat. When we cut cane, it isn't to fill someone's pockets but to buy tractors and machines we never had before.

Last night I was listening to a re-broadcast of Fidel's speech at Vado del Yeso over the "Voice of Cuba." I heard his speech at the dedication of a new *reparto* in Oriente, and his latest speech, too, the one where he said we wouldn't reach the goal of 10 million tons of sugar. The people did more than their part but the leaders made mistakes about equipment and so on. When Fidel said that, Abelardo and Dámaso commented, "Sure, we knew that already. How could we make 10 million when so

---

40. Each grocery store serves a fixed number of people, since each household's food-ration book is good only in the store at which the family has chosen to register. This restriction (which does not apply to clothing and manufactured goods) facilitates the distribution of food in the correct amounts from the central warehouses to the stores.

many sugar mills in Havana and Matanzas were stopped for repairs part of the time?"

"Well," I said, "it still isn't any too clear to me. Maybe the cane they're cutting in Oriente isn't giving a high yield because they started cutting too soon. It would have yielded a higher percentage of sugar if they'd only waited fifteen more days before starting the harvest." That goal was something they thought up too rapidly, too lightly. Now the Cuban people should turn this setback into a victory by working all the harder.

I didn't cut cane this year so I can't tell what the conditions were. Not that I feel guilty about not going. I mean, one more person wouldn't have made any difference in making the 10 million. But I'd like to have taken part in this harvest because I enjoy working in the country. Flora held me back. She was afraid to stay in the *reparto* alone. They started cutting right near here and I said, "Just look at that! If I'd gone, I could have been working nearby. Both of us would have been better off. But no, you wanted me to stay and I was afraid to leave you alone."

I'd hoped for the 10 million. If we make the 10 million, I thought, we'll probably have a little more of everything, especially food. But the shortages will end, little by little, and we'll have enough of the essentials. Rice will be first. The rice ration is already 2 pounds more than it used to be. Our Prime Minister has said that by 1971 we'll have all the rice we need for our own consumption. Afterward will come soap, legumes, fats. We've seen the ration of fats increased in the last ten years. The same is true of some other articles. By 1975 or 1980 root vegetables and rice will be unrationed. We'll be able to freely buy clothing, household goods.... Our house will be bigger by 1972 or '73, I hope. A one-bedroom house for all of us is unhygienic. Besides, children grow and need a room of their own, especially girls.

I feel pretty optimistic about my future as a worker. Fidel Castro has said, "Wages will be revised, starting with the lowest." So some day I'll be earning a bit more and won't be in such a tight fix economically. I'll have a trade and a longer record as a militant in the Revolution. I hope to improve myself by the time I'm forty or forty-five. We'll have greater technical knowledge and more abundance by then and there'll be better planning so a worker won't have to go through so much red tape. He won't have to run around to so many places or see so many people to place his children in a *círculo*. He'll only have to go to his work center, fill in the forms, and his children will be accepted right away.

In a way those of us who live in Buena Ventura are set apart ... discriminated against. Set apart, because you can't expect people to change in such a short time. It's ten years since the triumph of the Revolution, with the Year of Education, the Year of Decisive Effort, and so forth, but these people are still mere children in their revolutionary development. I don't say this of everybody in Buena Ventura, but it's true of an awful lot of us. It's not the Revolution that discriminates against us or sets us aside. On the contrary, it has tried to erase our past and eliminate what was bad. Day by day the government does its best for poor people with low intelligence. It tries to win over those who cling stubbornly to their old ways. They sent us the best radio and television entertainers, those of the highest social and economic rank. They sent militiamen and the comrades with the most knowledge, to try to educate us and solve our housing problems.

In spite of this, we here in Buena Ventura are not a community. To build a real community there must be deep understanding and identification between neighbors. There should be sharing and mutual help, like between friends.

We had more community feeling in Las Yaguas, at least my family felt it for those who lived closest to us. People cared when somebody got sick. When one of us was sick, three or four neighbors stopped by every day to ask how we were. When *mamá* was in labor, a neighbor woman came to help deliver the baby. A neighbor always volunteered to take an injured child to the doctor. People were closer and got along better with each other there. There was a spirit you don't find here. I don't know what made the difference. Perhaps because we lived in the same place and were all poor together.

Here in Buena Ventura we all live in the same place, but each one feels alone. People act as if they'd gone to a lot of trouble if they so much as say hello. In Las Yaguas nobody interfered with your private life, but here, if they see you fairly often, they want to butt into your life.

The new system of life helped divide families who were on friendly terms with each other because so many neighbors were sent to different *repartos*. I had a lot in common with a family that now lives in Bolívar. In Las Yaguas I'd visit them practically every day and often eat there. But the new barrios are so far apart that now sometimes two whole months pass without my going to see them. So even if our standard of living is higher than it used to be, some of us don't like living in Buena Ventura.

Now that I'm older, I like collective living and strong community ties. A fellow needs other people to talk with, somebody he can go to when a relative is sick or when he needs help. It's so disorganized here. Help is hard to come by, not because we're not all revolutionaries or because I'm an official of the CDR, but because so many of the neighbors are embittered. Why, when I go to them for help they're apt to greet me with, "What, are you coming to call me up for guard duty in that shitty Committee? You're nothing but a shit-eater." They protest and start arguments and try to make problems for me. Without a well-organized CDR Buena Ventura will never be a cooperating community, and with such attitudes we won't have a good Committee. What we have a lot of here is individualism, separatism, and backbiting.

Some people here are still a long way from the "new man." A "new man" must be free of the putrid mentality former governments left us. He will not live in evil but will enjoy what is good. He will have enough knowledge so he won't have to go through what I did. He won't know what it's like to go a whole day without eating, or with nothing but a pitcher of sugar water. He won't have to go to school barefoot, wearing torn pants, or push a cart to help out his parents. They won't have the troubles I had because I couldn't learn a trade.

The new man will also be a moral man without any of the bad thoughts we have now, like deciding what to buy on the black market, trying to buy another person's ration book, and so on. He won't have to spend time trying to get things because he'll have socks, pants, everything he needs.

My mind is still old-fashioned, full of the poverty, suffering, and evils I saw before the Revolution. The Cuban kids today who grow up with socialist minds are different. Their clothes, books, jobs are assured. They suffer no hardship. Anybody who wants to mind his own business and study has the opportunity. Of course there are a lot of boys and girls who don't want to study or work hard. All they think about is dancing at night, eating ice cream at Coppelia, hanging around La Rampa in jeans and miniskirts—and they believe everything will turn out well in the end.

Modern fashion is a great problem but it's more tolerable in a young man than in a young girl. A woman loses prestige when she wears revealing clothes. If I see a girl in a miniskirt, I turn my face away. I have no interest in looking at what belongs to another man. I should say not! Such skimpy skirts are shameful. When a woman sits down . . . imagine! To dress like that is to challenge a man. Of course, it depends on how the girl uses it. A studious responsible girl who does productive work may wear miniskirts simply to be in fashion. But the girl who's gone astray uses miniskirts for another reason. She wants to show off her legs, to "hand out the ham" as we say. She hopes to attract some man and get something out of him. When I figure out what a girl like that is up to, I cut her dead.

They used to call men who wore tight pants "queers," but now tight pants are very correct, as cowboy pants once were. I don't like those new styles—they make me feel badly dressed. And I don't like long hair falling over a man's eyes either. You ride along on a bus behind a mane of hair and think it belongs to a girl, then it turns out to be a fellow. There's no reason for that now that there are no more Rebels left in the Sierra.

Our more serious young people are dedicated to study and work. Of course there were dedicated young people in the past—in the Twenty-sixth of July Movement, in the student organizations, and in the forefront against the dictatorship. They were there to protest, organize strikes, stop traffic. But they're not like that today. Now they're concerned with self-improvement and the goals set for them by the Revolution. Some of them are members of the Communist Youth. I don't have any friends like that, but some of my comrades at work are candidates for membership. Their conduct is above reproach. They're good comrades, ready to help you when you need anything.

In the cane fields I had a comrade, a militant, who was aspiring to join the Party. When he saw me tired and out of breath he'd say, "Come on, comrade, I'll give you strength to go on." Then he'd give me a drink of water from his canteen and encourage me, "Go ahead, don't sit down. If you sit down you'll ache all over and have less energy." When we arrived at the shelter after the day's work, he'd heat water and say, "Have some of this hot water; there's plenty for us both." And he'd lend me his tin can so I could pour water over myself.

I have no ambition to join the UJC or the Party. I'm past the age to be a UJC member anyway. You have to be twenty-seven or less and I'm thirty-two. Certainly I'd like to be a Party member but I don't have the necessary qualities. To be merely an aspirant, you must begin by setting a good example. You must carry out the tasks assigned by the Party and the Revolution. An aspirant must conscientiously do his duty for the Revolution. He should be the one to take the first step and carry most of the responsibility.

Anyone who thinks Party members get special privileges is mistaken. Nobody here is given any privileges. The Party members I know live just like me. Their houses can't be better or have more luxuries; their ration books can't have any more in them. Their only privilege is to work harder than the rest for the advancement of the Revolution. Of course they do have an open ration book, because the Revolution wants them to have what they need to fulfill their tasks.[41] If a comrade from the Party needs extra help—to make his life easier so he can do better work—he gets it, just as everybody else does in those circumstances. But I don't believe Party members eat better or live better than the rest of us. How can they when there are no longer privileged people in Cuba?

Whatever privilege a comrade has today, he's won by hard work and good conduct. Anybody can get the same things by acting the same way. After all, militants sometimes work till 11:00 or 12:00 at night. They're more dedicated to work and don't have much time or spirit to spare for their homes. Their life is a little harder because they can't look back—they must go forward.

An ordinary worker is free to say, "No, I can't go where you want to send me for such-and-such a reason." A PCC[42] member or a Young Communist can't refuse a task that's set before him. If these comrades

41. We do not know what Salazar meant by "open" ration book. The rank-and-file Party members interviewed had the same ration books and lived no differently from non-Party members. However, Party members who also held high government office did have a higher standard of living.
42. *Partido Comunista de Cuba* (Communist Party of Cuba).

eat better than I do, they deserve to because they're making so many sacrifices.

I hope the time comes when I'm more integrated in the Revolution. I'm beginning to be because I'm interned in Guanajay. I have to put in a certain number of hours of volunteer work besides my regular workday. Perhaps I won't be able to participate in the sugar harvest next year, but my job at Guanajay is a first step toward contributing to the Revolution. I can't stay away from work one single day. When I have to take spade in hand and work on a Sunday, I'll do it. I'll keep working for the Revolution because the workers have the power now.

The scarcity we suffer now can't last forever. I give it another ten years because the Cuban people have shown they won't undergo hardships forever. But if things don't improve in the next ten years it won't kill us. We've survived ten years of Revolution already, haven't we?

Fidel said it: "These have been ten years of decisive effort, ten years of sacrifice. And if we have to put in ten more years of effort and sacrifice, we're willing to do it." I believe everybody who feels himself to be a revolutionary *is* willing.

PART IV

Gabriel Capote Pacheco

Chapter One

Abandoned

THE TRIUMPH OF THE REVOLUTION meant nothing to me. It made no difference to me who was in power. And yet, under the dictatorship my life was as bad as a man could have. At twenty I still couldn't read or write. For 10 *centavos* I'd break my back mopping and cleaning up stores all day. I'd see kids in the street, rich kids whose fathers were doctors and shop owners, and I'd sit and watch them and suffer. I'd look at myself, beaten down, dressed in rags, like a stray dog loose on the street.

I can't tell you what that did to me. I felt completely abandoned and humiliated. I used to sit and wonder what was going to become of me. I knew if I didn't find a decent job I'd have to steal, and all I had to look forward to was jail.

It was the Revolution that pulled me out of the swamp I was stuck in. It made a human being out of me. When I think of the things I went through as a child, it still makes me sad. I had so few moments of happiness. If I had died, I would have lost nothing.

It's in Victoria de las Tunas, Oriente, that my first recollections begin. *Mamá* went back to live there to be near her family after *papá* left us. We lived in a poor barrio, Agua Dulce, in a small, one-room house made of board and thatch. There was not one cement house there that I re- member, only board and thatch, thatch and board. We had hardly any furniture—a bed, an ironing board, a small table, a stool, nothing else.

Agua Dulce was a wasteland with a small river running through it. It was called White River, only it wasn't white, it was filthy. People dumped garbage and dirty water into it and I had to bathe there. Once I dived in and cut my head open. I was scared to go home so I put a piece of flour sacking over it and hid in an empty house. The cut was deep and

Gabriel Capote was interviewed ten times, twice by Ruth M. Lewis, three times by Oscar Lewis, and five times by research assistant Paola Costa. Capote's mother and stepfather, a Party member, were each interviewed once by Oscar Lewis. The twelve transcripts totaled 741 pages.

wouldn't stop bleeding. If they hadn't found me there, I would have died.

Mamá was sixteen when she married my father. He was twenty-six and was a soldier. They were married under civil law. *Mamá* bore him three children, my sister Rita, my brother Ernesto, who was two years younger, and I, Gabriel, the youngest. My father abandoned me five months after I was born, so I grew up without a father's love.

I can never be quite sure how old I am because I don't know when I was born. When I grew up and wanted to get married, I had to present my birth certificate to get a license. I went to the Registry Office in Banes where I was born, but they couldn't find my name inscribed there. I asked *mamá* and some of *papá*'s relatives, but none of them remembered when I was born. So then they figured out my age as best they could and decided I was probably born around 1941. I'm still not sure about the year, much less the month or the day.

My *mamá*, Ana María Pacheco, brought us up. I always think of her with love because of the sacrifices she made for us, and the more I loved her, the more I hated my father. After he left us she had to struggle hard to support us. She never had enough money but she wouldn't ask him for a thing. Only once she asked him for some money when I was in the hospital, dying of typhus. *Mamá* needed 11 *pesos* to pay for an injection, but when she asked my old man he told her, "Sure, I'll give you the money—after you go to bed with me." The bastard!

That story cut deep into my heart. God, I hated my father! From the time we were very small we'd had it pounded into us how evil our old man was. *Mamá* hated him so much she never had a kind word to say about him, only "that good-for-nothing, that skirt-chaser! I wish he were dead."

It made me suffer to see how hard she worked for us. In Victoria de las Tunas she was a servant and took in washing as well. One day she was ironing and suddenly began to cry. Rita and I were so frightened, we crawled under the table and started crying too. Whenever I think of Victoria de las Tunas, I see that picture of my sister and me crying under the table.

Mamá left us shut up at home, with Rita in charge, while she went to work. I never got to go to school because of that. I always blamed my lack of schooling on *papá*, but it was *mamá*'s fault too. She had no choice, she had to go out to work, but she could have sent us to school instead of leaving us locked up at home. We never went though, not Ernesto, nor Rita, nor I. When I asked her, "*Mima*, why don't you send me to school? I want to learn," she'd just cry. I guess she didn't set much store by schooling.

I wanted to go to school because at home Rita was forever walloping me.

She'd bang me on the head, kick me in the belly, punch me in the mouth, till I bled. Then Ernesto would go after her to make her leave me alone, and she'd whimper and beg, "Stop, stop, you're killing me."

Ernesto always defended me against Rita, until one day I walloped her myself. I was bigger by then. Wild, that's what we were. I can see that now. We had no training, no father, nobody to guide us except poor little *mima*.

Often *mamá* would go out at night with her sister, leaving us alone in the house. She didn't lock us in then; she'd just tell us how children who went out at night had their heads torn off and their hearts wrenched out, thinking that would keep us home, see? But there were lots of dance halls in our neighborhood, and the minute *mamá* left, Rita would slip out, with me straddling her hip, and go to dance with her partner. We'd get back home long before *mima*.

One night we were alone in the house and toward morning someone started pushing on the locked door, trying to get in. I was little then, four or five maybe, but I knew there was a woman in the barrio who did witchcraft and I was frightened. My sister kept telling me, "That woman has come to take you away because you're bad." Rita was holding me in her arms but I was really frightened.

Mamá would get back around daybreak and sometimes she'd be loaded down with food for us. More often than not that was the only meal we'd have that day. Many's the day we went hungry and had to scrounge a bit of food. The stores were full then—everywhere you looked there was plenty of everything—but you had to have money. The days when there was no money or food, *mamá* would give us sugar water and bread, and when that ran out she'd tell us stories to send us to sleep.

But I used to ache with hunger! Once, I remember, I was crying for a bite to eat. I kept begging *mamá* for food and she began to cry too. What did I know! I was just a kid without a thought in my head. I hadn't stopped to ask myself where the food would come from. That night *mamá* went out and came back with some chicken.

Mamá wouldn't tell us where she went those nights until once I asked her, "Where do you go at night, *mima*?" I was so insistent, in the end she told me she went to dances. Later on I found out what kind of dances they were—you know, where a man goes looking for a woman to spend the night with. But I never asked *mamá* about that. Why should I? What right had I? I know how she struggled to feed us; she often went hungry so we could eat. She made forty thousand sacrifices for us. She was a good mother and I love her dearly.

She went to a lot of those dances. One night she met a man at a dance and they fell in love. He was called Piche. He wasn't much to look at: he was partly bald and wore glasses. But he had a job as a bookkeeper, and compared to us he was terribly rich. *Mamá* went to live with him—they never got married—and she took all of us kids along. Piche lived in Puerto Padre, which is a long bus ride from Victoria de las Tunas.

Mamá bore Piche a son, Frank. After a while she began to quarrel with my stepfather because of the way he treated us. He was always beating me and he pushed my sister around, too. Ernesto was the only one of us he liked. In the end *mamá* left Piche and returned to Victoria de las Tunas. Our half-brother, Frank, remained with his father.

SEÑORA PACHECO:

I married quite young, at the age of sixteen. I'd been in love before, but I'd never had a sweetheart until I met Ernesto Capote, the father of my children. He was a soldier in Delicias, where I lived. He was about twenty-seven years old and very good-looking. My *mamá* and my brothers and sisters didn't like him because they didn't know his family. But I liked him a lot—his face and everything about him pleased me. He really was handsome.

So I got married in a civil ceremony and I went with my husband to Banes to live with his *mamá*. Her name is Claudia Batista. I never met his father. My husband went back to his post in Delicias and I stayed in Banes. I suffered horribly with that family because I was just a girl and didn't know what I know today. His sisters would flare up and hit me for the slightest thing. It was bad for me.

Then I had my first son, who was called Primo. When he was about a year old, I went to visit *mamá*, and my son died on me five days after I arrived. He wasn't dead a month when my daughter Rita was born. Then my husband left the Army and got a job in Banes, and I had two more children, Ernesto and Gabriel.

I never really knew my husband. How could I? I was a mere child when I married. He wasn't right in the head. All the money he got, he bet on the cockfights. It was horrible. Within seven months of Gabriel's birth I got a divorce. I couldn't put up with my husband anymore. He landed in Mazorra[1] and my brothers came to fetch me. That's when I began to work. I did an immense amount of work in those days.

I've had a lot of trouble and pain in life. When we children were still small my father left my *mamá* to go off with another woman. We were nine kids . . . my brother Lalo finished the job of raising us. He worked and was the big man in the family. The others married and scattered like rain, so he was the whole thing at home, and all the money he earned was for the house. He was strict and we fought a lot with him. Later he and my brothers helped me finish raising my children.

1. See Salazar, n. 13.

In the beginning, I helped *mamá* with the washing and ironing she took in. After that I went to work as a servant in a house in Victoria de las Tunas. And then I remarried. Gabriel was five years old and he won't remember that. My brother had a grocery store and this gentleman from Puerto Padre used to balance the books there, like a bookkeeper. I went to the store and he fell in love with me. He was that type of man, from an office, educated, in fact he only lacked the degree to be a lawyer. He also kept the accounts for the sugar mill. He truly was an educated man, a decent man from a good family, of good moral fiber, and very accomplished.

They call him Piche, but his name is Jesús Carrasco. He's a communist and was always going around with Dr. De León from Delicias, who was also a communist. Anyhow, I had a child by Piche, and the news of it came out in the papers when the child was born, but it had to be hidden a bit because Piche was a bully. He's still that way. At least he was the last time I saw him, when I went to see Frank, my bastard son, my youngest. It's a very expensive trip. The last time I went was four years ago, and now he must be eighteen or nineteen years old, maybe even twenty. Piche's sister raised him and has taught him well.

I didn't continue with Piche because he was mistreating my children, hitting them. I had the little girl with me and he didn't love her. He hit Gabriel when the child had a fever and there was an argument. I live for my children; he who doesn't love my children I can't love. That's why I left Piche. He was a good, moral man and all that, but his defect was that he was very strict, very nervous, and he liked everything to be a certain way. He wanted the children to understand instantly and children can't be that way. So for this reason I separated from him and went to Victoria de las Tunas, where *mamá* was living then. Piche told me, "The way we'll get back together will be if you leave that girl at home with your *mamá*," and I told him, "No, I don't leave any child of mine for anyone." So I separated from him forever and came to Havana.

I brought two children with me and left Gabriel with *mamá*. He must have been eight or nine years old at that time, a small boy. My husband's sisters lived in Havana but they didn't want to take me in because they said the children would be a bother. I had some money with me so I rented a room, and in two days a girl found me a job, working by the hour. I'd get up, wash and iron stuff I'd brought from my job, then I'd take the clothing back to work. Some families would help me out at times. I worked with one for a year and I did well then. When they left Cuba they gave me a lot of things to sell.

I found myself working on different jobs again, with men mistreating me. You know, the types who want you to do *that*. It didn't mean a thing, but I had to do it, you know what I mean?

CAPOTE:

One morning I woke up and found the bed covered with black copper *kilos.* "Where did all that money come from?" I asked.

My grandma was there and she told me, "Your *mamá* left it for you. She went to Havana last night with your brother and sister. She's gone to look for work. Those *kilos* are for you to spend as you please while she's away."

I burst into tears. *Mamá* had never left me alone before, not for any great length of time anyway. And she hadn't said anything about going to Havana. Still, when I saw all that money and thought of all the movies I could go to, I soon bucked up.

I went to live with Grandma then. She was very poor, too poor even to have a board house. Hers was made of nothing but palm thatch built over a clay floor. The walls were forever falling in and having to be repaired with more palm bark and leaves. It was just one room, like *mamá*'s—the privy was out back—and there was hardly any furniture, just a bed, I remember. Grandma wouldn't let me sleep in it because I pissed on her sheets. She was a very clean, neat, little old lady and spent a lot of time putting things straight.

I slept on the floor, and sometimes in my sleep I'd roll out through the gap between the thatch wall and the floor and wake up at the bottom of the ditch that ran around the house. Times like that I'd wonder if I'd ever know anything besides squalor, filth, and misery.

But Grandma loved me and I loved her too. I even called her *mamá* after a while. I don't know for how long *mamá* was away but it was years. And in all that time we had no news of her. She didn't write or send me money or clothes. When she did come back for me, I didn't recognize her. But I still love her, even though she did practically abandon me.

Grandma was a simple country woman from Oriente. All *mamá*'s family were country people. Grandpa worked on a farm while they were married. They separated when I was very small so I never got to know him. I heard tell of him though, and none of it was good. They say he was crazy for the women and spent every *centavo* he earned on them— and on drink.

After he left Grandma he got a job making rubber sandals, and he made enough money to invest some of it in a grocery store. He made a lot of money there but Grandma never saw a *centavo* from him. He didn't look out for his children, and as for grandchildren, we might never have been born.

In the end, my grandpa lost all his money when he took up with a woman who cleaned him out. He was old and sick by then. After the Revolution he came back to my grandma, but she'd have none of him. "Get out of here," she told him. He came to my *mamá*'s house then, and that was the first time I actually met him. He was just a little old man. *Mamá* sent him packing too. "So now you remember us, when you're sick and broke." We were living in Havana by then. He went to the new Lenin Hospital and that's where he died.

My grandma's name is Ana Canete. She's very slight and wears eyeglasses and is very, very old now, about a hundred, I guess. She bore eight children, six sons and two daughters. Uncle Jesús and Uncle Ramón lived with her, so of all my uncles, they're the ones closest to my heart. She kept house for them and they gave her whatever they earned. It wasn't much.

Jesús was a hunchback. When I was a little kid I asked Grandma, "How did Uncle Jesús get that hump on his back?"

"He was playing ball one day and the ball hit him right there. He's had that swelling ever since," she answered.

Jesús made a living taking care of fighting cocks, and he won a bit of money betting on the fights. He made spurs for the cocks too; they were 5 *pesos* a pair. When a bird was hurt so bad it had to be killed, they'd give it to him and he'd bring it home to us. Grandma would cook it with rice or make a fricassee.

Uncle Ramón worked breaking stones and loading them into trucks. Looking at that truck full of stones one day, I asked him, "Uncle, what do they pay you?"

"One *peso* for each truckload," he answered. It took him all day to crush that many stones! I thought, "You won't ever catch me crushing stone for 1 *peso* a day, no sir!"

I never knew my uncles Cuco and Lalo but I often visited Abel. He worked in a *ballu*. That's a place where prostitutes go. Abel's a queer. He'd drink and dance with the women but you could tell he wasn't straight. His manner and the way he talks give him away.

Uncle Julio spent most of his life in jail. He'd serve his time for some crime and no sooner was he out than he'd be arrested again. Once he went to work for a bank and tried to hold it up. That time they kept him in jail quite a while. He's a nice guy, once you get to know him. He enjoyed his food, I remember, and was always chewing Chiclets between meals. He was a sharp dresser and wore a cologne that was advertised in the magazines. He carried a pistol, too. There was an air of mystery about him. I'd look at him and think, "That's some uncle I've got!"

Irma, *mamá*'s sister, lived with my grandma until she married a policeman. When she had a baby, I'd go to visit her and watch while she fed him. Whenever she looked the other way I'd steal a handful of mashed tubers. That's how hungry I was.

Grandma took good care of me while *mamá* was away, but she was soft and easygoing and allowed me too much freedom. I did just what I pleased and went wherever my feet took me. I earned a bit of money this way and that and spent every *kilo* on the movies. I was always at the movies. If I had no money I'd ask people on the street for some. I'd say, "Hey, got a penny so I can see the picture?" I'd cry when I said it so a lot of them gave me the penny. I liked Tarzan and cowboy pictures best.

I'd come home late at night after everyone was asleep and find Grandma waiting up for me. "Where in the world were you?" she'd scold. I paid her no mind. I just kept on the same way. One time I stayed out all night and got home to find everyone in an uproar. They were afraid I'd drowned in the river. They'd searched along the bank for me and even called the police. As soon as I turned up, Grandma dragged me inside the house and spanked me with a piece of cardboard. It made a lot of noise but didn't hurt much.

"Yell," she told me under her breath. "I'm supposed to be practically killing you." I yelled good and loud so my uncles would hear. Then Grandma hugged me and told me to lie on her bed and stay there. She never punished me the way *mamá* did.

When we did something wrong *mamá* would tell us, "It's all right. I'm not going to do anything to you." And we'd forget all about it. But then, after we'd gone to bed, she'd let us have it right across the legs with a strap. She was very strict with us.

I needed a strong hand to guide me but as long as *mamá* was away I ran wild. I went around in rags, torn pants, no shirt, no shoes. I'd never worn underwear then. I felt like dirt, I looked like dirt, and my hair was long and full of lice. Once in a while I'd go to the river to wash myself but not often. Dirt didn't worry me.

Sometimes I had the most beautiful dreams in which I had lots of money and toys. Then in the morning I'd wake up and realize it wasn't true. Or I'd dream that I had 5 *pesos* hidden in one of my pockets, and when I woke up I'd look for the money.

As a child, I knew I had a father named Ernesto Capote who lived in Banes, but I wouldn't have known him if I'd seen him on the street. My brother Ernesto knew him and would visit him. One day Ernesto took me with him, but when I saw *papá* it was like meeting a stranger. I didn't feel like a son to him.

I know very little about my father's family, except that he was abandoned by his *papá* soon after he was born, and my grandmother, Claudia Batista, brought him up alone. *Papá* is a younger brother of Batista, the dictator . . . well, not a brother, but practically. Fulgencio Batista was the illegitimate son of Carmela Zaldívar—I don't know who the father was. *Papá*'s mother and Carmela Zaldívar were friends from La Güira in Banes and were as fond of each other as if they were family. When Carmela was dying, she gave Fulgencio to my grandmother, who raised him and gave him her name because the father, whoever he was, didn't acknowledge him.[2]

Fulgencio had a brother, Panchín Batista, who once ran for mayor of Marianao.[3] I can't remember the other brother's name, and I never did get to know Fulgencio. We were family but my *mamá* never talked about him. No one ever told me I was related to General Batista, but as I grew up I caught on from things that happened.

After *mamá* left me with her mother, I went by myself to visit *papá*. I had a bit of money from selling old bottles so I bought a bus ticket to Banes. I wanted to ask *papá* if I could live with him. Not that I was fonder of him than of Grandma, but he was a lot better off and I thought he'd be able to give me more to eat and maybe some decent clothes to wear.

My father's mother, Claudia, came to the door. She was the meanest witch in the world, the kind that would throw ashes in your eyes. "What are you doing here?" she asked.

"I came to visit *papá*."

"Oh, but he's in jail. Never mind, I'll take you there." This was before Batista's coup in 1952. I must have been seven or eight.

Claudia took me to the jail. "*Papá* . . ." I said when I saw him.

"What are you doing here with that crazy old hag?" he interrupted roughly. *Papá* had a screw loose somewhere. He was apt to get into a violent rage all of a sudden for no apparent reason. Weeping, his mother led me away.

Outside again, she gave me a small jar of *café con leche*. "Take it to your *papá*," she said. She thought he'd accept it from me, seeing how I was his son and all that. I went back to *papá* and gave it to him.

"Did you make this?"

"No, Grandma made it."

"Then I don't want it," he screamed, dashing it to the floor. "I don't want anything."

I don't know why *papá* was in jail that time, but I guess it must have been for fighting. He loved to fight. He said he used to be a pro boxer but I don't know if that's true. He fancied himself a ladies' man, and any woman in the street whose looks he liked he'd pat on the bottom, whether she was with a man or not. If she had a man with her, of course he'd sock

2. Fulgencio Batista's parents, Belisario Batista, a cane-cutter, and Carmela Zaldívar, were from Banes, Oriente, where Fulgencio was born in January, 1901. Carmela Zaldívar died when Batista was fourteen years old, but apparently he never had a foster mother. Edmund A. Chester, a public relations aide to Batista who wrote a highly favorable account of the dictator's life, says that Batista left home at age fourteen and went to work on the railroad, but that he continued to see his father and was never abandoned by him. (*A Sergeant Named Batista* (New York: Holt, 1954), pp. 1–14.)

3. Belisario Batista and Carmen Zaldívar had four sons: Fulgencio, Hermelindo, Juan, and Francisco, who was known as Panchín. Panchín was mayor of Marianao and later governor of Havana Province.

papá and then *papá* would have his fight—until the cops came and carried him off to jail. He was off his rocker, there's no doubt about it, so I went home.

In Victoria de las Tunas I hung out with a gang of seven or eight boys, all of them bad, just like me. I paid them a *kilo* a day each and in return they made me their leader. I scavenged for empty jars and bottles to sell so that, one way or another, I made enough to pay them.

We were full of mischief. We'd go to the pavilions where the dances were held—the same ones *mamá* used to go to. I was seven or eight and already understood life. I'd try to get in to dance, but they had this custom—after your first dance, they'd tap you on the shoulder and ask for a *medio* as an entrance fee. I never had the money and they'd tell me to beat it. My gang and I got back at them though, by gathering a heap of blossoms from a plant called fart-flower—because that's exactly how it smells, see? Then we'd take our slingshots and hurl handfuls of blossoms through the window. You can imagine how the place stank!

When the other boys in the neighborhood played pitchpenny, my gang and I would creep up behind them, and all of a sudden we'd break up the game and run off with the money. I stole sometimes, but from my own family. Once I took a coat from Grandma and sold it to Aunt Irma. And I stole a razor from Uncle Julio, too, but I sold it to a guy who knew my uncle. That was the only time I got caught.

One day I was playing with the boys when Grandma came and said, "There's a woman who wants to talk with you."

I saw a wealthy woman, beautiful, elegant, with long hair down to her waist. She kissed me and hugged me and called me "son." I still didn't recognize her.

"It's your *mamá*," Grandma told me. I kissed the lady then and ran all over the place shouting, "My *mamá*, my *mamá!*"

It hadn't crossed my mind that this lovely, well-dressed person could be my mother. The last time I'd seen her she'd looked countrified, a real *guajirita*, kind of quiet and mousy. She'd always had long hair but she'd never bothered to fix it. Now it looked beautiful. Her face was made up, her eyebrows plucked, and she was dressed in fine clothes. She even sat differently. I was so proud of her I took her all over the barrio showing her off. "This is my *mamá!*" People stared at her as if she were a multimillionairess.

She took me to get a haircut right away. She dressed me in new brown knickers and white shoes, so I looked like the son of rich parents. People who were used to seeing me in rags and full of lice didn't recognize me. They said, "You're Gabriel? That boy who runs around with a gang?"

"That's me," I said. "My *mamá* gave me these new clothes!"

People used to kick me around, but when they saw those fine new clothes, did they change! All of a sudden everyone was so nice and polite to me!

I told my gang, "I'm going away, boys. To Havana!" They were jealous—I could tell from the look in their eyes.

Grandma didn't go with us to the bus terminal. She said goodbye at the door of her house. She was crying as she hugged me, and she told *mamá* over and over, "Take good care of him."

We traveled to Havana by bus, just the two of us. There I was, all dressed up, traveling with a woman who looked like a princess. It was quite a trip. When I saw Ernesto and Rita again, we kissed and hugged—at least Ernesto and I did. I was never that fond of Rita.

Mamá was living with her third husband, a man called Durán, in an apartment in La Asunción. What an impression that apartment made on me! It was beautiful. It was in a cement building in a middle-class neighborhood; there wasn't a palm-thatched hut within a mile. We had furniture, plenty of food, clothes—there was even a shower. To go from a hut to this!

My life changed completely in La Asunción. *Mamá*'s husband didn't allow her to work and I didn't work either. There was no need. I had everything I needed right there. We lacked nothing. I had no problems—not one. I was happy! I had my meals at the proper time, went to bed when I was supposed to. I wasn't allowed out late at night. If I happened to stay out till midnight, *mamá* would whale me.

Right after I moved to La Asunción I started school. It was a private school run by a little old lady, and there were only about twenty of us—first-graders and kindergarten. I was older than the other kids, and because of that I didn't make any friends and was bored. I wanted to learn to read and write, because everyone kept telling me if I didn't, I'd never get a job. But I didn't learn a thing. I couldn't concentrate and I was very careless. In the end I decided, "I'm going to quit." I left after three months.

Pretty soon *mamá* was too broke to send me anyway. We lived with Durán just eight months, then *mamá* left him and we had to get out of that apartment and move to the bad part of La Asunción. Our new house was only ten blocks from the old one but—*ay, mi madre!*—it was the meanest, most miserable, most run-down shack I ever lived in. The floor was packed earth and we had to sleep on it because we didn't have a stick of furniture. *Mamá* paid 5 *pesos* a month for that dump.

We moved to the house on foot, wheeling the heavier stuff in a hand-cart. The house was on a hill but there was no road, no path. A truck couldn't have got up there. All the buildings in that area were made of wooden boards, with tarpaper roofs. Our house had just one room.

None of the houses there had running water but there was a spring nearby. The water came fresh out of the rock and we'd fill cans for drinking and bathing. I used to bathe in the pool that formed underneath. We had a latrine that was nothing more than a hole dug in the ground with a few boards laid across. What a letdown, to use that cesspit after we'd gotten used to a porcelain bowl where you had only to pull a little lever to flush it! "Why?" I asked myself. "Why should I have to go through such a change?"

I lost my sweetheart, Dora, because of that move. She was the first girl I had ever kissed. I was so shy I'd have to go hide somewhere to kiss her. That's as far as it went. I used to live better than Dora. I dressed well and she and her mother would see the tradesmen going into our place carrying half a hog at a time and all manner of stuff. They were impressed, I guess, and when I fell for Dora she must have thought she had it made. But, well, when we moved to the poor section, Dora changed completely and so did her mother. They chased me away from their house because we'd gone down in the world. I wasn't good enough for them any longer. They weren't exactly subtle about it and I understood right away. They were after my money, that's all.

Señora Pacheco:

I'd married Durán because I couldn't educate the kids at 20 or 30 *pesos* a head. He was working in Transportation and was a good man. We didn't knit too well together—his character was different from mine and the children's—but he helped me a lot. I got some money together with that man, because he earned a good salary, and I went to Victoria de las Tunas to get Gabriel.

Some three or four months after I brought Gabriel to Havana I was divorced again, because that man Durán said he wasn't going to be raising so many children who weren't his own. To my mind my children are the greatest, so I left him. Since then I don't believe in anyone. My children are my life.

Then Gabriel came down with typhus. I was earning 25 *pesos* a month as a cook, but when he got sick I couldn't work because I had to watch for his fever and change his clothes every day. He was in the hospital and they gave me two prescriptions for him. The poor child was dying and if I didn't get the medicines they were going to have to pack him in ice to bring down the fever. That's when I went to everyone in my husband's family for help.

Fulgencio Batista was President of the Republic at that time, and my husband's whole family was doing well. Fulgencio gave a *botella*[4] to my husband's mother, Claudia, because she used to wash and iron for him when they were neighbors in La Güira, a poor neighborhood of

---

4. Literally "bottle"; used idiomatically to mean a sinecure, usually obtained by political appointment.

Banes. Claudia Batista had the same last name as Fulgencio, but they're not family. Gabriel's father didn't tell me that Fulgencio was part of their family, only that they'd grown up together in the same neighborhood and that his mother happened to have the same surname. If they'd been family, the President would certainly have left them in a better way, you know, because what they were given was just a small job with a tiny salary. The father of my children got one, and so did his sister.

They all had money, but when I went to them with the prescriptions for Gabriel, they closed their doors on me and wouldn't buy the medicines. Gabriel's father had already left Mazorra but he was all mixed up. No one from his family helped, and they were all employed and doing well, so I have absolutely nothing to be thankful to those people for.

That situation went on for a whole month; no one would get the medicine for me and every third day I had to go out and hustle up 4 or 5 *pesos*. My neighbors were helping me—anything anyone gave was a help. I wasn't working then. It was horrible in the time of Batista, very hard.

I left the hospital almost crying, and a gentleman stopped his car and asked, "What's the matter?" So I told him and he said, "Don't worry. Is he so sick? Come here." He bought all the prescription medicines for the child, and I thanked him gratefully on the spot. From then on he bought me everything, and I was able to save my son through this man. That was so long ago and I was in such a desperate situation.

The man's name was Renato, but I don't recall his surname. I was living alone with my children in La Asunción; I had relations with him, but never in my room. Renato fell in love with me, but I wasn't in love. He told me he was a free man but that didn't interest me. I was suffering for my child and nothing more. I was in a terrible situation. Then in four months I began to work somewhere else and moved to another room, so I didn't see him anymore.

CAPOTE:
When Fulgencio Batista came to power, he began to do lots of favors for his relatives and friends. Back in Banes, he had my grandmother Claudia Batista's shack pulled down and built her and my *papá* a big cement house with every luxury. Behind it was a big patch of land where the old lady grew vegetables. Claudia was given money and a job, too. All her relatives got their monthly payoff without working. My *papá* got a gravy job as Minister of Public Works, Claudia herself was on the payroll as a piano teacher, and Panchín ran for mayor of Marianao. My *papá* got money every month, yet he didn't do any work.

Mamá never got any money from *papá* or from Batista, but she must have gotten something at election time because she always voted for the General, and she wouldn't have voted for somebody for no reason at all. She didn't get a monthly allowance like *papá* did, but I noticed that after she voted we had plenty of food at home. That happened only once though.

It was after we'd moved that I got typhus. There was a guy who sold tamales and one day I ate a whole lot of them. Next morning I felt terrible. I had diarrhea and kept vomiting. Poor *mima* cried; she was so scared and didn't know what to do. She had no one to help her. She went to see Panchín Batista and he sent his own private doctor to our house. The doctor looked at my eyes and told *mima*, "Take him to the hospital." They wrapped me up in a sheet and took me to the hospital in a taxi. My head wasn't clear but I remember lying in bed with a needle in my arm and a serum bottle beside the bed and looking at *mima* through a glass pane.

My fever wouldn't go down and for a time it looked as though I wouldn't make it. That's when *mamá* went to my *papá* to ask him for the money for the injection I needed and he tried to make her go to bed with him! No wonder she hates him so much. I have four kids myself now, and if I had to steal for them I'd do it. My father had a good job then and he knew I was dying, yet he refused. A man like that is no father; he's an animal!

Mamá got the money though. She was crying out in the street and a man in a car stopped to ask her, "What's your trouble, Señora?"

"My son is dying in the hospital and I can't raise 11 *pesos* for medicine."

"Get in," the man told her. "I'll buy you the medicine."

There was nothing my *mamá* wouldn't do for me. She did things no woman should do, but she had to do it, to save my life. After I got home I had dizzy spells for about a month, but I was soon back to my old ways, running loose in the street with the gang, up to no good.

It wasn't long before my brother and I met El Chino, the terror of the neighborhood. Ernesto met him first and they got to be good pals. El Chino came to our house and we gave him food, to win his friendship. The truth is, Ernesto was scared of him. So was I. He was the leader of a big gang of kids, all of them colored. Around there, any boy who knew what was good for him made friends with El Chino and his followers. My brother and I tried to stay out of their way.

There were lots of other tough characters who carried knives and smoked marijuana. Now that's something that never tempted me. I saw lots of people smoking marijuana but I wasn't even curious to take one puff. I was thirteen when I started smoking cigarettes. A friend and I bought some and went behind a building to smoke them. The first one made me dizzy and I didn't like it, but I kept it up. No marijuana! I never touched it. I figured it would only make me worse off than I was already.

Stealing—that did tempt me. Anything I saw lying loose that I could take without being caught, I took. Once I was up in a tree stealing mangoes. A policeman saw me and yelled, "Get down from there." I was arrested and they made me wash plates and scrub floors as punishment, just to scare me, see? But I never did anything serious. It never entered my head to break into a house.

I used to shoot craps. It was illegal but I never got caught. There was a big, strong, blond man who got people together to play. I'd play and lose.

I was surrounded by bad examples. You act the way the people around you act, no? Well, all my friends were poor kids, like me, and bad, like me. We were always up to mischief. We'd go to the rich sections and steal coconuts and mangoes. And we'd go to the movies and shoot things at people with our slingshots. Pure mischief, that's all it was. But I'd go to the homes of my friends and their parents would throw me out. "Get out. I don't want my boy to mess with you." I felt like nothing when they talked to me like that.

In La Asunción *mamá* earned a living washing clothes and doing spiritist work. She'd always been a spiritist. I'd seen her practicing her sorcery back in Victoria de las Tunas. I guess she learned it from her mother. Grandma always had a glass of water set up beside a little statue of the *Virgen de la Caridad,* the one with a boat and two little blacks at the foot.

Mamá went all out and actually did *santería* work. I don't know if she had much faith in it; she did it because she was short of cash. She had an altar with her two Indians on horseback, a glass of water, coconuts, bananas, forty thousand things set in front of it. We kids would swipe the bananas and eat them. *Mamá* would get mad but we had to eat something!

When one of her clients came to the house *mamá* would tell us to get lost. Ernesto and I would leave, but then we'd creep back and watch through the cracks between the boards of the house. *Mamá* would get out her pack of cards and put a glass of water on the table. She charged 50 *kilos* for a consultation and her clients would drop the coins into the glass she had set out. Then the clients would stand in the middle of the room and *mamá* would make the sign of the cross over them and sprinkle the floor with some kind of special alcohol. She'd take off her shoes and step into the puddles of alcohol, then put a flame to them. Her feet didn't burn, but she'd start jumping around. At that point Ernesto and I had to run off so they wouldn't hear us laughing.

One day I spilled *mamá*'s bottle of alcohol. It was her own concoction, but I, not knowing any better, filled it with common alcohol. Next time someone came, *mamá* burned her feet. She said, "*Ay!*" but added quickly, "That means the spirit is coming." She nearly killed me afterward.

After she'd gone through her rigmarole, *mamá* would deal her cards and give the client advice, such as, "So-and-so isn't deceiving you," or "You will be very happy together." She'd always say things to please them so they'd pay her more. Some of the things she said happened to come true—just dumb luck—and she kept on getting customers.

When the people left, *mamá* would fish out the coins from the water and send me off to the grocer's to buy food. On good days she'd earn at least 1.50 *pesos.* That was enough for a meal because in those times you could buy a lot with a *peso.* A big can of sardines cost 30-odd *kilos,* and with the rest of the *peso* you could buy enough rice and bananas to make a good lunch.

But there were bad days when we'd have not a bite of food. Many times we cried with hunger and then *mima* cried with us. One day I was searching desperately for food and my poor little mother cried because she didn't know what to do. I think I was sick or something and I was begging for something to eat, so *mima* gave me her breast to make me stop. I was eleven or twelve then. *Mima* didn't give the breast to Rita or Ernesto, so I guess it must have been because I was the youngest and the sickliest.

On bad days we'd wait around, desperate for a customer. If someone showed up, we kids would go outside thinking, "We're sure to eat today, anyway." We'd hang around and peek in through the cracks, trying to figure out how much money had been dropped into the glass. Sometimes *mamá* asked her clients to bring chickens or pigeons as sacrificial offerings, and they always landed in our cooking pot. *Mamá* bristles when I say that to her today. "Damn it, how can you say such a thing?" But it's the truth.

Another thing she'd do—she'd take orders for a certain kind of necklace that was supposed to have magical powers, then she'd buy a pack of seeds and string them up and charge 10 *pesos* a necklace because it was supposed to have been "worked over," see? She had herself quite a little racket there.

At one point *mamá* was doing so well we moved. She rented a big house with a glassed-in porch, a dining room, a bedroom, and an enormous bathroom with a shower. For a while we lived like the bourgeosie again, with running water and every luxury. We even had our own hallway. It was a beautiful house.

When we moved in, *mamá* bought a set of bedroom furniture—on the installment plan—real good quality. She bought a radio for 7 *pesos,* a lamp, an electric iron, and a blanket that we used as a bedspread. Pretty soon we ran out of money and couldn't keep up all the payments. The guy who sold us the blanket showed up.

"Listen, I'm going to pay you soon," I told him.

"Nothing doing," he said, and took it away. It was a beautiful blanket, thick and gold-colored, with big splashy flowers on it.

In the end, we couldn't pay the rent and the landlord put our furniture out on the street. We carried it right back in again but then we had to get out. We hired a truck to take the furniture and *mamá* sat in front with the driver, clutching the lamp and a few bundles.

We moved to Enamorados Street, in another poor, run-down area. But there were good houses nearby and *mamá* got a job as a servant about two blocks away. The lady's name was Marta. She was nice to me. She gave me a present on the Day of the Three Kings—two pistols and a cartridge belt. I was so thrilled I didn't know what to do. It was the first present I'd ever received. Usually when Three Kings Day came around I'd wake up in the morning, look under my bed, and find nothing there. I'd see the other kids with their toys but I never got any. Nobody ever gave me anything.

I used to run errands for Marta. That's how I met her daughter, Rosario. She was the first great love of my life. The moment I set eyes on her I fell madly in love. It was like climbing up to heaven without a ladder. She was a youngster about my age, eleven or twelve. Her breasts were just beginning to grow. She was very, very pretty. I never thought there was any chance for me. She was well-to-do, I was a nobody. But one day she turned up at my house.

"Why don't you come and watch television at my house?" she said.

"Because I'm not invited."

"Well, you're invited now."

She took me to her house, and while we watched television I started making love to her. It was a childish thing between us—it didn't go beyond kisses. I was still very ignorant about women.

One day her *mamá* was out. "Let's go to bed the way *papás* and *mamás* do," Rosario said.

"All right. Tell me what I'm supposed to do."

"First you take off your pants and I take off my dress," she explained. Step by step I did as she said until we were both stark naked. We got into bed under a blanket. I guess she must have seen her mother in action sometime. She didn't want me to go into her front so I turned her around and tried to get in behind. Then I got scared. I jumped out of bed and hurried into my pants. We stared at each other as if asking, "What is this thing we were about to do?"

Mamá didn't approve of my friendship with Rosario. "Don't start in there, boy. You don't want to go making love to that girl. Those are well-to-do people and what are you? It's looking for trouble."

Rosario's mother didn't like me. There was this other guy, Alfredo, who used to hang around Rosario. His father was chief of the local police precinct and Rosario's *mamá* was having an affair with him. She had her eye on Alfredo for Rosario. He had money . . . I was just a nobody.

One day Alfredo turned up at Rosario's house. "Beat it!" he told me. "Get out, and don't come back." He could talk like that to me, seeing how his father was a police chief. Rosario didn't open her mouth so I had to leave. But I felt bad.

I saw Rosario secretly for a while, but she left the country after the Revolution. Her father was a terrible murderer. He was one of Batista's officers and he killed people like a madman. Later he was executed by a firing squad in La Cabaña. It seemed right that they should have left after that.

Mamá lost her job with Marta, but somehow she always managed to keep a roof over our head and the wolf from the door. She went back to her work with the saints and all that, and when she had no customers she went to dances at night. She only went to dances when there was no food. She'd sell all her kitchen things first. It hurt me to see how she had to work to feed us. She went through so much, things no woman should have to go through, and I respect her for it. Once she was at death's door, from an abortion I think. I don't know that we'd have survived without her.

By then *mamá* had changed a lot. She looked poor and shabby. Her hair was still long, but it didn't fall down to her waist and it wasn't beautiful like when she came to get me in Victoria de las Tunas. You could see how much she'd suffered, just by looking at her.

Chapter Two

Ernesto, Rita, and My Old Man

WHILE FULGENCIO BATISTA was in power, *papá* lived some of the time in Banes and some of the time in Havana. One day I said to my brother, "Let's look up our old man." I hadn't seen him since I'd visited him in Banes. It so happened that day was payday and *papá* took us to barrio Colón, where he picked up his pay. It came in two moneybags tied together. "See how much I get paid?" he said, and he let me lift one of them.

As we walked through Colón, which was a prostitute's barrio, *papá* said, "See that place? That's where you go when you want to be with a woman." It wasn't exactly news to me. Later I often caught sight of him in that section. He was short and plump and had Indian hair and coloring. And on account of being crazy, he didn't have much luck with women.

Papá used to play with himself. I know, because when I stayed with him he'd go in the bathroom for a full hour. I stayed with him quite a few times. Lying in bed beside him, I heard him talking to himself and laughing aloud. Sometimes he'd get up and stare at me. Ernesto and I often visited him together, and we always went on payday because then he'd take us shopping. It was very embarrassing to shop with him. He'd walk into a store and ask for a pair of shoes.

"Do you need socks?" he'd ask us. Then, "Do you need pants?" He'd pick out a lot of things, and when they were all wrapped up he'd ask, "How much?"

"Twenty-five *pesos*."

"That's too much," he'd say, and walk out, leaving the poor clerk standing there with the parcel. Yet *papá* was very simpleminded. Anyone could cheat him. He'd pay 40 *pesos* for a ring worth 30 *centavos*. Ernesto and I felt sorry for him. After all, he was our father. But I had no love for him and he had none for us, either. He begat us because he wanted to have pleasure with *mamá*. He never came back to my *mamá*, never bought anything for her. Now and then he'd send 5 or 6 *pesos* home for

Rita, and he'd give money to Ernesto, who handed it to *mamá*. The shoes and socks were the only pleasures I got out of him.

When Ernesto and I went to see him he'd hug us and call us "sonny," but if we went too soon after the last visit we'd have to leave again in a hurry because he'd start talking crazy. He'd stare at us with a crazy look in his bloodshot eyes. "You are my sons," he'd say, "but you come here just to screw me up. I'll screw you up first and kill you, too." And he'd start flinging knives, razors, anything he could lay his hands on. We'd get scared and beat it, fast. He thought someone had hired us to kill him—he was really insane.

Papá showed up at our house one day and went for *mamá*. Ernesto leaped at him through the window and I followed close behind and we bashed him good. Well, hell, we couldn't just stand by and watch him kill her.

He had these violent fits, see? He always wore those necklaces the *santeros* use, to protect him with their magical powers. He was very handy with pistols and all kinds of firearms, and he kept getting into trouble and being picked up by the police. One time he stood in the street and started shooting off a machine gun. "I'm going to kill every damn Negro here!" he yelled. The cops came and picked him up.

I went to the station to ask about him, and the cop on guard told me, "Oh, he isn't here. He's up front with the lieutenant." I went to the office and there was *papá*, chatting with the lieutenant, friendly as you please. He was never put inside a jail during the dictatorship, no matter what he did. General Batista saw to that. *Papá* carried a card from him and another from Tabernilla,[5] addressed to the armed forces. It was kind of an instant reprieve.

Another time, *papá* got on a bus carrying a submachine gun and said to the passengers, "If anybody tries to get off this bus, I'll kill him." That's how crazy he was. The driver was so scared he was driving past all the bus stops. One of the passengers jumped out of the window and *papá* shot at him. The driver, like a clever man, turned a corner so the guy who had jumped was out of range. The driver stopped in front of a café and *papá* got out as if nothing had happened. A policeman ordered him to stop and let himself be searched. My old man tried to pull out his pistol and the policeman shot him twice in the belly—it was a monster of a scar!

Papá's relatives took me to see him in the hospital. I went along just so I could get a free bus ride, not because I cared, you hear? Hell, that same night I was out dancing rock and roll to Elvis Presley. That's how much I cared for my old man! I was born that way, I guess.

5. General Francisco Tabernilla, army chief of staff under Batista. He fled to the United States in late 1958.

There was a real tough punk who lived near *papá* in barrio Santa Felisa. He was what we call *jabao*, light-skinned but with kinky hair. One day my brother and I were riding through the park on the way to *papá*'s when this guy starts threatening Ernesto. "Hey, who do you think you are, *blanquito*? I'm not scared of you or your old man. I'm going to cut you in the ass."

My brother didn't even answer, so I walked up to him. "What's with you, *chico*?" His only answer was a tremendous kick in the shins that took me by surprise. I yelled with pain, "*Ay, ay, ay!*" When we told *papá* how that fellow had kicked me, he armed himself and went out looking for him. The punk was standing on a street corner when *papá* came up with his boxer's walk. *Papá* pulled out a gun, "Hey, *jabao*." When the guy saw him he got lost, but fast. He knew *papá* would have killed him and gone free afterward.

A few weeks later that very same guy killed my cousin Orlando. Orlando had wronged the guy's sister, and the punk went after him and demanded that he do right by her and say the child was his. Orlando refused and the punk stabbed him and kept stabbing until he was sure he was dead. He stabbed him twenty times in all. I went to the funeral, and when I saw him lying there I couldn't believe he was dead. *Ay, mi madre!* And I'd quarreled with that killer only a few days earlier.

One day *papá* showed up at home full of cuts and bruises. He was eating ice cream but was so upset he was chewing the paper cup it came in. "What happened?" I asked him.

"Ventura[6] caught me, and look how he beat me up." I could barely understand him because he couldn't talk properly. *Papá* was in the habit of peeping at women whenever he got the chance, and it seems he'd been peeping through the blinds of Ventura's house to spy on his wife and they caught him at it and beat him practically to death.

My Grandma Claudia and General Batista used to see each other, and she had his telephone number, too. When Batista got fed up with *papá* he said to Claudia, "I don't know what to do about Nesto." That was *papá*'s nickname. "Hardly a day goes by that someone doesn't call to say that Nesto is in some kind of trouble or in jail and they want me to get him out. I'm fed up. I'm going to have him committed to Mazorra so he'll leave me in peace." That's how *papá* lost his job and was dropped from the Army. They put him in Mazorra. Well, he really was crazy.

When *papá* mentioned Ventura the day he was beaten up, the name didn't mean a thing to me. Later on, after Batista fell, I heard they were

---

6. Colonel Esteban Ventura, an intelligence officer in the Havana police who became Batista's chief of police. Hugh Thomas refers to him as "a legendary death-dealer" (p. 942). Ventura fled to Miami in late 1958. The U.S. government refused Castro's request for extradition. (*Cuba: The Pursuit of Freedom*, pp. 1027, 1077.)

after Ventura and Carratalá[7] and I thought, "Hell, why Ventura?" But Ventura was one of Batista's killers.

I didn't know the first thing about what was going on in Cuba. I saw how the police beat up people, and the horrors they committed against the students, but none of that meant anything to me. I didn't give it a second thought because all I was interested in was my next meal. I'd no idea Batista was a dictator, that he had people killed and tortured. I used to pass behind the police station and I'd often hear people screaming in pain—it gave me the cold shivers—but I never thought Batista had anything to do with it. *Coño,* I was quite fond of him. I had no idea what he was really like. I was so ignorant, I was actually proud of *papá*'s connections with him.

I even kept telling the neighbors that *papá* was a relative of President Batista so they'd respect us. Everybody laughed at me. "Ah, come on," they'd say, "if that were true, would you be living the way you are?"

One day my sister quarreled with a boy in the barrio and the boy's father, who was a sergeant, bawled her out. *Mamá* faced right up to the man: "You be careful how you speak to my daughter because her father knows the General."

The sergeant laughed in her face. We felt humiliated, seeing how *mamá* had no kind of pull at all. So my sister wrote to Fulgencio Batista asking for an interview, hoping he would help us out somehow, and the General sent a telegram giving Rita an appointment. In La Asunción letters and telegrams were not taken directly to the house but were left at the grocery store to be picked up. When I went to get the telegram, the grocer hugged me and said, "*Now* I believe you know Batista. I used to think you were making it up because you folks live so poorly." From that day forward he treated me with respect.

I went with my sister to call on the General but we never got to see him. His staff was awfully polite but I think they must have received orders not to let us in. My sister got tired of waiting so we got up to go. "Come back tomorrow or the day after," they told her. But she didn't go back again.

As I got older I tried to find ways of making money. I never forgot something my Uncle Ramón once told me. He said, "Listen, Gabriel, when you kids get big, you should get your *mamá* some place to live, a little house or a room. Otherwise, when she's old she'll have to sleep on the street." That's how it was in the old days. So I began to work as soon as I could.

I did the lowest kind of labor. I searched along the streets and in

7. A police commander under Batista, Colonel Carratalá sought political asylum in the United States just before the Rebels' victory.

garbage cans looking for old bottles and jars that I washed and sold at a place in Marianao. I got 1 *kilo* for two soft-drink bottles, 1 *medio* for a liter milk bottle, and 3 *kilos* for a half-liter milk bottle. I gave *mamá* whatever I earned. That way I helped her out a bit.

My brother did the same. Often we'd work together collecting bottles and beef bones, which we sold by the sackful. We sold newspapers, lottery tickets, candy—anything at all. We made 1 *centavo* on a news-paper and I'd sell about forty or fifty of them a day. Newspapers were pretty dull then and didn't sell the way they do now. I had to walk a lot and get on at least six buses to sell one paper.

I sold candy on the buses, too. I'd buy a boxful of cream caramels, then I'd go down the street crying, "Caramels for a *kilo!*" When a bus came by I'd jump on. "Candy! Candy!" I'd call. A few passengers always bought some before I was put off. I liked selling things. People never paid me much attention, but when they bought from me it made me happy. I'd stop sometimes and watch the other kids of my age going to school and I'd think, "If it's such a big deal to study and learn, maybe I should go too. Then I could get a decent job." But I found other ways of making money.

I had a friend, Manuel, who was in love with my sister. He was a radio announcer. The owner of the radio station was a government employee and he had official license plates on his car. Manuel used that car for an advertising business he had. He mounted the car with a loudspeaker and drove around broadcasting ads for different stores.

I started helping Manuel and he gave me a percentage of the profits. We'd go to a drugstore, say, and offer our services. Manuel charged 2.50 an hour. If the drugstore owner agreed, we taped whatever he wanted to announce. "Tonight, Wednesday, the Luzdel Malecón drugstore will be open all night. Telephone number..." and so on. We'd drive three times around the block so the owner could hear his ad being broadcast, then Manuel would drive to another section of the city and approach another storekeeper. After that we'd go home for the day. Ten hours later we'd go to collect our pay without having lifted a finger.

We had another racket going, with a laundry. They gave us 100,000 cardboard fans advertising their services. We got rid of 100 fans and took the rest home.

My first real job was at the Marqués de la Torre coffee shop. I'd run errands for the proprietor, and I kept pestering him for a job until one day he said, "All right, all right. I pay 75 *kilos* a day." I'd been wearing myself out selling candy and all I earned was 40 *kilos* a day, so 75 *kilos* was a world of wealth to me. I agreed and started working right away. I worked over fifty hours a week. There were two of us employed there and we worked in shifts. I worked from 6:00 in the morning to 4:00 in the afternoon, when the other guy came in. When he didn't show up—

which was often—I'd work until midnight. Saturdays and Sundays we worked together all day because there were more customers.

The shop was in the lobby of a drugstore. There were no tables or chairs—just a small square floor space—because we didn't serve food, only coffee, cigarettes, Chiclets, and soft drinks. At first I had a hard time working the till because I couldn't read or write. But I knew that one cup of coffee was 3 *kilos,* so two were 6 *kilos* and so on. When I sold chewing gum and cigarettes, the clients always helped me add up the prices and figure out the change. They'd say to me, "Here's the money. Take out such-and-such an amount and give me such-and-such change."

I never got tips, except at Christmas when I put out my coin bank, as everyone else did, and the customers dropped *centavos* into it. I never got a raise either, and I worked there almost five years. That was longer than the other guy who worked there, but the owner gave *him* a raise.

"Hey, what about me?" I asked.

"I'm not giving you a raise. If you don't like it, you can quit."

I hated his guts for that, but I stayed on. The wages were enough for me and I always gave my old lady a bit of money, whatever I could afford.

He was a miserly *gallego,* that son-of-a-bitch owner! He was Cuban but he looked foreign, German—fair-skinned, blue-eyed, and close-cropped hair. He never gave me my lunch, and if I smoked a cigarette I had to pay for it. If my brother dropped in and I served him a small cup of coffee, I had to pay for that too.

Once *mamá* was ill and needed 30 *pesos* for medicine, food, and rent. They were always trying to evict us, but every time they put our furniture out in the street we carried it back in again. Well, I asked my boss to lend me 30 *pesos.* I offered to pay it back out of my wages in regular installments, but the old skinflint refused because there was only a lousy 2 or 3 *pesos* in the cash register. "I'll get even with you!" I thought.

The boss would spend the weekend in Guanabo, so every week, while he was away, I'd send my brother to buy 55 *kilos'* worth of coffee and sugar at the wholesalers—I paid for it out of my own money—and I'd prepare it and sell it in the café. I got the most out of my coffee; if it said a certain amount would make thirty cups, I'd put in a lot of extra water and some brown sugar and get fifty cups out of it. Customers would complain, "This coffee is kind of weak," but they drank it. That way I made a good profit on it. I made about 5 *pesos* a day, which was more than my boss ever made.

Instead of putting that money in the cash register, I kept it in a tin under the counter. Pretty soon the tin wasn't big enough to hold all the money I made in one day, so I got a cigar box as well. I made enough to buy a pair of boots and a pair of black pants, both new. When the owner came back on Monday, he never found much money in the register, but he didn't catch on. That way I got even with him, see?

After a while I started to steal money straight out of the cash register. Until then I'd been stealing decent, I mean it was his premises and his customers and all, but it was my own coffee and sugar I'd been making a profit on. During the day I'd open a flap on top of my boots and tip the drawer of the cash register so that the coins fell into them. At night when I left the place, I'd slip out through a little back door, real slow, because my boots were so full of money I could hardly walk. In time I could have bought the place out from under the owner. "Serves him right," I thought, "the exploiting son-of-a-bitch!" Vacations? Days off? Such things didn't exist for me as long as I worked for him. But I got my own back.

I was beginning to be self-conscious about things. I had no clothes to my name other than the ones I stood up in, a pair of black jeans patched with different colors, and a T-shirt with a horse on it. I had to stay indoors while they were being washed. One day this kid says to me, "Hey, Capote, why don't you change your clothes before they fall off you?" I hated him for that. He was a rich kid—his father owned a garage—and he had everything: clothes, food—everything.

My brother was very fussy about the way he looked. He never let the girls see him wearing a pair of torn pants. If he didn't have a decent pair, he'd stay home till he got some. Clothes always looked good on him. He was handsome, too, much better looking than I. He looked like a movie star—big and strong, with fine, white teeth and a beautiful shock of hair falling over his forehead.

I was jealous of Ernesto. I'd tell him, "You can make it with a chick quicker than I can because you're a good-looking guy. I can't hold a candle to you. I'm no good at all." He'd just stare at me when I said things like that. But it was true. All the women fell for him. Sometimes we'd go out together to eye the girls and Ernesto always managed to pick one up, but I couldn't get even a little old Negro girl to go along with me. I was only window-shopping, so to speak.

I was fool enough to confess to my friends that the girls never gave me a tumble. "Look, fellows," I'd ask, "what do I do to get a girl?"

"Have those teeth pulled out, for a start," they'd answer. "How can you expect any girl to want to kiss you with all those rotten teeth?" They were rotten, all black and broken and ugly. I got awfully depressed about them, but when I remembered the dentist, I'd forget how bad they were. I was terrified of having them pulled. I kept my foul teeth and Ernesto flashed smiles at the girls while I looked on.

He always had some little sweetheart or other and every one of them was crazy about him. When he left them they'd come crying to me, "Gabriel, your brother left me." Ernesto never told me much about his affairs, only who was the latest conquest. He was always very closemouthed about such things.

He's kind of a loner, my brother. He's much more serious and less sociable than I. He never liked liquor or cigarettes or even coffee. He'd shoot craps a little now and then and he had his own set of friends, and his women of course, but otherwise he kept very much to himself. He was always locked up in the house. He had a very nice voice and loved to sing to himself.

He goes in for playing with himself, too. I know, because once I caught him at it in the bathroom. I barged in while he was bathing and there he was with some magazines and postcards.

"Hey, you dirty pig, what are you up to?"

"Get out! Beat it!" he yelled at me. "Why do you have to come bothering me?"

I burst out laughing. "Tell me what you're doing!"

After that, when he stayed too long in the bathroom I'd knock on the door and yell, "Hurry up, jerk off and get out of there!"

One day he was sitting on the porch "eating the carrot" and looking at one of those magazines of his. I was looking over his shoulder and that day I started doing it myself. After that I did it morning, noon, and night. Ernesto warned me, "You should wait three hours after a meal before doing that. Otherwise you might die." So I kept watching the clock after every meal. It became a mania with me. I took good care not to be caught by *mamá* or my sister, and I never did it in front of my brother either. I was too ashamed. Besides, you have to be alone so you can think about the things that make you come. It doesn't work if you're with somebody else. I was quite small when I started, and I kept it up until I began to have relations with women. That was my only relief.

When my brother was about fifteen he got sick. I don't know whether he began to do—you know, what people do with their right hands—too soon after eating, or whether it was witchcraft. I don't really believe in those things, but . . . I remember how it happened. Ernesto and I were very hungry and decided to go out to eat. We went to Marianao, where the Red Bus route went down to the beach. There, under a big guacimo tree, we saw a little heap of copper *kilos*. We took them and went to the nearest grocery store and bought two black *coquitos*. We were walking along the beach eating the coconut sweets when suddenly Ernesto began to foam at the mouth. I laughed at him. "Look at you, brother. You're foaming at the mouth!" Then we went home.

The following day he woke me at dawn. He was jabbering in English, with his eyes turned up so only the white showed. His tongue was full of cuts and he foamed a bloody froth at the mouth. He didn't recognize any of us.

"Ernesto is dying, *ay*, he's dying!" my sister cried. She got a cab and we drove him to the Calixto García Hospital. They told us it was a good thing we'd rushed him right over because if we'd waited he'd have died.

Ever since that night my brother has had those epileptic fits. But he kept on being lucky with the women. He didn't go out as much though, so I was the one who grew up to be more experienced.

SEÑORA PACHECO:

My son Ernesto had epileptic fits from an embolism he suffered. And there I was alone, working. Sometimes I had to stay home from work for a day, so the lady I worked for would fight with me about it. She said she couldn't go on that way and would have to look for another girl to cook for her, but she'd put up with me because I knew how to cook, and was well-behaved and respectful and didn't fool around. *Vaya*, I worked hard on that job!

Then I got married again, to a man named Federico. I think he's a chemist. He must have been about sixty years old. That was before the Revolution began. I don't remember the date; I never remember things according to dates. I was working too, but Federico helped me a lot. He got me a house, as he earned a good salary and brought all of it home. Although he was old he was very well preserved. He got along well with me ... we were together for three years.

My little daughter was always ... well, she's seeing a psychiatrist now. She has a bad temper and Federico blamed everything possible on her. The old man also had a temper and he wanted to take her in hand, but I said, "No, she's my daughter, I'll handle her." All of my tragedies come about on account of my children, because for my part I've lived my whole life quiet and contented.

I really loved that man because he was with me for so long. He was a good man, a little quarrelsome but good. *Qué va!* No one is perfect and, well, there's no perfect life. You have your thing, the other has his. The trouble was all on account of my children, never on my account. I've had luck with men at times; if not for my children I would have been happy. I'd never have divorced again and remained alone in my house for so long. But my children are my life and I'd give my life for them.

CAPOTE:

My sister Rita had none of the freedom Ernesto and I had because *mamá* was very strict with her. *Mamá* wouldn't let her go out, even with other girls, without a chaperone. She was a good girl, my sister, not the kind that gets into trouble.

Rita was *mamá*'s favorite. *Mamá* was always buying her dresses, shoes, panties. Even when we lived in Victoria de las Tunas and my brother and I wore rags, my sister was a bit better dressed. Her shoes were cheap, her little dresses torn and dirty, and her hair in a snarl, but she had more than we did.

"Hey, what about us?" my brother and I complained.

"She's a girl. She needs all those things. A boy can get away with dressing any old way but a girl has to dress neatly."

When I finally got enough money to buy myself a pair of shoes, Rita was jealous and stomped on them and tried to scuff them. She was very aggressive. She fought with our old lady all the time, talking back and using bad words. She was nutty all her life, just like *papá*.

Once she entered a singing contest at the amphitheater—she thought she had such a great voice, see? It was one of those contests where anyone can have a go. First prize was a wristwatch, but every competitor got a free six-pack of malt beer or regular. They decided on the winner by the applause of the audience, and the smart ones brought along their friends and relatives from their barrio. It was always the one with the most supporters who won.

Most people went in for the contest to win the six-pack of beer, but my sister thought she could really sing. She must have thought she was a movie actress the way she sang that night, Mexican style. She was lousy! Then she got mixed up in the middle of the song and jumped to another one. People started booing and yelling, "Hey, come off it! Give us a break!" They had to ring the bell to make her stop. When she came back to her seat, I said to her, "You've got a nerve, getting up there and singing when all your voice is good for is selling vegetables in the street!"

Still, she got her six-pack of beer, which we all drank later at home. She must have been about seventeen or eighteen then. We were still living on Enamorados. Rita was very pretty at that time, with a cinnamon complexion, long black hair, and a slender figure. She only weighed a bit over 80 pounds. She was skin and bones. To see her fat face today, you'd never think she'd once been pretty. She weighs about 200 pounds now. I guess it must be some kind of illness because, hell, it isn't normal to gain over 100 pounds.

Rita met a young fellow, Lorenzo Espinosa, a corporal. We were real fond of him. He used to tell us about fighting the Rebels in the Sierra. At that time I didn't even know there were Rebels in the Sierra so I thought he was lying and kidded him when he spoke about it. I'd scarcely heard of Fidel or anything about a Revolution.

Lorenzo asked for my sister's hand and *mamá* agreed. They started buying sheets and things. Lorenzo would visit and sometimes he'd stay overnight. He'd have a few drinks with us, then he'd say, "*Ay*, I'm drunk and I have to stand guard in the morning!" So *mamá* would ask him to stay, and in the morning she'd make coffee for him before he left. We treated him like one of the family, see? We trusted him.

We thought Lorenzo was a decent guy, but one day I heard Rita confess to *mamá* that she was pregnant. Pretty soon she and Lorenzo started quarreling. He was a shameless sort of a guy and Rita was jealous and quick-tempered. In the end, he left and didn't come back. And after they'd bought the bedroom furniture and all! We never saw him again,

not even after his son was born. I swear! That guy turned out to be
exactly like *papá*.

Rita tried to get rid of the baby before he was born. There are places
here to do that. She went to one of them, and was waiting her turn when
the police arrived to raid the place, so she jumped out of a window, big
belly and all, and ran for it. After that she had to have the child but she
didn't want him.

What happened to Rita didn't mean a thing to Ernesto and me. People
more civilized than us would have gotten angry and put pressure on her
boyfriend. I guess my brother and I were no more than animals. Not
mima. She told my sister plenty and made her cry a lot, though it didn't
change things.

Rita loved that guy like life itself. She was miserable for a long time
after he'd left. There was this record we used to hear that Lorenzo liked
a lot. "Oh, thish beer ish sho tashty it goesh to my head. . . ." It was
supposed to be funny but Rita could never hear it without crying.

When she was eighteen years old she began to work as a domestic
servant. She earned 30 *pesos* a month and her food. After I got my job,
we were able to move to a better house on Enamorados. We weren't well
off, but at least we didn't go hungry, and I had some money in my
pocket.

Ernesto was working too, for a man called El Gallego. He had a nice
little business selling fruit. El Gallego was rich by our standards and
owned a good one-story house on a street near us. He was about thirty,
short and slight. He started taking meals with us and fell in love with Rita
and wanted to marry her. We were delighted. Not Rita. She didn't like
him and would have nothing to do with him. We kept pointing out to my
sister how rich he was and what a good husband he'd make.

El Gallego let us live in half of his house free of charge. The bathroom
was in his half of the house and he wouldn't let us use it. We used a
chamber pot, and when that was full we'd take a piece of paper up on the
flat roof and move our bowels up there. He kept his part of the house
locked. But he gave Rita the key, and when we were hungry we'd stuff
ourselves on his apples and grapes. I once took a sheet of his lottery
tickets and sold them at a bar. It didn't pay anything, but if that number
had happened to win he would have killed me.

There never was anything between Rita and El Gallego. One day she
said a dirty word in front of him and he got disgusted and stopped
courting her. He told us he was leaving and the rent for the place was 75
pesos.

"We sure as hell can't afford that," I told *mamá*, and we went back to
Enamorados Street.

When I was fourteen *mamá* was living with another husband, David—I
forget his last name. He was a sergeant in Batista's army, and whenever

someone so much as mentioned Fidel's name, he'd pull out his pistol and yell, "Damn him, where is he? I'll plug him full of lead!" He was very loyal to Batista. He wore a ring that had Batista's name on it. The dictator himself had given it to him.

Mamá and David lasted together two or three years, the final years of the dictatorship. He was a real good guy. He was very good to us kids and treated us like his own family. Christmas Eve he'd buy all the makings of a fiesta. I got to be very fond of him. But I was jealous of him, too. We lived in his one-room house, so when David came home in the evening, *mamá* would send us out to buy candy or take a walk around the barrio. I felt jealous, terribly jealous, to think of her alone in that house with that man. I'd think, "Why doesn't she marry him and settle down with him for good?" It was only after I grew up that I realized she could never keep a man.

The sergeant and I were quite chummy. I could talk frankly with him and we had long conversations. One day he asked me, "Have you ever laid a woman?"

"Why do you ask?" I said. I was trembling all over and my heart went *taca, taca, taca,* that's how nervous the conversation was making me. At that time I'd never known a woman. I didn't even know what a woman's body was like—her intimate parts, you know—where they were. Nobody had ever explained it to me. I thought whatever it was they had was right under the navel.

"I'm going to take you to a place where you can have a woman," David said. "It's about time you learned, but don't go telling your *mamá* about it, or I'll be in trouble."

He took me to a wonderful, luxurious place, not a brothel but a house that belonged to a friend of his, an army captain and his wife. In the living room he introduced me to them. "I want you to meet my friends." I just stood there quaking. Then he threw an arm around the captain's shoulder and led him to the other end of the room.

The woman was very pretty, about thirty or thirty-five.

"Have you ever been with a woman?" she asked. I said yes or no, I don't remember which. She led me into her bedroom, a pretty room with a beautiful bed. We sat on the bed together, she snuggling up close. I was shaking like a leaf.

"Shall I show you some pictures my son drew?" she said. They were colored drawings and every one of them showed a man with a man, doing things. I was embarrassed. I didn't say anything but I thought, "Hell, if I was going to draw pictures like these, I'd draw a man with a woman, or a woman with a woman, but not a man with another man."

We got to the end of the pictures, then she hugged me and kissed me. I went wild. I tugged at her blouse and her tight black skirt. I was so excited I tore it. She wore a girdle underneath and I tried to tear it off.

"Hold your horses, old boy," she said. "Don't be so savage. I'll be right back."

She swept back in, wearing a transparent negligee ... *Ay, mi madre!* She lay down and I tried to get into her, right under the navel where I thought it was supposed to go. No sooner did I realize that I was aiming at the wrong place than *bang!* I came.

Having laid my first woman, I began talking about sex with my friends at the coffee shop, and that loosened their tongues too. It was then that I began going to Colón, where you had only to walk down the street and the women would accost you, "Hey, *pipo*, come with me."

I got to be a regular customer. I'd go there every other day. It was a fever that got into me. Right after work I'd be off like a flash to Colón. I could afford it, too, with all the extra money I was making at the coffee stand during the weekends.

I remember one fat woman with a very pretty face. She had a pimp, a black, who always waited for her outside. One night I asked how much and she said, "One *peso* and fifty *centavos* for the usual, but for 2 *pesos* I'll do such-and-such." And she gave me a long list of the dirty things she'd do. I gave her the 2 *pesos* but she didn't do any of them. Next time I went to a beautiful blond. I got into her and *bang!* I was through. That night, at home, I noticed my undershorts were stained. "What's this?" I thought. Next day I told one of my friends. "Ay, *chico*, you've got an infection. Better have a penicillin shot right away." I took his advice and got cured in no time at all. The following week I was back in Colón.

In a little while I got into another mess. There's a little bug they call a crab louse; if you get one, you get thousands and thousands of them. I got them and I couldn't get rid of them. One day after bathing, I smeared myself with kerosene and had to get right back in the bath because it burned so. I had the crabs for about six years, but that didn't keep me away from the women.

Chapter Three

I Found My Way

I NEVER THOUGHT ABOUT the problems of my country. I had no interest in politics and never got to vote in an election. I remember how the politicians would rush about, asking everyone to vote. Then, on election day, I'd see the ballot boxes set up in corners and people voting but I just wasn't interested. What did I care who was elected mayor? I don't think we need any election now. What good would it do? We've got Fidel and the Central Committee and that's all we need.

I did absolutely nothing for the Revolution. Some friends of mine went out selling bonds and so on. They would talk to me and let me listen when they tuned in the "Voice of the Sierra," but it all went in one ear and out the other. While they were shooting it out I was peddling oranges in the street. I didn't have a thought in my head. I was just floating in the air, and that's the truth!

At the time of the attack on the Palace,[8] I was listening to the Marianao station. I went out into the street to watch the tanks and all. People were running everywhere. Someone said, "They killed Batista!"

I felt I owed the man some loyalty so I got on my bicycle and went around insulting Fidel, telling everybody, "It's a lie, the General couldn't fall, *chico,*" and I don't know what all. I can't imagine why I felt I had to talk that way. What had Batista ever done for me anyway?

At the time of the Triumph, I was still working at the coffee shop in

8. On March 13, 1957, a group of about eighty men attacked the Presidential Palace in Havana in an attempt to assassinate Batista. Most of the attackers were members of the *Directorio Revolucionario,* a university student group organized by José Antonio Echeverría. The rebels were able to penetrate the Palace but could not find their way to Batista's living quarters. In a simultaneous attack, the students took over Havana Radio, and Echeverría mistakenly broadcast the announcement of Batista's death. Shortly afterward Echeverría was fatally shot by police. An estimated thirty-five rebels and five Batista policemen were killed in the attack. The Castro forces were already involved in the Sierra campaign and were not a part of the *Directorio* action. Castro later criticized the attack as "a useless expenditure of blood," although today in Cuba the anniversary of the attack is celebrated and Echeverría is a famous martyr. (Thomas, *Cuba: The Pursuit of Freedom,* pp. 925 ff.)

the Marqués de la Torre drugstore. One day as I rode up—I owned a motorcycle then—a bunch of people surrounded me. One of them said, "Hey, don't hit the kid. He's a good guy." Then to me, "Unlock the store. We're going to smash everything in here."

That was a few days after the fall of the dictatorship, when people were flocking to the wealthy districts like Miramar and stealing and smashing everything they could lay their hands on and throwing things out the windows. In the end, the new government clamped down on pilferers and passed some rough laws against burglary and assault. Remember El Chino, the terror of La Asunción? When the Revolution triumphed, El Chino thought he could do as he pleased and went around assaulting people and burglarizing businesses. One day he was breaking into a grocery store when a police captain saw him and shot him dead.

Poor El Chino! He didn't know what the Revolution was all about. As for me, if it hadn't been for the Revolution I'd have ended up in jail. With the victory, I began to find a way for myself.

I worked at the Marqués de la Torre until the invasion of Playa Girón. Then, one Thursday, the owner said to me, "Gabriel, tomorrow I'm leaving at 3:00 in the morning to go to Guanabo for the weekend." Saturday and Sunday he was gone as usual, and Monday, Tuesday, Wednesday went by with no sign of him. On Thursday the money was giving out when the police came and told us he'd left the country. He'd torn up the whole inside of the drugstore and smashed his car and left a note saying, "Down with communism."

That happened just after the invasion at Girón. I was out of work for a while and then I got a job at the Paradiso Hotel, which was operated by INIT.[9] I was only mopping floors but I earned 86 *pesos* a month, my meals, and my laundry was done free. I worked eight hours a day, with one day off a week and fifteen days' paid vacation every five months. What a change from my job with that tightfisted *gusano!*

The plainclothesman at the Paradiso had it in for me. He hated me from the very first, I don't know why. I'd only worked there a week when he said to me, "Go to the office and ask the accountant to settle up with you. You're through here."

My eyes were full of tears because, hell, I was earning such good wages, and to lose a job like that for no reason at all. . . . I told the accountant, "Look, could you pay me? The *delegado* just fired me."

The manager was in the office talking to her and they both stared at me. "And what authority does a plainclothesman have to fire people?" he asked. "Go right back and tell him you stay on that job until further notice."

9. *Instituto Nacional de la Industria Turística* (National Institute of the Tourist Industry).

The employees liked the manager. When the hotel got a shipment of meat—this was before rationing—he'd call us all together and give us 5 or 6 pounds each. "Pay for it later," he'd tell us. But the guy turned out to be a CIA agent. He always carried a submachine gun and smoked Chesterfields, and he owned a 1948 Ford. He spoke perfect Spanish and had somehow got hold of an army captain's uniform. No one suspected a thing.

One day I was chatting with him in the office—he'd just offered me a Chesterfield—when four or five men armed with machine guns burst into the room. I thought, "Hell, what's going on?" They arrested him and took him away.

All the hotel employees got together and protested to INIT. The police called us to a meeting and told us the guy was a spy who had infiltrated the Party. He'd come from North America and had got himself a gun and a uniform—everything was so disorganized at first it was easy, see? He led a group of counterrevolutionaries and had killed two people in Oriente. That's why he was arrested and shot.

It was his wife who informed on him. He'd treated her badly. She used to go see him and he'd yell at her, "Get out, before I put a bullet in your head!" He was real mean and she got back by telling on him. Whether she was for the Revolution or not, I don't know.

We were living in Almendares then because just at the beginning of the Revolution *mamá* made a complicated deal and bought a house there. Right after we moved in I met Caridad. It was love at first sight. She was beautiful—tall, slender, big breasts, just my type. She had long chestnut hair, a small mouth, and a gold-capped tooth! I loved everything about her, right down to her big toe! She lived across the street and would stand in her doorway leaning up against the wall. I'd stand in mine and give her the eye. She ignored me. I liked that. It meant she was a good girl. One day I asked her, "Come to the movies with me?"

"I'll think about it," she said. And then, "All right, I'll go with you."

I got all dressed up and dusted my face with talcum. I took her to the Marianao theater and we sat in the balcony. She had brought her little nephew along so I bought a bag of oranges and said to him, "Here, eat these and mind your own business." But when I started to steal an arm around Caridad, he piped up, "Take your arm away, damn it!" He was only four or five years old but a real devil.

I whispered to him, "Listen, kid. I'm going to kiss your aunt and do forty thousand things to her, and if you interfere I'll throw you over the balcony. So watch it!"

I put my arm around Caridad again and twisted my head around and scowled at him. He didn't say a word. Then I kissed her. It was like floating up to heaven. I was barbarously in love with her. That same day I told her, "I'm in love with you. Tomorrow I'm going to your house to ask permission to marry you."

I went there the next day after work. Caridad lived with her mother, her older sister, and her little nephew. They gave me coffee and we talked. Then I said, "Señora, I like your daughter very much and I want to marry her." I was a bad lot but I spoke from the heart that time.

Caridad's mother accepted me right away. She didn't ask how much I earned, about my family, or anything. After that I saw Caridad every day. I'd rush home from work mad to see her. We'd go to the movies, or sometimes we'd go with her mother and her mother's lover to the night-clubs in Marianao and spend the evening drinking.

Caridad's parents were separated. Her *papá* lived in Old Havana, but he brought money every week. He'd had both legs amputated on account of gangrene but he had relations with his wife nonetheless. And she put the horns on him.

One day I was alone with the old lady, Caridad's mother, when she suddenly cried out, "*Ay, what a pain!*"

"Can I do anything for you?" I asked, just being polite.

"Yes, take that liniment and rub it in," she told me. *Coño!* By the time I'd got the lid off the liniment she'd lowered her dress and was lying face down on the bed. "Rub it here," she told me. While I rubbed, she kept moaning and looking at me slyly out of the corner of her eye. I stared at her openmouthed. She was middle-aged, about forty, but still pretty and in good shape.

I was breathing hard and the old bird asked me, "What's wrong with you, my boy?"

"Nothing . . . nothing . . . ," I gasped.

"The pain is lower down," she said. "You'll have to rub lower." Degenerate, that's what she was. Imagine! The mother of my sweetheart!

Caridad's sister Aida was no kid either. Her husband was in jail and she had her lovers too. Ernesto started calling on her, and one day when we were at their house together, Aida pulled out some money and gave it to Caridad. "Here, go out with Gabriel and buy some sandwiches. I'm hungry." She wanted us out of the way so she could be alone with Ernesto. Later on he told me, "While you were gone, we did sixty-nine right there in the armchair."

I never went to bed with Caridad. I had plenty of opportunity because her mother often got drunk as a dog and fell into a stupor. Caridad would wipe the vomit from her face with a handkerchief. But she never said a word about it.

Sometimes I used to wonder whether Caridad was a virgin, but I never put it to the test. I always intended to take her to the altar and marry her before having her. I never went very far with her and she never led me on. For the six or seven months we were sweethearts I did without sex. I didn't go to Colón even once.

She was so beautiful! I was proud just to be seen with her. One day this guy tried to touch my sweetheart. He had quite a reputation as a tough, and we were walking by when he said to me, "Look at him, carrying a little *taco* when he's so big and has such balls!" I pretended not to hear. "I shit on your mother's cunt!" he said.

I stopped and gave him a look. Then he reached out and touched Caridad. That made me blind with fury and I went at him with both fists. He grabbed my balls; he was practically pulling my life off. My nails were long and I tried to gouge his eyes. I hit him with my fists, left, right, left, right, until they pulled me away. If they hadn't, I would have killed him.

"Let's quit," he said, and he turned around and got lost as I strutted off.

Caridad and her *mamá* were *gusanas* and they thought I was a counter-revolutionary just like them. They'd tell me about their counter-revolutionary activities, about some guy who planted bombs and another who was selling bonds. I never said a word although I was against all those things.

I worked at the Paradiso Hotel until I joined the militia in 1962, at the time of the October crisis. I joined of my own free will because I was a revolutionary by then. I still didn't know a thing about politics, but I could see how everything had changed. I used to earn less than 30 *pesos* a month and was squeezed and exploited and taken advantage of. I used to be a nobody and I could see the difference in myself as a person. My family was better off too—we were all eating and working. I was beginning to understand what it was all about so I took the path of the Revolution.

In October we were told that the American invasion was expected any moment and that their ships were already close to our shores. No one said anything about any Russian missiles—not to me at least. People were lining up to volunteer. I hadn't volunteered for Playa Girón but I joined this line and gave my name. I wasn't expecting to have to start shooting without any training but I found myself mobilized for immediate action, with the American ships in sight of the coast.

The men I was with knew as much about fighting as I did, but morale was good. If we'd been told the Americans were landing, we would have rushed off to fight without a second thought. You'd hear someone say, "If I die, I just hope they give me credit for it." Or, "If something happens to me, my old lady will be left alone and my kids will be orphans. I'd be sorry about that, but what does it matter? We're born to die." They were great guys, all of them. I was still unmarried so I had no such worries. And I didn't think about *mamá*. She had survived so much in her life she'd survive anything.

I was sent to the hills for a month. We were assigned to guard an arsenal and the lieutenant put each of us at surrounding posts. "Boys," he said, "if I give the signal, that means there are rebels about."

"Rebels?" I thought. He went on, "If anybody turns up in this area, he's a rebel, so don't talk, shoot."

"Well, I'll be damned," I thought. "He means every word of it."

During the afternoon I was perfectly calm. Every little while I'd look over at the next post and see a sentry on duty there. But then night came, a dark, moonless night. *Ay, mi madre!* I wanted to climb into a hole and pull it down on top of me. I whistled to the other guy to make sure he was still at his post. I could see the headlights of a car some distance away and I felt like jumping the fence, taking to the road, and getting lost. There I was all alone, in a panic, wanting to run.

Then I heard footsteps. I was so scared the piss started to dribble out of me. I fell to the ground and crawled behind a coconut palm. I pushed the helmet further down on my head. "Who's there?" I said. No answer. They'd taught me to fire a machine gun and I remembered the instructions. I started shooting, *pa, pa, pa,* aiming at the place the sound came from, crying all the while, *"Ay, mami! Ay, mami!"*

My comrades came running: "What's up?" I told them and they searched the place where I'd heard the noise. There were footprints but no other sign. The lieutenant was sent to the brig for having left me alone guarding arms. If the place had been blown up it would have destroyed who knows how much.

I didn't hear about the Russian missiles until after I was in the Army. When they took them back to Russia I thought, "What a shitty thing they've done!" Cubans were very disappointed. I guess the Russians had been through enough wars already. Or maybe they're cowards. They really screwed us, leaving us unarmed. The Americans could have got in here and blown us all to hell, because we had nothing, just two or three dinky airplanes, a few tanks, nothing to speak of. Once we buy the missiles the Russians won't be able to take them away from us, because they'll be ours. Fidel said so in a speech.

After it was all over I got the nerve sickness. My personality changed. I got irritable and would explode at any little thing. I'd never been that way before. I'm a bit better now but still not back to normal.

I don't know how it was for the civilians during the crisis. In Havana all the men had enlisted and the women were standing in for them in the factories. The whole city was quiet but every building had a machine gun mounted on the roof. I don't know whether people felt scared. What we soldiers felt mostly was awfully hungry, because supplies were delayed.

The sergeant said, "The troops have to eat." We searched the countryside and found a farmer, a counterrevolutionary, who had sacks of beans stashed away, and we appropriated them. We ate an awful lot of beans waiting for those supplies.

When I volunteered for the Army I didn't tell Caridad I was going. She kept asking *mamá* where I was but *mima* covered up for me. A few weeks later I showed up at the barrio with my rucksack, submachine gun, and gas mask. I was wearing an army helmet and my boots were caked with mud. *Mamá* was waiting in line at the store when I showed up. "Here I am, *mima*," I said. I happened to turn my head a little.... "Caridad!" I cried.

"Gabriel!" She was too startled to say more. She just stood there staring, remembering all the things her *mamá* had told me. That's when we had our first quarrel.

"This is how it stands," I said. "I'm a revolutionary, so now you know."

Caridad and her family soon forgave me and we began planning for our marriage in earnest. We even set a wedding date, January 24, and started to buy a few things. I was still working as a janitor then and didn't earn much. One day Caridad's *mamá* took my hand and said, "What kind of work do you do?" I told her I was a waiter, but I think she had her doubts because I always smelled of creosote from mopping floors. Once I heard her say to Caridad, "Are you really going to marry that guy? He's nothing but a janitor, poor devil. What can he do for you?" I heard her through the door and it hurt.

There was this guy, Lino, who'd been Caridad's sweetheart before me, only I didn't know that. One day he came up to her on the street and said something fresh. I was just behind and hurried over. "What's with you? Did you lose something that looks like her?"

"Why don't you get lost?" he said in a nasty tone of voice. I was going to hit him but some passerby stopped me. "Just you wait," I thought. "Next time I catch you when I'm out on my motorbike, I'll run you over!"

Not long after that Lino came up to me again. "Look, *chico*, I'm willing to fight you any time you like," he said. "But there's something you should know because I hear you plan to marry Caridad. That girl was once my sweetheart, and take it from me, she's a tramp."

"Take care what you say about her ... ," I began, choking with rage.

"Wait! Let me have my say, then we can fight. Tonight Caridad is going to meet a pal of mine in the park. He told me so himself. I'll take you in my car, and if I'm lying you can kill me."

"You'd better be lying," I said, "because I love that woman like my life."

That night Lino drove me to the park. There she was with another man. She was wearing the white shoes I'd given her. I'd bought all the clothes she wore for her fifteenth birthday—shoes, dress, stockings, the lot. My hard-earned money I spent on her. I was crazy with rage and jealousy. If I'd had a gun I'd have shot the two of them.

"Wait, don't get out," Lino said. He drove around and turned the headlights full on them. I jumped out and went over to them. "Good evening, Caridad," I said.

"Gabriel!" she gasped. I could see her face change color and her eyes go blank.

I tried to keep calm but the guy said something and we began to fight. I nearly killed him because I was terribly jealous. Then, with my shirt all torn, I got back in the car and Lino drove me to her house in a hurry. Imagine, I'd been on the verge of tearing this guy's head off and he did me that favor!

It happened that Caridad's father was visiting her *mamá* when I showed up.

"Good evening," I said. "Some time ago, I came here to ask formally for your daughter's hand in marriage. Well, I'm formally returning her to you."

"But why? What happened?" I told them what their daughter was doing in the park—touching that fellow all over and letting him do the same to her, the brazen slut! Her *papá* was indignant. When Caridad came hurrying in a few minutes later, he reached out, crippled though he was, and smashed his fist down on her head. I started for her and would have beaten her—any man would lose his head after what I'd been through—but at the last minute I turned and ran out, crying.

I was due on guard that night, so I went straight to my post. Alone, with my submachine gun, I suddenly leaned my temple against the muzzle and put my finger on the trigger. "*Ay, mi madre!*" I thought, "why not press the trigger and get it over with?" But I pictured myself with my face all smashed up and put down the gun.

I went to the man in charge of our unit and told him I was leaving because I felt ill. I got out of uniform and left on my motorcycle. I drove like a maniac, racing by Coney Island at about 1,000 kilometers an hour. It's a wonder I didn't smash myself up.

I drove around all night thinking only of Caridad. When I got home at about 2:00 in the morning, she was standing in her doorway in a housecoat. "Gabriel!" she called, running over to me.

"Go to hell," I shouted. "I never want to see you again, you tramp! Damn your whoring mother!" And then we kissed. Imagine that, we kissed! But then all the hurt and humiliation came back to me and I told her, "My one wish for you is that you get a husband who makes you a big belly and kicks you out."

Well, it happened. She married and had a daughter and the guy beat her and kicked her out. Finally she went into the life. I was already married by then, otherwise I might have helped her because I still loved her. She's left Cuba now, so there's no chance. If she'd stayed she might have been a problem in my marriage, because for two years afterward I was still dying for her. I never wanted to be with my wife the way I wanted to be with Caridad. She was the woman I really loved, and that's the truth. And it's just as true that I'd have been miserable if I'd married her.

Caridad was a tramp, a born tramp. Her mother worked in a cabaret and then was a streetwalker. What chance did her daughter have? No. It would have been a misfortune if I'd married her. She was no good. If I saw her now, I'd try to hurt her just to get even for what she did to me.

Her brother took the whole family to the States. He left first by hiding in an oil drum on the docks for a month until a ship came in. Then he swam for it and that's how he escaped. Later, when Fidel said anyone who wanted to leave could go through Camarioca,[10] her brother came back for them.

There are still a lot of *gusanos* in Cuba but none of them are activists. Some of them listen to Fidel's speeches and afterward criticize him and tell stories against him. The Committee sets a loudspeaker out in the street so that people will have to hear all the speeches. I think that's a mistake. After all, Fidel says more than any of the others, and if you've heard him why bother with the rest?

There are all kinds of *gusanos*. Some even have a truly revolutionary attitude. They don't like the system and specifically disapprove of a number of things . . . like the way the schools are run, or their jobs. But they admit that good things have been done too. And they do their work well, volunteer to go to the country, and cooperate with the rest of us in every way. So I wouldn't say they're an obstacle to the Revolution, even if they would like to see a change of government. I know that many of those who now say they don't like our system would go out and fight for it if need be. Their consciences would make them. Many of them have told me so.

There used to be a counterrevolutionary gang called "Black Jackets." Most of them were rich men's sons, unhappy at having half their property taken from them. They'd go around beating up women and revolutionaries, but the people rose up to deal with it. They went after them with sticks and put an end to their barbarities.

10. In October, 1965, Castro announced that those Cubans who wanted to leave and had obtained the necessary authorization could do so by leaving through the port at Camarioca, a village 70 miles east of Havana. Most left in small private vessels piloted by relatives and friends who had already immigrated to the United States but were allowed to return to pick up other emigrants. A month after the Camarioca port was opened, the Varadero-Miami airlift went into effect. (For an account of the emigration from Camarioca, see Lockwood, *Castro's Cuba, Cuba's Fidel*, pp. 283 ff.)

Now the *gusanos* are cutting telephone wires and ripping up bus seats, but if you catch one of them at it, you may shoot him then and there and nothing will happen to you. You'll get arrested maybe, but that's all, because everyone knows how much sugar cane we had to cut to pay for those buses. If a *gusano* is convicted for ripping up bus seats, he'll get twenty years at a prison farm. I have no idea how many people are serving terms for counterrevolutionary activities, but I know a number of people who have relatives in jail. An uncle of mine I'd never met, a captain in Batista's navy, was sentenced to thirty years. They're scared now. They know the government means business, because once they're caught in counterrevolutionary activities they haven't a chance of escaping the firing squad. And they always get caught.

I was away in the Army a month and a half. I didn't have to give up my job. The government gave me mobilization leave and my usual pay. After demobilization I worked in the Hotel Madrid.

I was still illiterate and the only job I could do was mop floors. One day the manager called me to his office. "It's sad to see a young fellow like you mopping floors," he said. "Look, if you go to school and get some education—learn to read and write—I'll get you a promotion. You'll earn better wages as a waiter and you'll get tips, too."

I began school right away. An American couple who had come to help the Revolution were employees at the Madrid, and they taught those of us who couldn't read or write. I already knew the alphabet and could form syllables. A black girl lived right next to us in La Asunción and she gave my brother and me a lesson every time we brought her a pack of cigarettes. Later on, when I worked at the coffee shop, a woman who was a retired teacher used to come and drink coffee there. She helped me a bit more.

At the Madrid I went to class every day. I learned fast and soon found my feet. When I could write well enough to take down a customer's order, they appointed me a waiter and gave me an identity card saying "Occupation: Waiter." The first day on my new job I got 10 *pesos* in tips. But I didn't quit school. The manager told me, "You can work from 7:00 A.M. to 3:00 P.M. and go to school at night so you can finish your studies." I kept at it and got through sixth grade in three years.

I'm a waiter to this day, but that doesn't mean I don't pinch-hit for an absent dishwasher or elevator man, or mop floors if need be. Nobody orders me to do these things. I do them voluntarily.

Mamá is a thoroughgoing revolutionary. She'd lay down her life for the Revolution. During the October crisis she joined up as a *miliciana*. Fidel will do something and you can't say a word against it because she knows what the score is. She's still poor but she lives better than she ever did before. She lives like a human being. She has a little room of her own and doesn't pay rent, so I don't have to worry about her being evicted and left out on the street.

Mamá doesn't work anymore because of her bad back. Still, she does her guard duty, and sick as she is, she goes to combat training with her militia unit. She's forty-eight years old now, but she keeps herself in good shape. She's tall and stout with long fair hair and gray eyes. She's always primping and she likes to display pictures of herself when she was young. I look at them and tell her, "You're getting old, *mamá*." Then she pulls her skin tight and says it isn't so.

After the triumph of the Revolution, *mamá* met her present husband, Luis Fundora. They've been together for about five years; they never married. He fought in the war and is a member of the Party. Now he works in park maintenance in Miramar. *Mamá* is very happy with him though she's very jealous. She's always been that way—jealous of her own shadow. Her husband can be 100 miles away and she'll think she caught sight of him with another woman. It's too much! I tell her, "*Mamá*, you're nearly fifty—too old for that kind of thing. Forget your jealousy. It's no way to live."

We talk as equals now, as revolutionaries. It's not like talking to your mother. She'll say, "What's your opinion of such-and-such?" And we'll have a long conversation about politics. Before the Revolution we had nothing to talk about. Absolutely nothing.

SEÑORA PACHECO:

On the first of January, the first day of the Revolution, I was at home, alone with my children. I was employed at the time. I'd always worked as a domestic and never knew anything about the government or the Revolution, or anything except my work, and I barely had enough life in me for that. But I don't think I'll ever forget how the Revolution was. Look, it was ours! I wore a black skirt and a red pullover.[11] There was a car that went around with loudspeakers calling out all the people. And the people in the street were yelling *"Viva"* and things like that. I went out too, and then I went to visit the whole family.

After that I continued working, of course, and I worked at the same thing. I wasn't integrated or anything and that's the truth. I'm a frank person. I came to know about the Revolution through my children, during the October crisis. Then I understood, and I saw how people were changing the situation.

I became a *miliciana* but I still don't know how to read or write. I just bought myself a pair of glasses so I can attend some classes, because I

11. Black and red were the colors of the Twenty-sixth of July Movement.

really need to learn. What with washing and ironing and attending to the children when they were young, I didn't have a clear mind. It was impossible. And then my son Ernesto had epileptic fits and all that, so I just couldn't be studying. Now I can because I'm living in peace and my present husband is a good man.

CAPOTE:

I don't know where my brother would be without the Revolution. His life is very unhappy. At home we all used to think Ernesto would get a job and marry before I did, but it turned out just the opposite. I suppose it was because of his epileptic fits that he never made his way in the world. After the Triumph he got a job in MINCON as a construction worker, but they said he was a danger to his own life and to his *compañeros,* so they pensioned him off at 85 *pesos* a month. Imagine paying him so he'll stay home!

He can't even be in the militia. He volunteered but they turned him down. He isn't anything. He keeps to his room all day. Clothes, that's all he used to care about; now he doesn't even care about that. Those epileptic fits have all but destroyed him. He won't go out as long as he's expecting one. He tells us ahead of time when one is coming. Afterward I'll go to see him and he'll hug and kiss me with the tears running down his face. Sometimes he'll have two or three fits in a single day. Then he's so helpless he has to be fed. I feel so unhappy for him at those times. He's under medical treatment. They gave him some pills and he gets electroshock.

Ernesto got married about four years ago, to a *mulata.* She was a pretty girl when they married and she's skinny now, ugly, though a good woman. She loves Ernesto and has given him everything. She works in a textile factory and earns around 160 *pesos* a month.

Mamá says Ernesto shouldn't have a wife on account of his fits, but the doctor says he can have sex, though not too often. They have a baby daughter of eighteen months who goes to the *círculo* every day while her *mamá* works. At least she's safe there. Ernesto can't look after her.

My brother doesn't believe in witchcraft but his wife does, and she's taken him to the spiritists. He half believes, half disbelieves. He'll take an offering to the sorcerer—I don't know what the guy does with the stuff, maybe he smokes the tobacco and drinks the rum himself—but the fact is, each time Ernesto has gone he's been free of the fits for a long time afterward.

Ernesto's wife wants to get out of Cuba. All her family have left. Two of her brothers were killed trying to get away. They set out in a boat but the coastguards caught up with them and ordered them to turn back. They offered resistance and the guards sank the boat.

Ernesto could leave too, but he doesn't want to. He's a revolutionary like me. He's told me himself he'd take up arms if need be. I know his wife has spoken to him about leaving. She's put herself and their baby daughter on the waiting list. Ernesto told me, "She's free to go if she likes but she can't take my daughter." She has no business taking his child out of the country and I warned him not to sign any papers.

As for Rita, my sister, she's not right in the head. She's always been that way. It seems to me that being the firstborn, she was affected by *papá*'s insanity. She talks a lot of nonsense against the Revolution, about having no food or clothes, and yet she was always a poor devil, exploited all her life. I've no idea why she complains. If she'd been rich and used to good food, good clothes. . . . But the only clothes she ever had were those little dresses made out of flour sacks. She never had shoes, and dinner was only a piece of sweet potato or a bit of banana. There's not much now, but she eats more than she ever ate before.

She has a little apartment that doesn't cost her a cent. She used to have a house with a huge front porch and new doors and shutters. Then the Urban Reform Office asked her if she'd be willing to exchange it for a single room and she accepted, for no reason at all, and moved into a room that's practically ready to collapse! After that, the doctor gave her a letter saying she shouldn't make any decisions without her brothers' or mother's approval. When a doctor writes that kind of a letter about a patient it means she isn't in her right mind.

Rita has a husband who's black. I'm not prejudiced—I visit there and sit and chat with him—but in private I've asked my sister, "Why did you have to go marry that Negro?"

"Because I love him," she said.

"Well, if you love him that's all right," I told her. What else could I say? But I don't like it and I know *mamá* isn't happy about it either. *Mamá* herself has never had a black husband. *Papá* was Indian but there's a lot of difference between Indian and Negro.

Rita's husband is ashamed of his family because they're all blacks. You can imagine how he loves Rita. After all, she's Indian. He's a longshoreman and makes about 300 *pesos* a month. He's integrated in the Revolution and is in the militia—a very fine man. He'll do anything for Rita and is very good to her son, too. He bought her a new bed and chest of drawers for the bedroom and she even has him do the cooking. He's sweet as sugar. My sister tells *mamá* he beats her up, then I have to go see, but I always find them laughing and hugging and kissing. I've given up on them.

It's a miracle that Rita's son survived. She couldn't cope with the child. She neglected him when he was sick and didn't fix his food or dress or bathe him. She lost control and even hit him. The doctor prescribed sleeping pills for her because she was picking fights and being violent. So then she spent the entire day sleeping. She just turned the boy loose on the streets and people had to bring him back home.

It came to the attention of the block Committee, who called Rita before them. They told her she must take better care of her son and send him to school. It's the law here. If a child is kept out of school without good reason, the parents are taken before the People's Court and punished. They warned Rita, but she still didn't send him. So the Committee held a trial for her and I had to appear. I told them Rita wasn't normal and wasn't responsible for what she said. If it hadn't been for me she'd have been on a work farm or in Mazorra by now.

After that *mamá* took the child. She had his name put down in her ration book and she takes complete care of him. He goes to school every day and now the boy can read and write a little. You can see he's being taken care of. If he'd grown up under the dictatorship, it would have been a disaster. As for Rita, she's going to a psychiatrist and they've given her electroshock and everything.

Most of *papá*'s relatives left Cuba after Batista fell. As far as I know, only two or three of his brothers and sisters are still here. I've never been close to them and don't even know their names, although I do know where they live. My Grandmother Claudia stayed on with *papá* in Banes after my brother Ernesto got him out of Mazorra.

Papá died in Hurricane Flora.[12] Ernesto was staying in Victoria de las Tunas just then and *papá* went to visit him. When the hurricane was announced, my brother said, "You'd better stay the night and wait till the hurricane is over." *Papá* wouldn't hear of it. The buses back to Banes had stopped running, but he set out on foot and was drowned crossing the river. They found his corpse in a cane field a month later, completely destroyed. They identified him by his card. His mother survived him by only two days. She loved *papá* dearly. Crazy about him, she was.

My Aunt Nieves, *papá*'s sister, stayed on here although she was against the Revolution. She used to tell me, "Fidel's days are numbered—the Americans will land here any day now." She changed her tune when the revolutionary government moved her into a new house, a real mansion, with a hall about ten blocks long. You can bicycle in it. They already owned a radio–record player, refrigerator, television and all, but they used to live in a run-down shack in a *reparto* like Las Yaguas. Their house was due to be torn down, and one day Nieves tied a rope to the roof and tugged on it until the roof fell in. When the government came and saw the damage, they gave her that phenomenal mansion.

Nieves loves the Revolution now. She says, "I always knew Fidel was a good man. Look at the house the government gave me." She was lucky.

One of Nieves's sons is a great athlete. He's competed in races in Mexico and Canada. I thought he'd take the opportunity to defect, but

12. October, 1963.

he hasn't. He has courage, that guy, and he's a true communist, one of the best.

She has another son who wants to get out of Cuba but can't as long as he's of military age. Once he's twenty-eight he can go. Lots of people are dissatisfied and want to get out. Well, all you have to do is ask. If you're sick they keep you in Havana until your turn comes, but if you're in good health they send you to Camaguey to do farm work until you leave.[13]

At the moment my cousin is in hiding. Well, he stays in the house because he wants to dodge being called up. If they see you on the street without a job, they stop and ask you for your *carnet* and that way they catch you. My cousin works maybe a month at MINCON, where you don't need papers for part-time work. You do your work, get paid, and that's that, no questions asked. The rest of the time he stays home; they've already been there, looking for him.

13. In 1968 Castro announced a change in policy toward those Cubans waiting their turns to emigrate via the Varadero-Miami airlift (begun in November, 1965): "The *gusanos* are no longer on holiday, waiting three years, living at the expense of others, yearning for the day when they will enter the Yankee paradise. Not any more. The way to Miami now runs through the countryside, through the canefields, through work." (Quoted in Richard R. Fagen, Richard A. Brody, and Thomas J. O'Leary, *Cubans in Exile* (Stanford, Calif.: Stanford University Press, 1968), p. 157 n. 19.) In practice this meant that ablebodied men and women who had received places on the waiting list were sent to work in agriculture for a minimum wage, plus maintenance, for as long as two years prior to their departure. The airlift was terminated in November, 1971.

Chapter Four

Fina and My Children

AFTER I BROKE UP with Caridad my friends told me, "Don't go to whores, *chico*. Get yourself a girl of your own. It's cleaner and cheaper." So I started looking for a woman, any woman. I wasn't choosey. I used to go to the amusement park on my day off and that's where I met Fina, my wife. She was riding on the merry-go-round with her nephew. I gave her a look and she looked right back at me. She liked the look of me I guess. I dressed well in those days. I went up to her and said, "Will you permit me to pay for this ride?"

"Oh no, thank you. No, no, no!"

I insisted, she accepted, and then we chatted awhile. A little later I cornered her, pushed her against the wall, and started kissing her. She kissed me back but very shyly, hardly daring to look me in the face. I could see she was a good girl and that was the last thing I wanted just then. At that point my intentions were anything but good. I wanted to spend the night with her and that was all. I still had the crabs but I thought, "So what if she gets them? As long as she doesn't infect me with anything." I didn't give a damn what happened to her. But I didn't have the courage to ask her to sleep with me, so I just got lost.

One Sunday night about six weeks later I went back to the amusement park. Not to meet Fina—I didn't want to start anything with her—but to see what I could pick up, because the place just swarmed with broads on Sunday nights. Well, I ran into Fina again. She lived quite near the park. We started talking. She worked as a servant and was learning to read and write. I walked her to school a couple of times, just to act the gentleman. Then I stopped seeing her for a month or two.

One morning, before I got up, someone knocked at our door. I looked through a crack in the boards and saw Fina standing there. "Darn her!" I thought. And I said to *mamá*, "Tell her I'm not at home."

I don't know how she got hold of my address. I sure didn't give it to her. I lived a long way from the amusement park. She had to get on a bus to come see me.

"Please tell Gabriel that Fina called," she told *mamá*.

"Why the hell does she have to come pestering me?" I said to myself. "To hell with her. I don't like her."

Fina wasn't bad-looking, in fact sometimes she looked awfully pretty, but I didn't fancy her as a wife, a woman to make a home with. Not at that time. I wasn't even particularly attracted to her as a woman. I didn't like her mouth, her figure, the way she laughed. She talked all in a rush, *rrrrrr*, the way country people talk. And her walk! Even now when I see her walking I say to her, "Are you hurrying to milk a cow, girrrrl?" That makes her laugh. She was a typical *guajirita*, a little country girl whose every word and gesture showed she didn't know anything about anything.

But I still hadn't found a woman. One night I took Fina to a bar and ordered two highballs, thinking that after I'd got a few drinks into her I could take her anywhere and do anything.

"I don't drink," she said.

"Ah, come on kid, just one little drink."

"I'll have a soft drink." So I ordered her a soft drink and downed the two highballs myself. I kept looking at her legs. She had nice curvy legs, very pretty. Then we took a walk and I kissed her a few times. We walked right by a *posada* but I didn't take her in. I lost my nerve. I hailed a taxi and took her home.

Three days later I was walking her to school when a pal of mine drove by in his old junk heap, a Buick.

"Hey," I called, "drive us to Marianao Beach? C'mon kid, hop in," I told her. I took her to a bar, got real high, and from there we went to a *posada*. Fina didn't want to go in but I urged her. "Come on, *chica*, let's go. Ah, come on, darling!" That did the trick. When I called her "darling" she went in with me. She was still wearing her school uniform and carrying her books.

When we were in the room I kissed her. She lay down but didn't want to undress, so I took off her clothes myself. When she was wearing only her panties I said, "I'll give you a *medio* to buy candy if you take those off."

She said no, but I insisted and finally we did it. And then, what did I find but that Fina wasn't a virgin. A man can always tell. Was I surprised! *Coño*, I mean . . . she was a tramp.

I still didn't like her, even after we'd made love. Virgin or not, she hadn't had much experience. But I was satisfied. We spent the night together and next morning we got on the bus. I thought, "I'll get rid of her as quick as I can."

Then she started to cry. "*Ay*, what shall I tell *mamá* when I get home?" That made me feel sorry for her so I took her to a restaurant. It was still early and they hadn't cooked anything yet except broth with bread in it.

She ate that and drank a glass of water, as happy as if I'd invited her to a banquet. I looked her over and thought, "I don't have the heart to throw her out after I've ruined her." So I took her back to my house.

"What are you up to?" *mamá* asked me.

"Nothing, old lady," I told her. "I just brought my sweetheart home."

"Fine, it's time you got married," she said.

Two days later I went to see Fina's *mamá*. I walked in, a perfect stranger, and told her, "Fina is at home with me." She burst into tears.

"It's all right. She's all right." Pretty soon she accepted the situation and came to visit us. I was twenty-one. Fina was seventeen. She got pregnant almost right away.

We lived with my mother for a while and then we had to leave because Fina didn't get on with *mamá*. At first *mamá* said Fina was a good woman, but then . . . *mamá* is very jealous and likes a good fight, and Fina is a timid little country girl, not the kind that looks for trouble. She never complained but I could see what was going on. We went to my sister Rita's house in Marianao, and she gave us a room. But Rita mistreated Fina. She used her as a servant, made her clean the house and do all the shopping while she was pregnant. Once Rita locked her out of the house.

From there we went to Fina's sister Hilda's house in Cuatro Caminos. After a while Hilda told us, "You'll have to find a place of your own because I won't want a baby grabbing and throwing things." I didn't get on with her, and then her husband started asking me for money. So I began to look elsewhere.

By that time I was earning 86 *pesos* a month as a waiter and I'd saved up my tips, so we moved into a room in the Hotel Telégrafo, right in the heart of Havana. It cost 5 *pesos* a day and in the end my money ran out. We moved back to *mamá*'s for two months and I wrote to Holguín for work, thinking we could live at my *papá*'s house in Banes. He was still alive then. I got a transfer to Holguín, but to get there I had to take up a collection at my work center for the bus fare.

I started working as a waiter in a restaurant, but when I went to see *papá* in Banes, I found his mother's house full up. She'd rented out all the rooms. It was against the law for a private individual to rent out property. Besides, it was the biggest mistake of her life, because when she wanted the tenants out they wouldn't leave and the law backed them up.[14] I wanted to stay there while I looked for another place, but my Grandmother Claudia said, "So, you've come to gobble what little food we have. Listen, whatever I can scrape up to eat is for my son."

"Don't worry, Grandma. I'll be leaving soon," I answered.

Fina went to stay with her *mamá* at Ciego de Avila. Rationing had already begun and I went there once a week to bring my wife her ration

14. Cuban law prohibits the eviction of any tenant.

of milk, rice, and meat. I was pretty disgusted with that setup, I can tell you. I told Fina, "Now, let's see what we can do."

I got a transfer back to the Hotel Madrid in Havana and looked for someplace to live. By then little Gabriel, our first son, was born. His birth date is November 27, 1963.

One day while I was in the hotel kitchen pinch-hitting for one of the dishwashers, an official came to me and said, "Well, Gabriel, how are you?"

"How am I?" I answered. "I'm not at all happy. How can I be happy washing dishes here, with my wife and son way off in Ciego de Avila?" He went to the heads of INIT and put up a fight for me. Then the hotel manager came to me with a letter. "Here," he said. "Now you have a room, so stop pestering us."

I went right away to the address given in the letter. It was a converted hotel on Rayo. I handed the letter to the manager and he asked one of the employees to show me my room. After having nothing, that little room seemed like a palace. I felt as if I'd been given the whole world, that's how happy I was. It had a very long, narrow window. It was half of a larger room that had been divided in two, right down the middle of a double window so that each of the new rooms could have light and ventilation. It was furnished with a wardrobe with two mirrored doors, a dressing table, a bed with a mattress, two sheets, and two towels. There was a rocking chair, two night tables, and a sink with cold running water.

I went back to the Hotel Telégrafo, where I had stored a few things—water glasses, a frying pan, and some other cooking equipment—and took them to my new room. I spent the whole afternoon scrubbing everything with Fab, dusting the furniture till everything was clean and beautiful. Then I went back to work.

That night when I returned to sleep there, I kept looking at my lovely new room. The only light it had was a bare bulb on the wall. I lay down but couldn't sleep, thinking of my wife and how much I wanted her with me. I got up toward morning and took a bus to the Ciego de Avila terminal. I walked into her *mamá*'s house with the room key in my hand and showed it to Fina. "Look, love, they gave us a room!"

She began to cry and I gave her a kiss. "All right, old girl, let's pack up and get going." We took a bus back to Havana and slept in our new room that very night.

Little Gabriel was already a year old when I married Fina. I married her because of her nobility. When I saw what a good woman she was, I said to myself, "She'll have a rough time if anything happens to me." She'd have to run around like crazy to get even my retirement fund, and that worried me. If we were legally husband and wife she'd be taken care of.

I used to think Fina was a tramp because I knew I wasn't the first, but when I got to know her I realized she must have had a sad experience, a disappointment in love. She's so trusting, anyone can deceive her. I never asked her about her past. I didn't want to know, poor girl. It's *now* I care about.

We were married in the courthouse in Miramar. They wanted two witnesses so I called my work center and they sent over two waiters. Then, "Do you, so-and-so, accept so-and-so?" and "Yes." Everyone signed, we kissed, Fina went home, and I went back to work. I didn't bother with a party.

Our second son, Arelis, was born in June, 1965, when little Gabriel was eighteen months old. I said, "Well, and where will this one sleep?" The eldest boy, Gabi, slept in bed with us, but when the second was born, I bought Gabi a crib that cost me 64 *pesos* counting the mattress. But *bang!* my wife got pregnant again right away. Our third child, Haydée, was born in 1966. I did the best I could. I bought a baby mattress and put it on the floor. The new baby went in the crib, Arelis slept with us, and little Gabriel slept on the baby mattress. But he was still just a little thing and he'd roll off in the night and hit his head on the floor and start crying.

Then our bed broke. The spring gave and we each had to fit into the hollows as best we could. My ribs and chest hurt all day long because of that. But *mamá* gave us the box springs from her bed, and Frank, my half-brother, helped me carry it over to our house. People along the way yelled at us, "Bedbugs, bring water quick, bedbugs!" I'd yell back at them, "I bet you don't have half as good as this at home!" We took it upstairs and I set it on four wooden packing boxes to keep it off the floor.

Some time later a neighbor sold me a small folding bed for 13 *pesos*. It had no mattress though, and I couldn't get hold of one anywhere, so we covered the springs with rags. But the poor kids' backs are all marked from the springs.

Our youngest boy, Mario, was born two years after Haydée. He's nine months old now. People ask me, why did I have so many children? Well, I wanted to have them. I like children. The only problem is the way they live. They don't live like human beings. They live like pigs. We all do. The furniture is broken. The wardrobe is held together with boards from the broken bed. We not only don't have beds, we don't have a blanket. My wife and I have only a crib-size sheet to cover us, and we keep pulling it away from each other all night long. Fina always wakes up in the morning with a headache from the chill.

We cook on a small kerosene stove I bought for 8 *pesos*, and also on a tin filled with alcohol; they both stand on the dressing table. We keep the food on the two bedside tables. The rocking chair broke so there's no place to sit. I stand by the bed holding my plate and look at my children flopped down on the floor, eating like puppies.

And I hate the lack of privacy. Sometimes I've come home after being away in the country a month or two, wanting to be with my wife, only you can't have intercourse in front of kids—it's too ugly. We have to wait and do it at night with the light out and with an eye on the kids every minute, in case they wake up. The eldest is already wise to such things. Now and then he wakes up. He still likes to suck on a pacifier, which is something I don't like, but when I want to do something with Fina, I tell her to give it to him behind my back. She slips it to him and warns him, "Be sure your *papá* doesn't know you have it." So the kid turns to the wall to suck it.

My life was good and happy when there were only three of us—me, Fina, and little Gabriel. I had no worries then. I made almost 400 *pesos* a month in salary and tips, and with that much money we didn't have to stand in line to buy food. We'd eat at a restaurant practically every day. But when another baby was born it wasn't easy to go out anymore. Now it's a dog's life, all six of us crammed into that tiny room. When it's hot we practically melt. And then the mosquitoes and cockroaches... *ay!* That's no way to live. I've gotten up before daybreak and gone to sit in the park because I couldn't stand the mosquitoes.

The roof leaked so they tarred it over, and now the ceiling is cracked. The door to our room is falling apart; I patched it up with wood from a packing case. The bathroom is out in the hall and is always filthy. I don't want the kids using it so we have a chamber pot for them. Fina and I use the toilet but we bathe in our room in a tin tub with water out of a pail. I can bathe at my work center, and sometimes I bring one of my kids to the hotel and put him under the shower. They get scared at first because they aren't used to it, but then I have a hard time getting them out again.

Fina comes from very poor people. She was born in a little village called Barajagua, in Oriente. Her *papá* was a railroad switchman and was killed in a railroad accident when she was very small. Her folks are all good, noble-hearted people. There's no evil or malice in any of them. Everybody loves them. But they're quiet and keep to themselves. They're not like us. I mean, when I see one of my family we hug and kiss, but if one of Fina's relatives comes around she'll say, "Oh, how have you been?" and then she won't take a blind bit of notice of him. Sometimes I think she's a woman without blood. But they're all like that. They don't say much.

I'm the one who talks to Fina. She doesn't talk to me. She's not high-spirited like other girls—doesn't care about makeup, parties, dancing. Not once in six years has she said to me, "Take me dancing." And we've never been to a party, either. The only places I've taken her to are the beach, the movies, and Coney Island, where she'll get on the swings with the children.

Fina has five brothers and sisters, all revolutionaries except her brother Felo. Another one, José, is an extreme revolutionary. With him it's an illness. I mean, you may be a good revolutionary but you don't have to pull out a gun and start shooting people for talking tough on the buses! José was in the Rebel Army during the Revolution, and one day when there was an air attack, he ran to get arms and fell into an empty well. His head got badly hurt and hasn't been right since. The Army gave him a discharge and now he works in a factory.

Pedro is the youngest. He's part of the new generation that has this hell of a sickness . . . tight pants, fringe all over, the zipper in the back, and clusters of curls over the forehead. I asked one of those kids, "Hey, how do you manage to squeeze into those pants you're wearing?"

"No problem," says he. "I sprinkle talcum or flour or starch inside them so they'll slip on easy." God, what a sight! Nobody over thirty would dare to dress that way. Now miniskirts I like. They're pretty.

Well, my brother-in-law Pedro went around in tight pants and long hair and didn't have steady work. He did odd jobs, cleaning and so on, and earned a few *kilos* that way. Then, when he reached military age, the government put him in the Centennial Youth Column[15] and paid him 100 *pesos* a month to do farm work and study at the same time.

When a *columnista* gets out of service he has a job waiting for him and his future is assured—not like when I was young. This generation knows nothing of the evil my generation knew. They're pure. They don't know what it is to suffer for want of a decent shirt—they all get scholarships, to say nothing of thirty thousand other opportunities to get ahead.

Fina's sisters, Irene and Hilda, are both members of the CDR and the Women's Federation. They're both quite old—over thirty. Fina's *mamá* is a revolutionary too, except that she's a Jehovah's Witness. She and I didn't get along until about a year ago. She'd visit us and start ordering us about and fixing up our room the way she liked it, telling us to move this here and put that there. One day I told her off. "Go to hell, old lady," I said. "Stop giving orders around here. This is my house and I'll put the bureau where I damn well please." We hated each other's guts.

Then, on my last birthday, I hugged and kissed her for the very first time and—you wouldn't believe it—since then she's changed completely toward me. She invited us to dinner and we spent the day with her. She's skinny but full of energy. She'll bustle around, complaining in the most cheerful tone of voice, "I'm only an old woman, a living corpse!" What a character!

Little Gabriel would sometimes stay with Fina's *mamá*. One day I went to visit him there and he said, "*Papá*, I went to Jehovah."

"What!" I said. His grandmother had taken him to one of her religious meetings. I took him back home because I don't want him growing up to

15. See Barrera, n. 52.

be one of those Jehovah's Witnesses. I've looked in at some of their meetings and I don't like what I've seen. They start singing and end up screaming and humiliating themselves. I don't understand it. They preach that it's sinful to dance, for women to wear makeup, and all sorts of nonsense.

Fina isn't religious. She believes in the *Virgen de la Caridad,* but that's her business and I don't interfere. She isn't a fanatic and she never speaks to the kids about it. The only religion they've learned from us is when they sneeze, we say "Jesús!"

Fina once bought a figure of St. Barbara and I threw it out. I told her I didn't want the thing in the house. She was annoyed, although she didn't say a word. I know she has notions of her own, but she never goes to Mass and none of our children are baptized.

Fina never argues with me. That's why I love her, because she doesn't contradict me. She accepts all my decisions without a word. She'll ask me, "Are we going to my *mamá*'s house today?" I'll say, "No, today I have to go get a haircut," and she doesn't insist. My word is law.

When I have a problem or can't make up my mind about something, then I consult her. For instance, I asked what she thought about exchanging ten cans of milk for a blanket. She said, "Yes, do make the exchange." I would have done it even if she'd said no, because the kids needed a blanket badly, but I asked her because I was sure she'd agree. I go ahead and do what I decide, no matter what she says. But at least when I consult her, she knows ahead of time what I'm going to do.

Once I asked Fina, "Old girl, do you think it would be a good idea to exchange this room for a bigger one in Oriente?"

"But I don't like Oriente, *chico,*" she answered. "Remember how we hated it there? It's a horrible place. Besides, I've gotten used to Havana."

She convinced me and I gave up the idea. But that time I myself wasn't really sure I wanted to move.

Fina never went to school as a child but she's intelligent. She can barely read and can just about write a letter. She wrote to me when I was cutting cane but I was the only one who could understand it.

They never taught her anything at home, not even about women's work. I had to teach her, the way you teach a little child. I told her, "When you sweep the floor, be sure to sweep under the bed and the dresser and take the rest of the furniture out to the hall until you're through."

I put up two nails above the baby's crib and hung a cord between them; then I said to Fina, "Look, hang the baby's ironed clothes on this cord. Put the shirts here and the pants there. Put the used clothes over here. That way you can tell which are clean and which should be washed."

I do the children's school uniforms myself. I take them to the hotel, wash, starch, and iron them, and bring them home neatly wrapped in newspaper. The only thing Fina does is boil the starch for me. For all that, sometimes I don't find a pair of clean undershorts to wear. When that happens I let her have it.

"Damn it," I say. "You know I have four pairs of undershorts, two that I keep at work and two here. The minute I change, while I'm taking my bath, you should start washing the pair I take off and have them ironed by the time I need them. That isn't much to ask. Suppose some day I asked you to do something really difficult, what would you do then?"

She doesn't say a word; she just bursts into tears. She'll cry at the slightest thing. You just have to say "boo" and she'll start crying.

There was a girl who came to the house and helped herself to food, perfume, deodorant, and stockings that Fina had been saving carefully. She's allowed only a very few pairs on the ration card. Fina could see that the girl was taking things but she didn't say a word. I had to tell her, "Aren't you being foolish? Are you the mistress of this house or what? Why should you allow this woman to take this, that, and the other?" That made her cry, and I had to stroke her head and say, "Don't cry. It's nothing to cry over. Tell me what you think, or has the cat got your tongue?"

We never quarrel. I scold her when she does something wrong. Like when she tried to force a kid's arm through the sleeve of a shirt without unbuttoning the cuffs first. That really gets on my nerves. I tell her, "Listen, what's your head good for besides growing hair? If you don't unbutton the cuffs first, you're going to tear the shirt." I yell if she doesn't bathe the kids but she says she has too much to do. I tell her, "Make time somehow but the kids must be bathed every day.

After I've told her off, I stop and think how those kids drive her clear out of her head. The four of them drive me out of my head too, when I'm shut up in that room with them. And then I'm sorry I talked to her that way, because the truth is, Fina is still a little girl. Yet I don't think I'm a domineering husband. I'm very considerate of her and she has great respect for me. Respect, not fear. Sometimes she's just sitting there quietly and I say, "Hey, you!" That scares her. I once said to her, "You get terribly frightened when I yell at you, don't you?"

"You can believe that if you like. But you'll find out!"

No matter what she says, I'm straightening my wife out gradually. She can cook; nothing fancy, of course, just plain, homey meals. It isn't easy to cook a meal in the tiny space we use for a kitchen. And we don't have enough dishes either. I'd love to have the salad served out of a bowl the way they do at the restaurant, but we don't have a bowl, so it has to be served directly on our plates.

We really feel the food shortages at home. Who doesn't? Everything is scarce. You just have to make the best of what little there is. If you go hungry, it's lack of planning; there's no need for it, much less to starve. Planning meals is beyond Fina, but things get done a bit better when I'm at home. So I plan all the meals—that way we don't run out of food and we have more variety. Sometimes Fina will serve nothing but rice and beans every day for weeks. I tell her, "Look, let's have something else." So then we'll have rice and beans and fried beef for weeks. I have to point out that we have lots of other things to eat.

With good planning you can have meat every day of the week. As soon as I get the week's ration of meat, I cut it up and say. "This is for Monday, this for Tuesday." We store it in a neighbor's frigidaire and give him a can of milk in return. I tell Fina, "When you're running out of meat, stretch it with a bit of rice. If you don't have rice, use a potato."

I show Fina how to divide up the potatoes, the beans, and the bananas to make them last the week. We get 24 pounds of rice a month. I tell her, "You know exactly how much you get. Make it last the thirty days." Beans we stretch over lunch and supper. With bread and *café con leche*, that makes a meal. I tell my wife, "You can make beans, fried egg, and potato salad. If there are no potatoes, use up the cucumbers before they go bad on you. When you're out of one thing, use what you do have. But plan ahead so the kids at least will be fed."

We never go hungry. There's always something to eat. But I'd be lying if I claimed we can make the food last all week. Neighbors help each other out. Our neighbor Blanca often brings us gifts of bananas, *malanga*, squash, yucca, tomatoes, hot peppers, rice, and all sorts of things. We take her a plate of food now and then, not in exchange but for friendship's sake. When we have so many oranges that we know some will spoil, we give her some. We get along that way.

Each month I turn over my pay to my wife and I know it's in good hands. All I take out is 40 *centavos* a week for bus fare. Fina can't count money but she figures out in her own way and manages very well. There's always money left over at the end of the month. But the truth is, she'd be a mess without me. I know more than she does, see? I tell you, I don't know what she'd do without me. Sometimes I tell her, "Look, old girl, I know a few people who have four kids too, only the husband is a drunk, spends all his money on himself, and runs after other women. I'd like to know what you'd do with a husband like him!"

She never has a word to say in answer to that. I'm a good husband. I don't drink—a highball now and then, if necessary, kind of the way you'd take a laxative. And maybe I do chase after the women but I didn't start until we'd been together four years. And I go out only at night, after 9:00 or so, when the kids are asleep.

I started my first affair when Fina was pregnant with our third child, Haydée. I was going to the Workers' School[16] then, to study for fifth

---

16. *Educación Obrera-Campesina* (EOC), or Worker-Peasant Education, offered three courses of study: grades one through three; grades four through six; and secondary school

grade. I went with one of the cooks from the Hotel Madrid. The first day at school I said to him, "Say, Benito, look at that girl, *compadre!* What a lovely chick!" She was slender but curvy, with pink cheeks, great big eyes, and curly hair. She had a permanent wave. She must have been about twenty or twenty-two. That night I dreamed I was in bed with her. The next day I said, "Benito, I dreamed about that chick and we did this and that and forty thousand things."

"What a wild man you are!" Benito laughed.

I tried to start a conversation with her but she didn't give me a chance. One day there was a big fuss in school because the money for the soft drinks had disappeared. Just to show off in front of her, I pulled out 2 *pesos* and said, "Never mind, pay for them with this."

At the next examination I sat beside her. She leaned over and said, "Gabriel, how do you work out this problem?" I didn't know but I invented an answer out of thin air.

After that we talked. She told me her name was Lourdes. She was married and had a little girl of three. Her husband was a bus driver. He was wonderful, she said, and so jealous! I saw there wasn't much chance for me. But I noticed that she smoked mild cigarettes, so I bought a pack for her. She refused to take them.

Her brother was in school too. I made friends with him and started buying him soft drinks and cigarettes, thinking, "Now I'll stand a better chance with her."

Then a cousin of hers, Melba, came up from the country and began coming to school. Melba was hot stuff, the kind of girl who goes out with fellows just for the fun of seeing it flow. Fire, that's what she was. I didn't like her but I kind of suspected she was in love with me because she kept throwing me looks and fooling around with me.

One day she said, "Gabriel, how do you look upon Lourdes and me?"

"Why, as schoolmates of course."

"That's the way I look upon you, too," she said. "But Lourdes feels differently."

A chill went right through me; my guts kind of shrank and twisted up and my heart started to beat fast. It had never entered my head that Lourdes could be in love with me. I stole a look over where she was standing. Our eyes met and she hung her head. I went over to her. She said, "You know the bar at the corner? Go sit there. I'll pass by with my husband and my brother after school. My brother is sure to see you and say hello." She'd planned the whole thing.

(equivalent to the first year of basic secondary). Classes were held in factories, farms, and offices, usually in the evenings. Graduates of the secondary program were eligible for vocational schools or for the Worker-Peasant university-preparatory program. (*Cuba: El Movimiento Educativo, 1967/68* (Havana: Ministry of Education, 1968), pp. 15, 102–3. Also see Nelson P. Valdés, "The Radical Transformation of Cuban Education," in Bonachea and Valdés, eds., *Cuba in Revolution,* pp. 429–31.

I thought, "*Ay, mi madre!* and I went to the bar and waited. In a little while I saw her walk by casually with her husband, her daughter, her brother, and Melba. Her brother caught sight of me and said, "Hey, Gabriel!"

"Come on over," I urged him.

They all came to my table and her brother introduced us. "This is my sister Lourdes."

"Pleased to meet you," said I with a straight face. He introduced the others and I invited them all to sit down and eat with me. They put away beer and sandwiches worth 20 *pesos*—20 *pesos*, you hear!

The next day I told Lourdes, "I want to talk with you, alone."

"All right. Where shall we meet?"

"How about Central Park—tonight?" She agreed.

That night I borrowed a suit and some cologne from my brother and wore a pair of real sharp shoes and went to meet her at the park. Lourdes showed up looking so pretty, wearing a dress with a belt slung low around her belly. Beautiful! But she had her little girl and Melba in tow! But Melba said, "I'll take the kid for a stroll," and left me alone with Lourdes.

I walked her around a long while and she kept looking back over her shoulder. I told her, "Relax, kid, if your husband shows up I can deal with him. I've got a twenty-one on me."

"A what?"

"A gun. Loaded. You've got nothing to worry about."

I bought my first gun at the time of the October crisis and carried it everywhere after that. Mostly I wore it for show, but you never knew when you might be held up. A gun could be very handy.

Twice we passed a *posada* where I'd been before with a chick. I told her, "I want to go someplace where we can be alone, where nobody can see us, because I like you very, very much." The third time I walked right into the *posada* with her, nervous as all get-out. I paid at the desk and got the key to room 32. There we were, alone in the bedroom, and I couldn't do a thing. My body just didn't respond properly. "This doesn't happen to a man!" I kept saying. "What's wrong with me?"

"Don't be silly," she said kindly. "There's nothing wrong with you. You're nervous, that's all. Let's wait till tomorrow. Next day we went to the *posada* again and I functioned perfectly. It was beautiful.

After that I began to spend less time at home with Fina and my children. Lourdes's husband was a bus driver and had to take long trips to the interior, so he was hardly ever in Havana. I'd visit her at her home in the evenings. Sometimes I'd tell Fina I had a CDR meeting or was with my militia unit or had to stand guard and I'd stay the night. Fina never argued. She's just a simple little country girl so she never doubted my word, and I made sure she never had any evidence. When I don't come home at night, she knows I'm at a meeting. She says she doesn't mind.

One night Lourdes bit me on the neck and left a mark. I covered it with a cloth and for three days I went around complaining of a pain. Fina never dared lift the bandage to look. She's not jealous.

I often met Lourdes at the park, and one night somebody called Fina on the phone in our building to tell her, "Say, if you want to see your husband with another woman, go to Capitol Park. They're there now."

When I got home Fina told me about the call. I denied it. I'm sure it was Lourdes's husband who made the call, because once he caught Lourdes and me kissing in the park.

While I was away doing military training, Lourdes's husband went to my house and told Fina I was having an affair with his wife. I carried a photo of Lourdes and Fina showed it to him and he said it was his wife. When I got back, Fina asked me about it. I told her the photo belonged to Benito, at the hotel. She didn't believe me, so next time I saw Lourdes I told her, "Tell your husband I want to talk to him, man to man."

We met in front of the Reina theater and I said, "While I was in a trench risking my skin, you went to my wife and slandered me. You told her I was having an affair with your wife. You had no right to do that to me. Suppose my wife had miscarried because of what you told her, eh?" Fina was big with Haydée then. I told him, "You go straight to my house and tell my wife you lied to her!"

Well, would you believe it! He went to my house and told Fina, "Look, Señora, I was mistaken. Your husband is called Gabriel, just like my wife's lover, Gabriel Fraga. I was confused because I have the nerve sickness." He took a bottle of pills from his pocket and said, "See, I have to take these for my nerves."

Fina wasn't convinced, but she had to accept it, poor girl. She didn't quarrel with me or anything. As for Lourdes's husband, he tried to bribe me to leave Lourdes alone because he was crazy about her. He gave me a baby pacifier for Haydée and a box of cookies. He didn't know I was earning a lot of money in tips then and had been giving Lourdes 2 *pesos* a day. Lourdes's brother told him, "Look, *chico*, a real *macho* came along and took your wife from you, just like in the movies, and that's that. Beat it! Lourdes is fed up with you."

Instead he moved to Jovellanos, taking Lourdes with him, but she'd come back to Havana and we'd go to a hotel. One day she told me she'd left him. She said, "Look, Gabriel, I want a home with a man's warmth in it. I'm too young to spend the rest of my life this way."

"Well," I reminded her, "I told you from the very first I had a wife and three children and I told you I loved my wife like life itself."

She shrugged. "All right."

A few days later she called me at work. "Listen," she said. "I never want to see you again." And hung up on me. I felt kind of sad about it, but I was relieved, too.

I felt happy, *ay* . . . so happy, when I was with Lourdes. But then I'd think, "Right now my poor little wife is in that stinking room with the kids and here I am, instead of taking her out to the movies. Why am I doing this to her?" But I kept on doing it because I liked Lourdes. When I got home at midnight, I'd feel such remorse when Fina got up to prepare coffee for me.

Now whenever I have a free day, I stay home and help my wife with the kids. I horse around with them, punching and biting, and then we hug each other. Arelis and the older boy are forever hitting each other. I separate them and make them hug. "Brothers mustn't fight. They must love each other," I tell them. But no sooner is my back turned than they're at it again.

I also help Fina clean the house. I used to be ashamed at the idea that somebody might see me with a broom in my hand. Now it doesn't embarrass me at all. There I am, scrubbing the floor, emptying the chamber pot, cleaning the tub. I peel the vegetables and kill all the cockroaches that have found their way into the dressing table where we cook. I have to keep after those cockroaches because we have thousands of them. We don't have rats, but once two tiny mice got into the room somehow. I found a chewed-up heap of paper inside the closet, so I took everything out and poured boiling water into it. "Ah, that'll get rid of them," I thought. But that very night I heard them going *eeeee*.

In the afternoon Fina will take the baby out into the hall and play with him a bit. She loves all the children, but the little one, Mario, is her favorite. When she buys pants for him nobody can touch them. The pants little Gabriel is wearing I had to buy for him because Fina complained that Mario's milk came first. Everything is for the little one. If I scold him she tells me, "Don't be a brute!" Yet if I do the same with the others, she never says a word. The other children aren't jealous though. They never hit the baby.

Fina bathes the children every day, but when I'm home I wash them myself. Then Fina takes her bath and I take mine, while she prepares dinner. By the time I've mopped the puddles off the floor, supper is ready and we all flop down to eat, like a pack of dogs. Afterward we set up the folding bed—we pack it away during the day to make more room—and all six of us go off to the movies. We take bread, cookies, candy, soft drinks—practically a picnic. That's the way I spend my life.

Chapter Five

They Made Me a Militant

IN 1967 THE YOUNG COMMUNISTS called all the hotel workers, as well as the manager and an official from the union, to an assembly and asked us who wanted to join as a militant,[17] so I raised my hand. I raised my hand for everything in those days.

There were two of us from the Madrid, me and another guy called Nilo, who worked in the coffee shop. They said, "Are there any objections to Comrade Nilo?" A lot of people objected. They said he was rude and hot-tempered, and slow. When he got an order from a customer, he would hold it up as long as he could. The only reason he was nominated was because he was young and the UJC is a youth organization. They asked him, "Would you go to work in the country for two years?"

"No, no, I can't . . . I'm a sick man." So they turned him down.

Then, "Are there any objections to Comrade Capote?"

One of the workers jumped up and said, "Comrade Capote and I had an argument and he insulted me." Then I explained to the committee. "Excuse me. He's referring to the time he got into an argument with another comrade here and I told him not to create problems and to get on with his job." Then I turned to him and said, "Well, comrade, what have you to say to that?"

He started to answer but everybody shouted at him, "Hey, shut up, will you." It was plain all the other workers agreed with me and that the man simply bore a grudge against me. It's easy to get on bad terms with one or another of your comrades, but I'd been working with INIT since 1961 and I didn't have a single enemy there.

Experience and hard knocks teach you a lot. I've learned to tolerate my fellow workers and they tolerate me. None of them can say, "Gabriel isn't a good guy, he doesn't act right by us." For instance, when one of my comrades does something wrong, I don't report him to someone higher up. Instead I explain to him why he isn't supposed to do it and

17. In Cuba *militante* is a term of reference for a full member of the Party or Youth, as opposed to an *aspirante*, or candidate for membership.

what will happen if he's caught. I warn him that the next time I'll report him. I can give advice because I've had enough experience to think about the consequences of things.

After the meeting the UJC people told me, "We'll phone you soon to let you know whether you've been chosen."

I didn't have to wait long. That very night they phoned to say, "Gabriel, you've been chosen as a militant in our organization."

"All right," I said. I didn't attach much importance to it.

They made me a militant because they saw I was a worker who didn't watch the clock, who got along with his fellow workers, who was ready to defend the Revolution at all times. I'd worked in a lot of places, rebuilding damage done by the hurricanes, cutting cane, and so on.

We had a study group every Saturday, to discuss current politics and our international policy. I learned something in the short time I attended and I feel the need of it now. One of the things they emphasized was that we *habaneros* should try to be closer to the peasants, and to work with them more.

You don't have much choice about doing volunteer work. You almost *have* to go work in the country because your comrades pressure you into going. Practically everyone goes, and if you don't the fellows won't leave you in peace. They'll say, "So you want to take it easy, eh? Just do your work here and that's that? That's downright shameless, everybody should take a turn." They keep after you like that until they shame you into going.

When a task is assigned, the department heads—who are chosen from among the workers of each department in the hotel—are responsible for seeing that it's carried out. First they call a meeting of the workers in each department, then they make whatever decisions have to be made. When they need a certain number of people to go work in the country, each department head at the hotel meets with his workers and they decide together how many and who can best be spared at that time. If the hotel is full and they can't spare anyone, they say so. Or maybe they'll send one worker instead of three.

I had volunteered once, in 1964, to go away six months as a *permanente*, to cut cane. The harvest goes on for six or seven months until it's completely cut. I was married by then and my wife was pregnant, so she went to Ciego de Avila to be with her mother. I'd never done farm labor in my life before, but it wasn't very hard for me because I was used to rough work, being outdoors and sleeping on the ground. I didn't like it but it was a job, just like any other, and had to be done. I got my regular pay.

That summer three hurricanes hit Cuba and did as much damage as Flora. After one hurricane, an emergency meeting was called and we were told that the banana, onion, *malanga,* and potato harvests would be completely lost if they weren't picked immediately. So I raised my hand and went to work. Whole plantations of bananas had been knocked down by the hurricane, and we had to pick up the fruit from the ground before it rotted. We picked yams and *malanga* out of fields that were like lakes. We worked all hours, all through the night. Lights were put up. We worked in eight-hour shifts and broke our backs to save all we could because we knew the *malanga* we were picking would keep our children from going hungry, though all this was before I had four children.

I went on doing voluntary work after they made me a militant. I planted coffee around Havana. We'd go out sometimes for one month, sometimes for ten or fifteen days. It was like a guerrilla action the way we'd plant an area, then pick up our tents, climb on the truck, and move to another place.

I was planting coffee when we heard the news that they had killed Che. At first I thought it was a lie—I couldn't believe it. I didn't even know he was out of the country. But then Fidel spoke and we knew it was true.[18] Some people were saying that Che had been killed here by his own . . . that Fidel had had him killed. All kinds of rumors went around. I never believed any of it. It never crossed my mind that he had been sent to be killed, because, in a way, El Che was number one in Cuba. I never got to see him, but I read some of his *Bolivian Diary* and his farewell letter to his children, where he tells them that he has no money to leave them but that he leaves them his example. I get gooseflesh every time I read that letter because it's such a great and noble thing. He gave up everything . . . everything. It takes a lot of courage to do that. Listen, I wasn't even worthy to pick up his shoes, and that's the truth.

One day I got a phone call. "Capote, you have a special assignment." Fidel was giving a banquet for the public in the Plaza de la Revolución and I was to serve at the tables of the Central Committee. That day they pinned a card to my lapel and sent us in a car.

The square was filled with long tables. We started setting them and unloading boxes of apples and grapes. I suddenly noticed a strange movement of people around me. There I was, holding a box of grapes, when Fidel himself walked right past me. *Ay, mi madre!* I stood there, just staring. It gave me such a queer feeling inside to be that near a great man like Fidel. Imagine, a man who has the whole world in an uproar! I thought, "Well now, see what kind of a person I am to be right beside so great a man!" I looked at myself with more pride.

Then somebody, Armando Hart[19] I think, asked, "How's everything going here?"

---

18. Guevara was killed in Bolivia on October 8, 1967; Castro confirmed the rumors in a nationally broadcast speech on October 15.

19. The first national coordinator of the Twenty-sixth of July Movement and the former Minister of Education, Armando Hart Dávalos is a member of the Party's Political Bureau and one of the Revolution's principal ideologues.

"Fine, fine," I said. I got real jittery and kept dropping knives and forks. One of the fellows asked me, "Hey, what's the matter with you?"

"Nothing, nothing, I'm just kind of nervous," I said. He burst out laughing. But *coño*, that was the first time I'd worked at anything that important and it was a delicate situation for me.

Suppertime came. The Central Committee table was right by the plaza where Fidel makes his speeches, and one of the members asked why we waiters weren't drinking. I told him the captain of our Gastronomic Zone[20] had forbidden it. "Never mind that," he said. "Have a drink!"

"Here's my chance to taste champagne," I thought. I opened a big bottle and drank straight from it, *taca, taca, taca.* It was warm and tasted like fresh-sawed wood. I asked a comrade, "Marcelo, how much does a bottle of champagne cost?"

"Sixty *pesos*," said he.

"Well, I've just guzzled 60 *pesos*," I announced.

When I loaded my tray again I felt dizzy and my eyes fogged. "Marcelo! Marcelo!" I shouted.

"What's wrong?" he asked, hurrying over to me.

"Grab my tray, quick, before I drop it! I can't see."

He laughed. In about ten minutes I was terribly drunk. After a while the Gastronomic captain came to me and asked, "How come you guys are drinking? Don't you know that's forbidden?"

"See that guy there with his back to us?" I said, pointing. "He's the one who told us we could drink." That shut him up. We went on drinking and didn't finish until about 3:00 in the morning.

At the end of 1967, when Fina was pregnant with our youngest child, I couldn't go out to plant coffee as much as I wanted to. I told them I couldn't leave Fina, which was true, no? Well, then they started working on the *Cordón de la Habana* and I was chosen to head one of the groups I'd been taught how to plant coffee and was supposed to show the comrades in my group how to do it. The problem was, the work was to continue for months at a time. I told them, "Comrades, I can't go."

"Why not?"

"I have my children to think of. If I could commute to and from work every day, I'd be only too pleased to go." They said no, so I went to my work center and explained my situation at a meeting of the UJC.

I told them that before anything a good communist had to look out for his children and that I couldn't go on any mission with my children living like animals.

I'd written before, telling them that I couldn't go on living the way I

20. Gastronomic Services is the division of INIT responsible for food services in hotels, restaurants, and nightclubs.

was, but I always got the same answer. They realized my problem was bad—I'll say it was! Like climbing to the moon without a ladder—but they couldn't do anything right away. There were people worse off than I was. Every time I was put off like that, it was a blow. I tell you, they left me pretty sore! I work, struggle, and make sacrifices and then. . . . Do you know what it is to come home after fifteen days' work in the country and find a child of yours sick and sleeping on the floor like a dog?

Coño, I wasn't asking for privileges—I don't want a big house. I'd like to have what my mother has, that's all. A room where my children can sleep on a bed at night, where I can sit down to Christmas Eve supper at a proper table with my children around me. Instead they have to sit on the floor to eat their roast pork. It breaks my heart.

Because of the house we live in, I take a day off whenever I can so Fina can go out without having to tie up the kids. She ties them to the foot of the bed and locks them in when she goes out. She has to do it, otherwise they'd be running around in the street with the other kids and Fina doesn't want that because some of those kids are no good. She wants to keep them inside all the time, so she ties them up or spanks them with a belt and keeps them sitting in one spot. Once they were playing in that tiny room and one of them fell against the dressing table and a piece of iron went right through his cheek and came out inside his mouth. *Coño,* I got home all sweaty from standing guard to find something like that!

Another time one of them fell and hit his head and had to have stitches in his scalp. So now my wife ties them to the bed. They have no toys to speak of—a little toy truck, a few bottle caps and such, and they yell and scream. But they can make all the racket they want; my wife pays no attention. She says, "I feel bad tying them up, but I must so they won't kill themselves." Listen, I live on the third floor and the window is low. Suppose one of them fell out? If I should lose a child that way, I'd kill myself. I honestly think I'd do it. No, it's better to keep them tied up than risk an accident like that, because that's the most terrible thing that can happen to you.

One day Haydée cut herself on the broken spring of the mattress and had to be rushed to the emergency clinic. They stitched her up and sent her home. There were tears in my eyes that day. I went to my UJC sectional. It was after midnight but the secretary was there. Still weeping, I told her my problem. She got very angry at the way those people had fobbed me off with vague promises. She said, "We'll send a comrade to look at your room, and if those people do nothing to solve your problem, we'll take your case to the provincial committee."

I was heartened when the secretary showed so much feeling, and I waited eagerly for the comrade who was to see our room. Nobody came. I didn't hear another word from the secretary or from the sectional. I was disgusted and gave up.

They are the ones running the country. If they don't help me, who can I turn to? I won't go back to the *Poder Local*. What's the use? Going back there is just looking for trouble. To hell with them! My wife and I are resigned to putting up with this place until the building falls down. I wish I were Superman so I could make the whole damned thing collapse. Then they'd have to move us out. That's my last hope.

I heard about one building where one piece of wall just fell off, and within half an hour all the tenants had been relocated by Urban Reform. Our building is already crumbling, and every now and then I hammer a bit on the wall, hoping a piece will fall out. I keep working at it. Any day now it will happen.

We had some neighbors who had never done a thing for the Revolution, but one day the woman came to me and said, "They gave me a real good house." She said it ironically. She meant, "You folks are so damn revolutionary yet they don't give you a thing. We're not revolutionary, but look at us!" She already had a bigger room than we did. It's a funny world. Here I am, screwed up all my life and always making sacrifices, but people like them are doing fine.

Not long ago they gave a place to a couple of newlyweds. I thought, "Now how the hell did they get that? Who gave it to them?" It's all a matter of connections, see? If you have friends in high places you get what you want, and that's all there is to it. I've protested about *amiguismo* and pointed out cases where people got things easily, through the Labor Commission, I'm told. Well, but how did they get the Labor Commission to give it to them? I work in a first-class hotel but I don't get any favors. Those people work for the Party for their own convenience.

To hell with them! They aren't true revolutionaries. One day they'll be found out. I can't wait! You should see the homes the *Poder Local* people have. It's enough to turn you into the worst counterrevolutionary in the world.

Around the end of 1968 the military called me up. They wanted to send me to Camaguey for two years, with occasional visits home. I was to be incorporated into the Centennial Youth Column. The wages were only 100 *pesos* a month. They said they'd also take care of my gas and electric bills while I was away. Big deal! I pay only 1 *peso* a month for electricity and we don't use gas at home, so how would that make up for the big cut in my wages? I was earning 171 *pesos* a month—they had raised them 65 *pesos* when they abolished tipping.[21] It's true I'd have no expenses in the country, but so what? Still, I said, "Fine, I'll go as soon as you get my wife a job and give the kids scholarships." When they made me a militant the year before, I told them the same thing.

It's up to whoever sends you out—the UJC in my case—to ask for the

21. Tipping was abolished during the "revolutionary offensive" of 1968.

scholarships, then the provincial committee has to approve it. The UJC didn't refuse outright, but they told me it would be difficult. I wrote a letter to the office of the Prime Minister explaining my situation. Celia[22] was the one who answered. She wrote that the situation was difficult for me but all cases of the kind were being turned over to Urban Reform. "I'm sorry for you," she wrote. But *coño,* what's the use of being sorry for me? What good is that? They should come and see how we live.

I felt trapped, completely trapped. I'm a revolutionary and I'd be only too happy to go away for two years and serve my country, provided they gave my children scholarships. Otherwise they'd have to take me under arrest. They could put me away in La Cabaña for twenty years, but I wouldn't leave my children living under those conditions, and that's the truth.

Some of the comrades said to me, "What if there was a war and you were called up?"

"That's different," I told them. "In wartime you don't think of your kids or anything else. You know you have to fight, so you go out and fight. But I'm talking about now. There's no war now."

I was ready to lay down my life in case of aggression, without thought to children, wife, mother; so how was it possible that my children were living under those conditions? Damn it all, why should I make sacrifices when they won't do a thing for me? They made me a militant, which means you have all the right qualities, so why do they let my children sleep on the floor like dogs?

The military kept on pressuring me and finally I got a telegram at the hotel, ordering me to show up, ready to leave, wearing old clothes, and carrying toothpaste and my ration book. I would have let myself be killed before I obeyed that order!

I went to the lieutenant and explained my case. "That's too bad," he says. "Be ready to get on the bus to Camaguey at 4:00 this afternoon."

"Now what the hell is this?" I thought.

I went to Adolfo, one of the officers of the sectional, and told him the problem. "As a militant, you must forget about personal problems and go where you're sent," he answered.

I said to him, "Look, let's understand each other. You know that I have four kids; you know that I can't just abandon them, leave them sleeping on a filthy old mattress covered in rags, while I go off to the country for two years. That would be a living death. So you can kill me right now, but I won't go."

"Just go where you're sent," he told me. "We'll talk about your case later."

22. Celia Sánchez Manduley is a veteran of the Sierra campaign, Minister of the Presidency, and one of six women on the Central Committee of the Cuban Communist Party.

"Not on your life!" I said. "You'll talk nothing else over with me."

I went straight home and wrote a letter resigning from the UJC. This is what I wrote:

> Comrade, I feel I am not qualified to be a militant member of the Youth organization. It seems that a militant must do whatever he is ordered. If you say, "Go to the country," a militant must go, no matter what. But I have four children, living in terrible conditions, and I cannot take off and leave them at a moment's notice. It is a painful decision but I am turning in my Party card. Yours in the Revolution, Gabriel Capote.

I put the letter in an envelope together with my Party card and took it to the UJC sectional office myself. I said to the guy, "Here, give this to Adolfo."

About three months later I was called to the sectional. They asked me, "Why did you turn in your Party card?"

"You took your time about asking," I said. "There's no point in my being a militant if I can't do what's required. I can't, so I'd better get out."

They gave me six months' suspension, and after that, if my attitude didn't change, permanent suspension. That was a bad day for me. Six months later they called me in to talk over my case. I refused to go. I told them I'd already said all I had to say. That was the end of it. I cut myself free of the UJC and didn't want to have anything more to do with it. I always thought militants were supposed to help each other, but they saw me tearing myself to pieces for my children and not one hand was put out to help me. They turned their backs on me. They strangled me. I resigned in a moment of blindness. Later I regretted it.

At the beginning of 1969 I was transferred to the Capri Hotel. That was a tourist hotel and the employees there were hand-picked. They were all first-rate workers. I don't know whether those who work in hotels that are tourist centers are specially chosen, but about 70 percent of the workers there are revolutionaries. The rest are neutral—I mean, they aren't *gusanos*. Many of them owned hotels or bars before the Revolution, like one man I knew, Mendoza. He had his own bar, but it was expropriated by the government and he went on managing it at a salary. Then, after about a year, they made Mendoza the cashier, and the woman who'd once been his accountant became the manager. "Isn't that something?" he said to me. "That woman used to be my employee and now I'm a cashier under her!"

He was arrested later on, for stealing. I couldn't understand that man. If he saw an employee take a soft drink or a beer or eat something, he'd make out a charge slip and send him to the office to make him pay for what he'd taken.

One day I said to him, "*Chico,* who are you trying to impress? If a man eats a bite of pudding, it isn't going to break the bank. I'm a better revolutionary than you are but I don't go around fingering people."

When he was arrested for stealing, I said, "I don't believe it. Why should he steal? He earns 200 *pesos* a month, owns a 1957 Ford, and has a house with every luxury."

But the man was caught red-handed and was sentenced to two years in jail. It's a bitter thing to go to jail. I've known fellows who had to go through it and I know it's the worst thing there is, the very worst. So when I catch someone doing something wrong, I talk to him straight from my heart. "What'll become of your kids, *chico,* if you're locked up in jail?" I always stress the guy's kids, because that's what keeps a man straight more than anything. How do I know that? From experience, that's how.

At the Capri we serve lots of foreigners and sometimes we hear them criticize the Revolution but we don't argue. Our orders are not to pay any attention. We had some Chileans here who talked a lot of crap but I never interfered. I served them and kept my mouth shut.

It was a stroke of luck being transferred there. The Capri is twenty thousand times better than the Madrid Hotel, where I'd been working before. At the Madrid, as long as you wore a tie it didn't matter if your pants were clean, but at the Capri you have to be immaculate. You had to bust your guts filling the orders at the Madrid, but at the Capri they expect elegant service and you don't rush about slamming plates on the table. Somebody sits down in the restaurant and you take about an hour to serve him. You set every piece of silver in its proper place, bring a napkin... everything is done with tremendous style. I'm not over-worked as I was in the other place. To me that's a great improvement.

My wages stayed the same—171 *pesos.* I haven't been ill since I started this job a year ago, and I didn't lose a single day's pay because of absence. I keep two coin banks, one for my wife and one for me, so there's always some money in the house. Even without tips, I still have enough to buy whatever comes to the store.

We work in shifts, twenty-four hours at a stretch. I report in at 11:00 in the morning and leave the next day at 11:00 A.M., then I come in the next day at 11:00. I get one day off a week and a full month's vacation every year. That month they give me twice my usual salary. I always spend my vacation at home, right here in Havana. We don't go away because of the kids. There are too many of them and my relatives are too poor to keep us all for a whole month. In Havana we go to the beach, the movies, and the amusement park so the kids can ride the merry-go-round. And we visit my wife's mother and mine.

We hotel workers take turns working on holidays. I'm usually lucky—most years I spend Christmas Eve and New Year's Eve at home—but last year I worked at the Capri both Christmas and New Year's Eve. Christmas Eve, when the customers had gone, the waiters prepared a big table and all the hotel employees sat down to eat roast pork and drink. I got terribly drunk. We were normally forbidden to drink on the job, but that evening we all got drunk and nobody said anything.

On New Year's Eve I was at work when the fireworks were set off at the Plaza de la Revolución and I felt awfully sad. There was everybody kissing each other, and I wanted to fly home and kiss Fina and the children too, because that's the custom, no? I got home at 6:00 that morning, and we ate the twelve grapes.[23]

23. A New Year's Eve tradition in Latin America and Spain.

Chapter Six

More to Lose Now

THERE'S A LOT MORE FREEDOM in Cuba now. Take young people—I see boys and girls walking unchaperoned all over the city. In the old days the *papá* or *mamá* had to go along. And the youngsters go with whoever they please—black with white. Now *there's* a change! That's something you'd see only now and then before the Revolution. Today it's quite usual.

Only the other day I pointed out to a comrade at work, "Hey, look at that black with the white broad."

"If she were related to me, I'd kill him," he said. Lots of people—99 percent—feel that way.

When I come across a mixed couple I look the other way, even if it's a black woman and a white man. I don't like to see it. It doesn't look good.

A white woman who goes with a black loses her reputation. I'm no racist but I sure as hell wouldn't want a daughter of mine to marry a black. It would hurt me deeply. Now if a son of mine wanted to marry a Negro girl, that's all right. A man doesn't lose as much by such a marriage. But no one in Cuba wants his daughter to marry a black. I've even heard some black girl comrades at work say, "What! Me marry a Negro? I should say not, I'm black enough for two. When I marry, it will be to improve the race."

My brother's wife is a mulatto girl, and when she was pregnant he said, "My baby is going to have a lot of black in its makeup." But as it turned out she bore him a perfectly beautiful little girl. *Mamá* loves her pretty grandchild but I know she wishes the kid didn't have any black blood in her veins.

Today's youngsters are more wholesome, not evil-minded as we were. It doesn't bother them that whites and blacks can be good friends now. I think that's a fine thing but nobody can change my mind. You can't change overnight. Think of all the years we spent thinking blacks were inferior. In the old days, if a Negro showed up at a party for whites he'd be kicked out. Now they can go anywhere, and there's complete equality as far as jobs are concerned. But intermarriage . . . that's going too far.

I'm against women's liberation, too. Most of the older generation are. You ask any married man in Cuba what he thinks of women's liberation. "Never!" he'd say. "Not my wife." They'd be furious, that's what.

The Revolution gave women a lot more freedom by giving them jobs, so now they don't depend so much on their husbands. I think that's not right. And as for this business of married women going alone to work in the country—it won't do. I've known a number of them who have gone to work in the country and put the horns on their husbands. It's the truth. Women are weak, see? When a woman goes away without her husband, the chances are she'll be unfaithful to him. Even if she loves her husband, in a moment of weakness she'll make a slip and the harm's done. The closer she stays to him, the more children she bears him, the better.

I'll never let Fina spend a month away from me, or even a few days. Now a job right here in the city, that's different; that's all right, though I wouldn't much care for that, either. If Fina were to find a day job as a cook or a waitress, I'd allow her to take it. But I won't let her go to the country, never! When I have a vacation, I take Fina to Oriente to visit her relatives, even though that ruins my rest, no? But I do it to give her a change, to get out of the city. The remainder of the time I expect her to stay home and look after the house. She has plenty to do there. She owes herself to me and the children.

A woman who is unfaithful to her husband is a whore. If I ever caught my wife with another man I'd take a stick to her. I'd kill her. Either that or I'd walk the two of them at gunpoint, stark naked, to the nearest police station. These are your only choices. Otherwise you couldn't go out in the street without people pointing and saying you have the horns.

A man who stays with his wife after she's put the horns on him is not a man. I despise him. The Party looks down on such a man. He'd be kicked out of the Party if he stayed with her.

I don't know if they punish a man who is having an affair. It seems to me men have different rights from women. A man is a man, after all, and you expect those things to happen. And then a man doesn't lose like a woman from having an affair. I mean, a woman can get pregnant. That's why the whole barrio may know that a man is having an affair with another woman and nobody thinks the worse of him for it. They aren't even interested enough to gossip much about it. That's the way we Cubans are.

Even if a man has relations with another woman and his wife finds out about it, he can always pacify her by saying, "Look, that woman practically threw herself at my head, so what could I do?" If a woman gives me the opportunity, I take it. It doesn't mean a thing. I can have affairs with other women, but if I should ever catch my wife with another *macho....!* What is mine is mine and that's all there is to it. If a woman is unfaithful to her husband, that proves she doesn't love him.

Sure, I can see there's a contradiction there, because I love my wife and yet I have another woman. But no matter what people say, I'll die still saying I don't believe that women should have the same rights as men. No, no, no, it just won't do.

I don't go looking for affairs but ... things happen. Take this woman I have now—Margarita. She's separated—she put the horns on her husband—and was living with her mother and two children three doors down the hall from us. She's a beautiful woman, a Gypsy type, with long, straight black hair and a lovely figure, slender, with a round bottom. Very pretty.

She'd sit in a rocking chair at the bottom of the stair; every day I have to go up those stairs on the way to our room and I couldn't help seeing her. She'd slyly let her housecoat fall open so I could see her thighs. She'd look sideways at me and bat her eyelashes. I never meant to have anything to do with her but she kept flirting with me with those eyes of hers. Beautiful eyes she has!

She started visiting us and became friendly with my wife, doing her hair and everything. Fina's so countrified she didn't know how to do her hair or put on makeup until Margarita taught her. She showed Fina how to look her best for me.

My mother-in-law thinks the world of Margarita. When they meet she kisses and hugs her and says, "Look after Fina for me."

I never asked Fina to introduce her to me. I hadn't spoken a word to her till Fina went away to see her mother. I began to fix some things outside the room and Margarita came over to provoke me.

She sat on the windowsill and let her skirt hike up so that I could see her beauty spot, the one she paints on her thigh; real brazen she was, batting her eyelashes at me. I thought, "Now we'll see!" I wrote her a note and handed it to her. She fairly snatched it out of my hand. I had written, "Can I see you on Thursday?" But heck, we didn't wait that long. Margarita told me she wanted to see me on Tuesday.

We met in front of the Coppelia. That day Margarita confessed that she'd fallen in love with me because Fina had told her everything I do to her in bed. And Margarita repeated it to me word for word.

"Well, you see, I pressed Gabriel and he came...." *Coño,* Fina told her every blessed thing down to the most intimate, dirtiest details. I couldn't believe it. Fina is so shy, she won't talk to me, her own husband, about such things. In bed she's like a piece of meat spread out there. Yet the things she told Margarita! *Ay,* she's so simpleminded. When Margarita heard all those things, she thought to herself, "I'm going to have that *macho!*" Isn't that something! My wife courted the girl for me without even knowing it.

That girl! She's only twenty-one or so but she knows more about sex than a woman twice her age. Listen, she's taught me things I never heard of before. I went to Colón for years, but that broad does things in bed that would have amazed any of the whores in Colón. And she'll come right out and say anything. She makes my blood run cold. We're in bed and she'll say without any embarrassment at all, "Stick it in behind." That's one thing I don't like about her. When she gets so aggressive it kind of discourages me, understand? If a woman knows dirty words, she should at least pretend she doesn't. And then, I don't like to tell a woman to do something, thinking it's new to her, and have her tell me a whole world of things that I don't know. It kind of makes everything go down.

She has another lover—an old guy. He's nearly seventy. He lives with his wife but gives Margarita 200 *pesos* a month and brings her his meat ration. Once I asked her, "What do you do with him?" She told me, "I'll be the death of him one of these days." She stretches out on the bed, opens her legs, and says, "All right, old man, come on!"

I had to laugh, but I told her, "You're a cruel bitch! Poor old man."

She's a tramp, but I don't care. It's not as though I'm in love with her. There's no tie between us. I see her when I feel like laying her, that's all. About once every two weeks we go to a *posada*. Sometimes I pay, sometimes she pays. If I'm short of money she'll send for drinks and pay for them. When we leave, she goes home and I wait an hour or so and get there after her.

So far Fina hasn't suspected. Margarita took care of that. She told her, "Gabriel's not my type." She's scared to death Fina will find out. She never visits when I'm home, and she doesn't even look at me on the stairs. As for me, I've never even said hello to her inside the building or looked at her when she steps out in the hall. One day I asked her, "What I'd like to know is whether my wife puts the horns on me."

Margarita's answer made my hair stand on end. She said, "Gabriel, that woman loves you like life itself. She can't live without you. That's why I don't want to make trouble between you two. When you want to leave me, just tell me. I promise I won't make a scene."

She and Fina are still best friends. Margarita goes shopping for her and bathes the kids. But if I so much as shake a leg at Fina, next day Margarita will come and tell me, "I hear you did this-and-so to your wife last night." It hurts my feelings, I tell you. Why does my wife talk like that? Why should she want to show off at her age, and with four kids! She never talks that way to me. And she didn't tell me she talks to Margarita like that. She knows I'd slap her face.

Once I tried to make her tell me, "What was Margarita doing here?"

"Bathing the kids."

Coño, it's real nice of her to bathe my kids!

Aside from Lourdes and Margarita, who I had full-blown affairs with, I've had a lot of other women, mostly prostitutes. There was a girl I met when I was on guard duty near the Capitol. She was a deaf-mute. Another was a real midget. I met her at the Madrid Hotel. She wanted to go with me, and oh, you should have seen that little girl in action! A midget with the face of a dopey country girl, but she was really something in bed.

None of those women has anything to do with love. Lourdes I loved like life itself, but when it came to the point of choosing between her and my children, that was it. It was over. There isn't a woman in the world I'd leave Fina for. I've had some lovely broads, girls I was proud to be seen with, a thousand times better-looking than Fina, but I wouldn't leave her for the best of them. And listen, Fina is nothing to look at! Dark-skinned, short, talks like a country girl—but it makes no difference. I love her anyway. Or . . . at least . . . I don't know how to describe my feelings. It's not love after all these years. It's a very deep affection.

Fina is everything to me. She and the children are my life. I have three boys and a girl and I just want to bring them up in peace. I'm not interested in anything else. I can't go falling in love anymore. That's for kids. I feel like an old man that way. I think the two great loves of my life left me without illusions. I never again got that feeling of being up in the clouds. I don't feel that way about Fina, though I still want her, as much as if it was the first night. I do love her. She's like one of my own blood, like a piece of my own heart, as if she were my mother.

When I see my kids fucked up in the fuckingest way possible, I feel completely disillusioned with the Revolution on account of that. *Coño,* I'm not the blah, blah kind of revolutionary—all talk, no action. I make sacrifices! I do guard duty every Sunday from midnight to 5:00 the next morning. Those are dangerous hours. There are still plenty of robberies happening here, and I might have to deal with some dangerous criminal who might kill me, no? And after risking my life like that, to go home to find my kids sleeping on the floor. . . ! I feel the life go out of me.

Just the other day they sent me word that my wife was a bit sick, poor thing, and they prescribed vitamin B_{12} for her, and a lot of rest. But when I got home my poor little wife was out buying food. I knocked on the door and there was no one to open up, so I pried the transom open and jumped in through it and there was my littlest kid tied to the bed. I tell you, at times like that I feel closed in and helpless, and I lose faith. Sometimes I feel so bad I tell Fina that if I had a boat handy I just might get into it and sail away from Cuba. She tells me, "*Ay,* don't talk like that, *chico.*" She's so revolutionary she never complains about anything.

Fina and I are both members of the block Committee, but I won't let her stand guard. I'm not having her tie up the children just so she can stand guard. When they came calling for her I told them, "My wife can't leave the kids alone to go stand guard because there's nobody to take care of them."

The last time I did volunteer work was just over a month ago. I picked potatoes near Havana. I've been there several times, one day at a time, so I don't have to stay away from home. But I won't go away to the country to cut cane anymore. I can't leave my wife alone with four kids in that tiny room. She'd go crazy. It would be different if I had a house to live in, because then I could ask *mamá* to stay with Fina while I was away. But how can I ask *mamá* to go sleep in that dinky little room? Besides, what would she sleep on? No, they can't expect me to be off cutting cane while my children have no beds to sleep on.

Little Gabriel's school principal told me I should take him to see a psychiatrist. She says he doesn't act like other boys; he's restless and won't pay attention in class. She says it's the way he's been brought up—that the kids should be free to run around instead of being locked up, tied to the bed, in a stuffy little room.

All his school principals said the same. I transferred him twice. I wanted him to stay with his grandma in Almendares, where he'd live better and at the same time ease our burden a bit. It didn't work, though. He wasn't happy there. When I went to see him he said, "I want to go home, *papá*."

"*Chico*," I told him, "at home you don't even have a bed to sleep on. Grandma gives you a bed of your own and takes good care of you." But he always cried when I went away. Each time I went there I'd tell him, "This time I've come to get you." So he'd feel happy, see? But it didn't take him long to catch on.

In the end the poor kid refused to eat and got thin and sickly. When he came home from school he'd throw his uniform on the floor and dash down his shoes; he threw everything he could lay his hands on. His grandmother couldn't stand it any longer, so I told my wife, "I'm going to bring him home." He was transferred back to a school near us and the principal told us again that the kid needed psychiatric treatment.

At the nursery school they told me the same thing about Arelis and Haydée. Imagine, such little kids needing a psychiatrist already! If the littlest one stays in the room he's going to wind up the same way.

I haven't taken the kids to a psychiatrist yet because I haven't had the time. My wife went to the polyclinic and they told her to go back the next day for an appointment, but she let it slide.

What I have on my mind all the time now is a house. Sometimes, lying in bed with my wife, I'll say to her, "*Mima*, wouldn't it be wonderful if we could have a big house and see the children safe and running around!"

That's my dream. I want to see my kids living well and comfortably. I want to see them become something. I'll fight to see that they don't go through what I had to go through.

It gives me such pleasure to buy them toys on the Day of the Three Kings. Last Day of the Three Kings I bought my daughter a doll and a set of dishes, and the boys got two battery-run cars for 5 *pesos* each, a train, a helicopter, and a tricycle. I buy all the things I never had in my life. I watch the boys as they play with them and say to myself, "If they knew that I never had even one of those things!" It makes me proud. Sometimes I look at them wearing their clean long-sleeved shirts, owning two pairs of new shoes at a time, and I think, "*Coño*, their old man never could afford to wear a long-sleeved shirt when he was a boy!"

They're a lot better off than I was even if they do have to sleep on the floor. When I look back to before the Revolution I see how we've come forward. The only thing I really suffer over is having to tie the children to the bedpost. But except for that, I'm happy in every way. I lack nothing. I have a good wife, nice children.

Sometimes I say to Fina, "*Mima*, I hate to think that this happiness can end at any moment."

"Why?" she asks.

"Well, we're as contented and happy as we can be today, but suddenly, when you least expect it, there could be an explosion and something might happen to me." I've had nightmares about that. I'll dream we're being bombarded and I'll look up and see the sky full of planes. Right now we're living so calmly and yet we're in terrible danger. I believe we're going to have another war with the Americans. They may try another invasion, because they're not going to allow communism just 90 miles away. They are not going to permit it. And next time it may not turn out as it did at Playa Girón.

There's nothing the imperialists wouldn't give for Fidel's head. Lots of Cubans have left here and they're going to try to get back. I don't know . . . I listen to the radio and read the newspaper and it seems to me nobody is satisfied with what they have. If it's a communist country, lots of people in it are against communism. If it's a capitalist country, it's full of people who wish it were communist. They have nothing but fights, demonstrations, and strikes.

Even two countries working for the same cause can't get along. Take China and the Soviet Union—it isn't right for them to be always quarreling. The other day I heard in a foreign radio broadcast that China was preparing to fight the Soviet Union as well as the United States. Now if that isn't the damnedest thing! I blame them both, China and Russia equally. They should both be fighting against imperialism. They should be united, damn it. I don't really know what they're quarreling about.

Fidel spoke about that once. The Chinese tried to distribute some pamphlets here about their policies, but Fidel said here in Cuba he gives the orders. He made a speech about it.[24]

I don't want war. I want Cuba to live in peace, but they'll come back, the Americans, that's for sure. They won't leave us in peace as long as Cuba is communist. American ships were continually violating Cuban territorial waters. They'd come up close to the coast and do as much damage as they pleased. So we bought torpedo launches from China to defend ourselves. Now any enemy boat that enters our waters is sunk.

Today, anyone who thinks our government can be overthrown has another think coming! Before, we could offer no resistance, but how could they come now? They see our aviation displays and military parades and those little torpedo launches and they think twice about it!

If a war should come, I'd be very sorry for my children's sake, but should my number come up, I'll go to the front to die, because we can't just let all this be taken from us. During the October crisis, when I thought about that dog's life I led in my childhood, I took my machine gun and went up into the hills after those rebels without the slightest fear. I have even more to lose now, and if I went into battle today I'd fight with a lot more spirit. There are only two ways of taking the Revolution. Either you're not sympathetic or you are, even if it costs you your life.

24. See Barrera, n. 26.

Abbreviations

ANAP	*Asociación Nacional de Agricultores Pequeños* (National Association of Small Farmers)
CDR	*Comités de Defensa de la Revolución* (Committees for Defense of the Revolution)
CTC	*Confederación de Trabajadores de Cuba* (Confederation of Cuban Workers), reorganized as *Central de Trabajadores de Cuba* (Central Organization of Cuban Trade Unions)
CUJAE	*Ciudad Universitaria José Antonio Echeverría* (José Antonio Echevería University City)
D(G)OP	*Dirección (General) de Orden Público* (Department of Public Order)
DTI	*Departamento Técnico de Investigaciones* (Department of Technical Investigations)
FAR	*Fuerzas Armadas Revolucionarias* (Revolutionary Armed Forces)
FEU	*Federación Estudiantil Universitaria* (University Student Federation)
FMC	*Federación de Mujeres Cubanas* (Federation of Cuban Women)
INIT	*Instituto Nacional de la Industria Turística* (National Institute of the Tourist Industry)
INRA	*Instituto Nacional de Reforma Agraria* (National Institute of Agrarian Reform)
JUCEI	*Juntas de Coordinación, Ejecución e Inspección* (Boards of Coordination, Execution and Inspection)
MINCIN	*Ministerio de Comercio Interior* (Ministry of Domestic Trade)
MINCON	*Ministerio de Construcción* (Ministry of Construction)
MINFAR	*Ministerio de las Fuerzas Armadas Revolucionarias* (Ministry of the Revolutionary Armed Forces)
MININT	*Ministerio del Interior* (Ministry of the Interior)
MSR	*Movimiento Socialista Revolucionaria* (Revolutionary Socialist Movement)
OFICODA	*Oficina de Control para la Distribución de Alimentos* (Office for Control of Food Distribution)

ONDI   *Organización Nacional de Dispensarios Infantiles* (National Organization of Chidren's Clinics)

PCC   *Partido Comunista de Cuba* (Communist Party of Cuba)

PSP   *Partido Socialista Popular* (Popular Socialist Party)

UJC   *Unión de Jóvenes Comunistas* (Union of Young Communists)

UMAP   *Unidades Militares para Ayudar la Producción* (Military Units for Aid to Production)

Glossary

Abacuá	all-male Afro-Cuban secret society
aguardiente	an alcoholic drink, in Cuba made from sugar cane
arroba	twenty-five pounds
brujero	a sorcerer
caballería	land measure, approximately 33⅓ acres
carnet	worker's identification card
central	sugar-mill complex, including the adjoining cane fields
círculo infantil	nursery school
colonia	sugar-cane farm; some were owned by independent *colonos,* others were company-owned but operated by tenant farmers
colono	sugar-cane farmer; refers to all cane growers whether they own or rent their farms
comadre, compadre	terms used by a child's parents and godparents in addressing or referring to each other
consolidado	a general term of reference for any consolidated enterprise
Cordón de la Habana	the cultivated greenbelt encircling Havana
frente	term used to designate areas of responsibility within the Committees for Defense of the Revolution
gallego (a)	man or woman from Galicia, Spain; often used in the vernacular to refer to light-skinned people whether or not they are of Spanish descent
guajiro (a)	Cuban peasant, sometimes used derogatorily to mean a rustic
gusano	literally "worm," used in Cuba to refer to anyone who does not support the Revolution, from passive opponents to active counterrevolutionaries
isleño (a)	a native of the Canary Islands

jardín infantil	open-air nursery school
kilo	a *centavo*
malanga	*arum sagitae folium,* a root vegetable favored by Cubans
maltina	a bottled drink made of malt and other grains
maricón	slang term for homosexual
Mayombé	Afro-Cuban religious cult, also known as *Palo Monte*
mayombero	member of the *Mayombé* religious cult
medio	five *centavos*
ñáñigo	another name for the *Abacuá,* or one of its members
padrino	godfather
palero	member of the *Palo Monte* religious cult
Palo Monte	Afro-Cuban religious cult, also known as *Mayombé*
permanente	long-term volunteer for productive labor
peseta	one fifth of a *peso,* or 20 *centavos*
peso	Cuban currency maintained by the Castro government at the pre-1959 rate of 1 *peso* = 1 U.S. dollar until 1974, when the rate was changed to 1.25 *pesos* = 1 U.S. dollar
posada	lodging house where rooms are rented by the hour
real	ten *centavos*
Regla Conga	Afro-Cuban cult, also known as *Mayombé* or *Palo Monte*
Regla Ocha	Afro-Cuban religious cult, also known as *santería*
reparto	a suburb or subdivision of a city
santería	Afro-Cuban religious cult that combines Yoruban and Roman Catholic beliefs and traditions
santero (a)	priest-practitioner of the *santería* cult
santo	saint; in *santería* the Spanish word also embodies the African concept of spirit (*orisha*)
solar	a low-rent multiple-family structure, usually one story high, with one or more rows of single rooms or small apartments opening onto a central patio
yaguas	bark of the royal palm

Selected Bibliography

BIBLIOGRAPHIC NOTE

In a study such as this, the most important source materials are, of course, the interviews from which the life stories are constructed. However, due to the special nature of the Cuba project and to the peculiarities of doing field work in a socialist system, secondary sources and supplementary field materials took on special importance. Since this latter group of materials is not cited in the bibliography, we want to mention those which were most important in helping us better understand the life stories and write footnotes to the texts. Among supplementary field materials we most relied on were: observations of the CDRs in five *repartos* and interviews with officers and members; a conference with officials and interviews with eleven judges of the People's Courts and reports on six observed trials; a pilot study of the *jardines infantiles* and interviews with the program's directors; interviews with officials of *Poder Local;* interviews with Armando Torres, who led the drive to eliminate organized prostitution in Cuba; and special studies of household budgets and material inventories. Finally, there were the approximately 12,000 pages of interview material from informants not included in the three volumes of this series; these interviews verified and elaborated upon some of the information provided in the published life stories. All of the above-mentioned sources were of great value in providing details on the mechanics of daily life under Cuban socialism, which, as far as we know, are unavailable in published sources.

The following works from the appended selected bibliography have been of particular value to us. For historical background we relied most heavily on Hugh Thomas's *Cuba: The Pursuit of Freedom,* a study of the island from the English expedition in 1762 through the missile crisis of 1962, with heavy emphasis on the twentieth century. We consulted Philip Foner's two-volume study of Cuba from 1492 to 1895 (part of a projected multivolume series on Cuban-U.S. relations) for additional information on slavery, colonialism, and the War of Independence. Other sources of background information were: the classic study of the sugar and tobacco industries by Fernando Ortíz, one of Cuba's most famous sociologists; *Rural Cuba* (1950) by the North American sociologist Lowry Nelson; and Verena Martínez-Alier's study of Cuban women in the nineteenth century (1974). For understanding the terminology and explaining certain rituals and practices of the Afro-Cuban sects, the works of Lydia Cabrera and Romulo

Lachatañere were especially helpful. A good general discussion of education and social-welfare policies in Cuba during the first three decades of this century can be found in *Problems of the New Cuba; Report of the Commission on Cuban Affairs* (1935).

The *Atlas Nacional de Cuba,* a magnificent work compiled by the Cuban and Soviet academies of sciences, was most useful to us, particularly as a source for changing place names. Included among its many maps are graphic summaries of some of the Revolution's major achievements. In 1971 its text was translated from the Spanish and reprinted (without maps) by the U.S. Department of Commerce, Joint Publications Research Service.

For information on the general direction of the Revolution's social and economic policies during the first decade we consulted the following: the speeches, writings, and published interviews of Ernesto Guevara, Minister of Industry during the early 1960s; the firsthand account of this period written by Edward Boorstein, then an economic advisor to the Cuban government; and Theodore Draper's *Castroism: Theory and Practice* for its discussion of the early attempts (under Guevara's direction) at industrialization. The Cuban Economic Research Project (*A Study on Cuba,* 1965) published a concise, yet quite detailed, study of the direction of economic development under the Revolution (including some economic statistics for the period 1959–64) in a larger work that includes an economic history of the colonial and republican periods.

For the period 1959–69, the work of Carmelo Mesa-Lago (including that with Roberto Hernández) and that of Lionel Martin (the *Guardian*'s Cuba correspondent) were invaluable for an understanding of Cuba's labor policies. Richard R. Fagen's study of the CDRs is the most comprehensive single English-language work on that organization for the period 1961–65. For additional and more recent information on the CDRs, as well as the People's Courts (and information on other mass organizations, such as unions) we are indebted to David K. Booth for sending us his excellent unpublished Ph.D. thesis (University of Surrey, 1973), which was based on field work carried out in Cuba in 1969.

In Bonachea and Valdés's *Cuba in Revolution,* Ricardo Leyva's article on health care and Valdés's article on education were especially helpful. Government publications acquired in Cuba in 1969–70—general information bulletins, statistical reports, texts of laws, for example—provided invaluable detail, particularly on education policy. Finally, and most important, were the speeches and writings of Fidel Castro, from 1953 (*History Will Absolve me,* which contains a comprehensive statement of the Twenty-sixth of July Movement's original objectives) to 1976. Castro's speeches were a principal source of information to us on social and economic policies, for details on the implementation of laws and programs as well as on their successes and failures.

Because this series places great emphasis on daily life under the revolutionary system, we found especially helpful journalistic accounts which re-created the general atmosphere in Havana, and elsewhere in Cuba, during the first ten years and after. The most outstanding single work of this kind is *Castro's Cuba, Cuba's Fidel* by the photo-journalist Lee Lockwood. This very readable and informative book, which is based on Lockwood's lengthy interviews with Castro, serves as a good introduction to revolutionary Cuba. Ruby Hart Phillips, the *New York Times* correspondent in Cuba for almost thirty years, wrote two books describing changes in Havana during the two years after the Triumph. The first of these, *Cuba: Island of Paradox* (1959), an evocative account of the first weeks after the victory, was written before Ms. Phillips became a militant anti-Castroite. Three other notable journalistic treatments of life in Cuba in the mid- and late 1960s are Sutherland's *Youngest Revolution* (1969), Yglesias's *In the Fist of the Revolution* (1969), and Reckford's *Does Fidel Eat More than Your Father?* (1971). Overall, Sutherland's work is enthusiastically sympathetic, but it contains good, quite realistic appraisals of race relations and the women's movement during the Revolution's first eight years.

For the purpose of updating information in the life stories, the single most valuable source was the *Granma Weekly Review* (1971–76), an official compilation of each week's most important speeches and news stories, translated and reprinted from *Granma*, the official daily of the Communist Party. Cubanists who are interested in every nuance in the printed media that might indicate changes in policy or leadership will certainly prefer *Granma*, but the *Weekly Review* does contain the complete text of most major speeches, laws, and declarations, as well as articles on Cuban history (particularly on martyrs and revolutionary battles), coverage of international relations and visiting dignitaries, and sports news. The *Weekly Review* has the obvious disadvantage over the daily paper of being a collection of articles selected especially for foreign audiences, and the minor disadvantage of utilizing often stilted official translations.

BOOKS AND PAMPHLETS

Anuario Estadistico, Curso 1966–67. Havana: Ministry of Education, n.d.

Area Handbook for Cuba. Washington, D.C.: Government Printing Office, 1971.

Atlas Nacional de Cuba. Havana: Academy of Sciences of Cuba and Academy of Sciences of the U.S.S.R., 1970.

Bonachea, Rolando B., and Nelson P. Valdés, eds. *Cuba in Revolution.* New York: Anchor Books, 1972.

Booth, David K. "Neighbourhood Committees and Popular Courts in the Social Transformation of Cuba." Unpublished Ph.D. thesis, University of Surrey, 1973.

Boorstein, Edward. *The Economic Transformation of Cuba.* New York: Monthly Review Press, 1968.

Cabrera, Lydia. *El Monte.* Miami: Rema Press, 1968.

Castro, Fidel. *History Will Absolve Me.* Havana: Book Institute, 1967.

Los CDR en Granjas y Zonas Rurales. Havana: Dirección Nacional de los CDR, 1965.

Chapman, E. E. *A History of the Cuban Republic.* New York: Macmillan, 1927.

Chester, Edmund A. *A Sergeant Named Batista.* New York: Holt, 1954.

Constitución de la Republica de Cuba. Havana: Compañia Editora de Libros y Folletos, 1940.

Cuba: A Giant School. Havana: Ministry of Foreign Affairs, n.d.

Cuba: El Movimiento Educativo, 1967/68. Havana: Ministry of Education, 1968.

Cuban Economic Research Project. *A Study on Cuba.* Coral Gables: University of Miami Press, 1965.

Debray, Regis. *Revolution in the Revolution?* New York: Monthly Review Press, 1967.

Draper, Theodore. *Castroism: Theory and Practice.* New York: Praeger, 1965.

———. *Castro's Revolution: Myths and Realities.* New York: Praeger, 1962.

Fagen, Richard R. *The Transformation of Political Culture in Cuba.* Stanford, Calif.: Stanford University Press, 1969.

———, Richard A. Brody, and Thomas J. O'Leary. *Cubans in Exile.* Stanford, Calif.: Stanford University Press, 1968.

Ferguson, Erna. *Cuba.* New York: Alfred A. Knopf, 1946.

Foner, Philip S. *A History of Cuba and Its Relations with the United States,* vols. I (1492–1845) and II (1845–95). New York: International Publishers, 1962, 1963.

Fundamental Law of Cuba, 1959. Washington D.C.: Pan American Union, 1959.

La Educación en los Cien Años de Lucha. Havana: Book Institute, 1968.

García Alonso, Aida. *Manuela, la Mexicana.* Havana: Casa de las Americas, 1968.

Gillette, Arthur. *Cuba's Educational Revolution.* London: Fabian Research Series 302, June, 1972.

Halperin, Maurice. *The Rise and Decline of Fidel Castro.* Berkeley, Calif.: University of California Press, 1972.

Horowitz, Irving Louis, ed. *Cuban Communism.* New Brunswick, N.J.: Transaction Books, 1970.

Jahn, Jahnheinz. *Muntu: An Outline of the New African Culture.* New York: Grove Press, 1969.

Karol, K. S. *Guerrillas in Power.* New York: Hill and Wang, 1970.

Kenner, Martin, and James Petras, eds. *Fidel Castro Speaks.* New York: Grove Press, 1969.

Lachatañere, Romulo. *Manual de Santería.* Havana: Editorial Caribe, 1942.

Lavan, George, ed. *Che Guevara Speaks: Selected Speeches and Writings.* New York: Merit, 1967.

Leiner, Marvin, with Robert Ubell. *Children Are the Revolution: Day Care in Cuba.* New York: Viking Press, 1974.

Lewis, Oscar. *La Vida.* New York: Random House, 1965.

———. *A Study of Slum Culture: Backgrounds for La Vida.* New York: Random House, 1968.

Ley de Reforma Agraria. Havana, 1959.

Lockwood, Lee. *Castro's Cuba, Cuba's Fidel.* New York: Vintage, 1969.

MacGaffey, Wyatt, and Clifford R. Barnett. *Cuba: Its People, Its Society, Its Culture.* New Haven: HRAF, 1962.

Martínez-Alier, Verena. *Marriage, Class and Colour in Nineteenth Century Cuba.* Cambridge: Cambridge University Press, 1974.

Matthews, Herbert L. *The Cuban Story.* New York: Braziller, 1961.

———. *Fidel Castro.* New York: Simon and Schuster, 1969.

Memorias de CDR, 1962. Havana: Dirección Nacional de los CDR, 1963.

Memorias de CDR, 1963. Havana: Dirección Nacional de los CDR, 1964.

Mesa-Lago, Carmelo. *Cuba in the Seventies.* Albuquerque: University of New Mexico Press, 1974.

———. *The Labor Force, Employment, Unemployment and Underemployment in Cuba: 1899–1970.* Beverly Hills, Calif.: Sage Publications, International Studies Series, 1972.

———. *The Labor Sector and Socialist Distribution in Cuba.* New York: Praeger, 1968.

———, ed. *Revolutionary Change in Cuba.* Pittsburgh: University of Pittsburgh Press, 1971.

Nelson, Lowry. *Cuba: The Measure of a Revolution.* Minneapolis: University of Minnesota Press, 1972.

———. *Rural Cuba.* Minneapolis: University of Minnesota Press, 1950.

La Ofensiva Revolucionaria: Asamblea de Administradores Populares. Havana: Dirección Nacional de los CDR, 1968.

Ortíz, Fernando. *Cuban Counterpoint: Tobacco and Sugar.* New York: Alfred A. Knopf, 1947.

Phillips, Ruby Hart. *Cuba: Island of Paradox*. New York: MacDowell, Obolensky, 1959.

———. *The Cuban Dilemma*. New York: Ivan Obolensky, 1962.

Plan de la Escuela Semi-internado, El Cangre. Havana: Ministry of Education, n.d.

Problems of the New Cuba; Report of the Commission on Cuban Affairs. New York: Foreign Policy Association, 1935.

Randall, Margaret. *Mujeres en la Revolución: Conversa con Mujeres Cubanas*. Mexico, D.F.: Siglo Veintiuno Editores, 1972.

Reckford, Barry. *Does Fidel Eat More than Your Father?* New York: Praeger, 1971.

Silverman, Bertram, ed. *Man and Socialism*. New York: Atheneum, 1971.

Semi-internado de Primaria, Valle del Perú. Havana: Ministry of Education, 1968.

Superación y Recreación para Maestros de Montaña en Varadero. Havana: Ministry of Education, 1968.

Suárez, Andrés. *Cuba: Castroism and Communism, 1959–1966*. Cambridge, Mass.: MIT Press, 1967.

Sucklicki, Jaime. *University Students and Revolution in Cuba, 1920–1968*. Coral Gables: University of Miami Press, 1969.

Sutherland, Elizabeth. *The Youngest Revolution*. New York: Dial Press, 1969.

Taber, Robert. *M-26: The Biography of a Revolution*. New York: Lyle Stuart, 1961.

Thomas, Hugh. *Cuba: The Pursuit of Freedom*. New York: Harper and Row, 1971.

Valdés, Nelson P. *A Bibliography on Cuban Women in the Twentieth Century* (reprinted from *Cuban Studies Newsletter*, June, 1974).

Yglesias, José. *In the Fist of the Revolution*. New York: Vintage, 1969.

Zeitlin, Maurice. *Revolutionary Politics and the Urban Working Class*. Princeton: Princeton University Press, 1967.

ARTICLES

Bascom, William R. "The Focus of Cuban *Santería*," *Southwestern Journal of Anthropology*, Spring, 1950.

Berman, Jesse. "The Cuban Popular Tribunals," *Columbia Law Review*, Dec., 1969.

Butterworth, Douglas. "Grass-Roots Political Organization in Cuba: A Case of the Committees for the Defense of the Revolution," in Wayne A. Cornelius and Felicity Trueblood, eds., *Latin American Urban Research: Anthropological Perspectives on Latin American Urbanization*, vol. IV (Beverly Hills, Calif.: Sage Publications, 1974).

Dumont, René. "The Militarization of Fidelismo," *Dissent*, Sept.-Oct., 1970.

FitzGerald, Frances. "A Reporter at Large (Cuba)," *New Yorker*, Feb. 18, 1974.

Fox, Geoffrey E. "Cuban Workers in Exile," *Transaction*, Sept., 1971.

Halperin, Ernst. "Peking and the Latin American Community," *China Quarterly*, Jan.-Mar., 1967.

Hartman, Chester. "The Limitations of Public Housing: Relocation Choices in a Working Class Community," *AIP Journal*, Nov., 1963.

———. "Social Values and Housing Orientations," *Journal of Social Issues*, Apr., 1963.

Leiner, Marvin. "Cuba's Schools, Ten Years Later," *Saturday Review*, Oct. 17, 1970.

Lewis, Oscar. "Family Dynamics in a Mexican Village," *Marriage and Family Living*, Aug., 1959.

Martin, Lionel. A series of articles on the Vanguard Worker program and union reorganization, *Guardian*, May 10–July 5, 1969.

Mesa-Lago, Carmelo. "Economic Significance of Unpaid Labor in Socialist Cuba," *Industrial and Labor Relations Review,* Apr., 1969.

Morgan, Ted. "Cuba," *New York Times Magazine,* Dec. 1, 1974.

Nicholson, Joe, Jr. "Inside Cuba," *Harpers,* Apr., 1973.

Yglesias, José. "Cuba Report: Their Hippies and Their Squares," *New York Times Magazine,* Jan. 12, 1969.

———. "A Cuban Poet in Trouble," *New York Review of Books,* June 3, 1971.

JOURNALS AND PERIODICALS

Bohemia, 1968–70.
Centro de Estudios del Folklore del TNC, 1961.
Cuba Internacional, 1969–70.
Cuba Review, 1974–76 (*Cuba Resource Center Newsletter,* 1972–73).
Cuban Studies Newsletter, 1972–75.
Ediciones CDR, 1969–70.
Etnología y Folklore, 1966–68.
Granma, 1969–70.
Granma Weekly Review, 1971–76.
Obra, 1961.